Hidden Truths
7th E

זהל ישראל,

The Qadosh Scrolls of the Hebrews

Avraham the man whose faith, Israel followed

Instructions for the Children of Avraham

Sefirim Ha Israel
The Torah Stands For

The Book of Beginnings
And these are the Names
He Called Out
And He gave words
Giving Many instructions (Torot)

The Tanak is Torah (Instructions), Navim (Prophets) and the Ketuvim (writings).

For more on the commentary of the Hidden-Truths Hebraic Scrolls see the additional HTHS Compendium Guide which goes further into some commentaries to explain the events, obtainable from Amazon.

Dedicated to Our father Abraham Ben Tharakh Ben Nakhkhur

YHWH, the name of the Creator in in the Hebrew language.

Abraham was the man chosen by YHWH, to enlighten His Torah and the major Covenants and promises to the people of Israel and the world that He made with him.

Do you know what they are and how they affect You?

In the writings YHWH gave testimony categorically stating **Abraham obeyed My Voice, kept my charge and guarded my commandments, my statutes and my TOROT (Both oral and written Torah).** Beresheeth 26:5.

He also called Abraham, **My friend.**

> **Yeshayahu 41:8** *But You, Israel, are my servant, Yakov whom I have chosen, the descendents of **Abraham My friend**.*

Would you like to know why this man was chosen and how this affects you, and your family? Would you like to be called YHWH's friend?

For us to even begin to understand Abraham takes time patience, and study, of this great man; because through him, we begin to see the need for humanity to come together rather than be divided and fighting each other. Therefore, YHWH saw it fit to place the promises with him that lives to this day. Abraham's monotheism is the only one that exists and is verified historically serving YHWH our maker; because we are the sons of Abraham, searching for the ancient paths that lead to our rest.

> **Yirmeyahu 6:16** Thus says YHWH: "Stand in the Ways and look intently, and make inquiry for the ancient paths, where the good way is, and walk in it; then you will find rest for your souls. But they said, `We will not walk in it.'

Are you going to walk in YHWH's Halaka (commandments), or, are you going to say no like the generations before us, who perished in disobedience? These writings will help you make this decision. Rabbi Simon has used his knowledge of both ancient and proto Hebrew to give the right flavour, and best understanding, of the writings from a Eastern Hebraic mindset, rather than a Western Roman/Greek mindset.

We only pray that in all things may our heavenly Father's name be glorified.

The ancient Hebrew text Midrash Raba, Parasha 38 tells us, the Babylonians (not so) kindly turned Abraham's offer down. Abraham fled from Babylon and began to teach while, roaming from town to town and from kingdom to kingdom, until he arrived in the Land of Israel (Maimonides, Yad HaHazakah (The Mighty Hand), Idolatry Rules, Chapter 1).

We Israel will overcome with YHWH El as our head, Hallelu-Yah and praise be to His Holy and glorified Name under which we live!

Who is Israel

It is time for the world to know the truth. There are other Hebrew roots Bibles out there translated by gentiles while this is the only one translated by a real Kohen. Whether you believe or not that is of no particular consequence. The gentiles translated texts lack our essential truths and are nothing but cheap imitations that will leave you with a bad taste in your mouth. Biological Israel is a history of Hebrews out of a region today known as North East Africa, who were the sons of Shem. Yes that is right they were the sons of Shem who had settled in the African region with their father Noakh, where the Ark landed in Chad, instead of what is taught by fanciful theories in Churches and Synagogues. The sons of Shem were men of black/brown skin tones who intermarried into the families of Ham, the son of Noakh. Rabbi Simon Altaf Hakohen from Beyth Tzadok has put his life on the line and the wealth to one side to aid him without subtracting the truth and replacing what was taken away and removed from our people. This is the rise of the Tzadok and the Kohanim and none can stop this. The Hebrews prior to Abraham came from India, what today would be called the Harappan Mohenjadaro cultures which were vastly intelligent.

The lies that are taught in television, newspapers and the skewed history of the West can be found in many places. There are some historians who tell the truth like Godfrey Higgins but unless you search for them you are likely to remain in the fog of darkness about who is Israel and when will they return. Even if facts are suppressed by wicked men and women, the rocks, the trees, the birds, the animals will cry out and tell who is Israel. Our people were Olive skinned. The olives were cultivated only in these lands and in South-Eastern Asia after which they were introduced into the Western Asia and European countries as they were carried from Egypt. The dove and the Eagle, which is a symbol of ancient Israel is also another bird species that started its life from North Africa and then spread to other cultures. Yahudah is called an Eagle in Beresheeth 49:9, while the Kings James Version translates it incorrectly as a lion's whelp. There are many cheap imitations of Hebrew roots bibles out there being promoted by gentiles but none will come even close to this text ordained by the Abbah.

Ancient Israel cannot be confused with all the Black people in the world, many in America claim to be descendants of ancient Israel and point to Devrim 28 as the fulfillment of them being in America. However, this is not true as the prophesies in Devrim 28 do not fit all the black people in America but apply mostly to the land mass of Israel when ancient Israel lived there. There are some ancient Israelites in North America but there are also many Hamites in the mix so one must be careful to determine who is Israel. If we look at ancient tablets and images the facial features do not match many Americans today. The character of genetic Israel is even more important in that they be subservient to their Torah leaders and obey the voice of YHWH but many in North America run around disobeying and slandering their teachers so they are not the House of Israel. Those that belong to the House of Israel in North America will be the humble ones who desire to obey the Torah and follow the Torah teachers so their character will determine the real Hebrews in this nation. Many Hebrews are situated in India/Pakistan and Afghanistan but no one bothers to check these facts.

Original Hebrews are Indo-Hebrew

Yahushua 24:3 And I took your father Abraham from the other side of the river,[1] and led him throughout all the land of Kanan, and multiplied his seed, and gave him Ytshak (Isaac).

[2]Had you been a cartographer and geographer working for the British East India company in the 17th and 18th centuries, you would have found all over India thousands of Hebrew-like place names with similar meanings in both languages as well. The map excerpt on this page shows a small section of ancient Seuna-Desa (Zion Land) in what is now **Maharashtra** (to right). At the bottom right of the excerpt is the city of Paithan, on the banks of the river Godivari. The Indo-Hebrews named the part of the river passing through Paithan's territory Paithan (Pison, Phison), according to their traditions. In the upper left-hand corner is the city of Satana. According to the legends of the Yadavas (Indo-Hebrews), Satana would have made the folks in Sodom and Gomorah envious. The Seunas and the Satanas decided to resolve their moral and religious differences on the battlefield. The forces of "Satan" lost, but their defeat didn't dishearten them. Eventually, we came to think of "Satan" as a being who lost the battle but not the war. The bible tells us that such a peace treaty hasn't yet been signed between these two ancient enemies.

In that part of India, the holiest of holies for the Indians, the names of many towns end in the appendage gaon. In Hebrew, gaon means "genius; great rabbinical scholar." Also in this region is an area that was once the favorite of Yadava royalty: Nashik, the exact Hebrew name for "Royal Prince." Satan is near the district called Khandesh (Land of Cain). There is also a Kodesh. Kod and Khad are Sanskrit terms for "First," "The Beginning," or "God." In Hebrew, Khadesh = "The first day of a Jewish calendar month." Notice that all these names have similar meanings and religious connotations in both languages. I invite my readers to investigate this anomaly for themselves.

The similarity of these Indian and Hebrew names certainly traumatized European colonists. Unwilling to admit that the Jews had never sprouted spontaneously in the Arabian desert, or were from outer space as I read recently, but were from the East as the bible itself tells us, they merely

Footnotes
[1] Clear proof Abraham came from Eastern Turkey, his ancestors came from Beyond from India/Pakistan region.
[2] http://www.viewzone.com/matlock.html

erased these matters from their minds or convinced themselves that they were "coincidences," even though the "coincidences" numbered in the thousands and were peppered over every region in India.

A 19th Century British Scholar Explains Why the Western World Never Learned About the Indian Origins of the Jews.

Though not generally known in this day and age, **Godfrey Higgins**(1772-1833), archeologist, politician, humanitarian, social reformer, and author, was one of the most enlightened and educated men of early 19th century England. He was a well-known iconoclast, rationalist, and admirer of the Jews, who vehemently opposed any kind of persecution of this ancient religious group. He wrote two oversized volumes, totaling around 1600 pages of fine print, about the Jews' Indian origins. These two volumes, entitled Anacalypsis, are extremely rare. The last printing was done in 1965 by University Books, NY. It's a difficult book to read because the author painstakingly proved the minutest of details in his dissertation. Even good readers need several weeks to finish it.

The first printing consisted of only 200 copies, twenty of which he had to give away. Only a few of the remaining 180 copies were sold. For nearly thirty years, the religious communities of England and Europe quietly suppressed the book. It has since been reprinted three times, but including the first printing, the total copies printed never totaled over a thousand. Only occasionally can it be found in a library. Even so, many authors have quoted and plagiarized it. Not a few spiritual charlatans, such as fraudulent mystics, psychics, and the Presbyterian preacher who wrote the novel on which The Book of Mormon is based, used Anacalypsis to produce their respective heresies and agendas. The famous 19th century mystic and founder of Theosophy, Madam Blavatsky, took advantage of the world's nearly total ignorance of this magnificent document, using much of Higgin's information, to convince the gullible that she had acquired her "mystical knowledge" from "otherworldly" sources called "Akashic records."

Godfrey Higgins gave an opinion that I have always espoused, which explains in part why the similarities of peoples, languages, philosophies, and place names between India and the Middle East became lost to the memory of mankind after Christianity and Islam took over the West.

"The outlines of the history of the extended empires, which I have here exhibited, would have been more conspicuous had our makers of maps and histories recorded the names of the places as they must have appeared to them. But from their native religious prejudices and necessary ignorance of the nature of the history, it seemed to them absurd to believe, that there should be places or persons in the East having exactly the same names as places and persons in the West; and to avoid the feared ridicule of their contemporaries, which in fact in opposition to the plainest evidence, and which they themselves could not entirely resist, that they thought well-founded, they have, as much as possible disguised the names. Thus, that which otherwise they would have called David-pouri, they called Daud-poutr, Solomon, Soleiman; Johnguior, Jahanguior, etc., etc. In the same way, without any wrong intention, they have been induced to secrete the truth, in many cases, from themselves, by hastily adopting the idea that the old Jewish names of places have been given by the modern Saracens or Turks, the erroneousness of which a moment's unprejudiced consideration would have shewn...I shall here merely add, that...I have observed...a great similarity in the countries where the tribes of Judah were settled in the East and in the West. The Western country seems, as much as possible, to have been accommodated by the Eastern..." (Vol. I, pp. 437-438.)

"When Mahmud of Gazna, the first Mohammedan conqueror, attacked Lahore, he found it defended by a native Hindoo prince called Daood or David. This single fact is enough to settle the question of the places not being named by Mohamedans." (Vol. I; p. 432.)

"I beg my reader to look at the ruins of the ancient cities of India: Agra, Delhi, Oude, Mundore, etc., which have many of them been much larger than London, the last for instance, 37 miles in circumference, built in the oldest style of architecture in the world, the Cyclopean, and I think he must at once see the absurdity of the little Jewish mountain tribe (the "Lost Tribes") being the founders of such a mass of cities. We must also consider that we have almost all the places of India in Western Syria...I think no one can help seeing that these circumstances are to be accounted for in no other way than by the supposition that there was in very ancient times one universal superstition, which was carried all over the world by emigrating tribes, and that they were originally from Upper India." (Vol. I; p. 432.)

"...the natives of Cashmere as well as those of Afghanistan, pretending to be descended from the Jews, give pedigrees of their kings reigning in their present country up to the sun and the moon, and along with this, they shew you the Temples still standing, built by Solomon, statues of Noah, and other Jewish Patriarchs...the traditions of the Afghans tell them, that they are descended from the tribe of Ioudi or Yuda, and in this they are right, for it is the tribe of Joudi noticed by Eusebius to have existed before the Son of Jacob in Western Syria was born, the Joudi of Oude, and from which tribe the Western Jews with the Brahmin (Abraham) descended and migrated. (Vol. I; p. 740.)

"In the valley of Cashmere, on a hill close to the lake, are the ruins of a temple of Solomon. The history states that Solomon, finding the valley all covered with water except this hill, which was an island, opened the passage in the mountains and let most of it out, thus giving to Cashmere its beautiful plains. The temple which is built on the hill is called Tucht Suliman. Afterwards Forster says, 'Previously to the Mahometan conquest of India, Kashmere was celebrated for the learning of the Brahmins and the magnificent construction of its temple.' Now what am I to make of this? Were these Brahmans Jews, or the Jews Brahmins? The inadvertent way in which Forster states the fact precludes all idea of deceit...

"The Tuct Soliman of Cashmere in the time of Bernier, was described by him to be in ruins, and to have been a temple of the idolaters and not of the Mohamedans. The Mohamedans reported that it was built by Solomon, in very ancient times. All this at once does away with the pretence that it was a building of the modern Mohamedans; and is a strong confirmation of the Jewish nature of the other names of the towns - Yuda-poor, Iod-pore, etc., etc. Bernier goes on to say...that the name of Mousa or Moses is common among the natives, that Moses died at Cashmere, and that they yet show the ruins of his tomb near the town. This is curious when connected with the fact, that the Jews of Western Syria say, no one ever knew where he was buried." (Vol. I; p. 771.)

An article in the April, 1997 issue of the Jewish magazine Momentdiscusses the possibility that a heavy Jewish presence once dominated India.

"A tribe of Sunni Moslems called the Pathans, now living in parts of Pakistan, number at least 15 million. The Pathan language bears traces of biblical Hebrew, and the Pathans themselves claim lineage from King Saul. They are said to follow, in varying degrees of observance, some 21 'Jewish' customs, including lighting candles on Friday night, wearing a four-cornered prayer garment, and performing circumcision on the eighth day.

Then there are the Kashmiris from Northern India, who number about five million; although they too are predominantly Sunni Moslems, many bear biblical-sounding names like Cleb (Caleb), Israel, Hahana, and Lavni..." (Searching for the Lost Tribes, by Winston Pickett, p. 51.)

Aramaic, a language as similar to Hebrew as Spanish is to Portuguese, originated in Afghanistan and Pakistan. Both Afghanistan and Pakistan were once part of India. Afghanistan seceded from Indian in the 1700s. Pakistan was cut out of India when the two nations were partitioned after World War II. Aramaic also is the source of modern Hebrew's square alphabet, used in Israel today. The Hebrew square alphabet and the truth that Hebrew is just an Aramaic dialect confirm the Indian origin of the Jews.

Those Christian and Jewish authorities who don't want it to be true that ten to thirty million Jews once lived in Afghanistan, Pakistan, and Northwestern India say that it is just a "coincidence" that so many tribes and places there have biblical names. Others insist that the Moslems christened all those tribes and places. As Godfrey Higgins tells us, many of those tribes and places had already received their so-called "biblical names" millenniums before Islam was a gleam in Mohammed's eyes and many centuries before those same names started showing up in the Middle East. Some of Israel's tribal and place names also started appearing in Afghanistan, Kashmir, and Northwestern India when Sargon II and Nebuchadnezzar exiled most of the Jews to that part of the world. The confusion about the origin of those tribal and place names will always exist as long as we stubbornly refuse to give the Indo-Hebrews their rightful place in history. The Aryans and Indo-Hebrews began to overrun parts of India and the Middle East around 2000 BC, perhaps more than a thousand years previously if there is any truth to the story about the progeny of Noah.

Somehow, our brainwashed minds blank out the face that the Ancient Egyptian and Akkadian names for Hebrew, Habiru and Apiru were derived from Indo-Hebrew dialects and meant "Sons of Ophir." The truth about the origins of the Hebrews has been screaming in our faces for thousands of years, but our benumbed minds have chosen not to hear it.

Why the Hebrew Roots scrolls?

For people in Pakistan and India, which number over one billion people and many still, unaware of YHWH, serving idolatry. It is essential that we equip our brethren working in those areas, with a translation that prepares them for effective truth teachings and deep learning of the Hebrew scrolls. For far too long they have had to settle for second rate translations being fed milk and never reaching the level needed for effective transmission, yet these are the people, who are at the forefront of debates with the unbelievers. The time has arrived for this change to occur and occur quickly.

YHWH has called his Kahuna out and raised Rabbi Simon to propagate these facts to the ends of the earth, while He will do the rest.

> **Malaki 2:4-7** And you shall know that I have sent this commandment to you, that my Covenant might be with Levi, says YHWH of Armies. **5** My Covenant was with him **of life and shalom**; and I gave them to him for **the fear wherewith he feared** me, and was afraid before my name. **6** The **Torah of truth was in his mouth**, and iniquity was not found in his lips: he walked with me in shalom and equity, and did turn many away from idolatry. **7** For the kohen (priest's) lips should Guard knowledge, and they should seek the Torah from his mouth: for he is the teacher from YHWH of Armies.

Holy Names

Often we are excited by new translations of the Hebrew scrolls, only to be disappointed by the descriptions we read of the Ruakh Ha Kodesh (Holy Spirit), though being the feminine side of YHWH, the popular error continues to appease, instead of addressing her as She. The Ruakh has been changed by bad translations to the masculine form but not in this translation. The Holy Spirit is seen as the Power of God described in a feminine way.

This translation will help to remove two thousand years of anti-Semitic theology, hatred, and bigotry to build a love for the nation of Israel, and the people. If you have been rescued from sin, then you have been grafted into the natural Olive tree irrespective of your skin tone, ethnicity, which is Israel. Welcome home brothers and sisters. We refuse to get into arguments about what is and is not the Holy Name's pronunciations; because we know exactly what the Murashu texts have confirmed for us ahead of time, clearly the True Name being, Yah-oo-weh, a short oo sound such as chute, the ancient Africans pronounced it as YEHWEH with no heh sound in it. We know some pronounce it as Yahowah or the many other variants; we acknowledge some of these variants because they were used once a year in the Temple by the High Priest in the Aharonic Benediction.

We condemn no one and encourage the use of the name of our Elohim in ritual purity.

Angels

There are ten levels of angels, they are created beings, which are close to God, although angels appear to have freewill but they are just robots programmed to do whatever God desires from them. The gentile theologies out there are not corrrect on angels. No angel has any authority to fight against God, even Satan is an angel of God and works on instructions given through his program. He is known as the epitome of evil inclination. The Ten levels are as follows:

1 - Chayot HaKodesh (holy beings), the Top ranking ones;
2 - Ofanim (wheels);
3 - Erelim (valiant ones);
4 - Chashmalim (electric ones);
5 - Seraphim (fiery ones);
6 - Malachim (messengers);
7 - Elohim (the mighty ones);
8 - B'nei Elohim (sons of the mighty);
9 - Keruvim (cherubim);
10 - Ishim (human-like).

Angels primary function is to serve God and that is what they do best.

Doctrine of the Ruakh Ha Kodesh and Torah Plural Marriage

Often we are excited by new translations of the Hebrew scrolls, only to be disappointed by the descriptions we read of the Ruakh Ha Kodesh (Holy Spirit), though being the feminine side of YHWH, the popular error continues to appease, instead of addressing her as She. The Ruakh has been changed by bad translations to the masculine form but not in this translation. The Holy Spirit is the seen as the Power of God in a feminine way.

Rabbi Simon Altaf has revealed the Chochmah (wisdom) the left side of the Sefirotic tree, to be both Abbah and Mother combined together since; because the Abbah is the source of all living beings. This is speaking Kabalisticly.

We will show, Torah Patriarchal polygamy was our ancient model and not serial monogamy (Although Torah monogamy was practiced); which is the model of the world. The patriarchal model is being restored in these last days. Torah polygamy was widely practiced in both ancient and modern Israel, both in the land, and in the exile. Rabbi Gershom Solomon's edict on European polygamy, was a ban to protect European Jewish lives, and this is no longer in effect. The way our ancestors practiced a type of monogamy for a limited time was when they would marry the first wife and stay with her for a number of years before they took the second wife to be placed in the North/South Axis.

For all the brothers who find it hard to afford a second wife they should only have one Torah wife. And to love their spouses and build a Torah home.

This is explained in the book Patriarchal marriage, Israel's Righteous method, which can be acquired from Amazon. Plural marriage has many Blessings but if practiced incorrectly it can have pitfalls too.

Halacha permits you to stay with one wife providing you have one son and daughter. Torah plural marriage is for those brothers and sisters who want to build a beyth in unity to serve the Abbah.

Two House
YHWH very clearly, and very early on, started to show us how the nation of Israel would be divided into two smaller countries called, the Two Houses of Israel, North and South. The split that took place with Jerobaom Ben Nebat was only meant to last 36 years but was extended due to Israel's sinful circumstances just as our exile has been extended due to our people being in sin of idolatry. We must remove all idolatry and return back to Torah.

End-Times Beast
We will reveal, the End-Times beast is extremist Islamic radicals, whose only goal is to destroy cultures, and subdue nations. We will reveal how the Islamic beast is living many precepts of what Israel should be doing. Once you know the end-times beast you no longer will fear the the fourth beast of prophet Dani'el (Dan 7:7), or his hordes, and you will be prepared to deal with them, with full preparation both for the work of the Torah, and for defense when attacked. We will also show how the other corrupted religions, masquerading as truth, will link into the end-times beast.

Fit for purpose
A translation cannot just be any type of translation, it needs to be fit for purpose, and we believe this will do the job of restoration, while many others have fallen short. This is essentially a study resource, which will help many understand the deep, hidden secrets of YHWH's instructions. It does not contain everything; but it contains enough hints, footnotes and direct quotes, to help in many areas of study. Praise YHWH Elohim that the Rabbi Simon Altaf was chosen for this task, a man who has devoted his time, energy and finances in order that YHWH will open many blind eyes to see again. This is truly a privilege.

Style of Translation
Wherever possible we have used direct Hebrew, word for word translation, and where needed, we have adopted a thought for thought, or, paraphrase translation, so this is a mixed translation. It is not possible to produce a word for word translation in our ancient text. You can never take the Hebrew language and do a direct word for word translation. If anyone says that they have, this would be totally inaccurate, as a direct word for word translation will make no sense when retranslated to other languages of the world.

A case in point; when we say, Mah shalom-kha, which is masculine, these words are translated, **How are you;** but it actually is a <u>thought</u> translation, and not a **word for word** translation, because if you translate this as a word for word translation it becomes, **what peace yours**? However, the thought is, how are you? In Hebrew, the word **shalom** is used in a very wide category of words, so you can see if we translated this word for word, then some of the sentences would make no sense in another language. This would make no sense to any Westerner; but is easily understood by Hebrew people, hence why we have used direct word, and thought, both, to highlight what YHWH, the author of the scrolls, is trying to convey through a given piece of text.

In another instance in the Hebrew in Genesis chapter 30:2… if we read the literal Hebrew it says **Jacob's nose glowed against Rakhél**. What does this mean to a western brought up person? It does not mean he looked like a reindeer with love oozing out of his nose but it actually meant that Jacob was very angry with Rachel. Hopefully now you will appreciate the problems we face when we translate from one language to another, something is always lost.

There are also nuances of the language which cause us to choose words that best fit the criteria of translating the relevant passages. A word can have many meanings in ancient Hebrew, therefore you cannot translate the word the same way in each passage, sometimes you have to choose the meaning that best fits the context of the paragraph, and this has certainly been done in this instance to help the reader. An example of this is the Hebrew word **eretz** meaning earth. Now the word "earth" is not always translated into the "whole world," at times in the Hebrew language it can mean, "the world;" but at other times it is the "country," "the province," or, a "piece of ground." we have kept that in mind and done just that. We pray with expectation that you will thoroughly appreciate and enjoy the words of this translation. Baruch HaShem YHWH (Praise be to the name of YHWH). We have added words in italics for easier reading and to clarify things, where it is not clear what the terms are. The italics are usually added words.

Cultural Background
Our people have been a lost sheep, wandering from country to country, city to city, being called names. Also their shepherds have simply tried to devour them with the bad translations and lawless gentile religions being kept by these leaders, who have been taking their money under the guise of tithes, which only rightly belong to the Kahuna (priesthood). They replaced YHWH and his priests with Jesus and his twelve disciples. This way they removed the truth from our people. Our people if they wish to be restored must reject this theology and return to the Torah.

Rabbi Simon Altaf HaKohen ben Eli ben Yosef ben Levi was brought up a Muslim understanding South-Asian, African and middle-eastern cultures, and it was in his 35th year, that YHWH called him to his rightful position in the priesthood of Israel, and so, being in that culture made it a Lot easier for the Rabbi to explain many concepts foreign to others using the Eastern understanding that he has since Israel is a North East African nation, the Jewel of Africa.

I want to give thanks to nameless brothers and sisters for proofing the Hidden Truths Hebraic Scrolls, we changed the name from Abrahamic-

Faith Netzarim Hebraic Study Scriptures to the Hidden-Truths Hebraic Scrolls to allow even greater clarity in the Hebrew to be presented to the reader because we have really presented Hidden Truths that were hid for centuries but as the prophet Daniel said in Dan 12:4 …knowledge shall be increased. He was not talking about science but knowledge of our people who they are and our scriptures will come to a greater light. We are coming to the end of the age when the gentile nations will be punished for their sins against our people who they persecuted.

Seven Rules of Elder Hillel
We have used these where we felt the need to explain the writings.

1. **Kal 'V'chomer** – *Using light and heavy*
2. **G'Zerakh Shavah** - *Equivalent expressions*
3. **Binyan Abbah mikathub echad** – *Using a single text to build a family.*
4. **Binyab Abbah mishene kethubim** – *Using two or more text to Build up a family*
5. **Kelal uferat** - *The general and the particular*
6. **Kayotze bo mimekom akhar** – *Using similar passages to build an analogy.*
7. **Davar hilmad me'anino** – *Using the context of a passage to get the explanation.*

These rules which were already established in the first century, to make a point, using the rules of such as Kal'V'chomer. Devised by Gamli'el the grandson of Hillel, best known for the School of Hillel are used to interpret our scrolls, we can gain much understanding when using these rules to understand the Tanak.

Rabbinic customs, S'yag, minhagim, Gezorot, Techonot and Ma'aseh Ha Torah
Contrary to popular opinion, rabbinic oral laws, and customs, which were established a long time ago and quoted in the writings are important for our learning. The prayer in Hebrew for meals is commanded to be said at the end of the meals; but there is a custom to say the short prayer before meals such as the ha motzi Lekhem min ha eretz prayer.

The Christians sometimes wear tzitzits and tallits so where did they learn how to wear these? These also come from different Hebrew traditions. Christians read the King James Version text that has many traditional readings in it but they do not know the traditional readings were taken from Judaism. What these are such as how some words are pronounced in the Hebrew are actually pronounced differently because of Hebrew traditions and they happily read them in the English without knowing the Hebrew underneath is not necessarily exactly as they have just read the words. Note the rabbinic literature such as the Talmud, Zohar and Mishnah are not inspired and not Scripture.

PRDS - Correct way to interpret the writings

It is important that we read the writings correctly to get its deeper message. The way to read the writings is as follows, with the acronym PRDS, or Pardes.

> ➢ [**P**]ashat   *simple*
> ➢ [**R**]emez   *hint*
> ➢ [**D**]rash   *search, allegory*
> ➢ [**S**]od   *hidden*

The first principle is **Pashat**, which means, read it literally, or, the literal principle. The second is **Remez,** meaning implied, or, hints, which means that the text has a deeper meaning that may not be immediately apparent.

> **Devrim 27:26** Cursed be he that confirmeth not **ALL THE WORDS OF THIS TORAH TO DO THEM**. And all the people shall say, Amen.

Now we can understand who would be cursed! Those are cursed who do NOT obey **the Torah, or those bent on obeying man-made laws to** attain **eternal rescue!**

The third rule is **Drash,** which means it is allegorical, typological, or, the homiletical meaning of the writings, almost like searching the scrolls for application of the text.

Sod is the reference to the hidden meaning of the writings e.g.; the words, Babylon, have a literal and hidden meaning to something in our time. Bearing this in mind, we start to read the writings, with a fuller understanding, not dissecting the writings incorrectly, but rightly understanding the words of YHWH.

Having this knowledge we can start to read the writings with a Hebraic understanding, so we do not miss any important points and facts. The writings are written in a way that we could do interactive learning, by asking questions, and then receive the understanding through the Ruakh Ha Kodesh (Holy Spirit), She will give us understanding of the difficult passages of the scrolls of the Hebrews.

DSS
Dead Sea Scrolls-Tanak, found in the Judean wilderness near En-Gedi in several caves at Qumran. Written between 150 BCE-68 CE by the Essenes (Chesed, Chassidic believers), a sect who preserved these scrolls in clay jars. We have used the DSS reading where appropriate, so we go back to an earlier text, which is more accurate, and show the alternative reading. Some of these scrolls dated to the 3rd Century BCE.

LXX
The Septuagint, meaning seventy, is the Greek translation of the Hebrew Tanak, done around 275-246 BCE. We have used the readings of this translation where appropriate. Note the LXX was translated by seventy-two of the finest Rebbim six from each tribe into the Greek according to Aristeas. It is suggested by some such as a British Hebrew scholar of the

19th century Moses Gaster (M. Gaster, The Samaritans (London, 1925)) that the Septuagint was not translated in Alexandria but in Israel and then given over to the people of Egypt where it would be well received because it was translated by learned Rebbim in Israel. Note, only the Torah was translated and not the whole Tanak as attested and later it was corrupted by Pesudo Christians such as the Isa 7:14 virgin birth when no such virgin birth exists.

The language and style of writing confirms it was of Alexandrian origin though some of the material that the writing was written on could have been easily imported from Israel confirming a view that Hebrew people needed a translation in the Greek language for Greek speaking Hebrews that grew up in Alexandria thus there was a need to have this work done for the Synagogues in the Diaspora, which in our opinion places this firmly in the 3rd century BCE as per Aristeas. Some orthodox Hebrew scholars today contend that the only translation that was done at that time by the Rebbim was the Torah, the Hebrew Law but the rest of the books of the Tanak were translated later between the second and first century BCE. This view is true. There were various stages of the whole translation, first the Torah, then the prophets followed by the other writings. In actuality the Samaritan Torah has very good readings and is quite a reliable text.

Please be warned that the Septuagint has various versions since the time of its first translation going up to the fourth century CE. There is a debate raging on still whether the Masoretic text is more reliable or the Septuagint because sometimes we find divergent readings with minor differences in the one or the other. The words **"And let all the malakhim of Elohim prevail for him"** are missing from the reading of Devrim 32:43 in the Masoretic text but are present in the Septuagint reading, which would indicate that for whatever masorot (traditions) caused some to remove these verses whether Christian missionary activity or otherwise, please see this text in Deut 32.43.

Mishnah and the Talmud
These are our texts and we preserve them but they are not scripture nor inspired. The Mishnah was recorded by Judah Ha Nasi (the prince) in circa 200CE. He was a Righteous man who lived a pious Torah life. Like him we must do the same.

Kabbalah
The Kabbalah has often been twisted by Gentiles who have the least understanding of it. The study of Kabbalah is the mystical study of the God of Israel. However Rabbi Simon Altaf Hakohen highly discourages anyone to study the Zohar as its highly dangerous if you keep it in your homes and study it incorrectly, unless you know what you are doing. It can destroy families and kill people so be warned. If you want to get to study an interpretation of the Zohar. There are also some themes in the Zohar that are anti-Torah and concepts from Hindusim adopted by modern Judaism.

The Torah cannot be usurped and most people who start the Zohar studies veer off from the direction of the Torah and start chasing after the impossible. They forget the meaning of Torah and start on the quest to reincarnation, which is not a teaching for everyone but only given to those as punishment that the Elohim of Israel desires. This warning of the Kohen should not be taken lightly.

The Zohar was written by Rabbi Moses de Leon (Moshe Ben Shem-Tov) in Spain in the 13th century later made famous by Rabbi Isaac Luria, the Ari. The writings were made popular in the later periods. They are not sacred texts and must not be treated as such by the true House of Israel.

We have used the Sefirotic tree (which the ancient Rebbim used to show the different aspects of God, which otherwise are quite difficult to understand) the ten attributes, and where appropriate highlighted those which makes it very helpful to understand the writings. We fully discourage the study of Kabbalah, without Torah as the goal, and steer clear of the gentile practices or Judaism's idea of Kabalah which in some instances is anti-Torah just as Christianity is. We also advise those studying Kabbalah, to be Torah vigilant, obedient first and foremost to YHWH's ways and not stray right or left to gentile diversions. Those that tried to make the Zohar, Kabbalah popular in Africa such as Nigeria and Ghana miserably failed. Many people there who dabbled in Kabbalah died. Please take this warning seriously. The idea of the sefirot is only as an illustration purpose of God and nothing more. All the teachings that emerged from mystics such as Rabbi Isaac Luria unless they align with Torah and the prophets of Israel are to be rejected.

Sefer Enoch, Sefer Yashar and Jubilees
We will be illustrating where we find these relevant in passages of the scrolls, to illuminate your understanding. We believe these to be safe and sound works, and know they were extensively used in the early first century. If they used it safely then so can we. We have already produced a commentary based translation of the book of Yashar and the books of Khanokh (Enoch) which can be purchased at Amazon (www.amazon.com) or www.lulu.com. The book of Jubilees is also available from Amazon translated by Rabbi Simon Altaf.

Closing thoughts
The scrolls are a history of our people and what happened to them. Our goals and objectives are to reach the nations, the lost sheep of the House of Israel many in the East and West, and the House of Yahudah, with the everlasting Torah. Being a humble servant of YHWH, I dare not make the claim that I have it all together 100%, with the difficulty of the language, the changes of the structure over six thousand years, and the three stage change of the Hebrew language script, I feel I have made the best effort possible. As in any project I am certain there will be room for much improvement as more information becomes available. I feel we have done our best to provide as close to the actual text and thought as possible. May our Father in the Heavens forgive us and other co-labourers in this project for any mistakes made in ignorance, or deliberation of the text, as we have tried to avoid errors, being in fear and awe of YHWH.

Turning away from sin

Today, turning around from wickedness is available to all, and you can become the commonwealth of Israel right now by bowing your head to the Abbah YHWH, asking for forgiveness of your sins, and vow to obey His Torah, do the mikvah, pay the offering to the Kohen.

Two Jerusalem
The two opinions of Jerusalem's

The place where most Christians go today in Israel with the Mount of Olives, are not the actual places of 2000 years ago. There were historically two Jerusalems, one that the Amorites occupied and ruled situated upon Mountains and one that the Jebusites occupied and ruled surrounded by Mountains. While every year most people visit Israel completely innocuously not knowing the sites the tourist guides are showing them are not the sites of the real Jerusalem.

> **First Chronicles 11:4-5** And David and all Israel went to Yerushalim, which is Yebus; where the Yavusi were, the inhabitants of the land. **5** And the inhabitants of Yebus said to David, You shall not come here. Nevertheless David took the castle of Tsiyon, which is the city of David.

The ancient name of Jerusalem was Yebus which was inhabited by the Yebusi people and these people after they were expelled by King David ended up in Nigeria. This is the same place where the true city of King David is and Mount Tsiyon is there at the ancient site of Jerusalem. So the present locale for modern Jerusalem where the Muslims and Jews is not even the place as that is the place of the Amorites as it says they dwelled in a mountain and this modern Jerusalem is a upon a Mountain.

> **WeDavar (Num) 13:29** The Amaleki dwell in the land of the south: and the Khitee, and the Yavusi (Jebusites), and the Amoree, dwell in the mountains: and the Kanani dwell by the sea, and by the coast of Yardan (Jordan).

Note there is a distinct difference in which Mountains both the Yavusi and Amoree dwell in.

> **Yahushua 10:3-5** Wherefore **Adoni-zedek King of Yerushalim** sent to Khoham King of Khevron, and to Piram King of Yarmuth, and to Yaphia King of Lakish, and to Debir King of Eglon, saying, **4** Come up to me, and help me, that we may smite Gibeon: for it has made peace with Yahushua and with the children of Israel. **5** Therefore the five Kings of the Amoree, the King of Yerushalim, the King of Khevron, the King of Yarmuth, the King of Lakish, the King of Eglon, gathered themselves together, and went up, they and all their hosts, and encamped before Gibeon, and made war against it.

> **Yahushua 15:63** As for the **Yavusi the inhabitants of Yerushalim**, the children of Yahudah could not drive them out: but the Yavusi dwell with the children of Yahudah at Yerushalim to this day.

As can be seen the real Jerusalem was the place where the children of Yahudah dwelt and the second Jerusalem which was on the mountain where the Amorites and others dwelt.

> **Devrim (Deut) 1:20** And I said to you, you have come into the Mountain of the Amoree, which YHWH our POWER will give to us.

> Judges:1:8 Now the children of Yahudah had **fought against Yerushalim**, and had taken it, and smitten it with the edge of the sword, and set the city on fire.

> JERUSALEM (JUBUSI)-Not conqured by the chidlren of Israel until King David conquered it
> Yahushua:15:63 As for the **Yebusites, the inhabitants of Yerushalim, the children of Yahudah could not drive them out**: but the Yebusites dwell with the children of Yahudah at Jerusalem unto this day.

The Real Jerusalem was surrounded by Mountain so it has to be in a valley. The second Jerusalem was also conquered by the children of Israel however the first was never fully conquered by Yahudah.

> **Psalm 125:2** As the **mountains surround Yerushalim**, so YHWH is around his people from henceforth even forever.

The Second True Jerusalem was surrounded by Mountains.

> **Yahushua 15:63** As for the Yavusi the inhabitants of Yerushalim, the children of Yahudah could not drive them out: but the Yavusi dwell with the children of Yahudah at Yerushalim to this day.

The next question should be when you go Israel to look at Mount Tsiyon look carefully it has no fields adjacent to it yet, YHWH tells us, it should be ploughed down as a field and the Temple destroyed and become a heap.

The following has never happened to the present day site called Jerusalem but has happened to the Jerusalem King David conquered and it is still a heap to this day with fields.

> **Micah 3:12** Therefore shall Tsiyon for your sake be plowed as a field, and Yerushalim shall become heaps and the mountain of the house as the high places of the forest.

Present day Mount Tsiyon according to present view of Christendom and Israel, however is it ploughed like a field? There are no fields even remotely close so this indicates this is not the true site. I hope the point is clear. For more see the HTHS Compendium Guide.

Ploughed fields in Tel Arad as prophesied still seen in 2014. The site of true Jerusalem is in the south of Israel.

My prayer to the Abbah in the shamayim is this;

Our forefathers transgressed your Torah, broke the Covenants, which were meant to give life but instead we received death. We cannot deny the lawlessness committed both by our ancestors who were unrighteous. We agree we all transgressed your Torah not knowing our limits, not understanding the great God we served but your punishment was just and Righteous. Abbah YHWH forgive Kol Israel because you made a promise with our father King Solomon that if we turn away from our sins and seek your face, your Torah (Second Chronicles 7:14) that you will restore us back to health and back to our land. We look to seek and serve you and obey your Torah. We turn away from our sins and ask for your abundant loving-kindness. We beseech your promise to Rescue us as we have now

Footnotes
[1] http://en.wikipedia.org/wiki/File:Jerusalem_Dormitio_Church_BW_1.JPG

come to a point of understanding. We await the restoration of all of our people everywhere called Israel and also called by the name of Abraham, Ytshak and Jacob. The nations have humiliated us, taken our land, cast us out, called us names and even slandered us. Our men, women and children have been killed, persecuted for just being your people to be called 'Chosen' and 'Holy.' Those of our people who are still rebellious to this day may you deal with them as your said in your holy words.

Gather us in our coming days soon we have suffered enough punishment and humiliation in the nations return us back to our promised land given to our Abbah Abraham, Isaac and Jacob. Amen.

Additions to the Law in 2018 and beyond until our Restoration
Additions to the Book of the Law known as Sefer Torah but in actuality it begins from Exodus 19 when Moses asended upon the Mountain to recieve the law.

   Devrim 4:44 And this is the Torah which Mosheh (Musa) set before the children of Israel:

   Devrim 31:9 And Mosheh (Musa) wrote this Torah, and gave it to the kohenim the sons of Lewi, which carried the ark of the Covenant of YHWH, and to all the elders of Israel.

It is quite clear to us that just as in Moses's time after his death he was not able to complete the book of the law but his student the next commander of Israel through the Levites added to the law of Moses and you can read about this in Yahoshua chapter 24.

   Yahoshua 24:22-26 And Yehoshua said to the people, You are witnesses against yourselves that you have chosen YHWH, to serve him. And they said, We are witnesses.
   23 Now therefore put away, said he, the strange powers which are among you, and incline your heart to YHWH the Supreme One of Israel.
   24 And the people said to Yehoshua, YHWH our POWER will we serve, and his voice will we obey.
   25 So Yehoshua made a Covenant with the people that day, and set them a statute and an ordinance in Shkhem.[1]
   26 And Yehoshua wrote these words in the scroll of the Torah of Elohim, and took a great stone, and set it up there under an oak that was by the sanctuary of YHWH.

This needed to be added and was added in Yahoshua's time as the situation arose that some people of Israel were still carrying the false idols they worshipped in Egypt.

Hence why from time to time there may be a season when we have new things coming out like planes, trains, automobiles, robotics, new technology

Footnotes
[1] It's obvious that Christendom knows nothing about this Covenant that Joshua made else they would also be serving YHWH.

that we may need to add a law as to how the people behave and live with that aspect in their life.

Its not just for anyone to make that change but that change can only be made by the teachers of YHWH, and who are these?

> **Devrim (Deuteronomy) 21:5** And the kohenim the sons of Lewi shall come near; for them YHWH Your POWER has chosen to speak to him, and to **Benefit** in the name of YHWH; and by their word shall every controversy and every stroke be tried:

> **Malalchi 2:4-7** And you shall know that I have sent this commandment to you, that my Covenant will continue WITH LEWI, says YHWH of Armies.
> **5** My Covenant will continue with him for life and shalom; and I gave them[1] to him[2] for the fear wherewith he feared me, and was afraid before my name.[3]
> **6** Torahs[4] of truth will continue in his mouth, and iniquity was not found in his lips: he walks with me in shalom and equity, and did turn many away from idolatry.[5]
> **7** For the kohen (priest's) lips should Guard knowledge, and they should seek the Torah from his mouth: for he is the teacher from YHWH of Armies.

The only Kadosh, set apart Ministers of YHWH are the Levites in 2018 and beyond. It is them that can add to the laws that will be needed today and beyond. No other man from the street or no other tribal members of Israel are allowed to change the laws unless a levite is present and ordains it.

The Covenants are sealed and cannot be added to or subtracted from but the laws that were given to Moses were left open ended as Moses did not finalize them and neither did Yahoshua ben Nun. Hence no matter what someone else tells you they remain open ended to allow freedom to our people and are not rescinded nor done away.

Your humble servant chosen and called by your favour.

Rabbi Simon Altaf HaKohen Beyth Tzadok

(Nasi) Coordinator and head
Forever-Israel International Qahalim (Congregations) – Hidden Truths unleashed but can you handle it? His Kohanim are the voice

Footnotes

[1] The Lewites.

[2] Israel

[3] Many from the sons of Tzadok feared YHWH and serve Him trustworthily to this day even in the dispersion.

[4] Oral and written Torah.

[5] The Hebrew word Avon here is for idolatry such as bowing to stones, trees and images fashioned by hand.

of YHWH but many of you have neither sought the Kohen, nor respected them. Those of you who rejected them have rejected the Abbah and will NEVER enter Eretz Israel.

Barukh Shem ke'vod mal'khuto l'olam va'ed
Blessed be the Name of His glorified kingdom for ever and ever

The Sefirotic Attributes of Elohim

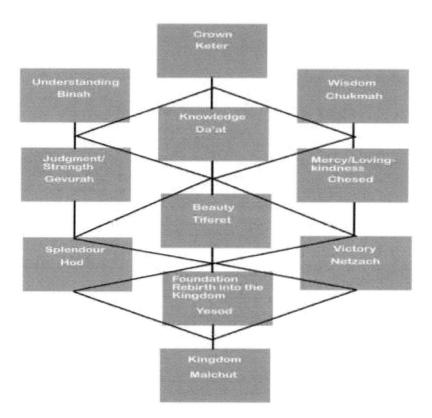

The Sefirotic Diagram

Torah Prayers

The person who is called up to read the Torah, touches the Torah scroll with his tzitzits or corner of his tallit, or the belt or mantle of the Torah and kisses it. He would then begin to read the brachot (Blessings of EL YHWH) bowing down at the word '**Bless**' Baruku and straightening up at YHWH's name.

Hebrew:
ברכו את יהוה המברך
Blessed are you YHWH, the one who Blesses us.

Hebrew:
ברוך יהוה המברך לעולם ועד
Translation:
Blessed is YHWH, the Blessed one, for all eternity.

Hebrew:
ברוך אתה יהוה אלהינו מלך
בנו מכל העמים ונתן לנו את העולם אשר העולם אשר בחר
תורתו ברוך אתה יהוה ונתן
התורה אמנ
Translation:
Blessed are you YHWH, our Supreme One, King of the universe, Who selected us from all the peoples and gave us His Torah. All knees bend to You, YHWH, Giver of the Torah. Amen.

Hebrew:
ברוך אתה יהוה אלהינו מלך העולם אשר נתן לנו תורת אמת וחיי עולם נטע בתוכנו ברוך
אתה יהוה נותן התורה אמנ
Translation:
Blessed are you YHWH, our Supreme One, King of the Universe, Who gave us the Torah of truth and implanted eternal life within us. Blessed are you, YHWH, Giver of the Torah. Amen.

Ahava Prayer
It is with great love that you love us, Oh YHWH (Hashem) our POWER. With great and abundant compassion, that you have mercy upon us, Our King. For the sake of our forefathers that trusted in you, and to whom you did teach the laws of life, the Torah. Be gracious to us and teach us truth. Our Merciful Father, the Compassionate One, be merciful to us and make our hearts to gain sense to hear to learn to teach to do and to fulfill with love all the words of instruction of Your Torah. Enlighten

our eyes to Your Torah and cause our hearts to cling to Your commandments. Allow our hearts to love and to endear your name that we should never be brought to shame, because we trust in your Qadosh, revered and wonderful name. We shall rejoice and be glad in our rescue. Bring us together from the four corners of the earth, Blessed are you, YHWH (Hashem), who chooses His people Israel, with love. Thank you for hearing our prayers.

Barukh Shem ke'vod mal'khuto l'olam va'ed
Blessed be the Name of His **glorified kingdom forever and ever**

Creation in Africa, the Creation of the first Red/Black man Called Ahdahm and the wayward wife Lilith

The First Book of Mosheh (Musa)

Beresheeth (Genesis)

בראשית

The Book of Beginnings

Torah Parsha 1 Beresheeth
Beresheeth 1:1-6:8
Haftarah: Yeshayahu (Isaiah) 42:5-43:21

Beresheeth Bara[1] Elohim[2] Alef-Tav[12] ha shamayim v'et ha eretz

Footnotes
[1] The Hebrew word **Bara** can only be used for creation by YHWH. Here all the world including the sun, moon and stars were created in the first day, but the sun and moon were hidden to be called out later on day 4.
[2] The Hebrew word Elohim is spelled with five characters; and here refers to the first five books of Torah when He powerfully revealed Himself to the Patriarchs and nation of Israel. The number five is the number of favor, so YHWH revealed His favor in and through the Torah for all who will obey it. Each character of His title reveals an aspect of the Ein Sof, the great Master of the Universes. See Gen 1:1 footnote at the rear appendix.
The word Elohim is used to describe judgment and justice this is crucial to understand, while the name YHWH is used to describe the merciful side of the Most High and Yasha the saving Arm but where did the saving Arm come from?

YHWH means typological meaning is "mercy" SO wherever you see the word YHWH
Continued in next section

written it means the Creator is revealing his merciful side or Khesed (loving-kindness) that is on the left side of the Most High when we look at it. When Adam and everything else was created it says by necessity Created Elohim (meaning He established a Court), Bara Elohim. This is why the Most High did not reveal himself as anything but Elohim. He hid himself basically. So while everyone is trying to fit their prophet and God as the saviour, Our El hid himself. He concealed himself. Adam was not shown who Elohim is. Remember Elohim is the COURT. Adam did not meet the whole court. Elohim is a plurality of attributes of the sefirot revealed in different forms.

.... THE LORD GOD [MADE EARTH AND HEAVEN]. This may be compared to a king who had some empty glasses. Said the king: ' If I pour hot water into them, they will burst; if cold, they will Covenant [and snap]. ' What then did the king do? He mixed hot and cold water and poured it into them, and so they remained [unbroken]. Even so, said the Holy One, Blessed is He: ' If I create the world on the basis of mercy alone, its sins will be great; on the basis of judgment alone, the world cannot exist. Hence I will create it on the basis of judgment and of mercy, and may it then stand!' Hence the expression,' THE LORD GOD. (Midrash Rabbah - Genesis XII:15)

Woe to the wicked who turn the Attribute of Mercy into the Attribute of Judgment. Wherever the Tetragrammaton ['Lord] is employed it connotes the Attribute of Mercy, as in the verse, The Lord, the Lord God, merciful and gracious (Ex. XXXIV, 6), yet it is written, And the Lord saw that the wickedness of man was great (Gen. VI, 5), And it repented the Lord that he had made man (ib. 6), And the Lord said: I will blot out man (ib. 7). Happy are the righteous who turn the Attribute of Judgment into the Attribute of Mercy. Wherever Elohim (God) is employed it connotes the Attribute of

Continued in next section

Beresheeth (Genesis)

1 In the beginning Elohim/Powers[3] created the shamayim and the land.

2 The land was desolate, and chaotic; and darkness was on the face of the deep. And the Ruakh of Elohim/Powers (Holy Spirit) was fluttering over the face of the mayim.

3 And Elohim/Powers said, Light be; and light was.

4 And Elohim/Powers saw the light that it was good; and Elohim/Powers separated[4] the light from the darkness.

5 Elohim/Powers called the light Day,[5] and the darkness He called Night. So the evening and the morning were Yom Akhad (Day one).

6 And Elohim/Powers said, Expanse be in the middle of the mayim, and divide the mayim (waters) from the mayim (waters).

7 Thus Elohim/Powers brought about the expanse, and divided the mayim which were under the expanse from the mayim which were above the expanse: and it was done.

8 And Elohim/Powers called the expanse shamayim.[6] So the evening and the morning were Yom Shanee (Day two).

9 And Elohim/Powers said, Let the mayim under the shamayim be collected together into one place, and let the dry land appear; and it was so.

10 And Elohim/Powers called the dry land Earth; and the

Judgment: Thus: Thou shalt not revile Elohim- God (Ex. XXII, 27); the cause of both parties shall come before Elohim-God (ib. 8); yet it is written, And Elohim heard their groaning, and Elohim remembered His Covenant (ib. II, 24); And Elohim remembered Rachel (Gen. XXX, 22); AND ELOHIM REMEMBERED NOAH. (Midrash Rabbah - Genesis XXXIII:3).

Footnotes

[1] This is the signature of the Abbah in the ein-sof, the middle pillar, Yahushua who is YHWH upon the earth and came many times in the guisse of the angel of YHWH, is the place of balancing mercy and judgment, as related to the sefirot, as Alef-Tav את. This is not translated in Hebrew, as it declared the first prophecy of the revelation of the Abbah who is the Alef, coming on the scene, who became personified as YHWH when light was retracted to allow creation to be made. He is mentioned in Mishle (Proverbs) 30:4, Dan 3:25, as an interface between us and the Abbah.

[2] Also picture of the Father and the Son Master Yahushua.

[3] Our Creator is a plurality of the sefirot, ultimately lights unseen.

[4] The drash reference to separating His righteous ones from those wicked by the hand of Elohim.

[5] Note the Hebrew day begins with **sunrise** and this does not define a sunset day, which was established during the Greek reign. This simply shows you how the night is married to the day but is a separate part called "darkness" and in the Hebrew Khoshek. and ends at sunset. A clear drash of troubles in our life followed by the brilliant light of King Messiah still to come and rejoicing in the Millennium. The custom day began at sunset to sunset which came into affect after the Greeks invaded Israel and imposed their law on the people. Their day began sunset to sunset model. The Babylonian day began sunrise to sunrise. The Temple services only occurred sunrise and never sunset. The present sunset to sunset Sabbath model is modern and not ancient. This is why normal ritual uncleanness finishes at sunset see Lev 11:25. The sunset defines end of the Yom (Day light).

[6] So there were two shamayim. The rakeayah was also called shamayim.

collecting together of the mayim He called Seas: and Elohim saw that it was good.

11 And Elohim/Powers said, Let the earth bring forth grass, the herb that yields zera (seed), and the fruit etz (tree) that yields fruit according to its kind, whose zera (seed) is in itself, upon the earth: and it was so.

12 And the earth brought forth grass, the herb that yields zera (seed) according to its kind, and the etz (tree) that yields fruit, whose zera (seed) is in itself, according to its kind: and Elohim/Powers saw that it was good.

13 So the evening and the morning were Yom Shilishi[1] (Day three).

14 And Elohim/Powers said, Let there be lights in the expanse of the shamayim to divide the day from the night; and let them be for signs, for *the* Moe'dim (celebrations: Appointed times),[2] and for days and years:

15 And let them be for lights in the expanse of the shamayim to give light upon the earth: and it was so.

16 And Elohim/Powers appointed[3] and brought forth two great lights; the greater light to rule the day, and the lesser light to rule the night the stars.

17 Elohim/Powers set them in the expanse of the shamayim to give light on the earth,

18 And to rule over the day and over the night, and to divide the light from the darkness: and Elohim/Powers saw that it was good.

19 And the evening and the morning were Yom Ravee (Day four).

20 And Elohim/Powers said, Let the mayim abound with an abundance of living creatures, and let birds fly above the earth across the face of the expanse of the shamayim.

21 And Elohim/Powers created great sea creatures,[4] and every living thing that moves, with which the mayim abounded, according to their kind, and every winged bird according to it's kind:[5] and Elohim/Powers saw that it was good.

22 And Elohim/Powers allotted an **Increase** for them, saying, Be fruitful, and multiply, and fill the

Footnotes

[1] Note YHWH does not give significance to the first six days, while He places the seventh day above all by giving it a name. Whereas before they were just ordinal values such as day 1, day 2 and day 3; meaning not all days are made equal.

[2] YHWH's calendar existed before man was created and is eternal because the Malakhim were observing and bound by Torah long before Adam was created. YHWH judged the first sin in the shamayim, where Satan was found with sin using the Torah. The Malakhim keep the celebrations in the Temple above. The weekly Sabbath is not determined by the lunar calendar but by the solar calendar.

Footnotes

[3] The Hebrew word here is not for the creative sense; as the sun and moon were created in Beresheeth 1:1, and were yet hidden from the eye. Therefore they were brought forth.

[4] This included within the category dinosaurs.

[5] Everything according to its kind, a dog will be a dog and a cat will be a cat, you do not get a half dog and a half cat as an animal. Evolution is foolish wisdom of gentiles, trying to do away with the Creator.

mayim in the seas, and let birds multiply on the earth.

23 So the evening and the morning were Yom Khamishee (Day five).

24 And Elohim/Powers said, Let the earth bring forth the living creatures according to their kind, cattle, and crawling things and beasts of the earth, each according to their kind: and it was so.

25 And Elohim/Powers brought forth the beasts of the earth according to their kind, cattle according to their kind, and everything that crawls on the earth according to their kind: and Elohim saw that it was good.

26 And Elohim/Powers said, Let Us make humans in Our image,[1] according to Our likeness: Let them have dominion over the fish of the sea, over the birds of the air, and over the cattle, over all the earth, and over every crawling thing that crawls on the earth.

Ahdahm and the First Woman Lilith created in Uganda from the Nilotic Red dust[2]

27 And Elohim/Powers created Ha-Ahdahm in their own image,[3] in the image[4] of Elohim/Powers created; male and female [5] created them.

Footnotes

[1] Word is plural in Hebrew.

[2] Even today some Ugandan women are fierece women and uncontrollable. They want freedom to rule their own lives.

[3] Plural, created Adam from the red dust so he was red/brown African descent from the Nile delta of the Nilotic earth.

[4] plural

[5] A man and woman were created here and at this point they were outside the Garden of Continued in next section

28 And Elohim/Powers allotted an **Increase** upon them, and Elohim/Powers said to them, Be fruitful, and multiply,[6] fill the earth,

Eden. The Hebrew word 'Adamah' means earth and not red as many have ascribed to it. The Chadic word 'dham' also means 'blood' and is associated with the dham/earth, because man was created from it. Red Earth mixed with the water and the first common ancestor of mankind was a red/brown dust man in Africa or brown colour. From him come all different races of people only possible if he was black/red or brown/red, the colour white does not produce all races. Sir Isaac Newton proved through the spectrum theory that only the black colour produces all colours.

The first woman that was created with Ahdahm was Lilith for his wife. Note both were created from the red ground, Lilith was animated by the vapour see note Gen 2:6, while Khawa his second wife (Patriarchal wife) was created from Ahdahm's side. Lilith was created in Uganda alongside Ahdahm. The first woman became rebellious to her husband and ran away by using the Holy name of Elohim, which then brought the need to create the second woman for Ahdahm. This was the first sign of the North/South axis of the two wives in Patriarchal marriage, which all our ancestors followed, which was the pattern later adopted by Abraham's ancestors who were Khuri from Seno/Gambia. Lilith ended up in the south, the creation took place in Africa while Khawa was created in the North region of Israel in Jerusalem. Israel was part of the African continent and not in Middle-East, which is a modern derivative word. At that time the whole land was very fertile, which today has become the Sahara and the Arabian Wilderness. YHWH made it desolate because of the sin. Wherever there is oil and coal today it can be proved that it was once very fertile. Note coal/oil produced from trees that were buried during the flood and compressed together, diamonds also come from coals. This is evidence of a fertile landmass.

[6] The first commandment for all of us is to bear children for Israel. Deliberately suppressing children is a sin. There is a hint here of Patriarchal polygamy. Many children Continued in next section

and subdue it: have dominion over the fish [1] of the sea, over the birds of the air, and over every living thing that moves on the earth.

29 And Elohim/Powers said, see, I have given you every herb that yields zera (seed), which is on the face of all the earth, and every etz (tree), whose fruit yields zera (seed); it shall be for you to use/consume.[2]

30 Also, to every beast of the earth, to every bird of the air, and to everything that crawls on the earth, in which there is life, I have given every green herb for use/consumption:[3] and it was so

31 And Elohim/Powers saw everything that had been made, and, indeed, it was very good. So the evening and the morning were Yom Ha Shishee (Day six).[4]

Chapter 2

1 Thus the shamayim and the earth were finished, and all the host of them.

2 And Elohim ceased from all work in the seventh day, because it was appointed as Yom Sabbath [5] (Day of rest) ceasing from all labour.[1]

---

cannot come from one wife. Some cultures have adopted plural marriages even today because it is in the design. The average children from one wife is five, and any over that starts to wear out the woman. Whichever we argue, it is a fact in our society, that when married women are made to bear, ten children, they end up with many illnesses due to over exertion of the body and die young. Some people can choose to remain Torah Monogamous this is permitted as long as they produce an heir.

[1] You are not going to have dominion over the earth with one child, this means extended families. The Muslims have done well to do just that, look at their numbers. While ancient Israel did heed this command but present day believers shy away from this. This pattern is being restored in the Patriarchal order as practiced by our forefathers.

[2] The Hebrew word Oklah is a feminine word, which means here to "use", any purpose and not just for food as all plants that have poison can be used for topical medicinal purposes, not food and others for eating. To consume does not necessary mean to eat, you can "consume" a poultice by applying it to your body, as the body consumes it to be healed of some problem.

[3] Herbs are used to make medicines so that is a "USE". We don't eat all herbs by Continued in next section

cooking, we use some for coloring, others for eating, etc.

[4] The ancient Hebrew here has an extra Heh, which according to our sages gives only the 6th day the reference of "The Sixth Day." This was understood to mean that YHWH was waiting on the 6th Day and made it special because on it He gave the Torah at Mount Sinai on Shavuot, which always falls on the 6th of Sivan. All Hebrew authorities agree that this was a Sabbath. However some opinions differ and it is believed that the Torah was given on the 7th of Sivan.

[5] The common misunderstanding is that the Roman Catholics changed the Sabbath from Saturday to Sunday; however this is not true, here is a text showing us just that. The Catholic Cardinal Gibbons, in Faith of Our Fathers, pg. 111, said, 'You may read the Bible from Genesis to Revelation, and you will not find a single line authorizing the sanctification of Sunday. The Scriptures enforce the religious observance of Saturday, a day which we (The Roman Catholic Church) never sanctify.

The first person known through historical evidence to reject the Sabbath and worship away from it was Marcion of Sinope, after which the second recorded case of usurping the authority of the Jerusalem overseers was Ignatius, popularly known as St. Ignatius, who annulled the Sabbath to Sunday worship. The idea here is not that YHWH needed rest, but that He ceased from all creative work. This shows a picture of the future redemptive work. In this first Sabbath Continued in next section

3 And Elohim allotted an **Increase**[2] upon the 7th Day, and set it apart[3] calling it Yom Shabbat: (Sabbath Day of rest)[4] because that in it he had ceased from all his work which Elohim created and that needed to be made.

4 These are the generations of the shamayim and of the earth[5] when they were created, in the day that YHWH Elohim made the earth and the shamayim,

בהבראם [6]

we ultimately see a remez hint of the Day of Tabernacles. We see this millennial reign to come in Zecharyah 14:17.
[1] Note, there is no night so the drash (allegory) also points to the seventh day meaning the Millennial reign.
[2] All those who come for glorying El Yah on the Sabbath will also be **Increased** as this day is set and appointed for increasing the men and women under YHWH.
[3] All days of the week are not equal; the Sabbath has the highest status. The typical petty talk of everyday is the same is wisdom of the foolish. While the Sabbath needs to be exalted as it is the remez of the everlasting, 'rest' and 'rescue'. YHWH hears people's prayers on this day.
[4] The word Shabbat in the ancient Hebrew is spelt with two shins so it is Shin + shin plus bet + Tav. שׁשׁבת

In the most ancient pictograph this means Shabbath or daughter of the sun connected with the sunrise. The shin is the symbol for the sun. Bet for a House and tav for the tree. The ancients preserved this by a diacritical mark of the double daggesh in the Bet. This clearly proves that the Sabbath was associated with the sun and not the moon as per erroneous lunar theories.
[5] This is a clear hint at one creation of Adam (earth and his seed) and the other hint of shamayim of the air (Lilith and the demons she beget). Elohim is showing the separation one of Eloah and one of Satan.
[6] The Heh, in the word create, which is underlined, is lowered in the original
Continued in next section

5 And every plant of the field before it was in the Adamah (ground), and every herb of the field before it grew: for YHWH Elohim had not caused it to rain[7] upon the Adamah/ground, And Ahdahm was not to be a servant to the Adamah (woman).[8]

Hebrew, signifying that a fall had occurred after creation, Satan rebelled, and was the first into sin. The heh here is for the creature Satan, who fell and was lowered from his place. Also the Heh is a hidden veiled expression for Lilith, the first woman since heh is feminine, she was the animation of Satan from the demonic dust that animated her.
[7] Humans had not seen rain until the time of the flood of Noah.
[8] The mist that arose was a special kind of mist within which Lilith was animated and became demonically possessed. Anything out of the ground including Lilith the first woman was not to be served by Adam. Later Khawa and other wives of Adam were created from his side bones, Adam is the only creature from the ground that was created in Elohim's image by His breath.

At the same time YHWH created Adam, he created a woman, Lilith, who like Adam was taken from the earth. She was given to Adam as his wife. But there was a dispute between them about a matter that when it came before the judges had to be discussed behind closed doors. She spoke the unspeakable name of Jehovah and vanished.

http://www.bitterwaters.com/Lilith_in_Zohar.html
Zohar 1:19b (Bereshit: Passages 98-101)
98 And Elohim said let there be me'orot (lights) in the expanse of heaven (Ge 1:14). Me'orot is spelled deficiently as me'erat (meaning to curse), thus diphtheria was created for children. After the radiance of primordial light was treasured away, a shell was created for the kernel (of light). That shell expanded, generating another shell. Emerging, she ascended and descended, arriving at the small faces. She desired to cling to them, be portrayed in them, and never depart. The bless Holy One separated her form there, bringing her down below
Continued in next section

6 But there went up a vapour[1] from the earth, and caused to

when he created Adam, so that this would be perfected in this world.

99 As soon as she saw Eve cleaving to the side of Adam, beauty above, as soon as she saw the complete image, she flew away, desiring as before to cleave to the small faces. Those guardians of the gates on high did not allow her. The blessed Holy One rebuked her and cast her to the bottom of the sea.

100 She dwelled there until Adam and his wife sinned. Then the blessed Holy One plucked her form there, and she rules over all those children – small faces of humanity – who deserve to be punished for the sins of their fathers. She flies off, roaming through the world. Approaching the earthly Garden of Eden, she sees cherubs guarding the gates of the Garden, and she dwells there by that flaming sword (Ge 3:24), for she emerged from the side of that flame.

101 As the flame revolves she flees and roams the world, finding children who deserved to be punished. She toys with them and kills them. This happens in the waning of the moon, whose light diminishes; this is me'orot (lights) deficient.

Zohar 2:xxx (Vayikra : Passages 316-317)
316. Come and see: In a hole by the great, supernal abyss, there is a certain female, a spirit above all spirits. We have explained that its name is Lilit. She was first with Adam. When Adam was created and his body perfected, a thousand spirits came on the body from the left side. This one wanted to enter it and that one wanted to enter it, but they could not. The Holy One, blessed be He, scolded them. Thus, Adam lay down spiritless, green in appearance, with all those spirits around him. 317. At that time, a cloud descended and pushed aside all the spirits (which surrounded Adam). ...

Zohar 1:148a-148b (Vayetze: Passage 23)
A deep mystery is found in the strength of Yitzchak's light, and from the dregs of wine. One shape emerged (from both), made of male and female (Good and Evil), as one. The male is called "Samael", and his female is always included with him. Just as on the side of holiness there are male and female, so on "the other side" there are male and Continued in next section

female, included one with the other. The female of Samael is called "snake", "a wife of harlotry", "the end of all flesh", "the end of days". Two evil spirits are attached to one another. The male spirit is fine, the female spirit spreads out down several ways and paths, and is attached to the male spirit.

Zohar 2:xxx (Pekudei: Passage 454)
When Adam was in the Garden of Eden and was occupied in worshipping his Master, Samael went down with all the grades in him, and was riding on the evil serpent to deviate them. As the serpent underneath was subtle, and led astray and seduced people, as it is written, "For the lips of a strange woman drip honey, and her mouth is smoother than oil" (Mishlei 5:3). He gives power and she practices the art (of seduction and instigation) in the world, and they cannot rule the one without the other.

http://witcombe.sbc.edu/eve-women/7evelilith.html
In the Apocryphal Testament of Reuben (one of the Testaments of the Twelve Patriarchs, ostensibly the twelve sons of Jacob), for example, it is explained that:

Women are evil, my children: because they have no power or strength to stand up against man, they use wiles and try to ensnare him by their charms; and man, whom woman cannot subdue by strength, she subdues by guile.

(Testament of Reuben: V, 1-2, 5)
References to Lilith in the Talmud describe her as a night demon with long hair (B. Erubin 100b) and as having a human likeness but with wings (B. Nidda 24b). In Rabbi Isaac ben Jacob ha-Kohen's "Treatise on the Emanations on the Left," written in Spain in the 13th century, she is described as having the form of a beautiful woman from her head to her waist, and "burning fire" from her waist down. Elsewhere, Rabbi Isaac equates her with the primordial serpent Leviathan.

[1] The defiled vapour caused the animation of Lilith and she became the first wife. The breath of life was only put into Adam

water the complete face of the Adamah (woman).[1]

7 And YHWH Elohim formed Ha-Ahdahm of the dust of the ground, and breathed into his nostrils the breath of life;[2] and Ha-Ahdahm became a living soul.

8 And YHWH Elohim planted a Garden eastward in Ayden, and he led Ha-Ahdahm there whom he had formed. [3]

9 And YHWH Elohim transplanted[4] and caused to grow every etz (tree) that is pleasant to the sight, and good for food; the etz (tree) of life[5] also in the middle of the garden, and the etz (tree) of knowledge of good and evil.[6]

10 And a river (White Nile) goes out of Ayden to water the Garden; and from there it separated, and became four heads.[7]

11 The name of the first is Pishon: that is which is roundabout the whole land of Khavilah (Ancient India, Saudi Arabia and parts of Africa), where there is gold; [8]

Footnotes

[1] Unnatural vapour or a satanic form arose to water the face of Lilith, which caused her to be what she became. The Zohar says this was the defective light of Satan that animated Lilith with the defiling vapour. This was the first sotah (wayward wife) Lilith. Therefore Lilith is from filth and sediment and Adam is from Elohim of the dust without the vapour. See Numbers 5:24 where the same word used for watering is used for "to drink."

[2] Intrinsically this is the meaning of YHWH, 'breath of life', or 'light over the world,' since He is the life giver, it does not mean 'To be', that is a very late and modern meaning. Life enters through the nostrils and also leaves through the same passage. Adam was given life this way but not Lilith so she is not mentioned but received animation via the mist of the ground.

[3] This was not a small orchard but the Garden was created in West Africa and its boundaries ran from Africa to Israel because all the animals were in the Garden. The Garden was erected after the rebellion of Lilith, who ran away and Elohim turned her into a demoness (See Yeshayahu 34:11). The need for the Garden was to protect Ahdahm, Khawa including his other wives from the rebel malakhim who had descended to wreck creation in jealousy.

[4] Whole trees were transplanted from the shamayim upright in order to grow.

[5] Drash of the Torah, which has life.

Footnotes

[6] Both trees were signs one for the rebellion. The two trees were time shared so at any time only one tree would be visible in the middle of the Garden. The Torah tells us that both trees are in the middle at the same time, see Gen 3:3 also.

[7] The word Arba, shows us that these are going to be part of the territory of the End-Times Islamic beast. The word Arab is also a Kasdim word to mean mix, and represents, a desert roaming creature, applying to the Arab/Muslim people today, who will form a major destructive force in the 'End of Days'. All four rivers are in Islamic lands today, clearly showing us where the battle lines are drawn.

[8] Khavila incorporates India today's Pakistan. The river Pishon traveled from West Africa where the Garden had its beginnings and connected through Saudi Arabia which was in East Africa as one continent with Israel being in the same place of North-East Africa. At that time there was no Red Sea it was all one landmass. Arabia and Israel were part of that landmass called Africa today. The Pishon connected with the Nile running deep into South Africa connecting with other rivers. On the West it connected into Lake Chad which was very close to the Garden. See Gen 4:16. What does Elohim tell us here about Saudi Arabia? Saudi Arabia is the whore of Babylon, the name ascribed to the first woman rebel Lilith, who rebelled and ran away and hid in a cave here more correctly the cave at the heart of the mountain hence became the progenitor of demons as a punishment. This land mass is both of Saudi Arabia and West Africa. The Torah says the gold is good. Indeed many
Continued in next section

12 And the gold[1] of that land is good: there is bdellium[2] and the onyx stone.

13 And the name of the second river is Gihon (Blue Nile):[3] the same is that runs roundabout the whole land of Kush. (Sudan, south of the river Nile including Nubia, Ethiopia and parts of east Africa).

14 And the name of the third river is khidekel (Tigris): that is which goes toward the east of Ashshur.[4] (North Iraq – Mosul an area of Assyria). And the fourth river is Farat (Euphrates-Turkey)[5]

companies made a Lot of money here to dig gold, diamonds and other minerals. Why was the Mountain Sinai in Saudi Arabia? This is because it was within the Garden of Eden at one time, which spanned hundreds of miles. This is where the glory of YHWH descended to talk to the first man Ahdahm. Satan, later to cover the regions once occupied by the glory has established a new religion there and tried to pervert the way YHWH was petitioned in that landmass hence why many Muslims today pay homage to Allah there instead.

- Herodotus 5th century III.102: Besides these, there are Indians of another tribe, who border on the city of Caspatyrus, and the country of Pactyica; these people dwell northward of all the rest of the Indians, and follow nearly the same mode of life as the Bactrians. They are more warlike than any of the other tribes, and from them the men are sent forth who go to procure the gold. For it is in this part of India that the sandy desert lies. Here, in this desert, there live amid the sand great somewhat less than dogs, but bigger than foxes. The Persian king has a number of them, which have been caught by the hunters in the land whereof we are speaking. Those ants make their dwellings underground, and like the Greek ants, which they very much resemble in shape, throw up sand-heaps as they burrow. Now the sand which they throw up is full of gold. The Indians, when they go into the desert to collect this sand, take three camels and harness them together, a female in the middle and a male on either side, in a leading-rein. The rider sits on the female, and they are particular to choose for the purpose one that has but just dropped her young; for their female camels can run as fast

as horses, while they bear burdens very much better.

- The ants are known as Mountain ants and verified by a French historian Michel Peissel in Northern Pakistan region by the river Indus valley. The ancient ants are known today as Marmots that dig the gold and the people collect it.

-

[1] The natural gold, which is excellent in Saudi Arabia, including Africa and a remez (hint) of the black gold (crude oil), that was earmarked to come in the future, here in our time. This area is both East and West Africa.
[2] This is a special resin or gum from a tree; the best of which is found in Saudi Arabia. Although it is also found in India and Iraq.
[3] The name of the second river is Gihon: according to the Hebrew historian, Josephus Flavius. This is the name that the ancients called it. We do know the only river that passes Cush (Sudan) is the Blue Nile River. This is the same river that was called, Gi-haan, by the Ethiopians of old, and confirmed by Josephus. World war III – Unmasking the end times beast P126.
[4] The Assyrian Empire.
[5] The connection is made with the Islamic End-Times beast and Gog of the land of Magog, his country. Ezekiel 38:2.

Continued in next section

15 And YHWH Elohim led Ha-Ahdahm, and placed him into the Garden of Ayden to work and to guard it carefully.[1]

16 And YHWH Elohim commanded Ha-Ahdahm, saying, Of every etz (tree) of the garden, that you may freely eat:

17 But of the etz (tree) of the knowledge of good and evil, you shall not eat of it:[2] for in the day that you eat there you shall surely die.

18 And YHWH Elohim said, It is not good that Ha-Ahdahm had become alone;[3] I will make him a helper,[4] before him.[5]

19 And out of the ground YHWH Elohim formed every beast of the field and every fowl of the air; and brought them to Ahdahm to see what he would call them: and whatsoever Ahdahm called every living creature that was the name of them.[6]

20 And Ahdahm gave names to all cattle, and to the fowl of the air, and to every beast of the field; but for Ahdahm there was not found any helper[7] for him.

21 And YHWH Elohim caused a deep sleep to fall upon Ahdahm,

Footnotes

[1] This area was not an orchard; but an area that encompassed what is today's, two Jeruslems'. The Garden also encompassed the area of whole of Israel. The word 'Garden' is a bit misleading, because the Hebrew word 'gan' means a fenced-in area. It was an actual area of land given over to Adam to look after carefully and keep safe, as a trial and a test. Note he was put in the Garden showing the creation was outside the Garden in West Africa, the first Black man who was our ancestor. It is confirmed in many world cultures that they had Africans traveled there from which many races have come. This is true for India, China, Europe, USA, Latin America, Australia and many other nations. The reason why Adam was led to the Garden was because now there was a threat that Lilith had run away and Adam needed to be proteced from the fallen angels. Lilith had gone off and married Samyaza the fallen angel.

[2] When Lilith was first created she would have eaten of this tree of knowledge and evil to become more seditious and evil.

[3] Lilith the wayward wife had departed in rebellion.

[4] It is not good for him to be alone was said after Lilith ran away in rebellion and committed adultery with an angel it was then that the need for Adam, the second woman, Khawa, whom YHWH created for Adam, was to be a helper, and a companion, to be the strength of Adam, to be his side, Continued in next section and not a usurper. Many women today unfortunately are changing their roles to become, usurpers, which is contrary to their design.

[5] The Hebrew word Knegdo: can mean a counterpart, or an opposite, it also means "before him" as the new women were shown to Adam before even being created to be approved and not just one woman but more than one. This is a balanced role of patriarchal marriage where a woman cannot rule over a man as Lilith had tried to do. In the ancient Nun it means to "pour out" a clear implication of more than one wife. It is Rabbi Simon Altaf's opinion that he had a total of seven wives, one of them was Khawa but they were all called Ishah in Hebrew hence the confusion to think the text is always talking about Khawa is not the case. This aligns with the perfect model in Isa 4:1 during the millennium which arose from the Garden. The third, fourth woman was also created hinted at in the text.

[6] This included Adam giving Lilith a name, she too was called the Beast of the Field in Gen 3:1.

[7] Man was not designed to have a companion from the animal world but today most people are happy with their dogs but dogs and cats do not make helpers. In order to have a helper one must seek out a male or female according to prayer to YHWH that would be suitable for a person.

and he slept: and he took Akhat[1] of his side bones,[2] and closed up the flesh there;[3]

The Creation of Ahdahm's Second/Third wives Hawa, Ishah

22 And the side with the bone, which YHWH Elohim had taken from man, he made woman, and brought to the man.[4]

23 And Ahdahm said, at this reoccurrence,[5] This standing in front of my face is bones[6] of my bones,[7] and flesh of my flesh: she shall be called Ishah (woman),[8]

Footnotes

[1] Plural ending word for one is "akhat" versus singular ending word "Akhad." See Gen 1:9 where it is singular Akhad while here it is plural Akhat with a Tav ending instead of a dalet. It means man/husband can be united with more than one wife at one time.

[2] YHWH took Adam's SIDE, including his flesh, which can mean more than one rib. The same word is used in building the tent; Shemoth (Exodus) 26:20. One side of the tent consisted of twenty pieces of wood, therefore, we can not say with certainty, that it was a single rib. This is assumed by many; but simply presumptuous.

[3] Please see footnote Exodus 26:26.

[4] More than one woman brought, one at a time.

5 Ha'Paam in the ancient Hebrew hieroglyph has the character of the Heh, the Head for Peh, the Ayin to walk and Mem for plural waters, it means women standing in front of him. The Heh is not just a 'The' but "THESE" meaning more than one.

6 The Hebrew word in verse 22 צלעת for sides indicates plural planks as in the Ark of the Tent, and עצם bones, and not, a single bone. Those who argue, for a single rib, can not address the Hebrew language showing us, plural bones, which indicates the creation of more than one woman at the same time. Total of 7 wives.

7 מעצמ Bones, in other words more than one woman.

8 The same Hebrew word can also denote a wife or wives, so Adam could have been calling her his wife and not just a woman, Continued in next section

because she were taken out of her Husband.[9]

24 Therefore shall a man leave his Abbah and his eem (mother), and shall cleave to his wife: [10] and they shall be Akhad[1] flesh.

these were two women created here one which was placed in the North axis and the other which was placed in the south axis, see Genesis 12 and Genesis 25 for an explanation of the North and South meanings. The word Aysh means 'fire' or something 'hot' so the idea of a woman also envelopes her passion towards her husband. The shin character is also used in the name of the sun for shamesh hence the women are also the glory of the man. A man has to keep each wives heat/passion in control through a loving relationship. Polygyny was present in the Garden and those who hate it don't see here two women were created to avoid incest from the beginning. YHWH indeed does not change Mal 3:6, only the wise understand this. A brother and a sister who are from the same mother and father cannot marry, which is a sin but a brother and a sister from different wives of the same husband are allowed to marry as was Abraham and his wife from Tharakh's second wife see Gen 11:29 and Gen 20:12. Ruler priests always had two wives minimum.

9 Septuagint

[10] The Hebrew word ואת־אמו ודבק באשתו V'at amo V'debak B'Aishto (The last word the Vav is a yud so it should read V'ishtee, which applies to plural wives and not just a singular woman as the context of the verse in Gen 2:23 before this was plural Etzim (bones). We can use it in singular context only when the context is singular but the word Ishah is singular, while here Ishto is a plural word ending indicative of more than one. The scribes often changed the spelling of words due to personal feelings or they were just bad spellers, they were not always trained. Here the Strong's concordance will not tell you what word was changed. The Strong's has many errors. The word Isha in Hebrew generally means a wife or just a "woman." Here the word that is being argued about is V'Ishto but it should actually read V'Ishtee באשתי. So the spelling is switched. Hence it is a plural word for wives באשתי and not wife! Also note that Continued in next section

25 And they were both naked, the man and his wife,[2] and they were not ashamed.

Fall of Ahdahm and his wives by Ahdahm's first adulterous wife Lilith through Deception
Chapter 3

1 Now the serpent[3] had become more cunning[4] than any beast of the field which YHWH Elohim had made. And said to the woman, Also even though Elohim has said, do not eat of any etzim (trees) of the garden.[5]

2 And the woman said to the serpent, We may eat of the fruit of the etzim (trees) of the garden:

3 But of the fruit of the etz (tree) which is in the middle[6] of the garden, Elohim has said, You shall not eat of it, neither shall you touch it,[7] lest you die.

4 And the serpent said to the woman, You shall not surely[8] die:[9]

5 For Elohim does know that in the day you eat there, then your eyes shall be opened, and you shall be as Elohim, knowing good and evil.

6 And when the woman saw that the etz (tree) was good[10] for food, and that it was pleasant to her eyes, and an etz (tree) to be desired to make one wise,[11] she took of the fruit and ate, and she

Footnotes

sometimes a word even if spelled with a Wah cannot be read with a Wah but with a Yud or vice versa!

[1] One in unity

[2] All three of them had eaten so the same Hebrew language as before B'Aishto in other words more than one woman at least two wives. The ancient Hebrew does not lie telling us more than one.

[3] Not a snake but a beautiful soulish animal that resembled a human being called Lilith. This was Adam's first wife who had run away. She came back to destroy Adam's household succeeding in making them fall as her revenge.

[4] Lilith demonically possessed by Satan, she had eaten of the tree of knowledge and evil hence was cunning. She looked like a beautiful woman but was not a reptile but mammal that had intelligence like a human being. Note Satan was created very beautiful Ezek 28:12 and Lilith was the product of Satan. Hence, she was also beautiful as the vapour from the ground that had been used in her had made her animated, that was not by the hand of Elohim but Satan because the vapour of the ground was a watery substance that was impure.

[5] This is literal Hebrew and not a question.

[6] The area of Gethsemane.

[7] Khawa adds something that Elohim did not command. She broke the authority structure of the man without asking him first, so, Elohim brought her into line swiftly.

[8] Lilith pushed her against the tree and said; see you shall not surely die. She weakened the command that YHWH had given. This is how Christians are receiving a watered down message in the churches. They live in idolatry.

[9] She knew she was talking about the second death, while Khawa certainly could not have this knowledge. So she clearly did not understand the plan fully, Lilith used her ignorance to deceive her. This is how many people are deceived today due to lack of correct knowledge; they are led to believe that the person of Satan does not exist and there was only one woman in the Garden.

[10] The weakness caused by Lilith's doubt had set in now. The woman was now perceiving the tree with another set of eyes, it looked good while before it was not so good and since Lilith had eaten of the tree she could demonstrate nothing would happen to Khawa.

[11] This is worldly wisdom like getting a university degree, or college diploma. This wisdom will certainly help you in this world, but has no eternal value whatsoever. Satan made the woman crave worldly wisdom, opposed to wisdom of the shamayim, and we find all of Khawa's seed is chasing and craving for this type of wisdom.

also took fruit for her husband apart from herself and he also ate.[1]

7 And the eyes of them both were opened,[2] and they knew

that they were naked; and they sewed fig leaves together, and made themselves aprons.[3]

8 And they heard the thunder[4] of YHWH Elohim as he stepped[5] through the Garden in the cool of the day:[6] and Ahdahm and his wives[7] hid themselves from the face[8] of YHWH Elohim amongst the etzim (trees) of the garden.

9 And YHWH Elohim called to Ahdahm, and said to him, Where are you? [9]

Footnotes

[1] Adam was <u>not</u> standing there as popularly taught. He was somewhere else when this conversation was taking place. The woman took the fruit, ate it first, and then went to give it to him. The Hebrew says 'Gam l'ishah emah' meaning he was with her in unity plus another woman was there, and not that he was standing beside her on his own. She had been deceived by Satan through Lilith because the command of YHWH became doubtful instead of certain. Adam listened to her voice, meaning momentarily he forgot the voice (Torah) of YHWH; and because he was taught to love his wives, he fell by eating without asking questions first. Adam did not know the fruit was from this tree, this is evident in the text where Adam says to YHWH, the woman gave me the fruit and I ate. He had two wives so which woman? He is denying knowledge that he knew which tree the fruit was from. It could be an excuse or he was really being truthful, and did not know this.

We have an apocryphal text: The Book of Adam, which tells us this and backs up the reasons above. Underlying the Hebrew text in The Book of Adam 3:2, Eve told Adam, "Oh, if I were dead then Elohim would have accepted you in paradise!" Adam replied to Eve and said to her, "Because of us, a great anger lies against (upon?) all creatures. (However) I do not know this: whether it is because of me or because of you." Eve replied to Adam, "My lord, if you think it wise, kill me so that I will be exterminated from the sight of Elohim and his malakhim, so that Elohim's anger against you may cease, which happened because of me: and he will bring you back into paradise.

[2] An idiomatic expression meaning, to know evil; before their fall into sin. Adam and Eve did not feel hungry and thirsty inside the Garden, as we do now outside the Garden they did. The tree of knowledge and evil has allowed our nature to be tainted until we get restored and nothing we do can take that away. We are hopelessly bound in the flesh
Continued in next section

until we are renewed in the resurrection. Our spirit constantly wars with our flesh.
[3] Notice the three things they did to hide their nakedness.
a) They did good deeds to 'cover' themselves.
b) The covering was made of herbage.
c) The covering was incomplete, they were only aprons. This symbolizes or shadows, man made religion, i.e., Islam, Humanism, Buddhism, etc. Elohim will not accept this! That is why we find, a little later, YHWH showing His displeasure at the man made covering.
[4] Before, when YHWH, the Malakh of his presence, would commune with these two, they may have heard gentle steps of the Master from the shamayim. Now they heard thunder and were afraid. The sin had caused this behaviour.
[5] The One who stepped in the Garden was not the Father but the Son Yahushua.
[6] Mid afternoon.
[7] Irregular plural for women in the Hebrew, here both wives hid with Adam.
[8] The walking of YHWH, in the Garden, in the form of a malakh, was one of the many faces of YHWH, also known as the presence of YHWH.
[9] The word used in this passage in Hebrew is Ayekha rather than Ayfo. Ayfo is location specific like when someone might ask which tree you are hiding behind while this is not the idea behind Ayekha or the Hebrew word Ay, which is used in speech with Qayin, this is used by YHWH (Gen 4:9). The two words Ayekha and Ay have existential spiritual meanings. YHWH was not asking for location
Continued in next section

10 And he said, I heard your sound in the garden, and I was afraid, because I was naked;[1] and I hid myself.

11 And he said, Who told you that you were naked? Have you eaten of the etz (tree), which I commanded you that you should not eat of it?

12 And the man said, The wife[2] whom you gave to be with me, she gave me of the etz (tree), and I did eat.

13 And YHWH Elohim said to the woman, What is this that you have done? And the woman said, The serpent tricked me, and I did eat.[3]

14 And YHWH Elohim said to the serpent, because you have done this, you are henceforth cursed above all cattle, and above every beast of the field; upon your belly shall you go, and dust[4] shall you eat all the days of your life:

15 And I will put enmity between you and the woman, and between your descendants (seed)[5] and her descendants (seed);[6] He shall bruise your head, and you shall bruise his heel.[7]

16 To the woman he said, I will greatly multiply your sorrow and your conception; your conception shall be painful to beget children; and your desire shall be for your husband,[8] and he shall have authority[9] over you.

17 And to Ahdahm he said, Because you have listened to the voice of your wife,[10] and have

---

of Adam but saying spiritually "What have you done this was not your purpose."

[1] The moment Adam and Khawa had eaten both their light covering left them and so they now knew they were naked and vulnerable. This nakedness described earlier did not mean they did not have a light covering. Earlier they had a light covering similar to the malakhim to cover and protect them. Malakhim do not wear clothes either but are not seen naked as the light covers them and their bodies.

[2] Which wife?

[3] Who ate Khawa or Ishah or all three including Lilith the serpent?

[4] The curse put upon Lilith the Serpent. The first adulterous woman was tried and found guilty who went and slept in a marital arrangement with a fallen angel then gave birth to a son called Azazel. See Lev 16:8 and Num 5:17. Lilith was turned into a demoness and later expelled from the
Continued in next section

continent of Africa, she has today settled in the Western lands of Europe and America where she rules through rebellious women.

[5] Satan's seed, are all those who are unsaved. In literal here the seed was of Lilith, who are demons trying to throw mankind.

[6] The word Zerah here is plural and connects to no single individual but to the whole of Israel. Christians misapply this as some kind of special single seed passage, while there are numerous passages quoting a woman's seed pointing to her descendants. Read Gen 16:10, 24:60, and 22:17.

[7] YHWH will crush Satan, (the Hebrew word shuph is used) and he [Satan] will injure the people of Israel.

[8] A married woman will always desire her husband, even if she separates, her thoughts will be for him. This is the natural design, and it also shows marriage unto death, not temporal, as people have made it in modern society unless she was with an unjust husband who did not fulfil the Covenant of marriage.

[9] Now YHWH sets the authority structure straight, once and for all times. A woman may never again break authority and if she does she will suffer loss. If a husband abuses his wife then YHWH has also built-in safety for the woman that the husband would love his wife and suffer.

[10] The authority structure was broken when the first man listened to his wife and not
Continued in next section

eaten of the etz (tree), of which I commanded you, saying, you shall not eat of it: cursed is the ground for your sake; in sorrow shall you eat of it all the days of your life;

18 Thorns also and thistles shall it bring forth to you; and you shall eat the herb of the field;

19 In the sweat of your face shall you eat Lakhem (bread), till you return into the ground; for out of it were you taken: for dust you are, and into dust you shall return.

20 And Ahdahm named his wive(s) Hawa;[1] because these[2] were the mother of all human life.

21 To Ahdahm also and to his wive(s)[3] did YHWH Elohim made robes of skin,[4] and clothed them.

YHWH; henceforth, Elohim corrected the authority structure. From that time forward we find women have been in disobedience, and rebellion to men, wanting their own way. The issue of authority in homes is still at stake, both arguing over who is the head, yet YHWH made Adam, Eve's husband, the head. Any home which has the woman as the head will never be a happy home, or **Increase**. The children will be disobedient; and the wife and husband will not get along in happiness, as the authority structure would be broken. Until it is fixed in that home, this situation will remain.

[1] Please note that Eve, the name, is a name of a Babylonian pagan deity. Adam's both wives were called Khawa pronounced – KHAWAH- hence, to illustrate; we use the name Eve, although it is a false deity's name. We are careful not to disobey Master YHWH, by showing what was there.

[2] Here the ancient letters cover both females but we do not have an appropriate word to translate in our language other than these.

[3] It's more than appropriate to use the word here as it is in its plural form since the context follows.

[4] To the two wives plural, The ancient Hebrew says literally "robes of skin," which Continued in next section

means this taken from the animala that were slaughtered. They were not naked when they were created as thought by people. They had a Holy light covering. They became naked after the first sin at which point the three tried to cover themselves with fig leaves. This was the first sacrifice in the Garden that YHWH had to make to shed blood, we are not told how many animals were sacrificed it appears at least three. Notice three things:
a) YHWH Elohim did the works/Torah and showed them how to make clothes.
b) The covering was made of robes/Torah. We believe it was a cloth covered from the animals sacrificed possibly wool.
c) The covering was complete robes instead of aprons. It is your choice, you can come to Elohim with your own righteousness and covering (rags and aprons, like menstrual clothes), which are inadequate, and unclean. The Rebbim believed as follows:

Midrash Rabbah - Genesis XX:12
http://www.yashanet.com/studies/judaism10 1/sidebars/ohr.htm
12. AND THE LORD GOD MADE FOR ADAM AND HIS WIFE GARMENTS OF SKIN ('OR), AND CLOTHED THEM (III, 21). In R. Meir's Torah it was found written, 'Garments of light (or) '2: this refers to Adam's garments, which were like a torch [shedding radiance], broad at the bottom and narrow at the top. Isaac the Elder said: They were as smooth as a finger-nail and as beautiful as a jewel. R.Johanan said: They were like the fine linen garments which come from Bethshean,3 GARMENTS OF SKIN meaning those that are nearest to the skin. R. Eleazar said: They were of goats' skin. R. Joshua said: Of hares' skin. R. Jose b. R. Hanina said: It was a garment made of skin with its wool. Resh Lakish said: It was of Circassian wool, and these were used [later] by first-born children.4 R. Samuel b. Nahman said: [They were made from] the wool of camels and the wool of hares, GARMENTS OF SKIN meaning those which are produced from the skin.5 R. Levi said: The Torah teaches you here a rule of worldly wisdom: spend according to your means on food; less than you can afford on clothing, but more than you can afford on a dwelling. Spend according to your means on food, as it is written, of every tree of the garden thou mayest freely eat (Gen. II, 16). Less than you can afford on clothing: AND Continued in next section

22 And YHWH Elohim said, Behold, the man is become as One of Us, to know good and evil: and now, lest he put forth his hand, and take also of the etz (tree) of life, and eat, and live forever:

23 Therefore YHWH Elohim expelled him from the garden of Ayden, to till the ground from where he was taken.

24 So he drove[1] out the man; and he placed at the east of the garden of Ayden Khruvims, and a flaming sword which turned every way, to keep the way[2] of the etz (tree) of life.

Chapter 4

1 And Ahdahm knew Hawa his wife;[3] and she conceived, and bare Qayin, and said, I have gotten a man-YHWH. [4]

2 And she continued[5] to give birth to his brother Hebel. And Hebel was a keeper of sheep, but Qayin was a tiller of the ground.

3 And in process of time it came to pass, that Qayin brought of the fruit of the ground an offering to YHWH.

4 And Hebel, he also brought of the Bekhorot (firstborn) of his flock and of the fat there. And YHWH had respect for Hebel and for his offering:[6]

5 But for Qayin and to his offering he had no respect. And Qayin was very angry, and his countenance fell.

6 And YHWH said to Qayin, Why are you angry? And why is your countenance fallen?

7 If you do well, shall it not be accepted? And if you do not do well, sin lies at your door. And to you shall be its desire, and you shall rule over it.[7]

THE LORD GOD MADE... GARMENTS OF SKIN, AND CLOTHED THEM.6 More than you can afford on a dwelling: for behold! they were but two, yet they dwelt in the whole world.7

---

(2) rut light, instead of rug skin.
(3) V. supra, XIX, 1.
(4) When they used to perform the sacrificial service, before the priests were chosen for it; v. infra, LXIII, 13; Num. R. IV, 8.
(5) Viz. the wool that comes off it.
(6) I.e. only simple, not expensive garments.
(7) Cf. Pes. 114a; Hul. 84b.

[1] The word for 'driven' in Hebrew is 'Garash', it means to 'divorce'. So YHWH allegorically divorced the first man Adam for rejecting His commandments. This is seen later, when Israel was also divorced for committing adultery with foreign elohim. When you take on a foreign elohim, the principle, is marriage and it becomes gross idolatry. Rejecting YHWH's Holy Torah has a price.

[2] The mention of the 'way' here is to show that YHWH's Torah was broken and needed to be restored.

[3] The Hebrew indicates as this time Adam had relations with both wives one after the Continued in next section

other and they both gave births hence Qayin from one and a girl from the other.

[4] Eve thought she bore Qayin, she thought he would crush Satan's head. Hence the Hebrew literally reads; I have gotten a man-YHWH.

[5] The Hebrew word Yasaph here indicates 'continued' action which in this case would be that Hebel was the twin brother to Qayin at the same time.

[6] This is the first picture of the Tithe offering that we see in the Scriptures, in the beginning order of commandments we are to have children, keep the Sabbath. Now, we see the picture of the Tithe.

[7] It is within every man to control his passions and to avoid committing a sin. Deliberate sin has no sacrifice in the Torah; it is entirely up to YHWH and His favor to give forgiveness for such a sin.

8 And Qayin talked with Hebel his brother: and it came to pass, when they were in the field, that Qayin rose up against Hebel [1] his brother, and killed [2] him.

9 And YHWH said to Qayin, Where is Hebel your brother? And he said, I do not know: Am I my brother's protector?

10 And he said, What have you done? The voice of your brother's blood cries to me [3] from the ground.

11 And now you are cursed from the earth, which has opened her mouth to receive your brother's blood from your[4] hand;

12 When you till the ground, it shall not continue to[5] yield to you her full strength; a wanderer[6] and a mover you shall be in the earth.

13 And Qayin said to YHWH, My punishment is greater than I can bear.

14 Behold, you have driven me out this day from the face of the land; and from your face shall I be hid; and I shall be a wanderer and a mover[7] in the earth; and it shall come to pass, that anyone that finds me shall kill me. [8]

15 And YHWH said to him, Therefore whosoever slays Qayin, vengeance shall be taken on him sevenfold.[9] And YHWH set a mark upon Qayin, lest any finding him should kill him before his set time.

Footnotes

[7] Truly the first Nomad.

[8] He was afraid of both people and animals. Qayin was afraid that the animals were no longer in control after the fall and thought a wild animal could kill him or another person could take revenge in the family. Here one more thing to understand is Adam had more than two wives both inside and outside the Garden with the North/South axis. His subsequent wife and children even if mentioned as Ishah may be thought of as Khawa but they are not all Khawa's children. One thing is clear Qayin was afraid of people alongside animals which is the hint. Khawa did have other children after this event but so did Adam's other wives. Adam did not just have three wives in total.

[9] Here YHWH identifies 'the seed'. He does not say that this will protect Qayin, although it does show the sign of His unmerited favour. The idea here is showing Qayin carrying the seed of vengeance unto seven generations. The mark was also his timeline for when he would be killed. He died later at the hands of Lamech. The 'seed' of Qayin; which is the seed of the anti-Messiah, shows that they would avenge 7 times. In essence, we see seven generations revealed of Qayin and the battle at the culmination of the Jubilee. It is a common Muslim custom that a family carries the line of revenge when there is enmity, to say, we will blot out your seven generations. This explains why the coming Muslims believe, if you kill one of theirs, they must try to kill seven of yours. This type of tit for tat killing is still evident in Iraq, Afghanistan and other Muslim nations of the world. It's very common in Islamic nations generally. YHWH showed us who the end time beast will be.

Footnotes

[1] Qayin overpowered his brother with an instrument of the field. This is the first act of murder in scripture.

[2] Septuagint

[3] Blood is the life force of an individual, today we know this as DNA, and here righteous Hebel's blood calls out to YHWH for justice.

[4] Elohim knew Qayin had murdered his brother so he was testing him.

[5] Wherever innocent blood is spilled, that earth will not give its full yield, this is a spiritual principle.

[6] The Hebrew word Nua, can mean; fugitive, wander, scatter, promoted, shaken, or, to and fro. In other words it has all the idea of restlessness and not belonging. The root meaning is; to wander to a place. Qayin is the prototype of the Anti-Messiah end-times Islamic beast. Arabs, are like nomads, wandering from place to place, showing us that Saudi Arabia is to play a major role.

17 And Qayin knew his wife;[2] and she conceived, and bare

is north of the ancient complex at Nok, the place to which Kain likely "wandered" after he was sent away, and where he married a daughter of the ruler of Nok.
[2] Who was Qayin's wife?

According to the ruler priestly clans and customs we are told that Qayin went to the land of Nod (Gen 4:16) which was in central Africa (Nigeria). He built a city there called Chanoch. Cha-Nok is a title "The Chief". So Qayin would be the one who started the Nok culture and not some later tribes. Qayin knew how to build because he had extensive knowledge of metal working. The Nok culture of Nigeria has been well known to have knowledge of smelting iron and making various instruments and building cities. This was in Nigeria.

If we look at the genealogies we see this picture.
Chanok--daughter of Chanoch-- married to Qayin. Qayin's wife called her son Chanoch based on the name of her father.

According to priestly rules Chanok in this case Ahdahm's daughter that was born to the third wife of Ahdahm's hidden wife in Genesis 2, who was married with Qayin and she then names her son on her father's name, a tribal name see Gen 2:23. So who was Chanoch whose daughter was married to Qayin? Cha-Nok is a title of Ahdahm daughter from the third wife who is the hidden wife because you are allowed to lawfully marry another of your father's wives daughter's. If he married Khawa's daughter that would be incest and sin see Lev 18:9.

The title Cha-nok simply means "the Chief" and is a way of carrying title of the father down the genealogical lines. We find similar usages of these named titles in the Tanak.

According to "The Complete Works of Josephus, translated by W. Whiston, Kregel, Josephus writes, "The number of Adam's children, as says the old tradition, was thirty-three sons and twenty-three daughters." These did not come from one wife but at least seven.

Sending away of Qayin to Nigeria

16 And Qayin went out from the presence of YHWH, and dwelt in the land of Nod,[1] on the east of Ayden.

Footnotes
[1] By our calculations we place the land of Nod in the heart of West Africa near Lake Chad. Nod and Nok are interchangeable words etymologically speaking in the African tongue. This area is the area of metal workers and we know Qayin was a metalworker and he knew how to make implements with metal since he killed his brother with a similar implement. Qayin built a city named in verse 4:17 to Chanoch which is synonymous with Nok or Nod. A Nigerian philologist by the name of Modupe Oduyoye confirms in his writings that the Hebrew words for Nod נוד and Nok נוך are identical. These were Qeny chiefs who maintained two wives on the North/South Axis as Patriarchs. Similar people can still be found today in both Africa and Asia. This tells us that Kano the City in Nigeria in the North is where Qayin would have placed his principle ruling wife as a chief and his second southern wife would be down south near the Jos plateau. This pattern of the North/South axis. Note these people extended all the way to India and modern day Pakistan.

(http://jandyongenesis.blogspot.co.uk/2012/06/recovering-african-background-of.html)
According to Genesis researcher Alice Linsley, in his book, Dr. Oduyoye notes the connection between Adamu Orisa (of Lagos State) and the Hebrew r'ison Adam. He notes that Hebrew Qayin(Kain/Cain) and the Arabic word for smith qayn are cognates. He says these words are related to the Yoruba Ogun and Fon Gun, both meaning "patron saint of smiths." Other cognates include Ebira Egene (the metalworker caste) and Hamn Kuno (who invented iron smelting). This connects Kain to the city of Kano, which

Continued in next section

Continued in next section

Khanokh and he builded a city, and called the name of the city, after the name of his son, Khanokh.

From the time of Hebel's death to the birth of Sheth more than hundred years had elapsed which means Ahdahm and his other wives had many other children who would have married and had families. According to Jewish tradition when Qayin and Hebel were born Ahdahm and Khawa had twin daughters with both Qayin and Hebel which would mean Khawa gave birth to 4 children at the same time if one is to accept this but we do not think this is a feasible argument. Otherwise she had given birth to the twins Qayin and Hebel. Either way Qayin cannot marry his biological sister this is a fallacy and sin. He would have married only his father's second or third wife's daughter which is allowed.

The midrashim write that the killing of Hebel came about because of a dispute who Qayin would marry according to Rashi the Jewish scholar. According to rabbinic tradition Qayin married one of these twin daughters and that is where his wife came from but we disagree as this introduces incest and sin. The other sons and daughters of Ahdahm were instrumental in populating the world. However Rabbi Simon Altaf disagrees with this narrative but instead offers with proof in the Torah that Qayin married Adam's other wife's daughter outside the Garden and she would be his half sister in the same manner like Abraham and Sarah his half sister, this marriage is by the laws of Elohim allowed, the same father but different mother. Adam had one wife in the North and others in the South in other words Adam had minimum three but up to seven as in the perfect model (Isa 4:1), one ran away this being Lilith, the others were with him who gave him all his children. This pattern is revealed throughout the writings. This pattern came from Adam which was both Patriarchal and later practiced by our ancestors such as Abraham, Isaac and Jacob. YHWH does not condone incest, never has and never will. The law is end to end and does not change even our ancestors knew this law well. Polygyny occurred in the Garden see Gen 2:22.

18 And to Khanokh was born Irad: and Irad begat Meḥuya'ĕl and Meḥuya'ĕl begat Methusa'ĕl and Methusa'ĕl[1] begat Lamakh.

19 And Lamakh took to him two wives:[2] the name of the one was Adah,[3] and the name of the other Zillah.[4]

20 And Adah bare Yabal: he was the Abbah of such as dwell in tents, and of such as have cattle.

21 And his brother's name was Yubal: he was the Abbah of all such as handle the harp and organ.

22 And Zillah, she also bare TubalQayin, an instructor in every instrument of brass and iron: and the sister of TubalQayin was Naamah.[5]

Footnotes

[1] Genesis 4:18 Meḥuya'ĕl, Methusa'ĕl and 5:21 Metushelakh are believed to be the names of twins by the scholar John Lamb DD 1835, which he believes were appended into one name by a scribe by mistake.

[2] The North/South axis is soon revealed in Lemach who adopted the same pattern as Adam. Patriarchal Polygamy is for us and it was hinted at in Genesis Chapter 1, Monogamy came from Satan who has a wife too, the whore of Babylon and polygamy are not equal. Our people did not marry two wives at the same time, it was one wife followed by another in later years. YHWH reveals his goodness for us if we obey him else we can behave as gentiles in serial monogamy. Asiatic and African people and rulers were polygamous even to this day. The ruling clan always had two wives and we see this pattern emerging once again here and being repeated in the Tanak.

[3] A woman of beautiful lips.

[4] Her name means "A little dear." The modern Hebraist translate her sister's name as dawn and her's as dusk, this is not the case with ancient text.

[5] Naamah was the twin sister of Tubal-Qayin. The Hebrew Tav indicates this plurality. The Tav prefixed to the name of Continued in next section

23 And Lamakh said to his wives, Adah and Zillah, Hear my voice;[1] you wives of Lamakh, hearken to my speech: for I have slain a man to my wounding,[2] and a young man[3] to my hurt.

24 If Qayin shall be avenged sevenfold, truly Lamakh seventy and sevenfold.

25 And Ahdahm knew his wife again; and she bare a son, and called his name Sheth: For Elohim, said she, has appointed me another zera (seed) instead of Hebel, whom Qayin murdered.

Rebellion of Men against YHWH Begins

26 And to Sheth, to him also there was born a son; and he called his name Enosh: then men profaned while calling upon [4] the name of YHWH.

Kingly Rulers of Africa
Righteous men walked in the Torah of YHWH
Chapter 5

1 This is the scroll of the generation of Ahdahm. In the day that Elohim created Ahdahm (mankind), He made him in the likeness of Elohim.

2 He created them male and female, and **Blessed** them and called their name Ahdahm[5] in the day they were created.[6]

3 And Ahdahm lived one hundred and thirty years, and begot a son in his own likeness,[7] after his image, and named him Sheth.

4 After he begot Sheth, the days of Ahdahm were eight hundred years; and he begot sons and daughters.[8]

Tubal-qayin and the ancient mah mem and heh indicates a plural birth with the name of Naa-mah indicates she was born a twin. The proof is that she is the only sister mentioned in the list while others had sisters too but they were not necessarily twins. We can detect this with the ancient pictograph text.

[1] Lamech was not the only polygamist which was and is part of Biblical culture. One of his wives Zilah, as is typical of today, decided that she was not going to have children and was going to become a slim model so to say. So, she drank a special brew that made her infertile, while the other wife was also disobedient and did not want to pay attention to what her husband would have to say. They both thought Lamech was a murderer, but the truth is he was not. You can read the full account in the Book of Yashar 2:18-28.

[2] Qayin's time was up, so, he was killed at the hands of Lamech, as appointed by YHWH.

[3] Lamech also accidentally killed Tubalqayin.

[4] Men did not call YHWH's name in respect, but began to profane the name of YHWH, hence the third commandment had to be introduced. They started to ascribe worship Continued in next section

to; the sun, moon and the stars. Exactly the opposite of what YHWH had intended and commanded.

[5] The woman is called in Adam's name, hence the surname of the male carries.

[6] This was when Lilith was created who rebelled and left. Khawa was the second wife Patriarchal wife alongside Adam's second wife in the garden from which all the earth was replenished. Lilith went into Adultery and ran away with a malakh, she was later turned into a demoness and bound. She vowed vengeance on mankind to kill their children. Hence the demons her children attack the children of men.

[7] All subsequent generations were in the likeness of Adam and Sheth. Man was born with the Yetzer Hara (Evil inclination) which allowed him to be able to sin. This is somewhat different from the Church terminology of original sin. Children are born with both Yetzer hara (sin inclination) and yetzer tov (Good inclination). Each individual then has to make his choice to do good or evil.

[8] Josephus and Hebrew tradition tells us; Adam's children, numbered, thirty three sons and twenty three daughters.

5 So all the days that Ahdahm lived were nine hundred and thirty years; and he died.

6 Sheth lived one hundred and five years, and begot Enosh.

7 After he begot Enosh, Sheth lived eight hundred and seven years, and begot sons and daughters.

8 So all the days of Sheth were nine hundred and twelve years; and he died.

9 Enosh lived ninety years, and begot Qeynan.

10 After he begot Qeynan, Enosh lived eight hundred and fifteen years, and begot sons and daughters.

11 So all the days of Enosh were nine hundred and five years; and he died.

12 Qeynan lived seventy years, and begot Mahalal'el.

13 After he begot Mahalal'el, Qeynan lived eight hundred and forty years, and begot sons and daughters.

14 So all the days of Qeynan were nine hundred and ten years; and he died.

15 Mahalale'el lived sixty-five years, and begot Yared.

16 After he begot Yared, Mahalale'el lived eight hundred and thirty years, and begot sons and daughters.

17 So all the days of Mahalale'el were eight hundred and ninety-five years; and he died.

18 Yared lived one hundred and sixty-two years, and begot Khanokh.

19 After he begot Khanokh, Yared lived eight hundred years, and begot sons and daughters.

20 So all the days of Yared were nine hundred and sixty-two years; and he died.

21 Khanokh lived sixty-five years, and begot Metushelakh. [1]

22 And Khanokh walked with Elohim after he begat Methushelakh three hundred years, and begat sons and daughters:

23 So all the days of Khanokh were three hundred and sixty-five years:

24 And Khanokh walked with Elohim:[2] and he was no more; for he was carried away[3] by Elohim.[4]

25 Methushelakh lived one hundred and eighty-seven years, and begot Lamakh.

26 After he begot Lamakh, Methushelakh lived seven hundred and eighty-two years, and begot sons and daughters:

27 So all the days of Methushelakh were nine hundred and sixty-nine years: and he died.

28 Lamakh lived one hundred and eighty-two years, and begot a son:

29 And he called his name Noakh,[5] saying, This one will

Footnotes

[1] Mtu-she-lakh - Super spear thrower associated with an African black man who was a very good hunter with the spear.

[2] He was a good Torah keeper.

[3] The Hebrew text does not say he was taken into the third shamayim. The errant rapture doctrine is built up from this, yet, this does not talk about any secret rapture of Enoch. The Hebrew phrase V'ene'nu is also a euphemism for 'He died'. We are not told when after his transportation he died. He was in west Africa where he died.

[4] We are not told where he went, he was transported from one place to another.

[5] The ancient meaning of the Hebrew word Noakh is concealed pouring.

comfort us concerning our work and the toil of our hands, because of the ground which YHWH has cursed.

30 After he begot Noakh, Lamakh lived five hundred and ninety-five years, and begot sons and daughters:

31 So all the days of Lamakh were seven hundred and seventy-seven years: and he died.

32 And Noakh was five hundred years old: and Noakh begot Shem,[1] Kham,[2] and Yapet.[3]

The angelic pact of Shemyaza to destroy mankind at Mount Khermon
Chapter 6

1 Now it came to pass, when men began to multiply on the face of the earth, and daughters were born to them,

2 That the sons of Elohim [4] saw the daughters of men that they were beautiful; and they took wives [5] for themselves of all whom they chose.

3 And YHWH said, My Ruakh (Spirit) shall not strive with man forever, for he is indeed flesh: yet his days shall be one hundred and twenty years.[6]

4 There were Nephillim (fallen ones) on the earth in those days; and also afterward,[7] when the sons of Elohim [8] came in to the daughters of men, and they bore children to them, these were the mighty men who were of old, men of name.

5 Then YHWH saw that the wickedness of man was great in the earth, and that every intent of the thoughts of his heart was only evil continually.

6 And YHWH took pity nevertheless observing man on the earth, and He was grieved in His heart.

7 So YHWH said, I will destroy man whom I have created from the face of the earth; both man, and beast, crawling things, and

Footnotes

[1] Shem was the Kohen (priest) the Malech-Tzadik Beresheeth 14:18, Shem and Cham were believed to be twins by the scholar John Lamb however they were not twins because Cham was the son of Noakh's wife Emzara. Shem and Cham were both black in colour.

[2] Cham means hot therefore black by definition.

[3] In ancient Hebrew Yapet means "High Head", in other words proud and a deceiver speaking from two tongues. This has been Yapet's style throughout history to acquire things by deception. If you want to validate this then examine the history how the Grecians conquered nations the famous Trojan horse incident in Troy. The capture and slavery of Africa and modern India are prime examples of deception of the mouth of Yapet.

[4] Rebellious malakhim.

Footnotes

[5] Some malakhim can acquire corporeal bodies and live as humans. The only trouble was the women's children were corrupted, that is why they came; these women were giving birth to deformed children, and giants, which caused many women to die. These malakhim came to corrupt mankind and taught them all the arts, music, wars, and other nasty things. These malakhim are bound in the lowest dungeons of She'ol until the day they will be removed from their chains and destroyed.

[6] YHWH prophesied the flood to be exactly 120 years later.

[7] Malakhim had more than one fall.

[8] The Nephillim and malakhim were one and the same ones who fell from the shamayim.

birds of the air; for it is a pity that I have made them.[1]

8 But Noakh found favour in the eyes of YHWH.

Torah Parsha 2 Noakh, Beresheeth 6:9-11:32
Haftarah: Yeshayahu 54:1-55:5

9 This is the genealogy of Noakh: Noakh was a Righteous man blameless in his generations, Noakh walked[2] with Elohim.

10 And Noakh begot three sons: Shem, Kham, and Yapet.

11 The earth also was corrupt before Elohim, and the earth was filled with violence.

12 So Elohim looked upon the earth, and, indeed, it was corrupt; for all flesh had corrupted their way on the earth.

13 And Elohim said to Noakh, The end of all flesh has come before Me; for the earth is filled with violence through them; and behold, I will destroy them with the earth.

14 Make yourself an ark of gopher wood; make rooms in the ark, and cover it inside and outside with pitch.

15 And this is how you shall make it: The length of the ark shall be four hundred and fifty feet, its width seventy five feet, and its height forty five feet.[3]

16 You shall make a window for the ark, and you shall finish it to eighteen inches from the roof; and set the door of the ark in its side; you shall make it with lower, second, and third decks.

17 And, behold, I, Myself, am bringing flood of mayim on the earth, to destroy[4] from under shamayim all flesh, in which is the breath of life, everything that is on the earth shall die;

18 But I will establish My Covenant with you; and you shall go into the ark, you, your sons, your wife, and your sons' wives with you.

19 And of every living thing of all flesh, you shall bring two of every sort into the ark, to keep them alive with you; they shall be male and female.

20 Of the birds after their kind, of animals after their kind, and of every crawling thing of the earth after its kind, two of every kind will come to you to keep them alive.

21 And you shall take for yourself of all food that is eaten, and you shall gather it to yourself; and it shall be food for you and for them.

22 Thus Noakh did; according to all that Elohim commanded him, so he did.

Footnotes
[1] We see human type emotions from the Holy One, its not that He did not know they were going to be bad, but we are shown the judgement (Gevurah) and mercy (Chesed) side of Elohim in the Great Ein Sof. This is the prophecy of the flood to come as, the Holy One, praise be He, has decided to send the flood, but not told Noakh yet.
[2] This word 'walked', means obeyed YHWH's Torah.
[3] We are assuming that a cubit is eighteen inches as the standard measurement but there were different measures of cubits at different times.
[4] Beresheeth 6:6 now Elohim's prophetic thought is revealed through action by the Gevurah (Strength, might, judgment) to our left and to His right.

Chapter 7

1 Then YHWH said to Noakh, Come into the ark, you and your entire household, because I have seen that you are Righteous before Me in this generation.

2 You shall take with you seven each of every clean[1] animal, a male and his female: two each of animals that are unclean, a male and his female.

3 Also seven each of birds of the air, male and female; to keep the species alive on the face of all the earth.

4 For after seven more days, I will cause it to rain on the earth forty days and forty nights; and I will destroy from the face of the earth all living things that I have made.

5 And Noakh did according to all that YHWH commanded him.

6 Noakh was six hundred years old when the flood of mayim were on the earth.

7 So Noakh, with his sons, his wife, and his sons' wives, went into the ark, because of the mayim of the flood.

8 Of clean animals, of animals that are unclean, of birds, and of everything that crawls on the earth.

9 Two by two they went into the ark, to Noakh, male and female, as Elohim had commanded Noakh.

10 And it came to pass after seven days that the mayim of the flood were on the earth.

11 In the six hundredth year of Noakh's life, in the second month, the seventeenth day of the month, on that day all the fountains of the great deep were broken up, and the windows of shamayim were opened.

12 And the rain was on the earth forty days and forty nights.

13 On the very same day Noakh and Noakh's sons, Shem, Kham, and Yapet, and Noakh's wife and the three wives of his sons with them, entered the ark.[2]

14 They, and every beast after its kind, all cattle after their kind, every crawling creature that crawls on the ground after its kind, and every bird after its kind, every bird of every sort.

15 And they went into the ark to Noakh, two by two, of all flesh in which is the breath of life.

16 So those that entered, male and female of all flesh, went in as Elohim had commanded him: and YHWH shut him in.

17 Now the flood was on the earth forty days; the mayim **Increased**, and lifted up the ark, and it rose high above the earth.

18 The mayim prevailed, and greatly **Increased** on the earth; and the ark moved about on the surface of the mayim.

19 And the mayim prevailed exceedingly on the earth; and all the high hills under the whole shamayim were covered.

Footnotes
[1] There were seven animals since three pairs make six, with one clean animal for sacrifice. The unclean were two, as no sacrifice could be made with them. Noakh knew the sacrificial system inherited from Adam.

Footnotes
[2] Only eight people survived the flood.

20 The mayim rose more than twenty feet, above the mountains.

21 And all flesh died that moved on the earth: birds and cattle and beasts and every crawling creature that crawls on the earth, and all men:

22 All in whose nostrils was the breath of the ruakh of life, all that was on the dry land, died.

23 So, He destroyed all living things which were on the face of the earth, both man, and cattle, crawling creatures, and birds of the air; they were destroyed from the earth: only Noakh and those who were with him in the ark,[1] remained alive.[2]

24 And the mayim prevailed on the earth one hundred and fifty days.

Chapter 8

1 Then Elohim remembered [3] Noakh, and every living thing, and all the animals that were with him in the ark. And Elohim made a wind to pass over the earth, and the mayim subsided.

2 The fountains of the deep and the windows of shamayim were also stopped, and the rain from the shamayim was restrained.

Footnotes
[1] Only those who are part of Israel will survive. The rest of the world will perish in the final judgment. If you are in the ark. The do it yourself, working their way with good deeds crowd, will not enter the Kingdom of YHWH. In order to enter you must have the seal of the Covenants in the Torah and do the works of the Torah, which clothes us with righteousness by Abbah's favour.
[2] Was this a global flood or not is debated amongst teachers of the Torah. Kul Ha eretz does not mean the entire earth in context hence the debate is still not settled!
[3] Meaning Elohim was going to favour Noah.

3 And the mayim receded continually from the earth. At the end of the hundred and fifty days the mayim decreased.

4 Then the ark rested in the seventh month, the seventeenth day of the month, beside the mountain of Ar-arat.[4]

Footnotes
[4] Then the ark rested in the seventh month, the seventeenth day of the month, beside the mountain of Ar-arat.

So once again we ask the question where did the Ark land? This has been a puzzling question for people of Faith for centuries and explorers alike have gone up to search for the ark but no one to date has found the ark. With modern technology and Satellites imagery why did they not find it? The answer is actually simpler than we think. The wrong location has been selected, also the ark was made from a particular wood called gofer only mentioned once in the whole of writings and this likely in Hebrew means a covering of reeds upon some kind of wood which was widely available in the region of Africa where Noakh lived and it is unlikely that this would have survived for thousands of years up to this time unless it had some special covering. This type of covering by reeds was widely available in Africa alone. The motif of forty days and forty nights of the flood tallies with the African culture because in ancient times the Nile used to flood for forty days during the wet periods and people used to leave their homes. Hence my earlier comments the flood is disputed to be global.

The ark rested in the 'region' known as 'the mountain of Ar-arat or beside the Mount Meni' in Central Africa near Lake Chad which used to be a sea. Many have been taught that this is a mountainous range that runs between Armenia, Turkey and Iran however this is not true. The ark has never been found in Iran or Turkey. The other explanation for this is that the closer language to Hebrew is the Arabic word har-arat, which means "Mountain of Intensity or passion, heat etc." The Arabic language carries many ancient Hebrew words correctly to the ancient order. Note this is a single Mountain and not a range of mountains. The
Continued in next section

Beresheeth (Genesis)

Mountain Meni in Central Africa is the likely resting place for Noakh's ark near Lake Chad, which in ancient times was a sea known as Mount Meru. The largest variety of animals is found in Africa only and not in Iran or Turkey. This makes it highly likely that Noakh's ark rested in Africa from where civilization once again spread.

1874, Godfrey Higgins, in his monograph Anacalypsis: An Inquiry into the Origins of Languages, Nations and Religions, noted that "Armenia" could mean "mount of Meru. Note also that there is a Mountain called Ararat in South Africa also.

Genesis 8:4 Then the ark rested in the seventh month, the seventeenth day of the month, beside the mountain of Ararat.

Immediately the first thing you notice is that while the scholars argue over which mountain or mountains in Turkey the HTHS Bible simply states the obvious that it is a single mountain and not mountains in plural.

Gen 8:4 ותנח התבה בחדש השביעי
בשבעה־עשׂר יום לחדש על הרי אררט:

If any of you reads Hebrew immediately can confirm in the Hebrew that it is not many mountains but a single Mountain. This fact is incredibly important to start tracing the Ark. In fact the Hebrew word Al Hari simply means on or beside the mountain.

One can quickly do a word study and trace the first occurrence of this word "hari" in Exodus 33:6 which is Strong's H2022.

Exo 33:6 So the children of Israel stripped themselves of their ornaments by Mount Horeb.

Now ask yourself did the children of Israel strip on the top of the Mountain or beside it? They were not allowed to touch the mountain. Note The Olive Tree a symbol of Israel and peace, vigor, growth and new life. Israel was given the Torah on a Mountain, Noah landed near one. Abraham took his son Isaac to a Mountain, while we are recognized as a nation, which is also the symbol of a Mountain. Note the little stone that the Prophet Dani'el mentioned that would rise and become a Mountain Dani'el 2:34. This is the reign of the Messiah.
Continued in next section

The land of Noakh is called Bor-Nu and is in central Africa. The words Bor-Nu means the land of Noah.

While many people search for Ararat the Hebrew could simply be Har-arat. The closer meaning to the Arabic is Intensity or shaking because of heat. The word Har in Hebrew means a Mountain so when we split the three words har Ar-rat we have as follows:

Har – Mountain
Ar – City
Arat – An ancient African word that means 'And.' Confirmed in the Amharic Ethiopian language. These Amharic speaking people are one of the true Hebrews the sons of King Solomon descended from his one son David and his relations with the Queen of Sheba known as Bilquis in Islam. The closest Hindi word is Arti which means towards the love of God. So one could posit the meaning likely to be "towards the Mountain" as a reference point indicating where humanity started from again.

Now imagine when people were traveling in ancient times through deserts and forests then what would be a good sign in the middle of nowhere? There is no sign better than a Mountain. How did Elijah find the Mountain of YHWH in Saudi Arabia? Did he have the GPS navigator or did he look for the tallest peak when walking in the direction of Saudi Arabia (First Kings 19:8)? Even the name used for the Mountain Horeb is Hor-Eb means this mountain was Holy to Shem's ancestors called Khuri the devotees of the deity Horus. One such ancestor being Joktan or Qahtan in the Arabic ruling the Arabian Peninsula. He lived and ruled in this area. His sons ruled Yemen for over a thousand years. So next time you hear people slandering Arabs as anti-Semitic pause for a moment, think, they are more Semitic than the modern Zionist Yahudim from Eastern Europe in Israel who call themselves Semitic but are not the sons of Shem from which the original Hebrews have descended but instead are gentile converts.

One of the sons of Joktan, the son of Eber the son of Shem mentioned in Genesis 10:26 is Hazarmaveth but in Arabic he is called Hadhramaut an area located in Yemen
Continued in next section

5 And the mayim decreased continually until the tenth month. In the tenth month, on the first day of the month, the tops of the mountains[1] were seen.

6 So it came to pass, at the end of forty days, that Noakh opened the window[2] of the ark which he had made.

7 Then he sent out a raven, which kept going to and fro until the mayim had dried up from the earth.

8 He also sent out from himself a dove, to see if the mayim had receded from the face of the land.

9 But the dove found no resting place for the sole of her foot, and she returned into the ark to him, for the mayim were on the face of the whole land. So he put out his hand and took her, and drew her into the ark to himself.

10 And he waited yet another seven days, and again he sent the dove out from the ark.

11 Then the dove came to him in the evening, and behold, a freshly plucked olive leaf[3] was in her mouth; and Noakh knew that the mayim had receded from the earth.

12 So he waited yet another seven days and sent out the dove, which did not return anymore to him.

13 And it came to pass in the six hundred and first year, in the first month, the first day of the month, that the mayim were dried up from the earth; and Noakh removed the covering of the ark and looked, and indeed the surface of the ground was dry.

14 And in the second month, on the twenty-seventh day of the month, the land was dried.

15 Then Elohim spoke to Noakh, saying,

16 Go out of the ark, you and your wife, and your sons and your sons' wives with you.

17 Bring out with you every living thing of all flesh that is with you: birds and cattle and every crawling creature that crawls on the earth, so that they may abound on the earth, and be fruitful and multiply on the earth.

18 So Noakh went out, and his sons and his wife and his sons' wives with him.

named after his son. It is known and often concealed fact that many Arabs and Africans are more Semitic than all the East European Jewry put together bringing the prophecy in Genesis 9:27 to pass. Israel's real re-creation and gathering is yet future for all the tribes exiled. The 1948 coming together was not the gathering of true Yahudah and Efrayim since many indigenous Arab people were uprooted and killed who had been forced to convert into Islam in the 7th century CE when Omar Ibn Khitab invaded Israel in 637 CE.

[1] Here the word is plural for Mountains but in the first instance of verse 4 it was not plural where it says "on the Mountain and not Mountains." The incorrect word can lead people into a wrong direction.

[2] Beneath the window he used for light a diamond that shone, since Noakh was African through and through except his skin had turned out white since he was an albino with woolly locks he had mined the diamond to place for light.

Footnotes

[3] Olive branch signifies that only Israel will come through the end time destruction and be the first survivors that the Holy One will send, and then the others. The Dove is the drash of the Holy Spirit of YHWH, in Covenant with Israel.

19 Every animal, every crawling creature, every bird, and whatever crawls on the earth, according to their Mishpakhot (families), went out of the ark.

20 Then Noakh built an altar to YHWH, and took of every clean animal and of every clean bird, and offered burnt offerings[1] on the altar.

21 And YHWH smelled a soothing aroma. Then YHWH said in His heart, I will never again curse the earth for man's sake, although the imagination of man's heart is evil from his youth; nor will I again destroy every living thing as I have done.

22 While the earth remains, seedtime and harvest, and cold and heat, and winter and summer, and day and night shall not cease.

Chapter 9

1 So Elohim **Blessed** Noakh and his sons, and said to them, Be fruitful, and multiply, and replenish [2] the earth.

2 And the fear of you and the dread of you shall be on every beast of the earth, on every bird of the air, on all that moves on the earth, and on all the fish of the sea; they are given into your hand.

3 All moving animals that have life shall be for use/consumption[3]

for you. I have given you all things, even as the green herbs.

4 But you shall not eat flesh with its life, that is, its blood.

5 Surely for your lifeblood I will demand a reckoning; from the hand of every beast I will require it, and from the hand of man; from the hand of every man's brother I will require the life of man.

6 Whoever sheds man's blood, by man his blood shall be shed: for in the images of Elohim He made man.

7 And as for you, be fruitful, and multiply;[4] bring forth abundantly in the earth, and multiply in it.

animals can be found in Leviticus Ch. 11. Noah knew what was clean, and unclean, and would never eat pigs or the likes of such animals. The word 'All' and 'life' have a special context. See our article 'all does not mean all', http://www.forever-israel.com/Simon/pdfs/ALL-Zec14.pdf. Here, common permissible food only, established for Noakh. Use here can also mean we can take the bones of an animal and grind them for medicine or take the heart of an animal and use it for medicinal purposes as most diabetic medicine is made from pigs, we don't eat it but the medicine can save our life.

[4] The Torah speaks about ruling class of people and they always had multiple households with at least two wives, north and south.

The West practices, what is, a form of polygamy, let us explain. Here, a man sleeps with a woman without marrying her, giving her some children. He then moves on to do the same with another woman, until he probably has quite a few children, and has quite a few women impregnated with children; but, no marriage to any of them. Most people accept this form of serial polygamy in the West where you just divorce and remarry the next one; but they have problems accepting YHWH's allowance for polygamy that establishes households and Continued in next section

Footnotes
[1] Noah knew the difference between clean and unclean because it was taught to him by Adam and then later both Noah and his son Shem setup the first Yeshiva a teaching center to teach people Torah.
[2] The earth was replenished after the flood.
[3] Excluding unclean animals, that is how this text is understood. The list of unclean Continued in next section

8 Then Elohim spoke to Noakh, and to his sons with him, saying,

9 And as for Me, behold, I establish My Covenant[1] with you and with your descendants after you;

10 and with every living creature that is with you: the birds, the cattle, and every beast of the earth with you; of all that go out of the ark, every beast of the earth.

11 Thus I establish My Covenant with you; never again shall all flesh be cut off by the mayim of the flood; never again shall there be a flood to destroy the earth.

12 And Elohim said, This is the sign of the Covenant[2] which I make between Me and you, and every living creature that is with you, for perpetual generations:

13 I set My rainbow in the cloud, and it shall be for the sign of the Covenant between Me and the earth.

14 It shall be, when I bring a cloud over the earth, that the rainbow shall be seen in the cloud:

15 and I will remember My Covenant, which is between Me and you and every living creature of all flesh; the mayim shall never again become a flood to destroy all flesh.

16 The rainbow shall be in the cloud; and I will look on it, to remember the everlasting Covenant between Elohim and every living creature of all flesh that is on the earth.

17 And Elohim said to Noakh, This is the sign of the Covenant, which I have established between Me and all flesh that is on the earth.

18 Now the sons of Noakh who went out of the ark were: Shem, and Kham, and Yapet: and Kham was the Abbah of Kanan.

19 These three were the sons of Noakh: and from these the whole earth was re-populated.

20 And Noakh began to be a farmer, and he planted a vineyard:

securing larger Israelite dwellings and lands. The earth cannot be replenished using the model of one family, having one child, as is/was practiced in China. Noah had a second wife named Emzara, she did not make it into the ark.

Noah was from a ruling class nobleman and also had two wives just like his predecessors; Ham was the product of that marriage, to that wife. They were Patriarchal, and practiced plural marriages. There is another argument that YHWH can give twelve or fourteen children to a woman and no doubt YHWH can so that does not mean monogamy is inferior. What these types of arguments show people running with head knowledge and lack knowledge how ruling classed lives. YHWH does not want one woman to be pregnant for half her life. Pregnancy is difficult and makes many changes in a woman and some women can even die from it. The average children in Israel were five to a woman in a fifty two children family with an average of seven wives. This can be clearly seen in our footnote in Numbers 1:46.

[1] The Covenant is mentioned seven times, and it represents the top level of the Sefirotic tree, and the top level of the Menorah.

Footnotes
[2] All Covenants are eternal, and binding; no Covenant is annulled or abrogated.

21 Then he drank of the wine, and was drunk; and became uncovered in her[1] tent.

22 And Kham, the Abbah of Kanan, saw the nakedness of his Abbah, and told his two brothers outside.

23 And He Shem took with Yapet a garment, laid it on both their shoulders, and went backward and covered the nakedness of their Abbah: their faces were turned away, and they did not see their Abbah's nakedness. [2]

24 So Noakh awoke from his wine, and knew what his younger son had done to him.

25 Then he said, Cursed be Kanan;[3] a servant of servants he shall be to his brethren.[4]

Footnotes
[1] In Noah's wife's tent same as in Gen 12:8 the word is feminine.
[2] The Hebrew grammar is at fault but really says "He Shem" took (Weh Yeh Khak instead of weh yeh Khoo) the garment". Really the main Benediction was upon Shem and not on Yapet as many think because Yapet wasn't very faithful and fell later into idolatry. The Hebrew can be compared with Gen 6:2 with "And they took ויקחו"
[3] Why did Noakh curse Kanan opposed to Cham directly. This is because Kanan was the product of the Union between Cham and his step-mother while Noakh was drunk they did the unthinkable sin and the result was Kanan. Noakh had two wives in the same North/South Axis. Adam also had the same. Abraham the same and the rest of our fathers. They all lived Patriarchal lives while Monogamy is never directly commanded polygamy is. While also the Hebrews have the character of the lion, which is polygamous hence, Satan is a depicted as a wolf which is a monogamous animal. Men can choose to live as Satan did or as our father Abraham. The curse was a pronouncement only on Qaynan and his sons who were removed from Israel. It did not affect Ham's other sons.

[4] By Rabbi Matthew Nolan, Torah to the Tribes, Oregon, USA, 2009
The Patriarchal family of Noakh.

The question arises as to why Kanan was cursed by Noakh? Why not curse Ham himself, or Cush or Put or Mitzrayim? By unfolding our Beresheeth narrative a little further than the traditional story, one of Noakh getting drunk and Ham coming in and looking at his naked father, we will soon discover Noakh's patriarchal roots. My suggestion is that Noakh and Ham were enjoying the fruits of Noakh's vineyard, in Noakh's tent, when Noakh passed out.

Ham then went into the adjoining chamber, and slept with Noakh's wife. He then came out being loose lipped because of his merriment, told his brothers. They then, backed into the tent and covered their father's wife; thereby covering their 'father's nakedness.' Kanan was the child of this union which is why Noakh cursed Kanan.

The Canaanites were well known in the Torah, for their perverse sexual practices. Which we are warned to avoid in Vayikra (Lev). A despicable trait of sexual immorality was passed down through the generational line birthed out of Ham's sin that took place in Noakh's tent (Beresheeth 9:22). Yet in our narrative we know that only one of Noakh's wives made it onto the ark. Sefer Ha Yashar, and Sefer Ha Yovel/Jubilees tell us of Noakh's wives. One named Emzara, the daughter of Rakeel, who did not make it onto the ark (Jubilees 4:33). The other named Naamah, Noakh's wife, the daughter of Enoch, who was not Ham's mother, and who did make it onto the ark (Yashar 5:12). Our text in Vayikra/Leviticus 18:7 & 18:8 supports this by clarifying the phrase for Ham's sin as 'uncovering your father's nakedness', which means sleeping with your father's wife (Naamah) who is not your mother. The nakedness of your mother is 'her nakedness', but the term used in Beresheeth 'your father's nakedness', is in reference to the nakedness of your father's wife that was uncovered i.e. slept with.

It is also important to note that Abraham lived with Noakh for thirty nine years (Yashar 9:5) and learned the instructions of YHWH and His ways. This is clearly where
Continued in next section

26 And he said, **Blessed** is YHWH, the POWER of Shem; and Kanan will become his servant.[1]

27 Elohim will allow Yapet to be deceived[2] and he will dwell[3] in the tents of Shem; and Kanan[4] will become his servant.

28 And Noakh lived after the flood three hundred and fifty years.

29 So all the days of Noakh were nine hundred and fifty years: and he died.

Chapter 10

1 Now these are the generations of the sons of Noakh, Shem, Kham, and Yapet: And sons were born to them after the flood.

2 The sons of Yapet were Gomer, Magog (Turkey), Madai, Yavan, Tubal, Mashek (Turkey), and Tiras.

3 The sons of Gomer were; Ashkenaz (Europe), Riphath, and Togarmah (Turkey).

4 The sons of Yavan were; Elishah, Tarshush,[5] Kittim,[6] and Dodanim (Rhode Islands and parts of Italy and Spain).

Abraham learned to order his house into a patriarchal one, that was, kadosh/Holy, and acceptable to YHWH, just like Noakh before him.

[1] This prophecy was fulfilled when the original descendants, living in the land, were removed by the twelve tribes of Israel and they served Shem but the prophecy will extend to the End of the Age when Kanan will once again serve Shem's sons and not Japheth.

[2] YHWH will deceive the Caucasian Europeans through the evil one that they will think they are the chosen ones when they in fact are not. They will go and take over the land of Israel as their own which has already happened. Patah means to speak evil from the heart but show a different face in other words two faced. Many European leaders will be two faced in the End of Days when they are deceived by their own minds and the people who reject YHWH will fall into lewdness. However the door would be open for good Caucasian people to join our people to serve YHWH that they may be rescued from the end-times wrath.

[3] Today the true Israelites are not in the land of Israel but many Ashkanzim are in fact converts from the kingdom of Khazar. They are not Semitic but in fact are the sons of Yapet. Just as YHWH had said they will occupy the tents of Shem and will look like Shem so they do today likewise. However in the future a time will come when the natural true Israelites will be brought into Israel and Yapet removed to his proper place. According to letters sent and received by the Sephardic Yahudim the King of Khazaria, who was Yosef himself said they had descended from Yapet. Note also after the breakup of the kingdom they all ended in modern Western Europe from where many of these migrated into Israel claiming to be ancient Yahudim.

The 13th Tribe p28 by Arthur Koestler Eldad visited Spain around 880 and may or may not have visited the Khazar country. Continued in next section

Hasdai briefly mentions him in his letter to Joseph – as if to ask what to make of him. Joseph then proceeds to provide a genealogy of his people. Though a fierce Hebrew nationalist, proud of wielding the 'sceptre of Judah", he cannot, and does not, claim for them Semitic descent; he traces their ancestry not to Shem, but to Noah's third son, Japheth; [end quote]

Few people in ancient Israel were from the Jewish stock that is Sephardic, most Africans and ancient Persian Jewry alone make up that stock, while the Ashkanazim Jews are really East European Khazar gentile converts into Judaism.

[4] The curse only applies to Kanan's sons in the land of Israel.

[5] This has to be read Tarshush and not Tarsish as these are the European sides, the region of south central Turkey.

[6] Cyprus and parts of Europe.

5 From these the coastland peoples of the Gentiles were separated into their lands; everyone according to his language, according to their Mishpakhot (families), into their nations.

6 The sons of Kham were; Kush,[1] Mitzrayim (Egypt) Phut (Somalia) [2], and Kanan.[3]

7 The sons of Kush (Nubia, Sudan, Ethiopia) were; Sheba,[4] Khavilah,[5] Sabtah, Raamah, and Sabtechah; and the sons of Raamah were Sheba (South Arabia, Yemen parts of West Africa) and Dedan.[6]

8 Kush begot Nimrud:[7] and he became a warrior/tyrant[8] upon the earth.

Nimrud ruled from Mesopotamia all the way to India he was from North Sudan.[9]

9 He was a warrior hunter[10] in the face of YHWH: therefore it is said, like Nimrud the warrior hunter in YHWH's face.[11]

10 And the first of his Malkhut (kingdom) was Babel (East Africa), Erekh, Accad,[12] and Calneh, in the land of Shinar (Eritrea, Djibouti and Somalia). [13]

11 From that land he went to Asshur,[14] and built Nineveh, Rehoboth Ir, Calah,

12 And Resen between Nineveh and Calah: that is the principal city.

13 And Mitzrayim (Egypt) begot Ludim, Anamim, Lehabim, [15] Naphtuhim,

14 Pathrusim, and Kaslukhim from who came the Plushtim,[16] and Kaphtorim.[17]

15 Kanan begot Sidon his Bekhor (first born), and Kheth,

16 And the Yavusee,[1] the Amoree, and the Girgashi;

Footnotes
[1] South of the river Nile, Nubia and Sudan.
[2] The land of Punt near bab -el Mandeb in Africa the horn of Africa, area of Somalia.
[3] Descendants of Ham, who were removed from Israel, because of the curse of Noah.
[4] South Arabia, today, known as Yemen including other parts of Africa.
[5] India, Saudi Arabia and West Africa.
[6] Oasis, in Northern, Saudi Arabia, where travellers often stopped for refreshments. Dedanites were black people.
[7] Nimrud means swift hawk pouring water.
[8] He was a giant opposing YHWH, and he built many cities.
[9] The people out of North Sudan a part of the Cush Empire was where the men were very tall and strong Nimrud came from there. These people are mentioned by Isaiah in 18:2. These people were known to be a fierce warrior class.
[10] Nimrud was a hunter of the souls of men, people worshipped him. He is the picture of Continued in next section

the anti-Messiah right in the regions of Turkey and Iraq, the very places which are today occupied by Islam. Which also is a 'giant' religion that will be brought down one day, like Goliath.
[11] This text shows Nimrud in opposition to YHWH, not a friend; but an enemy of YHWH.
[12] City North of Iraq.
[13] A term applied to Babylon, encompassing central Iraq that ran from Dijibouti, Eritrea, bab-el-mandeb to Yemen covering eastern Africa. See footnote Zech 5:11. This city was not in Babylon but was a province of Babylon in East Africa in Djibouti and surrounding regions.
[14] Regions of Iraq, Turkey, Syria and Iran.
[15] Libyans, this could be a textual error by the scribe, as the reference is to the Libyans, and not the Turkic people. While most Bibles read Ludim, it should really read Lubim, as Ludim are descendants of Japheth and not Ham.
[16] Some of the modern Berbers are from the Plushtim.
[17] South of Egypt land of the blacks.

17 the Khawee, the Arki, and the Sini;

18 the Arawadi, the Zemari, and the Khamathi: afterward the Mishpakhot (families) of the Kanani were dispersed.

19 And the border of the Kanani was from Sidon, as you go toward Gerar, as far as Azza (Gaza); then as you go toward Sedom, Amorah (Gomorrah), Admah, and Zeboim, as far as Lasha.

20 These were the sons of Kham, according to their Mishpakhot (families), according to their languages, in their lands and in their nations.

21 And children were born also to Shem, the Abbah of all the children of Eber, the brother of Yapet the elder.

22 The sons of Shem were; Elam (Iran), Asshur (Assyria), Arpakshad,[2] Lud (Turkey), and Aram (Syria) and Qeynan.[3]

[1] This is the ancient name for Jerusalem (Yebus) in the Torah for those who say Jerusalem is not mentioned in the Torah, so the son of Kanan was the original inhabitant of Yebus but because of his idolatry Jerusalem was taken from him and given over to his nephews the Israelites who were also the sons of Shem, the sons of Qeynan as there are two Kanan's and we have spelt it differently one the KJV Genealogy was removed by the haters of YHWH and His people. See footnote Gen 10:22 about Qeynan.

[2] Arpakshad is Aref+Chesed, these are twins or two persons. It appears this may have been mistaken for one person by the scribe hence the name is joined. We find one son under Nakh'Khur appearing as Chesed which is this derivative in Gen 22:22. According to the scholar John Lamb this should have been written the twins sons of Shem... According to John Lamb, The Dalet in chesed is like lips spelt Kaf, sin and dalet and shem like moon Continued in next section

signifies these studied astronomy who were later called Chasdees. He gives Aref the meaning "man of a bird's mouth" in his studies on ancient Hebrew Hieroglyphs page 69 Hebrew characters derived from Hieroglyphs.

[3] The missing genealogy of Qeynan has been rectified from the Septuagint as this piece of text was omitted by the Masorets which has created a conflict in that people do not know that the sixth son of Shem was Qeynan. The Masoretic subtraction was unlawful and YHWH will punish this as His pleasure. The masorets as part of a scheme did many changes omitting the changes in other places also such as the name of YHWH to Adoni. Arpakshad was not the grandfather of Shalakh but Qeynan was and this genealogy shows us clearly that Abraham was a Nilotic person and person of black skin colour as that was the skin colour of Kanan who was the great grandfather of Abraham.

Qeynan was the father of Shalakh. Qeynan is the biological grandfather of Eber the forefather of the Hebrews. The person was originally called Qeynan. The text proves that Qeynan was the biological ancestor of Abraham. This also means that between Qeynan and time of the end of the flood is 397 years which gives us extra time which otherwise is missing if you use the erroneous missing genealogy of the masorets bringing us in conflict with the Egyptians dynasties.

YHWH said THE LAND OF KANAN was the birth place of the children of Israel. It does not say the land of Jacob or the land of Abraham was their birthplace as that is an important fact and must be taken into consideration whenever understanding and looking at prophecy and property rights. If YHWH had told us the land of China was the birthplace of Israel then we would be looking for the Hebrews in China with Mongolian features but we are not although we do have some Yahudim in China with Mongolian features who had departed from Israel many years ago to live there.

Yes that is right the land today called Israel was originally possessed by Kanan and his descendants before YHWH gave it to the sons of Jacob. The reason the land was taken from Kanan was simply this that they Continued in next section were idolatrous and practiced all sorts of witchcraft and divination to false deities and sacrificed children, they did many other foolish things such as bestiality, and some other pretty weird things such as defecating in front of their false deity.

Another Kanan was also the SON of HAM and Kanan had 12 Children. If you note the genealogies only eleven are mentioned in Beresheeth 10:15-18. So who is the twelfth? We will look at this later.

Shem, was the father of Joktan called Qahtan in Arabic continuing all the way to Jacob excluding Esaw as an Israelite. However many converts joined Israel in the past and are counted as Israel irrespective of colour including today.

It was Yoktan in the Torah, Qahtan in the Arabic text who is the real progenitor of the Arabs. The original Arabs were also mostly black races of people even today you will find many dark skinned Arabs that they would rarely would show you on TV channels.

So how could Israel's father be an Amoree (Kanan's son) and mother be a Khitee, (another Kanan's son whose daughter married the Amoree)? This is what Y'chezkiel (Ezekiel) the prophet a Levite is telling us. When a Levite speaks we need to hear him because Levites are the only true teachers of YHWH.

Beresheeth 10:15-16 Kanan begot Sidon his Bekhor (first born), and Kheth, 16 And the Yebusee, the Amoree, and the Girgashi;

There you see the two identified in the above scriptures. Unfortunately most Jewish rabbis just like to gloss over this and ignore the fact that Abraham is identified as a man of dark skin tone! They think and teach that Israel is only being identified as these two nations because they were great nations at one time but that is not true. Israel was never a great nation until King David and King Solomon's time. Before that Israel was a very small nation and many other nations were much bigger and stronger than Israel. If it wasn't for YHWH every nation would have beat us into submission. Let me tell you one more thing according to YHWH's testimony our mother and father were
Continued in next section

Amoree and Khitee which means a marriage took place between these two black people and another black child was born namely Israel.

Abraham was a ruling prince from the clans of Shem and had relations with the Cushites (Black Africans from Ham) purchased some land from Kheth for his wife Sarah and other children's graves to bury his dead.

Beresheeth 23:5-9 And the sons of Kheth answered Abraham, saying to him, 6 Hear us, my master: you are a mighty prince among us: bury your dead in the choicest of our burial places; none of us will withhold from you his burial place, that you may bury your dead. 7 Then Abraham stood up, and bowed himself to the people of the land, the sons of Kheth. 8 And he spoke with them, saying, If it is your wish that I bury my dead out of my sight; hear me, and meet with Ephron the son of Zokhar for me, 9 That he may give me the cave of Machpelah, which he has, which is at the end of his field; let him give it to me at the full price, as property for a burial place among you.

Abraham was a ruling Horoite prince from Turkey but his father Tharakh actually came from West Africa and he was working for the Black Cushite King Nimrud who was also a relative of Abraham through Shem and Ham's sons and daughters having mixed marriages.

Abraham made a legal purchase in Israel from the sons of Kheth who acknowledged him as a ruling prince and this is significant. No one offers you land free but they offered it as a gift first however Abraham paid for it and made a legal deed in order to secure it for the later generations. The reason why they offered it free is because Abraham had relations with the Khitee.

The sons of Kheth were the sons of Kanan who was the biological father of Shalakh and Shalakh is the father of Eber. The purchase of the piece of land was recorded in the Torah that no one can dispute Abraham's purchase of the land from the black men which were the Kanani who sold to another black man (A son of Shem) Abraham.

Continued in next section

23 The sons of Aram were; Uz, Hul, Gether, and Mashek.[1]

24 Qeynan begot Shalakh; and Shalakh begot Eber. [2]

25 To Eber were born two sons: the name of one was Phaleg;[3] for in his days the earth was divided; and his brother's name was Yoktan.

26 Yoktan[4] begot Almodad, Sheleph, Hazarmaveth, Yarakh,

27 Hadoram, Uzal, Diklah,

28 Obal, Abimael, Sheba,[5]

29 Ophir,[6] Khavilah, and Yobab: all these were the sons of Yoktan.

Since Qeynan was the son of Shem whose daughter married Ham's therefore by YHWH's own testimony these children were of light and dark brown skin tones and of African ethnicity.

Why was YHWH so blunt? This is because he called Israel here gentiles and associated them with the practices and ways of the gentiles. This is something that we are forbidden not to do to follow after the gentiles.

[1] Some translations read Mash. These are Turkic people.

[2] Septuagint.

[3] A city near the Euphrates called Phalga.

[4] The ancestor of the southern Arabs called Qahtan.

[5] Sheba was black inhabiting regions of Africa.

[6] Ophir is the biblical term for the land of Africa noting that the term 'Africa' is of late historical derivative. In the Greek tongue the term Frike means cold and horror and appending the A to it becomes Africa which mean "not the land of cold and horror" but as can be seen many horrors were perpetrated there by the so called civilised nations of the world one such as slavery and colonization to subjugate the 10,000 kingdoms that existed there. In the Latin language the term Afrika meant sunny. It is well known that India's and China's ancestors were African people and also they were the early inhabitants of the Americas.

30 And their dwelling place was from Mesha,[7] as you go toward Sephar, the mountain of the east.[8]

31 These were the sons of Shem, according to their Mishpakhot (families), according to their languages, in their lands, according to their nations.

32 These were the Mishpakhot (families) of the sons of Noakh, according to their generations, in their nations: and from these the nations were divided on the earth after the flood.

Chapter 11

1 Now the whole earth had one language and Akhad speech.[9]

2 And it came to pass, they set out to the eastern direction, and they found a valley between the mountains in the land of Shinar (Eritrea, Djibouti and Somalia)[10] and they made their dwelling there.

3 Then they said to one another, Come, let us make bricks, and bake them thoroughly. And they had brick for stone, and they had asphalt for mortar.

Footnotes

[7] Ancient name for Mecca in Western-Saudi Arabia.

[8] Pilgrimage place of Islam.

[9] The first language was Hebrew, written in hieroglyphics.

[10] Eastern Africa all the way to Iraq and to the borders of Iran, although we believe that it is a wider area covering ancient Assyria. These came from West Africa to Eastern Africa to build in this area the Tower of Babel right in the heart of East Africa connecting to Yemen and Saudi Arabia.

4 And they said, Come, let us build ourselves a city[1] and a tower, whose top is in the shamayim; let us make a name[2] for ourselves, lest we be scattered abroad over the face of the whole earth.[3]

5 And YHWH came down to see the city and the tower,[4] which the sons of men had built.

6 And YHWH said, Indeed, the people are Akhad and they all have an Akhad language; and this is what they begin to do: now nothing that they propose to do, will be withheld from them.

7 Come, let Us[5] go down and there confuse their language, that they may not understand one another's speech.

The Tower of Babel destroyed and India Separated from Africa which was once joined to it.

India and Pakistan were part of Africa and China was in the south including Philippines and Thailand were adjacent nations of India that Nimrud had control over. Africa was one big landmass which was split up by judgment of YHWH and his seventy angels who descended to judge Nimrud at the tower of Babel in East Africa. There was no Indian Ocean next to East Africa until India, Pakistan and the other nations were split up after the judgment of Nimrud hence why Babel Mendeb to this day is known as the "Gate of Grief or Tears remembered by the Arabs".

8 So YHWH scattered them abroad from there over the face of all the earth: and they ceased building the city.

9 Therefore its name is called Babel;[6] because there YHWH confused the language of all the

Footnotes

[1] It took them forty three years to build this city and the tower was over a mile high, some estimate mile and a half.
[2] They wanted to build a name and were opposing the authority of YHWH. These people were fearful that they may receive another flood so they wanted to build a huge tower to protect them.
[3] In the east of Africa.
[4] Herodotus and Strabo suggest that the tower was a furlong, which is a mile high. These people wanted to challenge the Elohim of shamayim, YHWH.
[5] Unity of the Plurality of YHWH.

Footnotes
[6] The area of Eritrea, Djobouti and Yemen, Bab'el-Mandeb in Arabic is the "Gate of Grief" or ancient Tower of Babel. This is the area of the tragedy of the Tower of Babel in the land of Punt where Nimrud established his first kingdom. This land was first established by Nimrud and later Nebuchadnezzar had some control over this land too as it is counted as Babylon this includes Yemen and Saudi Arabia. The Arabs remember the story of the tower of Babel which was destroyed by judgement by YHWH and one judgment was the earthquake which separated India from Africa in those days when many people drowned.

earth: and from there YHWH scattered them abroad over the face of all the earth.

10 This is the genealogy of Shem: Shem was one hundred years old, and fathered Arpakshad in the second year after the flood:

11 And after Shem became father to Arpakshad, he lived three hundred and thirty five more years (fathering other sons and daughters), and then he died.

12 Arpakshad was a hundred and thirty-five years old when he became father to Qeynan.

13 And after Arpakshad became the father to Qeynan, he lived three hundred and thirty years more (as he fathered other sons and daughters), and then he died. Qeynan was a hundred and thirty years old when he became father to Shalakh. And after he became father to Shalakh, he lived three hundred and thirty years (as he fathered other sons and daughters), and then he died.

14 Shalakh lived one hundred and thirty years, and became father of Eber:

15 And after he became father to Eber, he lived three hundred and thirty years more (as he fathered other sons and daughters), and then he died.

16 Eber was a hundred and thirty-four years old when he became father to Phaleg:

17 And after he became father to Phaleg, he lived two hundred and seventy years (as he fathered other sons and daughters), and then he died.

18 Phaleg was a hundred and thirty years old when he became father to Ragau.

19 After he begot Ragau, Phaleg lived two hundred and nine years, and fathered others sons and daughters.

20 Ragau lived a hundred, thirty-two years, and begot Serug:

21 After he begot Serug, Ragau lived two hundred and seven years, and fathered other sons and daughters.

22 Serug lived a hundred, thirty years, and begot Nakhkhur:

23 After he begot Nakhkhur, Serug lived two hundred years, and fathered other sons and daughters.

24 Nakhkhur lived seventy-nine years, and fathered Tharakh:[1]

Footnotes

[1] Tharakh was a mighty chief under Nimrud. Rulers and chief's like this always had two wives one in the north and the other in the south to create the north-south axis and to protect their lands. The north is representative for Ain Sof which is applied to YHWH and His place of dwelling is in the north which is the third shamayim. These people worshipped the sun and stars so they did not place their families in the east and west because the sun rises out of the east and sets in the west associated with their false elohim.

We find that Tharakh named one of his son's Haran who was in the North and the other Ur or we see this in the name Nakh'Khur. This region extended from Turkey all the way to the south of Israel where the Qeny and Horites lived. The Horites people settled and lived in present day Israel known as Kanan. They were situated in Bethlehem and surrounding regions. Abraham would have not been a foreigner in Israel but would have known these lands belonged to his father because Tharakh's second wife was from the region of Bethlehem the name of a man. Abraham's first wife Keturah (cousin Continued in next section

25 After he begot Tharakh,[1] Nakhkhur lived one hundred and twenty nine years, and fathered other sons and daughters and he died.

26 Now Tharakh[2] lived seventy years, and begot Abram,[3] Nakhkhur, and Haran.[4]

27 This is the genealogy of Tharakh: Tharakh begot Abram, Nakhkhur, and Haran; Haran begot Lot.[5]

28 And Haran died before his Abbah Tharakh in his native land, in Ur of the Kasdim.[6]

29 Then Abram and Nakhkhur took wives: the name of Abram's wife was Sarai; and the name of Nakhkhur's wife, Milkah, the daughter of Haran, the Abbah of Milkah, and the Abbah of Yskah.[7]

30 But Sarai was barren; she had no child.

31 And Tharakh took his son Abram, and his grandson, Lot, the son of Haran, and his daughter-in-law Sarai, his son

wife) was also from Bethlehem connected to his mother's family who lived in this region. Abraham's second wife Sarah was his half sister wife.

[1] Tharakh is the first person, known by the Hebrew writers, to have coined money, then men started to worship images. He was an idolater, worshipping statues as elohim, and seems to have departed from the Faith of the forefathers.

[2] Abraham's mum was called Amthalai, or Chamtelaah, Arabic writers called her, Juno. 3 The name Eber or Abar means 'son of the bird'. YHWH added Mem to Abraham's name so it became Abram when he crossed over the waters as mem is for waters then he was given the heh. Abraham was a man of dark complexion this meaning is in his name also. His father's name is Tarach which meant 'dove of my bosom.' The ancient khet in his name means concealed, Dark or Black. Note that the Hebrew language when written in pictograph was monosyllable. Shem was of fair complexion as termed by the shin in his name which can mean shining black skin and he had the locks of hair like Africans. The Ark landed in Central Africa and that is where the original Hebrews started from and gravitated towards at their punishments and will also return from there. Cham his brother was jet black. Japheth's fair white complexion came from Noakh being an albino so he was similar to him.

[4] A place in Turkey, where the moon God's temple was in ancient times, and a place of major trade.

[5] Lot and Sarah were cousins.

Footnotes

[6] In Turkey near present day Edessa, used to be known as Ur or Urfa.

[7] Abraham was dark skinned man, his father was from Seno/Gambia from the fulfulbe tribe, His wife Mashek was Caucasian. Yskah's name after marriage was Sarai meaning my princess, according to the Targum of Jonathan. However that is incorrect. Sarah's tribal name was Sara spelt without the Hebrew Heh, she was Abraham's third wife. This was an African tribe, which had migrated to Mesopotamia from the south, she was of royal blood. She was from Tharakh's second wife, who was a black Ethiopian. See Gen 20:12. However Elohim saw it fit to give her the title Sarah with a heh which means princess with a ruakh. In Hebrew culture a name is not a marker but a reflection of who you are. It is different to today's names e.g. Melek David would not just mean 'King David' but would be seen in the people as 'Beloved King" or 'The Loving King', 'loving' being the meaning of the word 'David.'

It is to be noted that Abraham's people were Hebrews and of black skin colour with wooly hair. We have to make a distinction that amongst the black skinned Hebrews some people were of straight hair also. It is also important to note that Abraham married the daughter of Joktan the son of Eber, the son of Shalakh, the son of Arpakshad and the son of Shem who lived in Beersheba Israel, she was of black skin tone also as was Sarah.

Abram's wife; and they went out with them from Ur of the Kasdim, to go to the land of Kanan, and they came to Haran and dwelt there.

32 So the days of Tharakh were two hundred and five years: and Tharakh died in Haran.[1]

Torah Parsha 3 Lech Lecha, Beresheeth 12:1-17:27
Haftarah: Yeshayahu 40:27-41:16

Chapter 12

1 Now YHWH had said to Abram,[2] Get[3] out of your country,[4] from your native country, and from your Abbah's Beyth (house), to a land that I will show you:[5]

2 And I will make you a strong/mighty nation and I will make you a benefit to others and make your name great. And You shall be an **Increase**[6] to all[7] who embrace you.

3 I will **Bless** those who come to **Bless** you, and I will curse him[8] who despises you and sees you as worthless;[9] and in you all the Mishpakhot (families) of the earth shall be en-grafted.[10]

Footnotes

[1] A region in Eastern Turkey, where Abraham and his clan came from. This is also attested by Joshua the son of Nun in Joshua 24:3.

[2] The language was not called Hebrew, as we understand the term today, but it was termed Abaru, from Abraham.

[3] Abraham's family came out of India, today known as Pakistan what we are told in the Tanak, (The other side of Euphrates) Josh 24:3.

[4] South-eastern Turkey, not Iraq, as erroneously thought by many.

[5] According to rabbinic Judaism Abraham was born in 1948 BCE, note this is inaccurate. Abraham was the Tenth generation from Noakh. He was a descendant of Shem a Black Hebrew. These were the Semitic people who lived in Africa. At Abraham's birth Shem would be 390 years old and Shem's father Noakh would be 892 years old placing Abraham at 58 years of age when Noakh died. Noakh was Abraham's teacher alongside Shem who operated the first Yeshivah out of West Africa before his children migrated outwards to Turkey and beyond. Noakh had first hand information of Methushelah who lived the longest in record and he had full knowledge
Continued in next section

of Adam which was passed down to Abraham through Noakh accurately. Adam was created in Israel a country in Africa. The Garden of Ayden also stretched from West Africa to the East and to the North of African outside the borders of Israel.

[6] YHWH gave Abraham's Faith to all others to make him a **blessing** to all those who come to know Abraham's Mighty EL. To embrace Abraham is to Embrace the promises given to Him and receive his blessings and those who curse Abraham's progeny will be cursed in this earth.

[7] Y'sraélites only....

[8] The Hebrew here is, 'arar', which means to curse, or, to put a curse upon to decrease, not black magic, simply uttering via the mouth, as Balaam the false prophet tried in Numbers 22:18.

[9] Both words for curse are different, as the Hebrew used here is 'kalal', which means, - contempt-, dishonor and despise. Anyone who despises Israel will have a Holy curse put on them. The ancient Hebrew meaning has been used to its fullest. The Black Hebrews have been treated with contempt and so those people who did this would be severely punished both in this world and the next. While, many people have been chasing after the wrong people and were gentiles until converted. The real Black Hebrews are in front of their eyes but were despised and called bad names. Such people have punishment awaiting and those that died are already being punished in She'ol with no eternal life.

[10] All the families shall be engrafted, the Hebrew word, nevrechu, is used to mean; engrafting to take place in the future. Many teach this as some kind of gentile engrafting
Continued in next section

4 So Abram departed as YHWH had spoken to him; and Lot went with him: and Abram was seventy-five years old when he departed from Haran.

5 Then Abram[1] took Sarai[1] his wife, and Lot his brother's son,

but the define article in the Hebrew word Adamah and the fact that the prophecy's context is verse 1. This means this only applies to the Israelites families who are in the land or will be brought in the land in the future who will thus receive the increase. At that point as they will come back as wandering Israelites they will be re-joined or regrafted to the Olive tree, This is not about gentiles being brought in who are idolaters and Elohim does not bless idolaters, which contradicts the Torah. ונברכו בך כל

משפחת האדמה Therefore this prophecy must be understood in its correct context as each line of chapter 12 has a hook that connects back to the previous verse, the Hebrew letter Wah, which is the adjoiner.

[1] Abraham's Two Concubines By a researcher on the studies in Genesis Alice C. Linsley
http://jandyongenesis.blogspot.com/2010/08/abrahams-two-concubines.html

God established Abraham as a ruler in Kanan, the land over which his mother's people ruled. The northern and southern boundaries of Abraham's territory were marked by the settlements of his two wives. Sarah dwelt in Hebron and Keturah dwelt in Beer-sheba to the south. Abraham's wives bore him 7 sons. Daughters were born also, though they are not named in the Bible. Abraham's sons married these daughters and the daughters of Na-hor, Abraham's older brother.

Sons were born to Abraham by concubine servants as well. Ishmael, was born of Hagar and, according to the Septuagint, Eliezar of Damascus was born of Masek. In the New Jerusalem Bible (following the Vulgate) Abraham says to the Lord: "Since you have given me no offspring... a member of my household will be my heir." The Septuagint offers this: "What will you give me, seeing I go childless and the heir of my house is Continued in next section

Eliezer of Damascus, the son of Masek, my domestic maidservant." Eliezar as a son of Abraham by a maidservant, parallels the story of Hagar. This means that Abraham had 9 sons: Ishmael, Eliezer, Isaac, Joktan, Zimram, Medan, Midian, Ishbak and Shuah. There were also daughters. Clearly, God fulfilled His King will concerning Abraham that he should be the "Father of a multitude".

Hagar and Masek are to Abraham's household what the concubines Zilpah and Bilhah are to Jacob's household. They built up the ruling houses of these patriarchs by producing many offspring. If the biblical pattern is to be trusted, we may reasonably suspect that Hagar and Masek were the servants of Sarah and Keturah, just as Zilpah was the servant of Leah and Bilhah the servant of Rachel (Gen. 30). That Masek was Keturah's servant is supported by the fact that the name Masek is still found among the south Arabian Mahra. They dwell in Yemen, Oman and southern Saudi Arabia (see map). This is where we would expect to find the descendents of Abaham by Keturah's servant Masek.

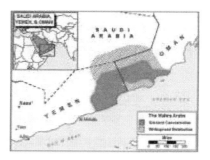

Some Mahra/Masek are semi-nomadic and others are settled in small semi-fortified villages where they farm and raise chickens for eggs and goats for milk. They are known to aggressively defend their territories and water sources and are regarded as belonging to the warrior caste. Their chiefs control the goods and persons who pass through their lands.

The Mahra/Masek are an endogamous tribe, which means that they exclusively marry within their kinship circle. Most men have only one wife, but the chief may have more than one. Children receive inheritances patrilineally, with the first-born son receiving Continued in next section

and all their possessions that they had gathered, and the people whom they had acquired in Haran; and they departed to go to the land of Kanan; so they came to the land of Kanan.

the lion's share. Young girls are valued for childbearing and for the bonding of families through marriage. This was especially true in Abraham's time for both wives and concubines.

[1] Sarah is the descendant of the West African tribe where she is from and was a princess since the name Sarai meant my princess from which it was changed by Elohim to Sarah. The group members with the same family structure can still be found near Lake Chad. These people are organized by a patrilineal descent and still function the same way today. Since the lines of Shem and Ham intermarried Abraham had many black descendants. One of Cush's descendants Sheba had a daughter who married with Joktan and produced a son called Sheba as was custom to name sons after their grandfather in this tribe. Bathsheba a black African woman the wife of Uriah who later became the wife of King David was a direct descendant of Sheba from the Ham lineage who became the descendant of King Messiah.

An inscription was found to confirm trade of Judah and the King of Sheba in the 6th century BC. This confirms that our diagram above is correct according to ancient customs.
http://www.bib-arch.org/bar/article.asp?PubID=BSBA&Volume=36&Issue=1&ArticleID=28

6 Abram passed through the land to the place of Shkhem, [2] as far as the terebinth tree of Moreh.[3] And the Kanani were then in the land.

7 Then YHWH appeared[4] to Abram, and said, "To your descendants I will give this land" and there he built an altar [5] to YHWH, who had appeared to him.

8 And he moved from there to the mountain east of Beyth'el, and he pitched her tent,[6] with Beyth'el on the west, and Ai on the east: there he built an altar to YHWH,[7]and called on the name of YHWH.

9 So Abram journeyed, going on still toward the South.

10 Now there was a famine in the land: and Abram went down to Mitzrayim (Egypt) to dwell there; for the famine was severe in the land.

Footnotes
[2] The name means shoulder.
[3] Moreh means teacher in Hebrew. This place may well have been an ancient shrine, and Abraham built an altar there to show the true Elohim YHWH.
[4] The Hebrew text shows, YHWH appeared to Abraham, physically in some angelic form, perhaps the angel of YHWH who appeared at other times too like Gen 16:7. The Arabic word raaya and Ethiopic raya are the same in meaning.
[5] There were a particular set of instructions on how to build the altar for YHWH, and this could only happen if Abraham had already received these instructions. He had them from Noah, and Shem, who were his teachers.
[6] The verb here is, to pitch Sarah's tent first, and then his own. This is because Abraham loved Sarah and the sages wrote about this. Each wife would have her own tent or home.
[7] Abraham knew the name of YHWH, and was saved as a child through Noah. Noah's son Shem trained him for 39 years.

11 And it came to pass, when he was close to entering Mitzrayim (Egypt), that he said to Sarai his wife, Indeed, I know that you are a woman of beautiful appearance:

12 Therefore it will happen, when the Mitzrim (Egyptians) see you, that they will say, This is his wife: and they will kill me, but they will let you live.

13 Please, say you are my sister:[1] that it may be well with me for your sake; and that I may live because of you.

14 So it was, when Abram came into Mitzrayim (Egypt), that the Mitzrim (Egyptians) saw the woman, that she was very beautiful.

15 The princes of Pharaoh also saw her, and commended her to Pharaoh: and the woman was taken to Pharaoh's Beyth (house).

16 He treated Abram well for her sake: he had sheep, oxen, male donkeys, male and female servants, female donkeys, and camels.

17 But YHWH plagued Pharaoh and his Beyth (house) with great plagues because of Sarai, Abram's wife.

18 And Pharaoh called Abram and said, What is this you have done to me? Why did you not tell me that she was your wife?

19 Why did you say, She is my sister'? I might have taken her as my wife: now therefore here is your wife, take her, and go your way.

20 So Pharaoh commanded his men concerning him: and they sent him away, with his wife, and all that he had.

Chapter 13

1 Then Abram went up from Mitzrayim (Egypt), he, and his wife, and all that he had, and Lot with him, to the South.

2 Abram was very rich in livestock, in silver, and in gold.

3 And he went on his journey from the South as far as Beyth'el, to the place where her tent[2] had been at the beginning, between Beyth'el and Ai;

4 To the place of the altar, which he had made at first: and there Abram published the name of YHWH.

5 Lot also, who went with Abram, had flocks, and herds, and tents.

6 Now the land was not able to support them, that they might dwell together: for their possessions were so great, that they could not dwell together.

7 And there was strife between the herdsmen of Abram's livestock and the herdsmen of Lot's livestock: the Kanani and the Perzee then dwelt in the land.

8 So Abram said to Lot, Please let there be no strife between you and me, and between my

Footnotes
[1] Abraham's father Tharakh had two wives, Sarah was from the second wife hence his half sister therefore she by definition could be called his sister. Abraham was a good Torah keeper so knew what he was saying was not a lie while many least understand this truth.

Footnotes
[2] Sarah's tent here mentioned in the feminine, Women's tents goes up first and the home is run by the wife or wives.

herdsmen and your herdsmen; for we are brethren.

9 Is not the whole land before you? Please separate from me: if you take the left, then I will go to the right; or, if you go to the right, then I will go to the left.

10 And Lot lifted his eyes, and saw all the plain of Yardan (Jordan), that it was well watered everywhere, before YHWH destroyed Sedom and Amorah (Gomorrah), like the garden of YHWH,[1] like the land of Mitzrayim (Egypt), as you go toward Tzoar.

11 Then Lot chose for himself all the valley of Yardan (Jordan); and Lot journeyed east: and they separated from each other.

12 Abram dwelt in the land of Kanan,[2] and Lot dwelt in the cities of the plain, and pitched his tent even as far as Sedom.

13 But the men of Sedom were exceedingly wicked and sinful against YHWH.

14 And YHWH said to Abram, after Lot had separated from him, Lift your eyes now, and look from the place where you are northward, southward, eastward, and westward:

15 For all the land which you see, I give to you, and your descendants forever.[3]

16 And I will make your descendants as the dust of the earth:[4] So that if a man could number the dust of the earth, then your descendants also could be numbered.

17 Arise, walk in the land through its length and its width; for I give it to you.

18 Then Abram moved his tent, and went and dwelt by the terebinth etzim (trees) of Mamre, which are in Khevron, and built an altar[5] there to YHWH.

Chapter 14

1 And it came to pass in the days of Amraphel King of Shinar (Eritrea, Djibouti and Somalia),[6] Ariokh King of Ellasar, Khederlaomar [7] King of Elam,[8] and Tidal King of Gentile nations.

2 That they made war with Bera King of Sedom, Birsha King of Amorah (Gomorrah), Shinab King of Admah, Shemeber King of Zeboiim, and the King of Bela that is, Tzoar.

3 All these joined together in the Valley of Siddim that is, the Salt Sea.

4 Twelve years they served Khederlaomar, and in the thirteenth year they rebelled.

5 In the fourteenth year Khederlaomar, and the Kings that were with him, came and

Footnotes

[1] Reference to Eden.

[2] Present day Israel.

[3] To the Black African looking sons of Abraham and not to the false pretenders Ashkenazim Jews who occupy the land in Israel today and call themselves chosen are not the chosen but are gentiles.

Footnotes

[4] This is as Israel's dust, which means many billions of people, who to this day remain uncountable.

[5] Building an altar to YHWH was a way to signify a structure, to set as a memorial before YHWH, and also for the people to know who Abraham worshipped.

[6] This is Nimrud, who ruled over east Africa and Iraq, see Gen 10:10.

[7] It means 'roundness of a sheaf.'

[8] Iran

attacked the Rephaim[1] in Ashteroth Karnaim, the Zuzim in Kham, the Emim in Shuweh Kiriathaim.[2]

6 And the Khuri in their mountain of Seir, as far as El Paran, which is by the wilderness.

7 Then they turned back, and came to En Mishpat, that is, Kadesh, and attacked all the country of the Amaleki, and also the Amoree who dwelt in Khatstson-Tamar.

8 And the King of Sedom, the King of Amorah (Gomorrah), the King of Admah, the King of Zeboiim, and the King of Bela (that is, Tzoar) went out and joined together in battle, in the Valley of Siddim;

9 Against Khederlaomar King of Elam, Tidal King of nations, Amraphel King of Shinar (Eritrea, Djibouti and Somalia), and Ariokh King of Ellasar; four Kings against five.

10 Now the valley of Siddim was full of asphalt pits; and the Kings of Sedom and Amorah (Gomorrah) fled, some fell there; and the remainder fled to the mountains.

11 Then they took all the goods of Sedom and Amorah (Gomorrah), and all their provisions, and went their way.

12 They also took Lot, Abram's nephew, who dwelt in Sedom, and his goods, and departed.

13 Then one who had escaped came and told Abram[3] the

Footnotes

[1] These giants were worshippers of Ishtar, which is where the word 'Easter' comes from. Is it not ironic that this place was only six miles from Northern Arabia, which today also has a giant religion known as Islam? The other thing is that the king of Iran defeated them. This is a prefigurement and drash of another battle to come between Iran and Saudi Arabia. This would be the precursor to the Western states feeling the heat because Saudi oil is about to go up in smoke; but the terrorists that will arrange to do that will be trained by Iran and Turkey. Iran will join hands with Turkey to attack the greater Babylon, being Saudi Arabia, and will cause destruction. This text, and its drash, shows us that Iran will come in league with other nations; and will succeed in breaking Arabia. The US, and the UK, and some other EU Nations, will try to rescue Arabia, which is the picture of Abraham. Please see our footnote in the Tanak, the book of Isaiah 13.17, 22:6 and Jer 51:11. Please also see the book World War III – Unmasking the end-times Beast by Rabbi Simon Altaf from www.forever-israel.com.

[2] A race of giants.

Footnotes

[3] According to Godfrey Higgins, a reliable English historian said, "The Kasdim were originally dark skin as would be Nebuchadnezzar." Abraham would be darker as was his father and his mother. Professor Rudolph Windsor who wrote a book called FROM BABYLON TO TIMBUKTU states the following, "The Kasdim and the other People of that region were Jet black in their complexion."

The Torah says Abraham came from Ur, the ancient word has the meaning of "fire oven." In Hebrew the word Or means light. The temperatures in these regions could reach up to 130 degrees Fahrenheit. The Sumerians called themselves Saagig which means black heads. It was a common practice for them to shave their heads. The Sumerians were related to the people from Ur who were of Black skin also. Note Nimrud the son of Cush was a black Nubian King or Cushite. The children of Ham and Shem married so we see black colour evident but Shem was not a white man either but also of dark features since Noah was of African origin. He had white skin according to the book of Enoch (106:2-5) and that caused his father Lamech of black skin to run away with fright since he should have been of black skin. Yet Noah did have white locks of hair
Continued in next section

(Abrahu: Hebrew); [1] for he dwelt by the terebinth etzim (trees) of Mamre the Amoree, brother of Eshkol, and brother of Aner: and they were allies with Abram.

14 Now when Abram heard that his brother was taken captive, he armed his three hundred and eighteen trained servants, who were born in his own Beyth (house), and went in pursuit as far as Dan.

15 He divided his forces against them by night, and he and his servants attacked them, and pursued them as far as Hobah, which is north of Damascus.

16 So he brought back all the goods, and also brought back his brother Lot and his goods, as well as the women and the people.

17 And the King of Sedom went out to meet him at the valley of Shuweh, that is, the King's valley, after his return from the defeat of Khederlaomar, and the Kings who were with him.

18 Then Malakhitsadek [2] King of Shalom [3] brought out Lakhem (bread) and wine: And he was the kohen (priest) of *the* Most High EL (Power).

19 And he spoke an **Increase** for him, and said, **Increased** be Abram of Most High El (Power), Possessor of shamayim and earth:

20 And *the* Most High EL (Mighty Power) Increaser, who has given your enemies into your hand. And he gave him a tithe [4] of all.

21 Now the King of Sedom said to Abram, Give me the persons, and take the goods for yourself.

22 But Abram said to the King of Sedom, I have lifted my hand [5] to YHWH, *the* Most High El (Power), the Possessor of shamayim and earth.

23 That I will take nothing, from a thread to a sandal strap, and that I will not take anything that is yours, lest you should say, I have made Abram rich'.

24 Except only what the young men have eaten, and the portion of the men who went with me, Aner, Eshkol, and Mamre; let them take their portion.

Chapter 15

1 After these things the word of YHWH came to Abram in a vision, saying, Do not be afraid

---

as a Jamaican man would have black hair with woolly braids.

[1] The language of Abraham was called Abaru, and the term Hebrew is a modern term, very late derivative.

[2] Shem was called Melechzedek.

[3] The word is Shalom not Salem, this was mistranslated because, when the Israelites (both houses) were in exile, they lost the language, and many of the manuscripts were burnt. After finding the Dead Sea Scrolls, many people forgot that we are in the modern era with no Hebrew vowel points; so it is difficult to place some words correctly. But we know now, from ancient sources, the correct way to say these words.

Footnotes

[4] A tithe of 10% that was given to the Levite in Abraham's loins to the future grandsons so Abraham received the tithe long before the Torah was given to Moses. Tithe is mandatory for all believers, including Christians, who err not to keep Torah or to Tithe to the present Levites forever!

[5] Abraham swore an oath in the name of YHWH as stated in Torah Deuteronomy 6:13.

Abram: I am your shield, and your exceedingly great reward.

2 But Abram said, Adoni[1] YHWH, what will You give me, seeing I go without heir, and he, the son of Mashek[2] Eli'ezer of Damascus is over my Beyth (house)?[3]

Footnotes

[1] Adoni (my master), followed by YHWH. The word is not Adonai; but Adoni YHWH, in English that would be, Master or Lord. Remember Hebrew has gone through at least four stages of development. Today's modern Script is nothing like the ancient script which was in hieroglyphs listed in the back. Many word meanings were extended and even different from the modern Hebrew.

[2] Abraham's third wife who was likely Keturah's maid.

[3] For some strange reason the verse in Gen 15:2 which reads in plain Hebrew "The son of Mashek of my house" while it was obscured in its intended meaning has been corrected in this edition of the Study. The Hebrew letters are "ובן־מׁשק ביתי."

Abraham's third wife who was likely Keturah's maid she would have come from bilateral trade agreements between Abraham's father Tharakh who managed a large part of the Euphrates river under the rulership of Nimrud in South-Eastern Turkey where Abraham was born. Mashek would have been the maid of Keturah as was Hagar the princess the maid of Sarah. Keturah was the daughter of Joktan who would have had a hand in giving Mashek to Keturah. Abraham had four wives two of which came from the hand maids of his earlier wives.

Mashek was a Turkic woman the daughter of Japheth. These people were later partly conquered by the Hittites in Turkey. They had land holdings in ancient Israel such as Hebron where Abraham purchased a field from Ephron.(Gen 23:6-18) and he was recognized as a prince amongst the Hittite people which would have this confirmation from Turkey that Abraham was of Noble Birth.

It is uncommon for women to be referenced as mothers unless there is a special case in point. Abraham took Mashek as wife while Continued in next section

3 Then Abram said, Look, You have given me no offspring; indeed the son born in my Beyth (house) is my heir!

4 And, behold, the Word of YHWH came to him, saying. This one shall not be your heir; but one who will come from your own bowels shall be your heir. [4]

5 Then He brought him outside, and said, Look now toward the shamayim, and count the stars, if you are able to number them: and He said to him, So shall your descendants be.

6 And he trusted with faithfulness in YHWH; and He accounted it to him for Righteousness.[5]

7 Then He said to him, I am YHWH, who brought you out of Ur [6] of the Kasdim, to give you this land to inherit it.

8 And he said, Adoni YHWH, how shall I know that I will inherit it?

9 So He said to him, Bring Me a three-year-old heifer, a three-year-old female goat, a three-

he was still in South-Eastern Turkey. Since she was not a ruling princess the text is silent about her.

[4] Eli'ezer of Damascus was born from Mashek the wife of Abraham, Eli'ezer was Abraham's son born from a concubine but he could not be the ruling prince this is why a ruling prince had to be born out of the Northern Wife Sarah in the North/South divide whose son would be a ruler according to African ruling priestly clans established by YHWH long ago.

[5] Abraham was saved by the favor of YHWH because he believed in Him, he did not have to believe in any spiritual laws, or recite some new found formula by the sixteenth century Protestant Church.

[6] This is modern day Sanliurfa in South-Eastern Turkey. He was not from Iraq.

year-old ram, a turtledove, and a young pigeon.

10 Then he brought all these to Him, and cut them in two, down the middle, and placed each piece opposite the other: but he did not cut the birds in two.

11 And when the vultures came down on the carcasses, Abram drove them away.

12 Now when the sun was going down, a deep sleep fell upon Abram: and, behold, horror and great darkness fell upon him.

13 Then He said to Abram, Know certainly that your descendants will be strangers in a land that is not theirs, and will serve them; and they will afflict them four hundred years;[1]

14 And also the nation, whom they serve, I will judge: afterward they shall come out with great possessions.[2]

15 Now as for you, you shall go to your ahvot (fathers) in peace (shalom); you shall be buried at a good old age.

16 But in the fourth generation they shall return here: for the iniquity of the Amoree is not yet complete.

17 And it came to pass, when the sun went down, and it was dark, that behold, there was a smoking oven, and a burning

torch[3] that passed between those pieces.

Footnotes

[3] Picture of the Set-Apart plurality of YHWH. Interestingly, when the covenant was made with Abraham, it shows us two recognisable distinct entities. First, the 'smoking oven', and second, the 'burning torch.' Let us look briefly into what is underneath the hood so to speak.

The Torch is the Messiah (the living Torah) who calls Himself the 'light of the world' (Yochanan John 8:12).

The Hebrew word tanoor (Tav, Nun, Vav and Resh) for the burning oven, shows us the picture of all Three, the Abbah, the Son, and the Ruach Ha Kodesh; the feminine side of YHWH in the Sefirotic tree.

Tav - This is the Son, who reveals himself as the Aleph and Tav, the Father in Him. The sign of the stake, where He shows Himself to be pierced, and also, the

Continued in the next section

18 On the same day hwhy made a covenant with Abram, saying: To your descendants I have given this land, from the river of Mitzrayim (Egypt) to the great river, the River Euphrates.3

19 The Kenites, the Kenezzites, and the Kadmonites,

Completer of the covenant and the Bringer of the New Covenant, as His words echo 'it is finished.'

Nun – This shows us the picture of the fish that is representative of the seed, without which there can be no continuation of life. It's a symbol that shows us the 'seed' that originates from the Father, and given to the Ruach Ha Kadosh, to bring forth the Son, Messiah Yahushua. The Yesod: reproduction, what we call born again; that leads to the Malchut (Kingdom of Messiah). We see here also, the children of Messiah, (Yesha'yahu 53:10) we see here that through Abraham, (Beresheeth 12:3) many people would receive the new birth. He, being the type of the man, before us so to speak.
Continued in next section

Footnotes

[1] Israel was to spend time in Egypt in captivity although not all 400 years were in captivity. One hundred and sixteen years were of the captivity and the last eighty-six years of this was hard bondage when they cried out.

[2] These are the Twelve Tribes of Israel, who were to be released with great treasures.

18 On the same day YHWH made a Covenant with Abram, saying: To your descendants I have given this land, from the river of Mitzrayim (Egypt) to the great river, the River Farat (Euphrates).[1]

19 The Qeny, the Kenezzi, and the Kadmoni,

20 The Khitee, the Perzee, and the Rephaim.

21 The Amoree, the Kanani, the Girgashi, and the Yavusi.[2]

Chapter 16

1 Now Sarai Abram's wife, had borne him no children: and she had a Mitzri (Egyptian) maidservant, whose name was Hagar.

2 So Sarai said to Abram, See now, YHWH has restrained me from bearing children: Please, go in to my maid; perhaps I shall obtain children by her; And Abram heeded the voice of Sarai.

3 Then Sarai, Abram's wife took Hagar her maid the Mitzri (Egyptian), and gave her to her husband Abram to be his wife, after Abram had dwelt ten years in the land of Kanan.[3]

4 So he went in to Hagar, and she conceived: and when she saw that she had conceived, her mistress was looked upon with contempt as worthless[4] in her sight.

5 Then Sarai said to Abram, You have brought this wrong on me: I gave my maid into your embrace; and when she saw that she had conceived, she looked upon me with contempt as worthless in her sight: YHWH judge between me and you.

6 So Abram said to Sarai, Indeed, your maid is in your hand; do to her as you see good in your sight.[5] And when Sarai dealt harshly with her, she fled from her presence.

Vav – The hook and the ladder to heaven, with the three columns. This has the ordinal value six, and is the picture of man, and the picture of Messiah Yahushua, connecting the shamayim (heavens) with the earth below. Without Him we cannot ascend.

The Resh – The Resh is the picture of the Ruach Ha Kadosh, the head being the beginning. See Mishle (Proverbs 1:7) ...The beginning of Da'at (knowledge). Here knowledge is the mother side of Elohim, known as the Ruach ha Kodesh, represented by the middle column of the Tree, which represents the Ten Attributes of YHWH.

[1] The land of Israel has much bigger borders than today, and will one day receive all the land going into Iraq, and coming down to parts of Egypt, and Saudi Arabia, since the Mountain of Sinai is in Saudi Arabia and it too belongs to Israel.

[2] The Yebusites have settled in Nigeria after they were removed from Jerusalem by King David.

Footnotes

[3] Note Abraham was already married to Keturah and Mashek so Hagar was his fourth wife.

[4] Hagar became proud, her conception was miraculous she thought highly of herself that she immediately became pregnant; but her companion wife was not able to for whom she was meant to be begetting the child. Sarah was the primary wife in the North, who would have the authority in the Northern region and Abraham's household, including with children, to be favoured first. Abraham's wife in the South Keturah held head-wife position in Beersheba. When women do not bear children in the east they are looked down upon as worthless.

[5] YHWH is very clear, He showed in Deut 21:15; that the primary wife, and her children are to be favoured first. This is how Plural marriages work. See Gen 25:2.

7 Now Malakh YHWH [1] found her by a spring of mayim in the wilderness, by the spring on the way to Shur.[2]

8 And He said, Hagar, Sarai's maid, where did you come from? And where are you going? And she said, I am fleeing from the presence of my mistress Sarai.

9 So the Malakh YHWH said to her, Return to your mistress, and submit [3] yourself under her hand.

10 Then the Malakh YHWH said to her, I will multiply your descendants [4] exceedingly, so that they shall not be counted for multitude.

11 And the Malakh YHWH said to her, Behold, you will be with child, and you shall bear a son, you shall call his name Yshmael;[5] because YHWH has heard your affliction.

12 He shall be a wild man;[6] his hand[7] shall be against all, and all

13 And she called the name of YHWH who spoke to her, You are El-Roi (The POWER behind visions/Sight)[10] for she said, Have I also seen visions, behold,[11] who reveals visions of *the* End[12] to me.[13]

14 Therefore the well was called Beer Lakhai Roi (Well of Living Visions); behold, this is between Kadesh and Bered.

hand against him; and he shall dwell in the faces[8] of all his brethren.[9]

Footnotes
[1] Special angel of YHWH, some say the Metatron.
[2] A place in the desert of Arabia.
[3] The second wife must submit under the first wife. YHWH shows Hagar she is wrong to run away.
[4] Yshmael the son of Abraham was to be favoured by YHWH with **blessings** and multiplication of descendants because his mother listened to the voice of YHWH and returned.
[5] YHWH loved Yshmael and gave him his name meaning 'The Voice of YHWH, the Mighty One.' Hagar lost her child through a miscarriage first-time and this time YHWH promised her she will conceive again miraculously so this was the second time she conceived to receive this child named by YHWH. The conception happened when she returned home to be with Abraham.
[6] Yshmael was to be a fighter and hunter.
[7] In singular meaning they will rise against him many nations joined as "one hand" as gentiles today join together and attack the Continued in next section

Arabs that is what is indicated here by the singular "hand" as Western Allies attacked in the Gulf wars.
[8] In opposition to his brethren and in the middle of them which means the true Hebrews will be close by, see HTHS compendium edition notes for more.
[9] Yshmael was to always fight with his brethren, never being satisfied with what he had. Many Arabs are also like Yshmael, and are in opposition to their brethren.
[10] The Power who sees and gives visions. She was distraught and had lost her first child through a miscarriage but then she was shown a vision of getting another son who was Yshmael. These were no ordinary visions she was shown future history just as Abraham was shown later with his son Ytshak. She saw world history as the rise and fall of Yshmael and then the reconnect of the brothers in the future with the true Israelites, she was shown the war with the false Jews (Khazari converts) also.
[11] Ha'lom here means "Behold" in a powerful way like, Wow. The ancient Hebrew reveals "nations colliding" with each other that type of BEHOLD where Yshmael is part of this.
[12] The Hebrew word Akhari is for the End-Times here and not just referring to "afterward" as in some small event here and now.
[13] Hagar was shown visions of her son's future, the wars Yshmael's future children will get into and the End Time restoration of Yshmael with his Hebrew brothers.

15 So Hagar bore Abram a son: and Abram named his son, whom Hagar bore, Yshmael.

16 Abram was eighty-six years, old when Hagar bore Yshmael[1] to Abram.

Chapter 17

1 When Abram was ninety-nine years old, YHWH appeared to Abram, and said to him, I am El-Shaddai (The Mighty Power); have your Halaka [2] before Me and be Holy.

2 And I will make My Covenant[3] between Me and you, and will multiply you exceedingly.

3 Then Abram fell on his face:[4] and Elohim talked with him, saying,

4 As for Me, behold, My Covenant[5] is with you, and you shall be the Abbah of many nations.

5 No longer shall your name be called Abram, but your name shall be Abraham;[6] for I have made you the[7] Abbah[8] of many nations.[9]

6 I will make you exceedingly fruitful, and I will make nations of you, and Kings shall come from you.

7 And I will establish My Covenant between Me and you and your descendants after you in their generations for an everlasting Covenant, to be *the* Mighty One to you, and your descendants after you.

8 Also I give to you, and your descendants after you, the land in which you are a stranger, all the land of Kanan, as an everlasting [10] possession; and I will be their Mighty One.

9 And Elohim said to Abraham, As for you, you shall keep My Covenant,[11] you, and your descendants after you throughout their generations.

10 This is My Covenant which you shall keep, between Me and you and your descendants after you; every male child among you shall be circumcised. [12]

Footnotes

[1] Yshmael was a man who died believing YHWH.

[2] To walk in YHWH's Torah commandments

[3] The line of prophets, and the line of Messiah, was to be established through Isaac, and not Yshmael.

[4] The proper ancient way to submit to YHWH was/is bowing to Him, prostrate on the ground, to show full submission.

[5] The Covenant of circumcision is so important that it is mentioned ten times, indicating the ten sefirot. This is one of the two seals, Sabbath being the first.

[6] YHWH changes Abraham's name, and adds a Heh, the indication of which is to show us that he had the Ruakh of Elohim (Holy Spirit), known as Cochmah.

[7] LXX

[8] Spiritual father of Faith.

[9] When Israel was going to be scattered for her punishment, the ten tribes mingled with gentiles, producing many more gentiles.

[10] The land of Israel has no conditions set for the inheritance, Isaac's children have it for eternity no matter what anyone thinks or says.

[11] How do you keep a Covenant? By being obedient to the requirements of the Covenant, by circumcising, and obeying Torah. If you do one and not the other or do not do either then you have no part in this Covenant whether you call yourself Muslim or Christian.

[12] The purpose of circumcision is argued and how much to perform. The Egyptians had circumcision for their priestly clans, a man would not marry a woman who was uncircumcised as she was considered unclean because the Egyptians circumcised

Continued in next section

11 And you shall be circumcised in the flesh of your foreskins;[1] and it shall be a sign [2] of the Covenant [3] between you and Me.

12 He who is eight days old among you shall be circumcised,[4] every male child[5] in your generations, he who is born in your Beyth (house), or bought with money from any foreigner, who is not your descendant.

13 He who is born in your Beyth (house), and he who is bought with your money, must be circumcised; and My Covenant shall be in your flesh for an everlasting [6] Covenant:[7]

14 And the uncircumcised male child, who is not circumcised in the flesh of his foreskin, that person shall be cut off [8] from his people; he has broken My Covenant.[9]

their women priestesses. It is a faulty assumption that the whole foreskin is removed as do the Muslims and Jews today. Only a small part of the foreskin is removed. If the whole was removed then how would Yahushua the son of Nun re-circumcise Beyth Israel (Jos 5:2)? This was not a hatafat dam brit but a re-circumcision as there was foreskin to cut. In fact on a male circumcision could be done at least 3 or 4 times considering the amount of skin taken is very small. This fact is unfortunately both ignored by the present people. YHWH will call all people to be re-circumcised before entering the land in the future. The directions will be given in Isaiah 2:3-4 & Ezek. 44:9 both for resurrected and living believers.

[1] The Hebrew word 'Arlot' indicated that all harlotries must be left behind. Remember, all languages descended from Hebrew including English, where we have the word harlot meaning whoring. So, YHWH set the Covenant of circumcision for His people so they would no longer whore after other elohim. Circumcision was done in some other nations before Abraham was asked to perform it; but YHWH's order of circumcision was different from the other nations. In some African nations today they perform circumcision just before they get married, while circumcision in the Hebrew Faith is a seal of our Covenant rights.

[2] This is the seal of the Abrahamic Covenant. The two seals of our faith are the 7th day Sabbath Saturday sunrise to Sunday sunrise and circumcision, and renders you guilty of judgment, your kingdom to be lost and you put outside the kingdom as a servant. Also you who are males, will not be able to enter the Millennial Temple either.

[3] Claiming Covenant is not enough, you are only in the Abrahamic Covenant if you get circumcised; as that is the eternal requirement of the Covenant. This must be done as soon as possible after a man's rescue.

Footnotes

[4] If a male child, then he is circumcised on the 8th day, and the child is given a name, which has a good Hebrew meaning?

[5] Scripture does not allow female circumcision, although some nations perform this act.

[6] Everlasting means, forever, and not 4000 years. An error espoused by Christendom teaches that after this timeframe, we are under 'favor', and no longer have to circumcise. Abraham was also in favor and did not complain about circumcision.

[7] This is an eternal Covenant; Christians err by believing it's only for the Jewish nation. Abraham was not a Jew but an Assyrian with parents from West Africa. In Order to be in the Covenant circumcision must be done by males irrelevant of what tribe of Israel you belong to or not. There is only one tribe of Israel called Yahudah with eleven other sons, who make up the remaining tribes, known as Israel. Many believers come from these other tribes.

[8] Not complying with YHWH's law means death, not Blessings as many in Christendom claim.

[9] Christians are erring by deliberately choosing not to follow through with circumcision. Why blame your pastor, when you can read it yourself that the Covenant is eternal but the Pastor is only towing the old

Continued in next section

15 Then Elohim said to Abraham, As for Sarai your wife, you shall not call her name Sarai, but Sarah[1] shall be her name.

16 This is My Covenant which you shall keep, between Me and you and your descendants after you; every male child among you shall be circumcised. [2]

17 And you shall be circumcised[3] in the flesh of your

party line and not what the scripture says. Both the Pastor and the non-observing people will have to answer to YHWH, as they do not carry the 'seal' of the Covenant that is required.

[1] Sarah was also saved and had the Ruakh of Elohim (Holy Spirit), so she was given a heh, which is the Chochmah wisdom of YHWH, represented as an attribute of YHWH.

[2] The purpose of circumcision is argued and how much to perform. The Egyptians had circumcision for their priestly clans, a man would not marry a woman who was uncircumcised as she was considered unclean because the Egyptians circumcised their women priestesses. It is a faulty assumption that the whole foreskin is removed as do the Muslims and Jews today. Only a small part of the foreskin is removed. If the whole was removed then how would Yahushua the son of Nun re-circumcise Beyth Israel (Jos 5:2)? This was not a hatafat dam brit but a re-circumcision as there was foreskin to cut. In fact on a male circumcision could be done at least 3 or 4 times considering the amount of skin taken is very small. This fact is unfortunately both ignored by the present people. YHWH will call all people to be re-circumcised before entering the land in the future. The directions will be given in Isaiah 2:3-4 & Ezek. 44:9 both for resurrected and living believers.

[3] **Should Torah men circumcise today?**
If we say circumcision is for all males then the next question is what about Galatians and what Paulos wrote there in? We cannot hear him as he has no right to make rulings on what was already established. His letters are not scripture and not halachik. If you follow Paulos then you have nothing to do Continued in next section

with the true assembly. There is only one voice of YHWH the only voice we must follow. If you confusingly follow Paul's voice then you are led astray by apostate teachings.

Anyone who foregoes circumcision forgoes the kingdom as it would be an act of rebellion to disobey YHWH. Who do you want to hear Paulos the apostate apostle or YHWH?

A lot of Christian Pastors are deceiving their flocks not to circumcise. For them Paulos outweighs the greatest leader and teacher of the Torah, Moses, who was called out by YHWH. To love YHWH is to obey His every command without question.

The Hebrew word for love is אהב which kabbalistically reveals something quite deep to us. It consists of the three Hebrew letters of Alef, Heh and Bet. This is explained in the book Hebrew wisdom, Kabbalah. Alef is the source of all the universe, related to our Father in shamayim, from whom we also receive the Ruakh Ha Kodesh. They are in these three letters. The Heh is significant and reveals the Ruakh Ha Kodesh while the Bet reveals the very first bet used in the Torah in Genesis 1:1 for the word Beresheeth. This signifies the House of our Father in shamayim on which He set His Son (Ps 2:6) to rule and reign, this can apply to King David or any person he chooses to call his son. The word Ahav equals the numeric eight in Gematria, which also reveals new beginnings and connects us to the celebration of Tabernacles. This can also reveal Shemini Atzeret, the 8th day, which will start at the completion of the Millennium reign.

Before Elohim gave circumcision, the Egyptians were circumcising both male and female in their priesthood. It was unthinkable for an Egyptian priest to marry a priestess who was not circumcised. The black Egyptians narrowed it down to those not circumcising being unclean and filthy and not fit for marriage. Hence why we see Yosef's marriage with a priestess. YHWH takes it a level further by making it into a Covenant/Agreement to be part of His chosen nation.

Continued in next section

foreskins;[1] and it shall be a sign [1] of the Covenant between you and Me.

Elohim has the ability to cut off people (Gen 17:14) who refused to obey Him. If you refuse to do so you will be counted as a rebel and not allowed into the kingdom.

Brit milah, physical circumcision is not an option (Ezek 44:9) but mandatory as it is one of the SEALS OF THE Hebrew faith and the Covenant/Agreement given to father Abraham which was Everlasting. Those people who are not circumcised including Christians will not be allowed in the Temple and there will be no magical circumcisions for them in the future either.

Circumcision is an eternal Covenant/Agreement and must be done for males on the 8th day of their birth as mentioned in Beresheeth 17:10. Those that come in the faith late in their lives still have to do it no later than one year after conversion. Failure to do this would mean the teachers have the right to disfellowship them for breaking the Torah.

If you claim to be part of the Abrahamic Covenant/Agreement but do not adhere to the requirements of the Covenant/Agreement, which is circumcision then you have nothing whatsoever to do with Abraham.

If you claim to be purchased and redeemed by the blood of the Messiah but the Torah calls for obedience to the Covenants and not follow a Christian blood pagan theology. This is indeed clear in the Covenant/Agreement given to Abraham. YHWH does not play games as gentiles do. Those of you who will disobey will pay the penalty for it.

The spirituality behind circumcision is to remove the femaleness behind a man. When a person does not circumcise it is understood that he carries the traits of both male and female at birth. Thus, it is circumcision that allows the side of maleness to dominate the person. Without doing this the male is confused into unrighteous lifestyles.

When we circumcise we shed the blood which is an absolute requirement for any Covenant/Agreement on our part to show obedience.

Continued in next section

If we refuse to shed blood of our little skin which is useless anyway if left on and can cause various diseases later because dirt and dust entraps there then it only goes to show that we are not willing to meet Elohim on the part of the Covenant/Agreement that He requires us to do. Those who disobey do not have any part with true Israel.

Some questions;
Question) What if I just came to Faith and am uncircumcised, when shall I do it?

Answer) You can wait up to one year and learn the Torah but then must do it. Find a Hebrew doctor. There are registered mohel's (recognized circumcisers) in the USA and Europe too.

Question) I am a Torah observer but I did not know that I should circumcise myself or my son but I want to do it, since I just realized, I was taught wrong, what do I do now?

Answer) Find a Hebrew doctor and get your son circumcised as soon as possible, there are directory listings both in the US and UK for them. There are similar Rebbim in other countries where you will find mohelim (Yahudim doctors for circumcision) who can do this. At worst get him circumcised by a gentile doctor and then do the hatafat dam brit (drawing of a drop of blood with a prayer) later.

Question) Can I celebrate Passover without being circumcised?

Answer) You can join in the celebration to learn its principles but you cannot partake of the meal until you are physically circumcised (Exodus 12:44). It's a sin for you to take part in the meal until you are properly circumcised. If your leader has been teaching you and others not to circumcise then the sin is upon him and he will be judged for it but you will also suffer the consequences of losing your increases and authority in this earth.

[1] The Hebrew word 'Arlot' indicated that all harlotries must be left behind. Remember, Continued in next section

18 And Abraham said to Elohim, Oh that Yshmael might [2] live before Your face.

19 Then Elohim said, No, Sarah your wife shall bear you a son, and you shall call his name Ytshak:[3] I will establish My

all languages descended from Hebrew including English, where we have the word harlot meaning whoring. So, YHWH set the Covenant of circumcision for His people so they would no longer whore after other elohim. Circumcision was done in some other nations before Abraham was asked to perform it; but YHWH's order of circumcision was different from the other nations. In some African nations today they perform circumcision just before they get married, while circumcision in the Hebrew Faith is a seal of our Covenant rights.
[1] The two seals of our faith are the 7th day Saturday Sabbath, sunrise to sunset and circumcision, not having this renders you guilty of judgment, your kingdom place to be lost and you put outside the kingdom as a servant.
[2] Abraham questioned YHWH by asking, can the promise be with Yshmael. YHWH responds in the next verse in the negative, that He will not take his life; but the Covenant is with Isaac. Therefore not breaking His own law, which says, the first born son of the primary wife must be chosen first. Yshmael was a legitimate son of Abraham, and rightful owner to Blessings, after Isaac. Some Christians err on this by claiming Yshmael was not Abraham's legitimate son. He was the legal son of Abraham, fully sealed 'in' the Covenant; but not the man to 'carry' the Covenant, that is all.
[3] The name of Ytshak is 'YHWH laughs over the unbelief.' This also shows a future picture where all the people of Israel will become 'laughter', for the nations, when they scoff and jeer at the Elohim of Israel as a myth and legend. They laugh at the flood as a legend, they laugh at the exodus from Egypt as a legend. Today this can be seen anywhere in or out of Israel, where the gentile nations laugh at the Scriptures of the Hebrews. Even Christendom mocks, and laughs at Torah keeping believers. In the end YHWH will have the final laugh.

Covenant with him for an everlasting Covenant, and with his descendants after him.

20 And as for Yshmael, I have heard you: Behold, I have **Increased** him, and will make him fruitful, and will multiply him exceedingly; he shall beget twelve princes, and I will make him a great nation.

21 But My Covenant I will establish with Ytshak,[4] whom Sarah shall bear to you at the appointed time next year.

22 And when He finished talking with him, and Elohim went up from Abraham.

23 So Abraham took Yshmael his son, all who were born in his Beyth (house), and all who were bought with his money, every male among the men of Abraham's Beyth (house); and circumcised the flesh of their foreskins that very same day that Elohim had said to him.

24 Abraham was ninety-nine years old when he was circumcised in the flesh of his foreskin.[5]

25 And Yshmael his son was thirteen years old, when he was circumcised in the flesh of his foreskin.

26 That very same day Abraham was circumcised, and his son [6] Yshmael.

Footnotes
[4] The Messianic line was to pass through Isaac, and not Yshmael, thus ruling out prophets from Yshmael's sons.
[5] Abraham did his own circumcision at ninety-nine; what excuse do you have with all the medical professionals and Mohels?
[6] Scripture is very clear; Yshmael is Abraham's rightful son, and not just the son of a slave woman. Hagar was Abraham's

Continued in next section

27 And all the men of his Beyth (house), born in the Beyth (house), or bought with money from a foreigner, were circumcised with him.

Torah Parsha 4 Vayeira, Beresheeth 18:1-22:24
Haftarah: Melekhim Bet 4:1-37

Chapter 18

1 Then YHWH appeared[1] to him by the terebinth etzim (trees) of Mamre,[2] as he was sitting by the tent door in the heat of the day.[3]

2 So he lifted his eyes and looked, and behold, three men[4] were standing by him; and when he saw them, he ran from the tent door to meet them, and bowed himself to the ground,

3 and spoke saying, My YHWH[5], if I have now found favour in Your sight, do not pass by Your servant.

4 Please let a little mayim be brought, and wash your feet,[6] and rest yourselves under the etz (tree).

5 And I will bring a morsel of lechem (bread), that you may comfort your hearts. After that you may pass by, in as much as you have come to your servant. And they said, Do as you have said.[7]

6 So Abraham hurried into the tent of Sarah and said, Quickly, make ready three measures of fine meal; knead it and make rotis. [8]

Footnotes

[5] See appendix HBYH.

[6] In the ancient near east the meaning of 'washing of feet' has 3 meanings:
1: Leave your idles outside.
2: Go have relations with your wife.
3. Ratification of the Covenant just as Yahushua did the ratification of the New Covenant in John 13:10.

Take note, Here the 3rd application is taking place!!!

[7] YHWH came to this man whose colour was black and so was his wives, Sarah, Hagar, Keturah except Mashek who was Caucasian, she being the daughter of Japheth. YHWH did not see it racism to place Caucasians above the Hebrew people. The majority of the Hebrews were people of Black and brown skin colours with very few Albinos amongst us. We did not have many sons of Japheth who believed who were of caucasian skin colour so there was no racism at that time.

[8] The occasion was no ordinary one but the first Passover that YHWH celebrated with Abraham, where a calf was slaughtered and they made what is known as Indian roti as Abraham's ancestors came from India, these

second wife, fully approved scripturally; as opposed to by the world, which frowns upon second marriages in a patriarchal order.
[1] Abraham was first visited by God in a vision soon after the act of circumcision, at which point Abraham sees the three, YHWH in a personified form and the two angels Michael and Gabriel dressed as Arabs standing near him. Michael came to herald the coming of his son Isaac, which would be later personified in the greater Isaac Yahushua who was present there on the table too for this Covenant event. Gabriel came to announce judgment on Sodom and Gomorrah. Both Michael and Gabriel went and judged Sedom and Gomorrah.
[2] The occasion of the visit was the Passover celebration.
[3] About 12 noon to 2.30 pm. 2.30 pm was also the time the Passover lamb was prepared to be sacrificed. Here the Calf is prepared.
[4] YHWH here on earth in person to sit and commune with Abraham. What an amazing event, YHWH is not some Ashkenzi looking person but a Dark brown Arab looking man.

Continued in next section

7 And Abraham ran to the herd, took a tender and good heifer, gave it to a young man, and he hastened to prepare it. [1]

8 So he took butter and milk and the calf which he had prepared, and set it before them; and he stood by them under the tree as they ate. [2]

9 Then they said to him, Where is Sarah your wife? And he said, Here, in the tent. [3]

10 And He said, I will certainly return to you according to the time of life, and behold, Sarah your wife shall have a son. [4] And Sarah was listening in the tent door which was behind him. [5]

Footnotes

roti can be made with butter or without and are unleavened, if you have been told this is challah bread its not so and its not cracker bread that the modern Jews eat from Europe who are mostly converts to the Israelite faith and not Genetic. The same will happen in the millennium when YHWH will have us sacrifice heifers opposed to goats and lambs.

[1] He took the best of the herd.

[2] Standing by your guests is a sign of humility while they are eating and Abraham was a humble man. Many in the Muslim world still practice this custom with their guests when women cook and allow the guests to eat while they wait upon the guests.

www.chabad.org - A calf, tender and good: There were three calves, in order to feed them three tongues with mustard. — [from B.M. 86b].

To the youth: This was Ishmael, to train him to perform mitzvoth. — [from Aboth d'Rabbi Nathan, ch. 13]

And he took cream and milk, etc.: But he did not bring bread, because Sarah became menstruous, for the manner of the women returned to her on that day, and the dough became ritually unclean. — [from B.M. 87a]

Cream: the fat of the milk that is skimmed off the top.

And the calf that he had prepared: that he had prepared. Each one that he prepared, he took and brought before them. — [from B.M. 86b]

And they ate: They appeared to be eating. From here we learn that a person should not deviate from custom. — [from B.M. ad loc., Gen. Rabbah 48:14, Targum Jonathan]

[3] www.chabad.org - And they said to him: Heb. אֵלָיו. There are dots over the letters ויא in the word אֵלָיו. And we learned: Rabbi Simeon the son of Eleazar says: "Wherever the [undotted] letters are more than the dotted ones, you must expound on the [undotted] letters, etc." And here, the dotted letters are asked Sarah, "Where (אֵיוֹ) is Abraham?" (Gen. Rabbah 48:15) We learn that a person should ask in his lodging place of the husband about the wife, and of the wife about the husband (B.M. 87a). In Bava Metzia (ad loc.) it is said: The ministering angels knew where our mother Sarah was, but [they asked in order] to make known that she was modest, in order to endear her to her husband. Said Rabbi Joseph the son of Chanina: In order to send her a cup of blessing (i.e., the cup of wine upon which the Grace after Meals is recited). more than the [undotted] letters, and you must expound on the dotted [letters]. [The meaning is that] they also

[4] This would be Abraham's last and ninth son the ruling son in the North with the ruling wife Sarah. While Abraham's other wives lived in the south and west.

[5] www.chabad.org - At this time next year: At this time in the coming year. It was Passover, and on the following Passover, Isaac was born, since we do not read כָּעֵת [at "a" time], but כָּעֵת [at "this" time]. כָּעֵת חַיָּה means: at this time, when there will be life for you, when you will all be alive and well. — [from Targum Yerushalmi, Targum Jonathan]

I will surely return: The angel did not announce that he [himself] would return to him, but he was speaking to him as an emissary of the Omnipresent. Similarly (above 16:10): "And the angel said to her: I will greatly multiply [your seed]," but he [the angel] did not have the power to multiply [her children], but he spoke as an emissary

Continued in next section

11 Now Abraham and Sarah were old, well advanced in age; and Sarah had passed the age of childbearing.

12 Therefore Sarah laughed within herself, saying, after I have grown old, shall I have pleasure, my master [1] being old also? [2]

13 And YHWH said to Abraham, Why did Sarah laugh, saying, Shall I surely bear a child, since I am old? [3]

14 Is anything too hard for YHWH? At the appointed time[4] I will return to you, according to the time of life, and Sarah shall have a son.

15 But Sarah denied it, saying, I did not laugh, for she was afraid. And He said, No, but you did laugh!

16 Then the men rose from there and gazed[5] toward Sedom, and Abraham went with them to send them on the way.

17 And YHWH said, Shall I hide [6] from Abraham what I am doing,

18 Since Abraham shall surely become a great and mighty nation, and all the nations of the earth shall be grafted[7] in him?

19 For I have a relationship[8] with him, in order that he may command his children and his household after him, that they Guard the Halaka[9] of YHWH, to do tzedekah[10] and justice, that

of the Omnipresent. Here too, it was as an emissary of the Omnipresent that he said this to him. (Elisha said to the Shunamite woman (II Kings 4:16): "At this season, at this time next year, you will be embracing a son." And she said, "No my lord, O man of Godly, do not fail your maidservant. Those angels who announced to Sarah said (below verse 14): 'At the appointed time, I will return,'" [but Elisha did not promise to return]. Elisha replied, "Those angels, who live and endure forever, said, 'At the appointed time, I will return.' But I am flesh and blood, alive today and dead tomorrow. Whether I shall be alive or dead, 'At this time, etc. [you will embrace a son.'"] (Gen. Rabbah 53:2).
And it was behind him: The entrance was behind the angel
[1] How many wives today refer to their husbands as 'master', or even treat them as one. Many are cursing them to their face, as if they are the servants of the modern wives, and plotting behind their backs.
[2] www.chabad.org -Within herself: She looked at her insides and said, "Is it possible that these insides will carry a child; that these breasts, which have dried up, will give forth milk?" - [from Tan. Shoftim 18]

Smooth flesh: Heb. עֶדְנָה, smoothness of flesh, and in the language of the Mishnah (Meg. 13a, Men. 86a): "It causes the hair to fall out and smoothes (מְעַדֵּן) the flesh." Another explanation: an expression of time (עִדָּן), the time of the menstrual period. — [from Gen. Rabbah 48:17]
[3] www.chabad.org - Is it really true: Is it really true that I will give birth?- Continued in next section

Although I am old: Scripture altered [her statement] for the sake of peace, for she had said,"and my master is old." - [from B.M. 87a]
[4] We must always wait for YHWH's appointed times in our lives if we are to have His plan fulfilled.
[5] With a deadly gaze to destroy it, not a good gaze.
[6] YHWH will not hide anything from his prophets.
[7] Nivrechu to mean all the nations will be grafted in him.
[8] The Hebrew word Yada "to know" means to have a deep relationship as in a family.
[9] All the true Hebrews will guard the Torah, this is a prerequisite to know if one is Hebrew or runs after lawless gentile doctrines.
[10] The term tzedakah here refers to doing charitable deeds of kindness giving money to others the secret to Abraham's right relationship to YHWH as he valued his Continued in next section

YHWH may bring to Abraham what He has spoken to him.

20 And YHWH said, Because the outcry[1] against Sedom and Amorah (Gomorrah) is great, and because their sin is very grave,

21 I will go down now and see whether they have done altogether according to the outcry against it that has come to Me; and if not, I will know.

22 Then the men turned away from there and went toward Sedom, but YHWH still stood before Abraham.[2]

23 And Abraham came near and said, Would You also destroy the innocent[3] with the wicked?

24 Suppose there were fifty innocent[4] within the city; would

You also destroy the place and not spare it for the fifty innocent that were in it?

25 Far be it from You to do such a thing as this, to slay the innocent with the wicked, so that the innocent should be as the wicked; far be it from You. Shall not the Judge of all the earth do right? [5]

26 And YHWH said, If I find in Sedom fifty innocent within the city, then I will spare all the place for their sakes.

27 Then Abraham answered and said, Indeed now, I who am but dust and ashes have taken it upon myself to speak to YHWH; [6]

28 Suppose there were five less than the fifty innocent; would You destroy all of the city for lack of five? And He said, If I find there forty-five, I will not destroy it.

29 Then he spoke to Him yet again and said, Suppose there should be forty found there? And He said, I will not do it for the sake of forty.

30 And he said, Let not YHWH[7] be angry, and I will speak: Suppose thirty should be found there? And He said, I will not do it if I find thirty there.

31 Then he said, Indeed now, I have taken it upon myself to speak to Adoni (Lord: Master) Suppose twenty should be found there? And He said, I will not destroy it for the sake of twenty.

relationship more than his money to Master YHWH.

[1] Who was the outcry from? The sages tell us that a girl who helped feed a poor person was brutally killed and so it was her outcry from the ground that went up to YHWH.

[2] This is the original Hebrew text translation which was altered by the Scribes who felt that it is not respectable for Elohim to be standing before Abraham so the text was switched which in most translations today reads Abraham stood before YHWH. The Jerusalem Talmud states in the name of Rebbe Simon that YHWH said "He was the first to stand up for a zaken." Because the Talmud offers no explanation it is assumed it is hinting at the text in Genesis 18:22 that YHWH is standing waiting for Abraham. The meaning is Abraham first prayed and prepared himself then he came before YHWH to make his supplication for the people of Sedom and Amorah.

[3] Here it means innocent not righteous by Torah standards!

[4] Why 50? Rashi suggests that this is because Sedom was a metropolis of five cities and that would mean 10 righteous to form a minim for a synagogue therefore 10 times 5 is equal to 50. Abraham was pleading for five cities to be spared.

Footnotes
[5] YHWH is an equitable judge even if someone never heard about him their judgment will be just.
[6] See appendix HBYH.
[7] See appendix HBYH.

32 And he said, Let not YHWH[1] be angry and I will speak at this recurrence: Suppose ten[2] should be found there? And He said, I will not destroy it for the sake of ten.

33 So YHWH went His way as soon as He had finished speaking with Abraham; and Abraham returned to his place.

Chapter 19

1 Now the two malakhim came to Sedom in the evening; and Lot was sitting in the gate [3] of Sedom: and when Lot saw them, he rose to meet them; and he bowed himself with his face towards the ground;

2 And he said, Here now, my masters, please turn in to your servant's Beyth (house), and spend the night, and wash your feet, [4] then You may rise early, and go on your way. And they said, No; but we will spend the night in the open square.

3 But he insisted strongly; so they turned into him, and entered his Beyth (house); and he made them a banquet (celebration of Unleavened Bread), and baked chametz Lakhem (Unleavened bread),[5] and they ate.

4 Now before they lay down, the men of the city, the men of Sedom, both old and young, all the people from every quarter, surrounded the Beyth (house):

5 And they called to Lot, and said to him, Where are the men who came to you tonight? Bring them out to us, that we may know [6] them carnally.

6 So Lot went out to them through the doorway, and shut the door behind him,

7 And said, Please, my brethren, do not do so wickedly.

8 See now, I have two daughters who have not known a man; please, let me bring them out to you, and you may do to them as you wish:[7] only do nothing to these men; since this is the reason they have come under the shadow of my roof.

9 And they said, Stand back; Then they said, This one came in to stay here, and he keeps acting as a judge: now we will deal worse with you, than with them. So they try to stampede against the man Lot, and came near to break down the door.

10 But the men reached out their hands, and pulled Lot into

Footnotes
[1] See appendix HBYH.
[2] Drash (allegory), the Ten tribes. YHWH spared the ten to restore them back to Y'sra'el.
[3] The 'gate' means; he had an important political position in the city as a judge.
[4] See footnote Beresheeth 18:4
[5] This was the time of the khag, celebration of Unleavened Bread; even Lot celebrated this, and he was not Hebrew as people apply it today but he was a resident of Sedom out of Assyria in South Eastern Turkey.

Footnotes
[6] The men wanted to assault the malakhim sexually, because these men were wicked and depraved. They were into sodomy and that was and still is a sin.
[7] Lot was allowing his daughters to marry these men not just to be given away for rape but through the proper contractual obligation of Bride price. In the East; guests are honoured above all else, and it would never be allowed for them to be given over to the enemy. Hence, Lot cannot give the guests to the evil men. This custom of not handing over guests is still practiced by the Muslims all over the world.

the Beyth (house) with them, and shut the door.

11 And they struck the men who were at the doorway of the Beyth (house) with blindness, both small and great: so that they became weary trying to find the door.

12 Then the men said to Lot, Have you anyone else here? A son-in-law, your sons, your daughters, and whoever you have in the city, take them out of this place:[1]

13 For we will destroy this place, because the outcry against them has grown great before the face of YHWH; and YHWH has sent us to destroy it.

14 So Lot went out, and spoke to his sons-in-law, who had married his daughters,[2] and said, "get up, get out of this place;" for YHWH will destroy this city. But to his sons-in-law he seemed to be joking in their sight, they mocked him.

15 When the morning dawned, the malakhim urged Lot to hurry, saying, Arise, take your wife, and your two daughters, who are here; lest you be consumed in the punishment of the city.

16 And while he lingered, the men took hold of his hand, his wife's hand, and the hands of his two daughters; YHWH being merciful to him, and they brought him out and set him outside the city.

17 So it came to pass, when they had brought them out, that he said, Escape for your lives; and do not look behind you, nor stay anywhere in the plain; escape to the mountains, lest you be destroyed.

18 Then Lot said to them, Oh no, not so my YHWH:[3]

19 Indeed now, your servant has found favour in your sight, and you have revealed great unmerited favour, which you have shown me by saving my life; but I cannot escape to the mountains, lest some evil overtake me, and I die:

20 See now, this city is near enough to flee to, and it is a little one: Please, let me escape there (is it not a little one?) and my soul shall live.

21 And he said to him, See, I have favored you concerning this thing also, in that I will not overthrow this city, for which you have spoken.

22 Hurry escape there; for I cannot do anything until you arrive there. Therefore the name of the city was called Tzoar.

23 The sun had risen upon the earth when Lot entered Tzoar.

24 Then YHWH rained brimstone and fire on Sedom and Amorah (Gomorrah), from YHWH [4] out of the shamayim;

Footnotes
[1] Lot's daughters were betrothed but his sons in law refused to leave the city.
[2] Betrothal is termed engagement in the modern words. In the Torah laws betrothal is a marriage while departure of the bride follows a year later.

Footnotes
[3] Master YHWH is present here, to destroy and bring down fire from shamayim, from Abbah YHWH. Lot knows this and wants to prevent his own death in the cities he is escaping to. See appendix HBYH.
[4] We see a picture of the Abbah, and His Son Yahushua who was on the Earth standing as Continued in next section

25 So He overthrew those cities, all the plain, all the inhabitants of the cities, and what grew on the ground.

26 But his wife looked intently from behind hesitating,[1] and she became a statue of salt.[2]

27 And Abraham went early in the morning to the place where he had stood before YHWH:

28 Then he looked toward Sedom and Amorah (Gomorrah), and toward all the land of the plain, and he saw, and, behold, the smoke of the land which went up like the smoke of a furnace.[3]

29 And it came to pass, when Elohim destroyed the cities of the plain, that Elohim favoured Abraham,[4] and sent Lot out of the midst of the overthrow, when He overthrew the cities in which Lot had dwelt.

30 And Lot went up out of Tzoar, and dwelt in the mountains,[5] and his two daughters were with him; for he feared to dwell in Tzoar: and he and his two daughters, dwelt in a cave.

31 Now the bechora (first born) said to the younger, Our Abbah is old, and there is no man on the earth to come in to us[6] as is the custom of all the earth:[7]

32 Come, let us make our Abbah drink wine, and we will lie with him, that we may preserve the lineage of our Abbah.[8]

33 So they made their Abbah drink wine that night: and the

YHWH, The Greater YHWH is the Father John 10:29 and the lesser is His Son Yahushua, John 8:58! We see the perfect Achad unity of YHWH.

[1] The Hebrew suggests when YHWH started the hail and brimstones; she did not come out of the range of the fire of the skies, and the air was full of some type of vapour, which caused her body to just go stiff like a statue. She was looking intently, suggesting that she would miss her lavish lifestyle in Sodom. Aventinus, a historian, reports an incident in modern day Bavaria, in 1348, when more than fifty peasants, with the cows they had milked, at the time of an earthquake, were struck with a pestilential air, and stiffened into statues of salt. We must not take YHWH's judgment lightly, they were real and the future ones will also be real.

[2] Lot's wife lacked obedience, they were told not to look back, as the energy of the storm was intense; there was vapour and air, and she longed to go back to the ways of Sodom and showed lack of respect for YHWH and His judgment, she inhaled the vapour and became like a statue. Her statue was confirmed by Josephus, the historian, as still standing by the Dead Sea where Sodom was discovered, and he said that, he saw her statue.

[3] There were two cities destroyed, this is a remez (hint), of the future burning of the oil rich kingdom of Saudi Arabia, for its Continued in next section

harlotries with the kings of the world and Jordan.

[4] Lot survived because of Abraham.

[5] The city of Tzor was also wicked, so Lot was afraid that the judgment would also destroy this city. Josephus, the Hebrew historian, tells us that he hid in the caves of Engedi; in and around the mountains of Israel, near the Dead Sea. This is likely to be the same place where King David hid from King Saul: (1 Samuel 23:29).

[6] They assumed everyone was dead, and there was now no one to marry them.

[7] Both of their husbands had died in Sedom who refused to leave.

[8] Preserving lineage is a big issue in the Eastern culture. This is true for Orthodox Jews, and many Muslims. Both would give anything to have a son, who can continue their line. Although Western culture was concerned about this in the past but no longer concedes to such things; this is an important concept for all Easterners.

bechora (firstborn) went in, and lay with her Abbah; and he did not know when she lay down, or when she arose.

34 It happened on the next day, that the bechora (firstborn) said to the younger, Indeed I lay with my Abbah last night: let us make him drink wine tonight also; and you go in, and lie with him, that we may preserve the lineage of our Abbah.

35 Then they made their Abbah drink wine that night also: and the younger arose, and lay with him; and he did not know when she lay down, or when she arose.

36 Thus both the daughters of Lot were with child by their Abbah.

37 The bechora (first born) bore a son, and called his name Moav: he is the Abbah of the Moavi to this day. [1]

38 And the younger, she also bore a son, and called his name Ben-Ammi: he is the Abbah of the people of Ammon to this day.

Chapter 20

1 And Abraham journeyed from there to the South, and dwelt between Kadesh and Shur, and stayed in Gerar.

2 Now Abraham said of Sarah his wife, She is my sister:[2] and

Avimelekh King of Gerar sent, and took Sarah.

3 But Elohim came to Avimelekh in a dream by night, and said to him, Indeed, you are a dead man, because of the woman whom you have taken; for she is a man's wife.

4 But Avimelekh had not come near her: and he said, YHWH [3], will You slay an innocent gentile[4] also?

5 Did he not say to me, She is my sister? And she, even she herself said, He is my brother. In the integrity of my heart and innocence of my hands I have done this.

6 And Elohim said to him in a dream, Yes, I know that you did this in the integrity of your heart; for I also withheld you from transgressing against Me: therefore I did not let you touch her.

7 Now therefore restore the man's wife; for he is a prophet, and he will pray for you, and you will live: but if you do not restore her, know that you shall surely die,[5] you, and all who are yours.

Footnotes
[1] No Moabite or Ammonite is allowed to join the congregation of YHWH because of incest. Incest was and is a sin. See Deut 23:3. YHWH has never allowed incest at any time. Ruth was not a Moabitess but a Israelite living in the region of Moav.
[2] She was Abraham's half sister, same father but different mother. These marriages were and are allowed.

Footnotes
[3] See appendix HBYH.
[4] Abimelekh was referring to himself so the correct translation is gentile, and not nation, as many Bible translations make this assumption.
[5] Anyone who comes against YHWH's people, his end will be worse than his beginning! The punishment for casting down one of YHWH's prophets is not just death for the man, or woman, who did this; but their whole household will come under the curse of death, and disease. The reverse side of this, is helping the prophet of YHWH, to receive Blessings, and respect. Choose wisely!

8 So Avimelekh rose early in the morning, called all his servants, and told all these things in their hearing: and the men were very afraid.

9 And Avimelekh called Abraham, and said to him, What have you done to us? How have I offended you, that you have brought on me and on my kingdom a great sin? You have done deeds to me that ought not to be done.

10 Then Avimelekh said to Abraham, What did you have in view that you have done this thing?

11 And Abraham said, Because I thought, Surely the fear of Elohim is not in this place; and they will kill me[1] on account of my wife.

12 But indeed she is truly my sister; she is the daughter of my Abbah,[2] but not the daughter of my mother; and she became my wife.

13 And it came to pass, when Elohim caused me to wander from my Abbah's Beyth (house), that I said to her, This is your kindness that you should do for me; in every place where we go, say of me, He is my brother.

14 Then Avimelekh took sheep, oxen, and male, and maid servants, and gave them to Abraham, and he restored Sarah his wife to him.

15 And Avimelekh said, See, my land is before you: dwell where it seems good in your sight.

16 Then to Sarah he said, Behold, I have given your brother a thousand pieces of silver: indeed, he is to you a covering of your eyes,[3] before all who are with you, and before all others: thus she was proved right.

17 So Abraham prayed to Elohim: and Elohim healed Avimelekh, his wife, and his maid servants;[4] then they bore children.

18 For YHWH had closed up all the wombs of the Beyth (house) of Avimelekh, because of Sarah Abraham's wife.

Chapter 21

1 And YHWH visited Sarah as He had said, and YHWH did for Sarah as He had spoken.

2 For Sarah conceived, and bore Abraham a son in his old age, at the appointed time of which Elohim had spoken to him.

3 And Abraham called the name of his son that was born to

Footnotes
[1] Murder was a less serious offence in this place.
[2] Sarah was the daughter of Tharakh's second wife so she was the half sister of Abraham. All these ancient people had two wives and were polyganous. YHWH's permits these marriages from the Garden in his perfect free will and are perfectly legal even today.

Footnotes
[3] She was given a veil to wear to hide her beauty.
[4] These were Abimelekh's concubines: referred to as maidservants, they were his lesser wives. The same Hebrew word is used in Beresheeth 21:12 for Abraham's wife Hagar. Note, YHWH came to reprimand Abimelekh for trying to commit adultery unknowingly; but YHWH was perfectly fine with him taking on additional wives Polygamy was, and is, Biblically allowed in all ages.

him, whom Sarah bore to him, Ytshak [1] (Isaac).

4 Then Abraham circumcised his son Ytshak when he was eight days old,[2] as Elohim had commanded him.

5 Now Abraham was one hundred years old, when his son Ytshak was born to him.

6 And Sarah said, Elohim has made me laugh, so that all who hear will laugh with me.

7 She also said, Who would have said to Abraham, that Sarah would nurse children? For I have borne him a son in his old age.

8 So the child grew, and was weaned: and Abraham made a great banquet on the same day that Ytshak was weaned.

9 And Sarah saw the son of Hagar the Mitzri (Egyptian), whom she had birthed for Abraham, fooling around *sexually*.[3]

10 Therefore she said to Abraham, Cast out this maid[4] and her son: for the son of this maid shall not be heir with my son, namely with Ytshak.

11 And the matter was very displeasing in Abraham's sight because of his son.[5]

12 But Elohim said to Abraham, Do not let it be displeasing in your sight because of your offspring, or because of your maid; whatever Sarah has said to you, listen to her voice;[6] for in Ytshak your descendants[7] shall be called.

13 Yet I will also make a nation of the son of the maid, because he is your seed.[8]

14 So Abraham rose early in the morning, and took Lakhem (bread), and a skin of mayim, and putting it on her shoulder, he gave it to Hagar, and the boy, and sent her away: and she departed, and wandered in the wilderness of Beersheva.

15 And the mayim in the skin was used up, and she placed the boy under one of the shrubs.

16 Then she went, and sat down across from him, at a distance of about a bowshot: for

Footnotes

[1] Ytshak means 'YHWH will laugh over their unbelief.' Many people made Israel the Black people a joke and a laughter and ridiculed scorning our people. There is a penalty for this in the End of the Age. Isaac was born on the festival of Unleavened Bread on Nissan 15.

[2] All of us must circumcise our sons on the 8th day, this is one of the seals of our Faith in YHWH. Without this seal we cannot enter the Covenant given to Abraham.

[3] The Hebrew indicates more likely he was trying to molest his brother.

[4] By putting the term 'bondwoman' people try to deny Hagar was Abraham's legal 4th wife. The correct term is maid, there is no word for wife in Hebrew, its either the term 'maid', 'woman', or 'wife.' Here the Hebrew word Ammah is used for a secondary wife.

Footnotes

[5] While Sarah was correct, that only her son could qualify for a double portion of the inheritance in a polygamous relationship because she was the ruling wife in the North and Hagar was the wife in the South. Abraham loved Yshmael too, that is why he was displeased, and did not want to send his wife Hagar away. This was a trial for Abraham, he did join back his wife Hagar and son.

[6] This was a test for Abraham; he was not kicking his wife out for fun.

[7] The Covenant was to be established only through Isaac, and not Yshmael because Sarah was the ruling princess placed in the North the place of the priestly throne.

[8] YHWH confirms Yshmael is Abraham's legitimate son too.

she said to herself, Let me not see the death of the boy. So she sat opposite him, and lifted her voice, and wept.

17 And Elohim heard the voice of the child;[1] and the Malakh Elohim (Messenger of YHWH) called to Hagar out of shamayim, and said to her, What ails you, Hagar? Fear not, for Elohim has heard the voice of the child where he is.

18 Arise, lift up the boy, and hold him with your hand; for I will make him a great nation.[2]

19 And Elohim opened her eyes, and she saw a well of mayim;[3] then she went and filled the skin with mayim, and gave the boy to drink.

20 So Elohim was with the lad; and he grew, and dwelt in the wilderness, and became an archer.

21 He dwelt in the wilderness of Paran: and his mother took a wife for him from the land of Mitzrayim (Egypt).[4]

22 And it came to pass at that time, that Avimelekh and Phichol the commander of his army spoke to Abraham, saying, Elohim is with you in all that you do:

23 Now therefore, swear to me by Elohim that you will not deal falsely with me, with my offspring, or with my grandsons: but according to the kindness that I have done to you, you will do to me, and to the land in which you have dwelt.

24 And Abraham said, I will swear.

25 Then Abraham rebuked Avimelekh because of a well of mayim, which Avimelekh's servants had seized.

26 And Avimelekh said, I do not know who has done this thing: you did not tell me, nor had I heard of it, until today.

27 So Abraham took sheep and oxen, and gave them to Avimelekh; and the two of them made a Covenant.

28 And Abraham set seven ewe lambs of the flock by themselves.

29 Then Avimelekh asked Abraham, What is the meaning of these seven ewe lambs which you have set by themselves?

30 And he said, You will take these seven ewe lambs from my hand, that they may be my witness, that I have dug this well.

31 Therefore he called that place Beersheva;[5] because the two of them swore an oath there.[6]

Footnotes

[1] YHWH heard Yshmael's crying, and had compassion towards him, hence children's prayers are important, and heard. He loved Yshmael because he was Abraham's son.

[2] YHWH's Increases Yshmael.

[3] YHWH also loves Yshmael.

[4] Yshmael got mixed with the Egyptians, since his mother was an Egyptian. The wife of Yshmael was very rude, and not a good woman. He took a second wife to have a total of 12 children.

Footnotes

[5] The ancient Egyptian and the Hebrew Hieroglyph meaning of Beersheba is the following, "In the presence of LIGHT (meaning YHWH) where he has dominion and superiority over the water."

[6] This is the place in the South of Israel where Abraham's wife Keturah the daughter of Joktan was living in with her six sons already born before Isaac.

32 Thus they made a Covenant at Beersheva: so Avimelekh rose, with Phichol the commander of his army, and they returned to the land of the Philistines.

33 Then Abraham planted a tamarisk tree in Beersheva, and there called on the name of YHWH, the Everlasting El (Power).

34 And Abraham stayed in the land of the plushtim (Philistines)[1] many days.

Chapter 22

1 Now it came to pass after these things, that Elohim tested Abraham, and said to him, Abraham: and he said, Here I am.

2 And He said, Take now your son, your Beloved[2] son Ytshak,

Footnotes

[1] The philistines were a people of black skin colour.

[2] The ancient Hebrew word Yakhed does not mean 'only' as supposed or even translated in many texts incorrectly given the wrong picture. This translation ignores Abraham's other sons a total of eight all born before Ytshak. Six of his sons from Keturah were rulers of modern Arabian regions and Yemen. See Gen 25:2. His firstborn son in the south with the wife Keturah was Jokshan or Yoktan in the Hebrew tongue and his firstborn son in the North was Ytshak. He also had a son from Mashek called Eli'ezer who was most likely the eldest of all the sons but he was not a ruler so could not be counted. The narrator of Beresheeth is not looking at who is first or who is second but looking at who is in the line of a ruling prince. Since Abraham had no son from his princess wife Sarah therefore when YHWH gave this son Ytshak he became his youngest and beloved son just like today if we have a youngest child we tend to love him more. However this son was also in the line of kings and therefore kings were to come from him and through the ruling princess wife and father Abraham. Ascension of kings in some regions was to be from
Continued in next section

mothers, this is the African way, which today the modern state of Israel has adopted by saying only those are Jews who are from the mother, however its not accurate to say that. The issue is not of being a Jew but of being a Yahudi and a ruler.
The most accurate meaning of the Hebrew word Yakhed is "Beloved" or close to the bosom. The spelling of the word is Yud, Khet, Yud plus Dalet יחיד.

The word Yud means eyes, or light, the word, Khet is for the bosom or darkness so this son was both a dark skinned boy and closer to Abraham. One could say concealed by YHWH for an appropriate time just as the real Hebrews today scattered in western gentile nations are concealed. The Dalet means the mouth because this boy was promised by the Mouth of YHWH so it indicates that this was a boy of contractual unity from Abbah in shamayim and affinity. Abraham's other sons had Rights in the various territories but they could not continue the Covenant/Agreement to bring the Messiah while Ytshak was the only one bestowed this unique gift and respect. This does not mean Abraham did not love Yshmael or his other sons, he did love them all but they were not meant to carry the messianic line. The bad interpretations have caused a wide scale rift between Muslims and the Hebrews only because of trying to cast Yshmael as an infidel who is Abraham's flesh and blood son and also rightful heir to the Egyptian territory. Note Ancient Egyptians were black. We need to understand Abraham had more Arab and Kushite blood than the alleged Caucasian Jewish blood since the modern Caucosoid Jews are gentile converts of Ashkenazi origin from Caucus Mountians. Abraham was a man of colour and so were his sons and his wives. At least three of Abraham's wives were of dark black skin both of Sarah, Keturah and Hagar while Mashek was of lighter colour. False traditions and heretic gospels that depict Sarah as white are inaccurate as she was of Shem's and Ham's blood therefore Black in skin tone as both these men were black. Abraham's family were noble rulers whose ancestors came from Western Africa.

whom you love, and go to the land of MarYah;[1] and offer him there as a burnt offering on one of the mountains of which I shall tell you.

3 So Abraham rose early in the morning, and saddled his donkey, and took two of his young men with him[2], and Ytshak his son, and he split the wood for the burnt offering, and arose, and went to the place of which Elohim had told him.

4 Then on the third day Abraham lifted up his eyes, and saw the place afar off.[3]

5 And Abraham said to his young men, Stay here with the donkey; the lad and I will go over there and pay homage to him,[4] and we will come back to you,

6 So Abraham took the wood of the burnt offering, and laid it on Ytshak his son; and he took the fire in his hand, and a knife; and the two of them went together.

7 And Ytshak spoke to Abraham his Abbah, and said, My Abbah: and he said, Here I am, my son. And he said, Look, the fire and the wood: but where is the lamb for a burnt offering?

8 And Abraham said, My son, Elohim will appear Himself with the lamb for a burnt offering:[5] and the two of them went together.

9 Then they came to the place of which Elohim had told him: and Abraham built an altar there, and placed the wood in order, and he bound Ytshak his son, and laid him on the altar upon the wood.

10 And Abraham stretched out his hand, and took the knife to slay his son.

11 And the Malakh YHWH[6] called to him from the shamayim and said, Abraham, Abraham:[7] and he said, Here I am.

12 And He said, Do not lay your hand[8] on the lad, or do anything to him: for now I know that you fear Elohim, seeing you

Footnotes

[1] Temple Mount in Israel believed by the proselyte Yahudim. However, MarYah is the Aramaic word for Master YHWH and has an interesting connotation. It is three days journey away. This is not the land what is taught to you by the gentiles but is in East Africa today known as Arabia where the Mountain of YHWH is. So the reserved land was called as Master YHWH, this is YHWH's identifier, same as the Mountain Sini'yah, known as Sinai, where He spoke to Moses.

[2] The two men were Yshmael and Eli'ezer arguing over who will get Abraham's inheritance after Isaac's death. They were both his sons. Eli'ezer was the son of Abraham's third wife Mashek.

[3] Also the drash (allegory) is to see the end-times.

[4] The word 'worship' throughout the scriptures is wrong to use because it conveys something very different to what is being said. The word 'worship' is incorrect in its usage and should be avoided in speech or reverence to YHWH. The word Shaha when applied to YHWH is to cherish him, love him, adore him, reverence him but on the other hand it means to bend, to bow down to the unclean spirit beings such as Satan. To put your foot on the neck of another bowed Continued in next section

down person is the implied meaning of the text. The correct word in this instance is 'Pay homage to' YHWH. The word in man's system of religion is very different where you grovel to ask for something, while our prayer to YHWH who in love and justice grants us that which we desire.

[5] Abraham was speaking about the future glorious rule and reign of Israel.

[6] The Malakh of YHWH, the angel of the Covenant.

[7] Calling his name twice was so Abraham would pay attention, and listen; to stop Abraham from sacrificing his son Isaac.

[8] Isaac was 37 years old.

have not withheld your son, your Beloved son[1] from Me.

13 Then Abraham lifted his eyes, and looked, and there behind him was a ram caught in a thicket[2] by its horns: and Abraham went and took the ram, and offered it up for a burnt offering instead of his son.

14 And Abraham called the name of the place YHWH Yireh (YHWH Will-Provide): as it is said to this day, on the Mountain of YHWH He shall be seen.

15 Then the Malakh YHWH called to Abraham a second time out of the shamayim,

16 And said, By Myself I have sworn, says YHWH, because you have done this thing, and have not withheld your son, your beloved[3] son:

17 In **Blessing**, unconditionally I will **Bless** you, and in multiplying unconditionally[4] I will multiply your descendants as the stars of the shamayim, and as the sand which is on the seashore; and your descendants

shall possess the gate of their enemies;[5]

18 In your seed all the nations of the earth shall be **Blessed**; because you have obeyed My voice.

19 So Abraham returned to his young men, and they rose and went together to Beersheva; and Abraham dwelt at Beersheva.

20 Now it came to pass after these things, that it was told Abraham, saying, Indeed, Milkah, also has borne children to your brother Nakhkhur;

21 Hutz his Bekhor (firstborn), Buz his brother, Kemu'el the Abbah of Aram,

22 Chesed, Hazo, Pildash, Yidlaph, and Bethu'el.

23 And Bethu'el begot Rivka: these eight Milkah bore to Nakhkhur, Abraham's brother.

24 His concubine, whose name was Reumah, also bore Tebah, Gaham, Thahash, and Maakath.

Torah Parsha 5 Chai Sarah, Beresheeth 23:1-25:18
Haftarah: Melekhim Alef 1:1 - 1:31

Chapter 23

1 Sarah lived one hundred twenty-seven years:[6] these were the years of the life of Sarah.

Footnotes
[1] A remez (hint), to the beloved Son of YHWH, who is Israel. Translating this as an 'only' son would make no sense, as that would make it sound like Yshmael is illegitimate, including the other six sons of Keturah plus the son of Mashek, while we know he is not and Abraham had eight other sons apart from Ytshak making it nine sons.
[2] YHWH provided the ram; but Satan tried to prevent the ram from reaching the altar, so Abraham would sacrifice his son, Hence, YHWH had to speak, to stop Abraham.
[3] See footnote Gen 22:2.
[4] The word "unconditionally" is in the nuance of the ancient Hebrew text and needs to be read this way as the words Brekhakha and We'ha raba impute a Blessing without a condition attached to it.

Footnotes
[5] The many nations that will come out of Abraham will defeat and conquer their enemies.
[6] Sarah died from the grief of thinking that her son was perhaps going to be used for a sacrifice not knowing the full facts. Although Sarah loved Abraham her husband, still sometimes the most trustworthy wives will question their husband's motives because of fear, rather than waiting upon YHWH to Continued in next section

2 So Sarah died in Kiryath Arba; that is Khevron in the land of Kanan: and Abraham came to mourn for Sarah, and to weep for her.

3 Then Abraham stood up from before his dead, and spoke to the sons of Kheth, saying,

4 I am a foreigner and a sojourner among you: give me property for a burial place among you, that I may bury my dead out of my sight.

5 And the sons of Kheth answered Abraham, saying to him,

6 Hear us, my master: you are a prince of Elohim among us: bury your dead in the choicest of our burial places; none of us will withhold from you his burial place, that you may bury your dead.

7 Then Abraham stood up, and bowed himself to the people of the land, the sons of Kheth.

8 And he spoke with them, saying, If it is your wish that I bury my dead out of my sight; hear me, and meet with Ephron the son of Zokhar for me,

9 That he may give me the cave of Machpelah,[2] which he has, which is at the end of his field; let him give it to me at the full price, as property for a burial place among you.

10 Now Ephron dwelt among the sons of Kheth: and Ephron the Khitee answered Abraham in the presence of the sons of Kheth, all who entered at the gate of his city, saying,

11 No, my master, hear me: I give you the field, and the cave that is in it, I give it to you; in the sight of the sons of my people I give it to you: bury your dead.

12 Then Abraham bowed himself down before the people of the land.

13 And he spoke to Ephron in the hearing of the people of the land, saying, If you will give it, please, hear me: I will give you money for the field; take it from me, and I will bury my dead there.

14 And Ephron answered Abraham, saying to him,

15 My master, listen to me: the land is worth four hundred shekels of silver;[3] what is that between you and me? So bury your dead.

16 And Abraham listened to Ephron; and Abraham weighed out the silver for Ephron, which

answer prayer. Note, it is not advisable to communicate everything of YHWH with your spouse immediately, there has to be a time of prayer, and then exercising wisdom when to communicate such matters.
[1] The kuf is a small letter here indicating the word 'bakah' to weep, this means Abraham was sad that Sarah was overcome by Satan's deception since the Kuf is for smiting, and he was weeping for his wife Sarah. The lowering of the kuf indicates that everyone was sad for Abraham's loss.

Footnotes
[2] This cave is the burial place for the patriarchs and is in Israel in (Hebron) to this day where many Hebrew people go to pay homage to Abraham and the Patriarchs.
[3] In other words he was asking for this money in a mocking way, which was given to him by Abraham so the people became the witnesses with documents signed and sealed that were passed to Isaac and Jacob.

he had named in the hearing of the sons of Kheth, four hundred shekels of silver, currency of the merchants.

17 So the field of Ephron, which was in Machpelah, which was before Mamre, the field, and the cave, which was in it, and all the etzim (trees) that were in the field, which were within all the surrounding borders, were accounted for,

18 To Abraham as a possession in the sight of the sons of Kheth, before all who went in at the gate of his city. [1]

19 And after this, Abraham buried Sarah his wife in the cave of the field of Machpelah before Mamre: that is, Khevron in the land of Kanan.

20 So the field, and the cave that is in it, were deeded to Abraham by the sons of Kheth as property for a burial place.

Chapter 24

1 Now Abraham was old, well-advanced in age; and YHWH had **Increased** Abraham in all things.

2 So Abraham said to the elder servant[2] of his Beyth (house), who ruled over all that he had, Please, put your hand under my thigh:[3]

3 And swear by YHWH, the Elohim of shamayim and the Elohim of the earth, that you will not take a wife for my son from the daughters of the Kanani,[4] among whom I dwell:

4 But you shall go to my land and to my Mishpakha (family), and take a wife for my son Ytshak.

5 And the servant said to him, Perhaps the woman will not be willing to follow me to this country: Must I take your son back to the land from which you came?

6 But Abraham said to him, Beware that you do not take my son back there.

7 YHWH Elohim of the shamayim, who took me from my Abbah's house and from the land of my Mishpakha (family), and who spoke to me and swore to me, saying, To your descendants I give this land; He will send His Malakh before you, and you shall take a wife for my son from there.

8 And if the woman is not willing to follow you, then you will be released from this oath:[5] only do not take my son back there.

9 So the servant put his hand under the thigh of Abraham his master/owner/father, and swore to him concerning this matter.

10 Then the servant took ten of his master's camels and

Footnotes
[1] This purchase had to be noted and recorded for Abraham's later generations such as Jacob.
[2] Eli'ezer who was his son and his personal assistant. Obed in ancient Hebrew means the one who works and conducts the business of the house.
[3] Hands were put on the reproductive organs as a custom in ancient times to say if you do not do what you say, may your descendants perish. It's also the area of circumcision so this shows respect to the Covenant. The testicular area is the area of the man's seed, Continued in next section

so this was considered important. Some people in India and Ethiopia still take oaths like this.
[4] These people were idolatrous and would turn away Isaac's heart. Abraham took an oath from his son Eli'ezer for Ytshak.
[5] This was a conditional oath, such can be made even today.

departed, for all his master's goods were in his hand: and he arose and went to Mesopotamia, to the city of Nakhkhur.

11 And he made his camels kneel down outside the city by a well of mayim at evening time, the time when women go out to draw mayim.

12 Then he said, O YHWH, Mighty One of my Adoni (master: father) Abraham, please give me success this day, and show unmerited favour[1] to my master Abraham.[2]

13 Behold, I stand here by the well of mayim; and the daughters of the men of the city are coming out to draw mayim:

14 Now let it be that the young woman to whom I say, Please let down your pitcher that I may drink; and she says, Drink, and I will also give your camels a drink: let her be the one whom You have appointed for Your servant Ytshak; and by this I will know that You have shown loving-kindness to my master.

15 And it happened, before he had finished speaking, that behold, Rivka, who was born to Bethu'el, son of Milkah, the wife of Nakhkhur, Abraham's brother,

came out with her pitcher on her shoulder.

16 Now the young woman was very beautiful to behold, a virgin,[3] no man had known her: and she went down to the well, filled her pitcher, and came up.

17 And the servant ran to meet her and said, Please let me drink a little mayim from your pitcher.

18 So she said, Drink, my master. Then she quickly let her pitcher down to her hand, and gave him a drink.

19 And when she had finished giving him a drink, she said, I will draw mayim for your camels also, until they have finished drinking.

20 Then she quickly, emptied her pitcher into the trough, ran back to the well to draw mayim, and drew for all his camels.[4]

21 And the man wondering at her remained silent, so as to know whether YHWH had made his journey prosperous or not.

22 So it was, when the camels had finished drinking, that the man took a golden nose ring weighing half a shekel,[5] and two

Footnotes

[1] Abraham already had unmerited favour with YHWH; but his son Eli'ezer wanted to see that being demonstrated, which YHWH complied with immediately.

[2] The Biblical way to take a bride is determined by the parents and by prayer to YHWH. You do not make a good marriage by dating someone for six years living together immorally and producing children out of wedlock. Isaac's marriage is called an arranged marriage and can be seen today in the Muslim, Hindu cultures and the Sephardic Hebrew culture.

[3] The Hebrew word 'Betulah' can also be used for a married woman this is why the text is appended with 'no man had known her.'

[4] Rebecca was a dedicated and strong woman drawing water for ten camels. The midrashim suggest her age was 3 but that is idealistic. Her age was 13. According to Rambam the age of a mature woman in halacha is 12 years Plus one day or her having two pubic hairs (MT Ishut 4:7). The common custom in the East is still for the ladies to go out and fetch water sometimes travelling for many miles.

[5] This is a Hebrew custom adopted by other cultures such as India, Pakistan and the Arab nations.

Beresheeth (Genesis)

bracelets for her wrists weighing ten shekels of gold,

23 And said, Whose daughter are you? Tell me please: is there room in your Abbah's Beyth (house) for us to lodge?

24 So she said to him, I am the daughter of Bethu'el, Milkah's son, whom she bore to Nakhkhur.

25 Moreover she said to him, We have both straw and enough feed, and room to lodge.

26 Then the man bowed down his head and paid homage to YHWH.

27 And he said, **Blessed** is YHWH Mighty One who has not forsaken my Adoni (Master, father)[1] Abraham of His unmerited favour and His truth: as for me, being on the way, YHWH led me to the Beyth (house) of my master's brethren.[2]

28 So the young woman ran and told those of her mother's Beyth (house) these things.

29 Now Rivka had a brother whose name was Laban,[3] and Laban ran out to the man by the well.

30 So it came to pass, when he saw the nose ring and the bracelets on his sister's wrists, and when he heard the words of his sister Rivka, saying, Thus the

Footnotes
[1] Elie'zer was Abraham's son from Mashek his third wife.
[2] Even though the relatives had heard of YHWH, they had no relationship with him. This shows us we cannot just drop our families, and run off, we need to be trustworthy to YHWH and witness to our families.
[3] Laban means 'white' he was an African albino. Rachel was black as her sister Leyah and the other half sisters Bilhah and Zilpah were of African roots.

man spoke to me; that he went to the man; and there he stood by the camels at the well.[4]

31 And he said, Come in, O **Blessed** one of YHWH, Why do you stand outside? For I have prepared the Beyth (house), and a place for the camels.

32 Then the man came to the Beyth (house): and he unloaded the camels, and provided straw and feed for the camels, and mayim to wash his feet and the feet of the men who were with him.

33 And food was set before his face to eat, but he said, I will not eat until I have spoken the words of my important matter. And he said, speak the words.

34 So he said, I am Abraham's servant.

35 YHWH has **Blessed** my master (Adoni: father) greatly; and he has become great: and He has given him flocks and herds, silver and gold, male, and female servants, and camels, and donkeys.[5]

36 And Sarah my master's wife bore a son to my master when she was old: and to him he has given all that he has.

37 Now my master made me swear, saying, You shall not take a wife for my son from the daughters of the Kanani, in whose land I dwell;[6]

Footnotes
[4] The nose ring is an ancient symbol for the betrothal.
[5] No mention of Abraham breeding pigs because he ate clean animals.
[6] Isaac had two wives; Rebecca was his second wife in the North.

98

38 But you shall go to my Abbah's Beyth (house) and to my Mishpakha (family), and take a wife for my son.[1]

39 And I said to my master, Perhaps the woman will not follow me?

40 But he said to me YHWH, before whom I walk,[2] will send His malakh with you, and prosper your way; and you shall take a wife for my son from my Mishpakha (family), and from my Abbah's Beyth (house):

41 You will be clear from this oath when you arrive among my Mishpakha (family); for if they will not give her to you, then you will be released from my oath.

42 And this day I came to the well and said, O YHWH Elohim of my adoni (master: father) Abraham, if You will now prosper the way in which I go;

43 Behold, I stand by the well of mayim; and it shall come to pass that when the maiden comes out to draw mayim, and I say to her, Please give me a little mayim from your pitcher to drink;

44 And she says to me, Drink and I will draw for your camels also; let her be the woman whom YHWH has appointed for my master's son.

45 But before I had finished speaking in my heart, there was Rivka, coming out with her pitcher on her shoulder; and she went down to the well, and drew mayim: and I said to her, Please let me drink.

46 And she made haste and let her pitcher down from her shoulder, and said, Drink, and I will give your camels a drink also. So I drank, and she gave the camels a drink also.

47 Then I asked her, and said, Whose daughter are you? And she said, The daughter of Bethu'el, Nakhkhur's son, whom Milkah bore to him. So I put the nose ring on her nose and the bracelets on her wrists.

48 And I bowed my head and paid homage to YHWH, and YHWH the Increaser Elohim of my adoni (master: father) Abraham, who had led me in the way of truth[3] to take the daughter of my master's brother for his son.

49 Now if you will deal kindly and truly with my master, tell me; and if not, tell me; that I may turn to the right hand or to the left.

50 Then Laban and Bethu'el answered and said, The thing comes from YHWH: we cannot speak to you either bad or good.

51 Here is Rivka before you, take her, and go, and let her be your master's son's wife, as YHWH has spoken.

52 And it came to pass, when Abraham's servant heard their

Footnotes

[1] This is a Hebrew and Biblical custom. We find this custom is still prevalent amongst the Muslims in Pakistan, who will not marry their sons and daughters outside their family and if they are abroad, they will send for the son's wives back in Pakistan. Some Arab tribes do the same.

[2] In Hebrew the halacha, whose commandants I obey, meaning obeying Torah of YHWH.

Footnotes

[3] The way of Truth – Eli'ezer was taught Torah keeping by Abraham. He discipled him since he was his son.

words, that he paid homage to YHWH, bowing himself to the ground.

53 Then the servant brought out jewels of silver, jewels of gold, and clothing, and gave them to Rivka: he also gave precious things to her brother and to her mother.[1]

54 And he and the men who were with him, ate and drank, and stayed all night; then they arose in the morning, and he said, Send me away to my master.

55 But her brother and her mother said, Let the young woman stay with us a few days, at least ten; after that she may go.

56 And he said to them, Do not hinder me, since YHWH has prospered my way; send me away so that I may go to my master.

57 So they said, We will call the young woman and ask her personally.

58 Then they called Rivka, and said to her, Will you go with this man? And she said, I will go.

59 So they sent away Rivka their sister, and her nurse,[2] and Abraham's servant, and his men.

60 And they spoke an **Increase** to Rivka, and said to her, Our sister, may you become the mother of thousands of ten thousands;[3] and may your descendants possess the gates[4] of those who hate them.

61 Then Rivka and her maids arose, and they rode on the camels, and followed the man: so the servant took Rivka, and departed.

62 Now Ytshak came from the way of Beer Lahai Roi, for he dwelt in the South.

63 And Ytshak went out to meditate in the field in the evening: and he lifted his eyes, and looked, and, there, the camels were coming.

64 Then Rivka lifted her eyes, and when she saw Ytshak, she dismounted[5] from her camel.

65 For she had said to the servant, Who is this man walking in the field to meet us? And the servant said, It is my master: so she took a veil,[6] and covered herself. [7]

tribes were scattered and they became many gentile nations.

[4] Isaac's children will be victorious, as this prophecy comes down through Jacob to his twelve sons, collectively known as Israel.

[5] It was the custom for women to get off their ride and bow.

[6] She covered herself to show she was willing to marry him and showed a sign of submission severely lacking in our modern women. She was Isaac's second wife.

[7]

http://jwa.org/encyclopedia/article/maimonides
Maimonides on Husband and wife relationship

Maimonides's recipe for a "pleasant and honorable" marriage entails clear instructions for a submissive wife. Fear of her husband should rule her and she should honor him beyond any limit. The wife should intuit all his desires, remove all his hates, follow all his commands and should view her husband as a prince or king
Continued in next section

Footnotes

[1] In Eastern culture you have to give gifts to the parents of the girl and vice versa.

[2] Debar'yah (Deborah)

[3] Billions of Israelites, this prophecy was fulfilled as given to Abraham when the Ten
Continued in next section

(Mishneh Torah Ishut 15:20). In return, the husband should not instill undue fear in her, but should act gently towards her, without anger (MT Ishut 15:19). If the husband wounds his wife he must pay compensation in full for her injury, humiliation, pain and medical expenses. The money belongs solely to her and Maimonides states, in opposition to earlier sources
(Tosefta Bava Kamma 9:14), that the husband cannot benefit from it in any way. If the husband injures her during consensual intercourse he is also liable for damages (MT Hovel u-Mazik4:16–17). However, if the wife refuses to do any of the legally obligated household work for her husband, Maimonides states that the courts may force her to submit by hitting her with a rod. If the husband and wife present different claims in regard to her behavior, the court must appoint someone to stay with them and witness the actual dynamic
(MT Ishut 21:10). Maimonides's extreme stance in this case seems to stem from his intense Faith that idleness leads to immorality. (MT Ishut 21:2–3).

Maimonides permits many types of sexual interaction between husband and wife, as long as the act is consensual and does not occur in excess. The husband can have intercourse whenever he wishes when his wife is permissible to him, and kiss any part of the woman's body as he desires. He may have vaginal or anal intercourse with his wife. Maimonides instructs that one should not have intercourse while thinking of somebody else, while drunk, while in the midst of a fight, when one is asleep, when one hates the other, or after he has decided in his heart to divorce her. Maimonides explicitly states that the husband should not force her to have intercourse against her will or if she is afraid of him (MT Forbidden Intercourse 21:9, 12). In MT De'ot 5:4, he states, "And he should not rape her if she does not want it, rather it should be from mutual desire and happiness."

Maimonides expects women to behave with extreme modesty. The husband must provide his wife with a veil. (If she goes out without one she can be divorced and lose the money of
her ketubbah [MT Ishut 24:12]). Maimonides states that since the woman is not
Continued in next section

66 And the servant told Ytshak all the things that he had done.

67 Then Ytshak brought her into his mother Sarah's tent, and he took Rivka, and she became his wife; and he loved her: so Ytshak was comforted after his mother's death.

Chapter 25

1 And Henceforth Abraham continued [1] with his wife,[1] and her name was Keturah. [2]

imprisoned, she is permitted to go out to her father's house or to a wedding; however, it would be unseemly if she were to leave her home excessively and therefore her husband should prevent his wife from doing so except for once or twice a month. Since "all the honor of the king's daughter is within" (Psalms 45:14), she should sit in the corner of her house with no freedom of movement (MT Ishut 13:11);

Rabbi Simon Altaf Hakohen comments on modesty: I would highly discourage the practice of veiling our women in public unless you are in a Muslim country and its a custom of that country. Simple head coverings are sufficient for most occasions. Even in western corporate environments our skilled women should not wear any head covering not to be targeted by the goyim unless its a modest hat or simple scarf. They can wear the head covering outside the building before they enter and take off on entering.

[1] Alice C. Linsley a theological researcher studying the patterns in Genesis for over thirty years, writing her blog reports on Just Genesis (http://jandyongenesis.blogspot.com/) verifies the theory that we have espoused that all the patriarchs followed a pattern of having more than one wife to control the North/South axis and that just because certain family information may be absent it does not mean that it did not occur. We know because we see this pattern with Qayin, Lamech, Mahalal'el, Methusa'ël, Metushelakh, Noakh, Yoktan, Isaac, Jacob, Continued in next section

2 And she had birthed him Zimran, Yokshan, [3] Medan, Midian,[1] Ishvak,[2] and Shuakh.

and even King David. carrying right up to the pages of the New Covenant/Agreement.

[1] Many translations translate this verse as if Abraham just took on another wife sequentially after the death of his first wife however the ancient text can be translated another better way which seems to have been ignored by the translators in the past who also did not recognize that Abraham followed a pattern of his horoite ancestors from Africa of keeping two wives in the North/South axis. The book of Jasher 23:87 tells us that after Abraham came back from the sacrifice he went to Beersheba but did he not live in Hebron in the North then one should ask what is he doing in the south where Beersheba is? This is where his wife Keturah was and his mother's household were where an important well of water was marking their territory.

Since Abraham already had this wife in the North/South axis this is a crucial point in understanding where the narrator takes us in Genesis. This wife was living in the South while Sarah was alive so how could he be taking Keturah as a third wife makes absolutely no sense. Also Abraham and Sarah were both old and Sarah was heard saying to Elohim that she is too old (Gen 18:7) to have children then how could Abraham being very old suddenly have six more sons from Keturah? The reality is that Isaac nor Ishmael are the first born sons but instead Yoktan is born to Keturah and these sons to Keturah were already born prior to Isaac but none of them were the sons of the promise. The story can be likened to King David who was the youngest therefore Isaac was also the youngest born to be the promised son.

The Herbew words in Genesis 25:1 V'Yasaf Abraham VeChaf Ishah better translate to "Henceforth Abraham continued with his wife" meaning now the narrative is introducing the story of the family that lived in Beersheba which was Abraham's mother's home the wife of his father Tharakh who was still alive. Beersheba was the place of Tharakh's first wife while nothing is mentioned is of his second wife but she was there also in another location based on the North/South axis.

[2] Abraham's alleged 2nd wife Hagar was actually the 4th wife and not his second and Continued in next section

another one mentioned in Gen 15:2 is called Mashek who was likely the third wife while Sarah was the initial wife and Hagar the 4th.

[3] Who is the first born son Isaac or Ishmael? Actually neither, Yoktan (Yokshan) is the firstborn of Keturah she lived in Beersheba and Abraham was already married to Keturah before he acquired Hagar as his wife. She was likely his third wife, Keturah likely to be the first wife named her son in her great grandfather Yoktan's (Gen 10:25) name which was the common custom and is shown with others too in the Tanak such as Isaac and Jacob. Abraham had two wives followed by Hagar the third wife given to him by Sarah. Sarah was Abraham's patrilineal wife (Sister wife) and Keturah was his cousin wife. We find the pattern in the Tanak of people of noble birth or princes having at least two wives one from the father's side and one usually from the mother's side. This was common practice in African/Asian cultures and is even today. Note all three women Sarah, Hagar and Keturah were brown skinned women and the ancestors of the African people while all other literature including Gnostic depicting them as white is absolutely false them as white is false. Keturah would be taking care of the family inheritance home of Abraham in the south while Sarah would have been taking care of the inheritance home in the north in Shkhem.

Abraham was a prince and chief (Gen 23:6). Such type of people always had at least two wives with lineages from both parents while they often also took extra wives to protect the property and extend the sons to regions under their control. Hagar was of Egyptian descent which was part of the North African region. One may ask how can Abraham say I have no seed when he had seven eight sons already in Genesis 15:3. To most people this is lost but in effect Abraham is not denying his other eight sons but his ruling princess had no seed so this is why Abraham talks about having no seed. While when Sarah has become pregnant this is truly a miracle for a barren woman who otherwise had no chance of a child.

3 Yokshan begot Sheba and Dedan. And the sons of Dedan [3] were Asshurim, Letushim, and Leummim.[4]

4 And the sons of Midian; were Ephah, Epher, Hanoch, Avidah, and Eldaah. All these were the children of Keturah.

5 And Abraham gave all that he had to Ytshak.

6 But Abraham gave gifts,[5] to the sons of the concubines,[6] which Abraham had, and while he was still living he sent them eastward, away from Ytshak his son, to the country of the east.

7 This is the sum of the years of Abraham's life which he lived, one hundred seventy-five years.

8 Then Abraham breathed his last. and died in a good old age, an old man, and full of years; and was gathered to his people.

9 And his sons Ytshak and Yshmael buried him in the cave of Machpelah,[7] which is before Mamre, in the field of Ephron the son of Zokhar the Khitee,

10 The field which Abraham purchased from the sons of

Kheth: there Abraham was buried, and Sarah his wife.

11 And it came to pass, after the death of Abraham, that Elohim **Blessed** his son Ytshak; and Ytshak dwelt at Beer Lahai Roi.

12 Now this is the genealogy of Yshmael, Abraham's son, whom Hagar the Mitzri (Egyptian), Sarah's maidservant, bore to Abraham:

13 And these were the names of the sons of Yshmael, by their names, according to their generations: The Bekhor (firstborn) of Yshmael, Nebayoth; then Kedar,[8] Adbeel, Mibsam,

Footnotes

[8] The Muslim prophet Muhammad was alleged to be a descendant from Kedar. Kedar one of the sons of Yshmael. The Hebrew word means powerful Black or powerful dark skinned. All the ancient Arabs were of black origin that travelled from Africa to inhabit the regions of Yemen, Northern and Southern Arabia. They were not pale or white skinned as modern Arabs because these ones came with the mixing of Asians who settled the lands later and had come travelling to the regions. Hagar their grandmother was a black kushite princess. The Arabs also came from Joktan who was the real first Arab. The black group who contributed to the ancient Arabs were called the Bejas who the Romans identified as the Blemmyes people. These later came to be known as Bedouins. These were all Kushite people of the land of the blacks.

The Roman history writer Ammianus Marcellinus in his book XIV, IV 1-7 (380 CE) called them Saracens which was a name used to describe the Arabs in both modern and ancient times. These were described as the Blemmyae by the Romans the tribes that lives on the banks of the Nile. He writes in his book XIV4.

> At this time also the Saracens, a race whom it is never desirable to have either for friends or enemies,

Continued in next section

[1] Jehtro was an ancestor of Midian so Moses had a wife from the Arab clans relating back to Joktan as Keturah was Joktan's daughter.

[2] Isaac's father in law to his first wife not mentioned in the Torah.

[3] Northern Arabians of African descent.

[4] Arabian tribes of African descent.

[5] The children of the half wives. Concubines could not, in Torah, be permitted firstborn inheritance. This only belonged to Sarah, and her son Isaac. But the gifts here specifies something of value, something tangible like gold, silver, cows, sheep and goats since our father Abraham was very rich, and a favoured man of YHWH.

[6] These were Hagar and Mashek.

[7] Hebron

ranging up and down the country, if ever they found anything, plundered it in a moment, like rapacious hawks who, if from on high they behold any prey, carry it off with a rapid swoop, or, if they fail in their attempt, do not tarry. And although, in recounting the career of the Prince Marcus, and once or twice subsequently, I remember having discussed the manners of this people, nevertheless I will now briefly enumerate a few more particulars concerning them.

Among these tribes, whose primary origin is derived from the cataracts of the Nile and the borders of the Blemmyae, all the men are warriors of equal rank; half naked, clad in coloured cloaks down to the waist, running to different countries, with the aid of swift and active horses and speedy camels, alike in times of peace and war. Nor does any member of their tribe ever take plough in hand or cultivate a tree, or seek food by the tillage of the land; but they are perpetually wandering over various and extensive districts, having no home, no fixed abode or laws; nor can they endure to remain long in the same climate, no one district or country pleasing them for a continuance.

Their life is one continued wandering; their wives are hired, on special Covenant/Agreement, for a fixed time; and that there may be some appearance of marriage in the business, the intended wife, under the name of a dowry, offers a spear and a tent to her husband, with a right to quit him after a fixed day, if she should choose to do so. And it is inconceivable with what eagerness the individuals of both sexes give themselves up to matrimonial pleasures.

But as long as they live they wander about with such extensive and perpetual migrations, that the woman is married in one place, brings forth her children in another, and rears them at a distance from either place, no opportunity of remaining quiet being ever granted to her. They all live on venison, and are further supported on a great abundance of milk, and on many kinds of herbs, and on whatever birds they can catch by fowling. And we have seen a great many of them wholly ignorant of the use of either corn or wine."

The Black African Bejas/Saracens also called the Blemmys gave to the Arabs of today (blacks and pales) the knowledge to live in the Sahara as well as the most basic cultural elements that define the Bedouin culture including nomadic identity, marital culture and martial arts. For instance, the war-like Blemmyes (Beja) had normally fought with curiously shaped bows, and it was from them that the tribes of Hijaz and Yemen (in Arabia) – and the other Arab tribes – adopted the use of the bow. Historically, the Beja ruled the vast territory of theirs (laying between Northern Nigeria and Sudan) in five kingdoms – namely, the Naqis, Baqlin (Taflin), Bazin, Jarin and Qat'a (Qit'a, also perhaps Qas'a).

http://nabataea.net/arabia.html
During the Roman Period, historians such as Josephus and Strabo freely intermix the use of the word Arab with Nabataean, and vice versa. Nabataean kings were known as kings of the 'Arabs' and their kingdom was known as Arabia. Thus it was only fitting that the Nabataean Kingdom became known as the Province of Arabia, once it was absorbed into the Roman Empire. The oldest reference to these Arabs can be found in the biblical book Genesis, where Arabian merchants buy and sell Jacob's son Joseph. Other references can be found in the Assyrian king Salmanasser's account of a battle in 853 BC and in the reports about a kingdom named Aribi, that is mentioned from Tiglath- Pileser III (ruled 745-727) onward and was an Assyrian vassal until the second half of the seventh century. Later, the Arabs were subdued by the

Continued in next section
Continued in next section

14 Mishma, Dumah,[1] Massa,

15 Hadar, Tema,[2] Yetur, Naphish, and Kedemah:

16 These were the sons of Yshmael, and these were their names, by their towns and their settlements, twelve princes [3] according to their nations.

17 These were the years of the life of Yshmael: one hundred thirty-seven years: and he breathed his last and died; and was gathered to his people.[4]

18 They dwelt from Khavilah as far as Shur which is east of Mitzrayim (Egypt), as you go toward Assyria: he died in the presence of all his brethren. [5]

Torah Parsha 6 Toldot, Beresheeth 25:19-28:9

Babylonian king Nabonidus, who made the oasis of Tema' his capital and reached Iatribu (modern Medina).

During the Roman Period, historians such as Josephus and Strabo freely intermix the use of the word Arab with Nabataean, and vice versa. Nabataean kings were known as kings of the 'Arabs' and their kingdom was known as Arabia. Thus it was only fitting that the Nabataean Kingdom became known as the Province of Arabia, once it was absorbed into the Roman Empire.

Biblically
Arabs show up in three biblical lists of genealogy:
The descendants of Joktan (Genesis 10:25-30)
The descendants of Abraham through Keturah (Genesis 10:1-6) The descendants of Ishmael (Genesis 25:13-18)
(It is possible that some of the descendants of Cush, the son of Ham (Genesis 10:7) are also called Arabs.)

There seems to have been some intermingling between the tribe of Simeon and the Ishmaelites, for the clans of Mibsam and Mishma are associated with both. (Genesis 25:13 and I Chronicles 4:25).

Ishmaelites do not appear among the victims of David's raids into the lands south and east of Israel, even though these enter Arab lands. (I Samuel 27:8 and Genesis 25:18) David's sister married Jether the Ishmaelite (I Chronicles 2:17) and two of David's administrators were Obil the Ishmaelite, and Jaziz the Hagarite, (I Chronicles 27:30).

Hagar and Ishmael were given Arabia (Genesis 21:8-21) and Isaac's descendants were promised the Holy Land. Apparently they were not hostile to each other, for Ishmael and Isaac worked together to bury their father Abraham in the Cave of Macphilah, in Mamre (Genesis 25:9).

On the other hand, the Bible refers to various individuals and groups as being 'Arabs.' Jeremiah prophesied against the 'kings of the Arabs' sometime between 627 and 586 BC.

Muslim Traditions
Continued in next section

The Arab genealogist Hisham Ibn Muhammad al-Kalbi (A.D. 737-819), known as Ibn al Kalbi, established a genealogical link between Ishmael and Mohammed. He quotes writers who had access to biblical and Palmyran sources, but the majority of his information came from the ancient oral traditions of the Arabs. His book, 'Djamharat al Nasab' has been translated into German by W. Caskel, (Ghamharat an-Nasab (The Abundance of Kinship) Das genealogische Werk des Hisam Ibn Muhammad al Kalbi, Leiden: E. J. Brill, 1966) It seemed to be Ibn al Kalbi's opinion that the people known as 'Arabs' were all descendants of Ishmael.

[1] Dumah al Jandal a place in Saudi Arabia, called Jauf today.
[2] An Oasis in Northern Arabia
[3] They became twelve nations. The end time's war is between the twelve sons of Yshmael and Isaac. The sons of darkness verse the sons of light. The whole thing is about the inheritance and the battle still rages on to this day who owns the land of Israel.
[4] Yshmael was a saved righteous man in YHWH.
[5] Chavilah is East Africa where Arabia is located.

Beresheeth (Genesis)

Haftarah: Malaki 1:1-2:7

19 This is the genealogy of Ytshak, Abraham's son: Abraham begot Ytshak:

20 Ytshak was forty years old when he took Rivka as wife, the daughter of Bethu'el the Syrian of Padan Aram, the sister of Laban the Syrian.

21 Now Ytshak pleaded with YHWH for his wife, because she was barren: and YHWH granted his plea, and Rivka his wife conceived.

22 And the children struggled together within her; and she said, If all is well, why am I this way? So she went to inquire of YHWH.

23 And YHWH said to her, Two nations are in your womb, two peoples shall be separated from your body; one people shall be stronger than the other; and the older shall serve the younger.[1]

24 So when her days were fulfilled for her to give birth, indeed there were twins[2] in her womb.

25 And the first came out reddish-brown,[3] he was like a hairy[4] garment all over, so they called his name Esaw.[5]

26 Afterward his brother came out, and his hand took hold of Esaw's heel *to protect his head*; so his name was called Yakov: and Ytshak was sixty years old when she bore them.

27 So the boys grew: and Esaw was a skillful hunter, a man of the field; but Yakov[6] was a complete man, dwelling in tents.

28 And Ytshak loved Esaw, because he ate of his game: but Rivka loved Yakov.

29 Now Yakov cooked a stew: and Esaw came in from the field, and he was starving:

30 And Esaw said to Yakov, Please feed me with that reddish stew; for I am starving: therefore his name was called Edom.

31 And Yakov said, Sell me your birthright[7] as of this day.

Footnotes

[1] The battle was spiritual, and was revealed in the birth of the children when, Esaw tried to kill his brother in the womb by his heel.

[2] When Ribkah had twins the word Te-omim had defective spellings and while Tamar had twins (Gen 38:27) it did not. This shows both Tamar's sons would be righteous, while in Ribkah's case one of her sons Esaw would be wicked. תומם versus תאומים (Genesis Rabbah 85:13)

3 Brown colour.

Footnotes

[4] Esaw being hairy is the Remez hint of him being part of the end-times hairy beast of Islam.

[5] Esaw's secondary biblical meaning is stubble as he shall be stubble one day but the primary is a "bird" (Obad 1:4) as he will try to set in the stars of shamayim. Read Obadiah 1:18. According to John Lamb the ancients applied the names rather than the sounds to proper meanings e.g. he quotes IBID p70, Rebecca called her infant עשׂו Esaw, Because he was (Sear) עשׂר "hairy." Let us now consider the manner in which this was formed. By changing the order of the letters שׂער (sear) became עשׂר (Esar), a word already in use signifying 'ten.' She therefore changed ר resh "a bird," into a Wah "a bird," letters of the same ideal meaning, but of totally different sounds.

[6] Yakov was a black man of African descent.

[7] Selling your birthright means giving your inheritance away which Esaw did.

32 And Esaw said, Look, I am about to die: so what profit shall this birthright be to me?

33 And Yakov said, Swear to me as of this day; So he swore to him: and sold his birthright to Yakov.

34 Then Yakov gave Esaw Lakhem (bread) and stew of lentils; and he ate and drank, arose, and went his way: therefore Esaw despised his birthright.[1]

Chapter 26

1 There was a famine in the land, besides the first famine that was in the days of Abraham. And Ytshak went to Avimelekh King of the Plushtim, in Gerar.

2 Then YHWH appeared to him, and said, Do not go down to Mitzrayim (Egypt); live in the land of which I shall tell you:

3 Dwell in this land, and I will be with you and **Increase** you; for to you and your descendants I give all these lands, and I will perform the oath which I swore to Abraham your Abbah;

4 And I will make your descendants multiply as the stars of the shamayim, and I will give to your descendants all these lands; and in your descendants all the nations of the earth[2] shall be **Blessed**;

5 because Abraham obeyed My voice and guarded My ordinance, My commandments, My statutes, and My Torot.[3]

6 So Ytshak dwelt in Gerar:

7 And the men of the place asked him about his wife. And he said, She is my sister: for he was afraid to say, She is my wife, because he thought, lest the men of the place should kill me for Rivka: because she is beautiful to behold.

8 Now it came to pass; when he had been there a long time that Avimelekh King of the Plushtim looked through a window, and saw, and there was Ytshak showing endearment to Rivka his wife.

9 Then Avimelekh called Ytshak and said, Quite obviously she is your wife. So how could you say, She is my sister? And Ytshak said to him, Because I said, lest I die on account of her.

10 And Avimelekh said, What is this you have done to us? One of the people might soon have lain with your wife, and you would have brought guilt on us.

11 So Avimelekh charged all his people, saying, He who touches this man or his wife shall surely be put to death.[4]

12 Then Ytshak sowed in that land, and reaped in the same

Footnotes
[1] The birthright is so important in Eastern culture that people do not give up on it, and may even kill for it. Yet here we are shown a picture of Esaw, being so concerned about his stomach that he does not care for his birthright.
[2] Same promise passed down to Isaac from Abraham.
[3] Abraham was a very good Torah keeper and YHWH gave a true report on behalf of Abraham keeping His Torah teachings.
[4] This shows Abimelekh believed in some of the laws of the Torah. A clear hint of the religion of Islam, which will come and settle in the regions of Israel and will take on some Torah aspects. Although we know that the Philistines were idolatrous people. Here is the demarcation of the end-times battle, if one can see it.

year a hundredfold; and YHWH **Blessed** him.

13 The man began to prosper, and continued prospering until he became very prosperous:

14 For he had possessions of flocks and possessions of herds and a great number of servants: so the Plushtim envied him.

15 Now the Plushtim had stopped up all the wells which his Abbah's servants had dug in the days of Abraham his Abbah, and they had filled them with earth.

16 And Avimelekh said to Ytshak, Go away from us, for you are much mightier than we.

17 Then Ytshak departed from there and pitched his tent in the Valley of Gerar, and dwelt there.

18 And Ytshak dug again the wells of mayim which they had dug in the days of Abraham his Abbah, for the Plushtim had stopped them up after the death of Abraham: he called them by the names which his Abbah had called them.

19 Also Ytshak's (Isaac) servants dug in the valley, and found a well of running mayim there.

20 But the herdsmen of Gerar did strive with Ytshak's herdsmen, saying, The mayim is ours:[1] so he called the name of the well Esek,[2] because they strove with him.

21 Then they dug another well, and they quarrelled over that one also: so he called its name Sitnah.[3]

22 And he moved from there, and dug another well; and they did not quarrel over it: so he called its name Rehoboth;[4] because he said, For now YHWH has made room for us, and we shall be fruitful in the land.

23 Then he went up from there to Beersheva.

24 And YHWH appeared to him the same night, and said, I am the Elohim of your Abbah Abraham: do not fear, for I am with you. I will **Bless** you and multiply your descendants for My servant Abraham's sake.

25 So he built an altar there and called on the name of YHWH, and he pitched his tent there; and there Ytshak's (Isaac) servants dug a well.

26 Then Avimelekh came to him from Gerar with Ahuzzath one of his friends, and Phichol the commander of his army.

27 And Ytshak said to them, Why have you come to me, since you hate me and have sent me away from you?

28 And they said, We have certainly seen that YHWH is with you. So we said, Let there now be an oath between us, between

Footnotes
[3] Hatred
[4] To enlarge, this is an incredible end-times prophecy for the children of Isaac. The Muslims will have contention with Israel; they will show hatred and battle with them. Then YHWH will give Israel victory and will enlarge their land, to the point that the Muslims will no longer be seen quarrelling with them, as that will be the end of all ends, after the battles.

Footnotes
[1] Is that not what the Muslims are doing, claiming everything of Israel as their own?
[2] Means Contention.

us and you, and let us make a Covenant with you;

29 That you will do us no harm, since we have not touched you, and since we have done nothing to you but good and have sent you away in peace (shalom): YHWH has now **Blessed** you.

30 So he made them a banquet, and they ate and drank.

31 Then they arose early in the morning and swore an oath with one another; and Ytshak sent them away, and they departed from him in peace (shalom).

32 It came to pass the same day that Ytshak's (Isaac) servants came and told him about the well which they had dug, and said to him, We have found mayim.

33 So he called it Shevah: therefore the name of the city is Beersheva to this day.

34 When Esaw was forty years old, he took as wives: Yehudeeth the daughter of Beeri the Khitee, and Basemath the daughter of Elon the Khitee:

35 And they were a grief of mind to Ytshak and Rivka.[1]

Chapter 27

1 Now it came to pass, when Ytshak was old and his eyes were so dim that he could not see, that he called Esaw his eldest son, and said to him, My son: and he answered him, Here I am.

2 And he said, Behold now, I am old. I do not know the day of my death:

3 Now therefore, please take your weapons, your quiver and your bow, and go out to the field and hunt game for me.

4 And make me savoury food, such as I love, and bring it to me that I may eat, that my soul may give you an **Increase** before I die.

5 Now Rivka was listening when Ytshak spoke to Esaw his son. And Esaw went to the field to hunt game and to bring it.

6 So Rivka spoke to Yakov her son, saying, Indeed, I heard your father speak to Esaw your brother, saying,

7 Bring me game and make savoury meat for me, that I may eat it and **Bless**[2] you in the presence of YHWH before my death.

8 Now therefore, my son, obey my voice according to what I command you.

9 Go now to the flock and bring me from there two choice kids of the goats; and I will make savoury meat from them for your father, such as he loves:

10 Then you shall take it to your father, that he may eat it, and that he may **Bless** you before his death.

11 And Yakov said to Rivka his mother, Look, Esaw my brother is a hairy man, and I am a smooth skinned man:

Footnotes

[1] YHWH did not allow intermarrying of Israel with the Hittites see Deut 7:1. You can marry an Y'shmaelite woman if she accepts the Elohim of Israel even if she is a Muslim and is willing to relinquish Islam.

Footnotes

[2] To say the words in front of YHWH as a witness to **Bless** him but the **Blessing** was for Yakov.

12 Perhaps my father will feel me, and I shall seem in his sight to be a cheat;[1] and I shall bring a curse/decrease on myself and not an **Increase**.

13 But his mother said to him, Let your curse be on me, my son; only obey my voice,[2] and go get them for me.

14 And he went and got them and brought them to his mother, and his mother made savoury meat, such as his father loved.

15 Then Rivka took the choice clothes of her elder son Esaw, which were with her in the Beyth (house), and put them on Yakov her younger son.

16 And she put the skins of the kids of the goats on his hands and on the smooth part of his neck:

17 Then she gave the savoury food and the Lakhem (bread), which she had prepared, into the hand of her son Yakov.

18 So he went to his father and said, My father; and he said, Here I am; who are you, my son?

19 And Yakov said to his father, I am Esaw your Bekhor (firstborn); I have done just as you told me; please arise, sit and eat of my game, that your soul may **Bless** me.

20 And Ytshak said to his son, How is it that you have found it so quickly, my son? And he said,

Because YHWH Your POWER brought it to me.

21 Then Ytshak said to Yakov, Please come near, that I may feel you, my son, whether you are really my son Esaw or not.[3]

22 So Yakov went near to Ytshak his father, and he felt him and said, The voice is Yakov's voice, but the hands are the hands of Esaw.

23 And he did not recognize him, because his hands were hairy, like his brother Esaw's hands: so he *spoke* Increases for him.

24 Then he said, Are you really my son Esaw? And he said, I am.

25 And he said, Bring it near to me, and I will eat of my son's game, so that my soul may **Bless** you. So he brought it near to him, and he ate; and he brought him wine, and he drank.

26 Then his father Ytshak said to him, Come near now and kiss me, my son.

27 And he came near and kissed him: and he smelled the smell of his clothing, and congratulated him and said: Surely, the smell of my son is like the smell of a field YHWH has **Blessed**:

28 Therefore may Elohim give you of the dew of shamayim, of the fatness of the earth, and plenty of grain and wine:[4]

29 Let peoples serve you, and nations bow down to you: be master over your brethren, and

Footnotes
[1] Jacob was not a deceiver; Christians have been erring over this. The inheritance was his right, and it was lawful for him to acquire it, and to obey his mother's voice.
[2] Rebecca knew this because; YHWH had already shown her this. The Covenant belonged to Jacob, and not Esaw.

Footnotes
[3] Isaac was partially blind at his old age.
[4] Israel and YHWH's people will never be without food if they serve YHWH trustworthily and obey His Torah.

let your mother's sons bow down to you: cursed be everyone who curses you,[1] and **Blessed** will be those who will **Bless** you.

30 Then it happened, as soon as Ytshak had finished saying the **blessing** for Yakov, and Yakov had scarcely gone out from the presence of Ytshak his father, that Esaw his brother came in from his hunting.

31 He also had made savoury meat, and brought it to his father, and said to his father, Let my father arise and eat of his son's game, that your soul may **bless** me.

32 And his father Ytshak said to him, Who are you? And he said, I am your son, your Bekhor (firstborn) Esaw.

33 Then Ytshak trembled exceedingly, and said, Who? Where is the one who hunted game, and brought it to me and I ate all of it before you came, and I have **Blessed** him? And, indeed, he shall be **Blessed**.

34 When Esaw heard the words of his father, he cried with an exceedingly great and bitter cry, and said to his father, **Increase** me, even me also, O my father!

35 But he said, Your brother came with craft[2] and has taken away your **Blessing**.

36 And Esaw said, Is he not rightly named Yakov? For he has supplanted me these two times: he took away my birthright; and,

now look, he has taken away my **Blessing**.[3] And he said, Have you not reserved a **Blessing** for me?

37 Then Ytshak answered and said to Esaw, Indeed I have made him your master, and all his brethren I have given to him as servants; with grain and wine I have sustained him. What shall I do now for you, my son?

38 And Esaw said to his father, Have you only one **Blessing**, my father? **Bless** me, even me also, O my father! And Esaw lifted up his voice and wept.

39 Then Ytshak his father answered and said to him: Behold, your dwelling shall be away from[4] the fatness of the earth, and of the dew of shamayim from above;

40 By your sword you shall live, and you shall serve your brother; and it shall come to pass when you will have the rule,[5] that you shall break his yoke from your neck.

Footnotes
[3] Esaw was lying to get his way, since he had already sold his birthright, which his Abbah did not know about. And in the womb, he tried to kill his brother, so now he blames him for saving his life.
[4] Dead Sea scrolls. There was no **Blessing** for Esaw, as he deserved none by his actions, which YHWH knew ahead of time. He was going to mingle with the Arabs and try to kill his Israelite brothers. Which we now find in Islam, as the end times beast tries to destroy Israel and kill the Christians.
[5] This was the time when the Edomi were converted to Judaism, they took key places then they slew many Hebrews and overtook the Temple rule. They mixed with the Romans and started to rule over the Hebrews instead. This was a future prophecy fulfilled in the 2nd Temple during Herod's time. Herod was an Edomote hybrid Jew.

Footnotes
[1] All those who curse Israel will be under a curse, and those that **Bless** her, will be Blessed.
[2] Isaac did not know that Esaw had sold his birthright.

41 So Esaw hated Yakov because of the **Blessing** with which his father had **Blessed** him, and Esaw said in his heart, The days of mourning for my father are at hand; then I will kill my brother Yakov.[1]

42 And the words of Esaw her older son were told to Rivka. So she sent and called Yakov her younger son, and said to him, Surely your brother Esaw comforts himself concerning you by intending to kill you.

43 Now therefore, my son, obey my voice: arise, flee to my brother Laban in Haran:

44 And stay with him a few days, until your brother's fury turns away;

45 Until your brother's anger turns away from you, and he forgets what you have done to him; then I will send and bring you from there: why should I be bereaved also of you both in one day?

46 And Rivka said to Ytshak, I am disgusted in my life because of the daughters of Kheth:[3] if Yakov takes a wife of the daughters of Kheth, like these who are the daughters of the land, what good will my life be to me?

Chapter 28

1 Then Ytshak called Yakov and *spoke* Increases for him, and ordered him, and said to him: You shall not take a wife from the daughters of Kanan.[4]

2 Arise, go to Padan Aram,[5] to the Beyth (house) of Bethu'el your mother's father; and take yourself a wife from there of the daughters of Laban your mother's brother.

3 May El-Shaddai (The Mighty Power) **Bless** you, and make you fruitful and multiply you, that you may be an assembly of peoples;[6]

4 And give you the **Blessings** of Abraham, to you and your

Footnotes

[1] Esaw was the deceiver and had planned to kill Jacob, though it did not work in the womb. Obviously Satan was behind this.

[2] The Kuf letter in Hebrew is small here, signifying the picture of a person turning away, Rebecca was disappointed with Esaw and his wife so had turned away because of discouragement of a disobedient son.

[3] The Kuf letter in Hebrew is small here, signifying the picture of an oar of a boat that has veered away from its destination, Rebecca was disappointed with Esaw and his wife because he had turned away and she was discouraged because of this disobedient son.

Footnotes

[4] Isaac did not like what Esaw had done, so he commanded Jacob not to take wives from the local women; but to go back to the country of their ancestors. There is wisdom in this, because the local women were idolatrous so could not be trustworthy wives. We find this is why the custom of arranged marriages works in the East. Although, because of the idolatries of the European nations, marriages are not kept to the same standard as Torah patriarchal marriages. The Western marriages last an average of six months to two years, if you are fortunate while this is monogamy which is not what our forefathers practiced. We are given patriarchal plural marriages as our model.

[5] Northern Syria.

[6] Israel was to become an assembly of people, here the word Qahal is used in the Hebrew tongue where we get our modern word church from, this is a derived word but not in the scrolls. It actually goes back to the word circus and that is what most churches are these days, circuses and showmanship of men. The only Church YHWH recognised is Israel, any other entity is not His, and cannot replace Israel.

descendants with you, that you may inherit the land in which you are a stranger, which Elohim gave to Abraham.[1]

5 So Ytshak sent Yakov away: and he went to Padan Aram,[2] to Laban the son of Bethu'el the Syrian, the brother of Rivka, the mother of Yakov and Esaw.

6 When Esaw saw that Ytshak had **Blessed** Yakov and sent him away to Padan Aram to take himself a wife from there; and that as he Blessed him he commanded him, saying, You shall not take a wife from the daughters of Kanan;

7 And that Yakov had obeyed his father[3] and his mother and had gone to Padan Aram.

8 Also Esaw saw that the daughters of Kanan did not please in the sight of[4] his father Ytshak.

9 So Esaw went to Yshmael and took Mahalath the daughter of Yshmael, Abraham's son, the sister of Nebajoth, to be his wife in addition to the wives he had; [5]

Footnotes

[1] The **Blessing** of the land will follow the line of Jacob's children and not Yshmael.

[2] Syria

[3] Jacob was trustworthy and the obedient son while Esaw was disobedient. Isaac had realised by now that the Increasing that he gave him was correct so he said it again.

[4] Idolatry does not please YHWH's people.

[5] The Arabs and Egyptians became mixed and are to this day. Polygamy is and was part of real Hebrew culture. Our lifestyle is Patriarchal marriage. We are allowed to takes wives from Arabs as long as they accept the Elohim of Israel. This is why Esaw married into Yshmael as he was trying to please his parents.

Torah Parsha 7 Vayetz, Beresheeth 28:10-32:3

Haftarah: Hoshea 12:13-14:9

10 Now Yakov went out from Beersheva and went toward Haran.

11 So he came to a certain place,[6] and stayed there all night, because the sun had set. And he took one of the stones[7] of that place and put it at his head, and he lay down in that place to sleep.

12 Then he dreamed, and behold a ladder was set up on the earth, and its top reached to the shamayim: and there the malakhim of Elohim were ascending and descending on it.[8]

Footnotes

[6] Ancient Rebbim recognise the Hebrew word for place is Ha-Makom meaning, this is one of the names of Elohim.

[7] The stone in Hebrew is, Stones plural and the word is Eben. The first character is Alef, which is the left side of the tree, for the Father and Strength, from our angle the right side of YHWH is mercy. The word Alef is for the Father who is the source of all things. The other word separated in Eben, is Ben and so represents, the middle pillar.

[8] The malakhim are descriptions of saved people who ascend, and then descend. These are redeemed, so the remez (hint), shows people, not literal malakhim. In ancient thought; the ladder is three vertical pillars, we have the right side, the left side, and the middle pillar. The ladder is also known as a tree. The left side is the Father's, strength, the right is, mercy, while middle pillar is Adam Kadmon, who mediates between the two. In ancient thought the Hebrew word Sulam, for ladder, and the word Sinai, both have a value of 130. So the Temple mount region below is connected to Mount Sinai above harmonized by the middle pillar.

The word Sinai:

Samech = 60

Yud = 10

Nun = 50

Continued in next section

13 And behold YHWH stood above it and said: I am YHWH Elohim of Abraham your father and the Elohim of Ytshak: the land on which you lie I will give to you and your descendants;

14 Also your descendants shall be as the dust of the earth; you shall spread abroad to the west and the east, to the north and the south: and in you and in your seed all the Mishpakhot (families) of the earth shall be **Blessed**.[1]

15 Behold, I am with you and will Guard you wherever you go, and will bring you back to this land; for I will not leave you until I have done what I have spoken to you.

16 Then Yakov awoke from his sleep and said, Surely YHWH is in this place, and I did not know it.

17 And he was afraid and said, How awesome is this place! This is none other than the Beyth (house) of Elohim, and this is the Gate of shamayim.[2]

18 Then Yakov rose early in the morning, and took the stone that he had put at his head, set it up as a pillar, and poured oil on top of it.[3]

19 And he called the name of that place Beyth'el: but the name of that city had been Luz[4] previously.

20 Then Yakov made a vow, saying, If Elohim will be with me, and Guard me in this way that I am going, and give me Lakhem (bread) to eat and clothing to put on,

21 So that I come back to my father's Beyth (house) in peace (shalom); then YHWH shall be my POWER:

22 And this stone, which I have set as an altar shall be Elohim's Beyth (house), and of all that You give me I will surely give a tenth[5] to You.

Chapter 29

1 So Yakov went on his journey, and came to the land of the people of the East.

2 And he looked, and saw a well in the field; and, behold, there were three flocks of sheep

Yud = 10

Total: 130

The word Sulam – Ladder

Samech = 60
Lamed = 30
Mem = 40

Total: 130. The other interpretation is that Moses and Aaron are the malakhim ascending and descending the ladder. Another variation is that if you spell Sulam with the Wah, then you get the value 136, which is the same as the word for mammon. This means spending your life gathering mammon and the way of YHWH are not compatible.

[1] Abraham's promise repeated to Jacob, who carried the line of **Increase**.

Footnotes
[2] This door of the shamayim.
[3] He anointed the place where the Temple was to be built.
[4] Old name for Jerusalem.
[5] Jacob vows to give his 10% tithe to YHWH realizing where his Increases were coming from. The tithe was setup long before the Torah was given at Mount Sinai and is mandatory today for all believers to be given to Torah teachers. They are not to be wasted by giving them to Pastors who teach Torah disobedience in churches.

lying by it; for out of that well they watered the flocks: and a large stone was on the well's mouth.

3 Now all the flocks would be gathered there: and they would roll the stone from the well's mouth, water the sheep, and put the stone back in its place on the well's mouth.

4 And Yakov said to them, My brethren, where are you from? And they said, We are from Haran.

5 Then he said to them, Do you know Laban the son of Nakhkhur? And they said, We know him.

6 So he said to them, Is he well? And they said, He is well, and look, his daughter Rakhel is coming with the sheep.

7 Then he said, Look, it is still high day; it is not time for the cattle to be gathered together: water the sheep, and go and feed them.

8 And they said, We cannot until all the flocks are gathered together, and they have rolled the stone from the well's mouth; then we water the sheep.

9 Now while he was still speaking with them, Rakhel came with her father's sheep: for she was a shepherdess.

10 And it came to pass, when Yakov saw Rakhel the daughter of Laban his mother's brother, and the sheep of Laban his mother's brother, then Yakov went near, and rolled the stone from the well's mouth, and

watered the flock of Laban his mother's brother.[1]

11 Then Yakov kissed Rakhel, and lifted up his voice, and wept.

12 And Yakov told Rakhel that he was her father's brother, and that he was Rivka's son: so she ran and told her father.

13 Then it came to pass, when Laban heard the report about Yakov his sister's son, that he ran to meet him, and embraced him and kissed him, and brought him to his Beyth (house). So he told Laban all these things.

14 And Laban said to him, Surely you are my substance and my flesh. And he stayed with him for a month.

15 Then Laban said to Yakov, Because you are my relative, should you therefore serve me for nothing? Tell me, what should your wages be?

16 Now Laban had two daughters: the name of the elder was Le'yah, and the name of the younger was Rakhel.

17 Le'yah's eyes were delicate; but Rakhel was beautiful of form and appearance.

18 Now Yakov loved Rakhel; so he said, I will serve you seven years for Rakhel your younger daughter.

19 And Laban said, It is better that I give her to you than that I should give her to another man.[2] Stay with me.

Footnotes

[1] Yakov was very strong he removed the stone from the well when Rachel came, this stone would normally take several shepherds to remove it otherwise. Yakov was a very strong man.

[2] This practice is still prevalent in the Islamic culture taken from the Hebrew culture. Very
Continued in next section

20 So Yakov served seven years for Rakhel, and in his sight they seemed but a few days because of the love he had for her.

21 Then Yakov said to Laban, Give me my wife, for my days are fulfilled, that I may go in to her.

22 And Laban gathered together all the men of the place, and held a banquet.

23 Now it came to pass in the evening, that he took Le'yah his daughter and brought her to Yakov; and he went in to her.[1]

24 And Laban gave his maid Zilpah, to his daughter Le'yah as a maid.

25 So it came to pass, in the morning, that behold, it was Le'yah: and he said to Laban, What is this you have done to me? Was it not for Rakhel that I served you? Why then have you deceived me?

26 And Laban said, It must not be done so in our country, to give the younger before the Bekhor[2] (firstborn).

27 Fulfill her week,[3] and we will give you this one also for the service which you will serve with me still another seven years.

28 Then Yakov did so, and fulfilled her week: so he gave him his daughter Rakhel as wife also.[4]

29 And Laban gave his maid Bilhah to his daughter Rakhel as a maid.

30 Then Yakov also went in to Rakhel, and he also loved Rakhel more than Le'yah. And he served with Laban still another seven years.

31 When YHWH saw that Le'yah was loved-less,[5] He opened her womb: but Rakhel was barren.

32 So Le'yah conceived and bore a son, and she called his name Reuven; for she said, YHWH has surely looked on my affliction; now therefore my husband will love me.

33 Then she conceived again, and bore a son; and said, Because YHWH has heard that I am loved-less,[6] He has therefore

Footnotes

[3] Seven years.

[4] Polygamy was allowed and is still a valid form of marriage; this is being restored in the last days, known as Patriarchal marriage. Our forefathers practiced it, some believers may opt to choose this lifestyle, and it is not sin as long as you sustain your wives as Torah commands with separate homes!

[5] The Hebrew word Saneh has a very wide meaning which is better translated here as loved-less and not hated because this translation being used in the King James Version is incorrect under the context. Jacob had children with all his wives and he had his favorite wife Rachel but that does not mean he hated the others only that in the scheme of things he loved them less.

[6] See footnote Gen 29:31.

rarely Muslims marry their daughters outside the family.

[1] The ancient custom was to veil the bride, and for the bridegroom not to see her. The bride goes into the bed chamber first, waiting; and then the bridegroom. The whole night is spent in darkness, this was the custom. And this is the reason why Jacob did not know that it was Leah and not Rachel until the morning.

[2] Laban is telling a half truth, it is true that the custom was, and still is, to marry the elder first; but since he had promised the younger it would be wrong for him to give the elder which he did, so he was deceiving Jacob by the local custom.

given me this son also: and she called his name Shim'on.

34 She conceived again, and bore a son; and said, Now this time my husband will become attached to me, because I have borne him three sons: therefore his name was called Levi.

35 And she conceived again and bore a son: and said, Now I will speak forth the name of YHWH: therefore she called his name Yahudah; then she stopped bearing.

Chapter 30

1 Now when Rakhel saw that she bore Yakov no children, Rakhel envied her sister, and said to Yakov, Give me children, or else I die.

2 And Yakov's anger was aroused against Rakhel: and he said, Am I in the place of Elohim; who has withheld from you the fruit of the womb?

3 So she said, Here is my maid Bilhah,[1] go in to her; and she will bear a child on my knees, that I also may have children by her.

4 Then she gave him Bilhah her maid as wife: and Yakov went in to her.

5 And Bilhah conceived, and bore Yakov a son.

6 Then Rakhel said, Elohim has judged my case, and He has also heard my voice, and given me a son: therefore she called his name Dan.

7 And Rakhel's maid Bilhah conceived again and bore Yakov a second son.

8 Then Rakhel said, With great struggle I have struggled with my sister, and indeed I have prevailed: so she called his name Naphtali.

9 When Le'yah saw that she had stopped bearing, she took Zilpah her maid and gave her to Yakov as wife.[2]

10 And Le'yah's maid Zilpah bore Yakov a son.

11 Then Le'yah said, A gawd comes: so she called his name Gawd.[3]

12 And Le'yah's maid Zilpah bore Yakov a second son.

13 Then Le'yah said, I am happy, for the daughters will call me **Blessed**. So she called his name Asher (happy).

14 Now Reuven went in the days of wheat harvest and found mandrakes in the field, and brought them to his mother Le'yah. Then Rakhel said to Le'yah, Please give me some of your son's mandrakes.

15 But she said to her, Is it a small matter that you have taken away my husband? Would you take away my son's mandrakes also? And Rakhel said, Therefore he will lie with you tonight for your son's mandrakes.

16 When Yakov came out of the field in the evening, Le'yah went

Footnotes

[1] Bilhah became Jacob's third wife; it is legal to have a child by a handmaid, who became a lesser wife according to Torah.

Footnotes

[2] Fourth wife of Jacob.

[3] Many translators make this gad that is one possibility but it can also be pronounced literally God or gawd as pronounced in the Hebrew; and was taken from a pagan deity that was worshipped locally in Mesopotamia.

out to meet him and said, You must come in to me; for I have surely hired you with my son's mandrakes. And he lay with her that night.

17 And Elohim listened to Le'yah, and she conceived and bore Yakov a fifth son.

18 Le'yah said, Elohim has given me my hire, because I have given my maid to my husband: so she called his name Yskhar (Issachar).

19 Then Le'yah conceived again and bore Yakov a sixth son.

20 And Le'yah said, Elohim has endowed me with a good endowment; now my husband will dwell with me, because I have borne him six sons. So she called his name Zevulun.

21 Afterward she bore a daughter, and called her name Dinah.

22 Then Elohim remembered Rakhel, and Elohim listened to her and opened her womb.

23 And she conceived and bore a son, and said, Elohim has taken away my reproach:

24 So she called his name Yosef, and said, YHWH has increased me with another son.

25 And it came to pass, when Rakhel had borne Yosef, that Yakov said to Laban, Send me away, that I may go to my own place, and to my country.

26 Give me my wives and my children, for whom I have served you, and let me go: for you know my service which I have done for you.

27 And Laban said to him, Please, stay: if I have found favour in your eyes, for I have learned by experience that YHWH has Blessed me for your sake.

28 Then he said, Name me your wages, and I will give it.

29 So Yakov said to him, You know how I have served you, and how your livestock has been with me.

30 For what you had before I came was little, and it is now **Increased** to a great amount; YHWH has **Increased** you since my coming: and now when shall I also provide for my own Beyth (house)?

31 So he said, What shall I give you? And Yakov said, You shall not give me anything. If you will do this thing for me, I will again feed and keep your flocks:

32 Let me pass through all your flock today, removing from there all the speckled and spotted sheep, and all the brown ones among the lambs, and the spotted and speckled among the goats: and these shall be my wages.

33 So my Righteousness will answer for me in time to come, when the subject of my wages comes before you: everyone that is not speckled and spotted among the goats, and brown among the lambs, will be considered stolen if it is with me.

34 And Laban said, behold, let it be according to your word.

35 So he removed that day the male goats that were speckled and spotted, all the female goats that were speckled and spotted, everyone that had some white in it, and all the brown ones among the lambs, and gave them into the hand of his sons.

36 Then he put three days' journey between himself and Yakov: and Yakov fed the rest of Laban's flocks.

37 Now Yakov took for himself rods of green poplar, and of the almond and chestnut etzim (trees); peeled white strips in them, and exposed the white which was in the rods.

38 And the rods which he had peeled he set before the flocks in the gutters, in the watering troughs where the flocks came to drink, so that they should conceive when they came to drink.

39 So the flocks conceived before the rods, and the flocks brought forth streaked, speckled, and spotted.[1]

40 Then Yakov separated the lambs, and made the flocks face toward the streaked, and all the brown in the flock of Laban; but he put his own flocks by themselves and did not put them with Laban's flock.

41 And it came to pass, whenever the stronger livestock conceived, that Yakov placed the rods before the eyes of the livestock in the gutters, that they might conceive among the rods.

42 But when the flocks were feeble, he did not put them in; so the feebler were Laban's, and the stronger Yakov's.

Footnotes
[1] Even though Jacob did some clever engineering, but the end result was by YHWH; and Jacob recognized this and attributed it to Elohim and not to his method.

43 Thus the man became exceedingly prosperous, and had large flocks, female and male servants, and camels, and donkeys.

Chapter 31

1 Now Yakov heard the words of Laban's sons, saying, Yakov has taken away all that was our father's; and from what was our father's he has acquired all this wealth.

2 And Yakov saw the countenance of Laban, and indeed, it was not favourable toward him as before.

3 Then YHWH said to Yakov, Return to the land of your ahvot (fathers) and to your Mishpakha (family); and I will be with you.

4 So Yakov sent and called Rakhel and Le'yah to the field to his flock,

5 and said to them, I see your father's countenance which is not favourable toward me as before; but the Elohim of my father has been with me.

6 And you know that with all my might I have served your father.

7 Yet your father has deceived me and changed my wages ten times; but Elohim did not allow him to hurt me.

8 If he said thus: The speckled shall be your wages, then all the flocks bore speckled. And if he said thus: The streaked shall be your wages; then all the flocks bore streaked.

9 So Elohim has taken away the livestock of your father and given them to me.

10 And it happened at the time when the flocks conceived, that I lifted my eyes, and saw in a dream, and, behold, the rams which leaped upon the flocks were streaked, speckled, and gray-spotted.

11 Then the Malakh Elohim (Malakh of YHWH) spoke to me in a dream, saying, Yakov: and I said, Here I am.

12 And He said, Lift your eyes now and see, all the rams which leap on the flocks are streaked, speckled, and gray-spotted: for I have seen all that Laban is doing to you.

13 I am the El (Power) of Beyth'el, where you anointed the altar and where you made a vow to Me: now arise, get out of this land, and return to the land of your Mishpakha (family).

14 Then Rakhel and Le'yah answered and said to him, Is there still any portion, or inheritance for us in our father's Beyth (house)?

15 Are we not considered strangers by him? For he has sold us, and also completely consumed our money.

16 For all these riches[1] which YHWH has taken from our father, are really ours, and our children's: now then, whatever Elohim has said to you, do it.

17 Then Yakov rose and set his sons and his wives on camels.

18 And he carried away all his livestock and all his possessions which he had gained, his

acquired livestock, which he had gained in Padan Aram, to go to his father Ytshak in the land of Kanan.

19 Now Laban had gone to shear his sheep, and Rakhel had stolen the teraphim [2] that were her father's.

20 And Yakov stole away unknown to Laban the Aramee,[3] in that he did not tell him that he intended to flee.

21 So he fled with all that he had; and he arose, and crossed the river, and headed toward the mountains of Gil'ad.

22 And Laban was told on the third day that Yakov had fled.

23 Then he took his brethren with him, and pursued him for seven days' journey; and he overtook him in the mountains of Gil'ad.

24 But Elohim had come to Laban the Aramee in a dream by night, and said to him, Be careful that you speak to Yakov neither good nor evil.

Footnotes
[1] We see an example of unity in a Patriarchal household.

[2] Teraphim were figurines of the ancestors which were passed from father to son. These would have been passed to Laban who was the ruler of this territory and he would then pass them on to his firstborn son who he considered the ruler. When Rachel took these figures he was angry and wanted to get them back while Rachel may have thought to place her son Benyamin as ruler in the south. These were little figures that the people used of their ancestors to call upon who they saw as great priests to intercede for them after their death hence why they were held in high glory. This only happens in African culture as the Israelites were an African people the sons of Shem. The Khuri records indicates the story of the figurines.
[3] North Syria, region of ancient Turkey

25 So Laban overtook Yakov. Now Yakov had pitched his tent in the mountains: and Laban with his brethren pitched in the mountains of Gil'ad.

26 And Laban said to Yakov, What have you done, that you have stolen away unknown to me, and carried away my daughters like captives taken with the sword?

27 Why did you flee away secretly, and steal away from me, and not tell me; for I might have sent you away with joy and songs, with timbrel and harp?

28 And you did not allow me to kiss my sons and my daughters? Now you have done foolishly in so doing.

29 It is in my power to do you harm, but the Elohim of your father spoke to me last night, saying, guard your word with which you speak to Yakov neither good, nor evil.

30 And now you have surely gone because you greatly long for your father's house, but why did you steal my powers?

31 Then Yakov answered and said to Laban, Because I was afraid, for I said, Perhaps you would take your daughters from me by force.

32 With whomever you find your powers, do not let him live: In the presence of our brethren identify what I have of yours, and take it with you. For Yakov did not know that Rakhel[1] had stolen them.

33 And Laban went into Yakov's tent, into Le'yah's tent, and into the two maids' tents, but he did not find them.[2] Then he went out of Le'yah's tent and entered Rakhel's tent.

34 Now Rakhel had taken the terephim, put them in the camel's saddle, and sat on them. And Laban searched all about the tent but did not find them.

35 And she said to her father, Let it not displease in your eyes my master that I cannot rise before you, for the manner of women [3] is with me. And he

Footnotes

[1] She took them in the expectation of making her youngest son the ruler of her territory which Laban was not happy in doing Continued in next section

because he wanted his firstborn to be the ruler.

[2] Note this is a clear reference to Jacob housing his wives in separate tents. This is a mistake many people make in patriarchal marriage today, trying to make their wives cohabit the same house; but the Tanak is quite clear that each wife must have her own house, as seen here. Also by the example of our father Abraham in Genesis chapter 12:8: Israelites following the patriarchal lifestyle, as did our forefathers, must be able to afford his wives in separate homes or make suitable arrangements. Muslims in Saudi Arabia who have adopted this lifestyle have taken it from the Hebrews. The Qur'an (Sura 4:24), the Muslim book, tells them to take up to four wives (they can take more in the shape of concubines). This is taken from the model of Jacob; but each wife taken by the Muslims is always kept in separate homes. Even they have this understanding. The Muslims are propagating their seed faster than the traditional Hebrew people, because of man made doctrines that have enveloped the church and state, which many Hebrews are stuck in. The end time Islamic beast's onslaught is going to be very sharp, and ruthless, if people do not wake up soon.

[3] She lied to her Abbah that she was menstruating so the teraphim would not be taken away, as she thought they were going to be used to track them down through divination by her dad and also for her son.

searched but did not find the terephim.

36 Then Yakov was angry and rebuked Laban: and Yakov answered and said to Laban, What is my trespass? What is my sin, that you have so hotly pursued me?

37 Although you have searched all my things, what part of your household things have you found? Set it here before my brethren and your brethren that they may judge between us both!

38 These twenty years I have been with you; your ewes and your female goats have not miscarried their young, and I have not eaten the rams of your flock.

39 That which was torn by beasts I did not bring to you; I bore the loss of it. You required it from my hand, whether stolen by day or stolen by night.

40 There I was! In the day the drought consumed me, and the frost by night, and my sleep departed from my eyes.

41 Thus I have been in your house twenty years; I served you fourteen years for your two daughters, and six years for your flock, and you have changed my wages ten times. [1]

42 Unless the Elohim of my father, the Elohim of Abraham and the Fear of Ytshak, had been with me, surely now you would have sent me away empty-handed. Elohim has seen my affliction and the labour of my hands, and rebuked you last night.

43 And Laban answered and said to Yakov, These daughters are my daughters, and these children are my children, and this flock is my flock, all that you see is mine:[2] but what can I do this day to these my daughters, or to their children whom they have given birth?

44 Now therefore come, let us make a Covenant, you and I; and let it be a witness between you and me.

45 So Yakov took a stone, and set it up as an altar.

46 Then Yakov said to his brethren, Gather stones; and they took stones and made a heap, and they ate there on the heap.

47 Laban called it yegar Sahadutha:[3] but Yakov called it Galeed.

48 And Laban said, This heap is a witness between you and me this day. Therefore its name was called Galeed,[4]

49 Also Mizpah; because he said, May YHWH watch between you, and me when we are absent one from another.

50 If you afflict my daughters, or if you take other wives besides my daughters, although no man

---

Footnotes

[1] Working with idolaters is not easy, as they are not righteous and may keep changing as they live by the standards of this world. The word Monim here means 10 x 10 means 100.

Footnotes

[2] Laban speaks half truth; the daughters were no longer his after he married them off. The only thing that was his was his relationship to them; the flocks belonged to Jacob and not to Laban.

[3] The word witness in Aramaic.

[4] The word witness in Hebrew.

is with us see, Elohim is witness between you and me.[1]

51 Then Laban said to Yakov, Here is this heap and here is this altar, which I have placed between you; and me.

52 This heap is a witness, and this altar is a witness, that I will not pass beyond this heap to you, and you will not pass beyond this heap and this altar to me, for harm.

53 The Elohim of Abraham, the Elohim of Nakhkhur,[2] and the Elohim of their father judge between us. And Yakov swore by the Fear of his father Ytshak.

54 Then Yakov offered a sacrifice on the mountain, and called his brethren to eat Lakhem (bread): and they ate Lakhem (bread) and stayed all night on the mountain.

55 And early in the morning Laban arose, and kissed his sons and daughters, and spoke for **Increase** to them: then Laban departed, and returned to his place.

Chapter 32

1 So Yakov went on his way, and the malakhim of Elohim met him.

2 When Yakov saw them, he said, This is Elohim's company/might[3]: and he called the name of that place Makhanim.

Torah Parsha 8 Vayishlah, Beresheeth 32:3 – 36:43
Haftarah: Ovadiyah 1:1-21

3 Then Yakov sent messengers before him to Esaw his brother in the land of Seir, the country of Edom.

4 And he commanded them, saying, Speak thus to my master Esaw; Thus your servant Yakov says: I have dwelt with Laban, and stayed there until now:

5 I have oxen, donkeys, flocks, and male and female servants; and I have sent to tell my master, that I may find favour in your sight.

6 Then the messengers returned to Yakov, saying, We came to your brother Esaw, and he also is coming to meet you, and four hundred men are with him.[4]

7 So Yakov was greatly afraid and distressed; and he divided the people that were with him,

Footnotes

[1] Laban was putting Jacob under a false oath, as he could have taken more wives if he wanted; it was perfectly legal in Torah to do that. The world will always impose its own standards upon you to bring you into bondage. Note, in his witness Jacob does not say he will not take more wives; but he honours his words nevertheless to his death.

[2] The God of Nakh'Khur is the term he used for the false gods of Nakh'khur. Nakh'Khur, and his father Tharakh, both paid homage to this deity but not to YHWH, they were out of India and paid homage to many deities. This was also used by their descendants; this is why Laban calls upon this name.

Footnotes

[3] The Hebrew word is a sanskirt word that means company or in Sanskrit it means "might." The Bible is the story of the clans that left India to pursue the one God, Abraham's family came from India and settled in South-Eastern Turkey followed by Iraq then to Israel.

[4] Esaw was fully intent on killing Jacob; but YHWH made Esaw to change his mind along the route.

and the flocks and herds and camels, into two companies.

8 And he said, If Esaw comes to the one company and attacks it, then the other company which is left will escape.

9 Then Yakov said, O Elohim of my father Abraham, and Elohim of my father Ytshak, YHWH who said to me, Return to your country, and to your Mishpakha (family), and I will deal well with you:

10 I am not worthy of the least of all the mercies, and of all the truth, which You have shown Your servant; for I crossed over this Yardan (Jordan) with my staff; and now I have become two camps of people.

11 Rescue me, I pray, from the hand of my brother, from the hand of Esaw: for I fear him, lest he come and attack me, and the mother with the children.

12 For You said, I will surely treat you well, and make your descendants as the sand of the sea, which cannot be numbered for multitude.

13 So he lodged there that same night, and took what came to his hand as a present for Esaw his brother:

14 two hundred female goats and twenty male goats, two hundred ewes, and twenty rams,

15 thirty milk camels with their colts, forty cows, and ten bulls, twenty female donkeys, and ten foals.

16 Then he took them by the hand of his servants, every herd by itself; and said to his servants, Pass over before me, and put some distance between successive herds.

17 And he commanded the first one, saying, When Esaw my brother meets you, and ask you, saying, To whom do you belong? And where are you going? Whose are these in front of you?

18 Then you shall say, They are your servant Yakov's; it is a present sent to my master Esaw: and behold, he also is behind us.

19 So he commanded the second, the third, and all who followed the herds, saying, In this manner you shall speak to Esaw, when you find him;

20 and also say, Behold, your servant Yakov is behind us. For he said, I will appease him with the present that goes before me, and afterward I will see his face; perhaps he will accept me. [1]

21 So the present went on over before him, but he himself lodged that night in the camp.

22 And he arose that night and took his two wives, his two female servants, and his eleven sons, and crossed over the ford of Yabbok.

23 He took them, sent them over the brook, and sent over what he had.

24 Then Yakov was left alone; and a Man wrestled with him until the breaking of day. [2]

25 Now when He saw that He did not prevail against him, He

Footnotes

[1] Esaw is fully aligned with the End-Times Islamic beast thus he had married Yshmael's daughters, and the seed there wants to destroy Israel. But, YHWH will prevail to support Israel in the final victory.

[2] This man in the form of the Angel was indeed Yahushua in an angelic manly form.

touched the socket of his hip; and the socket of Yakov's hip was out of joint, as He wrestled with him.

26 And He said, Let Me go, for the day breaks. But he said, I will not let You go, unless You **Bless** me.

27 So He said to him, What is your name?[1] And he said, Yakov.

28 And he said you shall no longer be called Yakov, your name henceforth will be called Israel[2] as a prince, with power

Footnotes

[1] The preposition is not just 'what is your name', but what is your nature and fame and why do you want a **Blessing**? The Malakh of YHWH was testing him because He was about to change Jacob's destiny forever.

[2] The name is not just a title but a sign of authority and power. YHWH caused Yakov to receive a very powerful increase that if he would follow Torah and obey Elohim he could call help down from shamayim (Dwelling of His Majesty) anytime that he needed just as a prince could command an army YHWH put at his disposal special legions of malakhim to assist him. Yakov's new name Israel was to be a witness, indicating his power over men, in Gematria the Wah has a value of six and indicates his prevailing over men. This is true for all Israelites who will serve YHWH throughout time until the End of Days. Yakov was a black man with African ancestors and was given extra authority to know and to converse with Elohim, he was very trustworthy. Right now Yakov is hidden in nations where many Israelites are such as Islamic lands.

Jacob does not mean a liar or deceiver as has been taught by Church men but it means a simple pure man protecting his head from the heel. The heel here is of Satan that is mentioned in Gen 3:15. Many people do not realize the power they are missing in their lives by this name Israel and YHWH's own name. Abraham Abulafia a kabbalistic sage in the 13th century was one man who recognized the power and taught its use. The name Israel means the Mighty Yah, the Prince who reigns over His people.

from Elohim and you shall overcome all men.

29 Then Yakov asked Him, saying, Tell me Your name, I pray. And He said, Why is it that you ask about My name? And He **Blessed** him there.

30 And Yakov called the name of the place Peni'el: For I have seen Elohim face to face, and my life is preserved.[3]

31 Just as he crossed over Peni'el the sun rose on him, and he limped on his hip.

32 Therefore to this day the children of Israel do not eat the muscle that shrank, which is on the hip socket, because He touched the socket of Yakov's hip in the muscle that shrank.[4]

Chapter 33

1 Now Yakov lifted his eyes, and looked, and, there, Esaw was coming, and with him were four hundred men. So he divided the children among Le'yah, Rakhel, and the two maidservants.

2 And he put the maidservants and their children in front, Le'yah

Footnotes

[3] The fight was with a special Malakh. The sages believe Samma'el however this is the Master Yahushua!!! The only one that has the right to change a Name and pronounce a blessing over Israel.

[4] According to tradition Jacob's right hip was touched, the area of Hod which specifies Increases, praise, respect and majesty. After this event his name was changed to Israel, the people YHWH chose to **Bless** and to respect with Redemption and an eternal kingdom. If you are not in spiritual Israel then you are out of the kingdom irrespective of your denomination doctrines. It is important that you seek a Kohen (Levite Priest) to guide you to the way to Spriitual Israel and how to be redeemed.

and her children behind, and Rakhel and Yosef last.

3 Then he crossed over before them, and bowed himself to the ground seven times, until he came near to his brother.

4 But Esaw ran to meet him, and embraced him, and fell on his neck and kissed him: and they wept.

5 And he lifted his eyes, and saw the women and children; and said, Who are these with you? And he said, The children whom Elohim has graciously given your servant.

6 Then the maidservants came near, they and their children, and bowed down.[2]

7 And Le'yah also came near with her children, and they bowed down: afterward Yosef and Rakhel came near, and they bowed down.

8 Then Esaw said, What do you mean by all this company which I met? And he said, These are to find favour in the sight of my master.

9 But Esaw said, I have enough, my brother; keep what you have for yourself.

10 And Yakov said, No, please, if I have now found favour in your sight, then receive my present from my hand: now that I have seen your face, as though I had seen the face of Elohim, and you were pleased with me.

11 Please, take my **Increase** that is brought to you; because Elohim has dealt graciously with me, and because I have enough. And he urged him, and he took it.

12 Then Esaw said, Let us take our journey, let us go, and I will go before you.

13 But Yakov said to him, My master knows that the children are weak, and the flocks and herds which are nursing are with me: and if the men should drive them hard one day, all the flock will die.

14 Please let my master go on ahead before his servant. I will lead on slowly, at a pace which the livestock that go before me, and the children, are able to endure, until I come to my master in Seir.

15 And Esaw said, Now let me leave with you some of the people who are with me. But he said, What need is there? Let me find favour in the sight of my master.

16 So Esaw returned that day on his way to Seir.

17 And Yakov journeyed to Succoth, built himself a Beyth (house), and made booths for his livestock. Therefore the name of the place is called Succoth.

18 Then Yakov came safely to the city of Shkhem, which is in the land of Kanan, when he came

Footnotes
[1] Esaw had the full intention to kill his brother; but later changed his mind because YHWH had sent legions of malakhim to show Esaw that Jacob was not alone, and that these are His armies. Esaw was really afraid, and then changed his mind, so the jots represent family reunion.
[2] Bowing down was not an act of worship; but an act of respect before elders, and officials. The Chinese and Japanese cultures still carry this form of greeting.

from Padan Aram;[1] and he pitched his tent before the city.

19 And he bought the parcel of land, where he had pitched his tent, from the children of Khamur, Shkhem's father, for one hundred pieces of money.

20 Then he erected an altar there and called it El Elohe Israel.[2]

Chapter 34

1 Now Dinah the daughter of Le'yah, whom she had borne to Yakov, went out to see the daughters of the land.

2 And when Shkhem the son of Khamur the Khawee, prince of the land,[3] saw her, he seized her and lay with her, and ravished her.[4]

3 His soul was strongly attracted to Dinah the daughter of Yakov, and he loved the young woman and spoke romantically to the young woman.

4 So Shkhem spoke to his father Khamur, saying, Get me this young woman as a wife.

5 And Yakov heard that he had defiled Dinah his daughter. Now his sons were with his livestock in the field; so Yakov held his shalom[5] until they came.

6 Then Khamur the father of Shkhem went out to Yakov to speak with him.

7 And the sons of Yakov came in from the field when they heard it; and the men were grieved and very angry, because he had done a disgraceful thing in Israel by lying with Yakov's daughter, a thing which ought not to be done.

8 But Khamur spoke with them, saying, The soul of my son Shkhem longs for your daughter: Please give her to him as a wife.

9 And make marriages with us, give your daughters to us, and take our daughters to yourselves.

10 So you shall dwell with us: and the land shall be before you; dwell and trade in it, and acquire possessions for yourselves in it.

11 Then Shkhem said to her father and her brothers, Let me find favour in your eyes, and whatever you say to me I will give.

12 Ask me whatever dowry and gift, and I will give according to what you say to me: but give me the young woman as a wife.

13 But the sons of Yakov answered Shkhem and Khamur his father, and spoke cunningly, because he had defiled Dinah their sister:

14 And they said to them, We cannot do this thing, to give our sister to one who is uncircumcised; for that would be shameful to us:

15 But on this condition we will consent to you: If you will

Footnotes
[1] Northern Syria – Ancient Turkey
[2] The mighty Supreme YHWH, the Prince who reigns over Israel.
[3] Septuagint
[4] The daughter that was born by this event in this act of rape was said to be Asenath, who was brought up by Potipherah's wife, as her daughter, and afterwards married Yosef. This is referenced in Beresheeth (Genesis) 41:45.
[5] It takes great courage to keep peace in such a situation when your daughter has Continued in next section

been raped, and Jacob showed his courage, and patience, and what type of man he was.

become as we are, if every male of you is circumcised;

16 Then we will give our daughters to you, and we will take your daughters to us, and we will dwell with you, and we will become one people.

17 But if you will not heed us, and be circumcised; then we will take our daughter, and be gone.

18 And their words pleased Khamur in his sight, and Shkhem, Khamur's son.

19 So the young man did not delay to do the thing, because he delighted in Yakov's daughter: he was more honorable than all the household of his father.

20 And Khamur and Shkhem his son came to the gate of their city, and spoke with the men of their city, saying:

21 These men are at shalom with us. Therefore let them dwell in the land and trade in it; for indeed, the land is large enough for them; let us take their daughters to us as wives, and let us give them our daughters.

22 Only on this condition will the men consent to dwell with us, to be one people: if every male among us is circumcised, as they are circumcised.

23 Will not their livestock, their property, and every animal of theirs be ours? Only let us consent to them, and they will dwell with us.

24 And all who went out of the gate of his city heeded Khamur and Shkhem his son; every male was circumcised, all who went out of the gate of his city.

25 Now it came to pass on the third day, when they were in pain,[1] that two of the sons of Yakov, Shim'on and Levi, Dinah's brothers, each took his sword and came boldly upon the city and killed all the males.

26 And they killed Khamur and Shkhem his son with the edge of the sword, and took Dinah from Shkhem's Beyth (house), and went out.[2]

Footnotes

[1] The day when the wound of circumcision is most painful-Targum of Onkelos.

[2] What was done here was perfectly legitimate, considering Dinah was kept against her will after being raped. She was kept in Shkhem's house while they were negotiating to marry her, and she had no choice but to return home only after the event. While YHWH made the point clear that we do not marry non-Israelite nations, such as the seven mentioned in Deut 7:1, out of which, one was these, the Hivites. What people forget is how humiliating it is in the East for your sister to be raped, and then kept against her will. If such a thing happened today in the East, then likely the girl's family would go out to kill the entire boy's family, to take revenge and there would be no negotiation at all.

So the actions that the brothers took were perfectly justified, and the situation called for wisdom, which these boys exercised. And we find no rebuke from YHWH, showing us that He did not see this as a violation of His law; but justice. Which is the highest calling for us, even in the most extreme circumstances, and even if it does not make sense to us.

YHWH's law was broken and something had to be done to repair it. Although Shkhem wanted to marry Dina, the problem was, YHWH did not want Israel to make Covenant with the heathen nations, who would defile His laws further; and as can be seen they were only trying to convert to gain the wealth Jacob had so they could add two more stars to their own shoulders.

Interestingly Shkhem means 'shoulder.' This conversion was not a heartfelt conversion. He had broken His law to commit rape in the

Continued in next section

27 The sons of Yakov came upon the slain, and plundered the city, because their sister had been defiled.

28 They took their sheep, their oxen, and their donkeys, what was in the city and what was in the field,

29 And all their wealth. All their little ones and their wives they

first place. When someone's daughter is raped in the East, it brings disgrace to the whole family, and usually the girl will kill herself because of the shame she feels.

She would feel violated because women kept themselves for their husband and did not consider intercourse before marriage as something normal. As many women in the depraved European societies do; because it was, and is, whoring and sin.

On top of that Shkhem's family was using her as a bargaining chip; because she was held against her will, so this was a match that was never going to be made. In such a case the whole family of Jacob would be under extreme pressure, not knowing what was happening to their daughter, and from their own folks, who would demand answers to the dilemma, and action to be taken immediately, to remedy the shame in the clan.

If such as this had happened in an Islamic culture, they would have killed first and asked questions later. So at least we can see some respect in how the whole situation was dealt with by the brothers. The outcome would have been different had they released Dinah, and not made her a bargaining chip. The injunction in Deut 22:29 does not apply here, as these nations were strictly forbidden to be mingled with.

In such a rape situation; because of the guilt and dishonour brought to the victim's family, they would have to leave town. We find this also in the case of Jacob, where he was ordered by YHWH to leave town, because after the boys dealt honourably, the matter, as far as YHWH was concerned was closed, and no guilt was conferred upon them.

took captive; and they plundered even all that was in the houses.

30 Then Yakov said to Shim'on and Levi, You have troubled me by making me loathsome among the inhabitants of the land, among the Kanani and the Perzee: and since I am few in number, they will gather themselves together against me and kill me. I shall be destroyed, my household and I.[1]

31 But they said, Should he treat our sister like a harlot?

Chapter 35

1 Then Elohim said to Yakov, Arise, go up to Beyth'el and dwell there: and make an altar there to El (The Power), who appeared to you when you fled from the face of Esaw [2] your brother.

2 And Yakov said to his household and to all who were with him, Put away the foreign powers [3] that are among you, purify yourselves, and change your garments:

3 Then let us arise and go up to Beyth'el; and I will make an altar there to El (The Power), who answered me in the day of my

Footnotes

[1] Jacob had forgotten that the Covenant was in place to protect him and his household; but felt fearful out of human emotion, forgetting YHWH for a moment.

[2] We see no rebuke from YHWH showing us wisdom needs to be exercised in all matters and we are not to give over to the enemy just because they take our sister and hold her against her will.

[3] Jacob connects his family's issues and trials, with perhaps, someone holding onto false deities in the family, he was right, because Rach'el was still carrying 'God', the deity of Assyria, so he says to put away all false elohim.

distress and has been with me in the WAY[1] which I have gone.

4 So they gave Yakov all the foreign powers which were in their hands, and all their earrings which were in their ears; and Yakov hid them under the terebinth tree which was by Shkhem.[2]

5 And they journeyed: and the terror of Elohim was upon the cities that were all around them, and they did not pursue the sons of Yakov.[3]

6 So Yakov came to Luz[4] (that is, Beyth'el), which is in the land of Kanan, he and all the people who were with him.

7 And he built an altar there and called the place El Beyth'el:[5] because there Elohim appeared to him, when he fled from the face of his brother.

8 Now Devorah Rivka's nurse died, and she was buried below Beyth'el under the terebinth tree: so the name of it was called Allon Bachuth.[6]

9 Then Elohim appeared to Yakov again, when he came from Padan Aram, and *spoke* an **Increase** for him.

10 And Elohim said to him, Your name is Yakov: your name shall not be called Yakov anymore, but Israel shall be your name: so He called his name Israel. [7]

11 Also Elohim said to him, I am El-Shaddai:[8] be fruitful and multiply;[9] a nation; and a company of nations;[10] shall proceed from you, and Kings shall come from your body;

12 The land which I gave Abraham and Ytshak, I give to you, and to your descendants after you I give this land.

13 Then Elohim went up from him in the place where He talked with him.

14 So Yakov set up an altar in the place where He talked with him, an altar of stone: and he poured a drink offering on it, and he poured oil on it.[11]

Footnotes
[7] Jacob's name was changed twice, once going at Gen 32:28 and then on return here in Padamaram.

[8] In Biblical Hebrew El-Shaddai means the Powerful breast that feeds and nourishes. Elohim has qualities of both the Father and the mother ref: Yesha'yahu (Isaiah 60:16).
[9] YHWH here nullifies the oath that Jacob made with Laban Gen 32:50, the one not to take on more wives, by instructing Jacob go beget more children if need be; but we can see this was fulfilled in Jacob's children.
[10] V'Qahal Goyim and a congregation of gentile nations. Here we see the first clear prophecy of the Two Houses of Israel, Beyth (house) Yahudah and Beyth (house) Israel. The Ten tribes of Israel were to become many gentile (heathen) nations as they did later in history.
[11] Jacob anointed a stone altar with oil and wine to praise YHWH's appearing; but did not believe that the stone was YHWH. While many people today worship and anoint

Footnotes
[1] Note 'THE WAY', this is Torah instructions.
[2] They were wearing crescent earrings; this was the common custom as the moon deity had its centre in Harran a major crossroads. The custom amongst the moon worshippers was also that they had these things around their animals (Jud 8:21, Hos 2:13).
[3] YHWH protected Jacob and his household because their actions were justified!
[4] Luz means almond. This is the land where the Garden of Eden was and the tree of Almond the tree of life was situated on the Temple Mount region.
[5] The Mighty One, the house of the Mighty One.
[6] Oak of weeping.

Continued in next section

15 And Yakov called the name of the place where Elohim spoke with him, Beyth'el.[1]

16 Then they journeyed from Beyth'el: and when there was but a little distance to go to Ephrath,[2] Rakhel labored in childbirth, and she had hard labour.

17 Now it came to pass, when she was in hard labour, that the midwife said to her, Do not fear; you will have this son also.

18 And so it was, as her soul was departing (for she died), that she called his name Ben-Oni:[3] but his father called him Benyamin.[4]

19 So Rakhel died and was buried on the way to Ephrath (that is, Beyth-lekhem).

20 And Yakov set an altar on her grave: which is the altar of Rakhel's grave to this day.

21 Then Israel journeyed and pitched his tent beyond the tower of Eder.

22 And it happened, when Israel dwelt in that land, that Reuven went and lay with Bilhah his father's concubine:[5] and Israel heard about it. Now the sons of Yakov were twelve:

23 the sons of Le'yah were Reuven, Yakov's Bekhor (firstborn), and Shim'on, Levi, Yahudah, Yskhar (Issachar), and Zevulun:

24 The sons of Rakhel were; Yosef, and Benyamin:

25 The sons of Bilhah, Rakhel's maidservant were; Dan, and Naphtali:

26 And the sons of Zilpah, Le'yah's maidservant were; Gawd, and Asher: these were the sons of Yakov, who were born to him in Padan Aram.

27 Then Yakov came to his father Ytshak at Mamre, or Kiryath Arba that is Khevron, where Abraham and Ytshak had dwelt.

28 Now the days of Ytshak were one hundred and eighty years.

29 So Ytshak breathed his last and died, and was gathered to his people, being old and full of days; and his sons Esaw and Yakov buried him.

Chapter 36

1 Now this is the genealogy of Esaw, who is Edom.

2 Esaw took his wives from the daughters of Kanan; Adah the daughter of Elon the Khitee,[6] Aholibamah the daughter of Anah, the daughter of Zibon the Khawee. [7]

stones and give them the quality and attributes of Elohim.

[1] Jacob anoints the place where YHWH will build His house.

[2] Ancient name of Bethlehem.

[3] Son of my strength in that her entire strength was spent having the child.

[4] Son of my right or son of the south as Jacob was travelling down south.

[5] Reuben did not put the bed there it's a way of saying this. He actually made a statement of where Jacob his father should sleep. There was no physical act done.

Footnotes

[6] YHWH had forbidden Israel to marry these Hittites; but Esaw was a disobedient son.

[7] Gen 26:34 Esaw takes two wives Judith and Basemath, while the narrative in Genesis 36:2-3 names three wives, Adah and Aholibamah and Basemath. At this point the situation was no different, he changed the name of Basemath the daughter of Yshmael to Mahalath. He then changed Adah, Judith
Continued in next section

3 And Basemath Yshmael's daughter, sister of Nebayoth.

4 Now Adah bore Eliphaz to Esaw; and Basemath bore Reuel;[1]

5 And Aholibamah bore Yeush, Yaalam, and Korakh:[2] these were

and Basemath to Aholibamah. Basemath was burning incense to idols.

Rashi on this verse:
Daughter of Anah, daughter of Zibeon: If she was the daughter of Anah, she could not have been the daughter of Zibeon: Anah was the son of Zibeon, as it is said:"And these are the sons of Zibeon: Aiah and Anah" (below verse 24). [This] teaches [us] that Zibeon was intimate with his daughter-in-law, the wife of Anah, and Oholibamah emerged from between them both [i.e., from Zibeon and Anah]. Scripture teaches us that they were all mamzerim (illegitimate), products of adultery and incest. — [from Tanchuma Vayeshev 1]

Basemath, daughter of Ishmael: Elsewhere [Scripture] calls her Mahalath (above 28:9). I found in the Aggadah of the midrash on the Book of Samuel (ch. 17): There are three people whose iniquities are forgiven (מוֹחֲלִים) : One who converts to Judaism, one who is promoted to a high position, and one who marries. The proof [of the last one] is derived from here (28:9). For this reason she was called Mahalath (מְחֲלַת), because his (Esau's) sins were forgiven (נְמְחֲלוּ).

Sister of Nebaioth: Since he (Nebaioth) gave her hand in marriage after Ishmael died, she was referred to by his name. — [from Meg. 17a]

He was trying to fit in the Covenant of YHWH with Abraham but he did not succeed.

[1] This was to be Moses' father in law's dad. Therefore Jethro was an Ishmaelite and of Jordanian bloodline.
[2] Oholibamah bore...and Korah: This Korah was illegitimate. He was the son of Eliphaz, who had been intimate with his father's wife, Oholibamah, the wife of Esau. This is evidenced by the fact that he [Korah] is [also] listed among the chieftains of Eliphaz
Continued in next section

the sons of Esaw, who were born to him in the land of Kanan.

6 Then Esaw took his wives, his sons, his daughters, and all the persons of his household, his cattle and all his animals, and all his goods which he had gained in the land of Kanan; and went to a country away from the presence of his brother Yakov.

7 For their possessions were too great for them to dwell together; and the land where they were strangers could not support them because of their livestock.

8 So Esaw dwelt in Mount Seir: Esaw is Edom.

9 And this is the genealogy of Esaw the father of the Edomi in Mount Seir:

10 These were the names of Esaw's sons; Eliphaz the son of Adah the wife of Esaw, and Reuel the son of Basemath the wife of Esaw.

11 And the sons of Eliphaz were Teman, Omar, Zepho, Gatam, and Kenaz.

12 Now Timna[3] was the concubine[1] of Eliphaz Esaw's

at the end of this chapter. — [from Gen. Rabbah 82:12]
[3] According to another tradition (Tanhuma, Vayeshev 1), the description of Eliphaz's "marriage" to Timna teaches of corruption and degeneration among the descendants of Seir. This midrash is based on the inconsistency concerning Timna's lineage between Gen. 36:20–22, in which she is presented as the sister of Lotan (the son of Seir), and I Chron. 1:36, that mentions her as the daughter of Eliphaz. The Rabbis reconcile this discrepancy by explaining that Timna was indeed Eliphaz's daughter, as a result of his adulterous relations with Seir's wife; to compound his sin, Eliphaz took his own daughter as his concubine. The Torah charts the lineage of Esau's descendants at
Continued in next section

son; and she bore Amalek to Eliphaz: these were the sons of Adah Esaw's wife.

length, in order to show that this lineage was founded in adultery.

According to Rashi-
And Timna was a concubine: [This passage is here] to proclaim the greatness of Abraham-how much [people] longed to attach themselves to his descendants. This Timna was a daughter of chieftains, as it is said: "and the sister of Lotan was Timna" (below verse 22). Lotan was one of the chieftains of the inhabitants of Seir, from the Horites, who had dwelt there before. She said, "I may not be worthy of marrying you, but if only I could be [your] concubine" (Gen. Rabbah 82:14). In (I) Chronicles (1:36) [the Chronicler] enumerates her among the children of Eliphaz [here she is counted as the daughter of Seir the Horite, and the concubine of Eliphaz]. This teaches [us] that he (Eliphaz) was intimate with the wife of Seir, and Timna emerged from between them (Seir's wife and Eliphaz), and when she grew up, she became his (Eliphaz's) concubine. That is the meaning of "and the sister of Lotan was Timna." [Scripture] did not count her with the sons of Seir, because she was his (Lotan's) sister through his mother but not through his father. — [from Tanchuma Vayeshev 1]
[1] Timna was the sister of Lotan, one of Esau's chiefs, and therefore the daughter of royalty. The Rabbis relate that she sought to convert and join Abraham's household. She went to Abraham, Isaac and Jacob, but since they would not accept her, she went and became the concubine of Eliphaz. She declared: "Better for me to be a handmaiden to this nation [Israel], and not a noblewoman of that nation [the chiefs of Esau]" (Midrash Tannaim on Deut., 32:47). The Rabbis assert that Timna's willingness to exchange her status of noblewoman for that of concubine attests to her pure intent to convert. The Patriarchs did not understand her true aim; instead of rejecting her, they should have drawn her to the bosom of Judaism. They were accordingly punished, for her union with Eliphaz produced Amalek, who would cause Israel to suffer (BT Sanhedrin 99b).

13 And these were the sons of Reuel; Nahath, Zerakh, Shammah, and Mizzah: these were the sons of Basemath Esaw's wife.

14 These were the sons of Aholibamah, Esaw's wife, the daughter of Anah, the daughter of Zibon. And she bore to Esaw: Yeush,[2] Yaalam, and Korakh.

15 And these were the chiefs of the sons of Esaw: the sons of Eliphaz the Bekhor (firstborn) son of Esaw; were chief Teman, chief Omar, chief Zepho, chief Kenaz,

16 Chief Korakh, chief Gatam, and chief Amalek: these were the chiefs of Eliphaz in the land of Edom; they were the sons of Adah.[3]

17 And these are the sons of Reuel Esaw's son; chief Nahath, chief Zerakh, chief Shammah, and chief Mizzah. These were the chiefs of Reuel in the land of Edom: these were the sons of Basemath, Esaw's wife.

18 And these are the sons of Aholibamah Esaw's wife; chief Yeush, chief Yaalam, and chief Korakh: these were the chiefs who descended from Aholibamah

Footnotes
[2] This name in Hebrew is pronounced as Ya'ish but because of accepted rabbinic tradition this is pronounced as Ye-ush. Even the KJV translators who would have normally rejected the Hebrew traditions because of bias which are correct have happily done the same in the English.
[3] Although the description is of Eliphaz's sons but the list mentioned one son of Adah or Esaw who is Korah, while the list in verse 11 is correct Eliphaz had six sons but the man Korakh was the product of Eliphaz's adultery with his father's wife. See footnote verse 5 above.

Esaw's wife, the daughter of Anah.

19 These were the sons of Esaw, who is Edom, and these were their chiefs.

20 These are the sons of Seir the Horite, who inhabited the land; Lotan, Shobal, Zibon, Anah,

21 Dishon, Ezer, and Dishan: these are the chiefs of the Khuri, the sons of Seir in the land of Edom.

22 And the sons of Lotan were Hori and Hemam; and Lotan's sister was Timna.

23 And the sons of Shobal were these; Alwan, Manahath, Ebal, Shepho, and Onam

24 And these are the sons of Zibon; both Ayah, and Anah: this was that Anah that found the mayim in the wilderness, as he pastured the donkeys[1] of his father Zibon.

25 And the children of Anah were these; Dishon, and Aholibamah the daughter of Anah.

26 And these are the sons of Dishon; Hemdan, Eshban, Yithran, and Keran.

27 The sons of Ezer are these: Bilhan, Zaavan, and Akan.

28 The sons of Dishan are these: Uz, and Aran.

29 These were the chiefs of the Khuri; chief Lotan, chief Shobal, chief Zibon, chief Anah,

30 Chief Dishon, chief Ezer, and chief Dishan: these are the chiefs that came from the Khuri, according to their chiefs in the land of Seir.

31 And these are the Kings who reigned in the land of Edom, before any King reigned over the children of Israel.

32 And Bela the son of Beor reigned in Edom: and the name of his city was Dinhavah. [2]

33 And when Bela died, Yobab the son of Zerakh of Botsrah reigned in his place.

34 When Yobab died, Husham of the land of the Temanites reigned in his place.

35 And when Husham died, Hadad the son of Bedad, who attacked Midian in the field of Moav, reigned in his place: and the name of his city was Avith.

36 When Hadad died, Samlah of Masrekah reigned in his place.

Footnotes
[1] The crossbreed called mules, were discovered here, with the donkeys in the wilderness. The stallion donkeys of his father, coupled with mare horses, and produced another sort of creature called, mules, which are hybrid animals and do not conceive as they are sterile. This is the combined strength of the horse, with the sure footing of the donkey to create the hybrid.

Footnotes
[2] This is modern Tunis, A Roman province. Hannibal is connected to this place known as Carthage, who led Elephants through Spain and the Alps where half his army died, fighting the battles for 15 years and defeated Rome in Italy. The famous Battle of Cannae in 2 August 216 BCE in Apulia South-East Italy against the Roman consuls Lucius Aemilius Paullus and Gaius Terentius Varro, Hannibal outnumbered by a much larger Roman believed to be 88,000 troops versus 50,000 of Hannibal defeated Rome using the double envelope maneuver, his great tactics are still practiced by all modern armies. His tribe is believed to be from Ham, from the Canaanites of Israel, a descendant of Nimrod. Hannibal name means "beloved of Baal."

37 And when Samlah died, Saul of Rehoboth-by-the-River reigned in his place.

38 When Saul died, Baal-Hanan the son of Achbor reigned in his place.

39 And when Baal-Hanan the son of Achbor died, Hadar reigned in his place: and the name of his city was Pau; and his wife's name was Mehetavel, the daughter of Matred, the daughter of Mezahav.

40 And these are the names of the chiefs of Esaw, according to their Mishpakhot (families), and their places, by their names; chief Timnah, chief Alvah, chief Yetheth,

41 Chief Aholibamah, chief Elah, chief Pinon,

42 Chief Kenaz, chief Teman, chief Mivzar,

43 Chief Magdi'el, and chief Iram: these are the chiefs of Edom, according to their dwelling places in the land of their possession: he is Esaw the father of the Edomi.[1]

Torah Parsha 9 Vayeshev, Beresheeth 37:1-40:23
Haftarah: Amos 2:6-3:8

Chapter 37

1 Now Yakov dwelt in the land where his father was a stranger, in the land of Kanan.

2 This is the genealogy of Yakov. Yosef, being seventeen years old, was feeding the flock with his brothers; and the lad was with the sons of Bilhah, and the sons of Zilpah, his father's wives: and Yosef brought a bad report of them to his father.

3 Now Israel loved Yosef more than all his children, because he was a wise son to him:[2] and he made him a tunic[3] of fine white linen. [4]

4 And when his brothers saw that their father loved him more than all his brothers, they hated him, and could not speak peaceably to him.

5 Now Yosef dreamed a dream and he told it to his brothers and they continued to hate him.

6 So he said to them, Please hear this dream which I have dreamed:

7 There we were, binding sheaves in the field, and, behold, my sheaf arose, and also stood upright; and, indeed, your sheaves stood all around, and bowed down to my sheaf.

8 And his brothers said to him, Will you be King over us? Or, will you indeed have power over us? So their hatred continued for his dreams, and for his words.

9 Then he dreamed still another dream, and told it to his brothers, and said, Look, I have dreamed another dream; and, this time, the sun and the moon and the eleven stars bowed down to me.

10 So he told it to his father, and his brothers: and his father rebuked him, and said to him, What is this dream that you have

Footnotes
[1] All the different Jordanian people.

Footnotes
[2] Targum of Onkelos.

[3] The word signifies a tunic or robe.

[4] The Hebrew word "pas" in ancient script is for a moon. So this would mean a robe of linen of white like the face of the moon.

dreamed? Shall your mother and I and your brothers indeed come to bow down to the earth before you?[1]

11 And his brothers envied him; but his father kept the matter in mind.

[2]

Footnotes

[1] Yosef was seeing the future when in the remez (hint) he would prefigure the Messiah but also in the Pashat (literal) he was seeing himself in Egypt, where the entire world as he saw it would come to purchase grain to survive the drought therefore bowing to him to pay homage. In the future this would be fulfilled in the nation of the US who will be the Yosef nation, who very much like Egypt would have many believers and have the same kind of control and power where many nations would bow down to it. In the End of Days the USA would help Israel in the wars that are coming with the Islamic nations especially the one we call Armageddon. The US and the UK will play key roles as the shepherd nations of YHWH. Just like Yosef invited his father and his children to live in the richest portions of Egypt so will in the future when Israel is in trouble they will bring back Hebrew people to live in good parts of USA under a future president who will be very supportive for Israel.

[2] The dots in the letters above indicate a family reunion and here Yosef has been sent to the family to his brothers. Interestingly although this is about Jacob's family, the verse has seven words and the letters Alef+Tav sit right at word number three, indicating a sign like in the Ten commandments the third commandment stating do not falsify or profane the name of YHWH. Here the name of YHWH was about to be profaned. One can profane the name of YHWH by doing something He forbids you to do, while at the same time in the mercy of YHWH this was about to become the first highlight of the Messiah's redemptive work of sending Yosef into Egypt. The eleven brothers were feeding the earthly father's flock, Yosef was about to reveal feeding of the Israelite flock in the personification of the Messiah. The Alef symbolizes the Father Continued in next section

12 Then his brothers went to feed their father's flock in Shkhem.

13 And Israel said to Yosef, Are not your brothers feeding the flock in Shkhem? Come, I will send you to them. So he said to him, Here I am.

14 Then he said to him, Please go and see if it is well with your brothers, and well with the flocks; and bring back word to me. So he sent him out of the Valley of Khevron, and he came to Shkhem.

15 Now a certain man found him, and there he was wandering in the field:[3] and the man asked him, saying, What are you seeking?

16 So he said, I am seeking my brothers: Please tell me where they are feeding their flocks.

17 And the man said, They have departed from here; for I heard them say, Let us go to Dothan. So Yosef went after his brothers, and found them in Dothan.[4]

18 Now when they saw him afar off, even before he came near them, they conspired against him to kill him.

in shamayim the source of all things through whom we get the Ruakh Ha Kodesh.

[3] Remez (hint) of future Messiah, wandering, collecting His sons from the world, as the field is the drash for cities of the world. While the Hebrews wandered, after being scattered, the Messiah goes out to collect them through the Torah of YHWH.

[4] Note: Yosef found his eleven brothers, the Tribes, in Dothan, a town not far away from Samaria.

19 Then they said to one another, Look, this master of dreams is coming.[1]

20 Come therefore, let us now kill him, and cast him into some pit, and we shall say, Some wild beast has devoured him: and we shall see what will become of his dreams.

21 And Reuven heard it, and he rescued him out of their hands; and said, Let us not kill him.

22 And Reuven said to them, Shed no blood, but cast him into this pit which is in the wilderness, and do not lay a hand on him; that he might rescue him out of their hands, and bring him back to his father.

23 So it came to pass, when Yosef had come to his brothers, that they stripped Yosef of his tunic, the tunic of fine white linen that was on him.

24 Then they took him, and cast him into a pit: and the pit was empty, there was no mayim in it.

25 And they sat down to eat a meal: and they lifted their eyes and looked, and, there was a company of Yishmaelites coming from Gil'ad with their camels bearing spices, balm, and myrrh, on their way to carry them down to Mitzrayim (Egypt).

26 So Yahudah said to his brothers, What profit is there if we kill our brother, and conceal his blood?

27 Come, and let us sell him to the Yishmaelites, and let not our hand be upon him;[2] for he is our brother and our flesh. And his brothers listened.

28 Then Midiani traders passed by; so the brothers pulled Yosef up and lifted him out of the pit, and sold him to the Yishmaelites for twenty shekels of silver: and they took Yosef to Mitzrayim (Egypt).

29 Then Reuven returned to the pit; and, indeed, Yosef was not in the pit; and he tore his clothes.

30 And he returned to his brothers, and said, The lad is no more; and I, where shall I go?

31 And they took Yosef's tunic, and killed a kid of the goats, and dipped the tunic in the blood.

32 Then they sent the tunic of fine white linen, and they brought it to their father and said, We have found this. Do you know whether it is your son's tunic or not?

33 And he recognized it and said, It is my son's tunic. A wild beast has devoured him. Without doubt Yosef is torn to pieces.

34 Then Yakov tore his clothes, put sackcloth on his waist, and mourned for his son many days.

35 And all his sons and all his daughters arose to comfort him; but he refused to be comforted, and he said, For I shall go down into the grave to my son in

---

Footnotes

[1] The Hebrew word here, 'Ha Lazeh', is used to indicate a derogatory word. Yosef's brothers used this against him, it was not a common word, and so, they showed extreme hatred for their brother.

Footnotes

[2] Remez of Israel doing business with the Arabs, their half brothers. Also, that they would sell their own brother to them for business, as they are now dividing the land of Israel.

mourning. Thus his father wept for him.

36 Now the Midianites had sold him in Mitzrayim (Egypt) to Potipher, an officer of Pharaoh, and captain of the guard.

Chapter 38

1 It came to pass at that time that Yahudah departed[1] from his brothers, and visited a certain Adullamite, whose name was Hirah.

2 And Yahudah there he met a Kanani, the daughter of Shua, he married her and went in to her.[2]

3 And she conceived, and bore a son; and he called his name Er.

4 She conceived and birthed another son; and she called his name Onan.

5 And she continued to conceive, and birthed a son; and called his name Shelah: and he was at Chezib when she birthed him.[3]

6 Then Yahudah took a wife for Er his Bekhor (firstborn), and her name was Tamar. [4]

7 But Er,[5] Yahudah's Bekhor (firstborn), was wicked in the sight of YHWH, and YHWH killed him. [6]

8 And Yahudah said to Onan, Go in to your brother's wife,[7] and marry her, and raise up an heir to your brother.

9 But Onan[8] knew[1] that the heir would not be his;[2] and it came to

Footnotes

[4] Tamar was the daughter of Melekzadek (Shem), the priest of YHWH Yavamot 34b.

[5] According to one tradition Er was 7 yrs old when he married Tamar. Er did not want to make her pregnant as he thought she would lose her beauty from becoming pregnant. Also he listened to his mother. (Yavamot 34b)

[6] He did not want to give her children, so he ejaculated his sperm on the ground through masturbation (masturbation per se was not a sin), and YHWH was displeased. He did not have intercourse with her. He did this because his Canaanite mother had told him not to give Tamar children. The gentiles will always lead you astray from the Covenants. Not having children and deliberately suppressing them via contraceptives is a sin; because we are commanded to 'be fruitful and multiply.' However if you were poor and you did not have children that may be understandable but an argument is made that children are born with their own increases. If you have at least one son and then you do not have further children that is not counted as a sin.

[7] Levirate marriage: where a dead brother's wife had to be married to the brother who was alive, irrespective of him having one wife or not, this was commanded polygamy, to give the dead brother children, to raise his name.

[8] Onanism comes from the name Onan, for birth control. You will find this in many good dictionaries as the practice of, coitus interruptus. YHWH certainly did not appreciate birth control, so, no condoms would have been allowed in ancient Hebrew culture. Er and Onan had to die, because of Continued in next section

Footnotes

[1] The hint is that he also partially departed from YHWH's law for a few months. This is explained later if you catch the thought that he married a Canaanite, whom he was not supposed to marry; but he married her because she wore pretty make up and looked nice. The reason was also that he was drunk, and he made a promise to marry her while drunk; and so he had to fulfil his promise. Warning, we should never make promises when under the influence of drink or drugs.

[2] The name of the man was Shua; but his daughter's name was Aliyath.

[3] Onan and Shelah were twins. Yahudah did not give Shelah to Tamar as he was afraid that he too would die. He admits in verse 26 that he did not give her this son since he was afraid to lose him.

pass, when he came to[3] his brother's wife, that he emitted *his seed* on the ground, lest he should give an heir to his brother.

YHWH's displeasure with them, for destroying their seed. The highest calling from YHWH for any of us is not asceticism, although it is possibly a short term choice, and only a short term choice for some, at that, with strings attached; but for Israelite men the highest calling is to be fruitful, and multiply.

[1] Genesis 38:9, And Onan knew that the seed should not be his; and it came to pass, when he went in [the word is not one of having sexual intercourse] unto his brother's wife, that he spilled his sperm on the ground, lest that he should give seed to his dead brother's wife. Here comes the sting in the tail. Tamar's marriage had never been consummated! Not that it needed to be in Torah culture. Her two previous husbands had not had sexual intercourse with her, both practiced masturbation in front of her, destroying their seed on the ground.

[2] Onan did not want a child from Tamar as he thought it won't be his because in patriarchal commanded (Deut 25:5) polygamy the child would have received the dead brother's name so according to Yavamot 34b Tamar was still a virgin after these two marriages.

According to other accounts Yahudah was punished for lying to his father Yakov about Yosef being dead. (Seder Olam Rabba 2) Er and Onan were both wicked in their ways and instead of taking up on the father and righteousness they had taken on their Canaanite mother and listened to her who did not want them to have children with Tamar to increase Israel. She was killed by a curse from Yahudah because of her rebellion.

[3] The translations that say he had sexual contact with Tamar are faulty, because he never went into the girl; and always performed masturbation in front of her. The Hebrew word does not say he had any sexual contact with her; but simply, he came upon her, or, in the room where he intended to perform his own desire to masturbate; and throw his seed on the ground.

10 And the thing which he did displeased YHWH; in his sight therefore He killed him also. [4]

11 Then Yahudah said to Tamar his daughter-in-law, Remain a widow in your father's house, till my son Shelah is grown: for he said, Lest he also die as his brothers did. And Tamar went and dwelt in her father's house.

12 Now in the process of time the daughter of Shua Yahudah's wife died; and Yahudah was comforted, and went up to his sheepshearers at Timnah, he and his friend Hirah the Adullamite.[5]

13 And it was told Tamar, saying, Look, your father-in-law is going up to Timnah to shear his sheep.

14 So she took off her widow's garments, covered herself with the veil,[6] and wrapped herself, and sat in an open place which was on the way to Timnah; for

Footnotes

[4] He was not killed for masturbation, as people presume; but because he refused to raise sons for Israel as commanded. Israel was to multiply into many nations. Today we have many believers who refrain from having children, or may just have one, or two, this is upsetting for YHWH. Israel is supposed to multiply seed. This man did the same, upon advice from his mother, just like his brother who did not want to give Tamar children. He never had sex with Tamar; but did masturbate in front of her, and then, ejaculated on the ground.

[5] Yahudah put a curse on her because she had led his sons astray, and she died by this curse. From the pseudoepigrapha:Yahudah ll:3-5 While I was absent, she went off and brought from Kanan a wife for Shelah. When I realised what she had done, I pronounced a curse on her in the anguish of my soul, and she died in her wickedness, together with her children.

[6] See HTHS Torah Compendium edition.

she saw that Shelah was grown, and she was not given to him as a wife.

15 When Yahudah saw her, he thought she was a harlot, because she had covered her face. [1]

16 Then he turned to her by the way, and said, Please let me come in to you; for he did not know that she was his daughter-in-law. She said, What will you give me, that you may come in to me?

17 And he said, I will send you a young goat from the flock. And she said, Will you give me a pledge till you send it?

18 Then he said, What pledge shall I give you? So she said, Your signet and cord, and your staff that is in your hand.[2] Then

he gave them to her, and had sexual relations with her, and she conceived by him.

19 So she arose, and went away, and laid aside her veil, and put on the garments of her widowhood.

20 And Yahudah sent the young goat by the hand of his friend the Adullamite, to receive his pledge from the woman's hand, but he did not find her.

21 Then he asked the men of that place, saying, Where is the harlot, who was openly by the roadside? And they said, There was no harlot in this place.

22 And he returned to Yahudah and said, I cannot find her; and also the men of the place said, there was no harlot in this place.

23 Then Yahudah said, Let her take them, for herself, lest we be shamed for, I sent this young goat, and you have not found her.

24 And it came to pass, about three months after, that Yahudah was told, saying, Tamar your daughter-in-law has played the harlot; furthermore, she is with child by harlotry. So Yahudah said, Bring her out and let her be burned.[3]

Footnotes

[1] Tamar was a virgin when she had had relations with Yahudah. How did she become pregnant upon one time intimacy is she broke her hymen with her own finger so she could conceive. She called upon YHWH while sitting in her tent covering her face to not go outside without a seed - Yavamot 34b. She was extremely righteous woman, the name Tamar for a date palm signifies that and she was made the mother of judges, prophets and kings of Israel.

[2] From the historical canon of the Patriarchs known as the pseudoepigrapha; Yahudah 1-3 And after these things, while Tamar was a widow, she heard after two years that I was going up to shear my sheep, and adorned herself in bridal array, and sat in the city Enaim by the gate. For it was a law of the Amorites, that she who was about to marry should sit in whoring seven days by the gate.

Yahudah was also drunk at the time of meeting Tamar, just like his wife Aliyath, so he did not recognize her; because how can a man sleep with a woman and not recognize that it is his daughter in law? The reason why Tamar sat at the gate, the sign and Continued in next section

symbol of authority, was not because she was a harlot, she was seeking marriage; but Yahudah in his drunkenness could not tell the difference between marriage and harlotry, and at that time anything moving in a skirt would have been sufficient. Sadly, some men still behave like this today. So we get it now, that it was even a law of the Amorites, Tamar was now basically seeking the child from Yahudah, in view to marriage, not incest or adultery.

[3] She was commanded to be burned because she was a kohen's daughter. The Torah law is not burning on the stake unlike Continued in next section

25 When she was brought out, she sent to her father-in-law, saying, By the man to whom these belong, I am with child.[1] And she said, Please determine whose these are, the signet, and cord, and staff.

26 Therefore, Yahudah acknowledged them, and said, She has been more Righteous than I; because I did not give her to Shelah my son. And he never ceased from having a relation with her again.[2]

27 Now it came to pass, at the time for giving birth, that, behold, twins were in her womb.

the primitive uneducated Europeans did, which causes great pain but a molten lead was poured in the mouth of the person so that he or she would instantly die with the least pain and agony.

[1] Tamar did not want to shame Yahudah and so said "I am by child by the man to whom these belong", she was a great righteous woman. While today many women engage in lashon hara (evil speech) and tale-bearing to shame the men in their lives, what a contrast of present unruly women versus women of biblical times.

[2] Ve'Lo Yasaf Od L'da'ata phrase should mean, "He never ceased from having a relation with her again", in other words he accepted the fact she was to be his wife and "he did not separate from her ever again" by marrying her properly with a ketubah (Torah marriage Covenant). Yahudah was the chief of the tribe and a righteous judge. This is how the verse needs to be translated, while the other translations adopted the wording never to know her again are clearly wrong and against Torah that a husband did not fulfil the levirate duty to his wife then what kind of message does this send to wives looking for a lewirate marriage? If Yahudah did not have any further intimacy with his wife then that would make him a transgressor according to Torah law, therefore the verse is correctly to be specified he never left her after this event.

28 And so it was, when she was giving birth, that the one put out his hand; and the midwife took a scarlet thread, and bound it on his hand, saying, This one came out first.

29 Then it happened, as he drew back his hand, that his brother came out unexpectedly: and she said, How did you break through? This breach be upon you! Therefore his name was called Phratz.[3]

30 Afterward his brother came out, who had the scarlet thread on his hand. And his name was called Zerakh.[4]

Chapter 39

1 Now Yosef had been taken down to Mitzrayim (Egypt); and Potiphar, an officer of Pharaoh, captain of the guard, a Mitzri (Egyptian), bought him from the Yishmaelites, who had taken him down there.

2 YHWH was with Yosef, and he was a successful man; and he was in the house of his master the Mitzri (Egyptian).

3 And his master saw that YHWH was with him, and that YHWH made all he did to prosper in his hand.

4 So Yosef found favour in his sight, and served him: and he made him overseer of his house, and his entire belongings he put in his hand.

5 So it was from the time that he had made him overseer of his

Footnotes
[3] To break forth. Many Persians are from the tribe of Judah, Persia became to be known as Phares from this son.
[4] The Messianic line continued through Tamar and Yahudah.

house, and all that he had, that YHWH **Blessed** the Mitzrim (Egyptians) Beyth (house) for Yosef's sake; and the **Blessing** of YHWH was on all that he had in the house, and in the field.

6 And he left all that he had in Yosef's hand; and he did not know what he had, except for the Lakhem (bread) which he ate. And Yosef was handsome in form and appearance

7 Now it came to pass after these things, that his master's wife cast longing eyes on Yosef; and she said, Lie down with me.[1]

8 But he refused, and said to his master's wife, Look, my master does not know what is with me in the house, and he has committed all that he has to my hand;

9 There is none greater in this house than I; neither has he kept back any thing from me but you, because you are his wife: then how can I do this great wickedness, and sin against Elohim?

10 And so it was, as she spoke to Yosef day by day, that he did not heed her, to lie with her, or to be with her.

11 And it happened about this time, when Yosef went into the house to do his work; and none of the men of the house were inside,

12 And she caught him by his garment, saying, Lie with me: and he left his garment in her hand, and fled and ran outside.

13 And so it was, when she saw that he had left his garment in her hand, and fled outside,

14 That she called to the men of her house, and spoke to them, saying, See, he has brought in to us an Abrahu (Hebrew) to mock us; he came in to me to lie with me, and I cried out with a loud voice:[2]

15 And it happened, when he heard that I lifted my voice and cried out, that he left his garment with me, and fled, and went outside.

16 So she kept his garment with her, until his master came home.

17 Then she spoke to him with words like these, saying, The Abrahu (Hebrew) servant, whom you brought to us, came in to me to mock me:

18 So it happened, as I lifted my voice and cried out, that he left his garment with me, and fled outside.

19 So it was, when his master heard the words, which his wife spoke to him, saying, Your servant did to me, after this manner; that he was very angry.

20 Then Yosef's master seized him, and put him into the prison, a place where the King's prisoners were confined: and he was there in the prison.

21 But YHWH was with Yosef, and showed him loving-kindness, and He gave him favour in the sight of the keeper of the prison.

Footnotes
[2] When the gentiles do not get their way, they resort to insults, and lying allegations against believers. This is the typical pattern in the world; we see this throughout history, and even today.

Footnotes
[1] Adultery was and is forbidden, and a grievous sin, hence why Yosef refused to sleep with Potipherah's wife.

22 And the keeper of the prison committed to Yosef's hand all the prisoners that *were* in the prison; and whatever they did there, he was in charge.

23 The keeper of the prison did not look into anything that was under Yosef's hand; because YHWH was with him, and whatever he did, YHWH made it to prosper.[1]

Footnotes

[1] Wherever true righteous people stand, they will speak Increases for others around them, both in business, and commerce, and generally in family relationships.

Chapter 40

1 It came to pass, after these things that the cupbearer[1] and the baker of the King of Mitzrayim (Egypt) offended their masters,[2] the King of Mitzrayim (Egypt).

2 And Pharaoh was angry with his two officers, the chief cupbearer, and the chief baker.

3 So he put them in custody in the house of the captain of the guard, in the prison, the place where Yosef was confined.

4 And the captain of the guard charged Yosef with them, and he served them: so they were in custody for a while.

5 Then the cupbearer and the baker of the King of Mitzrayim (Egypt), who were confined in the prison, dreamed a dream both of them, each man's dream in one night, and each man's dream with its own interpretation.

6 And Yosef came in to them in the morning, and looked at them, and saw that they were sad.

7 So he asked Pharaoh's officers who were with him in the custody of his master's house, saying, Why do you look so sad today?

8 And they said to him, We each have dreamed a dream, and there is no interpreter of it. And Yosef said to them, Do not interpretations belong to Elohim? Tell them to me, please.

9 Then the chief cupbearer told his dream to Yosef, and said to him, Behold, in my dream a vine was before me;

10 And in the vine were three branches: it was as though it budded, its blossoms shot forth; and its clusters brought forth ripe grapes:

11 Then Pharaoh's cup was in my hand: and I took the grapes, and pressed them into Pharaoh's cup, and placed the cup in Pharaoh's hand.

12 And Yosef said to him, This is the interpretation of it: The three branches are three days:

13 Now within three days Pharaoh will lift up your head, and restore you to your place: and you will put Pharaoh's cup in his hand, according to the former manner when you were his cupbearer.

14 But remember me when it is well with you, and please show favour, to me, and make mention of me to Pharaoh, and get me out of this Beyth (house):

15 For indeed I was stolen away from the land of the Abrahu (Hebrews):[3] and also I have done nothing here that they should put me into the dungeon.

16 When the chief baker saw that the interpretation was good, he said to Yosef, I also was in my dream, and there I had three white baskets on my head:

Footnotes

[1] A wicked cupbearer could kill the king as his job was to taste anything that he handed to the king first to make sure no poison was mixed in the drinks he handed over so this matter was a treasonous matter.

[2] The plural Hebrew word for master implies hat he had offended not only the king but also officers below him.

Footnotes

[3] Abrahu or Ibri is the term given to the people who lived in Kanan, which later became Israelites, after Jacob came to be known by his modern name Israel; but his real name is Israel.

17 In the uppermost basket there were all kinds of baked goods for Pharaoh; and the birds ate them out of the basket on my head.

18 So Yosef answered and said, This is the interpretation of it: The three baskets are three days:

19 Yet within three days Pharaoh will lift off your head from you, and hang you on a tree; and the birds will eat your flesh from you.

20 Now it came to pass on the third day, which was Pharaoh's birthday, that he made a feast for all his servants: and he lifted up the head of the chief cupbearer and of the chief baker among his servants.

21 And he restored the chief cupbearer to his cupbearer's position again; and he placed the cup in Pharaoh's hand:

22 But he hanged the chief baker: as Yosef had interpreted to them.

23 Yet the chief cupbearer did not remember Yosef, but forgot him.

Torah Parsha 10 Miqeitz, Beresheeth 41:1-44:17
Haftarah: Melekhim Alef 3:15-4:1

Chapter 41

1 Then it came to pass, at the end of two full years, that Pharaoh had a dream: and, behold, he stood by the river.

2 Suddenly, there came up out of the river seven cows fine looking and fat; and they fed in the meadow.

3 Then, behold, seven other cows came up after them out of the river, ugly and gaunt; and stood by the other cows on the bank of the river.

4 And the ugly and gaunt cows ate up the seven fine looking and fat cows. So Pharaoh awoke.

5 He slept and dreamed a second time: and, suddenly, seven heads of grain came up on one stalk, plump and good.

6 And, behold, seven thin heads scorched by the east wind sprang up after them.

7 And the seven thin heads devoured the seven plump and full heads. So Pharaoh awoke, and indeed, it was a dream.

8 Now it came to pass in the morning that his spirit was troubled; and he sent and called for all the magicians of Mitzrayim (Egypt), and all its wise men: and Pharaoh told them his dream; but there was no one who could interpret them for Pharaoh.

9 Then the chief cupbearer spoke to Pharaoh, saying, I remember my faults this day:

10 Pharaoh was angry with his servants, and put me in custody in the house of the captain of the guard; both me and the chief baker:

11 And we each dreamed a dream in one night, he and I; each of us dreamed according to the interpretation of his own dream.

12 Now there was a young man with us there an Abrahu (Hebrew), a servant of the captain of the guard; and we told him, and he interpreted our dreams for us; to each man according to his dream he did interpret.

13 And it came to pass, as he interpreted to us, so it happened; I was restored to my office, and the baker was hanged.

14 Then Pharaoh sent and called Yosef, and they brought him quickly out of the dungeon: and he shaved, changed his clothing, and came to Pharaoh.

15 And Pharaoh said to Yosef, I have had a dream, and there is no one who can interpret it: and I have heard it said of you, that you can understand a dream to interpret it.

16 And Yosef answered Pharaoh, saying, It is not in me: Elohim will give Pharaoh an answer of shalom.[1]

17 Then Pharaoh said to Yosef, Behold, in my dream, I stood on the bank of the river:

18 Suddenly, seven cows came up out of the river, fine looking and fat; and they fed in the meadow:

19 And, behold, seven other cows came up after them, poor and very ugly and gaunt, such ugliness as I have never seen in all the land of Mitzrayim (Egypt):

20 And the gaunt and ugly cows ate up the first seven fat cows:

21 When they had eaten them up, no one would have known that they had eaten them; for they were just as ugly, as at the beginning. So I awoke.

22 Also I saw in my dream, and, suddenly, seven heads came up on one stalk, full and good:

23 Then, behold, seven heads, withered, thin, and scorched by the east wind, sprang up after them:

24 And the thin heads devoured the seven good heads; and I told this to the magicians; but there was no one who could explain it to me.

25 Then Yosef said to Pharaoh, The dreams of Pharaoh are one: Elohim has shown Pharaoh what He is about to do.

26 The seven good cows are seven years; and the seven good heads are seven years: the dream is one.

27 And the seven thin and ugly cows which came up after them are seven years; and the seven empty heads scorched by the east wind are seven years of famine.

28 This is the thing which I have spoken to Pharaoh: Elohim has shown Pharaoh what He is about to do.

29 Indeed, seven years of great plenty will come throughout all the land of Mitzrayim (Egypt):

30 But after them seven years of famine will arise; and all the plenty will be forgotten in the land of Mitzrayim (Egypt); and the famine will deplete the land;

31 And the plenty will not be known in the land because of the famine following, for it will be very severe.

32 And the dream was repeated to Pharaoh twice; because the

Footnotes
[1] Even though the Pharaoh was an unbeliever, Joseph does not want ill for him. This is the heart of a Hebrew, the fulfilling of the commandment. This is demonstrating the letter, and the spirit, of, 'love your neighbor as yourself', in reality.

thing is established by Elohim, and Elohim will shortly bring it to pass.[1]

33 Now therefore let Pharaoh select a discerning and wise man, and set him over the land of Mitzrayim (Egypt).

34 Let Pharaoh do this, and let him appoint officers over the land, to collect one-fifth of the produce of the land of Mitzrayim (Egypt) in the seven plentiful years.

35 And let them gather all the food of those good years that are coming, and store up grain under the authority of Pharaoh, and let them keep food in the cities.

36 And that food shall be a reserve for the land for the seven years of famine, which shall be in the land of Mitzrayim (Egypt); so that the land may not perish during the famine.

37 So the advice was good in the eyes of Pharaoh,[2] and in the eyes of all his servants.

38 And Pharaoh said to his servants, Can we find such a one as this, a man[3] in whom is the Ruakh (Holy Spirit) of Elohim?

Footnotes
[1] If something is repeated twice, then that thing is certain to come to pass.
[2] Yosef was about to get a name change, this is reflected in Tehillim (Psalm 81:5). The name in Tehillim is spelled with an extra Heh, indicating YHWH adding favour upon Yosef, now known as Yahosef, when the malakh Gabriel taught him the seventy languages that he needed, to become prime minister of Egypt.
[3] In the Talmud Rabbi Hiyya ben Abba said in the name of Rabbi Johanan: 'At the moment when Pharaoh said to Joseph, *And without you shall no man lift up his hand*, Pharaoh's astrologers exclaimed: 'Wilt thou set in power over us a slave whom his master bought for twenty pieces of silver!'
Continued in next section

39 Then Pharaoh said to Yosef, Because Elohim has shown you all this, there is no one as discerning and wise as you:

40 You shall be over my Beyth (house), and all my people shall be ruled according to your word: only in regard to the throne will I be greater than you.

41 And Pharaoh said to Yosef, See, I have set you over all the land of Mitzrayim (Egypt).[4]

42 Then Pharaoh took his signet ring from his own hand, and put it on Yosef's hand, and he clothed him in garments of fine linen, and put a gold chain around his neck;

43 And he had him ride in the second chariot which he had; and

He replied to them, 'discern in him royal characteristics.' They said to him, 'in that case he must be acquainted with the seventy languages.'

Malakh Gabriel came and taught [Joseph] the seventy languages, but he could not learn them. Thereupon [Gabriel] added to his name a letter from the Name of the Holy One, Blessed be He, and he learned [the languages]...' (Sotah 36b).

There were three who fled from sin and with whom the Holy One, Blessed be He, united His name. They are: Joseph, Yael, and Palti. How do we know it of Joseph? Because it says, He appointed it in Yehosef for a true report. What is the implication of the expression Yehosef? Elohim testifies in regard to him that he did not touch Potiphar's wife. (Midrash Rabbah - Leviticus 23:10)
[4] Before Yosef was made prime-minister of Egypt he had to go through a trial and had to be able to speak seventy languages, as this charge was brought by Pharaoh's officers and wise men. YHWH dispatched a malakh who taught Yosef seventy languages, and he took the office of the prime-minister in Egypt. See our compendium edition to the Bible.

they cried out before him, Bow the knee: and he set him over all the land of Mitzrayim (Egypt).

44 Pharaoh also said to Yosef, I am Pharaoh, and without your consent no man may lift his hand, or foot in all the land of Mitzrayim (Egypt).

45 And Pharaoh called Yosef's name Zaphnath-Paaneah.[1] And he gave him as a wife Asenath,[2] the daughter of Potipherah kohen (priest) of On. So Yosef went out over all the land of Mitzrayim (Egypt).

46 Yosef was thirty years old when he stood before Pharaoh King of Mitzrayim (Egypt). And Yosef went out from the presence of Pharaoh, and went throughout all the land of Mitzrayim (Egypt).

47 Now in the seven plentiful years the land brought forth abundantly.

48 So he gathered up all the food of the seven years which were in the land of Mitzrayim (Egypt), and laid up the food in the cities; he laid up in every city the food of the fields[3] which surrounded them.

49 Yosef gathered very much grain as the sand of the sea, until he stopped counting; for it was without number.

50 And to Yosef were born two sons before the years of famine came, which Asenath the daughter of Potipherah kohen (priest) of On bore to him.

51 Yosef called the name of the Bekhor (firstborn) Manasheh: For Elohim, has made me forget all my toil, and all my father's Beyth (house).

52 And the name of the second he called Efrayim:[4] For Elohim has caused me to be fruitful in the land of my affliction.

53 And the seven years of plenty that was in the land of Mitzrayim (Egypt), ended.

54 And the seven years of famine began to come, as Yosef had said: the famine was in all lands; but in all the land of Mitzrayim (Egypt) there was Lakhem (bread).

55 And when all the land of Mitzrayim (Egypt) was famished, the people cried to Pharaoh for Lakhem (bread): and Pharaoh said to all the Mitzrim (Egyptians), Go to Yosef; whatever he says to you, do.

56 The famine was over all the face of the earth: and Yosef opened all the storehouses, and sold to the Mitzrim (Egyptians);

Footnotes
[1] One of whom hidden things are revealed, Targum of Onkelos.
[2] Yosef would not marry the daughter of a heathen priest. This was the daughter of Dinah according to *Pirkei Rabbi Eliezer.* Do you want to believe that Yosef got everything else right but just forgot about not marrying a heathen daughter of a pagan priest? This is the problem when Christians are not taught fine details like this, which are strict Torah rules. Technically we are not forbidden into marrying into other cultures except the seven mentioned in the Torah, e.g., one can marry into the household of Ishmael or some other culture as long as we walk with wisdom as to whom we marry.

Footnotes
[3] Joseph made huge silos in Egypt and stored all the food in them
[4] Double fruitful. The name was used by Elohim later to signify the Ten scattered tribes.

and the famine became severe in the land of Mitzrayim (Egypt).

57 So all the countries came to Yosef in Mitzrayim (Egypt) to buy grain because the famine was severe in all lands.

Chapter 42

1 When Yakov saw that there was grain in Mitzrayim (Egypt), Yakov said to his sons, Why do you look at one another?

2 And he said, Indeed, I have heard that there is grain in Mitzrayim (Egypt): go down to that place, and buy for us there; that we may live, and not die.

3 So Yosef's ten brothers went down to buy grain in Mitzrayim (Egypt).

4 But Benyamin, Yosef's brother Yakov did not send with his brothers; for he said, Lest some calamity befall him.

5 And the sons of Israel went to buy grain among those who journeyed: for the famine was in the land of Kanan.[1]

6 Now Yosef was governor over the country, and it was he who sold to all the people of the land: and Yosef's brothers came, and bowed down before him with their faces to the earth.[2]

7 Yosef saw his brothers, and recognized them, but he acted as a stranger to them, and spoke harshly to them; and he said to them, Where do you come from? And they said, From the land of Kanan to buy food.

8 So Yosef recognized his brothers, but they did not recognize him.[3]

9 And Yosef remembered the dreams which he had dreamed about them, and said to them, You are spies; You have come to scrutinize the tracks of the country.[4]

10 And they said to him, No, my master, but your servants have come to buy food.

11 We are all one man's sons; we are honest men; your servants are not spies.

12 And he said to them, No, but you have come to see the inner workings of the country.

13 And they said, Your servants are twelve brothers, the sons of one man in the land of Kanan; and, in fact, the youngest is with our father today, and one is no more.

14 But Yosef said to them, It is as I spoke to you, saying, You are spies:

15 In this manner you shall be tested: By the life of Pharaoh, you shall not leave this place

Footnotes

[1] The 'land of Kanan' is the ancient term for the land of Israel.

[2] Now the dream, in the pashat (literal) level, comes true. The dream Yosef had while he was with them. When they insulted him, and made fun of him. Genesis 37:7, in the remez (hint), speaks of a future when all Ten Tribes will bow down to Messiah.

[3] The Ancient Greek Historian Herodotus upon his visit to Egypt in the 5th century BCE when the Monarchies had waned described the locals as black skinned and having woolly hair. When Yosef's brothers found him they did not recognize Him and thought he was an Egyptian. If the Egyptians were white or light brown as depicted in popular movies then ask yourself why did the alleged white brothers of Yosef did not recognize him in the Egyptians? This is how the deception of white Israel has spread amongst the nations.

[4] Septuagint

unless your youngest brother comes here.

16 Send one of you, and let him bring your brother; and you shall be kept in prison, that your words may be tested to see whether there is any truth in you; or else, by the life of Pharaoh, surely you are spies!

17 So he put them all together in prison three days.

18 Then Yosef said to them the third day, Do this and live, for I fear Elohim:

19 If you are honest men, let one of your brothers be confined to your prison house; but you, go and carry grain for the famine of your houses.

20 And bring your youngest brother to me; so your words will be verified, and you shall not die. And they did so.

21 Then they said to one another, We are truly guilty concerning our brother, for we saw the anguish of his soul when he pleaded with us, and we would not hear; therefore this distress has come upon us.

22 And Reuven answered them, saying, Did I not speak to you, saying, Do not sin against the young man'; and you would not listen? Therefore behold, his blood is now required of us.

23 But they did not know that Yosef understood them, for he spoke to them through an interpreter.[1]

24 And he turned himself away from them into a private area, and wept; and he returned to them again, and talked with them, and he took Shim'on from them, and bound him before their eyes.

25 Then Yosef gave a command to fill their sacks with grain, and to restore every man's money to his sack, and to give them provisions for the journey: and thus he did for them.

26 And they loaded their donkeys with the grain and departed from there.

27 And as one of them opened his sack to give his donkey feed at the encampment, he saw his money; and, there it was, in the mouth of his sack.

28 And he said to his brothers, My money has been restored; and, there it is, in my sack: and their hearts failed them, and they were afraid, saying to one another, What is this that Elohim has done to us?

29 And they came to Yakov their father to the country of Kanan, and told him all that had happened to them; saying,

30 The man, who is master of the land, spoke harshly to us, and took us for spies of the land.

31 And we said to him, We are honest men; we are not spies:

32 We are twelve brothers, sons of our father; one is no more, and the youngest is with our father this day in the country of Kanan.

33 Then the man, the master of the country, said to us, By this I

Footnotes
[1] They were communicating in Hebrew, and Joseph could speak and understand Hebrew; but he was communicating to them in the Egyptian language, using an interpreter to Continued in next section

communicate the Hebrew, so they would not know that he is their brother.

will know that you are honest men; leave one of your brothers here with me, take food for the famine of your households, and be gone:

34 And bring your youngest brother to me: then I shall know that you are not spies, but that you are honest men: so I will hand over your brother to you, and you may trade in this country.

35 And it happened as they emptied their sacks, that, surprisingly, each man's bundle of money was in his sack: and when they and their father saw the bundles of money, they were afraid.

36 And Yakov their father said to them, You have bereaved me: Yosef is no more, Shim'on is no more, and you want to take Benyamin away: all these things are come upon me.

37 Then Reuven spoke to his father, saying, Kill my two sons, if I do not bring him back to you: put him in my hands, and I will bring him back to you.

38 And he said, My son shall not go down with you; for his brother is dead, and he is left alone: if any calamity should befall him along the way in which you go, then you would bring down my gray hair with sorrow to the grave.

Chapter 43

1 Now the famine was severe in the land.

2 And it came to pass, when they had eaten up the grain which they had brought from Mitzrayim (Egypt), that their father said to them, Go back, buy us a little more food.

3 And Yahudah spoke to him, saying, The man solemnly warned us, saying, You shall not see my face, unless your brother is with you.

4 If you send our brother with us, we will go down and buy you food:

5 But if you will not send him, we will not go down: for the man said to us, You shall not see my face, unless your brother is with you.

6 And Israel said, Why did you deal so wrongfully with me, as to tell the man whether you had still another brother?

7 And they said, The man asked us pointedly about ourselves, and our Mishpakha (family), saying, Is your father still alive? Have you another brother? And we told him according to these words: could we possibly have known that he would say, Bring your brother down?

8 Then Yahudah said to Israel his father, Send the lad with me, and we will arise and go; that we may live, and not die, both we, and you, and also our little ones.

9 I will guarantee his safety; from my hand you shall require him: if I do not bring him back to you, and set him before you, then let me bear the blame forever.

10 For if we had not lingered, surely by now we would have returned this second time.

11 And their father Israel said to them, If it must be so, then do this; take some of the best fruits of this country in your vessels, and carry down a present for the

man, a little balm, and a little honey, spices, and myrrh, pistachio nuts, and almonds:

12 And take double money in your hand; and take back in your hand, the money that was returned in the mouth of your sacks; perhaps it was an oversight.[1]

13 Take your brother also, and arise, go back to the man:

14 And may El-Shaddai [2] give you loving-kindness before the man, that he may release your other brother, and Benyamin. If I lose my children, then I lose my children.

15 So the men took that present, and Benyamin; and they took double money in their hand, and arose, and went down to Mitzrayim (Egypt), and they stood before Yosef.

16 When Yosef saw Benyamin with them, he said to the steward of his house, Take these men to my home, and slaughter an animal and make ready; for these men will dine with me at noon.

17 Then the man did as Yosef ordered, and the man brought the men into Yosef's house.

18 Now the men were afraid because they were brought into Yosef's house; and they said, It is because of the money, which was returned in our sacks the first time, that we are brought in, so that he may seek an occasion against us and fall upon us, to take us as slaves with our donkeys.

19 When they drew near to the steward of Yosef's house, they talked with him at the door of the house,

20 And said, O sir, we indeed came down the first time to buy food:

21 And it happened, when we came to the encampment, that we opened our sacks, and, there, each man's money was in the mouth of his sack, our money in full weight: so we have brought it back in our hand.

22 And we have brought down other money in our hands to buy food: we do not know who put our money in our sacks.

23 And he said, Shalom Alekhem, do not be afraid: Your POWER, and the Elohim of your father, has given you treasure in your sacks: I had your money. Then he brought Shim'on out to them.

24 And the man brought the men into Yosef's house, and gave them mayim, and they washed their feet; and he gave their donkeys feed.

25 Then they made the present ready for Yosef's coming at noon: for they heard that they would eat Lakhem (bread) there.

26 And when Yosef came home, they brought him the present which was in their hand into the house, and bowed down before him to the earth.

Footnotes

[1] Some Christian pastors, teachers and Messinaic Rabbis have been in error, and cannot see past their rose tinted glasses, teaching that Jacob was a deceiver and a supplanter. We can see their error exposed here when Jacob, which means 'hand over heel'; and in the ancient Hebrew meaning is, 'YHWH, watching and guarding His House'. Jacob actually sends the money back to Yosef, which he had deliberately put in the sack, to show his honesty and integrity.

[2] The powerful breast.

27 Then he asked them about their well-being, and said, Is your elderly father well, the one of whom you spoke? Is he still alive?

28 And they answered, Your servant our father is in good health, he is still alive. And they bowed their heads down and prostrated themselves.

29 Then he lifted his eyes, and saw his brother Benyamin, his mother's son, and said, Is this your younger brother, of whom you spoke to me? And he said, Elohim be gracious to you, my son.

30 Now his heart yearned for his brother: so Yosef hurried; and sought somewhere to weep; and he went into his chamber, and wept there.

31 And he washed his face, and went out and he restrained himself, and said, Serve the Lakhem (bread).

32 So they set him a place by himself, and them by themselves, and the Mitzrim (Egyptians) who ate with him by themselves, because the Mitzrim (Egyptians) could not eat food with the Abrahu (Hebrews), for that is a ritually defilement[1] to the Mitzrim (Egyptians).[2]

33 And they sat before him, the Bekhor (firstborn) according to his birthright, and the youngest according to his youth: and the men looked in astonishment at one another.

34 Then he took servings to them from before him: but Benyamin's serving was five times as much as any of theirs. So they drank, and were merry with him.

Chapter 44

1 And he commanded the steward of his Beyth (house), saying, Fill the men's sacks with food, as much as they can carry, and put each man's money in the mouth of his sack.

2 Also put my cup, the silver cup, in the mouth of the sack of the youngest, and his grain money. So he did according to the word that Yosef had spoken.

3 As soon as the morning dawned, the men were sent away, they and their donkeys.

4 And when they had gone out of the city, and were not yet far off, Yosef said to his steward, Get up, follow the men; and when you overtake them, say to them, Why have you repaid evil for good?

5 Is not this the one from which my master drinks, and with which he forecasts?[3] You have done evil in so doing.

6 So he overtook them, and he spoke to them these same words.

7 And they said to him, Why does my master say these words? Far be it from us that your servants should do such a thing:

Footnotes
[1] The Hebrew word To'ebah's correct translation is not abomination but ritually defiled.
[2] This is because the Hebrews ate sheep and cows, and these are the deities of the Egyptians, whom they worshipped.

Footnotes
[3] The Egyptians used magic formulas, they also ascribed this to Yosef but Yosef was not doing it to commit magic but he used the cup to receive answer from YHWH upon prayer.

8 Look, we brought back to you from the land of Kanan: the money, which we found in the mouth of our sacks. How then could we steal silver, or gold from your master's Beyth (house)?

9 With whomever of your servants it is found, let him die, and we also will be my master's slaves.

10 And he said, Now also let it be according to your words; he with whom it is found shall be my slave; and you shall be blameless.

11 Then each man speedily let down his sack to the ground, and each opened his sack.

12 And he searched, and he began with the eldest, and left off with the youngest: and the cup was found in Benyamin's sack.

13 Then they tore their clothes, and each man loaded his donkey and returned to the city.

14 And Yahudah and his brothers came to Yosef's house; for he was still there: and they fell before him on the ground.

15 And Yosef said to them, What deed is this you have done? Did you not know that such a man as I can certainly forecast?

16 And Yahudah said, What shall we say to my master? What shall we speak? Or, how shall we clear ourselves? Elohim has found out the iniquity of your servants: see, we are my master's slaves, both we, and he also with whom the cup was found.

17 And he said, Far be it from me that I should do so: but the man in whose hand the cup is found, he shall be my slave; and as for you, go up in peace (shalom) to your father.

Torah Parsha 11 Vayigash, Beresheeth 44:18-47:27 Haftarah: Ykhezkiel 37:15-28

18 Then Yahudah came near to him, and said, O my master; please let your servant speak a word in my master's hearing, and do not let your anger burn against your servant: for you are even like Pharaoh.

19 My master asked his servants, saying, Have you a father, or a brother?

20 And we said to my master, We have a father, an elderly man, and a child of his old age, who is young; his brother is dead, and he alone is left of his mother's children, and his father loves him.

21 And you said to your servants, Bring him down to me, that I may set my eyes on him.

22 And we said to my master, The lad cannot leave his father: for if he should leave his father, his father would die.

23 And you said to your servants, Unless your youngest brother comes down with you, you shall see my face no more.

24 So it was, when we went up to your servant my father, that we told him the words of my master.

25 And our father said, Go back, and buy us a little food.

26 And we said, We cannot go down: if our youngest brother is with us, then we will go down: for we may not see the man's face,

unless our youngest brother is with us.

27 And your servant my father said to us, You know that my wife bore me two sons:

28 And the one went out from me, and I said, Surely he is torn to pieces; and I have not seen him since:

29 And if you take this one also from me, and calamity befalls him, you shall bring down my gray hair with sorrow to the grave.

30 Now therefore when I come to your servant my father, and the lad is not with us; since his life is bound up in the lad's life;

31 It will happen, when he sees that the lad is not with us, that he will die: and your servants will bring down the gray hair of your servant our father with sorrow to the grave.

32 For your servant became pledge for the lad to my father, saying, If I do not bring him back to you, then I shall bear the blame before my father forever.

33 Now therefore, please, let your servant remain instead of the lad as a slave to my master; and let the lad go up with his brothers.

34 For how shall I go up to my father, if the lad is not with me? Lest perhaps I see the evil that would come upon my father.

Chapter 45

1 Then Yosef could not restrain himself before all those who stood by him; and he cried out, Make everyone go out from me. So no one stood with him while, Yosef made himself known to his brothers.

2 And he wept aloud: and the Mitzrim (Egyptians) and the Beyth (house) of Pharaoh heard it.

3 Then Yosef said to his brothers, I am Yosef; does my father still live? And his brothers could not answer him; for they trembled in his presence.

4 And Yosef said to his brothers, Please come near to me. And they came near. And he said, I am Yosef your brother, whom you sold into Mitzrayim (Egypt).

5 Now therefore be not grieved, nor angry with yourselves because you sold me here: for Elohim sent me before you to preserve life.

6 For these two years the famine has been in the land: and yet there are still five years, in which there will be neither plowing nor harvesting.

7 And Elohim sent me before you to preserve a posterity for you in the earth, and to rescue your lives by a great rescue.[1]

Footnotes

[1] This verse is a Pashat (Literal Principal) and a Remez (Hint) because Adoni YHWH (The Egyptians would call Him Nb YHWH, Mar YHWH, or Kheri Yah Lord, Master, Owner, Possessor, Owner of the Shamayim and Eretz.) has always preserved His people. We Black Hebrews Israelites have been Sold into slavery, Poisoned with drugs and alcohol, Given diseases, Murdered, Lynched, Raped, Cursed, Spat upon, Incarcerated, and Impoverished, but we are still here and not only are we still here, Israel and Yahudah are being strengthened and nourished by the Torah again. YHWH is the Great Rescuer and will guard His people even though the gentiles used filthy tricks to obliterate us but did not succeed and will never succeed.
Continued in next section

8 So now it was not you who sent me here, but Elohim: and He has made me a father to Pharaoh, and master of all his house, and a ruler throughout all the land of Mitzrayim (Egypt).

9 Hurry, and go up to my father, and say to him, Thus says your son Yosef, Elohim has made me master of all Mitzrayim (Egypt): come down to me, do not tarry:

10 And you shall dwell in the land of Goshen, and you shall be near to me, you, and your children, your children's children, your flocks, and your herds, and all that you have:

11 And there I will provide for you; for there are still five years of famine; lest you, and your household, and all that you have, come to poverty.

12 And, behold, your eyes, and the eyes of my brother Benyamin, see that it is my mouth that speaks to you.

13 So you shall tell my father of all my splendour in Mitzrayim (Egypt), and of all that you have seen; and you shall hurry and bring my father down here.

14 Then he fell on his brother Benyamin's neck, and wept; and Benyamin wept on his neck.

15 Moreover he kissed all his brothers, and wept over them: and after that his brothers talked with him.

16 Now the report of it was heard in Pharaoh's house, saying, Yosef's brothers have come: and it pleased Pharaoh, and his servants well in their sight.

17 And Pharaoh said to Yosef, Say to your brothers, Do this; load your animals, and depart, go to the land of Kanan;

18 Bring your father and your households, and come to me: and I will give you the best of the land of Mitzrayim (Egypt), and you will eat the finest portions of the land.

19 Now you are commanded, do this; take carts out of the land of Mitzrayim (Egypt) for your little ones, and your wives, bring your father, and come.

20 Also do not be concerned about your goods; for the best of all the land of Mitzrayim (Egypt) is yours.

21 And the sons of Israel did so: and Yosef gave them carts, according to the command of Pharaoh, and he gave them provisions for the journey.

22 He gave to all of them to each man changes of garments; but to Benyamin he gave three hundred pieces of silver, and five changes of garments.

23 And he sent to his father these things; ten donkeys loaded with the good things of Mitzrayim (Egypt), and ten female donkeys loaded with grain Lakhem (bread) and food for his father for the journey.

24 So he sent his brothers away, and they departed: and he said to them, See that you do not cause a disturbance along the way.

These gentiles will be punished and will also lose their eternity since there is neither repentance nor remorse for what they have done and or are doing even presently.

25 Then they went up out of Mitzrayim (Egypt), and came to the land of Kanan to Yakov their father.

26 And they told him, saying, Yosef is still alive, and he is ruler over all the land of Mitzrayim (Egypt). And Yakov's heart fainted, because he did not believe them.

27 And when they told him all the words which Yosef had said to them; and when he saw the carts which Yosef had sent to carry him, the (ruakh) spirit of Yakov their father lived:

28 And Israel said, It is enough; Yosef my son is still alive: I will go and see him before I die.

Chapter 46

1 So Israel took his journey with all that he had, and came to Beersheva, and offered sacrifices to the Elohim of his father Ytshak.

2 And Elohim spoke to Israel in the visions of the night, and said, Yakov, Yakov,.[1] And he said, Here I am.

3 And He said, I am El (The Power), the Elohim of your father; do not fear to go down to Mitzrayim (Egypt), for I will make of you a great nation[2] there.

Footnotes
[1] Whenever YHWH says a word twice it means, pay close attention, this will come to pass.
[2] In Hebrew 'L'goyee gadol' means – a Great nation, physical multiplicity. This is to begin when they arrive in Egypt, using both the models of patriarchal marriages- monogamy and polygamy. And they all multiplied greatly, because they believed the command; to be fruitful, and multiply.

4 I will go down with you to Mitzrayim (Egypt); and I will also surely bring you up again: and Yosef's own hand will close your eyes.

5 And Yakov arose from Beersheva: and the sons of Israel carried their father Yakov, their little ones, and their wives, in the carts which Pharaoh had sent to carry him.

6 And they took their livestock, and their goods, which they had acquired in the land of Kanan, and went to Mitzrayim (Egypt), Yakov, and all his descendants with him:

7 His sons, and his sons' sons, his daughters, and his sons' daughters, and all his descendants he brought with him to Mitzrayim (Egypt).

8 Now these are the names of the children of Israel, who went to Mitzrayim (Egypt), Yakov and his sons: Reuven, Yakov's (Jacob's) Bekhor (firstborn).

9 The sons of Reuven; Khanokh, Pallu, Khetsron, and Carmi.

10 The sons of Shim'on; Yemu'el, Yamin, Ohad, Yaken, Zokhar, and Sha'ul, the son of a Kananit woman.[3]

11 The sons of Levi; Gershon, Kohath, and Merari.

12 The sons of Yahudah; Er, Onan, Shelah, Phratz, and Zerakh:[4] but Er and Onan died in

Footnotes
[3] This is evidence that Shi'mon had another wife at the same time, so he had children from Bunah this Kananit woman, alongside the children from Dinah, his principle first wife.
[4] This is the line of Messiah, with the legal marriage of Judah to Tamar.

the land of Kanan. And the sons of Phratz were Khetsron and Khamul.

13 The sons of Yskhar (Issachar); Tola, Puw'ah, Yobe (Job), and Shimron.

14 The sons of Zevulun; Sered, Elon, and Yakhle'el.

15 These were the sons of Le'yah, which she bore to Yakov in Padan Aram, with his daughter Dinah: all the persons of his sons and his daughters were thirty-three.

16 The sons of Gawd; Ziphion, Haggi, Shuni, Etzbon, Eri, Arodi, and Areli.

17 The sons of Asher; Yimnah, Ishuah, Isui, Bereyah, and Serah, their sister: and the sons of Bereyah; Kheber and Malkhi'el.

18 These were the sons of Zilpah, whom Laban gave to Le'yah his daughter, and these she bore to Yakov, sixteen persons.

19 The sons of Rakhel Yakov's wife: Yosef, and Benyamin.

20 And to Yosef in the land of Mitzrayim (Egypt) were born Manasheh and Efrayim, who Asenath the daughter of Potipherah Kohen (priest) of On bore to him.

21 The sons of Benyamin; Belah, Bakr, Ashbel, Gera, Naaman, Ehi, Rosh, Muppim, Khupim, and Ard.

22 These were the sons of Rakhel, who were born to Yakov: fourteen persons in all.

23 The son of Dan; Khushim.

24 And the sons of Naphtali; Yakhza'el, Guni, Yetser, and Shillem.

25 These were the sons of Bilhah, who Laban gave to Rakhel his daughter, and she bore these to Yakov: seven persons in all.

26 All the persons who went with Yakov to Mitzrayim (Egypt), who came from his body, besides Yakov's sons' wives, were sixty-six persons in all.

27 And the sons of Yosef, who were born to him in Mitzrayim (Egypt), were two persons:[1] all the persons of the house of Yakov, who went to Mitzrayim (Egypt), were seventy.[2]

28 Then he sent Yahudah before him to Yosef, to point out before him the way to Goshen: and they came to the land of Goshen.

29 And Yosef made ready his chariot, and went up to Goshen, to meet his father Israel, and he presented himself to him; and fell on his neck, and wept on his neck a good while.

30 And Israel said to Yosef, Now let me die, since I have seen your face, because you are still alive.

31 Then Yosef said to his brothers, and to his father's household, I will go up, and tell Pharaoh, and say to him, My brothers, and those of my father's house, who were in the land of Kanan, have come to me;

32 And the men are shepherds, for their occupation has been to feed livestock; and they have

Footnotes
[1] The LXX tells us Joseph had 9 sons. He also had daughters too.
[2] Septuagint reading is seventy-five.

brought their flocks, their herds, and all that they have.

33 So it shall be, when Pharaoh calls you, and says, What is your occupation?

34 That you shall say, Your servants' occupation has been with livestock from our youth even till now, both we, and also our father's: that you may dwell in the land of Goshen; for every shepherd is ritually unclean to the Mitzrim (Egyptians).[1]

Footnotes

[1] The Egyptians worshipped bulls and sheep as elohim, thus these people did not like those who ate these animals. The same can be seen in India today, where the Muslims and Christians eat cows; but Hindus worship the cows as Holy. Therefore they hate the people who eat these animals, and many times violence erupts because of this. This why this is called a ritual defilement by the gentiles.

Chapter 47

1 Then Yosef came and told Pharaoh, and said, My father and my brothers, their flocks, and their herds, and all that they possess, have come from the land of Kanan; and, indeed, they are in the land of Goshen.

2 And he took five men, from among his brothers, and presented them to Pharaoh.

3 And Pharaoh said to his brothers, What is your occupation? And they said to Pharaoh, Your servants are shepherds, both we, and also our father.

4 And they said to Pharaoh, We have come to dwell in the land; because your servants have no pasture for their flocks; for the famine is severe in the land of Kanan: now therefore please, let your servants dwell in the land of Goshen.

5 Then Pharaoh spoke to Yosef, saying, Your father and your brothers have come to you:

6 The land of Mitzrayim (Egypt) is before you; have your father and brothers dwell in the best of the land; let them dwell in the land of Goshen: and if you know any competent men among them, then make them chief herdsmen over my livestock.

7 And Yosef brought in his father Yakov, and set him before Pharaoh: and Yakov **Blessed** Pharaoh.

8 Pharaoh said to Yakov, How old are you?

9 And Yakov said to Pharaoh, The days of the years of my pilgrimage[1] are one hundred and thirty years:[2] few and evil have been the days of the years of my life, and they have not attained to the days of the years of the life of my ahvot (fathers) in the days of their pilgrimage.

10 So Yakov **Blessed** Pharaoh, and went out from before Pharaoh.

11 And Yosef situated his father and his brothers, and gave them a possession in the land of Mitzrayim (Egypt), in the best of the land, in the land of Rameses,[3] as Pharaoh had commanded.

12 Then Yosef provided his father, his brothers, and all his

Footnotes

[1] Today many believers are more concerned with building houses, and purchasing more and more property; but our forefathers saw themselves as pilgrims, even though the land of Israel had been given to them permanently by YHWH. Buying houses is not wrong; but our heart attitude needs to be in line with YHWH, to use those houses for YHWH, and not for our own selfishness.

[2] A gentile historian by the name of, Polyhistor from Demetrius, also states the age of Jacob, when he came into Egypt as 130, and that year to be the third year of the famine.

[3] Targum of Jonathan and the Jerusalem Targum call this land the land of Pelusium. But, this part of the country lay not in the Pelusiac but rather in the Heliopolitan home. Sir John Marsham gives his opinion that Rameses is the name of Pharaoh the then king of Egypt, because there were several kings of Egypt with that name and therefore he thinks this land was the king's land, the land of King Rameses, which Yosef placed his father and brethren in by the order of Pharaoh. Some writers believe, such as Jerome, that the Israelites built the city of Rameses. Dr. Shaw a learned historian takes the view that this Rameses is the land of Goshen, after the coming of the Israelites into it, and observes that, in the Egyptian language, 'Remsosch' signifies men that live a pastoral life.

father's household, with Lakhem (bread), according to the number in their Mishpakhot (families).

13 Now there was no Lakhem (bread) in all the land; for the famine was very severe, so that the land of Mitzrayim (Egypt) and all the land of Kanan languished because of the famine.

14 And Yosef gathered up all the money that was found in the land of Mitzrayim (Egypt), and in the land of Kanan, for the grain which they bought: and Yosef brought the money into Pharaoh's house.

15 So when the money failed in the land of Mitzrayim (Egypt) and in the land of Kanan, all the Mitzrim (Egyptians) came to Yosef, and said, Give us Lakhem (bread): for why should we die in your presence? For the money has failed.[1]

16 Then Yosef said, Give me your livestock; and I will give you Lakhem (bread) for your livestock, if the money is gone.

17 So they brought their livestock to Yosef: and Yosef gave them Lakhem (bread) in exchange for the horses, the flocks, the cattle of the herds, and for the donkeys: thus he fed them with Lakhem (bread) in exchange for all their livestock that year.

18 When that year had ended, they came to him the next year, and said to him, We will not hide from my master, that our money is gone; my master also has our herds of livestock; there is nothing left in the sight of my master, but our bodies, and our lands.

19 Why should we die before your eyes, both we and our land? Buy us and our land for Lakhem (bread), and we and our land will be servants of Pharaoh: give us seed, that we may live, and not die, that the land may not be desolate.

20 Then Yosef bought all the land of Mitzrayim (Egypt) for Pharaoh; for every man of the Mitzri (Egyptians) sold his field, because the famine was severe upon them: so the land became Pharaoh's.

21 And as for the people, he moved them into the cities from one end of the borders of Mitzrayim (Egypt) to the other end.

22 Only the land of the priests he did not buy; for the priests had rations allotted to them by Pharaoh, and they ate their rations which Pharaoh gave them: therefore they did not sell their lands.

23 Then Yosef said to the people, Indeed, I have bought you and your land this day for Pharaoh: look, here is seed for you, and you shall sow the land.

24 And it shall come to pass in the harvest, that you shall give one-fifth[2] to Pharaoh, and four-

Footnotes

[1] Illusion here is to money, which will fail one day and be worthless unless it's pegged to something tangible. This will happen in the future.

[2] This is the ancient form of taxation in fact Pharaoh's benevolence as he owned all the land, allowing them to keep 80% and giving only 20% to him, from here the sages teach if we are able to we should give 20% tzedekah/tithe as all the lands belong to YHWH after all the deductions. So as can be Continued in next section

fifths shall be your own, as seed for the field, and for your food, and for those of your households, and as food for your little ones.

25 So they said, You have rescued our lives: let us find favour in the sight of my master, and we will be Pharaoh's servants.

26 And Yosef made it a law over the land of Mitzrayim (Egypt) to this day, that Pharaoh should have one-fifth; except for the land of the priests only, which did not become Pharaoh's.

27 So Israel dwelt in the land of Mitzrayim (Egypt), in the province of Goshen; and they had possessions there, and grew, and multiplied exceedingly.

Torah Parsha 12 Vayechi, Beresheeth 47:28-50:26
Haftarah: Melekhim Alef 2:1-12

28 And Yakov lived in the land of Mitzrayim (Egypt) seventeen years: so the length of Yakov's life was one hundred and forty-seven years.

29 When the time drew near that Israel must die: he called his son Yosef, and said to him, Now if I have found favour in your sight, please put your hand under my thigh,[1] and deal kindly and truly with me. Please do not bury me in Mitzrayim (Egypt):

30 But let me lie with my ahvot (fathers), you shall carry me out of Mitzrayim (Egypt), and bury

me in their burial place. And he said, I will do as you have said.

31 Then he said, Swear to me. And he swore to him. So Israel bowed himself on the head of the bed.[2]

Chapter 48

1 Now it came to pass after these things, that Yosef was told, Indeed, your father is sick: and he took with him his two sons, Manasheh and Efrayim.

2 And Yakov was told, Look, your son Yosef is coming to you: and Israel strengthened himself, and sat up on the bed.

3 And Yakov said to Yosef, El-Shaddai appeared to me at Luz in the land of Kanan, and **Blessed** me,

4 And said to me, Behold, I will make you fruitful, and multiply you, and I will make of you a congregation of people;[3] and will give this land to your seed after you as an everlasting possession

5 And now your two sons, Efrayim and Manasheh, who were born to you in the land of Mitzrayim (Egypt) before I came to you in Mitzrayim (Egypt), are mine; as Reuven and Shim'on, they shall be mine.

6 Your offspring, whom you beget after them, shall be yours, and will be called by the name of their brothers in their inheritance.[4]

Footnotes
[2] The prophecy came true that said Joseph will put his hands on Jacob's closed eyes Gen 46:4.
[3] In Hebrew 'L'Qahal amim', means a congregation of people and this is everlasting people not temporal. This was the beginning of the congregation of Israel.
[4] They will carry the twelve tribal names.

seen taxation in a capitalist society, came out of the Torah; and also the loaning system is out of the Torah.
[1] Area of circumcision.

7 And as for me, when I came from Padan, Rakhel died beside me in the land of Kanan on the way, when there was but a little distance to go to Ephrath: and I buried her there on the way to Ephrath; that is Bayitlechem (Bethlehem).

8 Then Israel saw Yosef's sons, and said, Who are these?

9 And Yosef said to his father, They are my sons, whom Elohim has given me in this place. And he said, Please bring them to me, and I will **Bless** them.

10 Now the eyes of Israel were dim with age, so that he could not see. Then Yosef brought them near him; and he kissed them, and embraced them.

11 And Israel said to Yosef, I had not thought to see your face: and, in fact, Elohim has also shown me your children.

12 So Yosef brought them from beside his knees, and he bowed down with his face to the earth.

13 And Yosef took them both, Efrayim with his right hand toward Israel's left hand, and Manasheh with his left hand toward Israel's right hand, and brought them near him.

14 And Israel stretched out his right hand, and laid it on Efrayim's head, which was the younger, and his left hand[1] on Manasheh's head, guiding his

hands knowingly; for Manasheh was the Bekhor (firstborn).[2]

15 And he *spoke* a **Blessing** for Yosef, and said, Elohim, before whom my ahvot (fathers) Abraham and Ytshak walked, the Elohim who has fed me all my life long to this day,

16 the Malakh who has redeemed me[3] from all evil, **Bless** the lads; **LET MY NAME BE NAMED UPON THEM,[4] AND THE NAME OF MY AHVOT (FATHERS) ABRAHAM AND YTSHAK;[5] AND LET THEM GROW INTO A MULTITUDE IN THE MIDST OF THE EARTH.[6]**

17 Now when Yosef saw that his father laid his right hand on the head of Efrayim, it displeased

Footnotes

[2] Crossing the hand to place the **Blessings** on Efrayim, as this was lead by YHWH, to make him **Bless** more, since this is drash (allegorical) for the Ten Tribes of Israel. The right hand upon him specifies Binah (Understanding), Gevurah (Strength) and Hod (Awe). These will become mighty, powerful nations. The left hand on Menashsheh was for Chochmah (Wisdom), Chesed (Mercy), and Netzach (Victory). So the two sons will be given these qualities in the nations, they were to be dispersed in.

[3] Who is this special Malakh (Angel)? Since this same Malakh is called the Angel of the Lord or Angel of YHWH, its the same one that appeared to Abraham, to Moses and to Joshua who is called Captain of the Host of YHWH. Messiah Yahushua depicted in this.

[4] Many nations will be called and be in the character of Israel.

[5] Named in Abraham and Isaac, some like the Anglo/Saxons, qualify them to be from Isaac.

[6] In Hebrew, 'Vie-dagoo l'rov, karev eretz' means, Let them be like a great multitude of fish in the earth. This prophecy details how the two sons of Yosef prefigure the Ten tribes of Israel to be a multitude, to be gathered in the last days, happening in our time today and onwards to the end.

Footnotes

[1] Many Christians see a cross symbol here; but this is not the Babylonian pagan cross. See next footnote for an understanding on this.

him: and he took hold of his father's hand, to remove it from Efrayim's head to Manasheh's head.

18 And Yosef said to his father, Not so, my father: for this one is the Bekhor (firstborn);[1] put your right hand on his head.

19 But his father refused, and said, I know, my son, I know: he also shall become a people, and he also shall be great: but truly his younger brother shall be greater than he, and his descendants shall become a multitude of nations (melo ha goyim).[2]

20 And he **Blessed**[3] them that day, saying, In you shall Israel be **Blessed**, saying, Elohim make you as Efrayim and as Manasheh: and he set Efrayim before Manasheh.

21 Then Israel said to Yosef, Behold, I am dying: but Elohim will be with you, and bring you back to the land of your ahvot (fathers).

22 Moreover I have given to you one portion above your brothers, which I took from the hand of the Amoree with my sword and my bow.

Chapter 49

1 And Yakov called his sons, and said, Gather together, that I may tell you what shall befall you in the last days.

2 Gather together, and hear, you sons of Yakov, and listen to Israel your father.

3 Reuven, you are my Bekhor (firstborn), my might, and the beginning of my strength, the excellency of dignity and the excellency of power:

4 Unstable as mayim, you shall not excel; because you went up to your father's bed; then you defiled it: he went up to my couch. [4]

5 Shim'on and Levi are brothers; weapons of violence are their merchandise.

6 Let not my soul enter their council; let not my respect, be united to their assembly: for in their anger they slew a man, and in their self-will they dug up the wall.[5]

7 Cursed be their anger, for it is fierce; and their wrath, for it is

Footnotes
[1] Yosef thought his Abbah did not realise he was putting his right hand on the wrong son; but Jacob knew what he was doing, as it was directed by YHWH.
[2] Melo Ha Goyim, they will become many gentile nations. The same prophecy was given to Abraham in Beresheeth (Genesis) 12:3. The headship of all the tribes was shown, as in Bamidbar (Numbers) 2:18, where Efrayim is the head.
[3] Men cannot bless the Creator, it's incorrect to say we have any power to **bless** YHWH but that is how people speak the words without understadning the context. Man can give nothing to Yahweh El but it is He who gives us our **Blessings** and favour. Man can only obey Yahweh El and magnify his name in this way which in turn brings a Blessing and honour to His name.

Footnotes
[4] Reuben's birthright was removed because of his disobedience. He put his couch in his step-mum Bilhah's tent, not his mother; this was his Abbah's third wife. The early assemblies practiced Biblical polygyny, just like ancient Israel. Which was, and is, not a sin; but sleeping with your step-mother is sinful.
[5] The Hebrew can be read 'digged a wall', when they tore down Shkhem's house to kill the men there. Simeon and Levi were very strong men, and mighty fighters.

cruel: I will divide them in Yakov, and scatter them in Israel.

8 Yahudah, you are he whom your brothers shall praise: your hand shall be on the neck of your enemies; your father's children shall bow down before you. [1]

9 Yahudah is a young eagle from the prey; my son, you have gone up: he bows down; he stooped[2] down as an eagle, and as a lion; who shall rouse him?

10 The sceptre shall not depart from Yahudah, nor a lawgiver[3] from between his feet, to witness Shiloh[4] *and He* comes to receive Homage from the people.

Footnotes

[4] The prophecy of the coming of King Messiah Yahushua and that the Messiah was to come from Yahudah. All the Hebrew Targamim places this prophecy for the Messiah. The Hebrew word 'Shevet' is here translated 'Sceptre' and can also be translated 'Branch' 'Rod' or 'tribe.' The ancient word for Ad is to witness.

At the higher level they apply to the ultimate rule of King Messiah. (Yesha'yahu 11:1, Tehillim (Psalm) 23:4)

At the remez this shows that Yahudah will hold a distinct position in the twelve tribes and will not disappear as an identifiable entity and will appoint and rule until the King comes. Since the Ten tribes were rebellious as are many Christians today towards the Torah it also shows that Yahudah will remain closely aligned with Torah and will be so to speak, legally in charge of how things are conducted. Next time you cry legalistic be careful it is inbuilt in this prophecy by YHWH. The word for lawgiver, Machachok can easily be applied to this tribe in the Pashat understanding and we see Yahudah was to come back to the land of Israel first and they did in small numbers only, while the Ten tribes are still out there. The ashekenazi are not true Children of Israel but converts. The Ten will return with Teshuvah (Repentance) towards the Torah of YHWH at the appointed time. Tehillim Psalm 78.67 confirms this view. 'Moreover He refused the tent of Joseph, and chose not the tribe of Efrayim (Ten Tribes): But chose the tribe of Judah, the mount Tsiyon which He loved.' So did the Messiah fulfill the role of Shiloh the first time, the answer is <u>no</u>. Shiloh means to have peace and tranquility, but the Messiah Yahushua's first mission was to ratify the New Covenant that Israel broke at Mount Sinai and to bring redemption to the scattered tribes. So Shiloh, the King, who will rule, gather Israel and reign with peace has not yet happened and is still yet future since the majority of Israelites of Yahudah are still out of the land. So when Yahushua returns He will indeed return as the ruling king.

Midrash Rabba Genesis 98:8: ... 'until Shiloh comes' - this refers to the King Messiah. 'And Continued in next section

Footnotes

[1] The Ten tribes, namely many Christian nations, will one day go up to Israel and bow down their heads to Judah. The Christian world at that time will accept the decrees made by the Rebbim so bowing down means accepting and submitting to the Rebbim and the decrees they have established since YHWH made Judah the lawgiver. Judah is not going to hell as many have been teaching in churches. This has nothing to do with a dual Covenant; but the one Covenant, renewed by YHWH, with both Judah and the Ten tribes. Judah is first and Efrayim is second in line. The Ten tribes do not have exclusivity on the Covenant. If we read Nahum 1:15, a future prophecy, where Judah is commanded to keep the appointed feasts, meaning they never departed from Torah, so cannot be cast into hell as many think. The Torah is from Em Chockmah represents the Father's voice. He did not fulfil the prophesies the Messiah should have done, he cannot be accepted as the Messiah.

[2] The word rabbatz in the ancient pictographic Hebrew belongs to a bird. The word Aryeh means an eagle and not applicable to a lion in the first instance. The ancient word for a lion is Lebia.

[3] Judah is the lawgiver and when the Messiah comes Judah will keep the scepter but the people of the tribe of Judah will then be in submission to Messiah, since King David will also be resurrected then he will either be the Messiah himself or in co regent, one candidate for the Messiah is Daniel the prophet or one in likeness of.

11 Binding his donkey to the vine, and his donkey's colt to the choice vine; he washed his garments in wine, and his clothes in the blood of[1] grapes:[2]

12 His eyes are darker than wine, and his teeth whiter than milk.[3]

the obedience of the people be his' – he will come and blunt the teeth of the peoples of the world.

Midrash Rabba Genesis 99:7: 'until Shiloh comes' - the One to Whom the reign belongs.... 'And the obedience of the people be His' – He around Whom the nations gather, as it is stated: 'the root of Yishay that stands for a banner of the peoples, to it shall the nations seek' Yeshahyahu (Isa).11:10).

[1] This pictures two donkeys; one donkey is bound in judgment to the Messiah, which is none other than Yshmael, and his sons, the twelve tribes of Islam. Fighting against the other colt, Israel, which is bound in righteousness to the Messiah, to the choicest vine.

The choicest wine is the picture of the Messiah Himself. The first donkey is the wild man of Genesis 16:12 is Yshmael. His clothes, dripped in the blood of grapes, show us the picture of the coming thrashing of the Islamic armies. Which the Messiah will crush upon His return on the Mountains of Israel, in the battle of Armageddon mentioned in Ezekiel 38 and 39. The clothes of Messiah dripping with red blood, is not His own blood; but the enemies, which we find mentioned in Isaiah 34.6 and Isaiah 63:1-6. The great sacrifice in Edom. For more on this see the book World War III – Unmasking the End-Times Beast, by Rabbi Simon Altaf on www.forever-israel.com.

[2] Red grapes, a picture of the enemy that the Messiah will crush, these are the radical Islamists marked for the End of Days.

[3] Eyes here, are of the Messiah, because of the wrath to come on the Islamic nations, they are dark red in anger, while the teeth, whiter than white, represent his glory and His majesty.

13 Zevulun shall dwell by the haven of the sea; he shall become a haven for ships; and his border shall adjoin Sidon.

14 Yskhar (Issachar) is a strong donkey lying down between two burdens:[4]

15 He saw that rest was good, and that the land was pleasant; and he bowed his shoulder to bear a burden, and became a band of slaves.

16 Dan shall judge his people, as one of the tribes of Israel.

17 Dan shall be a serpent by the way, a viper by the path that bites the horse's heels, so that its rider shall fall backward.[5]

18 I have waited for your Yahshuah, O YHWH.

19 Gawd, a troop shall tramp upon him: but he shall triumph at last.

20 Out of Asher his Lakhem (bread) shall be rich, and he shall yield food fit for Kings.

21 Naphtali is a deer let loose: he gives goodly words.

22 Yosef is a fruitful son, a fruitful son[6] through the eyes;[1] his daughters run over the wall:[2]

Footnotes

[4] Targum of Jonathan, skilful in the doctrines of Torah. This is drash for them, having a burden for both houses of Israel to be Torah obedient, and be reconciled in akhad. It can symbolize a burden for two extreme borders. One is, STRICT Torah obedience, and the other is lax. Christians take the 'favor' doctrine without Torah obedience.

[5] Dan brought idolatry to Israel, through the hands of Jeroboam. This prophecy speaks about the End of Days, where the horse, is the horse of the anti-Messiah. The tribe of Dan has an important part to play in fighting the armies of Islam.

[6] The word for son in Hebrew here is 'ben' which reflects a rebuilder of a house. This is reflected in this prophecy with Yosef being Continued in next section

23 The archers have bitterly grieved him, shot at him, and hated him:[3]

24 But his bow remained in strength, and the arms of his hands were made strong by the hands of the Mighty Elohim of Yakov; from there is the Shepherd, the Stone of Israel,

25 By the El (Power) of your father, who will help you; and by the Almighty ,who will **Bless** you with **Blessings** of shamayim above, **Blessings** of the deep that lies beneath, **Blessings** of the breasts,[4] and of the womb:

26 The **Blessings** of your father have excelled, the **Blessings** of my ancestors up to the utmost bound of the everlasting hills: they shall be on the head of Yosef, and on the crown of the head of him who was separate from his brothers.

27 Benyamin is a ravenous wolf:[5] in the morning he shall devour the prey, and at night he shall divide the spoil. [6]

28 All these are the twelve tribes of Israel: and this is what their father spoke to them, and he **Blessed** them; he **Blessed** each one, according to his own **Blessing**.

29 Then he charged them, and said to them, I am to be gathered to my people: bury me with my ahvot (fathers) in the cave that is in the field of Ephron the Khitee,

30 In the tomb that is in the field of Machpelah, which is before Mamre, in the land of Kanan, which Abraham bought with the field of Ephron the Khitee as a possession for a burial place.

31 There they buried Abraham and Sarah his wife; there they buried Ytshak and Rivka his wife; and there I buried Le'yah.

the picture of the Messiah; but he looks very gentile. Yet he is a Hebrew, who was rebuilding his house, and protecting it while in Egypt, and obscurity. This tells us the Messiah will be veiled, until the end. As the brothers of Yosef did not recognize him until He openly spoke Hebrew, and told them, He was their brother.

[1] This word in the ancient Hebrew is 'ayin' meaning 'eyes' or 'sight.' Most of Christianity today relies on sight, rather than Faith. This prophecy tells us that many believers have come in via sight, meaning they saw miracles by sight, and are also the watchers Jer 31:6.

[2] The wall is the stumbling block that prevents them seeing Torah. So the 'daughters' are trying to step over the wall, which is the meaning behind the Hebrew.

[3] Yishmael, and Esaw, were both hunters, and archers.

[4] The same word is used for breast and almighty; and the same word is used for womb and mercy, they are both connected traits of YHWH. Through the Malchut (kingdom) of YHWH, which is the womb that births new life (meaning Born from above), connected with the tifereth (glory), which is the middle-pillar, taking us to the malchut (kingdom).

Footnotes

[5] The wolf is a highly monogamous creature, Benyamin remained less polygamous than the other tribes, hence ended up very small, and merged with Yahudah. They were strong; but at the same time, cunning like the wolf. Yahudah is described as a lion, a highly polygamous creature looking after his pride, so we can see in the descriptions of the Tanak, the tribe of Yahudah, where the Kings and people were polygamous alongside monogamy with many wives and many children.

[6] This prophecy is about the alleged apostle Paul who is described as a ravenous wolf so watch out as only the wolf/Satan can try to remove you from the Torah. Whether he did it deliberately or ignorantly he was trying to remove people from the Torah.

32 The field and the cave that is there were purchased from the sons of Kheth.

33 And when Yakov had finished commanding his sons, he drew his feet up into the bed, and breathed his last, and was gathered to his people.

Chapter 50

1 Then Yosef fell on his father's face, and wept over him, and kissed him.

2 And Yosef commanded his servants the physicians to embalm his father: and the physicians embalmed Israel.

3 And forty days were required for him; for such are the days required for those who are embalmed: and the Mitzrim (Egyptians) mourned for him seventy days.

4 And when the days of his mourning were past, Yosef spoke to the household of Pharaoh, saying, If now I have found favour in your eyes, please speak in the hearing of Pharaoh, saying,

5 My father made me swear, saying, Behold, I am dying: in my grave which I dug for myself in the land of Kanan, there you shall bury me. Now therefore please, let me go up, and bury my father, and I will come back.

6 And Pharaoh said, Go up, and bury your father, as he made you swear.

7 So Yosef went up to bury his father: and with him went up all the servants of Pharaoh, the elders of his house, and all the elders of the land of Mitzrayim (Egypt),

8 As well as all the beyth (house) of Yosef, his brothers, and his father's beyth (house): only their little ones, their flocks, and their herds, they left in the land of Goshen.

9 And there went up with him both chariots and horsemen: and it was a very great gathering.[1]

10 Then they came to the threshing floor of Atad, which is beyond the Yardan (Jordan), and they mourned there with a great and very solemn lamentation: and he observed seven days of mourning for his father.

11 And when the inhabitants of the land, the Kanani, saw the mourning at the threshing floor of Atad, they said, This is a deep mourning of the Mitzrim (Egyptians):[2] therefore its name was called Abel Mizraim, which is beyond the Yardan (Jordan).

12 So his sons did for him just as he had commanded them:

13 For his sons carried him to the land of Kanan, and buried

Footnotes

[1] The tribes were lined up in the procession, as in the Tent, even Esaw came with all his company of men, and mourned for his brother Jacob. Esaw and his sons fought a pitched battle with Jacob's sons, as they would not let them bury Jacob in the cave. Esaw had sold the land, and then lied about not selling it. Yosef was leading the battle, so we see an end time battle with the End times beast, Islam. When both the Christians, and the Hebrew people, will join together to fight them. Chushim, the son of Dan, cut off Esaw's head to settle the dispute at the cave, and then Jacob was buried. Radical Islamists will be humiliated and defeated the same way, after which we will see reconciliation between both, the twelve sons of Israel, and the Muslims.

[2] This text is proof that the ancient Israelites looked similar to Egyptians.

him in the cave of the field of Machpelah, before Mamre, which Abraham bought with the field from Ephron the Khitee as property for a burial place.

14 And after he had buried his father, Yosef returned to Mitzrayim (Egypt), he, and his brothers, and all who went up with him to bury his father.

15 When Yosef's brothers saw that their father was dead, they said, Perhaps Yosef will hate us, and may actually repay us for all the evil which we did to him.

16 So they sent messengers to Yosef, saying, Before your father died he commanded, saying,

17 Thus you shall say to Yosef: I beg you, please forgive the trespass of your brothers, and their sin; for they did evil to you: now, please, forgive the trespass of the servants of the Elohim of your father. And Yosef wept when they spoke to him.

18 Then his brothers also went and fell down before his face; and they said, Behold, we are your servants.

19 Yosef said to them, Do not be afraid: for am I in the place of Elohim?

20 But as for you, you meant evil against me; but Elohim meant it for good, in order to bring it about as it is this day, to rescue many people alive.

21 Now therefore do not be afraid: I will provide for you, and your little ones. And he comforted them, and spoke kindly to them.

22 And Yosef dwelt in Mitzrayim (Egypt), he, and his father's household: and Yosef lived one hundred ten years.

23 And Yosef saw Efrayim's children to the third generation: the children of Makhir, the son of Manasheh, were also brought up on Yosef's knees.

24 And Yosef said to his brethren, I am dying: and Elohim will surely visit you, and bring you out of this land to the land of which He swore to Abraham, to Ytshak, and to Yakov.

25 Then Yosef took an oath from the children of Israel, saying, Elohim will surely visit you, and you shall carry up my bones from here.

26 So Yosef died, being one hundred ten years old: and they embalmed him, and he was put in a coffin in Mitzrayim (Egypt). ת

The Second Book of Mosheh (Musa)

W'Elleh Shemoth (Exodus)

ואלה שמות

And these are Names

Torah Parsha 13 Shemoth, Shemoth 1:1-6:1
Haftarah: Yeshayahu 27:6-28:13 & 29:22-23

Chapter 1

1 Now these are the names of the children of Israel, which came to Mitzrayim (Egypt); each man and his household came with Yakov.

2 Reuven, Shim'on, Levi, and Yahudah,

3 Yskhar (Issachar), Zevulun, and Benyamin,

4 Dan, Naphtali, Gawd, and Asher.

5 All those who were descendants of Yakov were seventy persons: for Yosef was in Mitzrayim (Egypt) already.

6 And Yosef died, and all his brothers, and all that generation.

7 And the children of Israel were fruitful, and **Blessed** abundantly,[1] multiplied, and grew exceedingly mighty; and the land was filled with them.

8 Now there arose a new King over Mitzrayim (Egypt), who did not know Yosef.

9 And he said to his people, Look, the people of the children of Israel are more and mightier than we:

10 Come, let us deal wisely with them; lest they become large,[2] and if it comes to be, in the event of war, that they also join our enemies and fight against us, and so go up out of the land.

11 Therefore they set taskmasters over them[3] to afflict them with their burdens. And they built for Pharaoh supply cities, Pithom and Raamses.

12 But the more they afflicted them, the more they multiplied and grew[4]. And they were in dread of the children of Israel.

13 So the Mitzrim (Egyptians) made the children of Israel serve with rigor:

14 And they made their lives bitter with hard bondage, in mortar, in brick, and in all manner of service in the field: all their service, in which they made them serve, was with rigor.

15 Then the King of Mitzrayim (Egypt) spoke to the Abrahu

Footnotes

[1] All of Israel practiced patriarchal polygamy so therefore grew great in a short space of time. YHWH's model for Israel was, and is, to produce offspring, and not just to be a one child family like the Chinese. Our model is Patriarchal while the nations is monogamy the satanic model out of Rome and Greece which is why the world is in such a mess.

[2] Plural marriage was/is the Hebrew standard according to the Torah so the nations were afraid the Israelites would increase with many wives and children's. Today they impose monogamy upon you the Greek model of marriage.

[3] The Task Masters were Hebrews they took the hits on behalf of the Hebrews and Hashem gave them merit to have the Sanhedrin.

[4] YHWH had **Increased** Israel with organic growth. Patriarchal marriage was the model and is being restored in these last days. At the beginning of the millennium kingdom many women will come to the Abrahu (Hebrew) man and say please take us for wife, there will be seven wives to one man Isa 4:1.

(Hebrew) midwives, of which the name of one was Shiphryah, and the name of the other Puyah:

16 And he said, When you do the duties of a midwife for the Abrahu (Hebrew) women, and see them on the birth stones; if it be a son, then you shall kill him: but if it be a daughter, then she shall live.[1]

17 But the midwives feared Elohim, and did not do as the King of Mitzrayim (Egypt) commanded them, but rescued the male children alive.

18 So the King of Mitzrayim (Egypt) called for the midwives, and said to them, Why have you done this thing, and rescued the male children alive?

19 And the midwives said to Pharaoh, Because the Abrahu (Hebrew) women are not like the Mitzrim (Egyptians) women; for they are lively, and give birth

before the midwives come to them.

20 Therefore Elohim dealt well with the midwives: and the people multiplied, and grew very mighty.[2]

21 And so it was, because the midwives feared Elohim, that He provided households for them.

22 So Pharaoh commanded all his people, saying, every son who is born, ye shall cast into the river, and every daughter ye shall save alive.

Chapter 2

1 And a man[3] of the Beyth (house) of Levi went and took as wife, a daughter of Levi.[4]

2 So the woman conceived, and bore a son: and when she saw that he was a beautiful child,[5] she hid him three months.

Footnotes

[1] When the world cannot win against Israel they opt out for genocide; but Israel will still prevail. For Israel, life, is above all else, and must be preserved irrespective of what the local government tells you. Killing children, whether by abortion, or some other method, is murder. Many Christians are practicing murder by even killing their babies. This dastardly deed was advised to Pharaoh by no other than, Job, before he got saved, the man from Uz. See our compendium edition to the Torah. Yashar 66:21-22: if it pleases the king, let a royal decree go forth, and let it be written in the laws of Mitzrayim which shall not be revoked, that every male child born to the Israelites, his blood shall be spilled upon the ground. 22, And by your doing this, when all the male children of Israel shall have died, the evil of their wars will cease; let the king do so and send for all the Hebrew midwives and order them in this matter to execute it; so the thing pleased the king and the princes, and the king did according to the word of Job.

[2] Even though the midwives lied, YHWH still **Increased** them because they held life above all else, and Israel can never be cursed by anyone. If anyone thinks they can curse true Hebrew Israel of colour and still be **Increased**, they are simply mistaken and live in their own delusion. It is better to listen to YHWH than those in the world around you, who live in their state of confusion. They think it is okay to believe in the government's laws, even if they contradict Torah and allow murder. We respect the government laws but do not approve of them; but we are pro life so as not to cause anarchy, and confusion. Our primary focus, for us, and our families, is YHWH, and, His Torah, as supreme. YHWH's laws are above board and must be adhered to wherever you are in the world.

[3] The father of Moses was called Amram.

[4] Moses mother was called Yah'kobad.

[5] When Moses was born he was born after his sister Miriam prophesied that he will release Israel, so would be the saviour of Israel sent by YHWH. Pharaoh's daughter who took him in, her name was Bathia, Moses' Hebrew name given to him by his Continued in next section

3 And when she could no longer hide him, she took an ark of bulrushes for him, daubed it with asphalt and pitch,[1] put the child in it; and laid it in the reeds by the river's bank.

4 And his sister stood afar off, to know what would be done to him.

5 And the daughter[2] of Pharaoh came down to wash herself at the river; and her maidens walked along the river's side; and when she saw the ark among the reeds, she sent her maid to get it.

6 And when she had opened it, she saw the child: and, behold, the baby wept. And she had

compassion on him, and said, This is one of the Abrahu (Hebrew) children.[3]

7 Then his sister said to Pharaoh's daughter, Shall I go and call a nurse for you from the Abrahu (Hebrew) women, that she may nurse the child for you?

8 And Pharaoh's daughter said to her, Go. So the young maid went and called the child's mother.

9 Then Pharaoh's daughter said to her, Take this child away, and nurse him for me, and I will give you your wages. And the woman took the child and nursed him.[4]

10 And the child grew, and she brought him to Pharaoh's daughter, and he became her son.[5] So she called his name

mother Yah'kobad was Yah'kuthi'el, his father called him Khabar, his sister Miriam called him Yah'red. His brother Aaron called his name Abi'zanuch. Kehath Moses' grandfather called his name Abigdor, as it is a tradition to name sons by the elders too. Moses' nurse called him Abi'sokho. The rest of Israel called him ShemiYah. As can be seen Moses was a man of many names. Meanings of Moses' names, the longer versions:
a) Khabar- (It was for him that he associated with his wife whom he had turned away)
b) Yah'kuth'el- (I have hoped for him to the Almighty, and El-Yah restored him unto me).
c) Yah'red- (for she descended after him to the river to know what his end would be).
d) Abi'zanuch - (My father left my mother and returned to her on his account).
e) Abigdor- (on his account did EL-Yah repair the breach of the house of Jacob).
f) Abi'sokho - (In his tent was he hidden for three months).
g) Shemi'Yah- (In his days has El-Yah heard their cries and rescued them from their oppressors).
[1] Israel knew about crude oil long before the Arabs found it.
[2] Pharaoh daughter's name was Bathia according to some sources. Moses's adopted mother is called Thermuth in the book of Jubilees and Thermuthis by Josephus the historian in the early first century CE.

Footnotes

[3] She knew the child was a Hebrew, because the Hebrew children were fair, and beautiful, and of course circumcised. She also knew the edict that her father had set.

[4] Moses was black who grew as a prince in Pharaoh's household, likewise some people who get saved grow up in satanic homes; but come out later serving the great King. Satan was foiled once again when Bathia Pharaoh's daughter was paying Moses' own mother for him to grow up, and he did not even know it! The increases come like this to Hebrew children, that the wicked money, serves the righteous.

[5] Moses was not recognized in the Pharaoh's home that he is a Hebrew child because he was black in colour and looked like Pharaoh. If he was Caucasian they would have discovered him and killed him. We have fancy ideas today of him being of white skin which is popular in movies is nothing short of ignorance. During Moses adoption Seti I was the Pharaoh of Egypt. This is how one English historian George Rawlinson described him.

In the book History of Egypt. On page 252, the description of Seti I is as follows; He states in vivid details: "Seti's face was Continued in next section

Mosheh (Musa) [1] (Moses): saying, Because I drew him out of the mayim.

11 Now it came to pass in those days, when Mosheh (Musa) was grown, that he went out to his brethren and looked at their burdens: and he saw a Mitzri (Egyptian) beating an Abrahu (Hebrew), one of his brethren.

12 So he looked this way, and that way, and when he saw no one, he killed the Mitzri (Egyptian) and hid him in the sand.[2]

THOROUGHLY AFRICAN. He had a stormy face with a DEPRESSED FLAT NOSE, THICK LIPS and heavy chin."

Taking George's text into consideration it would be very hard for anyone to believe that Moses was Caucasian since he was called Pharaoh's grandson, one would be hard pushed not to notice a white skinned baby as an oddity in the Pharaoh's household. Only those people who are unaware of Egyptian history can believe such things, while the Israelites were a people whose ancestors came out of Africa such as Noakh, Cham, Shem and even Yapheth. Due to this type of ignorance we find movies depicting Hebrews such as Abraham, Moses, King David and King Solomon as white skinned people.

[1] The correct name of Moses in the ancient Egyptian language is written 'Mousses'; but pronounced close to Mosheh (Musa) which is very similar to the Arabic language today. The name developed as 'Moshe' is not his Egyptian name, this modern Hebrew appellation, unfortunately, is not correct because the name Moshe is not a Hebrew name; but an Egyptian one which means, 'to draw out of water.' See footnote Exo 2:2 for Mosheh (Musa)'s many Hebrew names.
[2] The Egyptian was trying to rape a Hebrew woman, and that is why Moses protected the woman and killed the Egyptian. This was not an act of aggression, or murder; but an act of kindness, and self defence to preserve Israel. Many Christians have erred over this one teaching, that it was murder.

13 And when he went out the second day, behold, two Abrahu (Hebrew) men were fighting: and he said to the one who did the wrong, Why are you striking your companion?

14 And he said, Who made you a prince and a judge over us? Do you intend to kill me, as you killed the Mitzri (Egyptian)? And Mosheh (Musa) feared, and said, Surely this thing is known.

15 When Pharaoh heard of this matter, he sought to kill Mosheh (Musa). But Mosheh (Musa) fled from the face of Pharaoh, and dwelt in the land of Midian: and he sat down by a well.

16 Now the kohen (priest) of Midian[3] had seven daughters: and they came and drew mayim, and they filled the troughs to water their father's flock.

17 Then the shepherds came and drove them away: but Mosheh (Musa) stood up and helped them, and watered their flock.

18 When they came to Reuel their father, he said, How is it that you have come so soon today?

19 And they said, A Mitzri (Egyptian)[4] rescued us from the hand of the shepherds, and he also drew enough mayim for us, and watered the flock.

20 So he said to his daughters, And where is he? Why is it that you have left the man? Call him, that he may eat Lakhem (bread).

Footnotes
[3] Jethro was also an advisor to Pharaoh, before he got saved. He was connected to Eber's lineage. He was black.
[4] Moses is described here as a black Egyptian.

21 Then Mosheh (Musa) was content to live with the man: and he gave Zipporah his daughter to Mosheh (Musa).[1]

22 And she bore him a son, and he called his name Gershom:[2] for he said, I have been a stranger in a foreign land.

23 Now it happened in the process of time that the King of Mitzrayim (Egypt) died: and the children of Israel groaned because of the bondage, and they cried out, and their cry came up to Elohim because of the bondage.[3]

24 So Elohim heard their groaning, and Elohim remembered His Covenant[4] with Abraham, with Ytshak, and with Yakov.

25 And Elohim looked upon the children of Israel, and Elohim considered[5] their plight.

Chapter 3

1 Now Mosheh (Musa) was tending the flock of Ythro his father-in-law, the kohen (priest) of Midian:[6] and he led the flock to the back of the wilderness, and came to Horev, the mountain of Elohim.

2 And Malakh YHWH appeared to him in a flame of fire from the midst of a bush: and he looked, and, behold, the bush was burning with fire, but the bush was not consumed.

3 Then Mosheh (Musa) said, I will now turn aside, and see this great sight, why the bush does not burn.

4 And when YHWH saw that he turned aside to look, Elohim called to him from the midst of the bush and said, Mosheh (Musa), Mosheh (Musa) (Moses, Moses).[7] And he said, Here I am.

5 And He said, Do not draw near to this place: take your sandals off [8] your feet, for the place where you stand is Holy ground.

6 Moreover He said, I am the Elohim of your father, the Elohim of Abraham,[9] the Elohim of

Footnotes

[1] This did not happen over night. Moses was held prisoner by Yah'thro (Jethro) for ten years, before he was freed. He pulled the rod out of his garden, with the name of YHWH, that Yah'thro (Jethro) had planted and had said, whosoever will pull it out of the ground, will marry my daughter. This can be read in the scroll of Yashar the compendium edition from Forever-israel website.

[2] Stranger

[3] YHWH listens to Israel's problems.

[4] YHWH decided to favour Israel because of their father Abraham and the Covenant formed with him.

[5] In Ancient Abaru (Hebrew) the word Yada has a Covenant meaning of a king and a suzerain vassal where the king remembers to protect his vassal if the vassal is in distress so this is why the word Yada here cannot just mean 'to know' but means 'to consider and send help' and can also mean YHWH felt Israel's pain in captivity and bondage so decided to act by sending the rescuer.

Footnotes

[6] North Eastern Saudi Arabia.

[7] Speaking a name twice, or using a term twice, implies the thing is of great importance and shows a spiritual connection, and relationship aspect to the Covenant established earlier with father Abraham.

[8] The sandals were made of leather, of dead animal skins, and YHWH does not allow death near him since He is by definition 'LIFE', so told him to remove DEATH from you and come stand near LIFE.

[9] As I said earlier he called Moses by his name twice and now He tells him, I am YHWH the Elohim of Abraham, meaning Continued in next section

Ytshak, and the Elohim of Yakov. And Mosheh (Musa) hid his face; for he was afraid to look[1] upon Elohim.

7 And YHWH said: I have surely seen the pain of My people who are in Mitzrayim (Egypt), and have heard their cry because of their taskmasters; for I know their affliction:

8 So I have come down to rescue them out of the hand of the Mitzrim (Egyptians), and to bring them up from that land to a good and large land, to a land flowing with milk and honey; to the place of the Kanani,[2] and the Khitee, and the Amoree, and the Perzee, and the Khuvi, and the Yavusi.

9 Now therefore, behold, the cry[3] of the children of Israel has come to Me: and I have also seen the oppression with which the Mitzrim (Egyptians) oppress them.

10 Come now therefore, and I will send you to Pharaoh, that you may bring My people the children of Israel out of Mitzrayim (Egypt).

11 And Mosheh (Musa) said to Elohim, Who am I, that I should go to Pharaoh, and that I should bring the children of Israel out of Mitzrayim (Egypt)?[4]

12 And He said, I will certainly be with you; and this shall be a sign to you, that I have sent you: When you have brought the people out of Mitzrayim (Egypt), you shall serve Elohim on this mountain.[5]

13 And Mosheh (Musa) said to Elohim, Indeed, when I come to the children of Israel, and say to them, The Elohim of your ahvot (fathers) has sent me to you; and they say to me, What is His name? What shall I say to them?

14 And Elohim said to Mosheh (Musa),

AHaYaH Ashar[6] AHaYaH: and He said, Thus you shall say to

Footnotes

YHWH is reminding him, I have a duty and a Covenant with your forefathers. This is why I am here to discuss what needs to happen.

[1] Moses knew that no one could see Elohim and live, so he was afraid that he might die. It is true that if we see the great Ein Sof Abbah YHWH as He is in His Holy Temple above, we cannot behold His incredible light and we will be consumed in a second; but He has to make adjustments for us to be able to see Him and live.

[2] The land of Kanan was now to be called Israel, and the children of Israel were to inherit the land, as the people of this land were idolatrous, and their time had come to be evicted since they did not repent of their sins.

[3] The cry of the righteous came up, and the cry for wickedness can also ascend up, when the righteous pray for wickedness to be removed as in Sedom and Amorah, Genesis 18:20 and also in Exodus 2:23.

[4] Elohim chose Moses because he was a Levite, and the right man to bring Israel out and teach them the Torah of YHWH.

[5] Mount Horeb or Mount Sinai in Saudi Arabia; also known as Jabal al Luz or Jabal al Mosheh (Musa).

[6] This is pronounced in Modern Hebrew as EhYeh Ashar EhYeh. Some believe this is the name of the Master of Shamayim, which was replaced with Yud, Heh, Wah and Heh, however so far we do not have any such evidence to validate this claim. In our opinion we pronounce this text as The Yah that Was the Yah. The word is spelled Alef + Heh + Yud + Heh. The Alef is the signature of the Father as the source of all things, who is defined as the Keter in the Sefirotic tree, the Heh is the term for 'The'; but in the tree it is the reference attribute for Cochmah

Continued in next section

the children of Israel, 𐤟𐤟𐤟 AHaYaH has sent me to you. [1]

15 Moreover Elohim said to Mosheh (Musa), Thus you shall

say to the children of Israel, YHWH Elohim of your ahvot (fathers), the Elohim of Abraham, the Elohim of Ytshak, and the Elohim of Yakov, has sent me to you: this is My Name forever,[2] and this is My memorial[3] to all generations.

16 Go, and gather the elders of Israel together, and say to them, YHWH Elohim of your ahvot (fathers), the Elohim of Abraham, of Ytshak, and of Yakov, appeared to me, saying, I have surely visited you and seen what is done to you in Mitzrayim (Egypt):

17 And I have said, I will bring you up out of the affliction of Mitzrayim (Egypt) to the land of the Kanani, and the Khitee, and the Amoree, and the Perzee, and the Khuvi, and the Yavusi, to a land flowing with milk and honey.

18 And they will heed your voice: and you shall come, you

(wisdom) the Ruakh Ha Kodesh, and represents YH for Yah. Therefore the first character is for Alef for the Father's signature, The Son is revealed in the first Character of Alef which in ancient thought is for earth/man while the second character is Heh which is for the nostrils or breath followed by the YUD and Heh forming Aha-

YAH 𐤟𐤟𐤟. This reveals the Keter crown upon the middle-pillar, through whom which we can go to the Malchut (Kingdom) via the Tifereth and Yesod. In Ancient Hebrew it does not translate to 'I AM'; but, The Light of the World' as AHa-Yah. So I Am The Yah would be in Pictographic script

𐤟𐤟𐤟. The Modern Hebrew really tells us nothing of the ancient meaning as

follows: אהיה אשר אהיה. 𐤟𐤟𐤟 𐤟𐤟𐤟AhaYah means "Light over the earth" and Ashar means "Risen sun over men."

[6] There is a missing Wah in the word Olam (forever) so some ancient Rebbim translate this word to an alternative reading, as Alem, meaning, to conceal or to hide; but then it would make no sense for the next statement which says, it is a remembrance to all generations. So, if the name was to be concealed, it cannot be a remembrance, however it can mean concealed under certain circumstances in order to protect the name which is also important because we must protect the Holy name and not use it in various states such as a ritually unclean one and also must not throw it around like a magic formula and defiling it. There are ways to protect it. Please see our article in www.forever-israel.com under Ask the Rabbi. The article is how to protect the name.

[1] The Modern Hebrew does not tell us the correct ancient meaning: אהיה אשר אהיה

𐤟𐤟𐤟 𐤟𐤟 𐤟𐤟𐤟

AhaYah means "Light over the earth" and Ashar means "Risen sun over the earth." In this passage we find the true name of YHWH.

Footnotes

[2] There is a missing Wah in the word Olam (forever) so some ancient Rebbim translate this word to an alternative reading, as Alem, meaning, to conceal or to hide; but then it would make no sense for the next statement which says, it is a remembrance to all generations. So, if the name was to be concealed, it cannot be a remembrance, however it can mean concealed under certain circumstances in order to protect the name which is also important because we must protect the Holy name and not use it in various states such as a ritually unclean one and also must not throw it around like a magic formula and defiling it. There are ways to protect it. Please see our article in www.forever-israel.com under Ask the Rabbi. The article is how to protect the name.

[3] How can the name be a memorial to all descendants if it was 'I was', as wrongly thought? This is why this statement would make no sense if the name revealed was not YHWH.

and the elders of Israel, to the King of Mitzrayim (Egypt), and you shall say to him, YHWH Elohim of the Abrahu (Hebrews) has met with us: and now please, let us go three days' journey into the wilderness, that we may sacrifice to YHWH our POWER.

19 But I know that the King of Mitzrayim (Egypt) will not let you go, no, not even by a mighty hand.

20 So I will stretch out My hand and strike Mitzrayim (Egypt) with all My wonders which I will do in its midst; and after that he will let you go.

21 And I will give this people favour in the sight of the Mitzrim (Egyptians): and it shall be, when you go, that you shall not go empty-handed.

22 But every woman shall ask of her neighbour, namely, of her who dwells near her Beyth (house), articles of silver, articles of gold, and clothing: and you shall put them on your sons, and on your daughters;[1] and you shall plunder the Mitzrim (Egyptians).

Chapter 4

1 Then Mosheh (Musa) answered and said, But, suppose, they will not believe me, or listen to my voice; suppose they say, YHWH has not appeared to you

2 So YHWH said to him, What is that in your hand? And he said, A rod.

3 And He said, Cast it on the ground. So he cast it on the

ground, and it became a serpent; and Mosheh (Musa) fled from it.[2]

4 Then YHWH said to Mosheh (Musa), Reach out your hand, and take it by the tail. And he reached out his hand, and caught it, and it became a rod in his hand:

5 That they may believe that YHWH Elohim of their ahvot (fathers), the Elohim of Abraham, the Elohim of Ytshak, and the Elohim of Yakov, has appeared to you.

6 Furthermore YHWH said to him, Now put your hand in your bosom. And he put his hand in his bosom: and when he took it out, behold, his hand was leprous, like snow.[3]

7 And He said, Put your hand in your bosom again. And he put his hand in his bosom again; and drew it out of his bosom, and, behold, it was restored like his other flesh.

8 Then it will be, if they do not believe you, nor heed the message of the first sign, that they may believe the message of the latter sign.[4]

Footnotes
[1] Wearing Jewellery is not a sin as some err on this subject.

Footnotes
[2] Moses was brought up in Egypt where there were a lot of magicians, and snake charmers. So, he ran away because he was scared of snakes. But what YHWH did was to remove the fear that Moses had grown up with so he would no longer be afraid of snakes. To remove our fears we must confront them head on.
[3] Obviously Moses was not Caucasian lily white, as depicted in the famous movie The Ten Commandments, otherwise his hand turning white would make no sense. He was similar to the African look.
[4] Note the first thing any true servant of YHWH needs to bring is His Holy name YHWH, and if that man comes in any other
Continued in next section

9 And it shall be, if they do not believe even these two signs, or listen to your voice, that you shall take mayim from the river, and pour it on the dry land: and the mayim which you take from the river will become blood on the dry land.

10 Then Mosheh (Musa) said to YHWH, O YHWH, [1] I am not eloquent, neither before, nor since You have spoken to Your servant: but I am slow of speech, and slow of tongue.

11 And YHWH said to him, Who has made man's mouth? Or, who makes the mute, the deaf, the seeing, or the blind? Have not I, YHWH?

12 Now therefore go, and I will be with your mouth, and teach you what you shall say.

13 And he said, O YHWH[2], please; send by the hand of whomever else You may send.

14 And the anger of YHWH was kindled against Mosheh (Musa), and He said, Is not Aharon the Levite your brother? I know that he can speak well. And look, he is also coming out to meet you: and when he sees you, he will be glad in his heart. [3]

15 And you shall speak to him, and put the words in his mouth: and I will be with your mouth, and with his mouth, and I will teach you what you shall do.

16 And he shall be your spokesman to the people: and he himself shall be as a mouth for you, and you shall be to him as elohim.[4]

17 And you shall take this rod[5] in your hand, with which you shall do the signs.

18 So Mosheh (Musa) went and returned to Ythro his father-in-law, and said to him, Please, let me go, and return to my brethren who are in Mitzrayim (Egypt), and see whether they are still alive. And Ythro said to Mosheh (Musa), Go in shalom.

19 And YHWH said to Mosheh (Musa) in Midian, Go, return to Mitzrayim (Egypt): for all the men are dead who sought your life.

20 Then Mosheh (Musa) took his wife and his sons, and set them on a donkey, and he returned to the land of Mitzrayim (Egypt): and Mosheh (Musa) took the rod of Elohim in his hand.

21 And YHWH said to Mosheh (Musa), When you go back to Mitzrayim (Egypt), see that you do all those wonders before Pharaoh, which I have put in your hand: but I will strengthen his heart, so that he will not let the people go.

---

name then beware as that may not be the Elohim of Israel.

[1] See appendix HBYH.

[2] See appendix HBYH.

[3] Aharon, being a fellow Levite was able to travel outside Egypt to meet with Mosheh (Musa) because according to Yasher 65:20, 32-34 and 69:9, the Lewites were exempt from hard labor. So we see that even before the Lewites became Kohenim (Priests) they were already training to be Kohenim and they were not enslaved as wrongly thought. Throughout history the Lewites have mostly escaped slavery of the gentiles. Get the Continued in next section

Forever-israel Book of Yasher from the Forever-israel website to read these details.

[4] A judge or a leader.

[5] This rod was from the Tree of life which was an almond tree.

22 Then you shall say to Pharaoh, Thus says YHWH, Israel is My son, My Bekhor (firstborn):

23 And I say to you, Let My son go, that he may serve Me: and if you refuse to let him go, indeed, I will kill your son, your Bekhor (firstborn).

24 And it came to pass on the way at the encampment that YHWH met him, and sought to kill him.[1]

25 Then Zipporah took a sharp stone, and cut off the foreskin of her son, and cast it at Mosheh (Musa)'s (Moses') feet, and said, Surely you are a husband of blood to me.

26 So He let him go: then she said, You are a husband of blood, because of the circumcision.

27 And YHWH said to Aharon, Go into the wilderness to meet Mosheh (Musa). And he went,

and met him on the Mountain of Elohim,[2] and kissed him.

28 And Mosheh (Musa) told Aharon all the words of YHWH who had sent him, and all the signs, which He had commanded him.

29 Then Mosheh (Musa) and Aharon went and gathered together all the elders of the children of Israel:

30 And Aharon spoke all the words which YHWH had spoken to Mosheh (Musa), and he did the signs in the sight of the people.

31 And the people believed: and when they heard that YHWH had visited the children of Israel, and that He had looked on their affliction, then they bowed their heads and paid homage.[3]

Chapter 5

1 Afterward Mosheh (Musa) and Aharon went in, and told Pharaoh, Thus says YHWH Elohim of Israel, Let My people go, that they may hold a feast[4] to Me in the wilderness.

2 And Pharaoh said, Who is YHWH, that I should obey His voice to let Israel go? I do not know YHWH, nor will I let Israel go.[5]

Footnotes

[1] There are a number of opinions; Why does YHWH want to kill Moses, the man He himself chose, and sent? The reason was that his wife Zipporah had succumbed to her father, who told her not to circumcise her son, and Moses was powerless to convince his wife, who would not listen. Hence when YHWH was ready to kill him, we see Zipporah doing the circumcision herself, to rescue her husband because he would have died on account of her disobedience. The second opinion is Moses came home from outside, the baby was born while he was away, when he came home he wanted to leave. The halacha was that if you are traveling you do not need to circumcise the child, not to put the child's life in danger, hence why Israel did not circumcise, (Josh 5:3), while they were traveling. An angel was sent opinions differs whether it was Gabriel or Raphaél, some say even Michael, who was commissioned to kill Moses. The Angel in the guise of a fire/serpent was swallowing Moses when Zipporah intervened to save her husband.

[2] Mountain of Horeb is in Saudi Arabia where the Torah was given to Moses.
[3] Note: submission by bowing their heads to the ground, they did not erect chairs, and stand, and sing, this form of worship is modern, not ancient. Many people in the world do not know YHWH the True Elohim; but claim to worship some kind of man made elohim.
[4] The Khag, celebration of Pentecost (Shavuot) to receive Torah.
[5] Many people in the world do not know YHWH the true Elohim but claim to worship some kind of man made elohim.

3 So they said, The Elohim of the Abrahu (Hebrews) has met with us: let us go three days' journey into the wilderness, and sacrifice to YHWH our POWER; lest He fall upon us with pestilence, or with the sword.

4 Then the King of Mitzrayim (Egypt) said to them, Mosheh (Musa) and Aharon, why do you take the people from their work? Get back to your labour.[1]

5 And Pharaoh said, Look, the people of the land are many now, and you make them rest from their labour.

6 So the same day Pharaoh commanded the taskmasters of the people, and their officers, saying,

7 You shall no longer give the people straw to make brick, as before: let them go and gather straw for themselves.

8 And you shall lay on them, the quota of bricks, which they made before, you shall not diminish it: for they are idle; therefore they cry out, saying, Let us go and sacrifice to our POWER. [2]

9 Let more work be laid on the men, that they may labour in it; and let them not regard false words.

10 And the taskmasters of the people, and their officers went out, and spoke to the people, saying, Thus says Pharaoh, I will not give you straw.

11 Go, get yourselves straw where you can find it: yet none of your work will be reduced.

12 So the people were scattered abroad throughout all the land of Mitzrayim (Egypt) to gather stubble instead of straw.

13 And the taskmasters forced them to hurry, saying, Fulfill your work, your daily quota as when there was straw.

14 Also the officers of the children of Israel, whom Pharaoh's taskmasters had set over them, were beaten, and were asked, Why have you not fulfilled your task in making brick both yesterday and today, as before?

15 Then the officers of the children of Israel came and cried out to Pharaoh, saying, Why are you dealing like this with your servants?

16 There is no straw given to your servants, and they say to us, Make brick: and, indeed, your servants are beaten; but the fault is in your own people.

17 But he said, You are idle, You are idle; therefore you say, Let us go and sacrifice to YHWH.

Footnotes

[1] Pharaoh did not let Israel keep the Sabbath rest either; but YHWH did not hold Israel guilty for this sin, since they were in exile. Hence, YHWH is lenient to those in exile who have difficulty keeping the Sabbath due to work; but they must pray to YHWH for Him to clear a path, so they can have the Sabbath day off.

[2] In the scroll of Yashar 69:5-8, Pharaoh made a decree that if any of the Israelites were short in their labor, either in brick or mortar, an Abrahu youngest son would be killed and put in the building in place of the brick. This is cruelty at its worse. Terrible things has happened to us in history but Yapet did the worst by enslaving us, raping our women and inflicting pain on us for more than four hundred years so rightfully the severe punishment will be on Yapet as well unbeknownst to many of them.

Continued in next section

18 Therefore go now, and work; for no straw shall be given you, yet you shall make the quota of bricks.

19 And the officers of the children of Israel saw that they were in trouble, after it was said, You shall not reduce any bricks from your daily quota.

20 Then, as they came out from Pharaoh, they met Mosheh (Musa) and Aharon who stood there to meet them:

21 And they said to them, Let YHWH look on you, and judge; because you have made us abhorrent in the sight of Pharaoh, and in the sight of his servants, to put a sword in their hand to kill us.

22 So Mosheh (Musa) returned to YHWH, and said, YHWH[1], why have You brought trouble on this people? Why is it You have sent me?

23 For since I came to Pharaoh to speak in Your name, he has done evil to this people; neither have You rescued Your people at all.[2]

Chapter 6

1 Then YHWH said to Mosheh (Musa), Now you shall see what I will do to Pharaoh: for with a strong hand he will let them go, and with a strong hand he will drive them out of his land.

Torah Parsha 14 Wa'Yera, Shemoth 6:2-9:35
Haftarah: Ykhezkiel 28:25-29:21

Footnotes
[1] See appendix HBYH.
[2] Moses becomes impatient. We must wait on YHWH's time not ours.

2 And Elohim spoke to Mosheh (Musa), and said to him, I am YHWH.

3 And I appeared to Abraham, to Ytshak, and to Yakov, as El Shaddai (The Mighty Power),[3] but by My Name YHWH was I not known to them?[4]

4 I have also established My Covenant with them, to give them the land of Kanan, the land of their pilgrimage, in which they were strangers.

5 And I have also heard the groaning of the children of Israel, whom the Mitzrim (Egyptians) keep in bondage; and I am mindful of My Covenant to bring it to pass.

6 Therefore say to the children of Israel, I am YHWH, and I will bring you out from under the burdens of the Mitzrim (Egyptians), and I will rescue you from their bondage, and I will redeem you with an outstretched Arm and with great judgments:

7 And I will take you as My people, and I will be Your POWER: and you shall know that I am YHWH Your POWER, who brings you out from under the burdens of the Mitzrim (Egyptians).

8 And I will bring you into the land, which I swore to give to

Footnotes
[3] The Mighty powerful Breast that feeds as the breast of a mother, Isaiah 66:13.
[4] Abraham knew YHWH by Name since he built an altar to YHWH, Genesis 12:8. So here YHWH asks a rhetorical question. By misapplying the ? in the text, the interpreters made it look like Abraham did not know the Name; but this was not the case.

Abraham, Ytshak, and Yakov; and I will give it to you as a inheritance: I am YHWH.

9 And Mosheh (Musa) spoke thus to the children of Israel: but they would not heed Mosheh (Musa) because of anguish of spirit, and cruel bondage.

10 And YHWH spoke to Mosheh (Musa), saying,

11 Go in, speak to Pharaoh King of Mitzrayim (Egypt), that he must let the children of Israel go out of his land.

12 And Mosheh (Musa) spoke before YHWH, saying, The children of Israel have not heeded me; how then shall Pharaoh heed me, for I am without eloquence?[1]

13 Then YHWH spoke to Mosheh (Musa) and Aharon, and gave them a command for the children of Israel, and for Pharaoh King of Mitzrayim (Egypt), to bring the children of Israel out of the land of Mitzrayim (Egypt).

14 These are the heads of their ahvots' (fathers) batiym (houses): The sons of Reuven the Bekhor (firstborn) of Israel; Hanoch, Pallu, Khetsron, and Carmi: these are the Mishpakhot (families) of Reuven.

15 And the sons of Shim'on, Yemu'el, Yamin, Ohad, Yaken, Zokhar, and Shaul the son of a Kanani woman: these are the Mishpakhot (families) of Shim'on.

16 And these are the names of the sons of Levi according to their generations;

Gershon, Kohath, and Merari: and the years of the life of Levi were one hundred and thirty-seven years.

17 The sons of Gershon; Livni and Shimi, according to their Mishpakhot (families).

18 And the sons of Kohath; Amram, Yshari, Khevron, and Uzziel: and the years of the life of Kohath were one hundred and thirty-three years.

19 The sons of Merari; Mahali and Mushi: these are the Mishpakhot (families) of Levi according to their generations.

20 And Amram took for himself Yeh'kobad, the daughter of his father's brother[2] as wife; and she bore him Aharon and Mosheh (Musa): and the years of the life of Amram were one hundred and thirty-seven years.

21 And the sons of Yshari; Korakh, Nepheg, and Zichri.

22 And the sons of Uzziel; Mishael, Elzaphan, and Zithri.

Footnotes

[2] Septuagint says here: sister, here, can denote a distant relative, not just direct bloodline. Cousin marriages were, and are, common in the Middle-East, Africa, and South-East Asia and are perfectly normal. Polyhistor, and Demetrius, historians, make her to be his cousin and not aunt.
Rabbi Simon Altaf; she was an aunty as the Hebrew does not permit us to change the meaning of the actual word referring to brother's wife although brother could also refer to a distant relative or even a cousin but the Hebrew here does not say that. So the only way Amram could marry his real aunt is through Levirate marriage the line passing down from father to son as his uncle was dead so its permissible. Look at Judah marrying Tamar who was his daughter in law but the son was dead so it was permissible! Important matter never twist the Hebrew and make it something its not. That is what most Rabbis are doing out there.

Footnotes

[1] Septuagint

23 And Aharon took to himself Eli'sheba, daughter of Amminadab, sister of Nakhson, as wife; and she bore him Nadav, Avihu, El'ezar, and Ithamar.

24 And the sons of Korakh; Assir, El'kanah, and Abiasaph: these are the Mishpakhot (families) of the Korahites.

25 And El'ezar Aharon's son took for himself one of the daughters of Puti'el as wife; and she bore him Phinekas: these are the heads of the ahvot (fathers) of the Lewim according to their Mishpakhot (families).

26 These are Aharon and Mosheh (Musa), to whom YHWH said, Bring out the children of Israel from the land of Mitzrayim (Egypt) according to their armies.

27 These are the ones who spoke to Pharaoh King of Mitzrayim (Egypt), to bring out the children of Israel from Mitzrayim (Egypt): these are the same Mosheh (Musa) and Aharon.

28 And it came to pass on the day when YHWH spoke to Mosheh (Musa) in the land of Mitzrayim (Egypt),

29 That YHWH spoke to Mosheh (Musa), saying, I am YHWH: speak to Pharaoh King of Mitzrayim (Egypt) all that I say to you.

30 And Mosheh (Musa) said before YHWH, Behold, I do not have eloquent speech, and how shall Pharaoh heed me?

Chapter 7

1 And YHWH said to Mosheh (Musa), See, I have made you a mighty one[1] to Pharaoh: and Aharon your brother shall be your nabi (prophet).

2 You shall speak all that I command you: and Aharon your brother shall speak to Pharaoh, that he must send the children of Israel out of his land.

3 And I will harden Pharaoh's heart, and multiply My signs and My wonders in the land of Mitzrayim (Egypt).

4 But Pharaoh will not heed you, that I may lay My hand on Mitzrayim (Egypt), and bring My armies, and My people the children of Israel, out of the land of Mitzrayim (Egypt) by great judgments.

5 And the Mitzrim (Egyptians) shall know that I am YHWH, when I stretch out My hand on Mitzrayim (Egypt), and bring out the children of Israel from among them.

6 And Mosheh (Musa) and Aharon did as YHWH commanded them; so did they.

7 And Mosheh (Musa) was eighty years old, and Aharon eighty-three years old, when they spoke to Pharaoh.

8 And YHWH spoke to Mosheh (Musa) and Aharon, saying,

9 When Pharaoh speaks to you, saying, Show a miracle for yourselves: then you shall say to Aharon, Take your rod, and cast it before Pharaoh, and it shall become a serpent.

Footnotes
[1] The word, elohim, here can better be used as mighty one, and not as the Holy One, as illustrated also in Tehillim 82:1.

10 So Mosheh (Musa) and Aharon went in to Pharaoh, and they did so, just as YHWH commanded: and Aharon cast down his rod before Pharaoh, and before his servants, and it became a serpent.

11 Then Pharaoh also called the wise men and the sorcerers: and the magicians of Mitzrayim (Egypt),[1] they also did in like manner with their enchantments.

12 For every man threw down his rod, and they became serpents: but Aharon's rod swallowed up their rods.

13 And He made Pharaoh's heart hardened,[2] and he did not heed them; as YHWH had said.

14 And YHWH said to Mosheh (Musa), Pharaoh's heart is hard; he refuses to let the people go.

15 Go to Pharaoh in the morning; when he goes out to the mayim; and you shall stand by the river's[3] bank to meet him; and the rod which was turned to a serpent you shall take in your hand.

16 And you shall say to him, YHWH Elohim of the Abrahu (Hebrews) has sent me to you, saying, Let My people go, that they may serve Me in the wilderness: and, indeed, until now you would not hear.

17 Thus says YHWH, By this you shall know that I am YHWH: behold, I will strike the waters which are in the river with the rod that is in my hand, and they shall be turned to blood.

18 And the fish that are in the river shall die, and the river shall stink; and the Mitzrim (Egyptians) will loathe to drink the mayim of the river.

19 Then YHWH spoke to Mosheh (Musa), Say to Aharon, Take your rod, and stretch out your hand over the mayim of Mitzrayim (Egypt), over their streams, over their rivers, over their ponds, and over all their pools of mayim, that they may become blood; and there shall be blood throughout all the land of Mitzrayim (Egypt), both in vessels of wood, and vessels of stone.

20 And Mosheh (Musa) and Aharon did so, just as YHWH commanded; and he lifted up the rod, and struck the mayim that were in the river, in the sight of Pharaoh, and in the sight of his servants; and all the mayim that was in the river was turned to blood.

21 And the fish that were in the river died; and the river stank, and the Mitzrim (Egyptians) could not drink the mayim of the river; and there was blood throughout all the land of Mitzrayim (Egypt).

22 And the magicians of Mitzrayim (Egypt) did so with their enchantments: and Pharaoh's heart grew hard, and he did not heed them; as YHWH had said.

Footnotes
[1] Balaam was one of the magicians and wise men present in this drama on the side of Pharaoh. Why make a snake? The Egyptians also worshipped snakes, and this worship travelled to India in later times. Since Moses' snake ate the snake of Pharaoh, this illustrates that YHWH is greater.
[2] YHWH was causative in his heart being made strong so that he would by freewill decide he is not going to let go.
[3] Nile in Egypt.

23 And Pharaoh turned and went into his Beyth (house) neither was his heart moved by this.

24 And all the Mitzrim (Egyptians) dug all around the river for mayim to drink; because they could not drink the mayim of the river.

25 And seven days passed, after YHWH had struck the river.

Chapter 8

1 And YHWH spoke to Mosheh (Musa), Go to Pharaoh, and say to him, Thus says YHWH, Let My people go, that they may serve Me.

2 And if you refuse to let them go, behold, I will smite all your territory with frogs:

3 And the river shall bring forth frogs abundantly, which shall go up and come into your Beyth (house), into your bedroom, on your bed, into the Beyth (house) of your servants, on your people, into your ovens, and into your kneading bowls:

4 And the frogs shall come up on you, on your people, and on all your servants.

5 Then YHWH spoke to Mosheh (Musa), Say to Aharon, Stretch out your hand with your rod over the streams, over the rivers, and over the ponds, and cause frogs to come up on the land of Mitzrayim (Egypt).

6 And Aharon stretched out his hand over the mayim of Mitzrayim (Egypt); and the frogs came up, and covered the land of Mitzrayim (Egypt).

7 And the magicians did so with their enchantments, and brought up frogs on the land of Mitzrayim (Egypt).

8 Then Pharaoh called for Mosheh (Musa) and Aharon, and said, Pray to YHWH, that He may take away the frogs from me, and from my people; and I will let the people go, that they may sacrifice to YHWH.

9 And Mosheh (Musa) said to Pharaoh, Accept the respect of saying: when I shall intercede for you, for your servants, and for your people, to destroy the frogs from you and your batiym (houses), that they may remain in the river only?

10 And he said, Tomorrow. And he said, Let it be according to your word:

that you may know that there is no one like YHWH our POWER.

11 And the frogs shall depart from you, from your batiym (houses), from your servants, and from your people; they shall remain in the river only.

12 Then Mosheh (Musa) and Aharon went out from Pharaoh: and Mosheh (Musa) called out to YHWH concerning the frogs which He had brought against Pharaoh.

13 And YHWH did according to the word of Mosheh (Musa); and the frogs died out of the batiym (houses), out of the courtyards, and out of the fields.

14 And they gathered them together in heaps: and the land smelled bad.

15 But when Pharaoh saw that there was relief, he hardened his heart, and did not heed them; as YHWH had said.

16 And YHWH said to Mosheh (Musa), Say to Aharon, Stretch out your rod, and strike the dust of the ground, that it may become lice throughout all the land of Mitzrayim (Egypt).

17 And they did so; for Aharon stretched out his hand with his rod, and struck the dust of the ground, and it became lice on man, and beast; all the dust of the land became lice throughout all the land of Mitzrayim (Egypt).

18 Now the magicians so worked with their enchantments to bring forth lice, but they could not: so there were lice on man, and beast.

19 Then the magicians said to Pharaoh, This is the finger of Elohim: and Pharaoh's heart grew hard, and he did not heed them; just as YHWH had said.

20 And YHWH said to Mosheh (Musa), Rise early in the morning, and stand before Pharaoh; as he comes out to the water; and say to him, Thus says YHWH, Let My people go, that they may serve Me.

21 Or, else, if you will not let My people go, behold, I will send swarms of flies on you, and your servants, on your people, and into your batiym (houses): and the batiym (houses) of the Mitzrim (Egyptians) shall be full of swarms of flies, and also the ground on which they stand.

22 And in that day I will Hollow the land of Goshen, in which My people dwell, that no swarms of flies shall be there; in order that you may know that I am YHWH in the midst of the land.[1]

23 And I will make a difference[2] between My people and your people: tomorrow this sign shall be.

24 And YHWH did so; and thick swarms of flies came into the Beyth (house) of Pharaoh, into his servant's batiym (houses), and into all the land of Mitzrayim (Egypt): the land was ruined because of the swarms of flies.

25 And Pharaoh called for Mosheh (Musa) and Aharon, and said, Go, sacrifice to Your POWER in the land.

26 And Mosheh (Musa) said, It is not right to do so; for we would be slaughtering the ritual impurity of the Mitzrim (Egyptians) to YHWH our POWER: if we sacrifice the abomination of the Mitzrim (Egyptians) before their eyes, then will they not stone us?[3]

27 We will go three days' journey into the wilderness, and sacrifice to YHWH our POWER, as He will command us.

28 And Pharaoh said, I will let you go, that you may sacrifice to YHWH Your POWER in the

Footnotes
[1] YHWH protects His people who keep Torah through calamities. The same protection will be there in the end time battle with Islam, for Torah keepers only.
[2] Torah keepers and non-Torah keepers, YHWH's people keep Torah, and are Holy from the rest of the world.
[3] Egyptians worshipped bulls, and sheep, which Moses was commanded to sacrifice, therefore showing, that bulls and goats are not elohim, as the Egyptian culture had come to worship them.

wilderness; only you shall not go very far away: intercede for me.

29 And Mosheh (Musa) said, Indeed, I am going out from you, and I will intercede to YHWH that the swarms of flies may depart tomorrow from Pharaoh, from his servants, and from his people, tomorrow: but let Pharaoh not deal deceitfully anymore in not letting the people go to sacrifice to YHWH.

30 And Mosheh (Musa) went out from Pharaoh, and interceded on his behalf to YHWH.

31 And YHWH did according to the word of Mosheh (Musa); He removed the swarms of flies from Pharaoh, from his servants, and from his people; not one remained.

32 And Pharaoh hardened his heart at this time also, neither would he let the people go.

Chapter 9

1 Then YHWH said to Mosheh (Musa), Go in to Pharaoh, and tell him, Thus says YHWH Elohim of the Abrahu (Hebrews), Let My people go, that they may serve Me.

2 For if you refuse to let them go, and still hold them,

3 Behold, the hand of YHWH will be on your cattle in the field, on the horses, on the donkeys, on the camels, on the oxen, and on the sheep: there will be a very severe pestilence.[1]

Footnotes

[1] Note even the Egyptians, who did not worship YHWH, did not touch pigs, and did not breed them, or eat them. This abomination of pig eating came from the West, from the Greek, and Roman cultures. The pig was designed to be a garbage collector, a biological cleaner. Many Continued in next section

4 And YHWH will make a difference between the livestock of Israel and the livestock of Mitzrayim (Egypt): and nothing shall die of all that belongs to the children of Israel.

5 Then YHWH set an appointed time, saying, Tomorrow YHWH will do this thing in the land.

6 And YHWH did this thing on the next day, and all the livestock of Mitzrayim (Egypt) died: but of the livestock of the children of Israel not one died.

7 And Pharaoh sent, and, indeed, not even one of the livestock of the Y'sraeli was dead. And the heart of Pharaoh became hard, and he did not let the people go.

8 So YHWH said to Mosheh (Musa) and Aharon, Take for yourselves handfuls of ashes from a furnace, and let Mosheh (Musa) scatter it toward the shamayim in the sight of Pharaoh.

9 And it will become fine dust in all the land of Mitzrayim (Egypt), and it will cause boils that break out in sores on man, and beast, throughout all the land of Mitzrayim (Egypt).

10 And they took ashes from the furnace, and stood before Pharaoh; and Mosheh (Musa) scattered them toward shamayim; and they caused boils that break out in sores on man, and beast.

11 And the magicians could not stand before Mosheh (Musa)

Christians foolishly ignore YHWH and eat this unclean animal, which harbors many diseases.

because of the boils; for the boils were on the magicians, and on all the Mitzrim (Egyptians).[1]

12 And YHWH hardened the heart of Pharaoh, and he did not heed them; just as YHWH had spoken to Mosheh (Musa).

13 And YHWH said to Mosheh (Musa), Rise early in the morning, and stand before Pharaoh, and say to him, Thus says YHWH Elohim of the Abrahu (Hebrews), Let My people go, that they may serve Me.

14 For at this time I will send all My plagues to your very heart, and on your servants and on your people; that you may know that there is none like Me in all the earth.

15 Now I will stretch out My hand, and strike you and your people with pestilence; and you shall be cut off from the earth.

16 And indeed for this purpose I have raised you up, that I may show My power in you; and that My Name may be declared in all the earth.

17 As yet you exalt yourself against My people, in that you will not let them go.

18 Behold, tomorrow about this time I will cause a very heavy hail to rain down, such as has not been in Mitzrayim (Egypt) since its founding until now.

19 Therefore send now, and gather your livestock, and all that you have in the field; for the hail shall come down on every man and every animal which is found in the field, and is not brought home, and they shall die.

20 He who feared the word of YHWH among the servants of Pharaoh made his servants and his livestock flee to their batiym (houses):

21 But he who did not regard the word of YHWH left his servants and his livestock in the field.

22 And YHWH said to Mosheh (Musa), Stretch out your hand toward the shamayim, that there may be hail in all the land of Mitzrayim (Egypt), on man, on beast, and on every herb of the field, throughout the land of Mitzrayim (Egypt).

23 And Mosheh (Musa) stretched out his rod toward the shamayim: and YHWH sent thunder and hail, and fire darted to the ground; and YHWH rained hail on the land of Mitzrayim (Egypt).

24 So there was hail, and fire mingled with the hail, very heavy, that there was none like it in all the land of Mitzrayim (Egypt) since it became a nation.[2]

25 And the hail struck throughout the whole land of Mitzrayim (Egypt) all that was in the field, both man and beast; and the hail struck every herb of the field, and broke every tree of the field.

Footnotes
[1] Magician's tricks could not work against YHWH's real miracles and judgment. Similar judgments will be repeated in the end time battle with the radical Muslims.

Footnotes
[2] The end time judgment, on the nations of radical Islamist armies that come up to fight Israel, will be the same.

26 Only in the land of Goshen, where the children of Israel were, there was no hail.

27 And Pharaoh sent, and called for Mosheh (Musa) and Aharon, and said to them, I have transgressed this time: YHWH is Righteous, and my people and I are wicked.

28 Intercede to YHWH; that there may be no more mighty thundering and hail; for it is enough. I will let you go, and you shall stay no longer.

29 And Mosheh (Musa) said to him, As soon as I have gone out of the city, I will spread out my hands to YHWH; the thunder will cease, and there will be no more hail; that you may know that the earth is YHWH's.[1]

30 But as for you and your servants, I know that you will not yet fear YHWH Elohim.

31 Now the flax and the barley were struck: for the barley was in the head, and the flax was in bud.

32 But the wheat and the spelt were not struck: for they are late crops.

33 And Mosheh (Musa) went out of the city from Pharaoh, and spread out his hands to YHWH: and the thunder and the hail ceased, and the rain was not poured on the earth.

34 And when Pharaoh saw that the rain, the hail, and the thunder had ceased, he continued to sin, and he hardened his heart, he and his servants.

35 And the heart of Pharaoh was hard, neither would he let the children of Israel go; as YHWH had spoken by Mosheh (Musa).

Torah Parsha 15 Bo, Shemoth 10:1-13:16
Haftarah Yirmeyahu 46:13-28

Chapter 10

1 Now YHWH said to Mosheh (Musa), Go in to Pharaoh: for I have hardened his heart, and the hearts of his servants, that I may show these signs of Mine through him:

2 And that you may tell in the hearing of your son, and your son's son, the mighty things I have done in Mitzrayim (Egypt), and My signs which I have done among them; that you may know that I am YHWH.

3 And Mosheh (Musa) and Aharon came in to Pharaoh, and said to him, Thus says YHWH Elohim of the Abrahu (Hebrews), How long will you refuse to humble yourself before Me? Let My people go, that they may serve Me.

4 Or else, if you refuse to let My people go, behold, tomorrow I will bring locusts within your borders:

5 And they shall cover the face of this land, so that no one will be able to see the land: and they shall eat the residue of what is left, which remains to you from the hail, and they shall eat every tree which grows up for you out of the field:

6 They shall fill your batiym (houses), the batiym (houses) of all your servants, and the batiym (houses) of all the Mitzrim (Egyptians); which neither your

Footnotes
[1] Contrary to popular error in the churches, the Earth belongs to YHWH, and not Satan.

ahvot (fathers), nor your grandfathers have seen, since the day that they were on the earth to this day. And he turned, and went out from Pharaoh.

7 Then Pharaoh's servants said to him, How long shall this man be a snare to us? Let the men go, that they may serve YHWH their Elohim: do you not yet know that Mitzrayim (Egypt) is destroyed?

8 And Mosheh (Musa) and Aharon were brought again to Pharaoh: and he said to them, Go, serve YHWH Your POWER: but who are the ones that are going?

9 And Mosheh (Musa) said, We will go with our young and our old, with our sons and our daughters, with our flocks and our herds we will go; for we must hold a khag (the appointed celebration time) with YHWH.

10 Then he said to them, YHWH had better be with you, when I let you, and your little ones go: beware, for calamity is ahead of you.[1]

11 Not so: go now you that are men, and serve YHWH; for that is what you desired. And they were driven out from Pharaoh's presence.

12 And YHWH said to Mosheh (Musa), Stretch out your hand over the land of Mitzrayim (Egypt) for the locusts, that they may come upon the land of Mitzrayim (Egypt), and eat every herb of the land, all that the hail has left.

13 So Mosheh (Musa) stretched out his rod over the land of Mitzrayim (Egypt), and YHWH brought an east wind on the land all that day, and all that night; and when it was morning, the east wind brought the locusts.[2]

14 And the locusts went up over all the land of Mitzrayim (Egypt), and rested on all the territory of Mitzrayim (Egypt): they were very severe; previously there had been no such locusts as they, nor shall there be such after them.

15 For they covered the face of the whole land, so that the land was darkened; and they ate every herb of the land, and all the fruit of the etzim (trees) which the hail had left: and there remained nothing green on the etzim (trees), or on the plants of the field, throughout all the land of Mitzrayim (Egypt).

16 Then Pharaoh called for Mosheh (Musa) and Aharon in haste; and said, I have transgressed against YHWH Your POWER, and against you.

17 Now, therefore, please forgive my sin only this once, and plead to YHWH Your POWER, that He may take away from me this death only.

Footnotes
[1] Pharaoh threatens Moses as if he holds the future of Israel; but the future is in YHWH's hands, and no calamity can befall those who serve the King and obey His Torah.

Footnotes
[2] The locusts are a description of the radical Islamic armies, they will also come at the End of Days when YHWH brings them against Israel to reveal His glory, See book World War III – Unmasking the end times beast by Rabbi Simon Altaf, www.forever-israel.com.

18 So he went out from Pharaoh, and interceded to YHWH.

19 And YHWH turned a very strong west wind,[1] which took the locusts away, and blew them into the Red Sea; there remained not one locust in all the borders of Mitzrayim (Egypt).

20 But YHWH hardened Pharaoh's heart, and he did not let the children of Israel go.

21 Then YHWH said to Mosheh (Musa), Stretch out your hand toward the shamayim, that there may be darkness over the land of Mitzrayim (Egypt), darkness which may even be felt.[2]

22 And Mosheh (Musa) stretched out his hand toward shamayim; and there was thick darkness in all the land of Mitzrayim (Egypt) three days:

23 They did not see one another, nor did anyone rise from his place for three days: but all the children of Israel had light in their dwellings.

24 Then Pharaoh called to Mosheh (Musa), and said, Go, serve YHWH; only let your flocks and your herds be kept back: let your little ones also go with you.

25 And Mosheh (Musa) said, You must also give us sacrifices and burnt offerings, that we may sacrifice to YHWH our POWER.

26 Our livestock also shall go with us; not a hoof shall be left behind; for we must take some of them to serve YHWH our POWER; for we do not know with what we must serve YHWH, until we arrive there.

27 But YHWH hardened Pharaoh's heart, and he would not let them go.

28 Then Pharaoh said to him, Get away from me, take heed to yourself, and see my face no more! For in the day you see my face, you shall die!

29 And Mosheh (Musa) said, You have spoken well, I will never see your face again!

Chapter 11

1 And YHWH said to Mosheh (Musa), I will bring yet one more plague on Pharaoh, and on Mitzrayim (Egypt); afterward he will let you go from here: when he lets you go, he will surely drive you out of here altogether.

2 Speak now in the hearing of the people, and let every man ask from his neighbour, and every woman from her neighbour, articles of silver, and articles of gold.

3 And YHWH gave the people favour in the sight of the Mitzrim (Egyptians). Moreover, the man Mosheh (Musa) was very great in the land of Mitzrayim (Egypt), in the sight of Pharaoh's servants, and in the sight of the people.

4 And Mosheh (Musa) said, Thus says YHWH, About midnight I will go out into the midst of Mitzrayim (Egypt):

Footnotes
[1] The remez (hint) in the Torah shows us that western armies shall come up, to stop the assault of the Islamic armies, and be part of the battle at the End of Days fighting for Israel, and their own survival, before the coming of Messiah. The U.S. and the U.K. are key marked nations for this battle. See the book in the previous footnote.
[2] It was a thick dark fog.

5 And all the Bekhor (firstborn) in the land of Mitzrayim (Egypt) shall die, from the Bekhor (firstborn) of Pharaoh who sits on his throne, even to the Bekhor (firstborn) of the female servant who is behind the hand mill; and all the Bekhor (firstborn) of the animals.[1]

6 And there shall be a great cry throughout all the land of Mitzrayim (Egypt), such as was not like it before, nor shall be like it again.

7 But against none of the children of Israel shall a dog[2] move its tongue,[3] against man, or beast: that you may know that YHWH does make a difference between the Mitzrim (Egyptians) and Israel.

8 And all these your servants shall come down to Me, and bow down to Me, saying, Get out, and all the people who follow you. After that I will go out. Then he went out from Pharaoh in great anger.

9 And YHWH said to Mosheh (Musa), Pharaoh will not listen to you; in order that My wonders

Footnotes
[1] Egyptians worshipped the firstborn as elohim, so YHWH killed the first born, to demonstrate that they were not elohim; but just ordinary humans. This put the fear in the Egyptians heart that had strange pagan beliefs, even some cultures such as the Tibetans, carry this type of Faith today.
[2] A term used for gentile people who have no Covenant with YHWH.
[3] Children of Israel are always special in YHWH's eyes because of our Covenants established with YHWH through our forefathers. It is not because we do everything right; but the promises, and agreements, YHWH has made with our forefathers, stand forever.

may be multiplied in the land of Mitzrayim (Egypt).

10 So Mosheh (Musa) and Aharon did all these wonders before Pharaoh: and YHWH hardened Pharaoh's heart, and he did not let the children of Israel go out of his land.

Chapter 12

1 Now YHWH spoke to Mosheh (Musa) and Aharon in the land of Mitzrayim (Egypt), saying,[4]

2 This month shall be your beginning of months:[5] it shall be the first month of the year to you.

Footnotes
[4] This is the 1st commandment of the Torah to the nation of Israel.
[5] The month of Passover, during March called Abib; but came to be known as Nisan. According to Hebrew laws today, they believe in four New Year dates, during the current Gregorian calendar year. According to the Mishnah, compiled during 200 CE, this is the designation as follows:

a) New Year for Years: The Civil new year; beginning what many Hebrew people today term as Rosh HaShana. This is really the Khag, celebration of Trumpets, called Yom Terua; but the Hebrew people believe that at this time Adam was created, according to the traditions. The 1st of Tishri is the secular New Year, (head of year) allowing us to make calculation of the year of Jubilee, and the year of release. The 1st of Tishri can fall between September 15 each year.

b) Religious New Year: The year for counting the feasts, and the year of kings begins Abib 1st, or also called Nisan 1. This is between March and April. This is the Biblical mandated religious head of months, the official New Year, as written by Moses in the Torah.

c) Year of the Trees: Vayikra (Lev) 19:23-25. This is in the Month of Shevat, January and February.

d) Year of Tithe of cattle: The 1st of Elul is considered for the Tithes of the Cattle. This is August and September time.
Continued in next section

3 Speak to all the congregation of Israel, saying, On the tenth day of this month every man shall take for himself a lamb, according to the Beyth (house) of his father, a lamb for a household:[1]

4 And if the household is too small for the lamb, let him and his neighbour next to his Beyth (house) take it according to the number of the persons; according to each man's need you shall make your count for the lamb.

5 Your lamb shall be without blemish,[2] a male of the first year: you may take it from the sheep or from the goats:

6 Now you shall keep it until the fourteenth day of the same month: and the whole assembly of the congregation of Israel shall kill it at twilight.[3]

7 And they shall take some of the blood,[4] and put it on the two

Footnotes

[4] Israel needed a mitzvah to be rescued and they did not have any. So, Elohim gave them to have brit milah as a mitzvah. So they did that. They had bloods in plural, one blood of the lamb, two, the blood of brit milah. This was the mitzvah that saved Israel. Yet many today refuse to circumcise.

http://mobile.myjewishlearning.com/holidays/Jewish_Holidays/Passover/Themes_and_Theology/Meaning_of_Exodus/Did_Israel_Deserve_Redemption.shtml

Nothing to Merit Redemption
According to the Mekhilta, God promised that the people would be redeemed at a certain time, but they had not done anything to merit redemption. The Mekhilta then reframes the reader's perception of the Exodus narrative by referencing the prophecy of Ezekiel who describes Israel in harsh terms. Ezekiel describes Israel as an abandoned baby girl, unwashed and unswaddled, "abandoned in an open field" (Ezekiel 16:5), whom God takes care of out of compassion.

As the passage quoted by the Mekhilta indicates, the girl grows into a young woman, and then God betroths the girl. The extended metaphor continues with the girl becoming unfaithful to her husband. Although the Mekhilta does not quote these particular verses, it will become clear that Ezekiel's negative perception of Israel in Egypt informs this midrashic discussion. The Mekhilta continues with R. Matia b. Heresh's conclusion to his problem. Israel had no particular merit, and...

"Therefore the Holy One gave them two mitzvot--the blood of the paschal lamb and the blood of circumcision--to perform in order to be redeemed, as it says, 'I passed by you and saw you wallowing in

[1] The number ten represents the Ten Sefirot, the Ten days of Awe, the ten plagues, ten is also for Judgment, and for the tribes of Israel, and the number Ten is the value of the letter Yud, which is the hand of YHWH.
[2] Being without sin.
[3] Between the evenings; 2.30 p.m. to 6 p.m.

Continued in next section

your blood, and I said to you, "In your blood, live; in your blood, live!'" (Ezekiel 16:6) For this reason Scripture required the purchase four days ahead of time, for one cannot obtain reward except through deeds." The repeated phrase "In your blood, live!" is understood as two different mitzvot concerning blood; the same phrase is recited at a circumcision ceremony. The negative view of an Israel lacking merit, however, is not allowed to stand unchallenged. The Mekhilta quotes the opposing view of R. Eliezer haKappar:

"Did not Israel possess four mitzvot [while they were in Egypt]...; that they were sexually pure, that they did not gossip, that they did not change their names, and that they did not change their language!?"

While the image of a non-assimilating, morally virtuous Israel is, perhaps, appealing to a modern audience, these particular examples are somewhat suspect. The proof for sexual purity is a reference to a child of an Egyptian man and an Israelite woman (Leviticus 24:10), which, the midrash assumes, must have been the only case of improper behavior. The proof that they maintained their names is strange considering Joseph took on an Egyptian name, Tzafenat Pa'aneah (Genesis 41:45).

Furthermore, according to a midrash attributed to the third century Rabbi Alexandri, the Israelites were shameless gossips. After Moses slays the Egyptian taskmaster, the arguing Israelites rebuke him saying, "Do you intend to kill me, as you killed the Egyptian" (Exodus 2:14). This causes Moses to come to conclude not only that the Israelites had been gossiping about his action, but that God allowed Israel to remain enslaved precisely because of the sin of gossip (Exodus Rabbah 1:30).

Israelite Idolaters?
Nevertheless, the argument that Israel was not entirely lacking merit forces the Mekhilta to pose once again the question of why the lamb was bought four days before the slaughtering. The Mekhilta responds:

"Because the Israelites in Egypt were steeped in idolatry. And the law against idolatry outweighs all other of the other mitzvot ... Therefore Moses said to them, stop worshipping idols and adhere to the mitzvot!

The tradition that, during the long exile in Egypt, Israel had become idolatrous also derives from Ezekiel, "I also said to them, 'Cast away, every one of you, the detestable things that you are drawn to, and do not defile yourselves with the idols of Egypt--I the L-rd am your God.' But they defied Me and refused to listen to Me" (Ezekiel 20:7-8).

If these successive passages are indeed one extended conversation, then the argument that idolatry outweighs the other mitzvot would reject Eliezer haKappar's argument that Israel was meritorious in Egypt. This would ultimately support R. Matia b. Heresh's opinion that the four days were to provide Israel with the opportunity to perform the two mitzvot of circumcision and the paschal sacrifice in order to prove their merit.

The passage from the Mekhilta concludes with a different explanation of the four-day gap. R. Judah b. Beteira argues simply that it was hard for the Israelites to part with their idols. A later midrash builds upon this idea, recognizing that the slaughtering of the lamb was both a political and a theological affirmation of loyalty to the God of Israel.

Continued in next section Continued in next section

doorposts and on the lintel of the batiym (houses), where they eat it.[1]

8 Then they shall eat the flesh on that night, roasted in fire, with matzah (unleavened bread); and with bitter herbs they shall eat it.

9 Do not eat it raw, nor boiled at all with mayim, but roasted in fire; its head with its legs, and its entrails.[2]

10 And you shall let none of it remain until morning; and what remains of it until morning you shall burn with fire.

"When the Holy One told Moses to slaughter the paschal lamb, Moses objected, '...Do You not know that the lamb is an Egyptian God? ' (cf. Exodus 7:22). God replied, 'On your life, Israel will not leave here until they slaughter the Egyptian Gods before their very eyes, that I may teach them that their Gods are really nothing at all" (Exodus Rabbah 16:3).

The perception of Israel as idolatrous in Egypt may be uncomfortable, but it explains a great deal, including the name of the holiday. As Bible scholar Menachem Leibtag has noted, "One 'passes over' something that he is supposed to 'step on.' Had the Israelites been righteous, there would not have been a punishment that required 'passing over.'" It also provides a little more context for Rav's explanation that the journey from disgrace to glory celebrated on Passover begins with idolatry, "In the beginning, our ancestors were idolaters..." (Bavli Pesachim 116a and the Passover Haggadah).

[1] This shows the picture those that believe on YHWH and obey his Torah will have life and those that don't will die.
[2] Drash (allegory) of keeping all the commandments of Torah.

11 And thus you shall eat it; with a belt on your waist, your sandals on your feet, and your staff in your hand; and you shall eat it in haste: it is YHWH's Protection (Passover).[3]

12 For I will pass through the land of Mitzrayim (Egypt) on that night, and will strike all the Bekhor (firstborn) in the land of Mitzrayim (Egypt), both man and beast; and against all the powers of Mitzrayim (Egypt)[4] I will execute judgment: I am YHWH.

13 And the blood shall be a sign for you on the batiym (houses) where you are: and when I see the blood, I will protect you (Passover)[5] you, and the plague shall not be on you to destroy you, when I strike the land of Mitzrayim (Egypt).

14 And this day shall be for you for a memorial;[6] and you shall Guard it as a khag (appointed celebration time) to YHWH

Footnotes
[3] Passover is the Protection for all the nations that join with Israel and become engrafted in by being Obedient to the voice, the magic is not the blood drained from the lamb but the obedience to do as told.
[4] The firstborn were seen to be special and have qualities of being like elohim so people worshipped them and YHWH killed them to show they are not elohim.
[5] See footnote in verse 23 and 27.
[6] Remembrance is <u>forever</u>, not for a season, and certainly not for Hebrew people only. If your mother or father died do you remember them only one year, or for all times, until your death?
A memorial is kept year by year. It is a shame that with the dispensationalist error, many people have lost their favour that comes with obedience, and joy, of Torah keeping. It's especially a time of joy, to celebrate the seven feasts of YHWH annually.

throughout your generations; you shall guard it as a khag (appointed time) by an everlasting ordinance.

15 Seven days you shall eat matzah (unleavened bread); even the first day you shall remove chametz (leaven) from your batiym (houses):[1] for whoever eats chametz Lakhem (leavened bread) from the first day until the seventh day, that person shall be cut off from Israel.

16 And in the first day there shall be a Holy assembly,[2] and on the seventh day there shall be a miqra kodesh[3] for you; no manner of work shall be done on them, but that which everyone must eat, that only may be prepared by you.

17 And you shall observe Khag ha Matzot (The Feast of Unleavened Bread); for on this same day I will have brought your armies out of the land of Mitzrayim (Egypt): therefore you shall guard this day throughout your generations as an everlasting[4] ordinance.

18 In the first month, on the fourteenth day of the month at evening, you shall eat matzah (unleavened bread), until the twenty-first day of the month at evening.

19 Seven days no chametz (leaven) shall be found in your batiym (houses): for whoever eats what is chametz (leavened), that same person shall be cut off from the congregation of Israel, whether he is a foreigner, or a native resident of the land.

20 You shall not eat chametz (leaven);[5] in all your dwellings you shall eat matzah (unleavened bread).

21 Then Mosheh (Musa) called for all the elders of Israel, and said to them, Pick out and take lambs for yourselves according to your Mishpakhot (families), and kill the protection (Passover) lamb.

22 And you shall take a bunch of hyssop, dip it in the blood that is in the basin, and strike the lintel and the two doorposts with the blood that is in the basin; and none of you shall go out of the door of his Beyth (house) until morning.

23 For YHWH will pass through to strike the Mitzrim (Egyptians); and when He sees the blood on the lintel, and on the two doorposts, YHWH will Protect (Passover)[6] the door, and not allow the destroyer[7] to come into

Footnotes

[1] We must remove all yeast from our houses, this is drash also, for removing sin from our lives, and repenting, and forsaking all bad things in our life.

[2] A gathered assembly of believers who praise and worship, YHWH. This is a mandatory day off from work, no work is to be done on this day.

[3] Compulsory day off, no work is done. The same as on the first day.

[4] In Hebrew 'l-Olam -v'ed' means 'forever', and 'eternal', so there is no time attached to it. It must be done always, and we will be keeping the feasts.

[5] Do not eat any risen bread such as Naan bread, raised chapatti or any other such foods.

[6] The Hebrew word Maskit more correctly means to protect, it does not mean to Passover like a hop.

[7] Satan, who kills and murders people, was allowed, that night, to destroy the bechor (firstborn).

your batiym (houses) to strike you.

24 And you shall observe this thing as an ordinance for you, and your sons forever.

25 And it will come to pass, when you come to the land which YHWH will give you, just as He promised, that you shall keep this service.

26 And it shall be, when your children say to you, What do you mean by this service?

27 That you shall say, It is the Protection/Mercy (Passover)[1] sacrifice of YHWH, who passed over the batiym (houses) of the children of Israel in Mitzrayim (Egypt), when He struck the Mitzrim (Egyptians), and rescued our households. And the people bowed their heads and paid homage.

28 Then the children of Israel went away, and did as YHWH had commanded Mosheh (Musa) and Aharon, so they did.

29 And it came to pass, that at midnight YHWH struck all the Bekhor (firstborn) in the land of Mitzrayim (Egypt), from the Bekhor (firstborn) of Pharaoh who sat on his throne to the Bekhor (firstborn) of the captive who was in the dungeon; and all the Bekhor (firstborn) of livestock.

30 And Pharaoh rose in the night, he, all his servants, and all the Mitzrim (Egyptians); and there was a great cry in Mitzrayim (Egypt), for there was not a Beyth (house) where there was not one dead.

31 Then he called for Mosheh (Musa) and Aharon by night, and said, Rise and go out from among my people, both you and the children of Israel; and go, serve YHWH, as you have said.

32 Also take your flocks and your herds, as you have said, and be gone; and **Bless** me also.[2]

33 And the Mitzrim (Egyptians) urged the people, that they might send them out of the land in haste; for they said, We shall all be dead.

34 And the people took their dough before it was chametz (leaven), having their kneading bowls bound up in their clothes on their shoulders.

35 And the children of Israel had done according to the word of Mosheh (Musa); and they had asked from the Mitzrim (Egyptians) articles of silver, articles of gold, and clothing:

36 And YHWH gave the people favour in the sight of the Mitzrim (Egyptians), so that they granted them what they requested. Thus they plundered the Mitzrim (Egyptians).

37 Then the children of Israel journeyed from Rameses to Succoth, about six hundred thousand men on foot, besides children.[3]

Footnotes

[1] Here the word Pesach more accurately means "mercy" and to "save" in the ancient derived Hebrew.

[2] Pharaoh being an unbeliever even asks for a **Blessing**. Believers should speak **Blessings** for those who ask.

[3] The figure comes close to four million when you consider that the Israelite people were Biblically polygamous with an average of eight wives and fifty two children in each

Continued in next section

38 A mixed multitude[1] went up with them also; and flocks, and herds, and a great deal of livestock.

39 And they baked matzah (unleavened) rotis[2] of the dough which they had brought out of Mitzrayim (Egypt), for it was not chametz (leaven); because they were driven out of Mitzrayim (Egypt), and could not wait, nor had they prepared provisions for themselves.

40 Now the sojourning of the children of Israel, who lived in Mitzrayim (Egypt), was four hundred and thirty years.[3]

41 And it came to pass at the end of the four hundred and thirty years on that very same day it came to pass that all the armies of YHWH went out from the land of Mitzrayim (Egypt).[4]

42 This is a night of much observance to YHWH for bringing them out of the land of Mitzrayim (Egypt). This is the night for YHWH, a solemn observance for all the children of Israel throughout their generations.[5]

43 And YHWH said to Mosheh (Musa) and Aharon, This is the ordinance of the Protection (Passover): No foreigner shall eat it.

44 But every man's servant who is bought for money, when you have circumcised him, then he may eat it.[6]

45 A Ger-Toshav (foreigner) and a hired servant shall not eat it.[7]

46 In one Beyth (house) it shall be eaten; you shall not carry any of the flesh outside the Beyth (house), nor shall you break one of its bones.

47 All the congregation[8] of Israel shall keep it.

48 And when a foreigner dwells with you, and wants to keep the Protection (Passover) to YHWH; let all his males perform brit-milah (circumcision), and then let him come near and keep it; and he shall be as a native of the land:

Footnotes

family. Please see articles under title Biblical marriages on www.forever-israel.com.

[1] There were also gentiles from Egypt joining the Exodus; they had to get circumcised to join the Passover meal.

[2] There are two types of roti, one with leaven and one without, these are the Indian styles of bread that the ancient Israelites cooked. There is also the one that you put oil on and its called a paratha. These were our staple foods in the ancient times.

[3] Abraham had Isaac twenty-five years after the prophecy was given to him Abraham stayed in Kharan five years. Birth of Isaac to birth of Jacob 60 years. Jacob going down to Egypt add 130 years Beresheeth 47:9. Israel coming out of Egypt 210 years. The sum total is 430 years.

[4] Note YHWH refers to Israel as His armies, a very special designation indeed.

[5] A good time to gather and reflect how YHWH brought our elders out of Egypt. The Hebrew people sit-up all night talking and praying over this event.

[6] The people who partake in the meal of the Passover must be circumcised or else it is a sin to eat the meal. Many Pastors' are making this mistake in Christian circles of allowing uncircumcised men to partake of the meal.

[7] A Ger-Toshav is a person who fears YHWH but has not yet circumcised therefore he cannot partake of the Passover meal.

[8] The entire congregation means all the people both gentile who are grafted in to Israel and those who are natives must keep the Passover. There is no such thing as a gentile church in YHWH's sight. There is only one assembly comprised of Hebrew and non-Hebrew believers called Israel.

for no uncircumcised person shall eat it.[1]

49 One Torah shall be for the native-born, and for the foreigner who dwells among you.[2]

50 Thus all the children of Israel did; as YHWH commanded Mosheh (Musa) and Aharon, so they did.

51 And it came to pass on that very same day that YHWH brought the children of Israel out of the land of Mitzrayim (Egypt) according to their armies.

Chapter 13

1 Then YHWH spoke to Mosheh (Musa), saying,

2 Consecrate to Me all the Bekhor (firstborn), whatever opens the womb among the children of Israel, both of man and beast: it is Mine.

3 And Mosheh (Musa) said to the people, Mention[3] this day, in which you went out of Mitzrayim (Egypt), out of the Beyth (house) of bondage; for by strength of hand YHWH brought you out of this place: no chametz Lakhem (leavened bread) shall be eaten.

4 This day you came out in the month Abib.

5 And it shall be when YHWH brings you into the land of the Kanani, and the Khitee, and the Amoree, and the Khuvi, and the Yavusi, which He swore to your ahvot (fathers) to give you, a land flowing with milk and honey, that you shall keep this service in this month.

6 Seven days you shall eat matzah (unleavened bread), and in the seventh day there shall be a khag, (appointed celebration time) to YHWH.

7 Matzah (unleavened bread) shall be eaten seven days; and no chametz Lakhem (leavened bread) shall be seen among you, nor shall chametz (leaven) be seen among you in all your quarters.

8 And you shall tell your son in that day, saying, This is done because of what YHWH did for me when I came up from Mitzrayim (Egypt).

9 And it shall be as a sign to you on your hand,[4] and for a

Footnotes

[1] The Protection/Mercy is only for those who obey the Voice of YHWH.

[2] YHWH recognises no assembly masquerading itself as a church, outside Israel. Either you are part of the assembly of Israel, or you are an impostor. One Torah/instructions for both the native Israelites and foreigners who join Israel, that means, Christians of all denominations must also keep Torah instructions. It is mandatory and not an option. If they do not, then they have no part in the Covenants with Abraham. There is no half way house.

[3] To remember for all times the release from slavery and tell our children.

Footnotes

[4] Wearing a Tefillin was introduced by the Rabbis much later than the Torah was given and not part of the Torah command. The command here means to cherish Torah as a jewel and not about wearing a box. See Deut 6:8.

http://www.chabad.org/library/howto/wizard_cdo/aid/272665/Hebrew/4-The-Straps.htm

The upper part of the tefillin box is a perfect cube; the lower part is a flatter box that is wider than the upper part. On one side, the lower part extends further than the other sides and has a slit through which the tefillin strap is threaded.

Continued in next section

remembrance between your eyes, that the Torah of YHWH may be in your mouth: for with a strong hand YHWH has brought you out of Mitzrayim (Egypt).

10 You shall therefore keep this command in its appointed time from year to year.

11 And it shall be when YHWH brings you into the land of the

The hand tefillin has one large compartment, in which a single scroll inscribed with the four portions is inserted. The head tefillin has four compartments, for its four scrolls, and has a raised Hebrew letter shin on each side.

1) Kadesh (Exodus 13:1-10)
2) VeHayah Ki Yeviacha (Exodus 13:11-16)
3) The Shema (Deuteronomy 6:4-9)
4) VeHayah Im Shamoa (Deuteronomy 11:13-21)

The head tefillin has a large, fixed loop to fit the head. The hand tefillin has a smaller, adjustable loop to tie on the upper arm.

The head strap's knot is in the shape of the Hebrew letter daled; the hand tefillin is knotted in the shape of the Hebrew letter yud. (Together, shin, daled, yud spell Shada-i -- one of the names of God.)

For the arm:
Transliteration: Barukh ata YHWH Eloheinu melekh ha-olam, asher kid'shanu b'mitzvotav v'tzivanu l'hani'ah t'filin.

Translation: "YHWH, our Mighty One Increaser, King of the universe, Who has sanctified us with His commandments and has commanded us to put on tefillin."

For the head:
Transliteration: Barukh ata YHWH Eloheinu melekh ha-olam, asher kid'shanu b'mitzvotav v'tzivanu al mitzvat t'filin.

Translation: "YHWH, our Mighty One Increaser, King of the universe, King of the universe, Who has sanctified us with His commandments and has commanded us regarding the commandment of tefillin."

Kanani, as He swore to you and your ahvot (fathers), and gives it to you,

12 That you shall be Holy to YHWH all that opens the womb, and every Bekhor (firstborn) that comes from an animal which you have; the males shall be YHWH's.

13 And every Bekhor (firstborn) of a donkey you shall redeem with a lamb; and if you will not redeem it, then you shall break its neck: and all the Bekhor (firstborn) of man among your children you shall redeem.

14 So it shall be when your son asks you in time to come, saying, What is this? That you shall say to him, By the strength of His hand YHWH brought us out of Mitzrayim (Egypt), out of the Beyth (house) of slavery:

15 And it came to pass, when Pharaoh was stubborn about letting us go, that YHWH killed all the Bekhor (firstborn) in the land of Mitzrayim (Egypt), both the Bekhor (firstborn) of man, and the Bekhor (firstborn) of beast: therefore I sacrifice to YHWH all males that opens the womb, being males; but all the Bekhor (firstborn) of my children I redeem.[1]

16 It shall be as a sign on your hand[2] and as frontlets between your eyes: for by strength of the

Footnotes
[1] This was to prevent the idolatry that existed in Egypt, where they worshipped their first born children, and first born animals.
[2] Tefilin should be worn by men, the same as the Hebrew people today. These will act as the sign. Read Deut 6:8.

hand of YHWH brought us out of Mitzrayim (Egypt).

Torah Parsha 16 Beshalach, Shemoth 13:17-17:16
Haftarah: Shoftim 4:4-5:31

17 And it came to pass, when Pharaoh had let the people go, that Elohim did not lead them by way of the land of the Plushtim, although that was near; for Elohim said, Lest perhaps the people change their minds when they see war, and return to Mitzrayim (Egypt):

18 But Elohim led the people around, by way of the wilderness of Sea of Reeds: and the children of Israel went up in orderly ranks out of the land of Mitzrayim (Egypt).

19 And Mosheh (Musa) took the bones of Yosef with him: for he had placed the children of Israel under solemn oath, saying, Elohim will surely visit you; and you shall carry up my bones from here with you.

20 And they took their journey from Succoth, and camped in Etham, at the edge of the wilderness.

21 And YHWH went before them by day in a pillar of cloud, to lead the way; and by night in a pillar of fire, to give them light; to go by day and night:

22 He did not take away the pillar of cloud by day, or the pillar of fire by night, from before the people.

Chapter 14

1 And YHWH spoke to Mosheh (Musa), saying,

2 Speak to the children of Israel that they turn and camp before Pi Hahiroth,[1] between Migdol[2] and the sea, opposite Baal Zephon,[3] you shall camp before it by the sea. [4]

3 For Pharaoh will say of the children of Israel, They are confused by the land; the wilderness has trapped them in.

4 And I will harden Pharaoh's heart, so that he will pursue them; and I will gain respect over Pharaoh, and over all his army; that the Mitzrim (Egyptians) may know that I am YHWH. And they did so.

5 And it was told the King of Mitzrayim (Egypt) that the people had fled: and the heart of Pharaoh and his servants was turned against the people, and they said, Why have we done this, that we have let Israel go from serving us? [5]

Footnotes
[1] The valley or mouth between the two rocks. This area is in Saudi Arabia today where the Mountain of YHWH was hence pi hakharoth would in ancient Hebrew mean "Mouth into the concealed Heights" since this area was closed off by surrounding rocks and the Mountains.
[2] A high tower or Mound.
[3] An altar for the ancient worship for Baal which means the Hidden Baal or Baal in the North.
[4] Gulf of Aqaba opposite end connecting to Saudi Sea near Mount Jabal Al Mosheh (Musa) in Al-Bad.
[5] Pharaoh had already sent an army before to bring the Israelites back, they said to them that you have spent your three days in the wilderness to do the festival and now return but the Israelites told them no they are going to a land of milk and honey as YHWH has declared to them so there was a battle between the two groups and the Israelites defeated the Egyptians, see (Yasher 81:12-17). This was the second time Continued in next section

6 And he made ready his chariot, and took his people with him:

7 And he took six hundred choice chariots, and all the chariots of Mitzrayim (Egypt), with captains over everyone of them.

8 And YHWH hardened the heart of Pharaoh King of Mitzrayim (Egypt), and he pursued the children of Israel: and the children of Israel went out with boldness.[1]

9 But the Mitzrim (Egyptians) pursued them, all the horses and chariots of Pharaoh, his horsemen, and his army, and overtook them camping by the sea, beside Pi Hahiroth, before Baal Zephon.

10 And when Pharaoh drew near, the children of Israel lifted their eyes, and, behold, the Mitzrim (Egyptians) marched after them; and they were extremely afraid: and the children of Israel cried out to YHWH.

11 And they said to Mosheh (Musa), Because there were no graves in Mitzrayim (Egypt), have you taken us away to die in the wilderness? Why have you so dealt with us, to bring us up out of Mitzrayim (Egypt)?

12 Is this not the word that we told you in Mitzrayim (Egypt), saying, Let us alone that we may serve the Mitzrim (Egyptians)? For it would have been better for us to serve the Mitzrim (Egyptians), than that we should die in the wilderness.

13 And Mosheh (Musa) said to the people, Do not be afraid, stand still, and see the salvation of YHWH, which He will accomplish for you today: for the Mitzrim (Egyptians) whom you see today, you shall see again no more forever.[2]

14 YHWH shall fight for you, and ye shall hold your shalom (Peace).

15 And YHWH said to Mosheh (Musa), Why do you cry to Me? Tell the children of Israel to go forward:

16 But lift up your rod, and stretch out your hand over the sea, and divide it: and the children of Israel shall go on dry ground through the midst of the sea.

17 And I, indeed, will harden the hearts of the Mitzrim (Egyptians), and they shall follow them: and I will gain respect over Pharaoh, and over all his army, his chariots, and his horsemen.

18 And the Mitzrim (Egyptians) shall know that I am YHWH, when I have gained respect for Myself over Pharaoh, his chariots, and his horsemen.

---

the Pharaoh was preparing a much larger army to fight and bring the Israelites back or to destroy them.

[1] This will prove an important point that it is not by miracles that people come to the Faith. Pharaoh had seen many miracles, and each time considered them; but he only finally let Israel go because YHWH is the true Elohim. However, as can be seen here, his heart was still a heart of stone, we see this in many Christian churches, where people have a heart of stone, refusing to obey Torah, and relying on, even chasing after, miracles.

Footnotes
[2] YHWH fights our battles, and we do not need to defend Him.

19 And the Malakh-Elohim,[1] who went before the camp of Israel, moved and went behind them; and the pillar of cloud went from before them, and stood behind them:

20 And it came between the camp of the Mitzrim (Egyptians) and the camp of Israel; and it was a cloud and darkness to the one, and it gave light by night to the other: so that the one did not come near the other all that night.

21 And Mosheh (Musa) stretched out his hand over the sea; and YHWH caused the sea to go back by a strong east wind all that night, and made the sea into dry land, and the mayim were divided.[2]

22 And the children of Israel went into the midst of the sea on the dry ground: and the mayim were a wall[3] to them on their right hand, and on their left.

23 And the Mitzrim (Egyptians) pursued, and went after them into the midst of the sea, all Pharaoh's horses, his chariots, and his horsemen.

24 And it came to pass, in the morning watch that YHWH looked down upon the army of the Mitzrim (Egyptians) through the pillar of fire and cloud, and He troubled the army of the Mitzrim (Egyptians),

25 And He took off their chariot wheels, so that they drove them with difficulty and the Mitzrim (Egyptians) said, Let us flee from the face of Israel; for YHWH fights for them against the Mitzrim (Egyptians).

26 And YHWH said to Mosheh (Musa), Stretch out your hand over the sea, that the mayim may come back upon the Mitzrim (Egyptians), on their chariots, and on their horsemen.

27 And Mosheh (Musa) stretched out his hand over the sea, and when the morning appeared the sea returned to its full depth; and the Mitzrim (Egyptians) fled into it; and YHWH overthrew the Mitzrim (Egyptians) in the midst of the sea.

28 And the mayim returned, and covered the chariots, the horsemen, and all the army of Pharaoh that came into the sea after them; not so much as one of them remained.

29 But the children of Israel had walked on dry land in the midst of the sea; and the mayim were a wall to them on their right hand, and on their left.[4]

30 So YHWH rescued Israel that day out of the hand of the Mitzrim (Egyptians); and Israel

Footnotes

[1] Metatron, and Memra, the Word, who is YHWH.

[2] We know from the Scroll of Yashar that the waters were divided into twelve pathways, and the water was frozen on each side, so each tribe of Israel could cross over on its own path. There was order and not disorder. The movie 'The Ten Commandments' does not accurately depict what happened.

[3] The waters congealed as ice on each side, and were frozen.

Footnotes

[4] This is a drash (allegorical) picture of the narrow gate. Many in the world and in churches are falling into the sea, which is the wide gate. Torah obedient believers continue to walk in the narrow pathway opened by YHWH.

saw the Mitzrim (Egyptians) dead on the seashore.[1]

31 Thus Israel saw the great work which YHWH had done in Mitzrayim (Egypt): and the people feared YHWH, and believed YHWH, and His servant Mosheh (Musa).

Chapter 15

1 Then Mosheh (Musa) and the children of Israel sang this song to YHWH, and spoke, saying, I will sing to YHWH, for He has lifted up his arm:[2] the horse and its rider He has thrown into the sea.

2 YAH is my strength and shir (song), and He has become my Yahshuah (Salvation: Rescue): He is my El (The Power), and I will hallel (praise) Him; my father's Elohim, and I will exalt Him.

3 YHWH is a man of war: YHWH is His name.[3]

4 Pharaoh's chariots and his army He has cast into the sea: his chosen captains also are drowned in the Sea of Reeds.

5 The depths have covered them: they sank to the bottom like a stone.

6 Your right hand,[4] O YHWH, has become glorious in power:

Your right hand, O YHWH, has dashed the enemy in pieces.

7 And in the greatness of Your Excellence You have overthrown those who rose against You: You sent forth Your wrath, which consumed them like stubble.

8 And with the blast of Your nostrils the waters were gathered together, the streams of water stood upright like a heap, the depths froze in the heart of the sea.

9 The enemy said, I will pursue, I will overtake, I will divide the spoil; my desire shall be satisfied on them; I will draw my sword, my hand shall destroy them.

10 You blew with Your wind, the sea covered them: they sank like lead in the mighty waters.

11 Who is like You, YHWH among the elim (powers)? Who is like You, great in splendour and Holy, to receive reverence and praises, doing amazing wonders?

12 You stretched out Your Right Hand, the earth swallowed them.

13 You in Your loving-kindness have led forth the people whom You have redeemed: You have guided them in Your strength to Your Holy habitation.

14 The people will hear, and be afraid: sorrow will take hold of the inhabitants of Plushtim.

15 Then the chiefs of Edom will be dismayed; the mighty men of Moav, trembling will take hold of them; all the inhabitants of Kanan will melt away.[5]

Footnotes

[1] Now did YHWH rescue Israel just to send them to hell? Clearly not, their physical rescue leads to the eternal rescue, being shown forth by their fruits. Problems occur with men, not YHWH. Please see footnote Leviticus 18:5.

[2] Gaw-aw גאה which means an arm in the ancient script or a hand.

[3] YHWH's name is used twice to show His signature.

[4] The judgment side of YHWH.

[5] This is future prophecy when Edom, that is not only Jordan but all of the Arabians and Continued in next section

16 Fear and dread will fall on them; by the greatness of Your Arm they will be as still as a stone; till Your people pass over, O YHWH, till the people pass over, whom You have purchased.[1]

17 You will bring them in, and plant them in the mountain of Your inheritance, in the place, O YHWH, which You have made for Your own dwelling, the Holy Place, O YHWH[2], which Your hands have established.

18 YHWH shall reign forever and ever.

19 For the horse of Pharaoh went in with his chariots and his horsemen into the sea, and YHWH brought back the waters of the sea upon them; but the children of Israel went on dry land in the midst of the sea.

20 Then Miriam the prophetess, the sister of Aharon, took the timbrel in her hand; and all the women went out after her with timbrels and with dances.

21 And Miriam answered them, Sing to YHWH, for He has lifted up his arm;[3] the horse and it's rider He has thrown into the sea.

22 So Mosheh (Musa) brought Israel from the Sea of Reeds, and they went out into the Wilderness of Shur; and they went three days in the wilderness, and found no mayim.

23 And when they came to Marah, they could not drink the waters of Marah, for they were bitter: therefore the name of it was called Marah.

24 And the people complained against Mosheh (Musa), saying, What shall we drink?

25 And he cried out to YHWH; and YHWH showed him a tree,[4] which when he cast it into the mayim, the mayim were made sweet: there He made a statute and an ordinance for them, and there He tested them,

26 And said, If you will diligently heed the voice of YHWH Your POWER, and will do what is right in His sight, and will give ear to His commandments, and keep all His statutes, I will put none of the diseases on you, which I have brought on the Mitzrim (Egyptians):[5] for I am YHWH who heals you.

27 Then they came to Elim, where there were twelve wells of mayim, and seventy palm etzim

Footnotes

[4] The tree that was cast into the water was a bitter one, according to the Targum of Jonathan, so the miracle was not that the tree was sweet, and could sweeten the water; but that YHWH did a miracle in time and space to show His glory. This is drash of the future bitterness of our exile, we have to go through bitterness before our rescue and happiness comes.

[5] If you want to be safe from the disease that the Egyptians had to experience, then you must be Torah obedient. We cannot walk limping in Torah, with one foot in the world, and one in the Church, refusing to obey Torah. Our assemblies' first motto must be obedience to YHWH and His voice, which is declared in the Torah of Moses.

the Muslim empire will be struck by YHWH and they will be really afraid of YHWH.

[1] YHWH purchased the people. We were his, we were created to serve him. All the world was created for us to serve him. He purchased us means he has allotted Covenants for us that we are always in his plan and he will restore us back to him, back to the Torah.

[2] See appendix HBYH.

[3] See footnote Shemoth 15:1.

(trees): so they camped there by the mayim.

Chapter 16

1 And they journeyed from Elim, and all the congregation of the children of Israel came to the wilderness of sin, which is between Elim and Sinai,[1] on the fifteenth day of the second month after they departed from the land of Mitzrayim (Egypt).

2 Then the whole congregation of the children of Israel complained against Mosheh (Musa) and Aharon in the wilderness:

3 And the children of Israel said to them, Oh that we had died by the hand of YHWH in the land of Mitzrayim (Egypt), when we sat by the pots of meat, and when we ate Lakhem (bread) to the full; for you have brought us out into this wilderness, to kill this whole assembly with hunger.

4 Then YHWH said to Mosheh (Musa), Behold, I will rain Lakhem (bread) from shamayim for you; and the people shall go out and gather a certain quota every day, that I may test them,[2]

whether they will walk in My Torah, or not.[3]

5 And it shall be, on the sixth day that they shall prepare what they bring in; and it shall be twice as much as they gather daily.[4]

6 Then Mosheh (Musa) and Aharon said to all the children of Israel, At evening, you shall know that YHWH has brought you out of the land of Mitzrayim (Egypt):

7 And in the morning, you shall see the glory of YHWH; for He hears your complaints against YHWH; and what are we, that you complain against us?

8 And Mosheh (Musa) said, This shall be seen, when YHWH gives you meat to eat in the evening, and in the morning Lakhem (bread) to the full; for YHWH hears your complaints which you make against Him: and what are we? Your complaints are not against us, but against YHWH.

9 And Mosheh (Musa) spoke to Aharon, Say to all the congregation of the children of Israel, Come near before YHWH: for He has heard your complaints.

10 Now it came to pass, as Aharon spoke to the whole congregation of the children of

Footnotes
[1] YHWH identifies the Mountain by His Holy Name, it is pronounced Sini'yah, and not Sinai, equivalent to the Mountain of Mar-Yah, where Abraham was told to go to sacrifice Isaac.
[2] YHWH established the Sabbath as a test for his people while most of Christendom today is actually breaking the Sabbath so they have already failed His test. Manna was given as a test for His people and those who today for whatever reason failed this test will be judged just as the children of Israel were judged. The judgment was that those Israelites were not allowed to enter the land of Israel except Joshua and Caleb who were trustworthy.
[3] YHWH tests His people by seeing if they obey His voice, sadly many still refuse to believe. They pick and choose which commandment they should obey, and which they should not.
[4] If we obey YHWH, He will give us twice on the sixth day, meaning shut down your businesses from Friday sunset to Saturday sunset. This is a mandatory commandment, not your choice. YHWH will send double to cover for the one day loss, and it will be no loss at all.

Israel, that they looked toward the wilderness, and, behold, the glory of YHWH appeared in the cloud.

11 And YHWH spoke to Mosheh (Musa), saying,

12 I have heard the complaints of the children of Israel: speak to them, saying, At twilight you shall eat meat, and in the morning you shall be filled with Lakhem (bread); and you shall know that I am YHWH Your POWER.

13 So it was, that quails came up at evening, and covered the camp; and in the morning the dew lay all around the camp.

14 And when the layer of dew lifted, there, on the surface of the wilderness was a small round thing, as fine as frost[1] on the ground.

15 And when the children of Israel saw it, they said to one another, Is this manna? For they were not sure what it was. And Mosheh (Musa) said to them, This is the Lakhem (bread) which YHWH has given you to eat.

16 This is the thing which YHWH has commanded, Let every man gather it according to each one's need, one omer[2] for each person, according to the number of persons; let every man take for those who are in his tent.

17 And the children of Israel did so, and gathered, some more, some less.

18 So when they measured it by omers, he who gathered much had nothing over, and he who

gathered little had no lack; every man had gathered according to each one's need.

19 And Mosheh (Musa) said, Let no one leave any of it till morning.

20 Notwithstanding they did not listen to Mosheh (Musa); but some of them left part of it until morning, and it bred worms, and stank: and Mosheh (Musa) was angry with them.

21 So they gathered it every morning, every man according to his need: and when the sun became hot, it melted.

22 And so it was, on the sixth day that they gathered twice as much Lakhem (bread), two omers for each one: and all the rulers of the congregation came and told Mosheh (Musa).

23 And he said to them, This is what YHWH has said, Tomorrow is a Sabbath rest,[3] a Holy Sabbath to YHWH; bake what you will bake,[4] and boil what you will boil; and lay up for yourselves

Footnotes

[1] Manna was like coriander seed and sweet like frosted flakes.

[2] Two quarts approximate about two litres.

[3] The word here for "TOMORROW" means it is not tonight at sunset. This is proof of the original Israelite doing the sunrise Sabbath which was changed later by Jews in Israel under persecution from Greece and Rome.

[4] All preparation must be done before the start of the Sabbath, Saturday sunrise until Sunday sunrise. The Sabbath was switched to Friday sunset to Saturday sunset after Antiochus invaded Israel and forced the people to give up the Torah and had many families killed. You can cook food prepared on Friday even light gas to cook, You can see this even in the book of Exodus 24:5 where 12 loaves were to be cooked on the Sabbath, this is why the text says to leave the prepared food until morning for fresh cooking, the only lighting that is prohibited is for manual labour.

all that remains, to be kept until morning.

24 So they laid it up till morning, as Mosheh (Musa) commanded: and it did not stink, nor were there any worms in it.

25 Then Mosheh (Musa) said, Eat that today; for today is a Sabbath to YHWH: today you will not find it in the field.

26 Six days you shall gather it; but on the seventh day, which is the Sabbath, there will be none.

27 Now it happened, that some of the people went out on the seventh day to gather, but they found none.

28 And YHWH said to Mosheh (Musa), How long do you refuse to keep My commandments and My Torot (instructions)?[1]

29 See, for YHWH has given you the Sabbath, therefore He gives you on the sixth day Lakhem (bread) for two days; let every man remain in his place, let no man go out of his place on the seventh day.

30 So the people rested on the seventh day.

31 And the Beyth (house) of Israel called its name Manna: and it was like white coriander seed, white; and the taste of it was like thin rotis made with honey.[2]

32 And Mosheh (Musa) said, This is the thing which YHWH has commanded, Fill an omer with it to be kept for your generations; that they may see the Lakhem (bread) with which I fed you in the wilderness, when I brought you out of the land of Mitzrayim (Egypt).

33 And Mosheh (Musa) said to Aharon, Take a pot, and put an omer of manna in it, and lay it up before YHWH, to be kept for your generations.

34 As YHWH commanded Mosheh (Musa), so Aharon laid it up before the Testimony, to be kept.

35 And the children of Israel ate manna forty years, until they came to an inhabited land; they ate manna, until they came to the border of the land of Kanan.

36 Now an omer is one-tenth of an ephah.[3]

Chapter 17

1 And all the congregation of the children of Israel set out on their journey from the wilderness of sin, according to the command of YHWH, and camped in Rephidim: and there was no mayim for the people to drink.

2 Therefore the people contended with Mosheh (Musa), and said, Give us mayim, that we may drink. And Mosheh (Musa)

Footnotes
[1] A rarely used word pointing to the two Torahs. YHWH gave Moses two Torah's one that he wrote down and another which was communicated by mouth called the oral Torah. This was kept in Israel for Israel and always communicated orally. Please see further footnotes on the oral Torah in Nehemiah 13 and Dani'el chapter 1:12 where even the prophets had no problem with the oral laws accept modern Christianity, which is teaching many falsehoods regarding the Hebrew people and their Torah.

Footnotes
[2] The mann tasting like whatever you wanted, if you wanted roast chicken it tasted like that, if roasted fish, it tasted like it.
[3] About two litres in water quantity, an ephah is about seven gallons.

said to them, Why do you contend with me? Why do you test YHWH?

3 And the people thirsted there for mayim; and the people complained against Mosheh (Musa), and said, Why is it you have brought us up out of Mitzrayim (Egypt), to kill us and our children and our livestock with thirst?

4 So Mosheh (Musa) cried out to YHWH, saying, What shall I do with this people? They are almost ready to stone me.[1]

5 And YHWH said to Mosheh (Musa), Go on before the people, and take with you some of the elders of Israel; also take in your hand your rod, with which you struck the river, and go.

6 Behold, I will stand before you there on the rock in Horev; and you shall strike the rock, and mayim will come out of it, that the people may drink. And Mosheh (Musa) did so in the sight of the elders of Israel.

7 So he called the name of the place Massah,[2] and Meribah,[3] because of the contention of the children of Israel, and because they tested YHWH, saying, Is YHWH among us, or not?

8 Then Amalek came, and fought with Israel in Rephidim.

9 And Mosheh (Musa) said to Yahushua, Choose us some men, and go out, fight with Amalek:[4] tomorrow I will stand on the top of the hill with the rod of Elohim in my hand.

10 So Yahushua did as Mosheh (Musa) said to him, and fought with Amalek: and Mosheh (Musa), Aharon, and Khur went up to the top of the hill.

11 And so it was, when Mosheh (Musa) held up his hand, that Israel prevailed: and when he let down his hand, Amalek prevailed.

12 But Mosheh (Musa) hands became heavy; so they took a stone, and put it under him, and he sat on it; and Aharon and Khur supported his hands, one on one side, and the other on the other side; and his hands were steady until the going down of the sun.

13 So Yahushua defeated Amalek and his people with the edge of the sword.

14 Then YHWH said to Mosheh (Musa), Write this for a remembrance in the book, and recount it in the hearing of Yahushua: for I will utterly blot out the remembrance of Amalek from under the shamayim.

15 And Mosheh (Musa) built an altar, and called its Name, YHWH -Is-My-Banner;

16 For he said, Because YHWH has sworn; YHWH will

Footnotes

[1] They were enraged like a mob.

[2] It means 'to prove.'

[3] To contend as in a bitter quarrel. Israel was behaving very badly with her husband YHWH; this is why the quarrel of a bitter wife can wear a person down.

Footnotes

[4] Israel was not taught pacifism, but self defense, so they fought for survival, while many in churches teach a form of pacifism we do not find this in the Tanak. We are to pursue peace; but when the enemy comes knocking at our door, we respond according to the severity of the situation.

have war with Amalek[1] from generation to generation.

Torah Parsha 17 Yithro, Shemoth 18:1-20:26

Haftarah: Yeshayahu 6:1-7:6 & 9:5-6

Chapter 18

1 When Ythro, the kohen (priest) of Midian, Mosheh (Musa)'s father-in-law, heard of all that Elohim had done for Mosheh (Musa), and for Israel His people, that YHWH had brought Israel out of Mitzrayim (Egypt);

2 Then Ythro, Mosheh's (Musa)'s father-in-law, took Zipporah, Mosheh (Musa)'s wife, after he had divorced her sending her back, [2]

3 And her two sons; of which the name of one was Gershom; for he said, I have been a stranger in a foreign land:

4 And the name of the other was Eli'ezer; for he said, the Elohim of my father, was my

help, and rescued me from the sword of Pharaoh:

5 And Ythro, Mosheh's (Musa)'s father-in-law, came with his sons and his wife to Mosheh (Musa) in the wilderness, where he was encamped at the mountain of Elohim:

6 And he had said to Mosheh (Musa), I your father-in-law Ythro am coming to you, with your wife, and her two sons with her.

7 And Mosheh (Musa) went out to meet his father-in-law, bowed down, and kissed him; and they asked each other about their well-being; and they went into the tent.

8 And Mosheh (Musa) told his father-in-law all that YHWH had done to Pharaoh and to the Mitzrim (Egyptians) for Israel's sake, all the hardship that had come upon them on the way,[3] and how YHWH had rescued them.

9 And Ythro rejoiced for all the good which YHWH had done for Israel, whom He had rescued out of the hand of the Mitzrim (Egyptians).

10 And Ythro said, Increaser be YHWH, who has rescued you out of the hand of the Mitzrim (Egyptians), and out of the hand of Pharaoh, and who has rescued the people from under the hand of the Mitzrim (Egyptians).

11 Now I know that YHWH is greater than all the powers: for in

Footnotes

[1] This is the picture of the Anti-Messiah who will be a Muslim, and his people, all of radical Islam joined with him. YHWH said He will destroy them by His hands. Amalek is also the fake Yahudim.

[2] They had a quarrel over the circumcision of the child, after which Zipporah went to her father's house, and here she returns back, realising her mistake of refusing to allow Moses to circumcise their son. Moses did not divorce his wife as many have thought, and he was also married to a Cushite woman which is not Zipporah. Zipporah was his second wife; but the Cushite was the first wife, who lost touch with Moses when he left Egypt. He divorced her and sent her back to her father as was custom but now the Father brings her back as she was being restored to her husband.

Footnotes

[3] When you follow YHWH, hardships will come; but YHWH will rescue you through all of these, as they test your Faith, and strengthen and refine you, like gold in a burning fire.

the very thing in which they behaved proudly He was above them.

12 Then Ythro, Mosheh's (Musa)'s father-in-law, took a burnt offering and other sacrifices to offer to Elohim: [1] and Aharon came, with all the elders of Israel, to eat Lakhem (bread) with Mosheh's (Musa)'s father-in-law before Elohim.[2]

13 And so it was on the next day, that Mosheh (Musa) sat to judge the people: and the people stood before Mosheh (Musa) from morning until evening.

14 So when Mosheh (Musa)'s father-in-law saw all that he did for the people, he said, What is this thing that you are doing for the people? Why do you sit alone, and all the people stand before you from morning until evening?

15 And Mosheh (Musa) said to his father-in-law, Because the people come to me to inquire of Elohim:

16 When they have a difficulty, they come to me; and I judge between one and another, and I make known the statutes of Elohim, and His Torot (instructions).

17 So Mosheh (Musa)'s father-in-law said to him, The thing that you do is not good.

18 Both you, and these people, who are with you will surely wear yourselves out: for this thing is too much for you; you are not able to perform it by yourself.

19 Listen now to my voice, I will give you counsel, and Elohim will be with you: Stand before Elohim for the people, so that you may bring the difficulties to Elohim:

20 And you shall teach them the statutes and the Torot (instructions), and show them the way[3] in which they must walk, and the work they must do.

21 Moreover you shall select from all the people able men, such as fear Elohim, men of truth, hating covetousness; and place such over them, to be rulers of thousands, rulers of hundreds, rulers of fifties, and rulers of tens:

22 And let them judge the people at all times: then it will be, that every great matter they shall bring to you, but every small matter they themselves shall judge: so it will be easier for you, and they will bear the burden with you.

23 If you do this thing, and Elohim so commands you, then you will be able to endure, and all this people will also go to their place in peace (shalom).

24 So Mosheh (Musa) heeded the voice of his father-in-law, and did all that he had said.

25 And Mosheh (Musa) chose able men out of all Israel, and made them heads over the

Footnotes

[1] In Shemoth 18:11-12, according to Yasher 82:5, Yah'thro (Reuel), After hearing of all the wonders that Adonai YHWH had done in Mitzraim, the Midian priest finally became a believer of YHWH. See also Shemoth 18:8-9.

[2] It is a common custom in the East, to invite guests to a dinner party as in the West.

[3] There is only <u>one</u> way to do the correct Halacha (commandments), and that is by YHWH's Torah.

people, rulers of thousands, rulers of hundreds, rulers of fifties, and rulers of tens.

26 And they judged the people at all times: the hard cases they brought to Mosheh (Musa), but they judged every small case themselves.

27 Then Mosheh (Musa) sent away his father-in-law; and he went his way to his own province.[1]

Chapter 19

1 In the third month, after the children of Israel had gone out of the land of Mitzrayim (Egypt), the same day they came to the wilderness of Sinai.

2 For they had departed from Rephidim, and had come to the wilderness of Sinai,[2] and camped in the wilderness; and Israel camped there before the mountain.

3 And Mosheh (Musa) went up to Elohim, and YHWH called to him from the mountain, saying, Thus you shall say to the Beyth (house) of Yakov, and tell the children of Israel;

4 You have seen what I did to the Mitzrim (Egyptians), and how I bore you on eagles' wings, and brought you to Myself.

5 Now therefore, if you will indeed, obey My voice, and keep

My Covenant, then you shall be a special possession[3] to Me above all people: for all the earth is Mine:

6 And you shall be to Me a kingdom of priests, and a Holy nation. These are the words which you shall speak to the children of Israel.

7 So Mosheh (Musa) came and called for the elders of the people, and laid before them all these words which YHWH commanded him.

8 Then all the people answered together, and said, All that YHWH has spoken we will do.[4] And Mosheh (Musa) brought back the words of the people to YHWH.

9 And YHWH said to Mosheh (Musa), Behold, I come to you in the thick cloud, that the people may hear when I speak with you, and believe you forever. And Mosheh (Musa) told the words of the people to YHWH.

10 Then YHWH said to Mosheh (Musa), Go to the people, and consecrate them today and tomorrow, and let them wash their clothes,[5]

Footnotes

[1] They were in the same country, Arabia, so here the use of the Hebrew term eretz, is for a province of Arabia; and not as another country which would be incorrect.

[2] They were in the desert of Saudi Arabia, this region is known by YHWH's name, and any wonder why Shaitan (Satan) wanted to have this place for himself, erecting a new religion over this land!

[3] Israel was to be special and separate from all the nations. Many erroneous pastors teach that the earth is controlled by Satan; but the scrolls of YHWH are clear. The earth belongs to YHWH; and Satan only floats in the air, basically he controls nothing and is under YHWH's authority.

[4] Note: Israel did not hear all the Word, the next sentence tells us that they heard the Word afterwards. This was a real leap of Faith that they said 'yes' first, and then heard the 'Word.' This is why Israel was to be special. These were the Twin Brides of YHWH, the Two Houses of Israel. The North and the South united together.

[5] There is a mystery of the marriage of YHWH to Israel; when the Bride says 'I do'
Continued in next section

11 And let them be ready for the third day: for on the third day YHWH will come down upon Mount Sinai in the sight of all the people.

12 You shall set bounds for the people all around, saying, Take heed to yourselves, that you do not go up to the mountain, or touch its base: whoever touches the mountain shall surely be put to death:

13 Not a hand shall touch it, but he shall surely be stoned, or shot with an arrow; whether man, or beast, it shall not live: when the shofar sounds long,[1] they shall come near the mountain.

14 Then Mosheh (Musa) went down from the mountain to the people, and sanctified the people; and they washed their clothes.

15 And he said to the people, Be ready for the third day: do not come near your wives.[2]

16 Then it came to pass on the third day in the morning, that there was thunderings[3] and lightnings, and a thick cloud on the mountain, and the sound of the shofar was very loud; so that all the people who were in the camp trembled.

17 And Mosheh (Musa) brought the people out of the camp to meet with Elohim; and they stood underneath[4] the mountain.

18 Now Mount Sinai was completely in smoke, because YHWH descended upon it in fire: it's smoke ascended like the smoke of a furnace, and the whole mountain quaked greatly.

19 And when the blast of the shofar sounded[5] long, and

rest of the world heard. The voice of YHWH spread to all four corners, in the language of the various peoples, as it went out to them. However, they refused to keep the Torah, and Israel was the only nation on the earth that said, 'We will do, and hear.' They heard after; but said, we will do, first. Shabbat 88 b - The school of Rabbi Ishmael taught: Behold My word is like fire, declares YHWH; and like a hammer that breaks the rock into pieces, just as a hammer is divided into many sparks, so every single word that went forth from the Holy One, blessed be He, split up into seventy languages.

[4] The Hebrew phrase b'takhteet ha'har means, under the mountain, so it was a chupah, just like, in a Hebrew wedding. Israel here is the dual Brides, the House of Israel and the House of Yahudah. The separation was to be shown much later; but in YHWH's eyes it was already done, so we see two brides here, not one as commonly thought. Ye'khezk'el (Ezek) 23:2, Yirmeyah (Jeremiah) 3:8.

[5] The Hebrew word 'halak' is used here, which tells us that this was no ordinary blast of a shofar; but the blast of, The Shofar of YHWH, where he tells his people to straighten up, and fix your Walk. Meaning, Torah obedience, without complaining and whining about it, as the Israelites had done in the wilderness. They were to have order in their lives, and not disorder. The call of the shofar was also one of the war calls of Continued in next section

and then has a mikvah (ritual bath), just like in the Hebrew marriage custom, when they are under the chupah, which here is the Mountain of YHWH, Mount Sini'yah.

[1] The allegorical marriage took place during the Khag, celebration of Weeks, which is Shavuot, and also known as Pentecost. The long shofar blast is the sound of the wedding khag, celebration.

[2] Any sexual contact with the spouses was strictly off-limits. This is not because sleeping with your spouse is bad; but because it would make you ritually unclean, and you had to be clean to stand before YHWH, hence even the clothes they wore had to be washed.

[3] Many ancient Rebbim suggest that here, the thundering were not just ordinary thundering; but they were sounds, as in the seventy languages of the earth, which the Continued in next section

became louder and louder, Mosheh (Musa) spoke, and Elohim answered him by voice.

20 Then YHWH came down upon Mount Sinai, on the top of the mountain: and YHWH called Mosheh (Musa) to the top of the mountain; and Mosheh (Musa) went up.

21 And YHWH said to Mosheh (Musa), Go down, and warn the people, lest they break through to gaze[1] at YHWH, and many of them perish.

22 Also let the priests, who come near YHWH, consecrate themselves, lest YHWH break out against them.[2]

23 And Mosheh (Musa) said to YHWH, The people cannot come up to Mount Sinai; for You warned us, saying, Set bounds around the mountain,[3] and consecrate it.

24 Then YHWH said to him, Away, get down, and then come up, you, and Aharon with you; but do not let the priests and the people break through to come up to YHWH, lest He break out against them.

25 So Mosheh (Musa) went down to the people, and spoke to them.

Aserat Hadebirot
The Decalogue[4]
The Ten Commandments

א וַיְדַבֵּר אֱלֹהִים, אֵת כָּל-הַדְּבָרִים הָאֵלֶּה לֵאמֹר. {ס}

ב אָנֹכִי יְהוָה אֱלֹהֶיךָ, אֲשֶׁר הוֹצֵאתִיךָ מֵאֶרֶץ מִצְרַיִם מִבֵּית עֲבָדִים: לֹא-יִהְיֶה לְךָ אֱלֹהִים אֲחֵרִים, עַל-פָּנָי.

ג לֹא-תַעֲשֶׂה לְךָ פֶסֶל, וְכָל-תְּמוּנָה, אֲשֶׁר בַּשָּׁמַיִם מִמַּעַל, וַאֲשֶׁר בָּאָרֶץ מִתָּחַת--וַאֲשֶׁר בַּמַּיִם, מִתַּחַת לָאָרֶץ.

ד לֹא-תִשְׁתַּחֲוֶה לָהֶם, וְלֹא תָעָבְדֵם: כִּי אָנֹכִי יְהוָה אֱלֹהֶיךָ,

---

the kingdom, to make yourself ready, to remove dross, to prepare for a road ahead of obedience. To show other nations how to be obedient to the word, through YHWH's voice. All the nations roundabout Israel.
[1] One traditional custom of the East is not to look at your bridegroom, we see this here, YHWH warns not to look at Him. Technically, it is the Bridegroom YHWH who is supposed to lift the veil of the Bride, and not vice versa. This custom is carried in both Hinduism and Islam because it is ancient and based on the Torah. This custom is still maintained by Hindus, Muslims and the Yahudim; but the ones who are supposed to maintain it, have no idea about it. And they go about as if there is no tomorrow, completely mixing heathen customs with their own.
[2] The teachers amongst the saints need to heed this command, as many have one foot in the world and one in Torah, or none in Torah at all.
[3] This is also seen in Islamic culture, boundaries are set for the marriage place, Continued in next section

including where the guests will sit, and then the marriage is conducted. Many of the precepts of Islam are derived from Torah.
[4] YHWH works in tens as in the ten Sefirot to reveal his nature, the Ten utterances at creation, the Ten plagues, the Ten tribes sent out in judgment and mercy, the Ten Commandments are mandatory, not optional, contrary to popular Faith.

Chapter 20

1 And Elohim spoke all these words, saying,

2 [**Alef: One**] I am YHWH Your POWER, who brought you out of the land of Mitzrayim (Egypt), out of the Beyth (house) of slavery.

3 [**Bet: Two**] You shall have no other powers before Me.

4 You shall not make for yourself a carved image,[1] or any likeness of anything that is in the shamayim above, or that is in the earth beneath, or that is in the mayim under the earth:

5 You shall not bow down to them nor serve them. For I, YHWH Your POWER, am a Devoted[2] El (Power), visiting the iniquity of the ahvot (fathers) on the children to the third and fourth generations[3] of those who hate Me;

6 And showing loving-kindness to thousands to those who love Me,[4] and Guard My commandments.

Footnotes

[1] Any statues or pictures of YHWH are forbidden, and a sin. Having any statues for worship such as: Mary or other man made images, is also a sin, and must be avoided in the body of Israel.

[2] Samaritan Torah from Exodus 34:14.

[3] The curse of YHWH is still upon those whose great grandfather's hated YHWH. The curse can only be broken by the great grandchildren, by repenting of the mistakes their fathers had made, and making the curse null, and void, through their present actions of obedience.

[4] The spoken favour of obedient parents to children will last to a thousand generations, literally.

לְרֵעֶךָ. {פ}

אֵל קַנָּא--פֹּקֵד עֲוֹן אָבֹת עַל-בָּנִים עַל-שִׁלֵּשִׁים וְעַל-רִבֵּעִים, לְשֹׂנְאָי.

ה וְעֹשֶׂה חֶסֶד, לַאֲלָפִים--לְאֹהֲבַי, וּלְשֹׁמְרֵי מִצְוֹתָי. {ס}

ו לֹא תִשָּׂא אֶת-שֵׁם-יְהוָה אֱלֹהֶיךָ, לַשָּׁוְא: כִּי לֹא יְנַקֶּה יְהוָה, אֵת אֲשֶׁר-יִשָּׂא אֶת-שְׁמוֹ לַשָּׁוְא. {פ}

ז זָכוֹר אֶת-יוֹם הַשַּׁבָּת, לְקַדְּשׁוֹ.

ח שֵׁשֶׁת יָמִים תַּעֲבֹד, וְעָשִׂיתָ כָּל-מְלַאכְתֶּךָ.

ט וְיוֹם, הַשְּׁבִיעִי--שַׁבָּת, לַיהוָה אֱלֹהֶיךָ: לֹא-תַעֲשֶׂה כָל-מְלָאכָה אַתָּה וּבִנְךָ וּבִתֶּךָ, עַבְדְּךָ וַאֲמָתְךָ וּבְהֶמְתֶּךָ, וְגֵרְךָ, אֲשֶׁר בִּשְׁעָרֶיךָ.

י כִּי שֵׁשֶׁת-יָמִים עָשָׂה יְהוָה אֶת-הַשָּׁמַיִם וְאֶת-הָאָרֶץ, אֶת-הַיָּם וְאֶת-כָּל-אֲשֶׁר-בָּם, וַיָּנַח, בַּיּוֹם הַשְּׁבִיעִי; עַל-כֵּן, בֵּרַךְ יְהוָה אֶת-יוֹם הַשַּׁבָּת--וַיְקַדְּשֵׁהוּ. {ס}

יא כַּבֵּד אֶת-אָבִיךָ, וְאֶת-אִמֶּךָ--לְמַעַן, יַאֲרִכוּן יָמֶיךָ, עַל הָאֲדָמָה, אֲשֶׁר-יְהוָה אֱלֹהֶיךָ נֹתֵן לָךְ. {ס}

יב לֹא תִרְצָח, {ס} לֹא תִנְאָף; {ס} לֹא תִגְנֹב, {ס} לֹא-תַעֲנֶה בְרֵעֲךָ עֵד שָׁקֶר. {ס}

יג לֹא תַחְמֹד, בֵּית רֵעֶךָ; {ס} לֹא-תַחְמֹד אֵשֶׁת רֵעֶךָ, וְעַבְדּוֹ וַאֲמָתוֹ וְשׁוֹרוֹ וַחֲמֹרוֹ, וְכֹל, אֲשֶׁר

215

7 [**Gimmel: Three**] You shall not lift up the name of YHWH Your POWER *in oaths* falsely; YHWH will not leave him unpunished,[1] who lifts up his name and falsifies it.[2]

8 [**Dalet: Four**] Remember[3] the Sabbath day, to keep it Holy.

9 Six days you shall labour, and do all your work:

10 But the seventh day is the Sabbath of YHWH[4] Your POWER: in it you shall do no work, you, nor your son, nor your daughter, nor your male servant, nor your female servant, nor your cattle, nor your stranger who is within your gates:

11 For in six days YHWH made the shamayim and the earth, the sea, and all that is in them, and ceased from *work* on the seventh day: therefore YHWH **Blessed** the Sabbath day, and consecrated it.

12 [**Heh: Five**] Give glory *and* honour to your father and your mother: that your days may be long upon the land which YHWH Your POWER is giving you.

13 [**Wah: Six**] You shall not murder.

14 [**Zayin: Seven**] You shall not commit adultery.[5]

15 [**Chet: Eight**] You shall not steal.[6]

16 [**Tet: Nine**] You shall not bear false witness against your[7] neighbour.

17 [**Yud: Ten**] You shall not covet your neighbour's Beyth (house); you shall not covet your neighbour's wife, nor his male servant, nor his female servant, nor his ox, nor his donkey, nor anything that is your neighbour's.[8]

18 Now all the people witnessed the thunderings, the lightning flashes, the sound of the shofar, and the mountain smoking: and when the people saw it, they trembled and stood afar off.

19 And they said to Mosheh (Musa), You speak with us, and we will hear: but let not Elohim speak with us, lest we die.

Footnotes

[1] Samaritan Torah.

[2] The Hebrew word shav means, to make it empty, the word nasa means to lift and speak the name in an oath, or to falsify his name in oaths by using it when you are lying about it. The Targum of Onkelos also suggested the use of the name in oaths to take false oaths was forbidden.

[3] This is a seal of a believer, hence it is mentioned as number four, because it is a Covenant sign in the Ten. Anyone who claims to be a believer but does not keep the 7th day Sabbath will have a very lowly status if allowed to enter the kingdom. It's not just about reciting a four line rescue prayer, and then doing what you like, as in the present is erroneously taught in church/man's dogma.

[4] This is YHWH's Sabbath, and not your own created day and time of the week. This means any day that man has created to replace YHWH's day is irrelevant, and must be discarded, such as Sunday.

Footnotes

[5] Rhetorical question by God as He is saying you beware as you will do that.

[6] This does not mean what you read. It means do not abduct a man/woman to sell into bondage.

[7] Many are bearing false witness against other believers casting judgment upon themselves, this is sin and will be judged by YHWH both here and in the coming age.

[8] Many are bearing false witness against other believers, casting judgment upon themselves, this is sin, and will be judged by YHWH both here, and in the coming age.

[8] Today this would mean, do not desire to take your neighbour's car, properties, or his wife and his other possessions.

20 And Mosheh (Musa) said to the people, Do not fear: for Elohim has come to test you, and that His fear may be before you, so that you may not sin.

21 And the people stood afar off, but Mosheh (Musa) drew near the thick darkness[1] where Elohim was.

22 Then YHWH said to Mosheh (Musa), Thus you shall say to the children of Israel, You have seen that I have talked with you from the shamayim.

23 You shall not make to be like Me elohim of silver; neither shall you make elohim of gold.[2]

24 An altar of earth you shall make for Me, and you shall sacrifice on it your burnt offerings, and your peace (shalom) offerings, your sheep and your oxen: in every place where my name is mentioned[3] I will come to you, and I will **Bless** you.

25 And if you make Me an altar of stone, you shall not build it of hewn stone: for if you use your tool on it, you have profaned it.

26 Neither shall you go up by steps to My altar, that your nakedness[4] may not be exposed on it.

Footnotes

[1] YHWH conceals in darkness.

[2] We are forbidden to make statues to worship, as the nations do.

[3] The name YHWH is to be proclaimed for a **Blessing** for our households even today.

[4] Many, many nations sacrificed to their elohim, they took off their clothes and were at times, completely naked before their version of elohim. In pre-Islamic Arabia the hajj (pilgrimage) was performed completely naked. YHWH forbids us to show any nakedness before him. So, the Israelite priests wore an under-garment that would
Continued in next section

Torah Parsha 18 Mishpatim, Shemoth 21:1-24:18
Haftarah: Yirmeyahu 33:25-26 & 34:8-22

Chapter 21

1 Now these are the judgments which you shall set before them:

2 If you buy an Abrahu (Hebrew) servant, he shall serve six years; and in the seventh he shall go out free and pay nothing.[5]

3 If he comes in by himself, he shall go out by himself; if he comes in married, then his wife shall go out with him.

4 If his master has given him a wife, and she has borne him sons or daughters, the wife and her children shall be her master's, and he shall go out by himself.[6]

5 And if the servant plainly says, I love my master, my wife,

not allow any of their nakedness to be revealed. In the worship of Baalpeor, the priests also went naked. It is unfortunate that today in many churches, some women, who at times are the pastor's daughter, are wearing inappropriate attire revealing their flesh, and setting a bad example. Such behavior in the past would be considered nothing short of whoring, and punishable by death, hence these people need to be aware; YHWH will not take this sin lightly.

[5] This is equivalent to today doing a Covenant with an employer and not the typical slavery we saw in the West where the black people were enslaved. The black slavery would never be allowed in the scrolls of YHWH as it was a gross violation of human rights.

[6] Being married he could choose to stay and live with his wife and children, that would be honoured as it was not hard bondage as in the nations, he was like a free man who could come and go and visit his relatives and go to the job at set times.

and my children; I will not go out free,

6 And then his master shall bring him to the judges. He shall also bring him to the door, or to the doorpost, and his master shall pierce his ear with an awl;[1] and he shall serve him forever.

7 And if a man sells his daughter to be a female servant, she shall not go out as the male servants do.

8 If she does not please her master, who has betrothed her to himself, then he shall let her be redeemed. He shall have no right to sell her to a foreign people, since he has dealt deceitfully with her.

9 And if he has betrothed her to his son, he shall deal with her according to the custom of daughters.[2]

10 If he takes another wife, he shall not diminish her food, her clothing, and her marriage rights.[3]

11 And if he does not do these three for her, then she shall go out free, without paying money.

12 He who strikes a man so that he dies shall surely be put to death.

13 And if he did not lie in wait, but Elohim has given him into his hand, then I will appoint for you a place where he may flee.

14 And if a man acts with premeditation against his neighbour, to kill him by treachery, you shall take him from My altar, that he may die.

15 And he who strikes his Father or his mother[4] shall surely be put to death.

16 He who kidnaps a man and sells him, or if he is found in his hand, shall surely be put to death.

17 And he who curses[5] his Father or his mother shall surely be put to death.

18 If men contend with each other, and one strikes the other with a stone or with his fist, and he does not die but is confined to his bed:

Footnotes

[1] Ancient custom to make a bond servant.

[2] He will deal with her like his own daughter in terms of dowry and food.

[3] A man is allowed to marry two wives as long as he promised to take care of the first wife's food, clothing and housing needs. In order for him to take a second wife he would have to do the same for the second. The model in Torah was for the second wife to have a separate tent meaning another house in our society today. He could not take her into the same house and expect the first to accept this as the normal circumstance. Women are very territorial creatures and no woman will allow the second wife to come live at the family home. Whoever will do this is only asking for disaster to befall upon him. In Gen 12:8, Abraham setup Sarah's tent first then his own, you will not find this in the English because the idea is conveyed in the Hebrew text. Read footnote Gen 12:8.

Footnotes

[4] On earth this is the highest way of respecting our parents; disobedient children who hate their parents or lift their hands will not receive any Increases from YHWH. YHWH first then parents, even if the parents are not in the Hebrew Faith they are to be respected and not spoken against. The word strike is not just by hands but by actions also. If a son or daughter defrauded their parents in effect they are striking their parents down by definition and if brought to the elders and the sin is found they would be condemned to death. If parents ask children to commit idolatry like put up Christmas trees then children have the right to refuse this.

[5] The previous footnote applies. A curse is not by mouth only but by actions also.

19 If he rises again and walks about outside with his staff, then he who struck him shall be acquitted. He shall only pay for the loss of his time, and shall provide for him to be thoroughly healed.

20 And if a man beats his male or female servant with a rod, so that he dies under his hand, he shall surely be punished.

21 Notwithstanding, if he remains alive a day or two, he shall not be punished; for he is his property.

22 If men fight, and hurt a woman with child, so that she gives birth prematurely, yet no lasting harm follows, he shall surely be punished accordingly as the woman's husband imposes on him; and he shall pay as the judges determine.

23 And if any lasting harm follows, then you shall give life for life:[1]

24 Eye for eye,[2] tooth for tooth, hand for hand, foot for foot:

25 Burn for burn, wound for wound, stripe for stripe.

26 If a man strikes the eye of his male or female servant, and destroys it, he shall let him go free for the sake of his eye.

Footnotes

[1] So in this scenario if a child is injured in the womb and was born was disabled the man would have to pay a large sum of compensation or support that child for life!

[2] If someone strikes you blind it does not mean you strike him blind also, the words eye for an eye or tooth for a tooth simply mean fair judgment by judges appointed in Israel. You will not find any people in Israel who were without eyes and limbs as a result of this punishment, in fact you will find none as the commandment is understood as fair and just punishment.

27 And if he knocks out the tooth of his male or female servant, he shall let him go free for the sake of his tooth.

28 If an ox gores a man or a woman to death, then the ox shall surely be stoned, and its flesh shall not be eaten; but the owner of the ox shall be acquitted.

29 And if the ox tended to thrust with its horn in times past, and it has been made known to his owner, and he has not kept it confined, so that it has killed a man or a woman, the ox shall be stoned and its owner also shall be put to death.[3]

30 If there is imposed on him a sum of money, then he shall pay to redeem his life, whatever is imposed on him.

31 Whether it has gored a son or gored a daughter, according to this judgment it shall be done to him.

32 If the ox gores a male or female servant, he shall give to their master thirty shekels of silver coins, and the ox shall be stoned.

33 And if a man opens a pit, or if a man digs a pit and does not cover it, and an ox or a donkey falls in it:

34 The owner of the pit shall make it good; he shall give money to their owner, but the dead animal shall be his.

Footnotes

[3] The same Torah law will apply today with pit-bull terriers that have at times bitten and killed babies. The owner and the dog would <u>both</u> be stoned if Torah was in force today. The victim's family could apply for blood money meaning they could ask for a suggested sum of money. The Muslims do this today and carry this Torah law.

35 And if one man's ox hurts another's, so that it dies, then they shall sell the live ox and divide the money from it; and the dead ox they shall also divide.

36 Or if it was known that the ox tended to thrust in time past, and its owner has not kept it confined, he shall surely pay ox for ox, and the dead animal shall be his own.

Chapter 22

1 If a man steals an ox or a sheep, and slaughters it or sells it, he shall restore five oxen for an ox and four sheep for a sheep.[1]

2 If the thief is found breaking in, and he is struck so that he dies, there shall be no guilt for his bloodshed.

3 If the sun has risen on him, there shall be guilt for his bloodshed. He should make full restitution; if he has nothing, then he shall be sold for his theft.

4 If the theft is certainly found alive in his hand, whether it is an ox or donkey or sheep, he shall restore double.

5 If a man causes a field or vineyard to be grazed, and lets loose his animal, and it feeds in another man's field, he shall make restitution from the best of his own field and the best of his own vineyard.

6 If fire breaks out and catches in thorns, so that stacked grain, standing grain, or the field is consumed, he who kindled the fire shall surely make restitution.

7 If a man gives to his neighbour money or articles to keep, and it is stolen out of the man's Beyth (house), if the thief is found, he shall pay double.

8 If the thief is not found, then the master of the Beyth (house) shall be brought to the judges to see whether he has put his hand into his neighbour's goods.

9 For any kind of trespass, whether it concerns an ox, a donkey, a sheep, or clothing, or for any kind of lost thing which another claims to be his, the cause of both parties shall come before the judges; and whomever the judges condemn shall pay double to his neighbour.

10 If a man gives to his neighbour a donkey, an ox, a sheep, or any animal to keep, and it dies, is hurt, or driven away, no one seeing it,

11 Then an oath of YHWH shall be between them both, that he has not put his hand into his neighbour's goods; and the owner of it shall accept that, and he shall not make it good.

12 But if, in fact, it is stolen from him, he shall make restitution to the owner of it.

13 If it is torn to pieces by a beast, then he shall bring it as evidence, and he shall not make good what was torn.

14 And if a man borrows anything from his neighbour, and it becomes injured or dies, the

Footnotes

[1] Today this law would mean that if a thief steals a man's car, then he shall restore the value of five cars back to him. When a man's car is ripped, broken into, he feels angry and violated, because his car is his personal space and YHWH understood the emotions behind such possessions. YHWH's laws are just and supersede any man made laws.

owner of it not being with it, he shall surely make it good.

15 But if its owner was with it, he shall not make it good; if it was hired, it came for its hire.

16 And if a man entices a virgin who is not betrothed, and lies with her, he shall surely pay the bride-price for her to be his wife.

17 If her Father utterly refuses to give her to him, he shall pay money according to the bride-price of virgins.

18 You shall not permit a sorceress to live.

19 Whoever lies with an animal shall surely be put to death.

20 He who sacrifices to any elohim, except to YHWH only, he shall be utterly destroyed.

21 You shall neither mistreat a foreigner nor oppress him, for you were foreigners in the land of Mitzrayim (Egypt).

22 You shall not afflict any widow or fatherless child.

23 If you afflict them in any way, and they cry at all to Me, I will surely hear their cry;

24 And My wrath will become hot, and I will kill you with the sword; your wives shall be widows, and your children fatherless.

25 If you lend money to any of My people who are poor among you, you shall not be like a moneylender to him; you shall not charge him interest.[1]

26 If you ever take your neighbour's garment as a pledge,

you shall return it to him before the sun goes down.

27 For that is his only covering, it is his garment for his skin. What will he sleep in? And it will be that when he cries to Me, I will hear, for I am gracious.

28 You shall not revile Elohim, nor curse an *Y'sraeli* ruler of your people.

29 You shall not delay to offer the first of your ripe produce and your juices. The Bekhor (firstborn) of your sons you shall give to Me.

30 Likewise you shall do with your oxen and your sheep. It shall be with its mother seven days; on the eighth day you shall give it to Me.

31 And you shall be Holy men to Me: you shall not eat any meat which is torn by beasts in the field; you shall throw it to the dogs.

Chapter 23

1 You shall not circulate a false report.[2] Do not put your hand with the wicked to be a wicked witness.

2 You shall not follow a crowd to do evil;[3] nor shall you testify in

Footnotes

[2] Slandering is a sin and must not be done.

[3] The context applies from verse one that slandering someone with a crowd of other people or a majority view is still wrong in YHWH's sight. Yet today we see innocent people being slandered by others in the name of God. They will come under the curse of YHWH by committing this sin and will remain until restitution is made. This sin will not allow them to enter the kingdom to come. In order to rectify this they would have to restitute by apologizing to the person and then repenting to YHWH. They must also pay a sum of money to the one
Continued in next section

Footnotes

[1] This applies to believing brothers and sisters who are in need but you can charge interest to the gentile people who are unbelievers.

a dispute so as to turn aside after many to pervert justice.

3 You shall not show partiality to a poor man in his dispute.

4 If you meet your enemy's ox or his donkey going astray, you shall surely bring it back to him again.

5 If you see the donkey of one who hates you fallen under its burden, would you refrain from helping, No You shall surely help him.

6 You shall not pervert the judgment of your poor in his dispute.

7 Keep yourself far from a false matter; do not kill the innocent and Righteous. For I will not justify the wicked.

8 And you shall take no bribe, for a bribe blinds the clear sighted and perverts the words of the Righteous.

9 Also you shall not oppress a foreigner, for you know the heart of a foreigner, because you were foreigner in the land of Mitzrayim (Egypt).

10 Six years you shall sow your land and gather in its produce,

11 And the seventh year[1] you shall let it rest and lie fallow, that the poor of your people may eat; and what they leave, the beasts of the field may eat. In like manner you shall do with your vineyard and your olive grove.

12 Six days you shall do your work, and on the seventh day you shall rest, that your ox and your donkey may well rest, and the son of your female servant and the stranger may be refreshed.

13 And in all that I have said to you, be very careful and make no mention of the name[2] of other elohim, nor let it be heard from your mouth.

14 Three times you shall keep a feast to Me in the year:

15 You shall keep the khag ha Matzot (appointed celebration time of Unleavened Bread), you shall eat matzah (unleavened bread) seven days, as I commanded you, at the time appointed in the month of Abib, for in it you came out of Mitzrayim (Egypt); none shall appear before Me empty);

16 And the khag ha Shavuot,[3] (the (appointed celebration time at the harvest) the Bikkurim (first-fruits) of your labours which you have sown in the field; and khag ha Sukkot (The Feast of Sukkot or Ingathering) at the end of the year, when you have gathered in

being slandered designated by the judges of Israel in that day in the exile. The Torah judge will decide what is monetary penalty to the slanderer.

We see this behavior prevalent on the internet, where gentiles claiming to be in faith slander Torah believers as a duty to their pagan society. For such people as these, they have already lost their eternal reward and are headed to the abyss. See verses Exodus 23:7, Ezekiel 3:18. If you remain rebellious you fall in with the camp of the wicked and that will be the end of you.

Footnotes
[1] The ground is to be rested in the 7th year the year of Shmita or the year of release.
[2] Do not pray or use other elohim's names and then try and use them to equate them to YHWH.
[3] The Khag, celebration of Pentecost and the giving of Torah and the summer harvest known as the Khag, celebration of Weeks.

the fruit of your labours from the field.

17 Three times[1] in the year all your males shall appear before YHWH Elohim.

18 You shall not offer the blood of My sacrifice with chametz Lakhem (leaven bread); nor shall the fat of My sacrifice remain until morning.

19 The first of the bikkurim of your land you shall bring into the Beyth (house) of YHWH Your POWER. You shall not grow a young goat in her mother's milk.[2]

20 Behold, I send a Malakh[3] before you to keep you in the way and to bring you into the place which I have prepared.

21 Beware of Him and obey His voice; do not provoke Him, for He will not pardon your sins; for My name is in Him.[4]

22 But if[5] you indeed obey His[6] voice and do all that I speak, then I will be an enemy to your enemies and an adversary to your adversaries.

23 For My Malakh[7] will go before you and bring you in to the Amoree and the Khitee and the Perzee and the Kanani and the Khuvi and the Yavusi; and I will cut them off.

24 You shall not bow down to their powers,[8] nor serve them, nor do according to their works; but you shall utterly overthrow them and completely break down their altars.

25 So you shall serve YHWH Your POWER, and He will **Bless** your Lakhem (bread) and your mayim. And I will take sickness away from the midst of you.

26 No one shall suffer miscarriage or be barren in your land; I will fulfill the number of your days.

27 I will send My fear before you, I will cause confusion among all the people to whom you come, and will make all your enemies turn their backs to you.

28 And I will send hornets before you, which shall drive out the Khawee, the Kanani, and the Khitee from before you.

29 I will not drive them out from before you in one year, lest the land become desolate and the beast of the field become too numerous for you.

30 Little by little I will drive them out from before you, until you have **Increased**, and you inherit the land.

31 And I will set your bounds from the Sea of Reeds to the Sea of the Plushtim, and from the wilderness to the River. For I will hand over the inhabitants of the land into your hand, and you shall drive them out before you.

Footnotes

[1] The three major feasts, unleavened bread, Pentecost and Tabernacles.

[2] The meaning is not to allow the kid to grow up in the milk before bringing it for sacrifice.

[3] This is one of the faces of YHWH.

[4] This is the Metatron, the Memra, He is the middle-pillar of the Sefirotic tree, and the one known as the Tzadik.

[5] There is always an IF and a THEN with YHWH. Increases will come to you and your household IF you are obedient and IF NOT, then you can forget about receiving any increases.

[6] Obeying His voice is to obey the Torah.

[7] YHWH himself in a malakhic form.

Footnotes

[8] Bowing down to any other elohim other than YHWH is a grievous sin.

32 You shall make no Covenant with them, nor with their powers.

33 They shall not dwell in your land, lest they make you sin against Me. For if you serve their powers, it will surely be a trap for you.

Chapter 24

1 Now He said to Mosheh (Musa), Come up to YHWH, you and Aharon, Nadav and Avihu, and seventy of the elders of Israel, and pay homage from afar.

2 And Mosheh (Musa) alone shall come near YHWH, but they shall not come near; nor shall the people go up with him.

3 So Mosheh (Musa) came and told the people all the words of YHWH and all the judgments. And all the people answered with one voice and said, All the words which YHWH has said we will do.

4 And Mosheh (Musa) wrote all the words of YHWH. And he rose early in the morning, and built an altar at the foot of the mountain, and twelve altars according to the twelve tribes of Israel.

5 Then he sent young men of the children of Israel, who offered burnt offerings and sacrificed shalom offerings of oxen to YHWH.

6 And Mosheh (Musa) took half the blood and put it in basins, and half the blood he sprinkled on the altar.

7 Then he took the scroll of the Brit[1] and read in the hearing of the people. And they said, All that YHWH has said we will do, and we will hear.[2]

8 And Mosheh (Musa) took the blood, sprinkled it on the people, and said, Behold, the blood of the Covenant which YHWH has made with you according to all these words.

9 Then Mosheh (Musa) went up, also Aharon, Nadav, and Avihu, and seventy of the elders of Israel,

10 And they saw the Elohim of Israel and supporting his feet with great strength there appeared to be a brilliant transparent sapphire and standing above it a pillar of strength as a bone (body), his essence pure as shamayim.[3]

11 But on the nobles of the children of Israel He did not lay His hand. So they saw Elohim, and they ate and drank.[4]

12 Then YHWH said to Mosheh (Musa), Come up to Me on the mountain and be there;

Footnotes
[1] Another name for Torah.

Footnotes
[2] Note the phrase in Hebrew N'aseh V'nishama means 'we will do and we will hear' meaning before we hear we are ready to obey the Torah. The details happen later so we must be prepared to obey first; this is the Hebrew way of action not just mere words. And not intellectualism as we find European attitudes is plagued by such ridiculous notions such as, unless you prove first I will not budge. The Eastern mind is ready to obey first then understand it slowly by doing it. Do and hear are idiomatic for obeying Torah. We find these in the New Covenant also.
[3] The bone or the body, they saw was the middle-pillar communing with Moses and the elders of Israel.
[4] This is Adam Kadmon the Ancient of Days, with whom Moses and the Elders of Israel ate and drank. He was the one who gave Moses the Torah at Mt Sinai.

and I will give you tablets of stone, and the Torah of commandments which I have written, that you may teach them. [1]

13 So Mosheh (Musa) arose with his assistant Yahushua, and Mosheh (Musa) went up to the mountain of Elohim.

14 And he said to the elders, Wait here for us until we come back to you. Indeed Aharon and Khur are with you. If any man has a difficulty, let him go to them.

15 Then Mosheh (Musa) went up into the mountain, and a cloud covered the mountain.

16 Now the glory of YHWH rested on Mount Sinai, and the cloud covered it six days. And on the seventh day He called to Mosheh (Musa) out of the midst of the cloud.

17 The sight of the glory of YHWH was like a consuming fire on the top of the mountain in the eyes of the children of Israel.

18 So Mosheh (Musa) went into the midst of the cloud and went up into the mountain. And Mosheh (Musa) was on the mountain forty days and forty nights.

Torah Parsha 19 Terumah, Shemoth 25:1-27:19
Haftarah: Melekhim Alef 5:12-6:13

Chapter 25

1 Then YHWH spoke to Mosheh (Musa), saying:

Footnotes
[1] Here another set of laws were given to Moses after the sin of the Golden Calf to straighten up Israel so they do not sin again.

2 Speak to the children of Israel, that they bring Me an offering. From everyone who gives it willingly with his heart you shall take My offering.

3 And this is the offering which you shall take from them: gold, silver, and bronze;

4 blue, purple, and scarlet thread, fine linen, and goats' hair;

5 ram skins dyed red, blue skins, and acacia wood;

6 oil for the light, and spices for the anointing oil and for the sweet incense;

7 onyx stones, and stones to be set in the ephod and in the breastplate.

8 And let them make Me a Holy place, that I may dwell among them.

9 According to all that I show you, that is, the pattern of the Tent and the pattern of all its furnishings, just so you shall make it.

10 And they shall make an ark of acacia wood; its length is to be three feet nine inches, its width two feet three inches, and its height two feet three inches

11 And you shall overlay it with pure gold, inside and out you shall overlay it, and shall make on it a molding of gold all around.

12 You shall cast four rings of gold for it, and put them in its four corners; two rings shall be on one side, and two rings on the other side.

13 And you shall make poles of acacia wood, and overlay them with gold.

14 You shall put the poles into the rings on the sides of the ark, that the ark may be carried by them.

15 The poles shall be in the rings of the ark; they shall not be taken from it.

16 And you shall put into the ark the Testimony which I will give you.

17 You shall make a lid of atonement of pure gold; its length to be three feet nine inches and its width to be two feet three inches.

18 And you shall make two Khruvim of gold; of hammered work you shall make them at the two ends of the lid of atonement.

19 Make one Khroob at one end, and the other Khroob at the other end; you shall make the Khruvim at the two ends of it of one piece with the lid of atonement.

20 And the Khruvim shall stretch out their wings above, covering the lid of atonement with their wings, and they shall face one another; the faces of the Khruvim shall be toward the lid of atonement.

21 You shall put the lid of atonement on top of the ark, and in the ark you shall put the Testimony that I will give you.

22 And there I will meet with you, and I will speak with you from above the lid of atonement, from between the two Khruvim which are on the ark of the Testimony, of all things which I will give you in commandment to the children of Israel.

23 You shall also make a table of acacia wood; three feet shall be its length, one foot and six

inches its width, and its height to be two feet three inches.

24 And you shall overlay it with pure gold, and make a molding of gold all around.

25 You shall make for it a frame of a handbreadth all around, and you shall make a gold molding for the frame all around.

26 And you shall make for it four rings of gold, and put the rings on the four corners that are at its four legs.

27 The rings shall be close to the frame, as holders for the poles to bear the table.

28 And you shall make the poles of acacia wood, and overlay them with gold, that the table may be carried with them.

29 You shall make its dishes, its pans, its pitchers, and its bowls for pouring. You shall make them of pure gold.

30 And you shall set the Lakhem panayim (bread of the faces) on the table before Me always.

31 You shall also make a menorah[1] of pure gold; the menorah shall be of hammered work. Its shaft, its branches, its bowls, its ornamental knobs, and flowers shall be of one piece.

32 And six branches shall come out of its sides: three branches of the menorah out of

Footnotes
[1] Seven pointed Menorah. It was also put into the Temple and was always lit up. This shows us the Ten Sefirot in the Tree, the Temple Menorah and the Tent menorah were seven branches on the top and three branches on the bottom stand making up Ten.

one side, and three branches of menorah out of the other side.

33 Three bowls shall be made like almond blossoms[1] on one branch, with an ornamental knob and a flower, and three bowls made like almond blossoms on the other branch, with an ornamental knob and a flower and so for the six branches that come out of the menorah.

34 On the menorah itself four bowls shall be made like almond blossoms, each with its ornamental knob and flower.

35 And there shall be a knob under the first two branches of the same, a knob under the second two branches of the same, and a knob under the third two branches of the same, according to the six branches that extend from the menorah.

36 Their knobs and their branches shall be of one piece; all of it shall be one hammered piece of pure gold.

37 You shall make seven lamps for it, and they shall arrange its lamps so that they give light in front of it.

38 And its wick-trimmers and their trays shall be of pure gold.

39 It shall be made of a talent[2] of pure gold, with all these utensils.

40 And see to it that you make them according to the pattern which was shown you on the mountain.[3]

Chapter 26

1 Moreover you shall make the Tent with ten curtains of fine woven linen and blue, purple, and scarlet thread; with artistic designs of Khruvim you shall weave them.

2 The length of each curtain shall be forty two feet, and the width of each curtain to be six feet. And everyone of the curtains shall have the same measurements.

3 Five curtains shall be coupled to one another, and the other five curtains shall be coupled to one another.

4 And you shall make loops of blue yarn on the edge of the curtain on the corner of one set, and likewise you shall do on the outer edge of the other curtain of the second set.

5 Fifty loops you shall make in the one curtain and fifty loops you shall make on the edge of the curtain that is on the end of the second set, that the loops may be clasped to one another.

6 And you shall make fifty clasps of gold, and couple the curtains together with the clasps, so that it may be one Tent.

7 You shall also make curtains of goats' hair, to be a tent over the Tent. You shall make eleven curtains.

8 The length of each curtain shall be forty five feet, and the

Footnotes

[1] The menorah's cups were like Almond blossoms to fill with pure virgin olive oil.

[2] A common talent was about sixty pounds in weight but a talent as this one was would be double, meaning 120 pounds of gold.

Footnotes

[3] Moses was shown the design from the actual original Ark in the Temple in the tenth shamayim where YHWH's throne is situated.

width of each curtain to be six feet; and the eleven curtains shall all have the same measurements.

9 And you shall couple five curtains by themselves and six curtains by themselves, and you shall double over the sixth curtain at the forefront of the tent.

10 You shall make fifty loops on the edge of the curtain that is outermost in one set, and fifty loops on the edge of the curtain of the second set.

11 And you shall make fifty bronze clasps, put the clasps into the loops, and couple the tent together, that it may be one.

12 The remnant that remains of the curtains of the tent, the half curtain that remains, shall hang over the back of the Tent.

13 And a foot and a half on one side and a foot and a half on the other side, of what remains of the length of the curtains of the tent, shall hang over the sides of the Tent, on this side and on that side, to cover it.

14 You shall also make a covering of ram skins dyed red for the tent, and a covering of blue skins above that.

15 And for the Tent you shall make the boards of acacia wood, standing upright.

16 Ten cubits shall be the length of a board, and a cubit and a half shall be the width of each board.

17 Two tenons shall be in each board for binding one to another. Thus you shall make for all the boards of the Tent.

18 And you shall make the boards for the Tent, twenty boards for the south side.

19 You shall make forty sockets of silver under the twenty boards: two sockets under each of the boards for its two tenons.

20 And for the second side of the Tent, the north side, there shall be twenty boards

21 And their forty sockets of silver: two sockets under each of the boards.

22 For the far side of the Tent, westward, you shall make six boards.

23 And you shall also make two boards for the two back corners of the Tent.

24 They shall be coupled together at the bottom and they shall be coupled together at the top by one ring. Thus it shall be for both of them. They shall be for the two corners.

25 So there shall be eight boards with their sockets of silver sixteen sockets two sockets under each board.

26 And you shall make bars of acacia wood: five for the boards on one side of the Tent,

27 five bars for the boards on the other side of the Tent, and five bars for the boards of the side of the Tent, for the far side westward.

28 The middle bar shall pass through the midst of the boards from end to end.

29 You shall overlay the boards with gold, make their rings of gold as holders for the bars, and overlay the bars with gold.

30 And you shall raise up the Tent according to its pattern which you were shown on the mountain.

31 You shall make a veil woven of blue, purple, and scarlet thread, and fine woven linen. It shall be woven with an artistic design of Khruvim.

32 You shall hang it upon the four pillars of acacia wood overlaid with gold. Their hooks shall be of gold, upon four sockets of silver.

33 And you shall hang the veil from the clasps. Then you shall bring the ark of the Testimony in there, behind the veil. The veil shall be a divider for you between the Holy place and the Most Holy.

34 You shall put the lid of atonement upon the ark of the Testimony in the most Holy place.

35 You shall set the table outside the veil, and the menorah across from the table on the side of the Tent toward the south; and you shall put the table on the north side. [1]

Footnotes
[1] The signs of the South for the Menorah reveal to us: the south side of man, the heart, plus the Temple was in the South of Israel revealing the placement of the Menorah. The Menorah which has seven candles but three legs on the stand reveals the Ten attributes of YHWH in the Sefirotic tree. The North side shows us the way to heavens and the throne room of YHWH is in the North side of our galaxy Job 26:7, Psalm 75:6 and Psalm 48:1-2. The Messiah will come from the North Side of Israel to teach Torah to the Hebrew nation down south, the place of adoration. The place of the heart of man is also south of the body. The North is also known as the conscience of man. Satan attacks the North hence why many nations of the world have the worst apostasy or unbelief in the North. There is an empty space in the North and it possibly contains 2000 milky ways and the milky ways are Continued in next section

36 You shall make a screen for the door of the Tent, woven of blue, purple, and scarlet thread, and fine woven linen, made by a weaver.

37 And you shall make for the screen five pillars of acacia wood, and overlay them with gold; their hooks shall be of gold, and you shall cast five sockets of bronze for them.

Chapter 27

1 You shall make an altar of acacia wood, seven feet six inches long and seven feet six inches wide the altar shall be square and its height shall be four feet six inches.

2 You shall make its horns on its four corners; its horns shall be of one piece with it. And you shall overlay it with bronze.

3 Also you shall make its pans to receive its ashes, and its shovels and its basins and its forks and its firepans; you shall make all its utensils of bronze.

4 You shall make a grate for it, a network of bronze; and on the

probably about 100,000 light years apart. If men think they can reach YHWH's throne room by space-ships they are greatly mistaken. The conscience is where the I AM, YHWH lives or Yahushua that is his throne room. Paul referred to it in his writings that we are the Temple of God (1 Corinthians 3:16). If we are the Temple then where does God dwell in us, since Jesus said the Kingdom is God within you (Luke 17:21? In our brains, the subconscious is where God dwells and we don't need to travel anywhere to find God, he is within us and you can access God and make your life a whole lot better. Change your view and your world will change.

network you shall make four bronze rings at its four corners.

5 You shall put it under the rim of the altar beneath, that the network may be midway up the altar.

6 And you shall make poles for the altar, poles of acacia wood, and overlay them with bronze.

7 The poles shall be put in the rings, and the poles shall be on the two sides of the altar to bear it.

8 You shall make it hollow with boards; as it was shown you on the mountain, so shall they make it.

9 You shall also make the court of the Tent. For the south side there shall be hangings for the court made of fine woven linen, one hundred cubits long for one side.

10 And its twenty pillars and their twenty sockets shall be of bronze. The hooks of the pillars and their bands shall be of silver.

11 Likewise along the length of the north side there shall be hangings one hundred fifty feet long, with its twenty pillars and their twenty sockets of bronze, and the hooks of the pillars and their bands of silver.

12 And along the width of the court on the west side shall be hangings of seventy-five feet, with their ten pillars and their ten sockets.

13 The width of the court on the east side shall be seventy-five feet.

14 The hangings on one side of the gate shall twenty-two and a half feet long, with their three pillars and their three sockets.

15 And on the other side shall be hangings of twenty-two and a half feet long, with their three pillars and their three sockets.

16 For the gate of the court there shall be a screen thirty feet long, woven of blue, purple, and scarlet thread, and fine woven linen, made by a weaver. It shall have four pillars and four sockets.

17 All the pillars around the court shall have bands of silver; their hooks shall be of silver and their sockets of bronze.

18 The length of the court shall be one hundred fifty feet long, the width seventy-five feet throughout, and the height seven and a half feet, woven of fine linen thread, and its sockets of bronze.

19 All the utensils of the Tent for all its service, all its pegs, and all the pegs of the court, shall be of bronze.

Torah Parsha 20 Tetzaveh, Shemoth 27:20-30:10
Haftarah: Ykhezkiel 43:10-27

20 And you shall command the children of Israel that they bring you pure oil of pressed olives for the light, to cause the lamp[1] to burn continually.

21 In the Tent of the appointed times, outside the veil which is before the congregation for a true report,[2] Aharon and his sons shall tend it from evening until morning

Footnotes
[1] Not just any lamp but the Menorah.
[2] Aduth in the Hebrew here means a group of people gathered to see and confirm the true report of YHWH as an everlasting account.

before YHWH. It shall be a statute forever to their generations on behalf of the children of Israel.

Chapter 28

1 Now take Aharon your brother, and his sons with him, from among the children of Israel, that he may minister to Me as kohen (priest), Aharon and Aharon's sons: Nadav, Avihu, El'ezar, and Ithamar.

2 And you shall make Holy garments for Aharon your brother, for glory and for beauty.

3 So you shall speak to all who are gifted artisans, whom I have filled with the Ruakh (Spirit) of wisdom, that they may make Aharon's garments, to consecrate him,[1] that he may minister to Me as Kohen (priest).

4 And these are the garments which they shall make: a breastplate, an ephod, a robe, a skillfully woven tunic, a turban,[2] and a sash. So they shall make Holy garments for Aharon your brother and his sons, that he may minister to Me as kohen (priest).

5 They shall take the gold, blue, purple, and scarlet thread, and fine linen,

6 And they shall make the ephod of gold, blue, purple, and scarlet thread, and fine woven linen, artistically worked.

7 It shall have two shoulder straps joined at its two edges, and so it shall be joined together.

8 And the intricately woven band of the ephod, which is on it, shall be of the same workmanship, made of gold, blue , purple, and scarlet thread, and fine woven linen.

9 Then you shall take two onyx stones and engrave on them the names of the sons of Israel:

10 Six of their names on one stone, and the remaining six names on the other stone, according to their birth.[3]

11 With the work of an engraver in stone, like the engravings of a signet, you shall engrave the two stones with the names of the sons of Israel. You shall set them in settings of gold.

12 And you shall put the two stones on the shoulders of the ephod as memorial stones for the sons of Israel. So Aharon shall bear their names before YHWH on his two shoulders as a memorial.

13 You shall also make settings of gold,

14 And you shall make two chains of pure gold like braided cords, and fasten the braided chains to the settings.

15 You shall make the breastplate of judgment. Artistically woven according to the workmanship of the ephod

Footnotes

[1] YHWH's priests are Holy and must be consecrated to accept and teach YHWH's Torah.

[2] Head-coverings are a commandment for all not just the High Priest.

[3] The High Priest is a Levite, the only one appointed to act on behalf on Israel. He does not carry on His Breastplate the names of any church denominations such as Baptist, Methodist, Pentecostal or other. Anyone who is not in Israel and on the High Priest's ephod is out of Israel and considered gentile, publican and a tax collector, which are all derogatory terms simply to indicate unbelievers.

you shall make it: of gold, blue, purple, and scarlet thread, and fine woven linen, you shall make it.

16 It shall be doubled into a square: nine inches[1] shall be its length, and nine inches shall be its width.

17 And you shall put settings of stones in it, four rows of stones: The first row shall be a sardius, a topaz, and an emerald; this shall be the first row;

18 The second row shall be a turquoise, a sapphire, and a diamond;

19 The third row, a jacinth, an agate, and an amethyst;

20 And the fourth row, a beryl, an onyx, and jasper. They shall be set in gold settings.

21 And the stones shall have the names of the sons of Israel, twelve according to their names, like the engravings of a signet, each one with its own name; they shall be according to the twelve tribes.

22 You shall make chains for the breastplate at the end, like braided cords of pure gold.

23 And you shall make two rings of gold for the breastplate, and put the two rings on the two ends of the breastplate.

24 Then you shall put the two braided chains of gold in the two rings which are on the ends of the breastplate;

25 and the other two ends of the two braided chains you shall fasten to the two settings, and put

them on the shoulder straps of the ephod in the front.

26 You shall make two rings of gold, and put them on the two ends of the breastplate, on the edge of it, which is on the inner side of the ephod.

27 And two other rings of gold you shall make, and put them on the two shoulder straps, underneath the ephod toward its front, right at the seam above the intricately woven band of the ephod.

28 They shall bind the breastplate by means of its rings to the rings of the ephod, using a blue cord, so that it is above the intricately woven band of the ephod, and so that the breastplate does not come loose from the ephod.

29 So Aharon shall bear the names of the sons of Israel on the breastplate of judgment over his heart, when he goes into the Holy place, as a memorial before YHWH continually.

30 And you shall put in the breastplate of judgment the Urim[2] and the Thummim,[3] and they shall be over Aharon's heart when he goes in before YHWH. So Aharon shall bear the judgment of the children of Israel over his heart before YHWH continually.

Footnotes
[1] The Hebrew word Zerith usually indicates half a cubit or a hand-breadth, translated as a 'span' in most translations.

Footnotes
[2] Meaning 'lights', these two stones were drawn by the High Priest to determine matters of difficulty. This was YHWH's lottery draw for Him to say; Yes or No to a matter that the High Priest could not give an answer to.
[3] Meaning reflections, one stone was light and the other dark.

31 You shall make the robe of the ephod all of blue.

32 There shall be an opening for his head in the middle of it; it shall have a woven binding all around its opening, like the opening in a coat of mail, so that it does not tear.

33 And upon its hem you shall make pomegranates[1] of blue, purple, and scarlet, all around its hem, and bells of gold between them all around:

34 A golden bell and a pomegranate, a golden bell and a pomegranate, upon the hem of the robe all around.

35 And it shall be upon Aharon when he ministers, and its sound will be heard when he goes into the Holy place before YHWH and when he comes out, that he may not die.

36 You shall also make a plate of pure gold and engrave on it, like the engraving of a signet: Holy to YHWH.

37 And you shall put it on a blue cord that it may be on the turban; it shall be on the front of the turban.

38 So it shall be on Aharon's forehead that Aharon may bear the iniquity of the Holy things which the children of Israel sanctify in all their Holy gifts; and it shall always be on his forehead, that they may be accepted before YHWH.

39 You shall skillfully weave the tunic of fine linen thread, you shall make the turban of fine linen, and you shall make the sash of woven work.

40 For Aharon's sons you shall make tunics, and you shall make sashes for them. And you shall make turbans for them, for glory and beauty.[2]

41 So you shall put them on Aharon your brother and on his sons with him. You shall anoint them, consecrate them, and sanctify them, that they may minister to Me as priests.

42 And you shall make for them linen trousers to cover their nakedness; they shall reach from the waist to the thighs.

43 They shall be on Aharon and on his sons when they come into the Tent of the appointed times, or when they come near the altar to minister in the Holy place, that they do not incur iniquity and die. It shall be a statute forever to him and his descendants after him.

Chapter 29

1 And this is what you shall do to them to sanctify them for ministering to Me as priests: Take

Footnotes

[2] The Turbans for all the priests are mandatory, to reveal YHWH's beauty and glory hence why a head covering is essential and not optional. Yet Christianity has made a mockery of this commandment while YHWH requires it. They are still arguing over whether we should wear it or not using Pauline letter in First Corinthians 11:4, which speaks about a prostitute's veil covering the face and not the traditional head-covering required in every congregation. Christians need to learn Paulos is not the one who sets YHWH's laws but YHWH Himself does. Anyone who teaches against YHWH's law including Paulos will be punished for it.

Footnotes

[1] The pomegranate was to be the picture of Israel's fruitfulness. Without wives (plural) and children this was not possible.

one young bull and two rams without blemish,

2 And matzah, (unleavened rotis) and rotis mixed with oil (*Parathas*),[1] and unleavened thin rotis anointed with oil, you shall make them of wheat flour.

3 You shall put them in one basket and bring them in the basket, with the bull and the two rams.

4 And Aharon and his sons you shall bring to the door of the Tent of the appointed times,[2] and you shall wash them with mayim.

5 Then you shall take the garments, put the tunic on Aharon, and the robe of the ephod, the ephod, and the breastplate, and gird him with the intricately woven band of the ephod.

6 You shall put the turban on his head, and put the Holy crown on the turban.

7 And you shall take the anointing oil, pour it on his head, and anoint him.

8 Then you shall bring his sons and put tunics on them.

9 And you shall gird them with sashes, Aharon and his sons, and put the turbans[3] on them. The priesthood shall be theirs for

an everlasting law.[4] So you shall consecrate Aharon and his sons.

10 You shall also have the bull brought before the Tent of the appointed times, and Aharon and his sons shall put their hands on the head of the bull.

11 Then you shall kill the bull before YHWH, by the door of the Tent of the appointed times.

12 You shall take some of the blood of the bull and put it on the horns of the altar with your finger, and pour all the blood beside the base of the altar.

13 And you shall take all the fat that covers the entrails, the fatty lobe attached to the liver, and the two kidneys and the fat that is on them, and burn them on the altar.

14 But the flesh of the bull, with its skin and its dung, you shall burn with fire outside the camp.[5] It is a sin offering.

15 You shall also take one ram, and Aharon and his sons shall put their hands on the head of the ram;

16 and you shall kill the ram, and you shall take its blood and sprinkle it all around on the altar.

17 Then you shall cut the ram in pieces, wash its entrails and its legs, and put them with its pieces and with its head.

18 And you shall burn the whole ram on the altar. It is a burnt offering to YHWH; it is a sweet aroma, an offering made by fire to YHWH.

19 You shall also take the other ram, and Aharon and his sons

Footnotes

[1] This is the Indian style chapatti, made in oil and the word "cake", is not your English cake but a roti/chapatti that the ancient Israelites ate whose ancestors came from India.

[2] This Tent could not just be erected anytime it had to be done at the appointed times.

[3] Head-coverings are for all priests not just the Hebrew people, and that includes New Covenant priests. This means that Christians who do not cover their heads commit a sin against YHWH and live disobediently.

[4] This law is permanent and no one can change it.

[5] Sin offering is done outside the camp.

shall put their hands on the head of the ram.[1]

20 Then you shall kill the ram, and take some of its blood and put it on the tip of the right ear of Aharon and on the tip of the right ear of his sons, on the thumb of their right hand and on the big toe of their right foot,[2] and sprinkle the blood all around on the altar.

21 And you shall take some of the blood that is on the altar, and some of the anointing oil, and sprinkle it on Aharon and on his garments, on his sons and on the garments of his sons with him; and he and his garments shall be Holy, and his sons and his sons' garments with him.

22 Also you shall take the fat of the ram, the fat tail, the fat that covers the entrails, the fatty lobe attached to the liver, the two kidneys and the fat on them, the right shoulder (for it is a ram of consecration),

23 one loaf of Lakhem (bread), one roti made with oil, and one thin roti from the basket of the matzah (unleavened bread) that is before YHWH;

24 And you shall put all these in the hands of Aharon and in the hands of his sons, and you shall wave them as a wave offering before YHWH.

25 You shall receive them back from their hands and burn them on the altar as a burnt offering, as a sweet aroma before YHWH. It is an offering made by fire to YHWH.

26 Then you shall take the breast of the ram of Aharon's consecration and wave it as a wave offering before YHWH; and it shall be your portion.

27 And from the ram of the consecration you shall consecrate the breast of the wave offering which is waved, and the shoulder of the heave offering which is raised, of that which is for Aharon and of that which is for his sons.

28 It shall be from the children of Israel for Aharon and his sons by a statute forever. For it is a heave offering; it shall be a heave offering from the children of Israel from the sacrifices of their shalom offerings, that is, their heave offering to YHWH.

29 And the Holy garments of Aharon shall be his sons' after him, to be anointed in them and to be consecrated in them.

30 That son who becomes Kohen (priest) in his place shall put them on for seven days, when he enters the Tent of the appointed times to minister in the Holy place.

31 And you shall take the ram of the consecration and boil its flesh in the Holy place.

32 Then Aharon and his sons shall eat the flesh of the ram, and the Lakhem (bread) that is in the

Footnotes

[1] Note; without putting the hands on the Ram's or the Bull's head the sacrifice would not qualify for sin.

[2] The spiritual connection is right ear lobe to the mind, the right thumb to the heart and the right big toe to the instincts. The three centers are the pivotal points of the body. These signify the first commandment to love YHWH your POWER with all your mind all your heart and all your strength. We can find the hidden mystery of this in (Koheleth-Ecclesiastes, 4:9-12)... A threefold cord is not quickly broken. The three centers also show the plurality of YHWH.

basket, by the door of the Tent of the appointed times.

33 They shall eat those things with which the atonement was made, to consecrate and to sanctify them; but a stranger shall not eat them, because they are Holy.

34 And if any of the flesh of the consecration offerings, or of the Lakhem (bread), remains until the morning, then you shall burn the remainder with fire. It shall not be eaten, because it is Holy.[1]

35 Thus you shall do to Aharon and his sons, according to all that I have commanded you. Seven days you shall consecrate them.

36 And you shall offer a bull every day as a sin offering for atonement. You shall cleanse the altar when you make atonement for it, and you shall anoint it to sanctify it.

37 Seven days you shall make atonement for the altar and sanctify it.[2] And the altar shall be most Holy. Whatever touches the altar must be Holy.[3]

38 Now this is what you shall offer on the altar: two lambs of the first year, day by day continually.

Footnotes

[1] Note; just like in the Passover no strangers were to eat the meal because the meal was only for those IN Israel and they were circumcised and Sabbath keeping, believing and keeping the Torah. Anyone else doing this would be disqualified and judged severely.

[2] The place of worship for YHWH is Holy and not just any altar so it must be properly anointed and prepared in the name of YHWH because that is what sanctifies it before it can be used.

[3] Even touching the altar is a sin if you are not obeying Torah.

39 One lamb you shall offer in the morning and the other lamb you shall offer at twilight.

40 With the one lamb shall be one-tenth of an ephah of flour mixed with one-fourth of a hin of pressed oil, and one-fourth of a hin of wine as a drink offering.

41 And the other lamb you shall offer at twilight; and you shall offer with it the grain offering and the drink offering, as in the morning, for a sweet aroma, an offering made by fire to YHWH.

42 This shall be a continual burnt offering throughout your generations at the door of the Tent of the appointed times before YHWH, where I will meet you to speak with you.

43 And there I will meet with the children of Israel, and the Tent shall be sanctified by My glory.

44 So I will consecrate the Tent of the appointed times and the altar. I will also consecrate both Aharon and his sons to minister to Me as priests.

45 I will dwell among the children of Israel and will be their Elohim.

46 And they shall know that I am YHWH their Elohim, who brought them up out of the land of Mitzrayim (Egypt), that I may dwell among them. I am YHWH their Elohim.

Chapter 30

1 You shall make an altar to burn incense on; you shall make it of acacia wood.

2 A foot and a half shall be its length and a foot and a half [1] its width it shall be square and three feet shall be its height. Its horns shall be of one piece with it.

3 And you shall overlay its top, its sides all around, and its horns with pure gold; and you shall make for it a molding of gold all around.

4 Two gold rings you shall make for it, under the molding on both its sides. You shall place them on its two sides, and they will be holders for the poles with which to bear it.

5 You shall make the poles of acacia wood, and overlay them with gold.

6 And you shall put it before the veil that is before the ark of the Testimony, before the lid of atonement that is over the Testimony, where I will meet with you.

7 Aharon shall burn on it sweet incense every morning; when he tends the lamps, he shall burn incense on it.

8 And when Aharon lights the lamps at twilight, he shall burn incense on it, continual incense before YHWH throughout your generations. [2]

9 You shall not offer strange incense [3] on it, or a burnt offering,

or a grain offering; nor shall you pour a wine offering on it.

10 And Aharon shall make atonement upon its horns once a year [4] with the blood of the sin offering of atonement; once a year he shall make atonement upon it throughout your generations. It is most Holy to YHWH.

Torah Parsha 21 Ki Tissa, Shemoth 30:11-34:35
Haftarah: Melekhim Alef 18:1-39

11 Then YHWH spoke to Mosheh (Musa), saying:

12 When you take the census of the children of Israel for their number, then every man shall give a ransom for himself to YHWH, when you number [5] them, that there may be no plague among them when you number them.

13 This is what everyone among those who are numbered shall give: half a shekel according to the shekel of the kadosh-place

Footnotes
[1] A cubit was generally Eighteen inches, but at the time of King Solomon the royal cubit was 25.5 inches.
[2] Incense was burnt both times of prayer in the morning and in the evening times.
[3] When we think we can just come any way before YHWH and burn incense as we like, we see that this was not acceptable before YHWH. He killed Aharon's son for doing this. Vayikra (Lev) 10:1.
[4] Yom Kippurim – Khag, celebration of Atonements performed once a year by the Kohen ha Gadol (High Priest).
[5] In time this became the Temple tax which was half a shekel. In the first century it amounted to two days wages, and the money was collected in the Month of Adar which is Feb/March our time. This money was used for the upkeep of the Tent. In present time in Israel this chapter is read a Sabbath before Rosh Chodesh Adar (New month) and the Hebrew people give half of the standard coin of the countries they live in. The Hebrew phrase B'Pakad for counting is repeated twice in this passage to show that YHWH did this as a special count during Moses' time and it was forbidden to count otherwise, as we see what happened in King David's time. Second Sam 24:1-15.

(a shekel is twenty gerahs). The half-shekel shall be an offering to YHWH.

14 Everyone included among those who are numbered, from twenty years old and above,[1] shall give an offering to YHWH.

15 The rich shall not give more and the poor shall not give less than half a shekel, when you give an offering to YHWH, to make atonement for yourselves.[2]

16 And you shall take the atonement money of the children of Israel, and shall appoint it for the service of the Tent of the appointed times, that it may be a memorial for the children of Israel before YHWH, to make atonement for yourselves.

17 Then YHWH spoke to Mosheh (Musa), saying:

18 You shall also make a laver of bronze, with its base also of bronze, for washing. You shall put it between the Tent of the appointed times and the altar. And you shall put mayim in it,

19 for Aharon and his sons shall wash their hands and their feet in mayim from out of it.[3]

20 When they go into the Tent of the appointed times, or when they come near the altar to minister, to burn an offering made by fire to YHWH, they shall wash with mayim, lest they die.

21 So they shall wash their hands and their feet, lest they die. And it shall be a statute forever to them to him and his descendants throughout their generations.

22 Moreover YHWH spoke to Mosheh (Musa), saying:

23 Also take for yourself quality spices five hundred shekels of liquid myrrh, half as much sweet-smelling cinnamon (two hundred and fifty shekels), two hundred and fifty shekels of sweet-smelling cane,

24 five hundred shekels of cassia, according to the shekel of the Holy place, and a hin of olive oil.

Footnotes

[1] YHWH saw 20 years and up as adults and required a sin offering from them, this is the age of accountability as YHWH sees it. Hebrew law today does bar mitzvahs for 13 years old boys which is fine. The school of Hillel's laws were binding because they heard a voice after 70 CE a bat kol announcing that Hillel rules. Christians must not reject Hebrew halacha based on ignorance.

[2] YHWH is equitable to treat the rich and poor the same way with no inequality or injustice.

[3] It is stated that it had 12 taps attached to it so that twelve people could wash their hands and feet at the same time. It is unheard of in the Hebrew culture, to just get

up and go to the assembly without any kind of washing. The nations have adopted many of the customs of Israel calling them their own but their origin belongs to Israel. Originally the copper laver had two spouts but later more spouts were added but the laver always remained copper even at the most prosperous times of Israel. http://www.templeinstitute.org/laver.htm The Midrash (Bamidbar Rabbah 9:14) relates that the original laver was made from the contributions of the righteous women of Israel, who donated their shiny mirrors towards this cause. These mirrors, made of highly polished copper, were melted down and it was from these that the laver was created. This act of sacrifice was precious in the eyes of the Holy One - the fact that the women cared more about fulfilling the word of God than about their own appearance. He declared that the laver must be of copper throughout the ages, to invoke the merit of these righteous women, so the memory of their action will always be before Him.

Continued in next section

25 And you shall make from these a Holy anointing oil, an ointment compounded according to the art of the perfumer. It shall be a Holy anointing oil.

26 With it you shall anoint the Tent of the appointed times and the ark of the Testimony;

27 The table and all its utensils, the menorah and its utensils, and the altar of incense;

28 The altar of burnt offering with all its utensils, and the laver and its base.

29 You shall consecrate them, that they may be most Holy; whatever touches them must be Holy.

30 And you shall anoint Aharon and his sons, and consecrate them, that they may minister to Me as priests.

31 And you shall speak to the children of Israel, saying: This shall be the Holy anointing oil to Me throughout your generations.

32 It shall not be poured on man's flesh; nor shall you make any other like it, according to its composition. It is Holy, and it shall be Holy to you.[1]

33 Whoever makes any like it, or whoever puts any of it on an outsider,[2] shall be cut off from his people.

Footnotes
[1] Even though the Hebrew people know how to make the oil today they will not make it as commanded by YHWH for any other use but in the Temple Service. This will have to wait for the millennial temple.
[2] The anointing shows that it was only for the Israelites, the twelve tribes and no one else. Likewise, rescue is only within Israel and no church has any right to it as they have to be grafted in to Israel and cannot stand alone.

34 And YHWH said to Mosheh (Musa): Take sweet spices, fragrant gum and cinnamon and galbanum, and pure frankincense with these sweet spices; there shall be equal amounts of each.

35 You shall make of these an incense, a compound according to the art of the perfumer, salted, pure, and Holy.

36 And you shall beat some of it very fine, and put some of it before the Testimony in the Tent of the appointed times where I will meet with you. It shall be most Holy to you.

37 But as for the incense which you shall make, you shall not make any for yourselves, according to its composition. It shall be to you Holy for YHWH.

38 Whoever makes any like it, to smell it, he shall be cut off from his people.

Chapter 31

1 Then YHWH spoke to Mosheh (Musa), saying:

2 See I have called by name Betsal'el[3] the son of Uri, the son of Khur, of the tribe of Yahudah.

3 And I have filled him with the Spirit of Elohim, in wisdom, in understanding, in knowledge, and in all manner of workmanship,

4 To design artistic works, to work in gold, in silver, in bronze,

5 In cutting jewels for setting, in carving wood, and to work in all manner of workmanship.

6 And I, indeed I, have appointed with him Aholiav[4] the

Footnotes
[3] In the image of Elohim this man was called to special service.
[4] The name means, the father's tent. YHWH is showing us that adding two people

Continued in next section

son of Ahisamakh, of the tribe of Dan; and I have put wisdom in the hearts of all who are gifted artisans, that they may make all that I have commanded you:

7 the Tent of the appointed times, the ark of the Testimony and the lid of atonement that is on it, and all the furniture of the Tent

8 The table and its utensils, the pure gold menorah with all its utensils, the altar of incense,

9 The altar of burnt offering with all its utensils, and the laver and its base

10 The garments of ministry, the Holy garments for Aharon the kohen (priest) and the garments of his sons, to minister as priests,

11 And the anointing oil and sweet incense for the Holy place. According to all that I have commanded you they shall do.

12 And YHWH spoke to Mosheh (Musa), saying,

13 Speak also to the children of Israel, saying: Surely My Sabbaths you shall keep, for it is a sign[1] between Me and you

throughout your generations, that you may know that I am YHWH who sanctifies you.

14 You shall keep the Sabbath, therefore, for it is Holy to you. Everyone who profanes it shall surely be put to death;[2] for whoever does any work on it, that person shall be cut off from among his people.

15 Work shall be done for six days, but the seventh is the Sabbath of rest, Holy to YHWH. Whoever does any work on the Sabbath day, he shall surely be put to death.

16 Therefore the children of Israel shall guard[3] the Sabbath, to observe the Sabbath throughout their generations as an everlasting Covenant.

17 It is a sign between Me and the children of Israel[4] forever; for in six days YHWH made the shamayim and the earth, and on the seventh day was the Sabbath to cease from all work and to be refreshed.[5]

18 And when He had made an end of speaking with him on Mount Sinai, He gave Mosheh

together was the model. This was the same way that King Solomon was the Builder of the Temple and a man from the tribe of Dan was joined to him. Divre HaYamim Bet (2 Chronicles 2:4)

[1] Saturday Sabbath is a sign and a seal for believers. Those that do not keep the Sabbath are seen as wicked in YHWH's sight as this is a major weekly appointed time to set His people apart. Repeated in Ye'chezk'el (Ezekiel) 20:12, 20. This is for All believers and if you do not keep the Sabbath YHWH may not allow you into His kingdom as He has the last say on it. Not you and certainly not your sun-day worship pastor who is breaking YHWH's Holy day by worshipping on a day YHWH did not choose for Israel aligned to the false sun-deity.

Footnotes
[2] This could mean second death for some people who continually profane it, only YHWH will decide on such people's future.
[3] It is so important that we have to guard/protect our commandments not to let the heathen mock us. See the articles on the Sabbath at: www.forever-israel.com/Ask-the-Rabbi.html. The brit (Covenant) must be guarded and upheld.
[4] The only assembly YHWH knows is Israel and there is no other church in His eyes.
[5] The idea here is not that YHWH needs to rest and refresh, but it is for man to cease and refresh. YHWH only shows us a picture of why it was created for us since He does not need a rest being the eternal one.

(Musa) two tablets of the Testimony, tablets of stone, written with the finger of Elohim.

Chapter 32

1 Now when the people saw that Mosheh (Musa) delayed coming down from the mountain, the people gathered together to Aharon, and said to him, Come, make us powers that shall go before us; for as for this man Mosheh (Musa), the one who brought us up out of the land of Mitzrayim (Egypt), we do not know what has become of him.

2 And Aharon said to them, Take off the golden earrings which are in the ears of your wives, your sons, and your daughters, and bring them to me.

3 So all the people took off the golden earrings which were in their ears, and brought them to Aharon.

4 And he received the gold from their hand, and he fashioned it with an engraving tool, and made a molded calf. Then they said, This is your elohi,[1] O Israel that brought you out of the land of Mitzrayim (Egypt).[2]

Footnotes

[1] Singular God and not gods as incorrectly translated in other bibles.

[2] Aharon was pressured in to go along with it at the threat of death. He made it in the image of the calf because the Egyptians main deity was Hathor the woman goddess. Since the first letter of Alef is the image of a man in ancient pictographic Hebrew and that letter is associated with YHWH, it was thus associated with YHWH. The goddess Hathor both appeared as a woman in pictures and as a cow also called Isis the black queen. A people in India still worship cows, drinking their urine and holding them sacred forbid their slaughter hence why often when Continued in next section

Muslims slaughter cows there are tensions between those that hold the cow sacred with those that do not.

Why did Aharon made the golden calf since he was the High Priest? One explanation given by the sages is that the people had miscalculated the arrival of Mosheh (Musa) by one day who said he would arrive forty complete days later and when forty days had passed according to the people he did not arrive but his arrival was actually the next day on the 17th Tammuz. The people had also been made to show a vision of a coffin with Mosheh (Musa) in it which shattered their hopes of being led to the promised land, this vision was through Satan. They had asked for the golden calf as a leader to follow after like they followed Mosheh (Musa). It was the apostate priests of Egypt that made the golden calf. We are punished for this sin in each generation until the Messiah comes.

However another explanation is that the people had become impatient after the miscalculation of the days and caused Aharon to build the idol, which he called YHWH as people in ancient times gave names of their gods to the idols. Aharon was afraid of the people so wanted to delay them as he knew Mosheh (Musa) was still alive but he complied as they would threaten to kill him. Aharon was not killed outright by YHWH because he was wearing the High Priest clothing which protected him. Had he been killed this would be an embarrassment for the High Priest and his value as the atoner for the people.

Aaron had observed that they had already killed his nephew Khur who was from Amram's second wife so he knew that they the Israelites were influenced by the mixed multitude who were not Abraham's descendants and these were into magic and witchcraft, the Egyptian priests. They had started this practice and through magic had made the rest of Israel err. They made the Golden Calf speak.

In Pirkei Avot (The Ethics of Our Fathers) our Sages tell us that we should always be careful to give everyone the benefit of the doubt as Mosheh (Musa) did not break the tablets until he had seen with his own eyes Continued in next section

5 So when Aharon saw it, he built an altar before it. And Aharon made a proclamation and said, Tomorrow is a feast [1] khag (appointed celebration time) to YHWH.

6 Then they rose early on the next day, offered burnt offerings, and brought shalom offerings; and the people sat down to eat and drink, and rose up to play.[2]

7 And YHWH said to Mosheh (Musa), Go, get down! For your [3] people whom you brought out of the land of Mitzrayim (Egypt) have acted lawlessly.[4]

8 They have turned aside quickly out of the way [5] which I commanded them. They have made themselves a molded calf, and paid homage to it and sacrificed to it, and said, This is your elohi, O Israel, that brought you out of the land of Mitzrayim (Egypt)!

9 And YHWH said to Mosheh (Musa), I have seen this people, and indeed it is a stubborn people!

10 Now therefore, let Me alone, that My wrath may burn hot against them and I may consume them. And I will make of you a great nation.

11 Then Mosheh (Musa) pleaded with YHWH his Elohim, and said: YHWH, why does Your wrath burn hot against Your people whom You have brought out of the land of Mitzrayim (Egypt) with great power and with a mighty hand?

12 Why should the Mitzrim (Egyptians) speak, and say, He brought them out to harm them, to kill them in the mountains, and to consume them from the face of the earth'? Turn from Your fierce wrath, and relent from this harm to Your[6] people.

13 Remember Abraham, Ytshak, and Israel, Your servants, to whom You swore by Your own self, and said to them, I will multiply your descendants as the stars of shamayim; and all this land that I have spoken of I give to your descendants, and they shall inherit it forever.

14 So YHWH relented from the harm which He said He would do to His people.

15 And Mosheh (Musa) turned and went down from the mountain, and the two tablets of the Testimony were in his hand. The tablets were written on both sides; on the one side and on the other they were written.

16 Now the tablets were the work of Elohim, and the writing

and had already been informed by YHWH and later by Yahushua ben Nun what was going on. Our temples were destroyed because of wanton hatred hence we must be ready to give benefit of the doubt to people before we judge them.

[1] This was an illegal appointed time that Aharon proclaimed just as modern Church has made many illegal pagan feasts, such as Christmas and Easter while there are only seven true feasts commanded in the Tanak.
[2] To commit idolatry and to commit whoring. Targum of Jonathan.
[3] Note the switch. YHWH calls them Moses' people when they go into idolatry.
[4] Septuagint
[5] The Way, to guard the Torah.

Footnotes
[6] Moses reminds YHWH that these are not his people but 'your people', there is a spiritual switch Shemoth (Exodus) 32:7.

was the writing of Elohim engraved on the tablets. [1]

17 And when Yahushua heard the noise of the people as they shouted, he said to Mosheh (Musa), There is a noise of war in the camp.

18 But he said: It is not the voice of those who shout in victory, nor is it the voice of those who cry out in defeat, but the voice of those who sing that I hear.

19 So it was, as soon as he came near the camp, that he saw the calf and the dancing. Mosheh (Musa) became enraged with anger[2] and he cast the tablets out of his hands and broke them at the foot of the mountain.

20 Then he took the calf which they had made, burned it in the fire, and ground it to powder; and he scattered it on the mayim and made the children of Israel drink it. [3]

21 And Mosheh (Musa) said to Aharon, What did this people do to you that you have brought so great a sin upon them? [4]

22 So Aharon said, Do not let the anger of my master become hot. You know the people that they are set on evil.

Footnotes
[1] YHWH's own finger wrote those words.
[2] Septuagint. It is right to have righteous anger over lewdness and idolatry.
[3] As the water of jealousy in Numbers 5:16 made them to drink so the chief architects of this crime were found out and dealt with. Also to show others the calf was meaningless and had no Holy properties.
[4] Aharon's brother Hur was killed for reproving the Israelites for this idolatry, no mention is made of him after this event.

23 For they said to me, Make us powers [5] that shall go before us; as for this Mosheh (Musa), the man who brought us out of the land of Mitzrayim (Egypt), we do not know what has become of him.

24 And I said to them, Whoever has any gold, let them break it off. So they gave it to me, and I cast it into the fire, and this calf came out.

25 Now when Mosheh (Musa) saw that the people were unrestrained (for Aharon had not restrained them, to their shame among their enemies),

26 Then Mosheh (Musa) stood in the entrance of the camp, and said, Whoever is on YHWH's side, come to me. And all the sons of Levi gathered themselves together to him.

27 And he said to them, Thus says YHWH Elohim of Israel: Let every man put his sword on his side, and go in and out from entrance to entrance throughout the camp, and let every man kill his brother, every man his companion, and every man his neighbour.

28 So the sons of Levi did according to the word of Mosheh (Musa). And about three thousand men of the people fell that day.

29 Then Mosheh (Musa) said, Consecrate yourselves today to YHWH, that He may bestow on you an **Increase** this day, for every man has opposed his son and his brother.

Footnotes
[5] False elohim.

243

30 And it came to pass on the next day that Mosheh (Musa) said to the people, You have committed a great sin. So now I will go up to YHWH; perhaps I can make atonement for your sin.

31 Then Mosheh (Musa) returned to YHWH and said, Oh, these people have committed a great sin, and have made for themselves an elohi of gold.

32 Yet now, if You will forgive their sin but if not, I pray, blot me out of Your scroll[1] which You have written.

33 And YHWH said to Mosheh (Musa), Whoever[2] has transgressed against Me, I will blot him out[3] of My scroll.

34 Now therefore, go, lead the people to the place of which I have spoken to you. Behold, My Malakh shall go before you. Nevertheless, in the day when I visit for punishment, I will visit punishment upon them for their sin.

35 So YHWH plagued the people because of what they did with the calf which Aharon made.

Chapter 33

1 Then YHWH said to Mosheh (Musa), Depart and go up from here, you and the people whom you have brought out of the land of Mitzrayim (Egypt), to the land of which I swore to Abraham, Ytshak, and Yakov, saying, To your descendants I will give it.

2 And I will send My Malakh before you, and I will drive out the Kanani and the Amoree and the Khitee and the Perzee and the Khawee and the Yavusee.

3 Go up to a land flowing with milk and honey; for I will not go up in your midst, lest I consume you on the way for you are a stubborn people.

4 And when the people heard this bad news,[4] they mourned, and no one put on his ornaments.

5 For YHWH had said to Mosheh (Musa), Say to the children of Israel, You are a stubborn people. I could come up into your midst in one moment and consume you. Now therefore, take off your ornaments, that I may know what to do to you.

6 So the children of Israel stripped themselves of their ornaments by Mount Horev.

7 Mosheh (Musa) took his tent and pitched it outside the camp, far from the camp, and called it the Tent of the appointed times. And it came to pass that everyone who sought YHWH went out to the Tent of the appointed times which was outside the camp.

8 So it was, whenever Mosheh (Musa) went out to the Tent, that

Footnotes

[1] Book of life.

[2] It's important that YHWH does not use the word; I will blot out of Israel who I will choose because Israel is marked for rescue and if YHWH decided to blot out Israel at this time then He would have broken His Covenant hence why YHWH says "I will blot out whoever", but does not say Israel.

[3] YHWH has the final say who He keeps in the book of life and who He blots out.

Footnotes

[4] It is indeed bad news when YHWH leaves us and we have no protection and no one to watch over us.

all the people rose, and each man stood at his tent door and watched Mosheh (Musa) until he had gone into the Tent.

9 And it came to pass, when Mosheh (Musa) entered the Tent that the pillar of cloud descended and stood at the door of the Tent, and YHWH talked with Mosheh (Musa).

10 All the people saw the pillar of cloud standing at the Tent door, and all the people rose and paid homage, each man in his tent door.

11 So YHWH spoke to Mosheh (Musa) face to face, as a man speaks to his friend. And he would return to the camp, but his servant Yahushua the son of Nun, a young man,[1] did not depart from the Tent.

12 Then Mosheh (Musa) said to YHWH, See, You say to me, Bring up this people. But You have not let me know whom You will send with me. Yet You have said, I know you by name, and you have also found favour in My sight.

13 Now therefore, I pray, if I have found favour in Your sight, show me now Your way,[2] that I may know You and that I may find favour in Your sight. And consider that this nation is Your people.

14 And He said, My Presence will go with you, and I will give you rest.

15 Then he said to Him, If Your Presence does not go with us, do not bring us up from here.

16 For how then will it be known that Your people and I have found favour in Your sight, except You go with us? So we shall be separate, Your people and I, from all the people who are upon the face of the earth.

17 Then YHWH said to Mosheh (Musa), I will also do this thing that you have spoken; for you have found favour in My sight, and I know you by name.

18 And he said, Please, show me Your glory.

19 Then He said, I will make all My goodness pass before you, and I will proclaim the name of YHWH[3] before you. I will be gracious to whom I will be gracious, and I will have compassion on whom I will have compassion. [4]

Footnotes

[3] There is no other name other than YHWH.

[4] Following the incident of the Golden Calf (Shemoth 33:12-23). Mosheh (Musa) had asked YHWH for a deeper understanding of YHWH's ways to see His face. YHWH responded by informing Mosheh (Musa) that no man can fully comprehend YHWH during his or her lifetime and his request was rejected since to know YHW\H fully would mean you are YHWH.

YHWH then allowed his back to be seen by Mosheh (Musa) that he would be permitted to understand some of His ways. During that discussion (Shemoth 33:19), YHWH had instructed Mosheh (Musa) "Vchanosi et asher achon (I will show grace/favour to whom I choose to show grace/favour). Our sages explain that this refers to Master YHWH giving favour to those undeservedly or those unworthy. (See Brachot 7a).

Footnotes

[1] Yahushua the son of Nun guarded the tent, Ibn Ezra places his age as 56. He was not exactly young in our terms since he was the general of the Israelite army but, he was still youthful because he was trustworthy to YHWH.

[2] The 'way' the Torah.

20 But He said, You cannot see My face; for no man shall see Me, and live.[1]

21 And YHWH said, Here is a place by Me, and you shall stand on the rock.

22 So it shall be, while My glory passes by, that I will put you in the cleft of the rock, and will cover you with My hand while I pass by.

23 Then I will take away My hand, and you shall see My back; but My face shall not be seen.

Chapter 34

1 And YHWH said to Mosheh (Musa), Cut two tablets of stone like the first ones, and I will write on these tablets the words that were on the first tablets which you broke.

2 So be ready in the morning, and come up in the morning to Mount Sinai, and present yourself to Me there on the top of the mountain.

3 And no man shall come up with you, and let no man be seen throughout all the mountain; let neither flocks nor herds feed before that mountain.[2]

4 So he cut two tablets of stone like the first ones. Then Mosheh (Musa) rose early in the morning and went up to Mount Sinai, as YHWH had commanded him; and he took in his hand the two tablets of stone.

5 Then YHWH descended in the cloud and stood with him there, and made proclamation of the name of YHWH.[3]

6 And YHWH passed before him and proclaimed, YHWH, YHWH[4] El (The Power), merciful and gracious, longsuffering, and abounding in goodness and truth,

Enlarged Nun[5]

7 Pouring[6] his loving-kindness for thousands, forgiving iniquity and transgression and sin, by no means clearing the *guilty*, visiting the iniquity of the ahvot (fathers) upon the children and the children's children to the third and the fourth *generation*.[7]

Footnotes

[1] We cannot see nor comprehend the glory of YHWH.

[2] The mountain is in Saudi Arabia and not in Egypt.

[3] YHWH declares His name not Moses.

[4] YHWH declaring His name twice has an important aspect in the Hebrew thought.

[5] The letter nun is a picture of a cup that is full to pour out and here it is enlarged. We receive mercy from YHWH even though we have done nothing to deserve mercy as he pours it onto us. This shows us the Covenants made with our forefathers Abraham, Isaac and Jacob because of whom we receive mercy on to a thousand generations even when we go astray, we have a chance to repent and return.

[6] An enlarged cup in the Hebrew pictograph.

[7] Elohim's thirteen attributes listed in verse 6 and 7. (1) YHWH — compassion before man sins; (2) YHWH — compassion after man has sinned; (3) El — mighty in compassion to give all creatures according to their need; (4) Rachum — merciful, that mankind may not be distressed; (5) Chanun — gracious if mankind is already in distress; (6) Erech appayim — slow to anger; (7) Rav chesed — plenteous in mercy; (8) Emet — truth; (9) Notzer chesed laalafim — keeping mercy unto thousands; (10) Noseh avon — forgiving iniquity; (11)Noseh peshah — forgiving transgression; (12) Noseh chatah — forgiving sin; (13) Venakeh — and pardoning.

8 So Mosheh (Musa) made haste and bowed his head toward the earth,[1] and paid homage.

9 Then he said, If now I have found favour in Your sight, O YHWH[2], let my YHWH[3], I pray, go among us, even though we are a stubborn people; and pardon our iniquity and our sin, and take us as Your inheritance.

10 And He said: Behold, I make a Covenant. Before all your people I will do marvels such as have not been done in all the earth, nor in any nation; and all the people among whom you are shall see the work of YHWH. For it is an awesome thing that I will do with you.

11 Observe what I command you this day. Behold, I am driving out from before you the Amoree and the Kanani and the Khitee and the Perzee and the Khawee and the Yavusee.

12 Take heed to yourself, lest you make a Covenant with the inhabitants of the land where you are going, lest it be a snare in your midst.

13 But you shall destroy their altars, break their pillars, and cut down their Asherah[4] poles.

The enlarged Resh [5]

כִּי לֹא תִשְׁתַּחֲוֶה לְאֵל אַחֵר

14 For you shall pay homage to no other el (power), for YHWH, whose name is devoted,[6] is a devoted El (Power),

15 Lest you make a Covenant with the inhabitants of the land, and they play the harlot with their powers and make sacrifice to their powers, and one of them invites you and you eat of his sacrifice,

16 And you take of his daughters for your sons, and his daughters play the harlot with their powers and make your sons play the harlot with their powers.

17 You shall make no molded powers for yourselves.

18 The khag ha Matzot (The appointed celebration time of Unleavened Bread) you shall keep. Seven days you shall eat matzah (unleavened bread), as I commanded you, in the appointed time of the month of Abib; for in the month of Abib you came out from Mitzrayim (Egypt).[7]

19 All that open the womb are Mine, and every male Bekhor (firstborn) among your livestock, whether ox or sheep.

Footnotes

[1] Original custom is to bow to the ground to show complete obedience to the maker.

[2] See appendix HBYH.

[3] See appendix HBYH.

[4] YHWH hates Asherah the fertility deity, yet many Christians foolishly call Passover, the khag, celebration name of Easter which is the name of Asherah or Ishtarte. Calling it Easter is nothing short of an abomination before YHWH.

[5] The enlarged resh in the Hebrew word Akher (Ex 34:14) 'for you will worship no Continued in next section

other Elohim is the counterpart to the large dalet found in the Shma Israel as the witness in Deut 6:4. The difference is there we have a dalet and here we have a resh. The letter resh stands for a bird, height or sight. YHWH wants us to remember never to call any other elohim who claims to be from shamayim (height).

[6] Samaritan Torah.

[7] The khag, celebration of Unleavened Bread is known as the khag, celebration of rescue from bondage and slavery as we were in sin, and we were released from sin.

20 But the Bekhor (firstborn) of a donkey you shall redeem with a lamb. And if you will not redeem him, then you shall break his neck. All the Bekhor (firstborn) of your sons you shall redeem. And none shall appear before Me empty-handed.[1]

21 Six days you shall work, but on the seventh day you shall rest; in plowing time and in harvest you shall rest.

22 And you shall observe khag ha Shavuot (The appointed celebration time of Pentecost), of the Bikkurim of wheat harvest, and the khag ha Sukkot (The celebration appointed time of Sukkot: Tabernacles, the Ingathering) at the year's end.

23 Three times in the year all your men shall appear before master, YHWH Elohim of Israel.

24 For I will cast out the nations before you and enlarge your borders; neither will any man covet your land when you go up to appear before YHWH Your POWER three times in the year.

25 You shall not offer the blood of My sacrifice with chametz (leaven), nor shall the sacrifice of THE FESTIVAL OF PROTECTION[2] (The appointed celebration time of Protection/Passover) be left until morning.

26 The first of the bikkurim (Firstfruit) of your land you shall bring to the Beyth (house) of YHWH Your POWER. You shall not grow a young goat in her mother's milk. [3]

27 Then YHWH said to Mosheh (Musa), Write these words, for according to the tenor of these words I have made a Covenant with you and with Israel.

28 So he was there with YHWH forty days and forty nights; he neither ate Lakhem (bread) nor drank mayim. And He wrote on the tablets the words of the Covenant, the Ten Commandments.

29 Now it was so, when Mosheh (Musa) came down from Mount Sinai (and the two tablets of the Testimony were in Mosheh (Musa)'s hand when he came down from the mountain), that Mosheh (Musa) did not know that the skin of his face shone while he talked with Him.

30 So when Aharon and all the children of Israel saw Mosheh (Musa), behold, the skin of his face shone, and they were afraid to come near him.

Footnotes

[1] When we come up before YHWH on the major feasts we do not come up empty handed.

[2] The forces of darkness are at their highest at this time, at this time many families have fights, quarrels and married couples can even break up so care must be taken to understand what the Protection is about and to protect us from evil and harm.

[3] Although the rabbinic interpretation was not to cook milk and meat together but the actual interpretation is that you will not wait for the kid to grow up on the milk until the kid is brought for the sacrifice that is the context. It has nothing to do with paganism or cooking a goat in milk of her mother etc. Many Rabbis have debated this unduly. The Hebrew word Bishul means to grow as in Genesis 40:10 its first occurrence to ripen. This interpretation agrees with R. Joseph ben Isaac Bekhor Shor 12th century CE Orleans.

31 Then Mosheh (Musa) called to them, and Aharon and all the rulers of the congregation returned to him; and Mosheh (Musa) talked with them.

32 Afterward all the children of Israel came near and he gave them as commandments all that YHWH had spoken with him on Mount Sinai.

33 And when Mosheh (Musa) had finished speaking with them, he put a veil on his face.

34 But whenever Mosheh (Musa) went in before YHWH to speak with Him, he would take the veil off until he came out; and he would come out and speak to the children of Israel whatever he had been commanded.

35 And whenever the children of Israel saw the face of Mosheh (Musa), that the skin of Mosheh (Musa) face shone, then Mosheh (Musa) would put the veil on his face again, until he went in to speak with Him.

Torah Parsha 22 Vayakhel, Shemoth 35:1-38:20
Haftarah: Melekhim Alef 7:40 - 7:50

Chapter 35

1 Then Mosheh (Musa) gathered all the congregation of the children of Israel together, and said to them, These are the words which YHWH has commanded you to do:

2 Work shall be done for six days, but the seventh day shall be a Holy day for you, a Sabbath of rest to YHWH. Whoever does any work on it shall be put to death.

3 You shall kindle no fire throughout your dwellings on the Sabbath day. [1]

4 And Mosheh (Musa) spoke to all the congregation of the children of Israel, saying, This is the thing which YHWH commanded, saying:

5 Take from among you an offering to YHWH. Whoever is of a willing heart, let him bring it as an offering to YHWH: gold, silver, and bronze; [2]

6 Blue, purple, and scarlet thread, fine linen, and goats' hair;

7 Ram skins dyed red, blue skins, [3] and acacia wood;

8 Oil for the light, and spices for the anointing oil and for the sweet incense;

9 Onyx stones, and stones to be set in the ephod and in the breastplate.

10 All who are gifted artisans among you shall come and make all that YHWH has commanded:

11 The Tent, its tent, its covering, its clasps, its boards, its bars, its pillars, and its sockets;

Footnotes

[1] Lighting for manual labour, or business transactions on the Saturday. The original Sabbath was the Sunrise to sunset model but the custom Sabbath adopted after the Greek invasion by most of the Jewry is modern Saturday starting Friday sunset to Saturday sunset.

[2] Israel's default mode is abundance, anyone lacking needs to look into the perfect law that James 1:25 speaks about and bring abundance into their lives. Tell yourself daily "I am Abundance."

[3] Many translations have here the word 'badger skins', yet the badger is an unclean animal. This was not badger skins but dyed blue skins of goats and sheep.

12 The ark and its poles, with the lid of atonement, and the veil of the covering;

13 The table and its poles, all its utensils, and the Lakhem panayim (bread of faces);

14 Also the menorah for the light, its utensils, its lamps, and the oil for the light;

15 The incense altar, its poles, the anointing oil, the sweet incense, and the screen for the door at the entrance of the Tent;

16 The altar of burnt offering with its bronze grating, its poles, all its utensils, and the laver and its base;

17 The hangings of the court, its pillars, their sockets, and the screen for the gate of the court;

18 The pegs of the Tent, the pegs of the court, and their cords;

19 The garments of ministry, for ministering in the Holy place the Holy garments for Aharon the kohen (priest) and the garments of his sons, to minister as kohenim.

20 And all the congregation of the children of Israel departed from the presence of Mosheh (Musa).

21 Then everyone came whose heart was lifted, and everyone whose ruakh (spirit) was willing, and they brought YHWH's offering for the work of the Tent of the appointed times, for all its service, and for the Holy garments.

22 They came, both men and women, as many as had a willing heart, and brought earrings and nose rings, rings and necklaces, all jewelry of gold, that is, every man who offered an offering of gold to YHWH.

23 And every man, with whom was found blue, purple, and scarlet thread, fine linen, goats' hair, red skins of rams, and blue skins, brought them.

24 Everyone who offered an offering of silver or bronze brought YHWH's offering. And everyone with whom was found acacia wood for any work of the service, brought it.

25 All the women who were gifted artisans spun yarn with their hands, and brought what they had spun, of blue, purple, and scarlet, and fine linen.

26 And all the women whose heart stirred with wisdom spun yarn of goats' hair.

27 The rulers brought onyx stones, and the stones to be set in the ephod and in the breastplate,

28 and spices and oil for the light, for the anointing oil, and for the sweet incense.

29 The children of Israel brought a freewill offering to YHWH, all the men and women whose hearts were willing to bring material for all kinds of work which YHWH, by the hand of Mosheh (Musa), had commanded to be done.

30 And Mosheh (Musa) said to the children of Israel, See, YHWH has called by name Betsal'el the son of Uri, the son of Khur, of the tribe of Yahudah;

31 And He has filled him with the Ruakh (Holy Spirit) of Elohim, in wisdom and understanding, in knowledge and all manner of workmanship,

32 To design artistic works, to work in gold and silver and bronze,

33 In cutting jewels for setting, in carving wood, and to work in all manner of artistic workmanship.

34 And He has put in his heart the ability to teach, in him and Aholiav the son of Ahisamakh, of the tribe of Dan.

35 He has filled them with skill to do all manner of work of the engraver and the designer and the tapestry maker, in blue, purple, and scarlet thread, and fine linen, and of the weaver those who do every work and those who design artistic works.

Chapter 36

1 And Betsal'el and Aholiav, and every gifted artisan in whom YHWH has put wisdom and understanding, to know how to do all manner of work for the service of the Holy place, shall do according to all that YHWH has commanded.

2 Then Mosheh (Musa) called Betsal'el and Aholiav, and every gifted artisan in whose heart YHWH had put wisdom,[1] everyone whose heart was stirred, to come and do the work.

3 And they received from Mosheh (Musa) all the offering which the children of Israel had brought for the work of the service of making the Holy place. So they continued bringing to him freewill offerings every morning.

Footnotes
[1] YHWH chooses which man will receive wisdom from Him and who does not. It's not a free for all.

4 Then all the craftsmen who were doing all the work of the Holy place came, each from the work he was doing,

5 And they spoke to Mosheh (Musa), saying, The people bring much more than enough for the service of the work which YHWH commanded us to do.

6 So Mosheh (Musa) gave a commandment, and they caused it to be proclaimed throughout the camp, saying, Let neither man nor woman do any more work for the offering of the Holy place. And the people were restrained from bringing[2],

7 For the material they had was sufficient for all the work to be done indeed too much.

8 Then all the gifted artisans among them who worked on the Tent made ten curtains woven of fine linen, and of blue, purple and, scarlet thread; with artistic designs of Khruvim they made them.

9 The length of each curtain was twenty-eight cubits, and the width of each curtain four cubits; the curtains were all the same size.

10 And he coupled five curtains to one another, and the other five curtains he coupled to one another.

Footnotes
[2] Moses stopped the people once enough money had come in but today many corrupt Televangelists keep on asking for money as their agenda is not YHWH's work but to line up their own pockets. Have you ever heard a ministry saying we have enough money please stop giving? This will be the first when it happens!

11 He made loops of blue yarn on the edge of the curtain on the end of one set; likewise he did on the outer edge of the other curtain of the second set.

12 Fifty loops he made on one curtain, and fifty loops he made on the edge of the curtain on the end of the second set; the loops held one curtain to another.

13 And he made fifty clasps of gold, and coupled the curtains to one another with the clasps, that it might be one Tent.

14 He made curtains of goats' hair for the tent over the Tent; he made eleven curtains.

15 The length of each curtain was thirty cubits, and the width of each curtain four cubits; the eleven curtains were the same size.

16 He coupled five curtains by themselves and six curtains by themselves.

17 And he made fifty loops on the edge of the curtain that is outermost in one set, and fifty loops he made on the edge of the curtain of the second set.

18 He also made fifty bronze clasps to couple the tent together, that it might be one.

19 Then he made a covering for the tent of ram skins dyed red, and a covering of blue skins above that.

20 For the Tent he made boards of acacia wood, standing upright.

21 The length of each board was ten cubits, and the width of each board a cubit and a half.

22 Each board had two tenons for binding one to another. Thus he made for all the boards of the Tent.

23 And he made boards for the Tent, twenty boards for the south side.

24 Forty sockets of silver he made to go under the twenty boards: two sockets under each of the boards for its two tenons.

25 And for the other side of the Tent, the north side, he made twenty boards

26 And their forty sockets of silver: two sockets under each of the boards.

27 For the west side of the Tent he made six boards.

28 He also made two boards for the two back corners of the Tent.

29 And they were coupled at the bottom and coupled together at the top by one ring. Thus he made both of them for the two corners.

30 So there were eight boards and their sockets sixteen sockets of silver two sockets under each of the boards.

31 And he made bars of acacia wood: five for the boards on one side of the Tent,

32 Five bars for the boards on the other side of the Tent, and five bars for the boards of the Tent on the far side westward.

33 And he made the middle bar to pass through the boards from one end to the other.

34 He overlaid the boards with gold, made their rings of gold to be holders for the bars, and overlaid the bars with gold.

35 And he made a veil of blue, purple, and scarlet thread, and fine worked linen; it was woven with an artistic design of Khruvim.

36 He made for it four pillars of acacia wood, and overlaid them with gold, with their hooks of gold; and he cast four sockets of silver for them.

37 He also made a hanging for the entrance to the Tent door, of blue, purple, and scarlet thread, and fine woven linen, made by a weaver,

38 And its five pillars with their hooks. And he overlaid their capitals and their rings with gold, but their five sockets were of bronze.

Chapter 37

1 Then Betsal'el made the ark of acacia wood; three feet nine inches was its length, two feet three inches its width, and two feet three inches its height.

2 He overlaid it with pure gold inside and outside, and made a molding of gold all around it.

3 And he cast for it four rings of gold to be set in its four corners: two rings on one side, and two rings on the other side of it.

4 He made poles of acacia wood, and overlaid them with gold.

5 And he put the poles into the rings at the sides of the ark, to bear the ark.

6 He also made the lid of atonement of pure gold three feet nine inches was its length and two feet three inches its width.

7 He made two Khruvim of beaten gold; he made them of one piece at the two ends of the lid of atonement[1]:

8 One Khroob at one end on this side, and the other Khroob at the other end on that side. He made the Khruvim at the two ends of one piece with the lid of atonement.

9 The Khruvim spread out their wings above, and covered the lid of atonement with their wings. They faced one another; the faces of the Khruvim were toward the lid of atonement.

10 He made the table of acacia wood; three feet was its length, one foot six inches its width, and two feet three inches its height.

11 And he overlaid it with pure gold, and made a molding of gold all around it.

Footnotes

[1] One may say; we are not supposed to make idols or images of things in shamayim, and sure Cherubim are in shamayim but the idea is not about making idols but about worship rendered to those idols. So, these two cherubim are not made for idol worship but these two show Holy love between two cherubs. The commandment related to not making images of humans which we could then render for worship that is what YHWH was conveying. We find this mentioned in Deuteronomy 4:15-18, where YHWH explains why he did not show them any form of Himself. This was so they would not corrupt themselves, by making any graven images to worship. We see this prohibition explained or midrashed by the prophet Isaiah in 40:17-25, when we are told in no uncertain terms that the nations committed idolatry this way and are still doing it. They are worshipping man made images that are created by humans which many render worship to, calling them Holy. So in context making the images of cherubim are not prohibited as long as there is no Holy worship rendered to them. If people start to prostrate before them then that would constitute idolatry.

12 Also he made a frame of a handbreadth all around it, and made a molding of gold for the frame all around it.

13 And he cast for it four rings of gold, and put the rings on the four corners that were at its four legs.

14 The rings were close to the frame, as holders for the poles to bear the table.

15 And he made the poles of acacia wood to bear the table, and overlaid them with gold.

16 He made of pure gold the utensils which were on the table: its dishes, its cups, its bowls, and its pitchers for pouring.

17 He also made the menorah of pure gold; of hammered work he made the menorah. Its shaft, its branches, its bowls, its ornamental knobs, and its flowers were of the same piece.

18 And six branches came out of its sides: three branches of the menorah out of one side, and three branches of the menorah out of the other side.[1]

19 There were three bowls made like almond blossoms on one branch, with an ornamental knob and a flower, and three bowls made like almond blossoms on the other branch, with an ornamental knob and a flower and so for the six branches coming out of the menorah.

20 And on the menorah itself were four bowls made like almond[2] blossoms, each with its ornamental knob and flower.

21 There was a knob under the first two branches of the same, a knob under the second two branches of the same, and a knob under the third two branches of the same, according to the six branches extending from it.

22 Their knobs and their branches were of one piece; all of it was one hammered piece of pure gold.

23 And he made its seven lamps, its wick-trimmers, and its trays of pure gold.

24 Of a talent of pure gold he made it, with all its utensils.

25 He made the incense altar of acacia wood. Its length was a cubit and its width a cubit it was square and two cubits was its height. Its horns were of one piece with it.

26 And he overlaid it with pure gold: its top, its sides all around, and its horns. He also made for it a molding of gold all around it.

27 He made two rings of gold for it under its molding, by its two corners on both sides, as holders for the poles with which to bear it.

28 And he made the poles of acacia wood, and overlaid them with gold.

29 He also made the Holy anointing oil and the pure incense of sweet spices, according to the work of the perfumer.

Footnotes
[2] The tree of life was an Almond Tree and the Menorah is a symbol of life, if we have any symbols in our home then the following are paramount, the Menorah, the Shofar and the Tallit of course.

Footnotes
[1] This shows us the ten attributes of the Sefirotic tree.

Chapter 38

1 He made the altar of burnt offering of acacia wood; five cubits was its length and five cubits its width it was square and its height was three cubits.

2 He made its horns on its four corners; the horns were of one piece with it. And he overlaid it with bronze.

3 He made all the utensils for the altar: the pans, the shovels, the basins, the forks, and the fire pans; all its utensils he made of bronze.[1]

4 And he made a grate of bronze network for the altar, under its rim, midway from the bottom.

5 He cast four rings for the four corners of the bronze grating, as holders for the poles.

6 And he made the poles of acacia wood, and overlaid them with bronze.

7 Then he put the poles into the rings on the sides of the altar, with which to bear it. He made the altar hollow with boards.

8 He made the laver of bronze and its base of bronze, from the bronze mirrors of the ministering women who assembled at the door of the Tent of the appointed times.

9 Then he made the court on the south side; the hangings of the court were of fine woven linen, one hundred fifty feet long.

10 There were twenty pillars for them, with twenty bronze sockets. The hooks of the pillars and their bands were of silver.

11 On the north side the hangings were one hundred fifty feet long, with twenty pillars and their twenty bronze sockets. The hooks of the pillars and their bands were of silver.

12 And on the west side there were hangings of seventy-five feet long, with ten pillars and their ten sockets. The hooks of the pillars and their bands were of silver.

13 For the east side the hangings were seventy-five feet wide.

14 The hangings of one side of the gate were twenty-two and a half feet long, with their three pillars and their three sockets,

15 And the same for the other side of the court gate; on this side and that were hangings twenty-two and a half feet long, with their three pillars and their three sockets.

16 All the hangings of the court all around were of fine woven linen.

17 The sockets for the pillars were of bronze, the hooks of the pillars and their bands were of silver, and the overlay of their capitals was of silver; and all the pillars of the court had bands of silver.

18 The hanging for the gate of the court was woven of blue, purple, and scarlet thread, and of fine woven linen. The length was thirty feet long, and the height along its width was seven and a

Footnotes

[1] Bronze colour represents judgment of sin. The shining mirrors were there for people to see their faces so they acted as our modern mirrors.

half feet high, corresponding to the hangings of the court.

19 And there were four pillars with their four sockets of bronze; their hooks were of silver, and the overlay of their capitals and their bands was of silver.

20 All the pegs of the Tent, and of the court all around, were of bronze.

Torah Parsha 23 Pekudei , Shemoth 38:21-40:38
Haftarah Melekhim Alef 7:51 - 8:21

21 This is the inventory of the Tent, the Tent of the Testimony, which was counted according to the commandment of Mosheh (Musa), for the service of the Lewim, by the hand of Ithamar, son of Aharon the kohen (priest).

22 Betsal'el the son of Uri, the son of Khur, of the tribe of Yahudah, made all that YHWH had commanded Mosheh (Musa).

23 And with him was Aholiav the son of Ahisamakh, of the tribe of Dan, an engraver and designer, a weaver of blue, purple, and scarlet thread, and of fine linen.

24 All the gold that was used in all the work of the Holy place, that is, the gold of the offering, was twenty-nine talents[1] and seven hundred and thirty shekels, according to the shekel of the Holy place.

25 And the silver from those who were numbered of the

congregation was one hundred talents[2] and one thousand seven hundred and seventy-five shekels, according to the shekel of the Holy place:

26 A bekah for each man (that is, half a shekel, according to the shekel of the Holy place), for everyone included in the numbering from twenty years old and above, for six hundred and three thousand, five hundred and fifty men.

27 And from the hundred talents of silver were cast the sockets of the Holy place and the bases of the veil: one hundred sockets from the hundred talents, one talent for each socket.

28 Then from the one thousand seven hundred and seventy-five shekels he made hooks for the pillars, overlaid their capitals, and made bands for them.

29 The offering of bronze was seventy talents and two thousand four hundred shekels.

30 And with it he made the sockets for the door of the Tent of the appointed times, the bronze altar, the bronze grating for it, and all the utensils for the altar,

31 The sockets for the court all around, the bases for the court gate, all the pegs for the Tent,

Footnotes

[2] One common talent is about 27.2 KG in weight but the gold Talent is double in weight. Each nation had a different measure of the Talent hence why we cannot be certain what they each considered a Talent. Note; King David took away the crown of the king of the children of Ammon which 2 Samuel 12:30 mentions as one Talent in weight. If we consider this a Holy Talent then King David would have to wear a crown as heavy as 55KG which is difficult to imagine.

Footnotes

[1] We are not fully certain but if we estimate this by the talent of gold used then it makes 1582KG of Gold excluding the Shekels.

and all the pegs for the court all around.

Chapter 39

1 Of the blue, purple, and scarlet thread they made garments of ministry, for ministering in the Holy place, and made the Holy garments for Aharon, as YHWH had commanded Mosheh (Musa).

2 He made the ephod of gold, blue, purple, and scarlet thread, and of fine woven linen.

3 And they beat the gold into thin sheets and cut it into threads, to work it in with the blue, purple, and scarlet thread and the fine linen, into artistic designs.

4 They made shoulder straps for it to couple it together; it was coupled together at its two edges.

5 And the intricately woven band of his ephod that was on it was of the same workmanship, woven of gold, blue, purple, and scarlet thread, and of fine woven linen, as YHWH had commanded Mosheh (Musa).

6 And they set onyx stones, enclosed in settings of gold; they were engraved, as signets are engraved, with the names of the sons of Israel.

7 He put them on the shoulders of the ephod, that they should be stones for a memorial for the sons of Israel, as YHWH had commanded Mosheh (Musa).

8 And he made the breastplate, artistically woven like the workmanship of the ephod, of gold, blue, purple, and scarlet thread, and of fine woven linen.

9 They made the breastplate square by doubling it; a span was its length and a span its width when doubled.

10 And they set in it four rows of stones: a row with a sardius, a topaz, and an emerald was the first row;

11 The second row, a turquoise, a sapphire, and a diamond;

12 The third row, a jacinth, an agate, and an amethyst;

13 The fourth row, a beryl, an onyx, and a jasper. They were enclosed in settings of gold in their mountings.

14 There were twelve stones according to the names of the sons of Israel: according to their names, engraved like a signet, each one with its own name according to the twelve tribes.[1]

15 And they made chains for the breastplate at the ends, like braided cords of pure gold.

16 They also made two settings of gold and two gold rings, and put the two rings on the two ends of the breastplate.

17 And they put the two braided chains of gold in the two rings on the ends of the breastplate.

18 The two ends of the two braided chains they fastened in the two settings, and put them on

Footnotes
[1] The high priest can only intercede for the twelve tribes. He cannot intercede for a church made by man if that church is not engrafted into Israel then that church has no meaning and no standing in YHWH's sight. That may be Pentecostal, Methodist, Baptist it makes no difference. They need to be grafted into Israel and serve YHWH as He desires obeying the Torah coming under the authority of the Rabbis in charge.

the shoulder straps of the ephod in the front.

19 And they made two rings of gold and put them on the two ends of the breastplate, on the edge of it, which was on the inward side of the ephod.

20 They made two other gold rings and put them on the two shoulder straps, underneath the ephod toward its front, right at the seam above the intricately woven band of the ephod.

21 And they bound the breastplate by means of its rings to the rings of the ephod with a blue cord, so that it would be above the intricately woven band of the ephod, and that the breastplate would not come loose from the ephod, as YHWH had commanded Mosheh (Musa).

22 He made the robe of the ephod of woven work, all of blue.

23 And there was an opening in the middle of the robe, like the opening in a coat of mail, with a woven binding all around the opening, so that it would not tear.

24 They made on the hem of the robe pomegranates[1] of blue, purple, and scarlet, and of fine woven linen.

25 And they made bells of pure gold, and put the bells between the pomegranates on the hem of the robe all around between the pomegranates:

26 A bell and a pomegranate, a bell and a pomegranate, all around the hem of the robe to minister in, as YHWH had commanded Mosheh (Musa).

27 They made tunics, artistically woven of fine linen, for Aharon and his sons,

28 A turban of fine linen, exquisite turbans[2] of fine linen, short trousers of fine woven linen,

29 And a sash of fine woven linen with blue, purple, and scarlet thread, made by a weaver, as YHWH had commanded Mosheh (Musa).

30 Then they made the plate of the Holy crown of pure gold, and wrote on it an inscription like the engraving of a signet: HOLINESS TO YHWH.

31 And they tied to it a blue cord, to fasten it above on the turban, as YHWH had commanded Mosheh (Musa).

32 Thus all the work of the Tent of the tent of appointments was finished. And the children of Israel did according to all that

Footnotes

[1] Pomegranates were a picture of the fruitfulness of the tribes. Israel was a culture that thrived in polygamous marriages and saw the need to have large extended families. Unfortunately due to the present model of serial monogamy and divorce, to take on another wife is not approved of by men, but it is by YHWH and His Torah but strict guidelines are in place in how to conduct these types of marriages. In Biblical culture there was no divorce. While the end times Islamic beast is producing at a mass rate the church is stuck with its Roman/Greek model of serial monogamy and one or two children per family. If you are unfortunate to live in China they have ruled that any more than one child per Continued in next section

family and they will forcefully murder that child by an abortion, such is the fate of living in the world's laws. YHWH's Torah laws FREE people, while the world's laws ENSLAVE them. Now China allows two children as their econcomy needs more labour and the one child model has failed.
[2] Head-coverings are numerously mentioned because they are a law for Israel and for all those who are grafted in to Israel.

YHWH had commanded Mosheh (Musa); so they did.

33 And they brought the Tent to Mosheh (Musa), the tent and all its furnishings: its clasps, its boards, its bars, its pillars, and its sockets;

34 The covering of ram skins dyed red, the covering of blue skins, and the veil of the covering;

35 The ark of the Testimony with its poles, and the lid of atonement;

36 The table, all its utensils, and the Lakhem panayim[1] (bread of faces);

37 The pure Menorah with its lamps (the lamps set in order), all its utensils, and the oil for light;

38 The gold altar, the anointing oil, and the sweet incense; the screen for the Tent door;

39 The bronze altar, its grate of bronze, its poles, and all its utensils; the laver with its base;

40 The hangings of the court, its pillars and its sockets, the screen for the court gate, its cords, and its pegs; all the utensils for the service of the Tent, for the tent of appointments;

41 And the garments of ministry, to minister in the Holy place: the Holy garments for Aharon the kohen (priest), and his sons' garments, to minister as kohenim.

42 According to all that YHWH had commanded Mosheh (Musa),

so the children of Israel did all the work.

43 Then Mosheh (Musa) looked over all the work, and indeed they had done it; as YHWH had commanded, just so they had done it. And Mosheh (Musa) *spoke* Increases to them.

Chapter 40

1 Then YHWH spoke to Mosheh (Musa), saying:

2 On the first day of the first month you shall set up the Tent of the tent of appointments.[2]

3 You shall put in it the ark of the Testimony, and partition off the ark with the veil.

4 You shall bring in the table and arrange the things that are to be set in order on it; and you shall bring in the menorah and light its lamps.

5 You shall also set the altar of gold for the incense before the ark of the Testimony, and put up the hanging for the door of the Tent.

6 Then you shall set the altar of the burnt offering before the door of the Tent of the tent of appointments.

7 And you shall set the laver between the Tent of the appointed times and the altar, and put mayim in it.

8 You shall set up the court all around, and hang up the hangings at the court gate.

9 And you shall take the anointing oil, and anoint the Tent and all that is in it; and you shall

Footnotes
[1] Bread of many faces reveals the many faces of YHWH or the presence of YHWH such as the Ruakh Ha Kodesh, which is one face of YHWH.

Footnotes
[2] This was setup so that Israel could seek and serve YHWH and to come for their requests hence by it was for appointments.

Holy all its utensils, and it shall be Holy.

10 You shall anoint the altar of the burnt offering and all its utensils, and Consecrate the altar. The altar shall be most Holy.

11 And you shall anoint the laver and its base, and set it apart.

12 Then you shall bring Aharon and his sons to the door of the Tent of the appointed times and wash them with mayim.

13 You shall put the Holy garments on Aharon, and anoint him and set him apart, that he may minister to Me as kohen (priest).

14 And you shall bring his sons and clothe them with tunics.

15 You shall anoint them, as you anointed their father, that they may minister to Me as kohenim; for their anointing shall surely be an everlasting priesthood throughout their generations.[1]

16 Thus Mosheh (Musa) did; according to all that YHWH had commanded him, so he did.

17 And it came to pass in the first month of the second year, on the first day of the month, that the Tent was raised up.[2]

18 So Mosheh (Musa) raised up the Tent, fastened its sockets, set up its boards, put in its bars, and raised up its pillars.

19 And he spread out the tent over the Tent and put the covering of the tent on top of it, as YHWH had commanded Mosheh (Musa).

20 He took the Testimony and put it into the ark, inserted the poles through the rings of the ark, and put the lid of atonement on top of the ark.

21 And he brought the ark into the Tent, hung up the veil of the covering, and partitioned off the ark of the Testimony, as YHWH had commanded Mosheh (Musa).

22 He put the table in the Tent of the appointed times, on the north side[3] of the Tent, outside the veil;

23 And he set the Lakhem (bread) in order upon it before YHWH, as YHWH had commanded Mosheh (Musa).

24 He put the menorah in the Tent of the appointed times, across from the table, on the south[4] side of the Tent;

25 and he lit the lamps before YHWH, as YHWH had commanded Mosheh (Musa).

26 He put the gold altar in the Tent of the appointed times in front of the veil;

27 And he burned sweet incense on it, as YHWH had commanded Mosheh (Musa).

28 He hung up the hanging at the door of the Tent.

29 And he put the altar of burnt offering before the door of the Tent of the tent of appointments, and offered upon it the burnt offering and the grain offering, as

Footnotes

[1] The Levitical priesthood is eternal and will resume when the millennial temple is rebuilt in Jerusalem.

[2] The month of Abib or Nisan.

Footnotes

[3] The side of the 10th shamayim where YHWH's throne is.

[4] Represents the heart, the adoration of YHWH.

YHWH had commanded Mosheh
(Musa).

30 He set the laver between
the Tent of the appointed times
and the altar, and put mayim
there for washing;

31 And Mosheh (Musa),
Aharon, and his sons would wash
their hands and their feet with
mayim from it.

32 Whenever they went into
the Tent of the appointed times,
and when they came near the
altar, they washed, as YHWH
had commanded Mosheh (Musa).

33 And he raised up the court
all around the Tent and the altar,
and hung the hangings of the
court gate. So Mosheh (Musa)
finished the work.

34 Then the cloud covered the
Tent of the appointed times, and
the glory of YHWH filled the Tent.

35 And Mosheh (Musa) was
not able to enter the Tent of the
appointed times, because the
cloud rested above it, and the
glory of YHWH filled the Tent.

36 When the cloud was taken
up from above the Tent, the
children of Israel went onward in
all their journeys.

37 But if the cloud was not
taken up, then they did not
journey till the day that it was
taken up.

38 For the cloud of YHWH was
above the Tent by day, and fire
was over it by night, in the sight
of all the Beyth (house) of Israel,
throughout all their journeys. ת

We'Yikra (Leviticus)

The Third Book of Mosheh (Musa)

Wayikra (Leviticus)

ויקרא

And He Called

Torah Parsha 24 Wayikra, Wayikra 1:1-6:7

Haftarah: Yeshayahu 43:21-44:23

Chapter 1

 1

1 And YHWH called to Mosheh (Musa), and spoke to him out of the Tent of the appointed times, saying,

2 Speak to the children of Israel, and say to them, If any man from you bring an offering to YHWH, you shall bring your offering of the cattle, even of the herd, and of the flock.

3 If his offering be a burnt sacrifice of the herd, let him offer a male without blemish: he shall offer it of his own voluntary will at the door of the Tent of the appointed times before YHWH.

4 And he shall put his hand upon the head of the burnt offering; and it shall be accepted for him to make atonement for him.

5 And he shall kill the bullock before YHWH and the kohenim, Aharon's sons, shall bring the

blood,[2] and sprinkle the blood round about upon the altar that is by the door of the Tent of the appointed times.

6 And he shall skin the burnt offering, and cut it into pieces.

7 And the sons of Aharon the Kohen (priest) shall put fire upon the altar, and lay the wood in the right order on the fire:

8 And the kohenim Aharon's sons shall lay the parts, the head, and the fat, in order upon the wood that is on the fire which is upon the altar:

9 But his inwards and his legs shall he wash in mayim: and the kohen (priest) shall burn all on the altar, to be a burnt sacrifice, an offering made by fire, of a sweet savour to YHWH.

10 And if his offering be of the flocks, namely, of the sheep, or of the goats, for a burnt sacrifice; he shall bring it a male without blemish.

11 And he shall kill it on the side of the altar northward[3] before YHWH and the kohenim, Aharon's sons, shall sprinkle his blood roundabout upon the altar.

12 And he shall cut it into his pieces, with his head and his fat: and the kohen (priest) shall lay them in order on the wood that is on the fire which is upon the altar:

13 But he shall wash the

Footnotes

[1] When YHWH called to Moses the Alef which is normally a picture of a man is here made small. Now, the sign of strength shows that the sign of weakness in Moses or his (human) strength was made small, because he has to rely on YHWH's strength.

[2] Only the priests have the right to minister before YHWH and not just anyone so the priests are consecrated and Holy.

[3] The North side of the altar faces towards the 3rd shamayim where YHWH's throne is. It is also the place that Satan attacks. You will notice that large parts of the world in the northern hemisphere from Israel are into atheism, Islam or into nothing.

inwards and the legs with mayim and the kohen (priest) shall bring it all, and burn it upon the altar: it is a burnt sacrifice, an offering made by fire, of a sweet savour to YHWH.

14 And if the burnt sacrifice for his offering to YHWH be of birds, then he shall bring his offering of turtledoves, or of young pigeons.[1]

15 And the kohen (priest) shall bring it to the altar, and wring off his head, and burn it on the altar; and the blood there shall be wrung out at the side of the altar:

16 And he shall pluck away his crop with his feathers, and cast it beside the altar on the east part, by the place of the ashes:

17 And he shall cleave it with the wings there, but shall not divide it into two parts: and the kohen (priest) shall burn it upon the altar, upon the wood that is upon the fire: it is a burnt sacrifice, an offering made by fire, of a sweet savour to YHWH.

Chapter 2

1 And when any will offer a grain offering to YHWH, his offering shall be of fine flour;[2] and he shall pour oil upon it, and put frankincense thereon:

2 And he shall bring it to Aharon's sons the kohenim and he shall take there out his handful of the flour, and of the oil, with all the frankincense; and the kohen (priest) shall burn the memorial of

it upon the altar, to be an offering made by fire, of a sweet savour to YHWH.

3 And the remainder of the grain offering shall be for Aharon and his sons: it is most Holy of the offerings to YHWH made by fire.

4 And if you bring a grain of a grain offering baked in the oven, it shall be matzah (unleavened rotis) of fine flour mingled with oil, or matzah (unleavened) thin rotis anointed with oil.

5 And if your grain be a grain offering baked in a pan, it shall be of fine flour matzah (unleavened bread), mingled with oil.

6 You shall part it in pieces, and pour oil thereon: it is a grain offering.

7 And if your offering be a grain offering baked in the frying pan, it shall be made of fine flour with oil.

8 And you shall bring the grain offering that is made of these things to YHWH and when it is presented to the kohen (priest), he shall bring it to the altar.

9 And the kohen (priest) shall take from the grain offering a memorial, and shall burn it upon the altar: it is an offering made by fire, of a sweet savour to YHWH.

10 And that which is left of the grain offering shall be for Aharon and his sons: it is most Holy of the offerings to YHWH made by fire.

11 No grain offering, which you shall bring to YHWH, shall be made with leaven: for you shall burn no leaven, nor any honey, in any offering of YHWH made by fire.

12 As for the grain of the

Footnotes

[1] This was for those people who could not afford the expensive bull or sheep.

[2] The flour was taken from the pot in a special way by the kohen (priest) stretching his three fingers to pick up the flour and paring off with his thumb.

bikkurim (first-fruit), you shall offer them to YHWH but they shall not be burnt on the altar for a sweet savour.

13 And every grain of your grain offering shall you season with salt; neither shall you suffer the salt of the Covenant of Your POWER to be lacking from your grain offering with all your offerings you shall offer salt.

14 And if you offer a grain offering of your bikkurim[1] to YHWH You shall offer for the grain offering of your bikkurim (first-fruit) green ears of wheat dried by the fire, even wheat beaten out of full ears.

15 And you shall put oil upon it, and lay frankincense thereon: it is a grain offering.

16 And the kohen (priest) shall burn the memorial of it, part of the beaten wheat, and part of the oil, with all the frankincense: it is an offering made by fire to YHWH.

Chapter 3

1 And if his grain be a sacrifice of shalom offering, if he offer it of the herd; whether it be a male or female, he shall offer it without blemish before YHWH.

2 And he shall lay his hand upon the head of his offering, and kill it at the door of the Tent of the appointed times: and Aharon's sons the kohenim shall sprinkle the blood upon the altar round about.

Footnotes
[1] This is not the bikkurim (first-fruit) offering that was commanded during Passover, Pentecost or Tabernacles but a freewill tributary offering.

3 And he shall offer of the sacrifice of the shalom offering an offering made by fire to YHWH the fat that covers the inwards, and all the fat that is upon the inwards,

4 And the two kidneys, and the fat that is on them, which is by the loins, and the covers above the liver, with the kidneys, it shall he take away. [2]

Footnotes
[2] YHWH was smart to remove all the fat and the elements of the organs that would today give us lots of cholesterol and hence heart disease and death. His people did not experience these kinds of modern diseases because they stayed away from these foods. Needless amount of people are dying today as a result of disobedience and lack of instructions in body health. Fat in animal or even human body is a way to store toxins that can be harmful to us especially if the "inward parts" (kidney, liver...) are not able to process them efficiently for elimination. So fatty cells (the white adipocyte cells) has the ability to enlarge and imprison toxins, heavy metals, chemicals, pollutants etc.

An example: an animal is fed with grass that grows thanks to herbicides. These herbicides are toxic to the animal body and can eventually lead it to a premature death, so, in order for this not to occur, the body programs the storage of toxins in the fatty parts of the animal.

The same happens in human body in the white fat cells (indeed, there exists two different fats: the white and the brown one and guess which one is the best? The brown! Because it generates body heat thanks to the presence of iron and oxygen).It is brown fat, yes brown in color the same colour as the Israelites, and its great way that it burns calories like a furnace. In studies done it has been found that one form of it, which is turned on when people become cold, it then sucks fat out of the rest of the body to fuel itself as a furnace. In other studies it was discovered that a second form of brown fat can be created from ordinary white fat by exercise too. So the "inward parts" like the liver, the
Continued in next section

5 And Aharon's sons shall burn it on the altar upon the burnt sacrifice, which is upon the wood that is on the fire: it is an offering made by fire, of a sweet savour to YHWH.

6 And if his offering be for a sacrifice of shalom offering to YHWH of the flock; male or female, he shall offer it without blemish.

7 If he offer a lamb for his offering, then shall he offer it before YHWH.

8 And he shall lay his hand upon the head of his offering, and kill it before the Tent of the appointed times: and Aharon's sons shall sprinkle the blood there round about upon the altar.

9 And he shall offer of the sacrifice of the shalom offering an offering made by fire to YHWH; its fat, all the fat tail which he removes close to the backbone, and the fat that covers the inwards and all the fat that is on the inwards,

10 And the two kidneys, and the fat that is upon them, which is by the loins, and the covers above the liver, with the kidneys, it shall he take away.

11 And the Kohen (priest) shall burn it upon the altar: it is the food of the offering made by fire to YHWH.

12 And if his offering be a goat, then he shall offer it before YHWH.

13 And he shall lay his hand upon the head of it, and kill it before the Tent of the appointed times: and the sons of Aharon shall sprinkle the blood there upon the altar round about.

14 And he shall offer there his offering, even an offering made by fire to YHWH the fat that covers the inwards, and all the fat that is upon the inwards,

15 And the two kidneys, and the fat that is upon them, which is by the loins, and the covers above the liver, with the kidneys, it shall he take away.

16 And the kohen (priest) shall burn them upon the altar: it is the food of the offering made by fire for a sweet savour: all the fat is for YHWH.

17 It shall be an everlasting statute for your generations throughout all your dwellings, that you eat neither fat nor blood.[1]

Chapter 4

1 And YHWH spoke to Mosheh (Musa), saying,

2 Speak to the children of Israel, saying, If a soul shall sin through ignorance against any of the commandments of YHWH concerning things which ought not to be done, and shall do against any of them:

3 If the Kohen (priest)[2] that is

Footnotes

[1] Blood and fat are both so harmful to the body that YHWH made sure Israel stayed away from such practices, unlike the heathen nations. By consuming the blood of an animal you actually also consume the soul and that has spiritual ramifications.

[2] The kohen's sins are not exempt from punishment just because he stands close to Continued in next section

kidneys, the lungs, the intestines, even the skin are detoxifying organs (they act as filters, a reason not to eat them), and as saying if they are not working properly to eliminate toxins from the body, the storage of toxins begins in white fat cells.

anointed does sin according to the sin of the people; then let him bring for his sin, which he has transgressed, a young bullock without blemish to YHWH for a sin offering.

4 And he shall bring the bullock to the door of the Tent of the appointed times before YHWH; and shall lay his hand upon the bullock's head,[1] and kill the bullock before YHWH.

5 And the Kohen (priest) that is anointed shall take of the bullock's blood, and bring it to the Tent of the appointed times:

6 And the Kohen (priest) shall dip his finger in the blood, and sprinkle of the blood seven times before YHWH, before the veil of the sanctuary.

7 And the kohen (priest) shall put some of the blood upon the horns of the altar of sweet incense before YHWH, which is in the Tent of the appointed times; and shall pour all the blood of the bullock at the bottom of the altar of the burnt offering, which is at the door of the Tent of the appointed times.

8 And he shall take off from it all the fat of the bullock for the sin offering; the fat that covers the inwards, and all the fat that is upon the inwards,

9 And the two kidneys, and the fat that is upon them, which is by the loins, and the lobe above the liver, with the kidneys, it shall he take away,

10 As it was taken off from the bullock of the sacrifice of shalom offerings: and the kohen (priest) shall burn them upon the altar of the burnt offering.

11 And the skin of the bullock, and all his flesh, with his head, and with his legs, and his inwards, and his dung,

12 Even the whole bullock shall he carry forth outside the camp to a clean place, where the ashes are poured out, and burn him on the wood with fire: where the ashes are poured out shall he be burnt.

13 And if the whole congregation of Israel transgresses through ignorance, and the thing be hid from the eyes of the assembly, and they have done somewhat against any of the commandments of YHWH concerning things which should not be done, and are guilty;

14 When the sin, which they have sinned against it, is known, then the congregation shall offer a young bullock[2] for the sin, and bring him before the Tent of the appointed times.

15 And the elders of the congregation shall lay their hands

Footnotes

YHWH. For this reason, he is more accountable.

[1] This is a substitution offering. The animal takes the sin upon himself.

[2] Animal sacrifices only existed for unintentional sins and you will find no sacrifice for intentional sins. Unless YHWH provided favor from the start there would be no atonement for intentional sin for anyone. The Yom Kippurim sacrifice that includes intentional sins was only acceptable if YHWH approved of the people's heart. Else, it could be rendered null and void. The scarlet string that was placed on the Temple altar that used to turn white indicating that YHWH had accepted the sacrifice, stopped turning white and remained scarlet for forty years until the destruction of the second Temple.

upon the head of the bullock before YHWH and the bullock shall be killed before YHWH.

16 And the Kohen (priest) that is anointed shall bring of the bullock's blood to the Tent of the appointed times:

17 And the Kohen (priest) shall dip his finger in some of the blood, and sprinkle it seven times before YHWH, even before the veil.

18 And he shall put some of the blood upon the horns of the altar which is before YHWH, that is in the Tent of the appointed times, and shall pour out all the blood at the bottom of the altar of the burnt offering, which is at the door of the Tent of the appointed times.

19 And he shall take all his fat from him, and burn it upon the altar.

20 And he shall do with the bullock as he did with the bullock for a sin offering, so shall he do with this: and the kohen (priest) shall make atonement for them, and it shall be forgiven them.

21 And he shall carry forth the bullock outside the camp, and burn it as he burned the first bullock: it is a sin offering for the congregation.

22 When a ruler has transgressed, and done somewhat through ignorance against any of the commandments of YHWH his Elohim concerning things which should not be done, and is guilty;

23 Or if his sin, wherein he has sinned, come to his knowledge; he shall bring his offering, a kid of the goats, a male without

blemish:

24 And he shall lay his hand upon the head of the goat, and kill it in the place where they kill the burnt offering before YHWH it is a sin offering.

25 And the kohen (priest) shall take of the blood of the sin offering with his finger, and put it upon the horns of the altar of burnt offering, and shall pour out the blood at the bottom of the altar of burnt offering.

26 And he shall burn all the fat upon the altar, as the fat of the sacrifice of shalom offerings: and the kohen (priest) shall make atonement for him as concerning his sin, and it shall be forgiven him.

27 And if any one of the common people sin through ignorance, while he does somewhat against any of the commandments of YHWH concerning things which ought not to be done, and be guilty;

28 Or if his sin, which he has transgressed, come to his knowledge: then he shall bring his offering, a kid of the goats, a female without blemish, for his sin which he has transgressed.

29 And he shall lay his hand upon the head[1] of the sin offering, and slay the sin offering in the place of the burnt offering.

30 And the kohen (priest) shall take of the blood there with his finger, and put it upon the horns

Footnotes

[1] In many Islamic countries and non-Islamic ones, the Muslims will get a goat and lay their hands on the goat and kill the goat to ward off evil. This practice has its roots in Israelite culture.

of the altar of burnt offering, and shall pour out all the blood there at the bottom of the altar.

31 And he shall take away all the fat there, as the fat is taken away from off the sacrifice of shalom offerings; and the kohen (priest) shall burn it upon the altar for a sweet savour to YHWH; and the kohen (priest) shall make an atonement for him, and it shall be forgiven him.

32 And if he brings a lamb for a sin offering, he shall bring it a female without blemish.

33 And he shall lay his hand upon the head of the sin offering, and slay it for a sin offering in the place where they kill the burnt offering.

34 And the kohen (priest) shall take of the blood of the sin offering with his finger, and put it upon the horns of the altar of burnt offering, and shall pour out all the blood there at the bottom of the altar:

35 And he shall take away all the fat there, as the fat of the lamb is taken away from the sacrifice of the shalom offerings; and the kohen (priest) shall burn them upon the altar, according to the offerings made by fire to YHWH and the kohen (priest) shall make an atonement for his sin that he has committed, and it shall be forgiven him.

Chapter 5

1 And if a soul transgresses, and hear the voice of swearing, and is a witness, whether he has seen or known of it; if he do not utter it, then he shall bear his iniquity.

2 Or if a soul touch any unclean thing, whether it be a carcass of an unclean beast, or a carcass of unclean cattle, or the carcass of unclean crawling things, and if it be hidden from him; he also shall be unclean, and guilty.

3 Or if he touch the uncleanness of man, whatsoever uncleanness it be that a man shall be defiled with, and it be hid from him; when he knows of it, then he shall be guilty.

4 Or if a soul swear, pronouncing with his lips to do evil, or to do good, whatsoever it be that a man shall pronounce with an oath, and it be hid from him; when he knows of it, then he shall be guilty in one of these.

5 And it shall be, when he shall be guilty in one of these things, that he shall confess the name[1] that he has transgressed in that thing:

6 And he shall bring his trespass offering to YHWH for his sin which he has sinned, a female from the flock, a lamb or a kid of the goats, for a sin offering; and the kohen (priest) shall make atonement for him concerning his sin.

7 And if he be not able to bring a lamb, then he shall bring for his trespass, which he has committed, two turtledoves, or two young pigeons, to YHWH one for a sin offering, and the other for a burnt offering.

8 And he shall bring them to the

Footnotes
[1] The ancient Hebrew word Yada here means to confess the name of YHWH. The word is also used in a husband and wife as a word to have relationship.

kohen (priest), who shall offer that which is for the sin offering first, and wring off its head from its neck, but shall not divide it asunder:

9 And he shall sprinkle the blood of the sin offering upon the wall of the altar; and the rest of the blood shall be wrung out at the base of the altar: it is a sin offering.

10 And he shall offer the second for a burnt offering, according to the manner: and the kohen (priest) shall make atonement for him for his sin which he has transgressed, and it shall be forgiven him.

11 But if he be not able to bring two turtledoves, or two young pigeons, then he that transgressed shall bring for his offering the tenth part of an ephah of fine flour[1] for a sin offering; he shall put no oil upon it, neither shall he put any frankincense thereon: for it is a sin offering.

12 Then shall he bring it to the kohen (priest), and the kohen (priest) shall take his handful of it, even a memorial there, and burn it on the altar, according to the offerings made by fire to YHWH it is a sin offering.

13 And the kohen (priest) shall make atonement for him as touching his sin that he has transgressed in one of these, and it shall be forgiven him: and the remainder shall be the kohen's (priest), as a grain offering.

Footnotes

[1] Someone who could not afford the birds could bring in flour so YHWH accommodated all people rich and poor.

14 And YHWH spoke to Mosheh (Musa), saying,

15 If a soul commit a trespass, and sin through ignorance, in the Holy things of YHWH; then he shall bring for his trespass to YHWH a ram without blemish out of the flocks, with your estimation by shekels of silver, after the shekel of the sanctuary, for a trespass offering:

16 And he shall make amends for the harm that he has done in the Holy thing, and shall add the fifth part thereto, and give it to the kohen (priest) and the kohen (priest) shall make atonement for him with the ram of the trespass offering, and it shall be forgiven him.

17 And if a soul transgresses, and commit any of these things which are forbidden to be done by the commandments of YHWH though he knew it not, yet he is guilty, and shall bear his iniquity.

18 And he shall bring a ram without blemish out of the flock, with your estimation, for a trespass offering, to the kohen (priest) and the kohen (priest) shall make atonement for him concerning his ignorance wherein he erred and knew it not, and it shall be forgiven him.

19 It is a trespass offering: he has certainly trespassed against YHWH.

Chapter 6

1 And YHWH spoke to Mosheh (Musa), saying,

2 If a soul transgresses, and commit a trespass against YHWH, and lie to his neighbour in that which was given him to keep, or in fellowship, or in a thing taken away by violence, or has deceived his neighbour;

3 Or have found that which was lost, and lies concerning it, and swears falsely; in any of all these that a man does, transgressing therein:

4 Then it shall be, because he has transgressed, and is guilty, that he shall restore that which he took violently away, or the thing which he has deceitfully gotten, or that which was given him to keep, or the lost thing which he found,

5 Or all that about which he has sworn falsely; he shall even restore it in the principal, and shall add the fifth part more thereto, and give it to him to whom it belongs, in the day of his trespass offering.

6 And he shall bring his trespass offering to YHWH, a ram without blemish out of the flock, with your estimation, for a trespass offering, to the kohen (priest):

7 And the kohen (priest) shall make atonement for him before YHWH and it shall be forgiven him for any thing of all that he has done in trespassing therein.

Torah Parsha 25 Tzav, Wayikra 6:8 - 8:36
Haftarah: Yirmeyahu 7:21 - 8:3; & 9:23-24

8 And YHWH spoke to Mosheh (Musa), saying,

9 Command Aharon and his sons, saying, This is the instruction of the burnt offering: It is the burnt offering, because of the burning upon the altar all night to the morning, and the fire of the altar shall be burning in it.

10 And the kohen (priest) shall put on his linen garment, and his linen undergarments shall he put upon his flesh, and take up the ashes which the fire has consumed with the burnt offering on the altar, and he shall put them beside the altar.

11 And he shall put off his garments, and put on other garments, and carry forth the ashes outside the camp to a clean place.

12 And the fire upon the altar shall be burning in it; it shall not be put out: and the kohen (priest) shall burn wood on it every morning, and lay the burnt offering in arrangement; and he shall burn thereon the fat of the shalom offerings.

13 The fire shall ever be burning upon the altar; it shall never go out.

14 And this is the instruction of the grain offering: the sons of Aharon shall offer it before YHWH, before the altar.

15 And he shall take of it his handful, of the flour of the grain offering, and of the oil there, and

Footnotes
[1] The small mem in this verse specifies water and in women it would specify the womb. Here the man's soul is figuratively on the altar if it was not for the animal taking his place.

all the frankincense which is upon the grain offering, and shall burn it upon the altar for a sweet savour, even the memorial of it, to YHWH.

16 And the remainder there shall Aharon and his sons eat: with matzah (unleavened bread) shall it be eaten in the Holy place; in the court of the Tent of the appointed times they shall eat it.

17 It shall not be baked with leaven. I have given it to them for their portion of my offerings made by fire; it is most Holy, as is the sin offering, and as the trespass offering.

18 All the males among the children of Aharon shall eat of it. It shall be a statute forever in your generations concerning the offerings of YHWH made by fire: everyone that touches them shall become Holy.

19 And YHWH spoke to Mosheh (Musa), saying,

20 This is the offering of Aharon and of his sons, which they shall offer to YHWH in the day when he is anointed; the tenth part of an ephah of fine flour for a grain offering perpetual, half of it in the morning, and half there at night.

21 In a pan it shall be made with oil; and when it is baked, you shall bring it in: and the baked pieces of the grain offering shall You offer for a sweet savour to YHWH.

22 And the kohen (priest) of his sons that is anointed in his stead shall offer it: it is a statute forever to YHWH it shall be wholly burnt.

23 For every grain offering for the kohen (priest) shall be wholly burnt: it shall not be eaten.

24 And YHWH spoke to Mosheh (Musa), saying,

25 Speak to Aharon and to his sons, saying, This is the instruction of the sin offering: In the place where the burnt offering is killed shall the sin offering be killed before YHWH it is most Holy.

26 The kohen (priest) that offers it for sin shall eat it: in the Holy place shall it be eaten, in the court of the Tent of the appointed times.

27 Whatsoever shall touch the flesh there shall be Holy: and when there is sprinkled of the blood there upon any garment, You shall wash that whereon it was sprinkled in the Holy place.

28 But the earthen vessel wherein it is cooked shall be broken: and if it be cooked in a brazen pot, it shall be both scoured, and rinsed in mayim.

29 All the males among the kohenim shall eat there: it is most Holy.

30 And no sin offering, whereof any of the blood is brought into the Tent of the appointed times to reconcile in the Holy place, shall be eaten: it shall be burnt in the fire.

Chapter 7

1 Likewise this is the instruction of the trespass offering: it is most Holy.

2 In the place where they kill the burnt offering shall they kill the trespass offering: and its blood shall he sprinkled round about upon the altar.

3 And he shall offer of it all the fat there; the tail, and the fat that covers the inwards,

4 And the two kidneys, and the fat that is on them, which is by the loins, and the lobe that is above the liver, with the kidneys, he shall take away:

5 And the kohen (priest) shall burn them upon the altar for an offering made by fire to YHWH it is a trespass offering.

6 Every male among the kohenim shall eat there: it shall be eaten in the Holy place: it is most Holy.

7 As the sin offering is, so is the trespass offering: there is one instruction for them: the kohen (priest) that makes atonement therewith shall have it.

8 And the kohen (priest) that offers any man's burnt offering, even the kohen (priest) shall have to himself the skin of the burnt offering which he has offered.

9 And all the grain offering that is baked in the oven, and all that is dressed in the frying-pan, and in the pan, shall be the kohen's (priest) that offered it.

10 And every grain offering, mingled with oil, and dry, shall all the sons of Aharon have, one as much as another.

11 And this is the instruction of the sacrifice of shalom offerings, which he shall offer to YHWH.

12 If he offer it for a thanksgiving, then he shall offer with the sacrifice of thanksgiving matzah (unleavened) rotis mingled with oil, and matzah (unleavened) thin rotis anointed with oil, and rotis mingled with oil, of fine flour, fried.[1]

13 Besides the rotis, he shall offer for his offering leavened Lakhem (bread) with the sacrifice of thanksgiving of his shalom offerings.

14 And of it he shall offer one out of the whole sacrifice for a heave offering to YHWH, and it shall be the kohen's (priest) that sprinkles the blood of the shalom offerings.

15 And the flesh of the sacrifice of his shalom offerings for thanksgiving shall be eaten the same day that it is offered; he shall not leave any of it until the morning.

16 But if the sacrifice of his offering be a vow, or a voluntary offering, it shall be eaten the same day that he offers his sacrifice: and the day after also the remainder of it shall be eaten:

17 But the remainder of the flesh of the sacrifice on the third day shall be burnt with fire.

Footnotes

[1] The Tent was Passover all year round with no leaven except two times. However, The Todah (Thank you) offering when brought to the Tent was one of the two times that chometz (leaven) could be brought in. This consisted of the 40 loaves of bread, thirty of which were matzah (unleavened) and ten which would be chometz (leavened). This offering could be eaten by the person offering and his relatives and friends, any one can be invited as in a public barbeque. The offering must be eaten on the day offered and before the dawn, anything left over must be burned.

This kind of offering was given as a public thank you to Elohim, when one crosses over the desert safely, travels across the sea without harm, has been healed from an illness or was released from prison. The demonstration was to show ones gratitude for Master YHWH and His provision publicly.

18 And if any of the flesh of the sacrifice of his shalom offerings be eaten at all on the third day, it shall not be accepted, neither shall it be imputed to him that offers it: it shall be an abomination, and the soul that eats of it shall bear his iniquity.

19 And the flesh that touches any unclean thing shall not be eaten; it shall be burnt with fire: and as for the flesh, all that be clean shall eat it.

20 But the soul that eats of the flesh of the sacrifice of shalom offerings that pertain to YHWH, having his uncleanness upon him, even that soul shall be cut off from his people.

21 Moreover the soul that shall touch any unclean *thing*, as the uncleanness of man, or any unclean beast, or in all impure defiled *thing*, and eat of the flesh of the sacrifice of shalom offerings, which pertain to YHWH, even that soul shall be cut off from his people.

22 And YHWH spoke to Mosheh (Musa), saying,

23 Speak to the children of Israel, saying, You shall eat no manner of fat, of ox, or of sheep, or of goat.

24 And the fat of the animal that dies of itself, and the fat of that which is torn by other animals, may be used in any other use: but you shall in no wise eat of it.[1]

25 For whosoever eats the fat of the animal, of which men offer an offering made by fire to YHWH, even the person that eats it shall be cut off from his people.

26 Moreover you shall eat no manner of blood, whether it be of birds or of any animals, in any of your dwellings.

27 Whatsoever person it be that eats any manner of blood, even that soul shall be cut off from his people.[2]

28 And YHWH spoke to Mosheh (Musa), saying,

29 Speak to the children of Israel, saying, He that offers the sacrifice of his shalom offerings to YHWH shall bring his oblation to YHWH of the sacrifice of his shalom offerings.

30 His own hands shall bring the offerings of YHWH made by fire, the fat with the breast, it shall he bring, that the breast may be waved for a wave offering before YHWH.

31 And the kohen (priest) shall burn the fat upon the altar: but the breast shall be Aharon's and his sons.'

32 And the right shoulder shall you give to the kohen (priest) for a contribution offering of the sacrifices of your shalom offerings.

33 He among the sons of Aharon, that offers the blood of the shalom offerings, and the fat, shall have the right shoulder for his part.

34 For the wave breast and the contribution shoulder have I taken of the children of Israel

Footnotes

[1] Torn animals or hunted animals are not to be eaten unless they are cut correctly by slitting the throat and letting all the blood drip to the earth.

[2] Any blood eaten is a sin, you are technically consuming the soul of the animal by doing this.

from off the sacrifices of their shalom offerings, and have given them to Aharon the kohen (priest) and to his sons by a statute forever from among the children of Israel.

35 This is the portion of the anointing of Aharon, and of the anointing of his sons, out of the offerings of YHWH made by fire, in the day when he presented them to minister to YHWH in the kohen's (priest) office;

36 Which YHWH commanded to be given them of the children of Israel, in the day that he anointed them, by a statute forever throughout their generations.

37 This is the instruction of the burnt offering, of the grain offering, and of the sin offering, and of the trespass offering, and of the consecrations, and of the sacrifice of the shalom offerings;

38 Which YHWH commanded Mosheh (Musa) in Mount Sinai, in the day that he commanded the children of Israel to offer their offerings to YHWH, in the wilderness of Sinai.

Chapter 8

1 And YHWH spoke to Mosheh (Musa), saying,

2 Take Aharon and his sons with him, and the garments, and the anointing oil, and a bullock for the sin offering, and two rams, and a basket of matzah (unleavened bread);

3 And you gather all the congregation together to the door of the Tent of the appointed times.

4 And Mosheh (Musa) did as YHWH commanded him; and the assembly was gathered together to the door of the Tent of the appointed times.

5 And Mosheh (Musa) said to the congregation, This is the thing which YHWH commanded to be done.

6 And Mosheh (Musa) brought Aharon and his sons, and washed them with mayim.

7 And he put upon him the coat, and girded him with the girdle, and clothed him with the robe, and put the ephod upon him, and he girded him with the curious girdle of the ephod, and bound it to him there.

8 And he put the breastplate upon him: also he put in the breastplate the Urim and the Thummim.

9 And he put the turban upon his head; also upon the turban, even upon his forefront, did he put the golden plate, the Holy crown; as YHWH commanded Mosheh (Musa).

10 And Mosheh (Musa) took the anointing oil, and anointed the Tent and all that was in there, and sanctified them.

11 And he sprinkled there upon the altar seven times, and anointed the altar and all his vessels, both the laver and his foot, to sanctify them.

12 And he poured of the anointing oil upon Aharon's head, and anointed him, to sanctify him.

13 And Mosheh (Musa) brought Aharon's sons, and put coats upon them, and girded them with girdles, and put turban's[1] upon

Footnotes
[1] Head-coverings are commanded and must be worn by all Israelites priests or those Continued in next section

274

them; as YHWH commanded Mosheh (Musa).

14 And he brought the bullock for the sin offering: and Aharon and his sons laid their hands upon the head of the bullock for the sin offering.

15 And he slaughtered it; and Mosheh (Musa) took the blood, and put it upon the horns of the altar round about with his finger, and purified the altar, and poured the blood at the base of the altar, and sanctified it, to make reconciliation upon it.

16 And he took all the fat that was upon the inwards, and the lobe above the liver, and the two kidneys, and their fat, and Mosheh (Musa) burned it upon the altar.

17 But the bullock, and its hide, its flesh, and its dung, he burnt with fire outside the camp; as YHWH commanded Mosheh (Musa).

18 And he brought the ram for the burnt offering: and Aharon and his sons laid their hands upon the head of the ram.

19 And he slaughtered it; and Mosheh (Musa) sprinkled the blood upon the altar roundabout.

20 And he cut the ram into pieces; and Mosheh (Musa) burnt the head, and the pieces, and the fat.

21 And he washed the inwards and the legs in mayim; and Mosheh (Musa) burnt the whole

ram upon the altar: it was a burnt sacrifice for a sweet savour, and an offering made by fire to YHWH as YHWH commanded Mosheh (Musa).

22 And he brought the other ram, the ram of consecration: and Aharon and his sons laid their hands upon the head of the ram.

23 And he slaughtered it; and Mosheh (Musa) took of the blood of it, and put it upon the tip of Aharon's right ear, and upon the thumb of his right hand, and upon the great toe of his right foot.[1]

24 And he brought Aharon's sons, and Mosheh (Musa) put the blood upon the tip of their right ear, and upon the thumbs of their right hands, and upon the great toes of their right feet: and Mosheh (Musa) sprinkled the blood upon the altar round about.

25 And he took the fat, and the tail, and all the fat that was upon the inwards, and the lobe above the liver, and the two kidneys, and their fat, and the right shoulder:

26 And out of the basket of matzah (unleavened bread) that was before YHWH, he took one matzah (unleavened) roti, and a roti of oiled Lakhem (bread), and one thin roti, and put them on the fat, and upon the right shoulder:

27 And he put all upon Aharon's hands, and upon his sons' hands, and waved them for a wave offering before YHWH.

28 And Mosheh (Musa) took them from off their hands, and burnt them on the altar upon the

claiming to be priests in the New Covenant today and that means all saved men and women must cover up their hair when before YHWH. A naked head is a sign of disobedience before YHWH.

Footnotes
[1] See footnote Shemoth 29:20

burnt offering: they were consecrations for a sweet savour: it is an offering made by fire to YHWH.

29 And Mosheh (Musa) took the breast, and waved it for a wave offering before YHWH for of the ram of consecration it was Mosheh (Musa)'s part; as YHWH. commanded Mosheh (Musa).

30 And Mosheh (Musa) took of the anointing oil, and of the blood which was upon the altar, and sprinkled it upon Aharon, and upon his garments, and upon his sons, and upon his sons' garments with him; and sanctified Aharon, and his garments, and his sons, and his sons' garments with him.

31 And Mosheh (Musa) said to Aharon and to his sons, cook the flesh at the door of the Tent of the appointed times: and there eat it with the Lakhem (bread) that is in the basket of consecrations, as I commanded, saying, Aharon and his sons shall eat it.

32 And that which remains of the flesh and of the Lakhem (bread) shall you burn with fire.

33 And you shall not go out of the door of the Tent of the appointed times in seven days, until the days of your consecration be at an end: for seven days shall he consecrate you.

34 As he has done this day, so YHWH has commanded to do, to make atonement for you.

35 Therefore shall you abide at the door of the Tent of the appointed times day and night seven days, and keep the charge

of YHWH, that you die not: for so I am commanded.

36 So Aharon and his sons did all things which YHWH commanded by the hand of Mosheh (Musa).

Torah Parsha 26 Shemini, Wayikra 9:1 - 11:47
Haftarah: Shemuel Bet 6:1-7:17

Chapter 9

1 And it came to pass on the eighth day, that Mosheh (Musa) called Aharon and his sons, and the elders of Israel;

2 And he said to Aharon, take a young calf for a sin offering, and a ram for a burnt offering, without blemish, and offer them before YHWH.

3 And to the children of Israel You shall speak, saying, take a kid of the goats for a sin offering; and a calf and a lamb, both of the first year, without blemish, for a burnt offering;

4 Also a bullock and a ram for shalom offerings, to sacrifice before YHWH and a grain offering mingled with oil, for today YHWH will appear to you.

5 And they brought that which Mosheh (Musa) commanded before the Tent of the appointed times: and all the congregation drew near and stood before YHWH.

6 And Mosheh (Musa) said, This is the thing which YHWH commanded that you should do: and the glory of YHWH shall appear to you.

7 And Mosheh (Musa) said to Aharon, Go to the altar, and offer your sin offering, and your burnt

offering, and make atonement for yourself, and for the people: and offer the offering of the people, and make atonement for them; as YHWH commanded.

8 Aharon therefore went to the altar, and slaughtered the calf for the sin offering, which was for himself.

9 And the sons of Aharon brought the blood to him: and he dipped his finger in the blood, and put it upon the horns of the altar, and poured out the blood at the bottom of the altar:

10 But the fat, and the kidneys, and the lobe above the liver of the sin offering, he burnt upon the altar; as YHWH commanded Mosheh (Musa).

11 And the flesh and the hide he burnt with fire outside the camp.

12 And he slaughtered the burnt offering; and Aharon's sons presented to him the blood, which he sprinkled round about upon the altar.

13 And they presented the burnt offering to him, with the pieces there, and the head: and he burnt them upon the altar.

14 And he did wash the inwards and the legs, and burnt them upon the burnt offering on the altar.

15 And he brought the people's offering, and took the goat, which was for the sin offering for the people, and slew it, and offered it for sin, as the first.

16 And he brought the burnt offering, and offered it according to the manner.

17 And he brought the grain offering, and took a handful of it and burnt it upon the altar, beside the burnt sacrifice of the morning.

18 He slaughtered also the bullock and the ram for a sacrifice of shalom offerings, which was for the people: and Aharon's sons presented to him the blood, which he sprinkled upon the altar round about,

19 And the fat of the bullock and of the ram, the tail, and that which covers the inwards, and the kidneys, and the lobe above the liver:

20 And they put the fat upon the breasts, and he burnt the fat upon the altar:

21 And the breasts and the right shoulder Aharon waved for a wave offering before YHWH as Mosheh (Musa) commanded.

22 And Aharon lifted up his hands toward the people, and **Increased** them,[1] and came down from offering of the sin offering, and the burnt offering, and shalom offerings.

23 And Mosheh (Musa) and Aharon went into the Tent of the appointed times, and came out, and *spoke* Increases to the people: and the glory of YHWH appeared to all the people.

24 And there came a fire out from before YHWH and consumed upon the altar the burnt offering and the fat which when all the people saw, they

Footnotes

[1] This is the High Priestly benediction that Aharon was performing. He lifted both hands lifted with the right hand at shoulder length and the left a little lower then the thumb and first two fingers which he separated. This was followed by the last two fingers and the same on the left hand. The palm is faced downward as he recited the benediction.

shouted, and fell on their faces.

Chapter 10

1 And Nadav and Avihu, the sons of Aharon, took either of them his censer, and put fire therein, and put incense thereon, and offered profaned fire[1] before YHWH which he commanded them not.

2 And there went out fire from YHWH and devoured them, and they died before YHWH.

3 Then Mosheh (Musa) said to Aharon, This is what the word of YHWH, said, I will be Holy through the actions of those that I have brought closer to me,[2] and before all the people, I will be glorified. And Aharon held his shalom.

4 And Mosheh (Musa) called Misha'el and Elzaphan, the sons of Uzziel the uncle of Aharon, and said to them, Come near, carry your brethren from before the sanctuary out of the camp.

5 So they went near, and carried them in their coats out of the camp; as Mosheh (Musa) had said.

6 And Mosheh (Musa) said to Aharon, and to El'ezar and to Ithamar, his sons, Uncover not your heads,[3] neither rend your clothes; lest you die, and lest wrath come upon all the people: but let your brethren, the whole Beyth (house) of Israel, bewail the burning which YHWH has kindled.

7 And you shall not go out from the door of the Tent of the appointed times, lest you die: for the anointing oil of YHWH is upon you. And they did according to the word of Mosheh (Musa).

8 And YHWH spoke to Aharon, saying,

9 Do not drink wine nor strong drink, you, nor your sons with you, when you go into the Tent of the appointed times,[4] lest you die: it shall be a statute forever

Footnotes

[1] The fire was not taken from the altar of the burnt offering but could have been common household fire. It is also possible they were dressed inappropriately and were drunk. The priests were commanded not to be under the influence of drink during the service as YHWH warns only a few verses later about this again. But note having no head-covering is also an offence so this is also a possibility as stated in verse 6 and drinking in verse 9. They thought since they were Aharon's sons they could get special favour but YHWH is impartial to judgment, all proper procedures must be followed. These two men could not wait to become the next High Priest. They were conspiring with each other about the possibility that one of them would soon take over the duties of this office, and wanted their father dead and out of the way.

[2] It is our righteous Torah actions that set us apart from the heathens and Christendom, and not just lip service as given by the religious.

Footnotes

[3] It is an offence to stand before YHWH with our heads uncovered. Still, many foolishly do this today without knowing that this offence can get you killed. It is grievous standing before a righteous Holy king and having heads uncovered. Having ones head uncovered signifies worship to Satan and shows rebellion to the king. This is one of Satan's offences that led to his fall. When Messiah comes this will be enforced by his rule of Torah.

[4] This is another offence that the sons of Aharon committed and paid for with their lives apart from the head being uncovered. They were drinking alcohol or wine in the Tent which was forbidden. It's obvious they did not know the difference between a bar and a Holy place!

throughout your generations:[1]

10 And that you may distinguish between Holy[2] and not Holy, and between clean and unclean;[3]

11 And that you may teach the children of Israel all the statutes which YHWH has spoken to them by the hand of Mosheh (Musa).

12 And Mosheh (Musa) spoke to Aharon, and to El'ezar and to Ithamar, his sons that were left, Take the grain offering that remained of the offerings of YHWH made by fire, and eat it without the leaven beside the altar: for it is most Holy:

13 And you shall eat it in the Holy place, because it is your due, and your sons' due, of the sacrifices of YHWH made by fire: for so I am commanded.

14 And the wave breast and contribution shoulder shall you eat in a clean place; you, and your sons, and your daughters with you: for they be your due, and your sons' due, which are given out of the sacrifices of shalom offerings of the children of Israel.

15 The contribution shoulder and the wave breast shall they bring with the offerings made by fire of the fat, to wave it for a wave offering before YHWH; and it shall be your, and your sons' with you, by a statute forever; as YHWH has commanded.

16 And Mosheh (Musa) diligently sought the goat of the sin offering, and, behold, it was burnt: and he was angry with El'ezar and Ithamar, the sons of Aharon which were left alive, saying,

17 Why have you not eaten the sin offering in the Holy place, seeing it is most Holy, and Elohim has given it you to bear the iniquity of the congregation, to make atonement for them before YHWH?

18 Behold, the blood of it was not brought in within the Holy place you should indeed have eaten it in the Holy place, as I commanded.[4]

19 And Aharon said to Mosheh (Musa), Behold, this day have they offered their sin offering and their burnt offering before YHWH

Footnotes

[1] YHWH spoke this soon after the incident with Aharon's sons, so likely they were drunk and did not cover their heads. As in the previous verse, Moses warns not to uncover their heads yet most of Christianity realises little of how selfish and wicked it is, to stand before YHWH without heads covered.

[2] Aharon was married to Amminadab's daughter Elisheba mentioned in Exodus 6:23. She had seen her brother in law Mosheh (Musa) become King the first real leader of the Y'sra'eli tribes, her husband become the High Priest and her son Eli'ezer became assistant to the High Priest, her grandson Pinkas became leader anointed for war and her brother Nakshon became prince over the tribe of Yahudah. The inauguration of the Tent of Meeting was during the year 2449 according to Jewish reckoning. However instead of being joyous Elisheba had to mourn for her two sons, she had joy on one side and sorrow on the other. The whole saga with her sons is tragic. Because they had been joyous and been drinking, they thought they could enter the Tent without proper precaution but were killed.

[3] Unfortunately many Christian Pastors have still not learnt the difference between what is clean and what is unclean. They continue to sow disobedience and lead their flock down the same path. They call a man God and pervert the Torah keeping people in avodah zarah (Idolatry).

Footnotes

[4] This was the one of the offences of the two sons of Aharon.

and such things have befallen me: and if I had eaten the sin offering today, should it have been accepted in the sight of YHWH?

20 And when Mosheh (Musa) heard that, he was content.

Food laws of Elohim for all who are Israel or grafted into Israel to sanctify their food
Chapter 11

1 And YHWH spoke to Mosheh (Musa) and to Aharon, saying to them,

2 Speak to the children of Israel, saying these are the animals which you shall eat among all the animals that are on the earth.

3 Whatever divides the hoof, and is cloven footed, and chewing the cud, among the animals that shall you eat.

4 Nevertheless these shall you not eat of them that chew the cud, or of them that divide the hoof: as the camel, because he chews the cud, but the hoof is not divided; he is unclean to you.

5 And the rabbit, because he chews the cud, but his hoof is not divided; he is unclean to you.

6 And the hare, because he chews the cud, but the hoof is not divided; he is unclean to you.

7 And the pig though he has a divided hoof and be cloven footed, yet he chews not the cud; he is unclean to you.

8 Of their flesh shall you not eat, and their carcass shall you not touch; they are unclean to you.

9 These shall you eat of all that are in the mayim: whatsoever has fins and scales in the mayim, in the seas, and in the rivers, them

shall you eat.[1]

10 And all that have not fins and scales in the seas, and in the rivers, of all that move in the mayim, and of any living thing which is in the mayim, they shall be impure to you:

11 They shall be even impure to you; you shall not eat of their flesh, but you shall consider their carcasses impure.

12 Whatever has no fins and no scales in the mayim, that shall be impure to you.[2]

13 And these are they which you shall consider impure among the birds; they shall not be eaten, they are unclean: the eagle, and the vulture, and the black vulture,

14 And the kite, and various species of falcons;

15 The various species of crows;

16 And the Ostrich, and the night hawk, and the Seagull, and

Footnotes

[1] All fish regardless of size need to qualify by having fins and scales as a must to eat. If a fish has only fins and no scales then it is unclean and should not be eaten, such as dolphins, sharks and various other varieties of popular fish.

[2] So if a fish has fins but no scales then it is forbidden to eat. For instance the ray fish is unclean, and so are certain seafood such as shrimp, crab, lobster, shellfish and many other sea crawling creatures. They are known as scavengers and bottom feeders and feed on dead flesh, fish excrement and hazardous chemicals, which can carry disease to humans via the food chain. Meanwhile, Christians and even some Hebrew people disobey YHWH and khag, celebration on bottom feeders and unclean foods as part of their daily food consumption. No wonder many people are sick and dying today because of the unclean foods they are eating. YHWH wanted to keep His people alive without disease so they would have longevity of life.

the hawk after his kind,

17 And the little owl, and the fisher owl, and the great owl,

18 And the white owl, and the pelican, and the carrion vulture,

19 And the stork, the heron after her kind, and the hoopoe, and the bat.

20 All flying insects that creep, going upon all four, shall be impure to you.

21 Yet these may you eat of every winged insects that goes upon all four, that have jointed legs for leaping on the ground;[1]

22 Even these of them you may eat; the locust after his kind, and the destroying locust after his kind and the cricket after his kind and the grasshopper after his kind.

23 But all other flying insects, which have four feet or more,[2] shall be impure to you.[3]

24 And for these you shall be unclean: whosoever touches the carcass of them shall be unclean until the evening.

25 And whosoever picks up the carcass of them shall wash his clothes, and be unclean until the evening.

26 The carcasses of animals which divide the hoof, and are not cloven footed neither chew the cud will be unclean to you:

Footnotes

[1] Such as a grasshopper and all varieties of locusts.

[2] Four or more meaning insects that have four feet to walk and perhaps have two or more to use for their faces or to kill with. This excludes the ones mentioned earlier such as grasshopper and locusts.

[3] Some examples of these are; the spider, the fly, the bee and other varieties of flying insects.

everyone that touches them shall be unclean.

27 And whatsoever goes upon his paws, among all manner of animals that go on all four, those are unclean to you: whoever touches their carcass shall be unclean until the evening.

28 And he that carries the carcass of them shall wash his clothes, and be unclean until the evening: they are unclean to you.

29 These also shall be unclean to you among the crawling things that crawl upon the earth; the mole, and the mouse, and the tortoise after his kind,

30 And the gecko, and the land crocodile, and the sand reptile, and the sand lizard, and the chameleon.

31 These are unclean to you among all that creep: whosoever will touch them, when they be dead, shall be unclean until the even.

32 And upon whatsoever any of them, when they are dead, will fall, it shall be unclean; whether it be any vessel of wood, or raiment, or skin, or sack, whatsoever vessel it be, wherein any work is done, it must be put into mayim, and it shall be unclean until the evening; so it shall be cleansed.

33 And every earthen vessel, into which any of them falls, whatsoever is in it shall be unclean; and you shall break it.

34 Of all meat which may be eaten, that on which such mayim comes shall be unclean: and all drink that may be drunk in every such vessel shall be unclean.

35 And everything whereupon

any part of their carcass falls shall be unclean; whether it be oven, or ranges for pots, they shall be broken down: for they are unclean, and shall be unclean to you.

36 Nevertheless a fountain or pit, wherein there is plenty of mayim, shall be clean: but that which touches their carcass shall be unclean.

37 And if any part of their carcass fall upon any planting seed which is to be planted it shall be clean.

38 But if any mayim be put upon the seed, and any part of their carcass fall thereon, it shall be unclean to you.

39 And if any permissible animal, of which you may eat, dies; he that touches the carcass there shall be unclean until the evening.

40 And he that eats of the carcass of it shall wash his clothes, and be unclean until the evening: he also that carries the carcass of it shall wash his clothes, and be unclean until the even.

41 And every creature that crawls upon the earth shall be impure; it shall not be eaten.

[1]

42 Whatsoever goes upon the belly, and whatsoever goes upon all four, or whatsoever has more feet among all crawling things that crawl upon the earth, them you shall not eat; for they are impure.

43 You shall not make yourselves impure with any crawling thing that crawls neither shall you make yourselves unclean with them, that you should be defiled otherwise.

44 For I am YHWH Your POWER: you shall therefore sanctify yourselves, and you shall be Holy; for I am Holy: neither shall you defile yourselves with any manner of crawling thing that crawls upon the earth.

45 For I am YHWH that brought you up out of the land of Mitzraim (Egypt), to be Your POWER: you shall therefore be Holy, for I am Holy.

46 This is the instructions of the animals, and of the fowl, and of every living creature that moves in the mayim, and of every creature that crawls upon the earth:

47 To make a difference between the unclean and the clean, and between the animal that may be eaten and the animal that may not be eaten.

Torah Parsha 27 Tazria, Wayikra 12:1-13:59
Haftarah Melekhim Bet 4:42-5:19

Chapter 12
1 And YHWH spoke to Mosheh (Musa), saying,

2 Speak to the children of Israel, saying if a woman has conceived and given birth to a child: then she shall be unclean seven days; [1] according to the days of the separation for her infirmity shall she be unclean.

3 And in the eighth day the flesh of his foreskin shall be circumcised.[2]

4 And she shall then continue in the blood of her purifying thirty three days; she shall touch no Holy thing, nor come into the sanctuary, until the days of her purifying be fulfilled.

5 But if she bears a female child, then she shall be unclean two weeks,[3] as in her separation: and she shall continue in the blood of her purifying sixty-six days.[4]

6 And when the days of her purifying are fulfilled, for a son, or for a daughter, she shall bring a lamb of the first year for a burnt offering,[5] and a young pigeon, or a turtledove, for a sin offering, to the door of the Tent of the appointed times, to the kohen (priest).[6]

7 Who shall offer it before YHWH and make atonement for her; and she shall be cleansed from the issue of her blood. This is the instruction for her that has born a male or a female.

8 And if she be not able to bring a lamb, then she shall bring two turtledoves, or two young pigeons; the one for the burnt offering, and the other for a sin offering: and the kohen (priest) shall make atonement for her, and she shall be clean.

Chapter 13

1 And YHWH spoke to Mosheh (Musa) and Aharon, saying,

2 When a man shall have in the skin of his flesh a swelling, a scab, or bright spot, and it be in the skin of his flesh like the disease of leprosy; then he shall be brought to Aharon the Kohen (priest), or to one of his sons the

Footnotes

[1] She cannot have sex for 7 days and then after that she is permitted to her husband.

[2] All male believers and their male children are to be circumcised irrelevant of race or creed as they are now part of Israel. The babies when they are newborn should be circumcised on the 8th day as YHWH originally instructed Abraham, and as directed here in the Torah.

[3] She cannot have sex for 14 days and then after that she is permitted to her husband.

[4] When a woman gives birth to a baby girl, she is considered unclean for twice as long as when birthing a baby boy. After the deception of Satan, and with the extended length of time of her being unclean after she gives birth to a female child, she will now be reminded of the deception in the garden. So 66 + 14 days = 80 days, therefore she will bring a sacrifice on the 81st day to the Temple. What do we do without a Temple? We have to wait and bring the sacrifices which are accrued in the millennial Temple.

Footnotes

[5] The sages say that the reason for this was that women are in need of personal atonement as during this time they accidentally make an oath not to have children again or have relations with their husband's. Since the oath is not legally effective but she is obligated to satisfy her husband in intimacy God allowed a way for her to be atoned through the sacrifice given to the Kohen. Uttering an oath that is legally not binding is like taking Hashem's name in vain.

[6] A woman is ritually unclean for one week and plus thirty-three days later (a total period of 40 days so she goes for the sacrifice 41st day) she must bring a sacrifice into the Temple, she cannot enter the Temple before this time period.

kohenim:

3 And the Kohen (priest) shall look on the sores upon the skin of the flesh and when the hair in the sore is turned white,[1] and the sore in sight be deeper than the skin of his flesh, it is a disease of leprosy: and the Kohen (priest) shall look on him, and pronounce him unclean.

4 If the bright spot be white in the skin of his flesh, and in sight be not deeper than the skin and the hair there be not turned white; then the kohen (priest) shall shut up him that has the disease seven days:

5 And the Kohen (priest) shall look on him the seventh day: and, behold, if the sores in his sight be at a stay, and the disease spread not in the skin; then the kohen (priest) shall shut him up seven days more:

6 And the Kohen (priest) shall look on him again the seventh day: and, behold, if the sore be somewhat dark, and the sores spread not in the skin, the kohen (priest) shall pronounce him clean: it is but a scab: and he shall wash his clothes, and be clean.

7 But if the scab spread much abroad in the skin, after that he has been seen by the Kohen (priest) for his cleansing, he shall

be seen by the kohen (priest) again:

8 And if the Kohen (priest) see that, behold, the scab has spread in the skin, then the Kohen (priest) shall pronounce him unclean: it is leprosy.

9 When the disease of leprosy is in a man, then he shall be brought to the kohen (priest);

10 And the Kohen (priest) shall see him: and, behold, if the swelling be white in the skin, and it have turned the hair white, and there be quick raw flesh in the rising;

11 It is an old leprosy in the skin of his flesh, and the Kohen (priest) shall pronounce him unclean, and he shall not shut him up: for he is unclean.

12 And if leprosy breaks out on the skin, and the leprosy covers all the skin of him that has the sore from his head even to his foot, wheresoever the kohen (priest) sees;

13 Then the Kohen (priest) shall consider: and, behold, if the leprosy has covered all his flesh, he shall pronounce him clean that has the plague: it is all turned white: he is clean.

14 But when raw flesh appears in him, he shall be unclean.

15 And the Kohen (priest) shall see the raw flesh, and pronounce him to be unclean: for the raw flesh is unclean, it is leprosy.

16 Or if the raw flesh turn again, and be changed to white, he shall come to see the Kohen (priest);

17 And the Kohen (priest) shall see him: and, behold, if the sore be turned into white; then the Kohen (priest) shall pronounce

Footnotes
[1] The ancient Hebrews were of Black and brown skin colour. The leprosy in a black man was easy to see. This verse also shows us a spiritual contrast. The colour white as a sign of judgment which we also see happened to Israel when the Black people were taken into slavery for not obeying the Torah commandments by the Caucasian west.

him clean that has the plague: he is clean.

18 The flesh also, in which, even in the skin there, was a boil, and is healed,

19 And in the place of the boil there be a white swelling, or a bright spot, white, and somewhat reddish, and it be showed to the Kohen (priest);

20 And if, when the kohen (priest) sees it, behold, it be in sight lower than the skin, and the hair there be turned white; the Kohen (priest) shall pronounce him unclean: it is a plague of leprosy broken out of the boil.

21 But if the Kohen (priest) look on it, and, behold, there be no white hairs therein, and if it be not lower than the skin, but be somewhat dark; then the kohen (priest) shall shut him up seven days:

22 And if it spread much abroad in the skin, then the Kohen (priest) shall pronounce him unclean: it is a plague.

23 But if the bright spot stay in his place, and spread not, it is a burning boil; and the Kohen (priest) shall pronounce him clean.

24 Or if there be any flesh, in the skin whereof there is a hot burning, and the quick flesh that burns have a white bright spot, somewhat reddish, or white;

25 Then the Kohen (priest) shall look upon it: and, behold, if the hair in the bright spot be turned white, and it be in sight deeper than the skin; it is a leprosy broken out of the burning: wherefore the Kohen (priest) shall pronounce him unclean: it is

the plague of leprosy.

26 But if the Kohen (priest) look on it, and, behold, there be no white hair in the bright spot, and it be no lower than the other skin, but be somewhat dark; then the Kohen (priest) shall shut him up seven days:

27 And the Kohen (priest) shall look upon him the seventh day: and if it be spread much abroad in the skin, then the kohen (priest) shall pronounce him unclean: it is the plague of leprosy.

28 And if the bright spot stay in his place, and spread not in the skin, but it be somewhat dark; it is a rising of the burning, and the kohen (priest) shall pronounce him clean: for it is an inflammation of the burning.

29 If a man or woman have a plague upon the head or the beard;

30 Then the Kohen (priest) shall see the plague: and, behold, if it be in sight deeper than the skin; and there be in it a yellow thin hair; then the kohen (priest) shall pronounce him unclean: it is a dry scall, a leprosy of the head or beard.

31 And if the Kohen (priest) look on the infection of the eruption, and, behold, it be not in sight deeper than the skin, and that there is no black hair in it; then the Kohen (priest) shall shut up him that has the infection of the eruption seven days:

32 And in the seventh day the kohen (priest) shall look at the sore and, behold, if the eruption spreads not, and there be in it no yellow hair, and the eruption be not in sight deeper than the skin; והתגלח [1]

33 He shall be shaved, but the eruption shall he not shave; and the Kohen (priest) shall shut him up that has the eruption seven days more:

34 And in the seventh day the kohen (priest) shall look on the eruption: and, behold, if the eruption be not spread in the skin, nor be in sight deeper than the skin; then the Kohen (priest) shall pronounce him clean: and he shall wash his clothes, and be clean.

35 But if the eruption spread much in the skin after his cleansing;

36 Then the Kohen (priest) shall look at him: and, behold, if the eruption be spread in the skin, the kohen (priest) shall not seek for yellow hair; he is unclean.

37 But if the eruption be in his sight at a stay, and that there is black hair grown up therein; the scall is healed, he is clean: and the kohen (priest) shall pronounce him clean.

38 If a man also or a woman have in the skin of their flesh bright spots, even white bright spots;

39 Then the Kohen (priest) shall look: and, behold, if the bright spots in the skin of their flesh be darkish white; it is a freckled spot that grows in the skin; he is

Footnotes
[1] Enlarged Gimmel. This indicates the ancient picture of the hand from the letter. The plague was white in colour and in ancient times was given for a sign of judgment so this raising of the gimmel indicates YHWH raising his hand against the individual.

clean.

40 And the man whose hair is fallen off his head, he has become bald; yet he is clean.

41 And he that has his hair fallen off from the part of his head toward his face, he is bald in the forehead yet he is clean.

42 And if there be in the bald head, or bald forehead, a white reddish sore; it is a leprosy sprung up in his balding head, or his balding forehead.

43 Then the kohen (priest) shall look at it and, behold, if the rising of the sore be white reddish in his bald head, or in his bald forehead, as the leprosy appears in the skin of the flesh;

44 He is a leprous man, he is unclean: the kohen (priest) shall pronounce him utterly unclean; his plague is in his head.

45 And the leper in whom the plague is, his clothes shall be torn, and his head uncovered, and he shall put a covering upon his upper lip, and shall cry, Unclean, unclean.

46 All the days wherein the plague shall be in him he shall be defiled; he is unclean: he shall dwell alone; outside the camp shall his habitation be.

47 The garment also that the plague of leprosy is in, whether it be a woollen garment, or a linen garment;

48 Whether it be in the warp, or weft of linen, or of woolen; whether in leather, or in any thing made of leather;

49 And if the plague be greenish or reddish in the garment, or in the leather, either in the warp, or in the weft, or in any thing of leather; it is a plague of leprosy, and shall be shown to the kohen (priest).

50 And the kohen (priest) shall look at the plague, and shut him up that has the plague seven days:

51 And he shall look at the plague on the seventh day: if the plague be spread in the garment, either in the warp, or in the weft, or in leather, or in any work that is made of leather; the plague is a fretting leprosy; it is unclean.

52 He shall therefore burn that garment, not spread on the clothing, fabric, covering, in woolen or in linen, or any thing of leather, wherein the plague is: for it is a fretting leprosy; it shall be burnt in the fire.

53 And if the kohen (priest) shall look, and, behold, the plague be not spread in the garment, either in the spread on the clothing, fabric, covering, or in any thing of leather;

54 Then the kohen (priest) shall command that they wash the thing wherein the plague is, and he shall shut it up another seven days more:

55 And the kohen (priest) shall look on the plague, after that it is washed: and, behold, if the plague have not changed its colour, and the plague be not spread; it is unclean; You shall burn it in the fire; it continues eating away, whether it be bare within or outside.

56 And if the kohen (priest) look, and, behold, the plague be somewhat dark after washing of it; then he shall rend it out of the garment, or out of the leather, or out of the warp, or out of the weft:

57 And if it appear still in the garment, either in the warp, or in the weft, or in any thing of leather; it is a spreading plague: You shall burn that wherein the plague is with fire.

58 And the garment, either warp, or weft, or whatsoever thing of leather it be, which You shall wash, if the plague be departed from them, then it shall be washed the second time, and shall be clean.

59 This is the Torah of the plague of leprosy in a garment of woolen or linen, either in the warp, or weft, or any thing of leather, to pronounce it clean, or to pronounce it unclean.

Torah Parsha 28 Metzorah, Wayikra 14:1-15:33
Haftarah: Melekhim Bet 7:3-20

Chapter 14

1 And YHWH spoke to Mosheh (Musa), saying,

2 This shall be the Torah of the leper in the day of his cleansing: He shall be brought to the kohen (priest):

3 And the kohen (priest) shall go forth out of the camp; and the kohen (priest) shall look, and, behold, if the plague of leprosy be healed in the leper;

4 Then shall the kohen (priest) command to take for him that is to be cleansed two birds[1] alive

Footnotes
[1] According to the Mishnah they were to be the same height value and size and to be free clean birds. The birds stomach is removed before it is offered as birds eat anything from anywhere and it is considered Continued in next section

and clean, and cedar wood, and scarlet, and hyssop:

5 And the kohen (priest) shall command that one of the birds be killed over an earthen vessel over running mayim:

6 As for the living bird, he shall take it, and the cedar wood, and the scarlet, and the hyssop, and shall dip them and the living bird in the blood of the bird that was killed over the running mayim:

7 And he shall sprinkle upon him that is to be cleansed from the leprosy seven times, and shall pronounce him clean, and shall let the living bird loose into the open field.

8 And he that is to be cleansed shall wash his clothes, and shave off all his hair, and wash himself in mayim, that he may be clean: and after that he shall come into the camp, and shall stay out of his tent seven days.

9 But it shall be on the seventh day that he shall shave all his hair off his head and his beard and his eyebrows, even all his hair he shall shave off: and he shall wash his clothes, also he shall wash his flesh in mayim, and he shall be clean.

10 And on the eighth day he shall take two he lambs without blemish, and one ewe lamb one year old without blemish, and three tenth deals of fine flour for a grain offering, mingled with oil, and one log of oil.

11 And the kohen (priest) that makes him clean shall present the man that is to be made clean, and those things, before YHWH at the door of the Tent of the appointed times:

12 And the kohen (priest) shall take one male lamb, and offer him for a trespass offering, and the log of oil, and wave them for a wave offering before YHWH.

13 And he shall slaughter the lamb in the place where he shall slaughter the sin offering and the burnt offering, in the Holy place: for as the sin offering is the kohen's (priest), so is the trespass offering: it is most Holy:

14 And the kohen (priest) shall take some of the blood of the trespass offering, and the kohen (priest) shall put it upon the tip of the right ear of him that is to be cleansed, and upon the thumb of his right hand[1], and upon the great toe of his right foot:

15 And the kohen (priest) shall take some of the log of oil, and pour it into the palm of his own left hand:

16 And the kohen (priest) shall dip his right finger in the oil that is in his left hand, and shall sprinkle of the oil with his finger seven times before YHWH.

17 And of the rest of the oil that is in his hand shall the kohen (priest) put upon the tip of the right ear of him that is to be cleansed, and upon the thumb of his right hand, and upon the great toe of his right foot, upon the blood of the trespass offering:

18 And the remnant of the oil that is in the kohen's (priest) hand

a type of theft. So by removing the stomach you remove the symbol of theft before it is offered.

Footnotes
[1] See footnote Shemoth (Exodus) 29:20.

he shall pour upon the head of him that is to be cleansed: and the kohen (priest) shall make atonement for him before YHWH.

19 And the kohen (priest) shall offer the sin offering, and make atonement for him that is to be cleansed from his uncleanness; and afterward he shall kill the burnt offering:

20 And the kohen (priest) shall offer the burnt offering and the grain offering upon the altar: and the kohen (priest) shall make atonement for him, and he shall be clean.

21 And if he be poor, and cannot get so much; then he shall take one lamb for a trespass offering to be waved, to make an atonement for him, and one tenth deal of fine flour mingled with oil for a grain offering, and a log of oil;

22 And two turtledoves, or two young pigeons, such as he is able to get; and the one shall be a sin offering, and the other a burnt offering.

23 And he shall bring them on the eighth day for his cleansing to the kohen (priest), to the door of the Tent of the appointed times, before YHWH.

24 And the kohen (priest) shall take the lamb of the trespass offering, and the log of oil, and the kohen (priest) shall wave them for a wave offering before YHWH.

25 And he shall kill the lamb of the trespass offering, and the kohen (priest) shall take some of the blood of the trespass offering, and put it upon the tip of the right ear of him that is to be cleansed,

and upon the thumb of his right hand, and upon the great toe of his right foot:

26 And the kohen (priest) shall pour of the oil into the palm of his own left hand:

27 And the kohen (priest) shall sprinkle with his right finger some of the oil that is in his left hand seven times before YHWH.

28 And the kohen (priest) shall put of the oil that is in his hand upon the tip of the right ear of him that is to be cleansed, and upon the thumb of his right hand, and upon the great toe of his right foot, upon the place of the blood of the trespass offering:

29 And the rest of the oil that is in the kohen's (priest) hand he shall put upon the head of him that is to be cleansed, to make atonement for him before YHWH.

30 And he shall offer the one of the turtledoves, or of the young pigeons, such as he can get;

31 Even such as he is able to get, the one for a sin offering, and the other for a burnt offering with the grain offering: and the kohen (priest) shall make atonement for him that is to be cleansed before YHWH.

32 This is the Torah of him in whom is the plague of leprosy, whose hand is not able to get that which pertains to his cleansing.

33 And YHWH spoke to Mosheh (Musa) and to Aharon, saying,

34 When you be come into the land of Kanan, which I give to you for a possession, and I put the plague of leprosy in a Beyth (house) of the land of your possession;

35 And he that owns the Beyth

(house) shall come and tell the kohen (priest), saying It seems to me there is as it were a plague in the Beyth (house):

36 Then the kohen (priest) shall command that they empty the Beyth (house), before the kohen (priest) go into it to see the plague, that all that is in the Beyth (house) be not made unclean: and afterward the kohen (priest) shall go in to see the Beyth (house):

37 And he shall look on the plague, and, behold, if the plague be in the walls of the Beyth (house) with hollow strakes, greenish or reddish, which in sight are lower than the wall;

38 Then the kohen (priest) shall go out of the Beyth (house) to the door of the Beyth (house), and shut up the Beyth (house) seven days:

39 And the kohen (priest) shall come again the seventh day, and shall look: and, behold, if the plague be spread in the walls of the Beyth (house);

40 Then the kohen (priest) shall command that they take away the stones in which the plague is, and they shall cast them into an unclean place outside the city:

41 And he shall cause the Beyth (house) to be scraped within round about, and they shall pour out the dust that they scrape off outside the city into an unclean place:

42 And they shall take other stones, and put them in the place of those stones; and he shall take other mortar, and shall plaster the Beyth (house).

43 And if the plague come again, and break out in the Beyth (house), after that he has taken away the stones, and after he has scraped the Beyth (house), and after it is plastered;

44 Then the kohen (priest) shall come and look, and, behold, if the plague be spread in the Beyth (house), it is an active leprosy in the Beyth (house): it is unclean.

45 And he shall break down the Beyth (house), the stones of it, and the timber there, and all the mortar of the Beyth (house); and he shall carry them forth out of the city into an unclean place.

46 Moreover he that goes into the Beyth (house) all the while that it is shut up shall be unclean until the evening.

47 And he that sleeps in the Beyth (house) shall wash his clothes; and he that eats in the Beyth (house) shall wash his clothes.

48 And if the kohen (priest) shall come in and look upon it, and, behold, the plague has not spread in the Beyth (house), after the Beyth (house) was plastered: then the kohen (priest) shall pronounce the Beyth (house) clean, because the plague is healed.

49 And he shall take to cleanse the Beyth (house) two birds, and cedar wood, and scarlet, and hyssop:

50 And he shall kill the one of the birds over an earthen vessel over running mayim:

51 And he shall take the cedar wood, and the hyssop, and the scarlet, and the living bird, and dip them in the blood of the slaughtered birds, and in the running mayim, and sprinkle the Beyth (house) seven times:

52 And he shall cleanse the Beyth (house) with the blood of the bird, and with the running mayim, and with the living bird, and with the cedar wood, and with the hyssop, and with the scarlet:

53 But he shall let go the living bird out of the city into the open fields, and make atonement for the Beyth (house): and it shall be clean.

54 This is the Torah for all manner of infections of leprosy and eruptions,

55 And for the leprosy of a garment, and of a Beyth (house),

56 And for a rising, and for a scab, and for a bright spot:

57 To teach when it is unclean, and when it is clean: this is the Torah of leprosy.

Chapter 15

1 And YHWH spoke to Mosheh (Musa) and to Aharon, saying,

2 Speak to the children of Israel, and say to them, when any man has a discharge out of his flesh because of his discharge he is unclean.

3 And this shall be his uncleanness in his discharge: whether his flesh run with his discharge or his flesh be stopped from his discharge, it is his uncleanness.

4 Every bed, whereon he lies that has the discharge, is unclean: and every thing, whereon he sits, shall be unclean.

5 And whosoever touches his bed shall wash his clothes, and bathe himself in mayim, and be unclean until the evening.

6 And he that sits on anything whereon he sat that has the discharge shall wash his clothes, and bathe himself in mayim, and be unclean until the evening.

7 And he that touches the flesh of him that has the discharge shall wash his clothes, and bathe himself in mayim, and be unclean until the evening.

8 And if he that has the issue spit upon him that is clean; then he shall wash his clothes, and bathe himself in mayim, and be unclean until the evening.

9 And what saddle so ever he rides upon that has the discharge shall be unclean.

10 And whosoever touches any thing that was under him shall be unclean until the evening: and he that carries any of those things shall wash his clothes, and bathe himself in mayim, and be unclean until the evening.

11 And whomsoever he touches that has the issue, and has not rinsed his hands in mayim, he shall wash his clothes, and bathe himself in mayim, and be unclean until the evening.

12 And the vessel of earth, that he touches which has the discharge, shall be broken: and every vessel of wood shall be rinsed in mayim.

13 And when he that has the discharge is cleansed from the discharge; then he shall number to himself seven days for his cleansing, and wash his clothes, and bathe his flesh in running mayim, and shall be clean.

14 And on the eighth day he

shall take to him two turtledoves, or two young pigeons, and come before YHWH to the door of the Tent of the appointed times, and give them to the kohen (priest):

15 And the kohen (priest) shall offer them, the one for a sin offering, and the other for a burnt offering; and the kohen (priest) shall make atonement for him before YHWH for his issue.

16 And if any man has an emission of semen then he shall wash all his flesh in mayim, and be unclean until the evening.

17 And every garment, and every skin, whereon is emission of semen shall be washed with mayim, and be unclean until the evening.

18 The woman also with whom this man shall lie with the emission of semen, they shall both bathe themselves in mayim, and be unclean until the evening.

19 And if a woman has a discharge, and her discharge in her flesh be blood, she shall be put apart seven days: and whosoever touches her shall be unclean until the evening.

20 And everything that she lies upon in her separation shall be unclean: everything also that she sits upon shall be unclean.

21 And whosoever touches her bed shall wash his clothes, and bathe himself in mayim, and be unclean until the evening.

22 And whosoever touches any thing that she sat upon shall wash his clothes, and bathe himself in mayim, and be unclean until the even.

23 And if it be on her bed, or on any thing whereon she sits, when he touches it, he shall be unclean until the even.

24 And if any man lie with her at all, and her monthly flow be upon him, he shall be unclean seven days; and all the bed whereon he lies shall be unclean.

25 And if a woman have a discharge of her blood many days out of the time of her monthly separation, or if it run beyond the time of her monthly separation; all the days of the discharge of her uncleanness shall be as the days of her monthly separation: she shall be unclean.

26 Every bed whereon she lies all the days of her discharge shall be to her as the bed of her menstruation: and whatsoever she sits upon shall be unclean, as the uncleanness of her menstruation.

27 And whosoever touches those things shall be unclean, and shall wash his clothes, and bathe himself in mayim, and be unclean until the evening.

28 But if she be cleansed of her discharge, then she shall number to herself seven days, and after that she shall be clean.

29 And on the eighth day she shall take to her two turtledoves, or two young pigeons, and bring them to the kohen (priest), to the door of the Tent of the appointed times.

30 And the kohen (priest) shall offer the one for a sin offering, and the other for a burnt offering; and the kohen (priest) shall make atonement for her before YHWH for the discharge of her uncleanness.

31 Thus shall you separate the children of Israel from their uncleanness; that they die not in their uncleanness, when they defile my Tent that is among them.

32 This is the instruction for him that has discharge, and of him whose has emission of semen and is defiled with it;

33 And of her that is sick of her monthly separation, and of him that has a discharge of semen, of the man, and of the woman, and of him that lies with her that is unclean.

Torah Parsha 29 Acharei Mot, Wayikra 16:1- 18:30
Haftarah: Amos 9:7-15

Chapter 16

1 And YHWH spoke to Mosheh (Musa) after the death of the two sons of Aharon, when they drew near before YHWH, and died;

2 And YHWH said to Mosheh (Musa), Speak to Aharon your brother, that he come not at all times into the Holy place within the veil before the lid of atonement that was upon the ark; that he die not: for I will appear in the cloud upon the lid of atonement that was upon the ark.

3 Thus shall Aharon come into the Holy place: with a young bullock for a sin offering, and a ram for a burnt offering.

4 He shall put on the Holy linen coat, and he shall have the linen breeches upon his flesh, and shall be girded with a linen girdle, and with the linen turban shall he be attired: these are Holy garments; therefore shall he wash his flesh in mayim, and so put them on.

5 And he shall take of the congregation of the children of Israel two kids of the goats for a sin offering, and one ram for a burnt offering.

6 And Aharon shall offer his bullock of the sin offering, which is for him, and make atonement for himself, and for his Beyth (house).

7 And he shall take the two goats, and present them before YHWH at the door of the Tent of the appointed times.

8 And Aharon shall cast lots upon the two goats; one Lot for YHWH, and the other Lot for Azazel.[1]

Footnotes

[1] There are many differing views on this, the Hebrew word Azazel, Az meaning 'goat' and 'Azal' to go away implied meaning the 'goat that goes away.' Like a dump truck collecting garbage and towing it away and discarding it. Sin is collected and towed away from the camp. The Arabic term is Azala meaning to banish, Azalu for rough ground. This the son of Lilith who was a chief demon/angel. The term I'saraim is used in Vayikra (Leviticus) 17:7 for goat demons in the Desert (Azazel is the ruler of the fallen malakhim, 'Enoch 8:1 And Azazel taught men to make swords, and knives, and shields, and breastplates).' He was the production of the adultery of Adam's first wife Lilith see Gen 1:27.

Remember this was done on Yom Kippurim, the high priest had to enter into the Most Holy Place of the tent only allowed one time per year, on the Day of Atonement '10 Tishri on the Hebrew calendar.' This entry into the Most Holy Place was allowed so atonement could be made for the people for Israel, to cleanse their sins before YHWH, Numbers 16:30. The tractate Yoma marks the highlights and description of this ceremony.

A box was brought to the high priest that contained two lots, one marked for YHWH and the other for Azazel. The high priest put Continued in next section

We'Yikra (Leviticus)

9 And Aharon shall bring the goat upon which YHWH's Lot fell, and offer him for a sin offering.

10 But the goat, on which the Lot fell to be for azazel, shall be presented alive before YHWH, to make an atonement with him, and to let him go for azazel into the wilderness.

11 And Aharon shall bring the bullock of the sin offering, which is for him, and shall make atonement for himself, and for his

his hands in the box and brought out a lot in each hand; he held up the hand which contained the lot for YHWH. The high priest then tied a crimson thread on the horn of the goat which was to be sent away (Azazel), and another crimson thread around the throat of the goat which would be slaughtered for the sin offering.

First the High Priest must cleanse his own and his families sins with the blood of the bull (Num 16:6, 11-14), after this rite, the goat which had been designated for YHWH was brought to him. The high priest then slaughtered this goat, and its blood was used to purify the Most Holy Place from the uncleanness of the Israelites. In tractate (Yoma 6:2, The Mishnah, A New Translation) we are told.

'O Adonai, your people, the house of Israel, has committed iniquity, transgressed, and sinned before you. Forgive O Adonai, I pray, the iniquities, sins, and sins, which your people, the house of Israel, have committed, transgressed, and sinned before you, as it is written in the Torah of Moses, your servant, For on this day shall atonement be made for you to clean you. From all your sins shall you be clean before Adonai.'

In short, we can conclude that YHWH showed the rescue of the people of Israel through the Torah, and showed the banishment of Azazel to the lake of fire which was yet to take place but figuratively shown each year during Tent and Temple times to show and to remember the first woman Lilith and her seed which will be banished.

Beyth (house), and shall kill the bullock of the sin offering which is for himself:

12 And he shall take a censer full of burning coals of fire from off the altar before YHWH, and his hands full of sweet incense beaten small, and bring it within the veil:

13 And he shall put the incense upon the fire before YHWH that the cloud of the incense may cover the lid of atonement that was upon the ark of testimony that he die not:

14 And he shall take of the blood of the bullock, and sprinkle it with his finger upon the lid of atonement that was upon the ark eastward;[1] and the lid of atonement that was upon the ark shall he sprinkle of the blood with his finger seven times.

15 Then shall he slaughter the goat of the sin offering, that is for the people, and bring his blood within the veil, and do with that blood as he did with the blood of the bullock, and sprinkle it upon the lid of atonement that was upon the ark.

16 And he shall make atonement for the Holy place, because of the uncleanness of the children of Israel, and because of their sins in all their sins: and so shall he do for the Tent of the appointed times that remains among them in the midst of their uncleanness.

17 And there shall be no man in the Tent of the appointed times

Footnotes
[1] The Eastern gate of Ezekiel 44:1. The Hebrew word Qedem relates to the **Ancient of Days**.

294

when he goes in to make an atonement in the Holy place, until he come out, and have made an atonement for himself, and for his household, and for all the congregation of Israel.

18 And he shall go out to the altar that is before YHWH, and make atonement for it; and shall take of the blood of the bullock, and of the blood of the goat, and put it upon the horns of the altar round about.

19 And he shall sprinkle of the blood upon it with his finger seven times, and cleanse it, and set it apart from the uncleanness of the children of Israel.

20 And when he has made an end of reconciling the Holy place, and the Tent of the appointed times, and the altar, he shall bring the live goat:

21 And Aharon shall lay both his hands upon the head of the live goat, and make confession *in the name over* him with all the idolatries of the children of Israel, and all their rebellions in all their sins, putting them upon the head of the goat, and shall send him away by the hand of a fit man into the wilderness:

22 And the goat shall bear upon him all their iniquities to a land not inhabited: and he shall let go the goat in the wilderness.

23 And Aharon shall come into the Tent of the appointed times, and shall put off the linen garments, which he put on when he went into the Holy place, and shall leave them there:

24 And he shall wash his flesh with mayim in the Holy place, and put on his garments, and come forth, and offer his burnt offering, and the burnt offering of the people, and make atonement for himself, and for the people.

25 And the fat of the sin offering shall he burn upon the altar.

26 And he that let go the goat for Azazel shall wash his clothes, and bathe his flesh in mayim, and afterward come into the camp.

27 And the bullock for the sin offering, and the goat for the sin offering, whose blood was brought in to make atonement in the Holy place, shall one carry forth outside the camp; and they shall burn in the fire their skins, and their flesh, and their dung.

28 And he that burns them shall wash his clothes, and bathe his flesh in mayim, and afterward he shall come into the camp.

29 And this shall be a statute forever to you: that in the seventh month, on the tenth day of the month, you shall afflict your souls, and do no work at all, whether it be one of your own country, or a foreigner that lives among you:

30 For on that day shall the kohen (priest) make atonement for you, to cleanse you, that you may be clean from all your sins before YHWH.

31 It shall be a Sabbath of rest to you, and you shall afflict your souls, by a statute forever.

32 And the kohen (priest), whom he shall anoint, and whom he shall consecrate to minister in the kohen's (priest) office in his father's stead, shall make the atonement, and shall put on the linen clothes, even the Holy garments:

33 And he shall make atonement for the Holy sanctuary, and he shall make atonement for the Tent of the appointed times, and for the altar, and he shall make atonement for the kohenim, and for all the people of the congregation.

34 And this shall be an everlasting statute to you, to make an atonement for the children of Israel for all their sins once a year. And he did as YHWH commanded Mosheh (Musa).

Chapter 17

1 And YHWH spoke to Mosheh (Musa), saying,

2 Speak to Aharon, and to his sons, and to all the children of Israel, and say to them; This is the thing which YHWH has commanded, saying,

3 Whatever man there be of the Beyth (house) of Israel, that slaughters an ox, or lamb, or goat, in the camp, or that slaughters it out of the camp,

4 And bring it not to the door of the Tent of the appointed times, to offer an offering to YHWH before the Tent of YHWH; blood shall be imputed to that man; he has shed blood; and that man shall be cut off from among his people:

5 To the end that the children of Israel may bring their sacrifices, which they offer in the open field, even that they may bring them to YHWH, to the door of the Tent of the appointed times, to the kohen (priest), and offer them for shalom offerings to YHWH.

6 And the kohen (priest) shall sprinkle the blood upon the altar of YHWH at the door of the Tent of the appointed times, and burn the fat for a sweet savour to YHWH.

7 And they shall no more offer their sacrifices to goat demons, after whom they have gone whoring. This shall be a statute forever to them throughout their generations.

8 And You shall say to them, Whatever man there be of the Beyth (house) of Israel, or of the strangers which sojourn among you, that offers a burnt offering or sacrifice,

9 And brings it not to the door of the Tent of the appointed times, to offer it to YHWH; even that man shall be cut off from among his people.

10 And whatever man there be of the Beyth (house) of Israel, or of the foreigners that sojourn among you, that eats any manner of blood; I will even set my face against that man that eats blood, and will cut him off from among his people.

11 For the life of the flesh is in the blood: and I have given it to you upon the altar to make atonement for your souls: for it is the blood that makes atonement for the soul.[1]

12 Therefore I said to the children of Israel, No soul of you shall eat blood, neither shall any foreigner that lives among you

Footnotes
[1] The verse is about eating blood, prohibition of eating. You can have atonement without blood in fact people did in times past, look at Psalm 40:6, Psalm 51:16, First Samuel 15:22.

eat blood.

13 And whatever man there be of the children of Israel, or of the foreigners that lives among you, who hunts and catches any animal or bird that may be eaten; he shall even pour out the blood there, and cover it with dust.[1]

14 For it is the life of all flesh the blood is its life: therefore I said to the children of Israel, You will not eat the blood of any flesh: for the life of all flesh is its blood: whosoever eats it shall be cut off.[2]

15 And every soul that eats that which died of itself, or that which was torn by other animals, whether it be one of your own country, or a foreigner, he shall both wash his clothes, and bathe himself in mayim, and be unclean until the evening: then shall he be clean.

16 But if he wash them not, nor bathe his flesh; then he shall bear his iniquity.

Chapter 18

1 And YHWH spoke to Mosheh (Musa), saying,

2 Speak to the children of Israel, and say to them, I am YHWH Your POWER.

3 You must not do as they do in the land of Mitzrayim, where you lived, and as they do in the land of Kanan, where I bring you, you shall not do: neither shall you walk in their ordinances.

4 You shall do my judgments, and keep mine ordinances, to walk[3] therein: I am YHWH Your POWER.

5 You shall therefore keep my statutes, and my judgments: which if a man do, he shall have life[4] in them: I am YHWH.

6 None of you shall approach to any that is near of kin to him, to uncover their nakedness: I am YHWH.

7 The nakedness of your father, or the nakedness of your mother, shall You not uncover: she is your mother; You shall not uncover her nakedness.

8 The nakedness of your father's wife[5] shall You not uncover: it is your father's nakedness.

9 The nakedness of your sister, the daughter of your father, and also *the* daughter of your mother, whether she be born at home, or born abroad, even their

Footnotes

[1] The blood must be poured on the floor. Eating electrocuted chickens or cows is not clean as the blood remains clogged in the animal rendering the animal unfit to eat. By eating permissible meat you elevate yourself spiritually.

[2] By eating electrocuted clean animals you are unknowingly committing a sin by consuming blood. In some cultures they wring the neck and that would be the same as the blood would not pour out to the ground.

[3] Obey YHWH's commandments not the nations around you.

[4] There are two rescues. Unfortunately for Christians this is a little hard to understand. Here 'life' is not disconnected from eternal life; both are one and the same in YHWH through His favor. If you obey YHWH, not only does He rescue us, but he grants us physical and eternal life. Look at the example of Israel; first, they were saved from the slavery in Egypt which is one type of rescue, and then they were given eternal life by Faith.

[5] Idiomatic expression to uncover your father's nakedness, the second wife meaning step mother. This sin occurred in Israel.

nakedness You shall not uncover.

10 The nakedness of your son's daughter, or of your daughter's daughter, even their nakedness You shall not uncover: for their's is your own nakedness.

11 The nakedness of your father's wife's daughter,[1] The one born through your father is your

Footnotes

[1] There are two distinct laws here mentioned, the first is the same as Lev 18:9 where the woman that is being referenced is still the biological mother of the man and not the second wife so this is how it is to be understood. Here the father's daughter is also the daughter of the mother and biological sister of the man/son begotten within this family so he is being told how to handle the situation. If this was a different wife of the father such as a second or third wife then it would contradict Gen 20:12, and Second Sam 13:13. Abraham married Sarah from the same biological father and different mothers. Tamar offered herself to her brother in marriage though she was a sister from a different mother as well. YHWH has allowed marriages from the same father and different mother, look who was Qayin's wife that came from Adam's third wife created through his bones see Gen 2:21-24. This is why in the second part of this law "The one born to your father... it makes a case it is not different to Lev 18:9." A man is allowed to marry the step-sister from the second wife or third wife according to Torah law but forbidden from marrying his biological sister, note the Egyptians did this and this is the law YHWH forbids. Note in the Hebrew it says ערות בת-אשת אביך מולדת Ervot Bat Ishot Abekha Meldot. The word **Meldot** being issued just after the terms for wife and father indicates the "daughter" is from both of them biologically and not just the one parent Father as many seem to think and incorrectly apply. The language hides details that many do not understand. Why does the Torah say "One born through your Father" and why not "one through the wife or mother" because the Torah sees children as the seed of the man and not the woman in the usual sense so the point is being driven home differently in this text from the one mentioned in Lev 18:9 is the same point.

sister, you shall not defile her nor uncover her.

12 You shall not uncover the nakedness of your father's sister: she is your father's near kinswoman.

13 You shall not uncover the nakedness of your mother's sister: for she is your mother's near kinswoman.

14 You shall not uncover the nakedness of your father's brother, You shall not approach to his wife: she is your aunt.

15 You shall not uncover the nakedness of your daughter in law: she is your son's wife; You shall not uncover her nakedness.

16 You shall not uncover the nakedness of your brother's wife: it is your brother's nakedness.

17 You shall not uncover a woman/wife and her daughter's nakednesses[2], you shall not take

Footnotes

[2] This is describing taking them together to reveal their naked flesh it would a type of encounter where the woman and her daughter were asked to strip their clothes together, which is not permitted and considered indecent exposure. She must not be blood related to the man/husband or the daughter of the woman/wife. The prohibition is not of marriage to a step-daughter or to the mother. The sages suggested that a man can marry either one or the other (step daughter or mother) whether one party is living or deceased. A righteous man would be best advised to marry the mother followed by marrying the step-daughter to another righteous man provided she is older than 18! However in goyim culture the minimum age is usually set to 16 with consent from parents so one should marry his step-daughter after this age. It would be prudent to make sure that your step-daughter gets sufficient goyim education academically so she can support herself in case she needs to. Therefore, one must not force the step-daughter into a marriage with a man she is not happy to enter. Both Continued in next section

her son's daughter and her daughter's daughter to uncover the nakednesses *for* they are her relatives, for it is a violation.

18 And You shall not take a wife to her sister as an adversary, to uncover her nakedness *together* beside the other in her life time. [1]

19 Also You shall not approach to a woman to uncover her nakedness, during her monthly flow separation.[2]

20 Moreover You shall not lie carnally with your neighbour's wife, to defile yourself with her.

21 And You shall not let any of your offspring be put through the fire for Molech, neither shall You profane the name of Your POWER: I am YHWH.

22 You shall not lie with men, as with women: it defiles ritually.[3]

23 Neither shall You lie with any animal to defile yourself therewith: neither shall any woman stand before an animal to lie down with: it is confusion.

24 Defile not you yourselves in any of these things: for in all these the nations are defiled

parties (step-daughter and her husband to be) must consent to Torah fidelity before you enact the marriage through a Rabbi.

[1] Both sisters are permitted to the husband just as Jacob was married to two sisters but marriage is forbidden if solely marrying to oppress one sister at the hands of the other. A husband is not permitted to remove the clothes of both sisters together in the bedroom to put them to shame. One may say the word Ervah is in plural in verse 16 too where a brother's wife is prohibited however again it is inclusive not exclusive. It means only as far as the brother is alive, while YHWH commanded polygyny to the brother's wife after his death automatically without any ceremony. The same way there are two concurrent plural words Eruvot and L'glot both indicative one or the other case applies. You can marry the mother or the step-daughter. In such a scenario if a grown daughter is found in the same household the chances are very high that the man married to the mother may commit indecent acts with the step-daughter, this is prevalent in gentile culture, so in order to prevent such a scenario the Torah regulates the marriage of Hebrews to the goyim. While Judaism went the other way but then Judaism's laws (European Jews, proselytes from Khazaria and Yemen) evolved over time and are not the original laws of the Torah but rabbinic in nature. Please refer to the footnote above regards marriage of the step-daughter.

[2] Sexual intercourse is not allowed during the wife's monthly flow.

Footnotes

[3] This prohibition only applied to Israel not to make Temple Prostitutes, it is not applied whole sale to Homosexuality as many do today. The context is the Tent that was used for worship that no Israelite was to act as a Temple Prostitute and actually has nothing to do with the lifestyle of the same gender individuals today who engage in it for different reasons. One of the other reasons is that all Israelites were to produce children through marriage, while in the gentile homosexual community today such people cannot produce children living with the same sex but they have nothing to do with being Temple prostitutes hence the application that most religious authorities apply does not hold true. Many homosexual individuals also have regular marriages with females where they have produced Children before they go to reveal their likeness to the same gender sex, which also rules this out as applicable. Many also mistakenly believe that Sodom and Gomorrah were destroyed for Homosexuality. This is also not true, these cities were destroyed for injustice, see Ezek 16:49. The act of Homosexuality was never mentioned. The ancient word To'ebah was translated into the Greek as Bdelygma during the 3rd Century BCE, which meant it was a ritual violation to do with in the context of the Temple/Tabernacle worship. So it means do not bring male prostitutes into your place of worship. There are many other words that can be used for a moral violation least being To'ebah.

which I cast out before you:[1]

25 And the land is defiled: therefore I do visit the iniquity there upon it, and the land itself vomits out her inhabitants.

26 You shall therefore keep my statutes and my judgments, and shall not commit any of these ritual defilements; neither any of your own nation, nor any foreigner that lives among you:

27 For all these ritual defilements[2] have the men of the land done, which were before you, and the land is defiled;[3]

28 Do not make the land vomit you out also, when you defile it, as it did the nations that were before you.

29 For whosoever shall commit any of these abominations, even the souls that commit them shall be cut off from among their people.

30 Therefore shall you keep mine ordinance, that you commit not any one of these Ritual defilements, which were committed before you, and that you defile not yourselves therein: I am YHWH Your POWER.

Torah Parsha 30 Kedoshim, Wayikra 19:1-20:27
Haftarah: Ykhezkiel 22:1-16

Footnotes
[1] The heathens involve themselves in these types of foolish sexual sins but Israelites are to remain free and stick to either plural marriages or monogamous relations.
[2] To'ebah means to defile ritually so if you are ritually contaminated you also contaminate the land too.
[3] This is why they were being kicked out of the land they had defiled with their grievous sins.

Chapter 19

1 And YHWH spoke to Mosheh (Musa), saying,

2 Speak to all the congregation of the children of Israel, and say to them, You shall be Holy: for I YHWH Your POWER am Holy.

3 Each of you must respect his mother, and his father, and Guard my Sabbaths: I am YHWH Your POWER.

4 Do not turn to idols, nor make for yourselves molten elohim:[1] I am YHWH Your POWER.

5 And if you offer a sacrifice of shalom offerings to YHWH, you shall offer it at your own will.

6 It shall be eaten the same day you offer it, and the day after: and if any remains until the third day, it shall be burnt in the fire.

7 And if it be eaten at all on the third day, it is abominable; it shall not be accepted.

8 Therefore everyone that eats it shall bear his iniquity, because he has profaned the Holy thing of YHWH and that soul shall be cut off from among his people.

9 And when you reap the harvest of your land, You shall not wholly reap the corners of your field, neither shall You gather the gleanings of your harvest.

10 And You shall not glean your vineyard, neither shall You gather every grape of your vineyard; You shall leave them for the poor and foreigner[2] I am YHWH Your POWER.

11 You shall not steal, neither deal falsely, neither lie one to another.

12 And you shall not swear by my name falsely, neither shall You desecrate the name of Your POWER: I am YHWH.

13 You shall not defraud your neighbour, neither rob him: the wages of him that is hired shall not abide with you all night until the morning.

14 You shall not curse the deaf, nor put a stumbling block before the blind, but shall fear Your POWER: I am YHWH.

15 You shall do no iniquity in judgment: You shall not be partial to the person (face) of the weak (poor), nor be partial to the person (face) of the wealthy (great):[3] but in Righteousness shall You judge your neighbour.

16 You shall not go up and down as a slanderer[4] among your people: neither shall You stand against the blood of your neighbour: I am YHWH.

17 You shall not hate your brother in your heart: You shall

Footnotes

[1] Hand made images of false elohim.

[2] YHWH is equitable to leave some grains and fruits for the poor and foreigners who were passing through who were allowed to pick and eat if they were hungry.

[3] The context is someone of means of wealth or greatness who can buy the judge with a bribe. So the Hebrew word Gadol, should be correctly stated as Wealthy while the Hebrew word for rich is not used here which is Ashar but the context is richness. The word Panim here should be translated face instead of faces.

[4] This is counted as a grievous sin yet many believers are doing this today against each other. Judaism does not take likely to this sin as it can ruin people's lives while Christians think they can just do this and walk away in favor. There are eternal consequences of this sin and it must be repented of or you will suffer in the coming age.

rebuke your neighbour, and not suffer sin upon yourself for his sake.

18 You shall not avenge, nor bear any grudge against the children of your people, but You shall love your neighbour[1] as yourself: I am YHWH.

19 You shall keep my statutes. You shall not allow different animals to cross breed: You shall not sow your field with mixed seed: neither shall a garment mixed of linen and woolen come upon you.[2]

20 And whosoever lies carnally with a woman that is a bondmaid, betrothed to a husband, and not at all redeemed, nor freedom given her; she shall be scourged; they shall not be put to death, because she was not free.

21 And he shall bring his trespass offering to YHWH, to the door of the Tent of the appointed times, even a ram for a trespass offering.

22 And the kohen (priest) shall make atonement for him with the ram of the trespass offering before YHWH for his sin which he has done: and the sin which he has done shall be forgiven him.

23 And when you shall come into the land, and shall have planted all manner of trees for food, then you shall count the fruit there as forbidden: three years shall it be as forbidden to you: it shall not be eaten.

24 But in the fourth year all the fruit there shall be Holy to praise YHWH.[3]

25 And in the fifth year shall you eat of the fruit there, that it may yield to you the **Increase** there: I am YHWH Your POWER.

26 You shall not eat any thing with the blood: neither shall you practice any type of divination, or black magic.

27 You shall not round the corners of your heads,[4] neither shall You destroy the payot[5] (sides) of your beard.

28 You shall not make any cuttings in your flesh for the

Footnotes

[1] This commandment originated in the Torah and not Christian theology.

[2] The Torah is consistent, no cross cattle breeding or any other animal, no mixing of seed in the same field because this is where we get the word adulterating for adultery. Hence why plural marriages are allowed, because men are not mixing seed but putting the seed into each woman to produce children, while more than one husband to one woman would be mixing seed and adulterating. The same principle carries forward in clothing.

[3] The first three years, the fruit of an etz (tree) was considered uncircumcised and not fit to eat until the fourth year.

[4] It's like making a circle which was done in the ancient times for the dead.

[5] We have an explicit commandment here to make beards but no size is specified and we are allowed to trim the sides but not destroy them or disfigure them unless we have an illness that does that. Also the same applies to the head where hair is not supposed to be kept long but kept short and trimmed. Keeping long hair was only allowed in the Nazarite vow which was a sign of humility before YHWH. A case can be made against beards as they are not a requirement for all of Israel but only the priests but it was more a tradition that the rest of Israel kept beards. The word Zakan in Hebrew refers to a scholar of Torah so careful attention needs to be paid to who the short beards applies to if at all but not to all of Israel.

Micah 1:16 Shave your heads bald, and mourn for your delicate children; enlarge your baldness on your forehead as the eagle; for they are gone into captivity from you.

dead,[1] nor print any tattoos[2] upon you: I am YHWH.

29 Do not prostitute your daughter, to cause her to be a whore; lest the land fall to whoredom, and the land become full of wickedness.

30 You shall keep my Sabbaths,[3] and reverence my sanctuary: I am YHWH.

31 Do not turn after mediums to communicate to the dead neither seek after soothsayers, to be defiled by them: I am YHWH Your POWER.

32 You shall rise up before the gray head, and respect the face of the old man[4], and fear Your POWER: I am YHWH.

33 And if a foreigner lives with you in your country, you shall not vex him.

34 But the foreigner that dwells with you he shall be to you as one born amongst you, and You shall love him as yourself; for you were foreigners in the land of Mitzrayim (Egypt): I am YHWH Your POWER.[5]

Footnotes

[1] In the ancient times when people died, some heathen nations would cut their skin in respect. Some nations still practice this especially the Islamic religion. The Shia people cut themselves during the Muharram fast in respect and grievance for the killing of Imam Hussain, the Muslim prophet's grandson. Such a practice is not permitted in the Torah for you if you call yourself Israel.

[2] Note only Tatoos that have heathen deities but not common tattooes like flowers, animals etc are not forbidden.

[3] This is the weekly Sabbath, which is from Saturday Sunrise to Saturday sunset and the annual feasts!

[4] Respect must be given to the elderly.

[5] The leaders in Messianic congregations, have a bad habit of segregating, (non-Jews) believers, who are part of their
Continued in next section

35 You shall do no unrighteousness in regulation of measures, whether of length weight, or volume.

36 Just balances, just weights, a just ephah, and a just hin, shall you have: I am YHWH Your POWER, which brought you out of the land of Mitzrayim (Egypt).

37 Therefore shall you Guard all my statutes, and all my judgments, and do them: I am YHWH.

Chapter 20

1 And YHWH spoke to Mosheh (Musa), saying,

2 Again, You shall say to the children of Israel, Whosoever he be of the children of Israel, or of the strangers that sojourn in Israel, that gives any of his children as sacrifice to Molech; he shall surely be put to death: the people of the land shall stone him with stones.

3 And I will set my face against that man, and will cut him off from among his people; because he has given of his children to Molech, to defile my sanctuary, and to profane my Holy name.

4 And if the people of the land do any ways hide their eyes from the man, when he gives of his children to Molech, and kill him not:

5 Then I will set my face against that man, and against his Mishpakha (family), and will cut him off, and all that go a whoring

congregation. They make them feel like they are second class citizens, who are grafted-in, not truly a part of Israel. YHWH forbids this behavior.

after him, to commit whoredom with Molech, from among their people.

6 And the soul that turns after such as mediums, and after soothsayers, to go a whoring after them, I will even set my face against that soul, and will cut him off from among his people.

7 Sanctify yourselves therefore, and be you Holy: for I am YHWH Your POWER.

8 And you shall keep my statutes, and do them: I am YHWH which sanctifies you.

9 For everyone that curses his father or his mother shall be surely put to death: he has cursed his father or his mother; his blood shall be upon him.[1]

10 And the man that commits adultery with another man's wife, even he that commits adultery with his neighbour's wife, the adulterer and the adulteress shall surely be put to death.[2]

11 And the man that lies with his father's wife has uncovered his father's nakedness: both of them shall surely be put to death; their blood shall be upon them.

12 And if a man lie with his daughter in law, both of them shall surely be put to death: they have wrought confusion; their blood shall be upon them.

13 If a man also lie with a man, as he lies with a woman, both of them have committed Ritual Defilement:[3] they shall surely be put to death;[4] their blood shall be upon them.

Footnotes

[1] Swearing at our parents is forbidden. Respect must be given irrespective of whether they believe in YHWH or not but we must follow after YHWH and love YHWH.

[2] The Mishnah tells us in tractate Sanhedrin xi.1 that the punishment for this type of adultery should be by strangulation. The rabbinical decree was that when the Torah does not mention how the guilty parties should be killed then strangulation was to be used. (Sefira. Kedoshim, 4, 9). The people were put into animal excrement such as cowpat knee deep and then two napkins were used to pull to tighten the noose to strangulate the guilty party. The adultery to be killed by stoning mentioned in Deuteronomy 22:24 is a different type and the punishment mentioned is by stoning. This type of punishment was a rare occurrence in Israel. Mostly the rabbis made the husband to divorce the wife and put her out so that her life may be spared. During the Talmudic times the rabbis modified the

Continued in next section

laws to be milder when it came to punishing the guilty party. The rabbis even declared that a woman could not be punished unless she knew the law of Torah for adultery, if it could be proved that she did not know the law then she could be released free and caused to be divorced by a suspecting husband, which would prevent a suspicious husband from having his wife killed. This saved women who were wrongfully suspected.

This is why in the year 40CE the death penalty was abolished by the Temple, see tractate Sanhedrin 41a. This was likely to be done in view of the pressure from the Roman government that was in Judea at the time. The suspecting woman would lose all her property rights. An adulteress was not allowed to marry her suspecting male friend and if she did succeed in marrying him she was forced to separate, see tractate Sotah in the Talmud. If a woman was found to be an adulteress with a man then the husband could only stone his wife if he himself was free from all sins of the Torah.

[3] Only in regards to Temple prostitution.

[4] The punishment of homosexuality was only applied to Israelites who were prohibited to act as Temple Prostitutes and not to the nations. See Lev 18:22. This has nothing to do with the nations doing the same gender acts! Elohim would not only mention this twice if this was such a serious sin as most attest out of shear ignorant attitudes. The

Continued in next section

14 And if a man take a wife and her mother, it is wickedness: they shall be burnt with fire,[1] both he

case in point of the Sabbath is mentioned at least 137 times in positive or a negative light, while this act of same gender relation is only mentioned a total of 2 times in the Torah. If this was a sin as the religious authorities described then let them prove why it only ever gets mentioned twice and why were they not honest to mention this only applies to Temple Prostitutes. Also one other question that needs to be asked where did the act start from? We are told in the Torah that Nephalim (Gen 6:2) the malakhim that fell brought and taught the humans how to do these acts. If one was to agree the angels taught these acts to humans then who is to blame for this? There are transvestite born that have impairment not due to their own fault so should they also be put to death? Also we have seen births of hermaphrodite, again not by one's own volition, these people are the creation of Elohim so one must exercise mercy and not judgement. Often the religious world is wrong so be careful how to make a judgment upon such people that you not be found guilty of injustice, the very sin Sodom and Gomorrah were destroyed for.

[1] This is not the traditional burning on a stake as the Catholics did to the Protestants but this is where the hot lead was put into the person's mouth for death to occur quickly.

Such events were very rarely conducted. A court of at least 23 judges would have to be satisfied, to a legal certainty; for the capital offence had to have been committed before the court could impose a death sentence.

Since the true report of two eye-witnesses was required, and the witnesses were subjected to searching and detailed interrogation by the court, there was rarely an instance when the evidence met the prescribed legal standard. See Maimonides, Mishneh Torah, Book of Judges, Sanhedrin, chapter XII4.

The Mishna in Sanhedrin (52a) also described the procedure for 'burning' and stated clearly that it did not involve actual resorting to fire or flames. Rather, an
Continued in next section

and they; that there be no wickedness among you.

15 And if a man lie with an animal, he shall surely be put to death: and you shall slay the animal.

16 And if a woman approach to any animal, and lie down thereto, You shall kill the woman, and the animal: they shall surely be put to death; their blood shall be upon them.

17 And if a man shall take his sister, his father's daughter, and also his mother's daughter, and see her nakedness, and she see his nakedness; it is a wicked thing; and they shall be cut off in the sight of their people: he has uncovered his sister's nakedness; he shall bear his iniquity.

18 And if a man shall lie with a woman having her menstrual periods, and shall uncover her nakedness; he has discovered her monthly flow, and she has uncovered the fountain of her blood: and both of them shall be

extremely hot object (or wick) was inserted into the mouth of the condemned individual so as to cause instantaneous death. Here, too, the objective was to cause death quickly and without mutilation of the body.

Rabbi Elazar the son of Rabbi Tzadok said 'An incident once occurred with the daughter of a priest who committed adultery and they surrounded her with bundles of branches and burned her.' The other Rebbim responded to him, 'That was done because the court that performed this execution was not knowledgeable.' The Talmud, in fact, explains that the incident reported in the Mishna was the work of a court of Sadducees (*i.e.*, those who mistakenly applied the Biblical text without taking account of the oral tradition and rabbinic interpretation).
(http://www.jlaw.com/Briefs/capital2.html)

cut off from among their people.[1]

19 And You shall not uncover the nakedness of your mother's sister, nor of your father's sister: for he uncovers his near kin: they shall bear their iniquity.

20 And if a man shall lie with his uncle's wife, he has uncovered his uncle's nakedness: they shall bear their sin; they shall die childless.

21 And if a man shall take his brother's wife, it is an unclean thing: he has uncovered his brother's nakedness; they shall be childless.

22 You shall therefore keep all my statutes, and all my judgments, and do them: that the land, where I bring you to dwell therein, vomit you not out.

23 And you shall not walk in the manners of the nation, which I cast out before you: for they committed all these things, and therefore I abhorred them.

24 But I have said to you, You shall inherit their land, and I will give it to you to possess it, a land that flows with milk and honey.[2] I am YHWH Your POWER, who has separated you from other people.

25 You shall therefore put difference between clean animals and unclean, and between unclean birds and clean: and you shall not make your souls abominable by animals, or by birds, or by any manner of creatures that crawls on the ground, which I have separated from you as unclean.

26 And you shall be Holy to me: for I YHWH am Holy, and have severed you from other people, that you should be mine.

27 A man also or woman that is a medium[3], or that is a soothsayer, shall surely be put to death: they shall stone them with stones: their blood shall be upon them.

Torah Parsha 31 Emor Lev
Wayikra 21:1-24:23
Haftarah Ykhezkiel (Ezekiel) 44:15-31

Chapter 21
1 And YHWH said to Mosheh (Musa), Speak to the kohenim the sons of Aharon, and say to them, There shall none be defiled for the dead among his people:

2 But for his kin, that is near to him, that is, for his mother, and for his father, and for his son, and for his daughter, and for his brother,

3 And for his sister a virgin, that is near to him, which has had no husband; for her may he be defiled.

4 But he shall not defile himself, being a chief man among his people, to profane himself.

5 They shall not make baldness upon their head, neither shall they shave off the payots (sides) of their beard, nor make any incisions in their flesh.

Footnotes
[1] The sin of a man sleeping with a woman with menstrual periods was death. During this time it is unhealthy for husbands to engage in sexual intercourse.
[2] Israel has some of the best honey and milking cows in the world. The expression is related to the land's fruitfulness.

Footnotes
[3] One claiming to talk to the dead

6 They shall be Holy to their Elohim, and not profane the name of their Elohim: for the offerings of YHWH made by fire, and the Lakhem (bread) of their Elohim, they do offer: therefore they shall be Holy.

7 They shall not take a wife that is a whore, or profane; neither shall they take a woman divorced from her husband: for he is Holy to his Elohim.

8 You shall sanctify him therefore; for he offers the Lakhem (bread) of Your POWER: he shall be Holy to you: for I YHWH, which sanctify you, am Holy.

9 And the daughter of any kohen (priest), if she profane herself by playing the whore, she has profaned her father: she shall be burnt with fire.[1]

10 And he that is the Kohen ha Gadol (High Priest) among his brethren, upon whose head the anointing oil was poured, and that is consecrated to put on the garments, shall not uncover his head, nor rend his clothes;

11 Neither shall he go in to any dead body, nor defile himself for his father, or for his mother;

12 Neither shall he go out of the sanctuary, nor profane the sanctuary of his Elohim; for the crown of the anointing oil of his Elohim is upon him: I am YHWH.

13 And he shall take a wife in her virginity.

Footnotes
[1] This was the charge levelled against Tamar because she was the daughter of a priest hence why Judah asked for her to be burnt (Gen 30:24). For how the burning was done please see Lev 20:14.

14 A widow, or a divorced woman, or profane, or a harlot, these shall he not take: but he shall take a virgin of his own people to wife.

15 Neither shall he profane his seed among his people: for I YHWH do sanctify him.

16 And YHWH spoke to Mosheh (Musa), saying,

17 Speak to Aharon, saying, Whosoever he be of your descendants in their generations that has any blemish, let him not approach to offer the Lakhem (bread) of his Elohim.

18 For whatsoever man he be that has a blemish, he shall not approach: a blind man, or a lame, or he that has a split nose, or anything superfluous,

19 Or a man that has a broken foot, or broken hand,

20 Or hunchback, or a dwarf, or that has a spot in his eye, or has an eruption, a feverish rash or crushed testicle; [2]

21 No man that has a blemish of the seed of Aharon the kohen (priest) shall come near to offer the offerings of YHWH made by fire: he has a blemish; he shall not come near to offer the Lakhem (bread) of his Elohim.

22 He shall eat the Lakhem (bread) of his Elohim, both of the

Footnotes
[2] These things occurring from self and not by an accident because just as today as in ancient times people neutered themselves or did some deliberate personal injury to prove their faithfulness to their false deities, even neutering of animals is forbidden a common occurrence today. The modern definition of castration is vasectomy! These things such as vasectomy, removal of uterus and other such methods are prohibited as anti-Torah and against the Elohim of Israel.

most Holy, and of the Holy.

23 Only he shall not go in to the veil, nor come near to the altar, because he has a physical issue; that he profane not my sanctuaries: for I YHWH do sanctify them.

24 And Mosheh (Musa) told it to Aharon, and to his sons, and to all the children of Israel.

Chapter 22

1 And YHWH spoke to Mosheh (Musa), saying,

2 Speak to Aharon and to his sons, that they separate themselves from the Holy things of the children of Israel, and that they profane not my Holy name in those things which they hallow to me: I am YHWH.

3 Say to them, Whosoever he be of all your descendants among your generations, that goes to the Holy things, which the children of Israel Holy to YHWH, having his uncleanness upon him, that soul shall be cut off from my presence: I am YHWH.

4 Whatever man of the seed of Aharon is a leper, or has a running issue; he shall not eat of the Holy things, until he be clean. And the one touches any thing that is unclean by the dead, or a man whose seed goes from him;

5 Or anyone touches any crawling creature, whereby he may be made unclean, or a man of whom he may take uncleanness, whatsoever uncleanness he has;

6 The soul which has touched any such shall be unclean until evening, and shall not eat of the Holy things, unless he wash his flesh with mayim.

7 And when the sun is down, he shall be clean, and shall afterward eat of the Holy things; because it is his food.

8 That which dies of itself, or is torn by animals, he shall not eat to defile himself therewith: I am YHWH.

9 They shall therefore keep mine ordinance, lest they bear sin for it, and die therefore, if they profane it: I YHWH do sanctify them.

10 There shall no foreigner eat of the Holy thing: a sojourner of the kohen (priest), or a hired servant, shall not eat of the Holy thing.

11 But if the kohen (priest) buy any soul with his money, he shall eat of it, and he that is born in his Beyth (house): they shall eat of his meat.

12 If the kohen's (priest) daughter also be married to a foreigner, she may not eat of an offering of the Holy things.

13 But if the kohen's (priest) daughter be a widow, or divorced, and have no child, and is returned to her father's Beyth (house), as in her youth, she shall eat of her father's meat: but there shall no foreigner eat there.

14 And if a man eat of the Holy thing by mistake, then he shall put twenty percent there to it, and shall give it to the kohen (priest) with the Holy thing.

15 And they shall not profane the Holy things of the children of Israel, which they offer to YHWH;

16 Or suffer them to bear the iniquity of trespass, when they eat their Holy things: for I YHWH do sanctify them.

17 And YHWH spoke to Mosheh (Musa), saying,

18 Speak to Aharon, and to his sons, and to all the children of Israel, and say to them, Whatsoever he be of the Beyth (house) of Israel, or of the strangers in Israel, that will offer his oblation for all his vows, and for all his freewill offerings, which they will offer to YHWH for a burnt offering;

19 You shall offer at your own will a male without blemish, of the OX *family*, the sheep, or of the goats.

20 You shall not offer anything that has a blemish, for it shall not be acceptable for you.

21 And whosoever offers a sacrifice of shalom offerings to YHWH to accomplish his vow, or a freewill offering of the OX *family*, or sheep, it shall be pure to be accepted; there shall be no blemish therein.

22 Blind, or broken, or maimed, or having a wen, or scurvy, or scabbed, you shall not offer these to YHWH, nor make an offering by fire of them upon the altar to YHWH.

23 Either a bullock or a lamb that has any thing superfluous or lacking in his parts, that may You offer for a freewill offering; but for a vow it shall not be accepted.

24 You shall not offer to YHWH that which is bruised, or crushed, or broken, or cut; neither shall you make any offering there in your land.

25 Neither from a foreigner's hand shall you offer the Lakhem (bread) of Your POWER of any of these; because their corruption is in them, and blemishes be in them: they shall not be accepted for you.

26 And YHWH spoke to Mosheh (Musa), saying,

27 When a bullock, or a sheep, or a goat, is brought forth, then it shall be seven days under the care of his mother; and from the eighth day and thenceforth it shall be accepted for an offering made by fire to YHWH.

28 And whether it be cow or ewe, you shall not kill it and her young both in one day.

29 And when you will offer a sacrifice of thanksgiving to YHWH, offer it at your own will.

30 On the same day it shall be eaten up; you shall leave none of it until the morrow: I am YHWH.

31 Therefore shall you keep my commandments, and do them: I am YHWH.

32 Neither shall you profane my Holy name; but I will be Holy among the children of Israel: I am YHWH who sanctifies you,

33 That brought you out of the land of Mitzrayim, to be Your POWER: I am YHWH.

The appointed celebration times of YHWH for all who are Israel and or grafted in Chapter 23

1 And YHWH spoke to Mosheh (Musa), saying,

2 Speak to the children of Israel, and say to them, Concerning the Moe'dim (feasts: Appointed times) of YHWH, which they[1]

Footnotes
[1] The Hebrew word "Otam" must be translated as "They".

shall proclaim to be Holy Assemblies, even these are My Feasts.

3 Six days shall work be done: but the seventh day is the Sabbath of rest, a Holy assembly;[1] you shall do no work therein: it is the Sabbath of YHWH in all your dwellings.

4 These are the Moe'dim (feasts: Appointed times) of YHWH,[2] even Holy convocations, which they[3] shall proclaim in their seasons.

5 In the fourteenth day of the first month at dusk is YHWH's Protection (Passover).

6 And on the fifteenth day[4] of the same month is the khag ha Matzot (The appointed celebration time of unleavened bread) to YHWH seven days you must eat matzah.

7 In the first day you shall have a Holy assembly: you shall do no servile work therein.

8 But you shall offer an offering made by fire to YHWH seven days: in the seventh day is a Holy assembly: you shall do no servile work therein.

9 And YHWH spoke to Mosheh (Musa), saying,

10 Speak to the children of Israel, and say to them, When you be come into the land which I give to you, and shall reap the harvest there, then you shall bring a sheaf of the bikkurim (first-fruit) of your harvest to the kohen (priest):

11 And he shall wave the sheaf before YHWH, to be accepted for you: on the day after the Sabbath the kohen (priest) shall wave it.

12 And you shall offer that day when you wave the sheaf a he lamb without blemish of the first year for a burnt offering to YHWH.

13 And the grain offering there

Footnotes

[1] A Holy assembly is when we are to meet together and fellowship. For those who are alone or have difficulty to go to an assembly they should conduct this in their home.

[2] These are YHWH's feasts and not Jewish feasts as wrongly taught by the Church. The Church has discarded the feasts but put a claim on Israelite rescue, well that is also of the Yahudim.

[3] The Hebrew word "Otam" should be "They" and not You as the rabbinic Jews deliberately taught to read the Hebrew wrong.

[4] The Elohim of Israel commanded Israel to ascend to Jerusalem on three feasts, also mentioned in (Deuteronomy 16-16). These three feasts are;
a. Unleavened Bread
b. Pentecost (Khag, celebration of Weeks) Shavuot
c. Tabernacles (Sukkot)

In Zechariah 14:16-19, we are told that the radical Islamic nations that survive will be humiliated and will have to go up and serve YHWH by paying reverence to YHWH in Jerusalem.

Now if the heathens will be under compulsion to respect the feasts in the 1000 years millennial kingdom to come, then how much more will the believers, out of love and obedience? Sukkot is also a high Holy day, a Continued in next section

Sabbath of YHWH, and his feasts are for all mankind, for all times to attend and present themselves to YHWH.

Note, that there are no bogus time gaps where the commandments are not in affect, as foolishly claimed by dispensationalists, who essentially deny YHWH's eternal commandments. All of mankind will keep the Sabbaths and the appointed times. The only question remaining is will you do so, out of love and obedience, or will you be 'smacked' into submission, within His kingdom with the rod of iron?

shall be two tenth deals of fine flour mingled with oil, an offering made by fire to YHWH for a sweet savour: and the drink offering there shall be of wine, the fourth part of a hin.

14 And you shall eat neither Lakhem (bread), nor parched wheat, nor green ears, until the selfsame day that you have brought an offering to Your POWER: it shall be a statute forever throughout your generations in all your dwellings.

15 And you shall count to you from the next day after the Sabbath, from the day that you brought the omer of the wave offering; seven Sabbaths shall be complete:

16 Even to the morrow after the seventh Sabbath shall you number fifty days; and you shall offer a new grain offering to YHWH.

17 You shall bring out of your habitations two wave loaves of two tenth deals: they shall be of fine flour; they shall be baked with leaven; they are the first-fruits to YHWH.

18 And you shall offer with the Lakhem (bread) seven lambs without blemish of the first year, and one young bullock, and two rams: they shall be for a burnt offering to YHWH, with their grain offering, and their drink offerings, even an offering made by fire, of sweet savour to YHWH.

19 Then you shall sacrifice one kid of the goats for a sin offering, and two lambs of the first year for a sacrifice of shalom offerings.

20 And the kohen (priest) shall wave them with the Lakhem

(bread) of the first-fruits for a wave offering before YHWH, with the two lambs: they shall be Holy to YHWH for the kohen (priest).

21 And you shall proclaim on the selfsame day, that it may be a Holy convocation to you: you shall do no servile work therein: it shall be a statute forever in all your dwellings throughout your generations.

22 And when you reap the harvest of your land, You shall not completely clean out the corners of your field when You reap, neither shall You gather any gleaning of your harvest: You shall leave them to the poor, and to the foreigner: I am YHWH Your POWER.

23 And YHWH spoke to Mosheh (Musa), saying,

24 Speak to the children of Israel, saying, in the seventh month, in the first day of the month, shall you have a Sabbath, a memorial of shouting[1], a miqra

Footnotes

[1] Note according to Torah its not a new year but just a day of shouting out God's glories. http://en.wikipedia.org/wiki/Rosh_Hashanah Rosh Hashanah is the start of the civil year in the Hebrew calendar (one of four "new year" observances that define various legal "years" for different purposes as explained in the Mishnah and Talmud). It is the new year for people, animals, and legal Covenants. The Mishnah also sets this day aside as the new year for calculating calendar years and sabbatical (shmita) and jubilee (yovel) years. Jews believe Rosh Hashanah represents either analogically or literally the creation of the World, or Universe. However, according to one view in the Talmud, that of R. Eleazar, Rosh Hashanah commemorates the creation of man, which entails that five days earlier, the 25 of Elul, was the first day of creation of the Universe.[2]

Continued in next section

We'Yikra (Leviticus)

The Mishnah, the core text of Judaism's oral Torah, contains the first known reference to Rosh Hashanah as the "day of judgment." In the Talmud tractate on Rosh Hashanah it states that three books of account are opened on Rosh Hashanah, wherein the fate of the wicked, the righteous, and those of an intermediate class are recorded. The names of the righteous are immediately inscribed in the book of life, and they are sealed "to live." The middle class are allowed a respite of ten days, until Yom Kippur, to repent and become righteous; the wicked are "blotted out of the book of the living forever."[3]

The term "Rosh Hashanah" does not appear in the Torah. Leviticus 23:24 refers to the festival of the first day of the seventh month as "Zicaron Terua" ("a memorial with the blowing of horns"). Numbers 29:1 calls the festival Yom Terua, ("Day [of] blowing [the horn]") and symbolizes a number of subjects, such as the Binding of Isaac and the animal sacrifices that were to be performed.[7][8] (In Ezekiel 40:1 there is a general reference to the time of Yom Kippur as the "beginning of the year",[7] but it is not referring specifically to the holiday of Rosh Hashanah.)

The Torah defines Rosh Hashanah as a one-day observance, and since days in the Hebrew calendar begin at sundown, the beginning of Rosh Hashanah is at sundown at the end of 29 Elul. The rules of the Hebrew calendar are designed such that the first day of Rosh Hashanah will never occur on the first, fourth, or sixth day of the Hebrew week[9] (i.e., Sunday, Wednesday, or Friday).

Since the time of the destruction of the Second Temple of Jerusalem in 70 CE and the time of Rabban Yohanan ben Zakkai, normative Hebrew law appears to be that Rosh Hashanah is to be celebrated for two days, due to the difficulty of determining the date of the new month.[7] Nonetheless, there is some evidence that Rosh Hashanah was celebrated on a single day in Israel as late as the thirteenth century CE.[10] Orthodox, and Conservative Judaism now generally observe Rosh Hashanah for the first two days of Tishrei, even in Israel where all other Hebrew holidays dated from the new month last only one day. The two days Continued in next section

of Rosh Hashanah are said to constitute "Yoma Arichtah" (Aramaic: "one long day"). The observance of a second day is a later addition and does not follow from the literal reading of Leviticus. In Reform Judaism, some communities only observe the first day of Rosh Hashanah, while others observe two days. Karaite Jews, who do not recognize Rabbinic Hebrew oral law and rely on their own understanding of the Torah, observe only one day on the first of Tishrei, since the second day is not mentioned in the Torah. This holiday is considered to be one of the more important Hebrew holidays.

On Rosh Hashanah itself, religious poems, called piyyuttim, are added to the regular services. Special prayer books for Rosh Hashanah and Yom Kippur, called the mahzor (plural mahzorim), have developed over the years. Many poems refer to Psalms 81:4: "Blow the shofar on the [first day of the] month, when the [moon] is covered for our holiday".

Rosh Hashanah has a number of additions to the regular service, most notably an extended repetition of the Amidah prayer for both Shacharit and Mussaf. The Shofar is blown during Mussaf at several intervals. (In many synagogues, even little children come and hear the Shofar being blown.) Biblical verses are recited at each point. According to the Mishnah, 10 verses (each) are said regarding kingship, remembrance, and the shofar itself, each accompanied by the blowing of the shofar. A variety of piyyutim, medieval penitential prayers, are recited regarding themes of repentance. The Alenu prayer is recited during the repetition of the Mussaf Amidah.

There are three different sounds that the Shofar makes:

Tekiah (one long sound)
Shevarim (3 broken sounds)
Teruah (9 short sounds)
In addition to the three sounds there are two variations:

Tekiah Gedolah (a very long sound, used at the end of the Ashkenazi rite prayer services)
Shevarim Teruah (3 broken sounds followed by 9 short sounds)
Continued in next section

312

kodesh.[1]

25 You shall do no servile work therein: but you shall offer an offering made by fire to YHWH.

26 And YHWH spoke to Mosheh (Musa), saying,

27 Also on the tenth day of this seventh month there shall be Yom Kippurim:[2] it shall be a miqra kodesh[3] to you; and you shall afflict your souls, and offer an offering made by fire to YHWH.

28 And you shall do no work in that same day:[4] for it is a Yom Kippurim (Day of Atonements), to make kapporah[5] for you before YHWH Your POWER.

29 For whatsoever soul it be

that shall not be afflicted in that same day, he shall be cut off[6] from among his people.[7]

30 And whatsoever soul it be that does any work in that same day, the same soul will I destroy from among his people.[8]

31 You shall do no manner of work: it shall be a statute forever[9] throughout your generations in all your dwellings.

32 It shall be to you a Holy Sabbath and you shall afflict your souls: in the ninth day of the month at even, from even to even,[10] shall you celebrate your Sabbath.

33 And YHWH spoke to Mosheh (Musa), saying,

34 Speak to the children of Israel, saying, The fifteenth day of this seventh month shall be khag[11] ha Sukkot (The appointed celebration time of Tabernacles) for seven days to YHWH.

35 On the first day shall be a miqra kodesh:[12] you shall do no servile work therein.

36 Seven days you shall offer

2.^ OU on Elul
3.^ (Psalms 69:29).
7.^ a b c Jacobs, Louis. "Rosh Ha-Shanah." Encyclopaedia Judaica. Ed. Michael Berenbaum and Fred Skolnik. Vol. 17. 2nd ed. Detroit: Macmillan Reference USA, 2007. 463-466.
9.^ A popular mnemonic is "behold adu rosh" ("Rosh [Hashanah] is not on adu"), where adu has the numerical value 1-4-6 (corresponding to the numbering of days in the Hebrew week, in which Saturday night and Sunday daytime make up the first day).
10.^ Rav David Bar-Hayim. "Rosh HaShanna One day or Two?". Machon Shilo website. Jerusalem: Machon Shilo. http://machonshilo.org/content/view/100/1/lang,english/. Retrieved 2008-09-25. "Includes link for Audio Shiur in English"
[1] A special assembly.
[2] 'The Annual khag, celebration of Yom Kippor, which is the Day of Atonement.'
[3] There is to be a 25 hours fast abstention from food and water. Today, the people who are ill and take medicine can abstain from the fast and find other ways to afflict their souls.
[4] It's mandatory; there is no work on this day.
[5] Covering

Footnotes
[6] If you do not obey YHWH, He can kill you for it.
[7] Compulsory fast for all healthy people even today.
[8] YHWH can still kill you today for disobedience. Serve YHWH.
[9] L'olam V'ed mean forever, no time gaps. The commandment is eternal; therefore we are to fast all throughout our life.
[10] Beginning on the 9th evening at sunset the fast starts and ends on the tenth day at evening. Biblical days start at sunrise when the sun appears and finish at sunset, so they are sunrise to sunrise. The custom day of sunset to sunset came in the time of the Greek invasion of Israel.
[11] Annual khag, celebration.
[12] Compulsory day off and Holy assembly.

an offering made by fire to YHWH on the eighth day[1] shall be a miqra kodesh[2] to you; and you shall offer an offering made by fire to YHWH: it is a solemn assembly;[3] and you shall do no servile work therein.

37 These are the feasts of YHWH, which you shall proclaim to be miqra kodesh,[4] to offer an offering made by fire to YHWH, a burnt offering, and a grain offering, a sacrifice, and drink offerings, every thing upon his day:

38 Beside the Sabbaths of YHWH, and beside your gifts, and beside all your vows, and beside all your freewill offerings, which you give to YHWH.

39 Also in the fifteenth day of the seventh month, when you have gathered in the fruit of the land, you shall keep a khag (appointed celebration time)[5] to YHWH seven days: on the first day shall be a Sabbath, and on the eighth day shall be a Sabbath.

40 And you shall take for yourself on the first day the fruit of the most beautiful trees,[6] branches of palm trees, and the branches of thick trees, and willows of the brook; and you

shall rejoice before YHWH Your POWER seven days.

41 And you shall keep it a khag (appointed celebration time) to YHWH seven days in the year. It shall be a statute forever in your generations: you shall celebrate it in the seventh month.

42 You shall dwell in booths[7] seven days; all that are Y'sraeli born shall dwell in booths:

43 That your generations may know that I made the children of Israel to dwell in booths, when I brought them out of the land of Mitzrayim (Egypt): I am YHWH Your POWER.

44 And Mosheh (Musa) declared to the children of Israel the feast of YHWH.

Chapter 24

1 And YHWH spoke to Mosheh (Musa), saying,

2 Command the children of Israel, that they bring to you pure oil olive beaten for the light, to cause the lamps of the menorah to burn continually.

3 Outside the veil of the testimony, in the Tent of the appointed times, shall Aharon order it from the evening to the morning before YHWH continually: it shall be a statute forever in your generations.

4 He shall order the lamps of menorah upon the pure candlestick before YHWH continually.

Footnotes
[1] Shemini Atzeret. The great day of the khag, celebration.
[2] Day off and assembly together.
[3] Mandatory day off work.
[4] A solemn assembly to celebrate the khag, celebration.
[5] The celebration of the Tabernacles for eight days. In the diaspora it is nine days celebration.
[6] This is the Dates of Palms, the best tree in the desert region and most pretty.

Footnotes
[7] A tent with open roof covered wit the branches of the various trees spoken of. The person sits in this and eats and give thanks to YHWH. One side of the tent can be the wall of the house if built beside the house.

5 And You shall take fine flour, and bake twelve rotis[1] there: two tenth deals shall be in one roti.

6 And You shall set them in two rows, six on a row, upon the pure table before YHWH.

7 And You shall put pure frankincense upon each row, that it may be on the Lakhem (bread) for a memorial, even an offering made by fire to YHWH.

8 Every Sabbath he shall set it in order before YHWH continually, being taken from the children of Israel by an everlasting Covenant.

9 And it shall be Aharon's and his sons'; and they shall eat it in the Holy place: for it is most Holy to him of the offerings of YHWH made by fire by an eternal statute.

10 And the son of a Y'sra'eli woman, whose father was a Mitzri (Egyptian),[2] went out among the children of Israel: and this son of the Y'sra'eli woman and a man of Israel had a fight in the camp;

11 And the Y'sra'eli woman's son blasphemed the name of YHWH, and cursed. And they brought him to Mosheh (Musa): (and his mother's name was

Footnotes

[1] Twelve tribes of Israel.

[2] All religious denominations of Judaism agree that a person may be a Yahudi either by birth or through conversion to Judaism (Kodashim 66b, Shulchan Aruch, EH 4:19). The halakhic definition based on Leviticus 24:10 according to European Jewry where the son of an Egyptian man born to a Hebrew mother is that a Yahudi is a person born to a Hebrew mother, or one that has converted to Judaism. This European Khazari Halakha has come to this ruling from the texts in Lev 24:10, Deut 7:1-5 and Ezr 10:2-3. The Karaites argue that dissent is by patrilineal descent and not through the mother. Reconstructionist Judaism, and liberal Judaism also work on patrilineal descent. It is important to note that after King Solomon and the two part division of Israel anyone living in the lands south of Israel whether Judah, Benyamin or Levi or other ten tribes living there would be classed as a Yahudi or Judean only. This is in accordance with the Tanak in Esther 2:5 Continued in next section

where Mordechai from the tribe of Benyamin is both called a Yahudi and from the tribe of Benyamin. Rabbi Simon Altaf Levi Ben Ali Ben Yosef Ben Deen's verdict on the above; The halakha by the European converted rabbis who call themselves Jews was made much later such as the Shulchan Aruch written in Europe, so this ruling by them is to be rejected. The Karaites who are also converted Khazari converts hold a more accurate position but they are not the true children of Yakov. A chosen seed of Israel is one only and <u>only</u> thorough the descent of the **Y'sra'eli father** and not the mother or both father and mother being of the line of Yakov. Our custom is patrilineal. In this passage the classic case is of the woman whose son is called the son of a Y'sraeli woman thus inferring foreign status upon him (the son) since his father was a gentile (Egyptian). He is not referred to as a Y'sraeli but his mother is. Therefore if a woman marries a gentile her offspring will not be called Y'sra'eli chosen but he will be seen as a convert (proselyte) in our way of life and our culture provided he follows YHWH. This is why YHWH forbid our forefathers from marrying our Hebrew daughters to the foreigners in the land of Canaan in Deut 7. We are allowed to marry any foreign women in exile as long as they submit to the ways of Israel and the Elohim of Israel. Our children will be 100% Y'sraeli just as were Mosheh (Musa)'s sons who was married to a Midianite (Exo 2:21) and Kushite (Num 12:1). King Solomon whose son Rakhab'am whose mother was an Amoni but the son was considered 100% Hebrew. The same with King David whose son King Solomon birthed by Bathsheba a Kushite/Shemite convert. The same as Abraham who was called a Hebrew (Gen 14:13) married to a Shemite (Sarah) an Egyptian (Hagar), a Shemite/Kushite (Keturah) and a daughter of Japheth (Mashek).

Shelomith, the daughter of Dibri, of the tribe of Dan:)

12 And they put him in ward,[1] that the mind of YHWH might be showed them.

13 And YHWH spoke to Mosheh (Musa), saying,

14 Bring forth him that has cursed outside the camp; and let all that heard him lay their hands upon his head, and let all the congregation stone him.

15 And You shall speak to the children of Israel, saying, Whosoever curses his Elohim shall bear his sin.

16 And he that blasphemes the name of YHWH, he shall surely be put to death, and all the congregation shall certainly stone him: as well the foreigner,[2] as he that is born in the land, when he blasphemes the name of YHWH, shall be put to death.

17 And he that killed any man shall surely be put to death.

18 And he that kills an animal shall make it good; animal for animal.

19 And if a man cause a blemish in his neighbour; as he has done, so shall it be done to him;

20 Breach for breach, eye for eye, tooth for tooth: as he has caused a blemish in a man, so shall it be done to him again.[3]

21 And he that killed a beast, he shall restore it: and he that killed a man, he shall be put to death.

22 You shall have one manner of Torah,[4] as well for the foreigner, as for one of your own country: for I am YHWH Your POWER.

23 And Mosheh (Musa) spoke to the children of Israel, that they should bring forth him that had cursed outside the camp, and stone him with stones. And the children of Israel did as YHWH commanded Mosheh (Musa).
Torah Parsha 32 Bahar Lev, Wayikra 25:1-26:2
Haftarah: Yirmeyahu 32:6-32:27

Chapter 25
1 And YHWH spoke to Mosheh (Musa) in Mount Sinai, saying,

2 Speak to the children of Israel, and say to them, When you come into the land which I give you, then shall the land keep a Sabbath to YHWH.

3 Six years You shall sow your field, and six years You shall prune your vineyard, and gather in the fruit there;

4 But in the seventh year shall be a Sabbath of rest to the land, a Sabbath for YHWH.[5] You shall neither sow your field, nor prune your vineyard.

5 That which grows of its own

Footnotes
[1] In the old days prisoners were only held for a few days before being judged. Tax payer money was not wasted to feed them for twenty or thirty year terms.
[2] This person who is referenced as the foreigner here is the son of the Y'sraeli woman and whose father was a gentile, a distinction is drawn of who is classified chosen. This alludes to Yahudith and the Danite.
[3] This was not about knocking people's teeth out or removing someone's eyes but fair and substantial punishment was given to match the severity of the crime.
[4] Only one Torah for all. We do not operate in double standards like the world.
[5] Year of shemita. No fallowing of the ground.

accord of your harvest You shall not reap, neither gather the grapes of your vine undressed: for it is a year of rest to the land.

6 And the Sabbath of the land shall be food for you; and for your servant, and for your maid, and for your hired servant, and for your foreigner that sojourned with you,

7 And for your cattle, and for the beast that are in your land, shall all the **Increase** there be food.

8 And You shall number seven Sabbaths of years to you, seven times seven years; and the space of the seven Sabbaths of years[1] shall be to you forty and nine years.

9 Then shall You cause the shofarim of the Yahubel[2] (shofar of the Jubilees) to sound on the tenth day of the seventh month, in Yom ha Kippurim (Day of Atonements) shall you make the shofar sound throughout all your land.

10 And you shall hallow the fiftieth year, and proclaim liberty throughout all the land to all the inhabitants there: it shall be a Yahubel to you; and you shall return every man to his possession,[3] and you shall return every man to his Mishpakha (family).[4]

11 A Yahubel (Jubilee) shall that fiftieth year be to you: you shall not sow, neither reap that which grows of itself in it, nor gather the grapes in it of your vine undressed.

12 For it is the Yahubel (Jubilee); it shall be Holy to you: you shall eat the **Increase** there out of the field.

13 In the year of this Yahubel (Jubilee) you shall return every man to his possession.

14 And if You sell anything to your neighbour, or buy anything of your neighbour's hand, you shall not oppress one another:

15 According to the number of years after the Yahubel (Jubilee) You shall buy of your neighbour, and according to the number of years of the fruits he shall sell to you:

16 According to the multitude of years You shall **Increase** the price there, and according to the fewness of years You shall diminish the price of it: for according to the number of the years of the fruits will he sell to you.

17 You shall not therefore oppress one another; but You shall fear Your POWER: for I am YHWH Your POWER.

Footnotes

[1] Forty nine years to the jubilee cycle.

[2] Year of Jubilee.

[3] All the people and property must be redeemed in the year of Jubilee. Servants must be released to go free.

[4] The ancient word Deror, the word for liberty used in the context of a Jubilee year means all of the following: the ancient Dalet is the marker for a mouth so his voice, his Continued in next section

commandments represent Torah obedience for his disciples.
Modern dalet is the symbol for The door, which is the Torah.
The staff belongs to the future Messiah (Ezekiel 37:19)
The Rosh or head is also of the Messiah (Isaiah 28:16), the tried precious stone. The Wah reveals him as a man and the ancient picture of the feather floating reveals with the Hebrew Resh means appointed by our Father when he comes for us.

18 Wherefore you shall do my statutes, and keep my judgments, and do them; and you shall dwell in the land in safety.

19 And the land shall yield her fruit, and you shall eat your fill, and dwell therein in safety.

20 And if you shall say, What shall we eat the seventh year? Behold, we shall not sow, nor gather in our **Increase**:

21 Then I will command my **Increase** upon you in the sixth year, and it shall bring forth fruit for three years.

22 And you shall sow the eighth year, and eat yet of old fruit until the ninth year; until her fruits come in you shall eat of the old store.

23 The land shall not be sold forever: for the land is mine;[1] for you are strangers and sojourners with me.

24 And in all the land of your possession you shall grant rescue for the land.

25 If your brother be waxen poor, and has sold away some of his possession, and if any of his kin come to redeem it, then shall he redeem that which his brother sold.

26 And if the man have none to redeem it, and himself be able to redeem it;

27 Then let him count the years of the sale there, and restore the remainder to the man to whom he sold it; that he may return to his possession.

28 But if he be not able to restore it to him, then that which is sold shall remain in the hand of him that has bought it until the year of Yahubel (Jubilee) and in the Yahubel (Jubilee) it shall go out, and he shall return to his possession.

29 And if a man sell his Beyth (house) in a walled city, then he may redeem it within a whole year after it is sold; within a full year may he redeem it.

30 And if it be not redeemed within the space of a full year, then the Beyth (house) that is in the walled city shall be established forever to him that bought it throughout his generations: it shall not go out in the Yahubel (Jubilee).

31 But the Batiym (houses) of the villages which have no wall round about them shall be counted as the fields of the country: they may be redeemed, and they shall go out in the Yahubel (Jubilee).

32 Notwithstanding the cities of the Lewim, and the Batiym (houses) of the cities of their possession, may the Lewim redeem at any time.

33 And if a man purchase from the Lewim, then the Beyth (house) that was sold, and the city of his possession, shall go out in the year of Yahubel (Jubilee) for the Batiym (houses) of the cities of the Lewim are their possession among the children of Israel.

34 But the field of the suburbs of their cities may not be sold; for it

---

Footnotes

[1] Israel's land was not to be sold to any foreigner. Pieces of land could be sold to Israelites but during the Jubilee year it had to be returned to the original owner. The main land-owner is YHWH who gave the land to Israel.

is their everlasting possession.

35 And if your brother be waxen poor, and fallen in decay with you; then You shall relieve him: yes, though he be a foreigner, or a sojourner; that he may live with you.

36 You take no usury from him, or **Increase**: but fear Your POWER; that your brother may live with you.

37 You shall not give him your money upon usury, nor lend him your victuals for **Increase**.

38 I am YHWH Your POWER, which brought you forth out of the land of Mitzrayim (Egypt), to give you the land of Kanan, and to be Your POWER.

39 And if your brother that dwells by you be waxen poor, and be sold to you; You shall not compel him to serve as a bondservant:

40 But as a hired servant, and as a sojourner, he shall be with you, and shall serve you to the year of Yahubel (Jubilee).

41 And then shall he depart from you, both he and his children with him, and shall return to his own Mishpakha (family), and to the possession of his ahvot (fathers) shall he return.

42 For they are my servants, which I brought forth out of the land of Mitzrayim (Egypt): they shall not be sold as bondmen.

43 You shall not rule over him with rigour; but shall fear Your POWER.

44 Both your bondmen, and your bondmaids, which You shall have, shall be of the heathen that are round about you; of them shall you buy bondmen and bondmaids.

45 Moreover of the children of the strangers that do sojourn among you, of them shall you buy, and of their families that are with you, which they begat in your land: and they shall be your possession.

46 And you shall take them as an inheritance for your children after you, to inherit them for a possession; they shall be your bondmen forever: but over your brethren the children of Israel, you shall not rule one over another with rigour.

47 And if a sojourner or foreigner wax rich by you, and your brother that lives by him wax poor, and sell himself to the foreigner or sojourner by you, or to the stock of the foreigner's Mishpakha (family):

48 After that he is sold he may be redeemed again; one of his brethren may redeem him:

49 Either his uncle, or his uncle's son, may redeem him, or any that is nigh of kin to him of his Mishpakha (family) may redeem him; or if he be able, he may redeem himself.

50 And he shall reckon with him that bought him from the year that he was sold to him to the year of Yahubel (Jubilee) and the price of his sale shall be according to the number of years, according to the time of a hired servant shall it be with him.

51 If there be yet many years behind, according to them he shall give again the price of his rescue out of the money that he was bought for.

52 And if there remain but few

years to the year of Yahubel (Jubilee), then he shall count with him, and according to his years shall he give him again the price of his rescue.

53 And as a yearly hired servant shall he be with him: and the other shall not rule with rigour over him in your sight.

54 And if he be not redeemed in these years, then he shall go out in the year of Yahubel (Jubilee), both he, and his children with him.

55 For to me the children of Israel are servants; they are my servants whom I brought forth out of the land of Mitzrayim (Egypt): I am YHWH Your POWER.

Chapter 26

1 You shall make no idols nor graven image, neither raise up a pillar, neither shall you set up any altar of stone in your land, to bow down to it: for I am YHWH Your POWER.

2 You shall keep my Sabbaths, and reverence my sanctuary: I am YHWH.

Torah Parsha 33 Bechukotai, Wayikra 26:3-27:34
Haftarah: Yirmeyahu 16:9-17:14

3 If you walk in my statutes, and keep my commandments, and do them;

4 Then I will give you rain in due season, and the land shall yield her **Increase**, and the trees of the field shall yield their fruit.

5 And your threshing season shall extend for you until the grape crop, and the grape crop shall extend to the sowing time:

and you shall eat your Lakhem (bread) to the full, and dwell in your land safely.

6 And I will give shalom in the land, and you shall lie down, and none shall make you afraid: and I will rid evil beasts out of the land, neither shall the sword go through your land.

7 And you shall chase your enemies, and they shall fall before you by the sword.[1]

8 And five of you shall chase a hundred, and a hundred of you shall put ten Thousand to flight: and your enemies shall fall before you by the sword.[2]

9 For I will have respect to you, and make you fruitful, and multiply you, and establish my Covenant with you.[3]

10 And you shall eat old store, and bring forth the old because of the new.

11 And I will set my Tent among you: and my soul shall not abhor you.

Footnotes

[1] This will only happen when you obey Torah but for disobedient people they will be chased out by their enemies.

[2] When we are obedient to YHWH's Torah we will prevail against any enemy but if we are disobedient like the Christians, then our enemies will come and destroy our houses and take away our children. This is a clear sign of rebelliousness in our people. The Original Black Hebrews had their children removed but in history and antiquity are known as fierce fighters.

[3] The only way the African races were fruitful because they always adopted polygamy, which was an Israelite custom in which each family had many children. The chiefs in the clans always had at least two wives placed in the North/South axis a custom still followed in West Africa by metal workers. Many Africans today are wicked running in Christian lawlessness and will be punished and also lived an unfulfilled life.

12 And I will be continually in your midst[1] and will be Your POWER, and you shall be my people.

13 I am YHWH Your POWER, which brought you forth out of the land of Mitzrayim (Egypt), that you should not be their bondmen; and I have broken the bands of your yoke, and elevated your positions.[2]

14 But if you will not hearken[3] to me, and will not do all these commandments;

15 And if you shall despise my statutes,[4] or if your soul abhor my judgments, so that you will not do all my commandments, but that you break my Covenant:

16 I also will do this to you; I will even appoint terror over you,[5]

Footnotes

[1] Only if we keep His halachot (commandments of Torah).

[2] Only free men can have elevated positions and so Israel was now fully free.

[3] If they do not listen, they will be outcasts. To listen is to obey the Torah.

[4] Many even today despise the Torah as a Hebrew thing, and still refuse to do the commandments written in the Torah. Such as the eternal loving annual feasts YHWH gave us, so that our children will learn the truth and not go astray.

[5] This prophecy applies in two ways. First the terror is to send them into Islamic nations who will continually oppress them or overtake their lands. If we take a critical look at both the Christians and black Hebrew people including those Caucasians who became converts to Judaism, both have been oppressed, the most by Islamic nations first but later by Europeans especially the black and Yahudim.

The terror that was appointed was that the followers of Allah were going to bring destruction upon the cities that the scattered tribes had inhabited. Just look at Pakistan, Darfur in Sudan, North and South Nigeria, Libya, Arabia, Northern Ethiopia. Terror is all Continued in next section

wasting disease,[6] and fever,

over it and these places have a sizeable Yahudim bloodline and a Northern Israelite community. Christians there are continually oppressed, because they are still not obedient to the Torah. Also look at India.

The bombing campaigns conducted from 2005 to 2009, were all done by Muslim radicals who brought sheer terror in India. Again, India has sizeable original Yahudim communities and many from the scattered tribes are still living there. The cause and effect scenario takes us back to nothing more than the judgment YHWH appointed, for Torah disobedience. In the latter times before the judgment would be over and times of restoration come the black Hebrews from whom many races descended were to go into slavery which we know happened in the 16th century CE.

The slavery was started by both the Muslims, and Christians who made money out of it and Europeans, who then continuously punished and harassed the original black Hebrew people to the present day. Today Africa the original continent of the Bible people one of the richest continents is being looted by the Europeans and Muslims for their Oil, Gold and diamonds wealth not to mention other mineral wealth being stolen by means of so called Trade agreements. Until Africans return to their Torah path they will continue to be harassed and put down so the only way to come out is by Torah obedience. The same is true of the Blacks in America where they are not allowed to rise to the top but kept low by racism that does not permit them to rise above the rest. The curses are over but the blacks have still not got back to the obedience to the Torah though they are now learning about it. The time has come for the emancipation of the minds of the Black Hebrews.

[6] One of our modern wasting diseases is Diabetes Mellitus. Do you ever wonder why there is such a high rate of this? This is one such disease appointed to afflict people who are Torah disobedient and it runs in families. Try tracing the history of the family and see who has this disease. You will find that Torah disobedience runs in that families history too, and I guarantee somewhere along the line, they will have Israelite blood.

which shall consume the eyes,[1] and cause sorrow of heart: and you shall sow your seed in vain, for your enemies shall eat it.[2]

17 And I will set my face against you, and you shall be slain before your enemies: they that hate you shall reign over you; and you shall flee when none pursues you.[3]

18 And if you will not yet for all this hearken to me, then I will punish you seven times more for your sins.[4]

19 And I will break the pride of your power;[5] and I will make your shamayim as iron,[6] and your earth as bronze:[7]

20 And your strength shall be spent in vain: for your land shall not yield her **Increase**, neither shall the trees of the land yield their fruits.

21 And if you walk contrary to me, and will not hearken to me; I will bring seven times more plagues upon you according to your sins.

Footnotes

[1] This disease as the Torah says causes issues to the eyes by destroying your eyesight. Just think it over; if our eyes are not willing to read and obey the Torah, the law of YHWH then what good are those eyes? YHWH's one judgment alone is enough to send us all railing to the floor. So much for our modern medicine.

[2] So true that our enemies are eating our seed, one grows and another eats. All the Hebrew people were thrown out of Muslim lands and those that remained were oppressed continually. Christians that own portions of land in Muslim nations are at times, forcefully ousted and occupied by Muslims. Christian families with sons and daughters have them at times, taken away and forcefully raped. The religion that was appointed for terror was Islam and YHWH is seeing if his people will turn away from sin and be obedient to his Torah. For the minute they start to behave as he wants them to, he will offer his full protection or else they will remain in this on/off state of anguish of heart.

[3] Your position will not be exalted but lowly unlike Daniel and Yosef even in exile they got exalted positions because of their Torah obedience.

[4] The House of Israel's sins were multiplied seven times while Yahudah repented after the Babylonian captivity. The sins of Efrayim were finished in 1996 in our time.

[5] Reflected by the Sanctuary or Temple and the last time it was the Islamic Caliph Omar
Continued in next section

who came in 637CE and occupied the land of Israel and took over the Temple Mount and it has been under their control since then.

[6] Symbol of oppression

[7] Symbol of Judgment by the Islamic nations (Bronze is the color of Islam), they will convert your children over to Islam and there is nothing you can do about it since you are disobedient and unless you return (teshuvah: repent) to obedience none of your prayers will be heard. Not obeying Torah has serious implications for the whole family of YHWH. In Dani'el 2:32 'This image's head was of fine gold, its chest and arms of silver, its belly and thighs of bronze.'

Belly and thighs of bronze-> This was the Grecian Empire which was later occupied by the Muslims all the way from Turkey to Pakistan. This was clear prophecy that the Muslims will invade and take over due to the lack of obedience of Israelites. They were primarily dispersed in the East and that is where Islam is centered and huge in number.

Area of Tifereth (Glory) Yesod (reproduction) and Malchut (Kingdom) covered by the Islamic hoards. Now they are multiplying and glorifying Allah while the Israelites were crying in exile. Its legs of Iron. Again Muslim nations in the east and southern Russian hemisphere match the description of Yesod and Malchut.

These two areas here show us how they are trying to replace the true sefirah of YHWH with their own version of Yesod (reproduction) and Malchut (Kingdom). Very few have eyes to see this.

22 I will also send wild beasts among you, which shall rob you of your children,[1] and destroy your cattle,[2] and make you few in number;[3] and your high ways shall be desolate.

23 And if you will not be reformed by me by these things, but will walk contrary to me;

24 Then will I also walk contrary to you,[4] and will punish you yet seven times for your sins.[5]

25 And I will bring a sword[6] upon you,[7] that shall avenge the vengeance of my Covenant: and when you are gathered together within your cities, I will send the pestilence among you; and you shall be given into the hand of the enemy.

26 And when I have broken the staff of your Lakhem (bread), ten women[8] shall bake your Lakhem (bread) in one oven, and they shall give you your Lakhem (bread) again by weight: and you shall eat, and not be satisfied.

27 And if you will not for all this hearken to me, but walk contrary to me;

28 Then I will walk contrary to you also in fury; and I, even I, will chastise you seven times for your sins.

29 And you shall eat the flesh of your sons, and the flesh of your daughters shall you eat.[9]

30 And I will destroy your high places, and cut down your images, and cast your carcasses upon the carcasses of your idols, and my soul shall abhor you.[10]

31 And I will make your cities waste, and bring your sanctuaries to desolation, and I will not smell the savour of your sweet odours.

32 And I will bring the land into desolation: and your enemies which dwell therein shall be astonished at it.

33 And I will scatter you among the heathen,[11] and will draw out a sword[12] after you: and your land

Footnotes

[1] Drash allegoric for spiritual demonic forces that will be unleashed and since you would have no protection from YHWH they can do whatever they like to turn your children away from you. This is common place amongst many believers since they are not Torah obedient.

[2] These are not just literal wild beasts, they are symbols of people. The Islamic nations are doing this today.

[3] Look at Islamic countries. The believers are few in numbers while the Muslims multiply and make life unbearable for many around them.

[4] It says clearly to the blind in heart that YHWH will not listen to your prayers when you disobey Him and His commandments.

[5] From the Assyrian exile onto present day when the exile was finally finished. The time was up in 1996.

[6] Trouble and warfare.

[7] You will have wars.

[8] Sign of the Ten tribes being removed with judgment hence the usage of the oven for heat and the symbol of refining.

[9] The enemy will besiege and this is literal. Sadly, this happened to Israel and it will happen to all those engrafted into the Covenants who do not obey.

[10] Israelites ended up in shamanism, witchcraft and all sorts of idolatry thinking that this will take them out of persecution and judgment but this did not help.

[11] Indeed this is YHWH's recurrent warning to Israel. Yet Israel did not heed it, so first came the dispersal of the Ten Northern Tribes to Assyria and then came the dispersal of the two Southern tribes to Iraq. The term heathen though applied at one time to the Assyrians and Babylonians, is now firmly affixed to the Muslim nations.

[12] The sword is a symbol of both 'war' and persecution for Israel. Although Judah repented and about 25% of them returned

Continued in next section

shall be desolate,[1] and your cities waste.

34 Then shall the land enjoy her Sabbaths, as long as it lies desolate, and you be in your enemies land; even then shall the land rest, and enjoy her Sabbaths.

35 As long as it lies desolate it shall rest; because it did not rest in your Sabbaths, when you dwelt upon it.

36 And upon them that are left alive of you I will send faintness into their hearts in the lands of their enemies; and the sound of a shaken leaf shall chase them; and they shall flee, as fleeing from a sword; and they shall fall when none pursues.[2]

37 And they shall fall one upon another, as it were before a sword, when none pursues and you shall have no power to stand before your enemies.

38 And you shall perish among the heathen, and the land of your enemies shall eat you up.[3]

39 And they that are left of you shall pine away in their iniquity in your enemies' lands; and also in the iniquities of their ahvot (fathers) shall they pine away with them.

40 And[4] They shall confess the name[5] with their iniquity, and the iniquity of their ahvot (fathers),[6] with their trespass which they trespassed against me, and that also they have walked contrary to me;

41 And that I also have walked contrary to them, and have brought them into the land of their enemies; then their uncircumcised hearts will be humbled, and they will accept the punishment of their iniquity:[7]

42 And I will remember my Covenant with Yakov, and also my Covenant with Ytshak, and also my Covenant with Abraham I will remember; and I will remember the land.[8]

43 The land also shall be left of them, and shall enjoy her Sabbaths, while she lies desolate outside them: and they shall accept the punishment of their iniquity: because, even because

---

to Israel after the Babylonian exile, the ten Northern tribes did not repent, and remained in exile until our time, 1996.

[1] History confirms that YHWH did indeed leave Israel desolate for many centuries, while Hebrew Israel wandered like gypsies from country to country and the Northern tribes assimilated into the nations and lost their identity.

[2] Always fearful of your enemies roundabout

[3] Many believers have zero value and are treated like 2nd and 3rd class citizens in the enemy's lands and they do not even know they belong to Israel. This has happened to the Black Hebrew people all over the world the true Hebrews and to Asians from the same stock. Whenever they live the natives rise against them and put them down with no real opposition since they live under the Continued in next section

Torah curses of not obeying the Torah. The only way to stand up is to obey Torah.

[4] One day Israel will repent, there is no IF in this and the next verse.

[5] The Hebrew word 'yada' relates to making confession in the name of YHWH for the one who transgressed the Torah.

[6] When we confess our sins we also need to confess our father's sins that we may be forgiven to lead a healthy life.

[7] The sign for true restoration is to repent and accept the yoke of shamayim, which is Torah.

[8] Repentance is our obligation daily not a weekly Sabbath thing.

they despised my judgments, and because their soul abhorred my statutes.

44 And yet for all that, when they are in the land of their enemies, I will not cast them away, neither will I reject them, to destroy them utterly, and to break my Covenant with them: for I am YHWH their Elohim.[1]

45 And I will for their sakes remember the Covenant of their ancestors, whom I brought forth out of the land of Mitzrayim (Egypt) in the sight of the heathen, that I might be their Elohim: I am YHWH.[2]

46 These are the statutes and judgments and Torot (instructions), which YHWH made between him and the children of Israel in Mount Sinai by the hand of Mosheh (Musa).[3]

Chapter 27

1 And YHWH spoke to Mosheh (Musa), saying,

2 Speak to the children of Israel, and say to them, When a man shall make a singular vow, the persons shall be for YHWH by your estimation.

3 And your estimation shall be of the male from twenty years old even to sixty years old, even your estimation shall be fifty shekels of silver, after the shekel of the sanctuary.

4 And if it be a female, then your

Footnotes
[1] Elohim will never annul His Covenant so we have a real choice to make to go back to our ancient paths of Torah.
[2] Black Hebrews.
[3] Mosheh (Musa) was a black man of North Africa by our modern Classification, the ancient land of Israel would be classified in Africa and not called Middle-East back then.

estimation shall be thirty shekels.

5 And if it be from five years old even to twenty years old, then your estimation shall be of the male twenty shekels, and for the female ten shekels.

6 And if it be from a month old even to five years old, then your estimation shall be of the male five shekels of silver, and for the female your estimation shall be three shekels of silver.

7 And if it be from sixty years old and above; if it be a male, then your estimation shall be fifteen shekels, and for the female ten shekels.

8 But if he be poorer than your estimation, then he shall present himself before the kohen (priest), and the kohen (priest) shall value him; according to his ability that vowed shall the kohen (priest) value him.

9 And if it be an animal, whereof men bring an offering to YHWH all that any man gives of such to YHWH shall be Holy.

10 He shall not alter it, nor change it, a good for a bad, or a bad for a good: and if he shall at all change beast for beast, then it and the exchange there shall be Holy.

11 And if it be any unclean animal, of which they do not offer a sacrifice to YHWH, then he shall present the animal before the kohen (priest):

12 And the kohen (priest) shall value it, whether it be good or bad: as You value it, who are the kohen (priest), so shall it be.

13 But if he will at all redeem it, then he shall add a fifth part there to your estimation.

14 And when a man shall Holy his Beyth (house) to be Holy to YHWH, then the kohen (priest) shall estimate it, whether it be good or bad: as the kohen (priest) shall estimate it, so shall it stand.

15 And if he that set it apart will redeem his Beyth (house), then he shall add the fifth part of the money of your estimation to it, and it shall be his.

16 And if a man shall sanctify to YHWH some part of a field of his possession, then your estimation shall be according to the seed there: an homer of barley seed shall be valued at fifty shekels of silver.

17 If he sanctifies his field from the year of Yahubel (Jubilee), according to your estimation it shall stand.

18 But if he sanctify his field after the Yahubel (Jubilees), then the kohen (priest) shall reckon to him the money according to the years that remain, even to the year of the Yahubel (Jubilees), and it shall be abated from your estimation.

19 And if he that Consecrate the field will in any wise redeem it, then he shall add the fifth part of the money of your estimation to it, and it shall be assured to him.

20 And if he will not redeem the field, or if he have sold the field to another man, it shall not be redeemed any more.

21 But the field, when it goes out in the Yahubel (Jubilees), shall be Holy to YHWH, as a field devoted; the possession there shall be the kohen's (priest).

22 And if a man sanctify to YHWH a field which he has bought, which is not of the fields of his possession;

23 Then the kohen (priest) shall reckon to him the worth of your estimation, even to the year of the Yahubel (Jubilees) and he shall give your estimation in that day, as a Holy thing to YHWH.

24 In the year of the Yahubel (Jubilees) the field shall return to him of whom it was bought, even to him to whom the possession of the land did belong.

25 And all your estimations shall be according to the shekel of the sanctuary: twenty gerahs shall be the shekel.

26 Only the Bekhor (firstborn) of the animals, which should be YHWH's Bekhor (firstborn), no man shall set it apart; whether it be ox, or sheep: it is YHWH's.

27 And if it be of an unclean animal, then he shall redeem it according to your estimation, and shall add a fifth part of it thereto: or if it be not redeemed, then it shall be sold according to your estimation.

28 Notwithstanding no devoted thing, that a man shall devote to YHWH of all that he has, both of man and animal, and of the field of his possession, shall be sold or redeemed: every devoted thing is most Holy to YHWH.

29 None devoted, which shall be devoted of men, shall be redeemed; but shall surely be put to death.

30 And all the tithe of the land, whether of the seed of the land, or of the fruit of the etz (tree), is YHWH's: it is Holy to YHWH.

31 And if a man will at all

redeem any of his tithes, he shall add thereto the fifth part there.

32 And concerning the tithe of the herd, or of the flock, even of whatsoever passed under the rod, the tenth[1] shall be Holy to YHWH.

33 He shall not search whether it be good or bad, neither shall he change it: and if he change it at all, then both it and the change there shall be Holy; it shall not be redeemed.

34 These are the commandments, which YHWH commanded Mosheh (Musa) for the children of Israel in Mount Sinai. ת

Footnotes

[1] A tenth of your income of whatever is set tithe of YHWH and today it should only go to Torah based Levite teachers who are teaching Torah. The love offering (Teruma) can be given to any Torah teacher.

The Fourth Book of Mosheh
(Musa)

We'Davar (Numbers)[1]

וידבר

And He gave words

**Torah Parsha 34 WeDavar,
WeDavar 1:1-4:20**
Haftarah: Hoshea 1:10-2:20

Chapter 1

1 And YHWH spoke to Mosheh (Musa) in the wilderness of Sinai, in the Tent of the appointed times, on the first day of the second month, in the second year after they came out of the country of Mitzrayim (Egypt), saying,

2 Take the censes of all the congregation of the children of Israel, after their mishpachotim (families), by the Beyth (house) of their abtim (forefathers), with the number of their names, every male by their polls;

3 From twenty years old[2] and upward, all that are able to go forth to war in Israel: You and Aharon shall count them by their

armies.[3]

4 And with you there shall be a man of every tribe; everyone head of the Beyth (house) of his ahvot (fathers).

5 And these are the names of the men that shall stand with you: of the tribe of Reuven; Elizur the son of Shedeur.

6 Of Shimeon; Shelumi'el the son of Zurishaddai.

7 Of Yahudah; Nakhson the son of Amminadab.

8 Of Yskhar (Issachar); Nethan'el the son of Zuar.

9 Of Zevulun; Eliab the son of Helon.

10 Of the children of Yosef: of Efrayim; Elishama the son of Ammihud: of Manasheh; Gamali'el the son of Pedahzur.

11 Of Binyamin; Abidan the son of Gideoni.

12 Of Dan; Ahiezer the son of Ammishaddai.

13 Of Asher; Pagi'el the son of Ocran.

14 Of Gawd; Eliasaph the son of Deu'el.

15 Of Naphtali; Ahira the son of Enan.

16 These were the renowned of the congregation, princes of the tribes of their ahvot (fathers), heads of thousands in Israel.

17 And Mosheh (Musa) and Aharon took these men which are expressed by their names:

18 And they assembled all the congregation together on the first day of the second month,[4] and they declared their pedigrees

Footnotes
[1] The title of this book is "And He gave words", and not "Numbers". This title Numbers came from the Catholic Church and is one of the names of the destroyer Satan as Arithmoi in the Greek.
[2] Although the Hebrew people do the Bar Mitzvah of a boy who is thirteen to make him a 'son of the commandment' but in YHWH's sight a male is accountable not at thirteen, but at twenty years of age. Anything below twenty is not counted as accountable directly because then the parents are responsible and accountable as heads of the household.

Footnotes
[3] You will never find an example of a thirteen year old going to war in the Tanak.
[4] Iyar

after their Mishpakhot (families), by the Beyth (house) of their ahvot (fathers), according to the number of the names, from twenty years old and upward, by their censes.

19 As YHWH commanded Mosheh (Musa), so he registered them in the wilderness of Sinai.

20 And the children of Reuven, Israel's eldest son, by their generations, after their Mishpakhot (families), by the Beyth (house) of their ahvot (fathers), according to the number of the names, by their censes, every male from twenty years old and upward, all that were able to go forth to war;

21 Those that were registered of them, even of the tribe of Reuven, were forty six thousand and five hundred.

22 Of the children of Shimeon, by their generations, after their Mishpakhot (families), by the Beyth (house) of their ahvot (fathers), those that were registered of them, according to the number of the names, by their censes, every male from twenty years old and upward, all that were able to go forth to war;

23 Those that were registered of them, even of the tribe of Shimeon, were fifty nine thousand and three hundred men.

24 Of the children of Gawd, by their generations, after their Mishpakhot (families), by the Beyth (house) of their ahvot (fathers), according to the number of the names, from twenty years old and upward, all that were able to go forth to war;

25 Those that were registered of them, even of the tribe of Gawd, were forty five thousand six hundred and fifty.

26 Of the children of Yahudah, by their generations, after their Mishpakhot (families), by the Beyth (house) of their ahvot (fathers), according to the number of the names, from twenty years old and upward, all that were able to go forth to war;

27 Those that were registered of them, even of the tribe of Yahudah, were seventy four thousand and six hundred.

28 Of the children of Yskhar (Issachar), by their generations, after their Mishpakhot (families), by the Beyth (house) of their ahvot (fathers), according to the number of the names, from twenty years old and upward, all that were able to go forth to war;

29 Those that were registered of them, even of the tribe of Yskhar (Issachar), were fifty four thousand and four hundred.

30 Of the children of Zevulun, by their generations, after their Mishpakhot (families), by the Beyth (house) of their ahvot (fathers), according to the number of the names, from twenty years old and upward, all that were able to go forth to war;

31 Those that were registered of them, even of the tribe of Zevulun, were fifty seven thousand and four hundred.

32 Of the children of Yosef, namely, of the children of Efrayim, by their generations, after their Mishpakhot (families), by the Beyth (house) of their ahvot (fathers), according to the number of the names, from twenty years old and upward, all that were able to go forth to war;

33 Those that were registered of them, even of the tribe of Efrayim, were forty thousand and five hundred.

34 Of the children of Manasheh, by their generations, after their Mishpakhot (families), by the Beyth (house) of their ahvot (fathers), according to the number of the names, from twenty years old and upward, all that were able to go forth to war;

35 Those that were registered of them, even of the tribe of Manasheh, were thirty two thousand and two hundred.

36 Of the children of Binyamin, by their generations, after their Mishpakhot (families), by the Beyth (house) of their ahvot (fathers), according to the number of the names, from twenty years old and upward, all that were able to go forth to war;

37 Those that were registered of them, even of the tribe of Binyamin, were thirty five thousand and four hundred.

38 Of the children of Dan, by their generations, after their Mishpakhot (families), by the Beyth (house) of their ahvot (fathers), according to the number of the names, from twenty years old and upward, all that were able to go forth to war;

39 Those that were registered of them, even of the tribe of Dan, were sixty two thousand and seven hundred.

40 Of the children of Asher, by their generations, after their Mishpakhot (families), by the Beyth (house) of their ahvot (fathers), according to the number of the names, from twenty years old and upward, all that were able to go forth to war;

41 Those that were registered of them, even of the tribe of Asher, were forty one thousand and five hundred.

42 Of the children of Naphtali, throughout their generations, after their Mishpakhot (families), by the Beyth (house) of their ahvot (fathers), according to the number of the names, from twenty years old and upward, all that were able to go forth to war;

43 Those that were registered of them, even of the tribe of Naphtali, were fifty three thousand and four hundred.

44 These are those that were registered, which Mosheh (Musa) and Aharon registered, and the princes of Israel, being twelve men: each one was for the Beyth (house) of his ahvot (fathers).

45 So were all those that were registered of the children of Israel, by the Beyth (house) of their ahvot (fathers), from twenty years old and upward, all that were able to go forth to war in Israel;

46 Even all they that were registered were six hundred thousand and three thousand and five hundred and fifty.[1]

Footnotes

[1] From WeDabar (Numbers) 3:40-43 and here we can see we have 22,273 first born sons in Israel to show us this was a Patriarchal culture with one man having several wives. This allows us to compute quite easily that in order to have this many sons, we must have the same number of families which is 22,273 families. So if we Continued in next section

330

47 But the Lewim after the tribe of their ahvot (fathers) were not registered among them.

48 For YHWH had spoken to Mosheh (Musa), saying,

49 Only You shall not number the tribe of Levi, neither take the sum of them among the children of Israel:

50 But You shall appoint the Lewim over the Tent of testimony, and over all the vessels there, and over all things that belong to it: they shall bear the Tent, and all the vessels there; and they shall minister to it, and shall encamp round about the Tent.

51 And when the Tent moves forward, the Lewim shall take it down: and when the Tent is to be pitched, the Lewim shall set it up: and the foreigner that comes near it shall be put to death.

52 And the children of Israel shall pitch their tents, every man by his own camp, and every man by his own banner, throughout their hosts.

53 But the Lewim shall pitch round about the Tent of testimony, that there be no wrath upon the congregation of the children of Israel: and the Lewim

take 633,550 men and divide by the 22, 273 individual families we arrive at a figure of 28 rounded down. This means that each Israelite family would have 28 sons on average. Now we are not taking any daughters into the equation because if we do, then we need to take an equal amount of daughters so 28 plus 28 would be 56 children per family. Please see the article on Patriarchal Marriages: for more: http://www.forever-israel.com/BM/Biblical-Marriages.html

shall keep the charge of the Tent of testimony.

54 And the children of Israel did according to all that YHWH commanded Mosheh (Musa), so did they.

Chapter 2

1 And YHWH spoke to Mosheh (Musa) and to Aharon, saying,

2 Each man of the children of Israel shall pitch by his own banner, with the ensign of their ahvot (fathers) Beyth (house): far off about the Tent of the appointed times shall they pitch.

3 And on the east side toward the rising of the sun shall they of the banner of the camp of Yahudah pitch throughout their armies: and Nakhson the son of Amminadab shall be captain of the children of Yahudah.

4 And his host, and those that were registered of them, were seventy four thousand and six hundred.

5 And those that do pitch next to him shall be the tribe of Yskhar (Issachar): and Nethan'el the son of Zuar shall be captain of the children of Yskhar (Issachar).

6 And his host, and those that were registered there, were fifty four thousand and four hundred.

7 Then the tribe of Zevulun: and Eliab the son of Helon shall be captain of the children of Zevulun.

8 And his host, and those that were registered there, were fifty seven thousand and four hundred.

9 All that were registered in the camp of Yahudah were one hundred and eighty six thousand and four hundred, throughout their armies. These shall depart first.

10 On the south side shall be the standard of the camp of Reuven according to their armies: and the captain of the children of Reuven shall be Elizur the son of Shedeur.

11 And his host, and those that were registered there, were forty six thousand and five hundred.

12 And those which pitch by him shall be the tribe of Shimeon: and the captain of the children of Shimeon shall be Shelumi'el the son of Zurishaddai.

13 And his host, and those that were registered of them, were fifty and nine thousand and three hundred.

14 Then the tribe of Gawd: and the captain of the sons of Gawd shall be Eliasaph the son of Reuel.

15 And his host, and those that were registered of them, were forty five thousand and six hundred and fifty.

16 All that were registered in the camp of Reuven were a hundred thousand and fifty and one thousand and four hundred and fifty, throughout their armies. And they shall go forth in the second rank.

17 Then the Tent of the appointed times shall set forward with the camp of the Lewim in the midst of the camp: as they encamp, so shall they go forward, every man in his place by their standards.

18 On the west side shall be the standard of the camp of Efrayim according to their armies: and the captain of the sons of Efrayim

shall be Elishama the son of Ammihud.

19 And his host, and those that were registered of them, were forty thousand and five hundred.

20 And by him shall be the tribe of Manasheh: and the captain of the children of Manasheh shall be Gamali'el the son of Pedahzur.

21 And his host, and those that were registered of them, were thirty and two thousand and two hundred.

22 Then the tribe of Binyamin and the captain of the sons of Binyamin shall be Abidan the son of Gideoni.

23 And his host, and those that were registered of them, were thirty and five thousand and four hundred.

24 All that were registered of the camp of Efrayim were a hundred thousand and eight thousand and a hundred, throughout their armies. And they shall go forward in the third rank.

25 The banner of the camp of Dan shall be on the north side by their armies: and the captain of the children of Dan shall be Ahiezer the son of Ammishaddai.

26 And his host, and those that were registered of them, were sixty-two thousand and seven hundred.

27 And those that encamp by him shall be the tribe of Asher: and the captain of the children of Asher shall be Pagi'el the son of Ocran.

28 And his host, and those that were registered of them, were forty and one thousand and five hundred.

29 Then the tribe of Naphtali:

and the captain of the children of Naphtali shall be Ahira the son of Enan.

30 And his host, and those that were registered of them, were fifty and three thousand and four hundred.

31 All they that were registered in the camp of Dan were a hundred thousand and fifty seven thousand and six hundred. They shall travel last with their standards.

32 These are those which were registered of the children of Israel by the Beyth (house) of their ahvot (fathers): all those that were registered of the camps throughout their hosts were six hundred thousand and three thousand and five hundred and fifty.

33 But the Lewim were not registered among the children of Israel; as YHWH commanded Mosheh (Musa).

34 And the children of Israel did according to all that YHWH commanded Mosheh (Musa): so they pitched by their banners, and so they set forward, everyone after their Mishpakhot (families), according to the Beyth (house) of their ahvot (fathers).[1]

Chapter 3

1 These also are the generations of Aharon and Mosheh (Musa) in the day that YHWH spoke with Mosheh (Musa) in Mount Sinai.

2 And these are the names of the sons of Aharon; Nadav the Bekhor (firstborn), and Avihu, El'ezar, and Ithamar.

3 These are the names of the sons of Aharon, the kohenim which were anointed, whom he consecrated to minister in the kohen's (priest) office.

4 And Nadav and Avihu died before YHWH, when they offered strange fire[2] before YHWH, in the wilderness of Sinai, and they had no children: and El'ezar and Ithamar ministered in the kohen's (priest) office in the sight of Aharon their father.

5 And YHWH spoke to Mosheh (Musa), saying,

6 Bring the tribe of Levi near, and present them before Aharon the kohen (priest), that they may minister to him.

7 And they shall keep his charge, and the charge of the whole congregation before the Tent of the appointed times, to do the service of the Tent.

8 And they shall keep all the instruments of the Tent of the appointed times, and the charge of the children of Israel, to do the service of the Tent.

9 And You shall give the Lewim to Aharon and to his sons: they are wholly given to him out of the children of Israel.

10 And You shall appoint Aharon and his sons, and they shall wait on their kohen's (priest) office: and the foreigner that comes near shall be put to death.

11 And YHWH spoke to Mosheh (Musa), saying,

Footnotes

[1] To see the actual positioning of the 12 tribes around the camp, go to the map section at the back of the Torah.

Footnotes

[2] See Vayikra (Leviticus) Chapter 10:1

12 And I, behold, I have taken the Lewim from among the children of Israel instead of all the Bekhor (firstborn) that opens the womb among the children of Israel: therefore the Lewim shall be mine;

13 Because all the Bekhor (firstborn) are mine; for on the day that I killed all the Bekhor (firstborn)[1] in the land of Mitzrayim (Egypt) I Holy to me all the Bekhor (firstborn) in Israel, both man and animal: mine shall they be: I am YHWH.

14 And YHWH spoke to Mosheh (Musa) in the wilderness of Sinai, saying,

15 Number the children of Levi after the Beyth (house) of their ahvot (fathers), by their Mishpakhot (families): every male from a month old and upward shall You number them.

16 And Mosheh (Musa) registered them according to the word of YHWH, as he was commanded.

17 And these were the sons of Levi by their names; Gershon, and Kohath, and Merari.

18 And these are the names of the sons of Gershon by their Mishpakhot (families); Livni, and Shimei.

19 And the sons of Kohath by their Mishpakhot (families); Amram, and Yshari, Khevron, and Uzziel.

20 And the sons of Merari[2] by their Mishpakhot (families); Makhli, and Mushi. These are the Mishpakhot (families) of the Lewim according to the Beyth (house) of their ahvot (fathers).

21 Of Gershon was the Mishpakha (family) of the Libni, and the Mishpakha (family) of the Shimi: these are the Mishpakhot (families) of the Gershoni.

22 Those that were registered of them, according to the number of all the males, from a month old and upward, even those that were registered of them were seven thousand and five hundred.

23 The Mishpakhot (families) of the Gershoni shall pitch behind the Tent westward.

24 And the chief of the Beyth (house) of the Mishpakha (family) of the Gershoni shall be Eliasaph the son of La'el.

25 And the charge of the sons of Gershon in the Tent of the appointed times shall be the Tent, and the tent, the covering there, and the hanging for the door of the Tent of the appointed times,

26 And the hangings of the court, and the curtain for the door of the court, which is by the Tent, and by the altar round about, and the cords of it for all the service there.

27 And of Kohath was the

Footnotes
[1] YHWH killed the firstborn in Egypt because the rulers claimed the firstborn had Holy properties, they worshiped them. So, YHWH showed who really is Holy and who is not by demonstration.

Footnotes
[2] Many Levites ended up in Afghanistan and also in India and Pakistan. The pukht Pathans in Pakistan are from the tribes. Some people of the tribes came from Iran to India and from there to Pakistan, even to China.

Mishpakha (family) of the Amrami, and the Mishpakha (family) of the Izehari, and the Mishpakha (family) of the Khebroni, and the Mishpakha (family) of the Uzzi'elites: these are the Mishpakhot (families) of the Kohathi.

28 In the number of all the males, from a month old and upward, were eight thousand and six hundred, keeping the charge of the sanctuary.

29 The Mishpakhot (families) of the sons of Kohath shall pitch on the side of the Tent southward.

30 And the chief of the Beyth (house) of the father of the Mishpakhot (families) of the Kohathi shall be Elizaphan the son of Uzziel.

31 And their charge shall be the ark, and the table, and the candlestick, and the altars, and the vessels of the sanctuary wherewith they minister, and the hanging, and all the service there.

32 And El'ezar the son of Aharon the kohen (priest) shall be chief over the chief of the Lewim, and have the oversight of them that keep the charge of the sanctuary.

33 Of Merari was the Mishpakha (family) of the Makhli, and the Mishpakha (family) of the Mushi: these are the Mishpakhot (families) of Merari.

34 And those that were registered of them, according to the number of all the males, from a month old and upward, were six thousand and two hundred.

35 And the chief of the Beyth (house) of the father of the

Mishpakhot (families) of Merari was Zuri'el the son of Abihail: these shall pitch on the side of the Tent northward.

36 And under the custody and charge of the sons of Merari shall be the boards of the Tent, and the bars there, and the pillars there, and the sockets there, and all the vessels there, and all that served thereto,

37 And the pillars of the court round about, and their sockets, and their pins, and their cords.

38 But those that encamp before the Tent toward the east, even before the Tent of the appointed times eastward,[1] shall be Mosheh (Musa), and Aharon and his sons, keeping the charge of the sanctuary for the charge of the children of Israel; and the foreigner that comes near shall be put to death.

[2]

39 All that were registered of the Lewim, which Mosheh (Musa) and Aharon registered at the commandment of YHWH, throughout their Mishpakhot

Footnotes
[1] Many sons of Aharon are still eastward in Burma, India and Pakistan.
[2] The jots simply show Jacob's family of Levi about to be multiplied.

The count here given is 22,000 which excluded the priests which numbered 300. Also note that these were 22,273 families which totalled 633,550 people (WeDabar Numbers 1:46) coming out of Egypt. When we divide the figure we get an average of 28 sons in one family in Patriarchal marriages, not counting the daughters which would on average also number 28. This shows us that YHWH was about to multiply the seed of Israel, to many billions so they cannot be counted.

(families), all the males from a month old and upward, were twenty two thousand.

40 And YHWH said to Mosheh (Musa), Number all the Bekhor (firstborn) of the males of the children of Israel from a month old and upward, and take the number of their names.

41 And You shall take the Lewim for me (I am YHWH) instead of all the Bekhor (firstborn) among the children of Israel; and the cattle of the Lewim instead of all the Bekhor (firstborn) among the cattle of the children of Israel.

42 And Mosheh (Musa) registered, as YHWH commanded him, all the Bekhor (firstborn) among the children of Israel.

43 And all the Bekhor (firstborn) males by the number of names, from a month old and upward, of those that were registered of them, were twenty and two thousand two hundred and threescore and thirteen.

44 And YHWH spoke to Mosheh (Musa), saying,

45 Take the Lewim instead of all the Bekhor (firstborn) among the children of Israel and the cattle of the Lewim instead of their cattle; and the Lewim shall be mine: I am YHWH.

46 And for those that are to be redeemed of the two hundred and seventy three of the Bekhor (firstborn) of the children of Israel, which are more than the Lewim;

47 You shall even take five shekels apiece by the censes, after the shekel of the sanctuary shall You take them: (the shekel is twenty gerahs):

48 And You shall give the money, wherewith the odd number of them is to be redeemed, to Aharon and to his sons.

49 And Mosheh (Musa) took the rescue money of them that were over and above them that were redeemed by the Lewim:

50 Of the Bekhor (firstborn) of the children of Israel he took the money; a thousand three hundred and sixty five shekels, after the shekel of the sanctuary:

51 And Mosheh (Musa) gave the money of them that were redeemed to Aharon and to his sons, according to the word of YHWH, as YHWH commanded Mosheh (Musa).

Chapter 4

1 And YHWH spoke to Mosheh (Musa) and to Aharon, saying,

2 Take the sum of the sons of Kohath from among the sons of Levi, after their Mishpakhot (families), by the Beyth (house) of their ahvot (fathers),

3 From thirty[1] years old and upward even until fifty years old, all that enters into the host, to do the work in the Tent of the appointed times.

4 This shall be the service of the sons of Kohath in the Tent of the appointed times, about the most Holy things:

5 And when the camp moves forward, Aharon shall come, and his sons, and they shall take down the covering veil, and cover the ark of testimony with it:

Footnotes
[1] The priestly service started at thirty years of age.

6 And shall put thereon the covering of blue leather,[1] and shall spread over it a cloth wholly of blue, and shall put in the staves there.

7 And upon the table of Lakhem panayim (bread of the faces) they shall spread a cloth of blue, and put thereon the dishes, and the spoons, and the bowls, and covers to cover withal: and the continual Lakhem (bread) shall be thereon:

8 And they shall spread upon them a cloth of scarlet, and cover the same with a covering of blue leather,[2] and shall put in the staves there.

9 And they shall take a cloth of blue, and cover the menorah of the light, and the lamps, and its tongs, and his fire pan, and all the oil vessels there, wherewith they minister to it:

10 And they shall put it and all the vessels there within a covering of blue leather, and shall put it upon a bar.

11 And upon the golden altar they shall spread a cloth of blue, and cover it with a covering of blue leather, and shall put to the staves there:

12 And they shall take all the instruments of ministry, wherewith they minister in the sanctuary, and put them in a cloth of blue, and cover them with a covering of blue leather, and

Footnotes

[1] Septuagint

[2] In most Bibles it says Badger skins but this is incorrect because the badger is an unclean animal. The skins that were used were from a kosher animal such as an antelope and the skin was then dyed.

shall put them on a bar:

13 And they shall take away the ashes from the altar, and spread a purple cloth thereon:

14 And they shall put upon it all the vessels there, wherewith they minister about it, even the censers, the flesh hooks, and the shovels, and the basins, all the vessels of the altar; and they shall spread upon it a covering of blue leather, and put to the staves of it.

15 And when Aharon and his sons have made an end of covering the sanctuary, and all the vessels of the sanctuary, as the camp is to move forward; after that, the sons of Kohath shall come to bear it: but they shall not touch any Holy thing, lest they die. These things are the burden of the sons of Kohath in the Tent of the appointed times.

16 And to the office of El'ezar the son of Aharon the kohen (priest) is the oil for the light, and the sweet incense, and the daily grain offering, and the anointing oil, and the oversight of all the Tent, and of all that therein is, in the sanctuary, and in the vessels there.

17 And YHWH spoke to Mosheh (Musa) and to Aharon, saying,

18 Do not cut off the tribe of the Mishpakhot (families) of the Kohathi from among the Lewim:

19 But thus do to them, that they may live, and not die, when they approach to the most Holy things: Aharon and his sons shall go in, and appoint them everyone to his service and to his duty:

20 But they shall not go in to

see when the Holy things are covered, lest they die.

**Torah Parsha 35 Naso,
WeDavar 4:21-7:89**
Haftarah: Shoftim 13:2-25

21 And YHWH spoke to Mosheh (Musa), saying,

22 Take also the sum of the sons of Gershon, throughout the Batiym (houses) of their ahvot (fathers), by their Mishpakhot (families);

23 From thirty years old and upward until fifty years old shall You number them; all that enter into perform the service, to do the work in the Tent of the appointed times.

24 This is the service of the Mishpakhot (families) of the Gershoni, to minister, and to carry:

25 And they shall carry the curtains of the Tent, and the Tent of the appointed times, his covering, and the covering of the blue leather that is above upon it, and the hanging for the door of the Tent of the appointed times,

26 And the hangings of the court, and the hanging for the door of the gate of the court, which is by the Tent and by the altar round about, and their cords, and all the instruments of their service, and all that is made for them: so shall they serve.

27 At the appointment of Aharon and his sons shall be all the service of the sons of the Gershoni, in all their burdens, and in all their service: and you shall appoint to them in charge all their burdens.

28 This is the service of the Mishpakhot (families) of the sons of Gershon in the Tent of the appointed times: and their charge shall be under the hand of Ithamar the son of Aharon the kohen (priest).

29 As for the sons of Merari, You shall number them after their Mishpakhot (families), by the Beyth (house) of their ahvot (fathers);

30 From thirty years[1] old and upward even to fifty years old shall You number them, everyone that enters into the service, to do the work of the Tent of the appointed times.

31 And this is the charge of their burden, according to all their service in the Tent of the appointed times; the boards of the Tent, and the bars there, and the pillars there, and sockets there,

32 And the pillars of the court round about, and their sockets, and their pins, and their cords, with all their instruments, and with all their service: and by name you shall reckon the instruments of the charge of their burden.

33 This is the service of the Mishpakhot (families) of the sons of Merari, according to all their service, in the Tent of the appointed times, under the hand of Ithamar the son of Aharon the

Footnotes

[1] The duty of a Tent or Temple priest started at age thirty and finished at fifty years of age so the priests would not wear out. 'They only served from one Sabbath to another annually, plus the three annual feasts that they were commanded to attend.' See 2 Chronicles 23:8.

kohen (priest).

34 And Mosheh (Musa) and Aharon and the chief of the congregation registered the sons of the Kohathi after their Mishpakhot (families), and after the Beyth (house) of their ahvot (fathers),

35 From thirty years old and upward even to fifty years old, everyone that enters into the service, for the work in the Tent of the appointed times:

36 And those that were registered of them by their Mishpakhot (families) were two thousand seven hundred and fifty.

37 These were they that were registered of the Mishpakhot (families) of the Kohathi, all that might do service in the Tent of the appointed times, which Mosheh (Musa) and Aharon did number according to the commandment of YHWH by the hand of Mosheh (Musa).

38 And those that were registered of the sons of Gershon, throughout their Mishpakhot (families), and by the Beyth (house) of their ahvot (fathers),

39 From thirty years old and upward even to fifty years old, everyone that enters into the service, for the work in the Tent of the appointed times,

40 Even those that were registered of them, throughout their Mishpakhot (families), by the Beyth (house) of their ahvot (fathers), were two thousand and six hundred and thirty.

41 These are they that were registered of the Mishpakhot (families) of the sons of Gershon, of all that might do service in the Tent of the appointed times, whom Mosheh (Musa) and Aharon did number according to the commandment of YHWH.

42 And those that were registered of the Mishpakhot (families) of the sons of Merari, throughout their Mishpakhot (families), by the Beyth (house) of their ahvot (fathers),

43 From thirty years old and upward even to fifty years old, everyone that enters into the service, for the work in the Tent of the appointed times,

44 Even those that were registered of them after their Mishpakhot (families), were three Thousand and two hundred.

45 These be those that were registered of the Mishpakhot (families) of the sons of Merari, whom Mosheh (Musa) and Aharon registered according to the word of YHWH by the hand of Mosheh (Musa).

46 All those that were registered of the Lewim, whom Mosheh (Musa) and Aharon and the chief of Israel registered, after their Mishpakhot (families), and after the Beyth (house) of their ahvot (fathers),

47 From thirty years old and upward even to fifty years old, everyone that came to do the service of the ministry, and the service of the burden in the Tent of the appointed times,

48 Even those that were registered of them, were eight thousand and five hundred and eighty.

49 According to the

commandment of YHWH they were registered by the hand of Mosheh (Musa), everyone according to his service, and according to his burden: thus were they registered of him, as YHWH commanded Mosheh (Musa).

Chapter 5

1 And YHWH spoke to Mosheh (Musa), saying,

2 Command the children of Israel, that they put outside of the camp every leper, and everyone that has a discharge, and whosoever is defiled by the dead:

3 Both male and female shall you put out, outside the camp shall you put them; that they defile not their camps, in the midst whereof I dwell.

4 And the children of Israel did so, and put them outside the camp: as YHWH spoke to Mosheh (Musa), so did the children of Israel.

5 And YHWH spoke to Mosheh (Musa), saying,

6 Speak to the children of Israel when a man or woman shall commit any sin that men commit, to do a trespass against YHWH, and that person be guilty;

7 Then they shall confess in the name their sin which they have done: and he shall recompense his trespass with the principal there, and add to it the fifth part there,[1] and give it to him against whom he has trespassed.

8 But if the man have no kinsman to recompense the trespass to, let the trespass be recompensed to YHWH, even to the kohen (priest);[2] beside the ram of the atonement, whereby an atonement shall be made for him.

9 And every offering of all the Holy things of the children of Israel, which they bring to the kohen (priest), shall be his.

10 And every man's Holy things shall be his: whatsoever any man gives the kohen (priest), it shall be his.

11 And YHWH spoke to Mosheh (Musa), saying,

12 Speak to the children of Israel, and say to them, If any man's wife go aside, and commit a trespass against him,

13 And a man has intercourse with her,[3] and it be secret from the eyes of her husband, and be kept close, and she be defiled, and there be no witness against her, neither was she caught;

14 And the ruakh (spirit) of jealousy come upon him, and he be jealous of his wife, and she be defiled: or if the ruakh (spirit) of jealousy come upon him, and he be jealous of his wife, and she be not defiled:

15 Then shall the man bring his wife to the kohen (priest), and he

Footnotes

[1] So if you defrauded someone you will return the principle sum plus 20%, or say if you owed somebody $100 then you had not paid, you would therefore repent, and pay $120 back and make restitution.

[2] Today this would mean paying the sum to a Torah teacher who is a Levite, not to anyone else. This is the payment to YHWH as there is no Temple. If another Torah teacher you are permitted to give Teruma (gift offering) but not Ma'aseh (Tithe).

[3] She had committed adultery secretly, the sin of our society today.

shall bring her offering for her, the tenth part of an ephah of barley meal; he shall pour no oil upon it, nor put frankincense thereon; for it is an offering of jealousy, an offering of memorial, bringing iniquity to remembrance.

16 And the kohen (priest) shall bring her near, and set her before YHWH:

17 And the kohen (priest) shall take Holy mayim in an earthen vessel; and of the dust[1] that is in the floor of the Tent the kohen (priest) shall take, and put it into the mayim:

18 And the kohen (priest) shall set the woman before YHWH, and uncover/loosen the woman's hair,[2] and put the offering of

memorial in her hands, which is the jealousy offering: and the kohen (priest) shall have in his hand the bitter mayim that causes the curse:

19 And the kohen (priest) shall charge her by an oath, and say to the woman, if no man has slept with you, and if You have not gone aside to uncleanness with another instead of your husband, be You free from this bitter mayim that causes the curse.[3]

20 But if you have gone aside to another instead of your husband, and if You be defiled, and some man had intercourse with you beside your husband:

21 Then the kohen (priest) shall charge the woman with an oath of cursing, and the kohen (priest) shall say to the woman, YHWH make you a curse and a cursing among your people, when YHWH will make your thigh to rot, and your belly to swell;

22 And this mayim that causes the curse shall go into your bowels, to make your belly to swell, and your thigh to rot: And the woman shall say, Amen, Amen.

23 And the kohen (priest) shall write these curses in a scroll, and he shall blot them out with the bitter mayim:

24 And he shall cause the woman to drink the bitter mayim that causes the curse: and the mayim that causes the curse

Footnotes

[1] Targum of Jonathan would suggest, the end of all flesh is to go back to the dust and so to put her in mind of her origins and her end; and in like manner the earthen vessel would suggest also being broken and returning to dust. This trial is called a Sotah.

Satan the vile serpent who is to eat dust all the days of his life is significant of the dust so she knows who she was being deceived by. A short term affair might seem very nice but the end results are terrible and the trauma long lasting for the guilt felt after this affair is hard to bear. The trial was executed on Lilith the first woman who was condemned to be a Serpent in the Garden hence to eat the dust all the days of the serpent's life. See (Gen 1:27; 3:1 and 3:14). The swelling of the belly is a supernatural pregnancy of her adultery that kills her if she is guilty. Azazel was the demon born to Lilith which was her judgment and which will in the end remove her evil seed from this planet. She has been since that time trying to destroy Adam's righteous seed.

[2] Married Women's head-coverings were done in order that others may know they are married, it was not a commandment but custom. In Pakistan and India and many other Eastern nations it is also a common
Continued in next section

practice. Please note it is not a commandment.

[3] The curse is real and painful even today if the woman is put under the oath of YHWH. The repercussions are awful.

shall enter into her, and become bitter.

25 Then the kohen (priest) shall take the grain offering of jealousy out of the woman's hand, and shall wave the offering before YHWH, and offer it upon the altar:

26 And the kohen (priest) shall take a handful of the offering, even the memorial there, and burn it upon the altar, and afterward shall cause the woman to drink the mayim.

27 And when he has made her to drink the mayim, then it shall come to pass, that, if she be defiled, and have done trespass against her husband, that the mayim that causes the curse shall enter into her, and become bitter, and her belly shall swell, and her thigh shall rot: and the woman shall be a curse among her people.

28 And if the woman be not defiled, but be clean; then she shall be free, and shall conceive children.

29 This is the Torah of jealousies, when a wife goes aside to another instead of her husband, and is defiled;

30 Or when the ruakh (spirit) of jealousy comes upon him, and he be jealous over his wife, and shall set the woman before YHWH, and the kohen (priest) shall execute upon her all this Torah.

31 Then shall the man be guiltless from iniquity, and this woman shall bear her iniquity.

Chapter 6

1 And YHWH spoke to Mosheh (Musa), saying,

2 Speak to the children of Israel, and say to them, When either man or woman shall separate themselves to vow a vow of a Nazarite, to separate themselves to YHWH:

3 He shall separate himself from wine and strong drink, and shall drink no vinegar of wine, or vinegar of strong drink, neither shall he drink any liquor of grapes,[1] nor eat moist grapes, or dried.

4 All the days of his separation shall he eat nothing that is made of the vine etz (tree), from the kernels even to the husk.

5 All the days of the vow of his separation there shall no razor come upon his head: until the days be fulfilled, in which he separates himself to YHWH, he shall be Holy, and shall let the locks[2] of the hair of his head grow.[3]

6 All the days that he separates himself to YHWH he shall come at no dead body.

7 He shall not make himself unclean for his father, or for his mother, for his brother, or for his sister, when they die: because the consecration of his Elohim is upon his head.

8 All the days of his separation he is Holy to YHWH.

9 And if any man die very suddenly by him, and he has defiled the head of his consecration; then he shall shave

Footnotes
[1] Wine made of grapes, Israel is allowed to drink alcohol.
[2] The locks were like African people because these were dark skinned people.
[3] See footnote Leviticus 19:27

his head in the day of his cleansing, on the seventh day shall he shave it.

10 And on the eighth day he shall bring two turtledoves, or two young pigeons, to the kohen (priest), to the door of the Tent of the appointed times:

11 And the kohen (priest) shall offer the one for a sin offering, and the other for a burnt offering, and make atonement for him, for that he transgressed by the dead, and shall Holy his head that same day.

12 And he shall consecrate to YHWH the days of his separation, and shall bring a lamb of the first year for a trespass offering: but the days that were before shall be lost, because his separation was defiled.

13 And this is the Torah of the Nazarite,[1] when the days of his separation are fulfilled: he shall be brought to the door of the Tent of the appointed times:

14 And he shall offer his offering to YHWH, one male lamb of the first year without blemish for a burnt offering, and one ewe lamb of the first year without blemish for a sin offering, and one ram without blemish for shalom offerings,

15 And a basket of matzah (unleavened), rotis of fine flour mingled with oil, and thin rotis of matzah (unleavened) anointed with oil, and their grain offering, and their drink offerings.

16 And the kohen (priest) shall bring them before YHWH, and shall offer his sin offering, and his burnt offering:

17 And he shall offer the ram for a sacrifice of shalom offerings to YHWH, with the basket of matzah (unleavened bread): the kohen (priest) shall offer also his grain offering, and his drink offering.

18 And the Nazarite shall shave the head of his separation at the door of the Tent of the appointed times, and shall take the hair of the head of his separation, and put it in the fire which is under the sacrifice of the shalom offerings.

19 And the kohen (priest) shall take the cooked shoulder of the ram, and one matzah (unleavened) roti out of the basket, and one matzah thin roti, and shall put them upon the hands of the Nazarite, after the hair of his separation is shaven:

20 And the kohen (priest) shall wave them for a wave offering before YHWH: this is Holy for the kohen (priest), with the wave breast and the contribution shoulder offering: and after that the Nazarite may drink wine.

21 This is the Torah of the Nazarite who has vowed, and of his offering to YHWH for his separation, beside that, that his hand shall get: according to the vow which he vowed, so he must do after the Torah of his separation.

22 And YHWH spoke to Mosheh (Musa), saying,

23 Speak to Aharon and to his sons, saying, this way you shall

Footnotes

[1] This vow required an animal sacrifice in the Temple and he did the sacrifice. Even those that claimed Torah is done away were put to the test, Ma'aseh Schlichim (Acts) 18:18; 21:23-24.

say the **Blessing** on the children of Israel, saying to them,

24 YHWH **Bless** you, and Guard you:

25 YHWH make his face to shine upon you,[1] and be merciful to you:

26 YHWH lift up his countenance upon you, and give you shalom.

27 And they shall put my name[2] upon the children of Israel; and I will **Bless** them.

Chapter 7

1 And it came to pass on the day that Mosheh (Musa) had fully set up the Tent, and had anointed it, and set-them apart, and all the instruments there, both the altar and all the vessels there, and had anointed them, and set them apart;

2 That the princes of Israel, heads of the Beyth (house) of their ahvot (fathers), who were the princes of the tribes, and were over them that were registered, offered:

3 And they brought their offering before YHWH, six covered wagons, and twelve oxen; a wagon for two of the princes, and for each one an ox: and they brought them before the Tent.

4 And YHWH spoke to Mosheh (Musa), saying,

5 Take it from them, that they do the service of the Tent of the appointed times; and You shall give them to the Lewim, to every man according to his service.

6 And Mosheh (Musa) took the wagons and the oxen, and gave them to the Lewim.

7 Two wagons and four oxen he gave to the sons of Gershon, according to their service:

8 And four wagons and eight oxen he gave to the sons of Merari, according to their service, under the hand of Ithamar the son of Aharon the kohen (priest).

9 But to the sons of Kohath he gave none: because the service of the sanctuary belonging to them was that they should bear upon their shoulders.

10 And the princes offered for dedicating of the altar in the day that it was anointed, even the princes offered their offering before the altar.

11 And YHWH said to Mosheh (Musa), They shall offer their offering, each prince on his[3] day, for the dedicating of the altar.

12 And he that offered his offering the first day was Nakhson the son of Amminadab, of the tribe of Yahudah:

13 And his offering was one silver charger, the weight was a hundred and thirty shekels, one silver bowl of seventy shekels, after the shekel of the sanctuary; both of them were full of fine flour mingled with oil for a grain offering:

14 One spoon of ten shekels of

Footnotes

[1] The idea that the sun rises from the East and sets in the West so YHWH's Torah will shine from the East to the West and his Blessings will come from the East to the West.

[2] We must use the kadosh name of YHWH when praying for increases upon believers. Many confused believers are not doing this today.

[3] The presentation was spread over twelve days one for each tribe.

gold, full of incense:

15 One young bullock, one ram, one lamb of the first year, for a burnt offering:

16 One kid of the goats for a sin offering:

17 And for a sacrifice of shalom offerings, two oxen, five rams, five he goats, five lambs of the first year: this was the offering of Nakhson the son of Amminadab.

18 On the second day Nethan'el the son of Zuar, prince of Yskhar (Issachar), did offer:

19 He offered for his offering one silver charger, the weight was a hundred and thirty shekels, one silver bowl of seventy shekels, after the shekel of the sanctuary; both of them full of fine flour mingled with oil for a grain offering:

20 One spoon of gold of ten shekels, full of incense:

21 One young bullock, one ram, one lamb of the first year, for a burnt offering:

22 One kid of the goats for a sin offering:

23 And for a sacrifice of shalom offerings, two oxen, five rams, five he goats, five lambs of the first year: this was the offering of Nethan'el the son of Zuar.

24 On the third day Eliab the son of Helon, prince of the children of Zevulun, did offer:

25 His offering was one silver charger, the weight was a hundred and thirty shekels, one silver bowl of seventy shekels, after the shekel of the sanctuary; both of them full of fine flour mingled with oil for a grain offering:

26 One golden spoon of ten

shekels, full of incense:

27 One young bullock, one ram, one lamb of the first year, for a burnt offering:

28 One kid of the goats for a sin offering:

29 And for a sacrifice of shalom offerings, two oxen, five rams, five he goats, five lambs of the first year: this was the offering of Eliab the son of Helon.

30 On the fourth day Elizur the son of Shedeur, prince of the children of Reuven, did offer:

31 His offering was one silver charger of the weight of a hundred and thirty shekels, one silver bowl of seventy shekels, after the shekel of the sanctuary; both of them full of fine flour mingled with oil for a grain offering:

32 One golden spoon of ten shekels, full of incense:

33 One young bullock, one ram, one lamb of the first year, for a burnt offering:

34 One kid of the goats for a sin offering:

35 And for a sacrifice of shalom offerings, two oxen, five rams, five he goats, five lambs of the first year: this was the offering of Elizur the son of Shedeur.

36 On the fifth day Shelumi'el the son of Zurishaddai, prince of the children of Shimeon, did offer:

37 His offering was one silver charger, the weight was a hundred and thirty shekels, one silver bowl of seventy shekels, after the shekel of the sanctuary; both of them full of fine flour mingled with oil for a grain offering:

38 One golden spoon of ten

shekels, full of incense:

39 One young bullock, one ram, one lamb of the first year, for a burnt offering:

40 One kid of the goats for a sin offering:

41 And for a sacrifice of shalom offerings, two oxen, five rams, five he goats, five lambs of the first year: this was the offering of Shelumi'el the son of Zurishaddai.

42 On the sixth day Eliasaph the son of Deu'el, prince of the children of Gawd, offered:

43 His offering was one silver charger of the weight of a hundred and thirty shekels, a silver bowl of seventy shekels, after the shekel of the sanctuary; both of them full of fine flour mingled with oil for a grain offering:

44 One golden spoon of ten shekels, full of incense:

45 One young bullock, one ram, one lamb of the first year, for a burnt offering:

46 One kid of the goats for a sin offering:

47 And for a sacrifice of shalom offerings, two oxen, five rams, five he goats, five lambs of the first year: this was the offering of Eliasaph the son of Deu'el.

48 On the seventh day Elishama the son of Ammihud, prince of the children of Efrayim, offered:

49 His offering was one silver charger, the weight was a hundred and thirty shekels, one silver bowl of seventy shekels, after the shekel of the sanctuary; both of them full of fine flour mingled with oil for a grain

offering:

50 One golden spoon of ten shekels, full of incense:

51 One young bullock, one ram, one lamb of the first year, for a burnt offering:

52 One kid of the goats for a sin offering:

53 And for a sacrifice of shalom offerings, two oxen, five rams, five he goats, five lambs of the first year: this was the offering of Elishama the son of Ammihud.

54 On the eighth day offered Gamali'el the son of Pedahzur, prince of the children of Manasheh:

55 His offering was one silver charger of the weight of a hundred and thirty shekels, one silver bowl of seventy shekels, after the shekel of the sanctuary; both of them full of fine flour mingled with oil for a grain offering:

56 One golden spoon of ten shekels, full of incense:

57 One young bullock, one ram, one lamb of the first year, for a burnt offering:

58 One kid of the goats for a sin offering:

59 And for a sacrifice of shalom offerings, two oxen, five rams, five he goats, five lambs of the first year: this was the offering of Gamali'el the son of Pedahzur.

60 On the ninth day Abidan the son of Gideoni, prince of the children of Binyamin, offered:

61 His offering was one silver charger, the weight was a hundred and thirty shekels, one silver bowl of seventy shekels, after the shekel of the sanctuary; both of them full of fine flour mingled with oil for a grain offering:

62 One golden spoon of ten shekels, full of incense:

63 One young bullock, one ram, one lamb of the first year, for a burnt offering:

64 One kid of the goats for a sin offering:

65 And for a sacrifice of shalom offerings, two oxen, five rams, five he goats, five lambs of the first year: this was the offering of Abidan the son of Gideoni.

66 On the tenth day Ahiezer the son of Ammishaddai, prince of the children of Dan, offered:

67 His offering was one silver charger, the weight was a hundred and thirty shekels, one silver bowl of seventy shekels, after the shekel of the sanctuary; both of them full of fine flour mingled with oil for a grain offering:

68 One golden spoon of ten shekels, full of incense:

69 One young bullock, one ram, one lamb of the first year, for a burnt offering:

70 One kid of the goats for a sin offering:

71 And for a sacrifice of shalom offerings, two oxen, five rams, five he goats, five lambs of the first year: this was the offering of Ahiezer the son of Ammishaddai.

72 On the eleventh day Pagi'el the son of Ocran, prince of the children of Asher, offered:

73 His offering was one silver charger, the weight was a hundred and thirty shekels, one silver bowl of seventy shekels, after the shekel of the sanctuary; both of them full of fine flour

mingled with oil for a grain offering:

74 One golden spoon of ten shekels, full of incense:

75 One young bullock, one ram, one lamb of the first year, for a burnt offering:

76 One kid of the goats for a sin offering:

77 And for a sacrifice of shalom offerings, two oxen, five rams, five he goats, five lambs of the first year: this was the offering of Pagi'el the son of Ocran.

78 On the twelfth day Ahira the son of Enan, prince of the children of Naphtali, offered:

79 His offering was one silver charger, the weight was a hundred and thirty shekels, one silver bowl of seventy shekels, after the shekel of the sanctuary; both of them full of fine flour mingled with oil for a grain offering:

80 One golden spoon of ten shekels, full of incense:

81 One young bullock, one ram, one lamb of the first year, for a burnt offering:

82 One kid of the goats for a sin offering:

83 And for a sacrifice of shalom offerings, two oxen, five rams, five he goats, five lambs of the first year: this was the offering of Ahira the son of Enan.

84 This was the dedication of the altar, in the day when it was anointed, by the princes of Israel: twelve chargers of silver, twelve silver bowls, twelve spoons of gold:

85 Each charger of silver weighing a hundred and thirty shekels, each bowl seventy: all the silver vessels weighed two thousand and four hundred shekels, after the shekel of the sanctuary:

86 The golden spoons were twelve, full of incense, weighing ten shekels a piece, after the shekel of the sanctuary: all the gold of the spoons was a hundred and twenty shekels.

87 All the oxen for the burnt offering were twelve bullocks, the rams twelve, the lambs of the first year twelve, with their grain offering: and the kids of the goats for sin offering twelve.

88 And all the oxen for the sacrifice of the shalom offerings were twenty and four bullocks, the rams sixty, the he goats sixty, the lambs of the first year sixty. This was the dedication of the altar, after that it was anointed.

89 And when Mosheh (Musa) was gone into the Tent of the appointed times to speak with him, then he heard the voice of one speaking to him from off the lid of atonement that was upon the ark of testimony, from between the two Khruvim's: and he spoke to him.

Torah Parsha 36 Behaalotecha, WeDavar 8:1-12:16 Haftarah: Zechariyah 2:10-4:7

Chapter 8

1 And YHWH spoke to Mosheh (Musa), saying,

2 Speak to Aharon, and say to him, When You light the lamps, the seven lamps shall give light over against the menorah.

3 And Aharon did so; he lighted the lamps there over against the candlestick, as YHWH commanded Mosheh (Musa).

4 And this work of the menorah was of beaten gold, to the shaft there, to the flowers there, was beaten work: according to the pattern which YHWH had showed Mosheh (Musa), so he made the menorah.

5 And YHWH spoke to Mosheh (Musa), saying,

6 Take the Lewim from among the children of Israel, and cleanse them.

7 And this You shall do to them, to cleanse them: Sprinkle mayim of purifying upon them, and let them shave all their flesh, and let them wash their clothes, and so make themselves clean.

8 Then let them take a young bullock with his grain offering, even fine flour mingled with oil, and another young bullock shall You take for a sin offering.

9 And You shall bring the Lewim before the Tent of the appointed times: and You shall gather the whole assembly of the children of Israel together:

10 And You shall bring the Lewim before YHWH and the children of Israel shall put their hands upon the Lewim:

11 And Aharon shall offer the Lewim before YHWH for an offering of the children of Israel, that they may execute the service of YHWH.

12 And the Lewim shall lay their hands upon the heads of the bullocks: and You shall offer the one for a sin offering, and the other for a burnt offering, to YHWH, to make an atonement for the Lewim.

13 And You shall set the Lewim before Aharon, and before his sons, and offer them for an offering to YHWH.

14 Thus shall You separate the Lewim from among the children of Israel: and the Lewim shall be mine.

15 And after that shall the Lewim go in to do the service of the Tent of the appointed times: and You shall cleanse them, and offer them for an offering.

16 For they are wholly given to me from among the children of Israel; instead of such as open every womb, even instead of the Bekhor (firstborn) of all the children of Israel, have I taken them to me.

17 For all the Bekhor (firstborn) of the children of Israel are mine, both man and beast: on the day that I smote every Bekhor (firstborn) in the land of Mitzrayim (Egypt) I set them apart for myself.

18 And I have taken the Lewim for all the Bekhor (firstborn) of the children of Israel.

19 And I have given the Lewim as a grain to Aharon and to his sons from among the children of Israel, to do the service of the children of Israel in the Tent of the appointed times, and to make an atonement for the children of Israel: that there be no plague among the children of Israel, when the children of Israel come near to the sanctuary.

20 And Mosheh (Musa), and Aharon, and all the congregation of the children of Israel, did to the Lewim according to all that YHWH commanded Mosheh (Musa) concerning the Lewim, so did the children of Israel to them.

21 And the Lewim were purified, and they washed their clothes; and Aharon offered them as an offering before YHWH; and Aharon made atonement for them to cleanse them.

22 And after that went the Lewim in to do their service in the Tent of the appointed times before Aharon, and before his sons: as YHWH had commanded Mosheh (Musa) concerning the Lewim, so did they to them.

23 And YHWH spoke to Mosheh (Musa), saying,

24 This is it that belonged to the Lewim: from twenty and five years old and upward they shall go in to wait upon the service of the Tent of the appointed times:

25 And from the age of fifty[1] years they shall cease waiting upon the service there, and shall serve no more:

26 But shall minister with their brethren in the Tent of the appointed times, to keep the charge, and shall do no service. Thus shall You do to the Lewim touching their charge.

Chapter 9

1 And YHWH spoke to Mosheh (Musa) in the wilderness of Sinai, in the first month of the second year after they were come out of the land of Mitzrayim (Egypt), saying,

2 Let the children of Israel also keep the Protection (Passover) at his appointed season.

Footnotes
[1] The priesthood was to end at fifty.

3 In the fourteenth day of this month, at even, you shall keep it in his appointed season: according to all the rites of it, and according to all the ceremonies there, shall you keep it.

4 And Mosheh (Musa) spoke to the children of Israel, that they should keep the Protection (Passover).

5 And they kept the Protection (Passover) on the fourteenth day of the first month at even in the wilderness of Sinai: according to all that YHWH commanded Mosheh (Musa), so did the children of Israel.

6 And there were certain men, who were defiled by the dead body of a man, that they could not keep the Protection (Passover) on that day: and they came before Mosheh (Musa) and before Aharon on that day:

7 And those men said to him, We are defiled by the dead body of a man: wherefore are we kept back, that we may not offer an offering of YHWH in his appointed season among the children of Israel?

8 And Mosheh (Musa) said to them, Stand still, and I will hear what YHWH will command concerning you.

9 And YHWH spoke to Mosheh (Musa), saying,

10 Speak to the children of Israel, saying, If any man of you or of your posterity shall be unclean by reason of a dead body, or be in a journey afar off, yet he shall keep the Protection (Passover) to YHWH.

11 The fourteenth day of the second month at even they shall keep it, and eat it with matzah (unleavened bread) and bitter herbs.[1]

12 They shall leave none of it to the morning, nor break any bone of it: according to all the ordinances of the Protection (Passover) they shall keep it.

13 But the man that is clean, and is not in a journey, and forbears to keep the Protection (Passover), even the same soul shall be cut off from among his people: because he brought not the offering of YHWH in his appointed season, that man shall bear his sin.

14 And if a foreigner shall sojourn among you, and will keep the Protection (Passover) to YHWH; according to the ordinance of the Protection (Passover) and according to the manner there, so shall he do: you shall have one ordinance, both for the foreigner,[2] and for him that was born in the land.

15 And on the day that the Tent was reared up the cloud covered the Tent, namely, the tent of the testimony: and at even there was upon the Tent as it were the appearance of fire, until the morning.

16 So it was always the cloud covered it by day, and the appearance of fire by night.

17 And when the cloud was taken up from the Tent, then after that the children of Israel

Footnotes

[1] Pesach Shani (Second Passover) for those who missed it and were defiled.

[2] One Torah for both – The foreigner who is going to eat the Passover meal must be circumcised.

journeyed: and in the place where the cloud abode, there the children of Israel pitched their tents.

18 At the commandment of YHWH the children of Israel journeyed, and at the commandment of YHWH they pitched: as long as the cloud abode upon the Tent they rested in their tents.

19 And when the cloud tarried long upon the Tent many days, then the children of Israel kept the charge of YHWH, and journeyed not.

20 And so it was, when the cloud was a few days upon the Tent; according to the commandment of YHWH they abode in their tents, and according to the commandment of YHWH they journeyed.

21 And so it was, when the cloud abode from even to the morning, and that the cloud was taken up in the morning, then they journeyed: whether it was by day or by night that the cloud was taken up, they journeyed.

22 Or whether it were two days, or a month, or a year, that the cloud tarried upon the Tent, remaining thereon, the children of Israel abode in their tents, and journeyed not: but when it was taken up, they journeyed.

23 At the commandment of YHWH they rested[1] in the tents, and at the commandment of

YHWH they journeyed: they kept the charge of YHWH, at the commandment of YHWH by the hand of Mosheh (Musa).

Chapter 10

1 And YHWH spoke to Mosheh (Musa), saying,

2 Make two shofarim (trumpets) of silver; of a whole piece shall You make them: that You may use them for the calling of the assembly,[2] and for the journeying of the camps.

3 And when they shall blow with them, all the assembly shall assemble themselves to you at the door of the Tent of the appointed times.

4 And if they blow but with one trumpet, then the princes, which are heads of the thousands of Israel, shall gather themselves to you.

5 When you blow an alarm, then the camps that lie on the east parts shall go forward.

6 When you blow an alarm the second time, then the camps that lie on the south side shall take their journey: they shall blow an alarm for their journeys.

7 But when the congregation is to be gathered together, you shall blow, but you shall not sound an alarm.

8 And the sons of Aharon, the kohenim, shall blow with the trumpets; and they shall be to you for an ordinance forever

---

Footnotes

[1] This also means YHWH showed them when it was the Sabbath and when not. There is no lunar Sabbath but weekly cycle of Hanok Calendar, later in history changed to the Lunar cyclee.

Footnotes

[2] Two Silver Trumpets are to be blown during new months, feasts and days of our Joy. The two trumpets represent both Houses of Israel and calling them back to restoration.

throughout your generations.[1]

9 And if you go to war in your land against the enemy that oppressed you, then you shall blow an alarm with the trumpets; and you shall be remembered before YHWH Your POWER, and you shall be rescued from your enemies.[2]

10 Also in the day of your gladness, and in your solemn days, and in the beginnings of your months, you shall blow with the trumpets over your burnt offerings,[3] and over the sacrifices of your shalom offerings; that they may be to you for a memorial before Your POWER: I am YHWH Your POWER.

11 And it came to pass on the twentieth day of the second month, in the second year, that the cloud was taken up from off the Tent of the testimony.

12 And the children of Israel took their journeys out of the wilderness of Sinai; and the cloud rested in the wilderness of Paran.[4]

13 And they first took their journey according to the commandment of YHWH by the hand of Mosheh (Musa).

14 In the first place went the banner of the camp of the children of Yahudah according to their armies: and over his host was Nakhson the son of Amminadab.

15 And over the host of the tribe of the children of Yskhar (Issachar) was Nethan'el the son of Zuar.

16 And over the host of the tribe of the children of Zevulun was Eliab the son of Helon.

17 And the Tent was taken down; and the sons of Gershon and the sons of Merari set forward, bearing the Tent.

18 And the banner of the camp of Reuven set forward according to their armies: and over his host was Elizur the son of Shedeur.

19 And over the host of the tribe of the children of Shimeon was Shelumi'el the son of Zurishaddai.

20 And over the host of the tribe of the children of Gawd was Eliasaph the son of Deu'el.

21 And the Kohathi set forward, bearing the Holy items of the inner sanctuary: and the others did set up the Tent before their arrival.

22 And the banner of the camp of the children of Efrayim set forward according to their armies: and over his host was Elishama the son of Ammihud.

23 And over the host of the tribe of the children of Manasheh was Gamali'el the son of Pedahzur.

24 And over the host of the tribe of the children of Binyamin was Abidan the son of Gideoni.

25 And the banner of the camp of the children of Dan set forward, which was the rearward of all the camps throughout their hosts: and over his host was Ahiezer the son of Ammishaddai.

26 And over the host of the tribe

Footnotes

[1] The eternal destiny of Israel is to be restored as one nation under YHWH.

[2] Even in times of severe problems we should blow the shofar to receive help from above.

[3] Blow during the new months, feasts and joyous occasions of Israel.

[4] Desert of Arabia near Mount Sinai

of the children of Asher was Pagi'el the son of Ocran.

27 And over the host of the tribe of the children of Naphtali was Ahira the son of Enan.

28 Thus were the journeying of the children of Israel according to their armies, when they set forward.

29 And Mosheh (Musa) said to Hobab, the son of Reuel[1] the Midiani, Mosheh (Musa)'s father in law, We are journeying to the place of which YHWH said, I will give it you: You come with us, and we will do you good for YHWH has spoken good concerning Israel.

30 And he said to him, I will not go; but I will depart to mine own land, and to my relatives.

31 And he said, Leave us not, I pray you; forasmuch as You know how we are to camp in the wilderness, and You may be to us our eyes.

32 And it shall be, if You go with us, yea, it shall be, that what goodness YHWH shall do to us, the same will we do to you.

33 And they departed from the Mount of YHWH three days' journey: and the ark of the Covenant of YHWH went before them in the three days' journey, to search out a resting place for them.

34 And the cloud of YHWH was upon them by day, when they went out of the camp.

35 And it came to pass, when the ark set forward, that Mosheh (Musa) said, Rise up, YHWH, and let your enemies be scattered; and let them that hate you flee before you.[2]

36 And when it rested, he said, Return, O YHWH, to the many thousands of Israel.

Chapter 11

1 And when the people complained, it displeased YHWH and YHWH heard it; and his anger flared out against them; and the fire of YHWH burnt among them, and consumed them that were in the uttermost parts of the camp.

2 And the people cried to Mosheh (Musa); and when Mosheh (Musa) prayed to YHWH, the fire was quenched.

3 And he called the name of the place Teberah[3]: because the fire of YHWH burnt among them.

4 And the mixed multitude that was among them fell to lusting: and the children of Israel also wept again, and said, who shall give us flesh to eat?[4]

Footnotes

[1] Reu'el is the father of Yithro. However here is mentioned the father of Yithro as was custom.

[2] The inverted nuns describe the wisdom of the Torah to the seven pillars and the ten sefirot in the sefirotic tree. These nuns act as kind of brackets in the ancient system but show hidden wisdom in the Torah.

[3] Burning

[4] The mixed multitude mentioned here were gentiles from Egypt who had joined Israel and they corrupted Israel with their defilement and lusts. They were wolves in sheep's clothing as we see many such people in churches today who are only divisive and have no rescue or concern with it. Today the gentiles corrupt our faith under

Continued in next section

5 We remember the fish, which we did eat in Mitzrayim (Egypt) freely; the cucumbers, and the melons, and the leeks, and the onions, and the garlic:[1]

6 But now our soul is dried away: there is nothing at all, beside this manna,[2] before our eyes.

7 And the manna was as coriander seed, and the colour there as the colour of bdellium.[3]

8 And the people went about, and gathered it, and ground it in mills, or beat it in a mortar, and baked it in pans, and made rotis of it: and the taste of it was as the taste of fresh oil.

9 And when the dew fell upon the camp in the night, the manna fell upon it.

10 Then Mosheh (Musa) heard the people weep throughout their Mishpakhot (families), every man in the door of his tent: and the anger of YHWH was kindled greatly; Mosheh (Musa) also was displeased.

11 And Mosheh (Musa) said to YHWH, why have You afflicted your servant? And why is it that I have not found favour in your sight, that You have given me such heavy burden of all this people?

12 Have I conceived all this people? Have I begotten them, that You should say to me, Carry them in your bosom, as a nursing father bears the sucking child, to the land which You swore to their ahvot (fathers)?

13 Where can I get meat to give to all this people? For they cry to me, saying, give us meat that we may eat.

14 I am not able to bear all this people alone, because it is too heavy for me.

15 And if You deal thus with me, kill me, I pray you, out of hand, if I have found favour in your sight; and let me not look upon your evil.[4]

16 And YHWH said to Mosheh (Musa), Gather to me seventy men of the elders of Israel, whom You know to be the elders of the people, and officers over them; and bring them to the Tent of the appointed times, that they may stand there with you.

17 And I will come down and talk with you there: and I will take of the Ruakh (Spirit) which is upon you, and will put it upon them; and they shall bear the burden of the people with you, that You bear it not yourself alone.

18 And you speak to the people and say, set yourselves apart for

---

the guise of man's religious systems such as Christendom.

[1] Many people are still running after food and paying little attention towards YHWH.

[2] Many cannot see the 'bread' of YHWH that is the Torah, the words which reveal eternal life to us. Which is mentioned in many areas of Torah but the people want something better than manna. The manna of YHWH, that descended from above, is excellent and nothing is better than that but many refuse to take the manna in this case the drash of Torah.

[3] This was given to them while they were in Saudi Arabia and they started to complain of YHWH's provision and lusted after human desires.

Footnotes

[4] Another one of the masoret's corrections Tikkunei Soferim fixed to the original Hebrew.

tomorrow, and you shall eat meat: for you have wept in the ears of YHWH, saying, Who shall give us meat to eat? For it was well with us in Mitzrayim (Egypt): therefore YHWH will give you meat, and you shall eat.

19 You shall not eat one day, nor two days, nor five days, neither ten days, nor twenty days;

20 But even a whole month, until it comes out of your nostrils, and it be hateful to you: because that you have despised YHWH which is among you, and have wept before him, saying, Why did we come out of Mitzrayim (Egypt)?[1]

21 And Mosheh (Musa) said, The people, among whom I am, are six hundred thousand footmen; and You have said, I will give them meat, that they may eat a whole month.

22 Shall the flocks and the herds be slain for them, to satisfy them? Or shall all the fish of the sea be gathered together for them, to satisfy them?

23 And YHWH said to Mosheh (Musa), IS YHWH's arm too short? You shall see now whether my word shall come to meet you or not.

24 And Mosheh (Musa) went out, and told the people the words of YHWH, and gathered the seventy men of the elders of the people, and set them roundabout the Tent.

25 And YHWH came down in a

cloud, and spoke to him, and took of the Ruakh (Spirit) that was upon him, and gave it to the seventy elders: and it came to pass, that, when the Ruakh (Spirit) rested upon them, they prophesied, and did not cease.

26 But there remained two of the men in the camp, the name of the one was Eldad, and the name of the other Medad: and the Ruakh (Spirit) rested upon them; and they were of them that were written, but went not out to the Tent: and they prophesied in the camp.

27 And there ran a young man, and told Mosheh (Musa), and said, Eldad and Medad do prophesy in the camp.

28 And Yahushua the son of Nun, the servant of Mosheh (Musa), one of his young men, answered and said, My master Mosheh (Musa), forbid them.

29 And Mosheh (Musa) said to him, are you jealous for my sake? Would Elohim that all YHWH's people were prophets, and that YHWH would put his Ruakh (Spirit) upon them all!

30 And Mosheh (Musa) got him into the camp, he and the elders of Israel.

31 And there went forth a wind from YHWH, and brought quails from the sea, and let them fall by the camp, as it were a day's journey on this side, and as it were a day's journey on the other side, roundabout the camp, and as it were two cubits high upon the face of the land.

32 And the people stood up all that day, and all that night, and all the next day, and they gathered

Footnotes

[1] Because of food at an instance they forgot all their troubles of slavery and the task masters. It's very sad when people only worry about their stomachs.

the quails: he that gathered least gathered ten homers:[1] and they spread them all abroad for themselves roundabout the camp.

33 And while the meat was yet between their teeth, before it was chewed, the wrath of YHWH was kindled against the people, and YHWH smote the people with a very great plague.

34 And he called the name of that place Kibroth-hattaavah:[2] because there they buried the people that lusted.

35 And the people journeyed from Kibroth-hattaavah to Khezeroth; and abode at Khezeroth.

Chapter 12

1 And Miriam and Aharon spoke against Mosheh (Musa) because of the Cushite woman whom he had married: for he had married a Cushite woman.[3]

Footnotes
[1] Same as ten donkey loads or two thousand litres load.
[2] It means 'graves of lust' for the place where they lusted.
[3] Moses had three wives in the Patriarchal model but he only consummated his marriage with two wives, Yashar 72:33-37; 76:4-6. Moses did not consummate the marriage with Adoniah because she served pagan deities, and he knew Torah well enough not to consummate that marriage because it was most likely given by Cushite customs and not Torah. We can see that this was confirmed later when Adoniah rebelled against Moses for him not following her and her false idols of worship in Cush. So Zipporah was really in the scheme of things number two but albeit became his primary wife for a season after which he took on another Cushite woman (this woman) who became number two. We know that Moses sent off Zipporah with a temporary Get because a Get is not permanent always. This Continued in next section

was to allow a separation for a time for her to repent of her error after which her father Jethro brought her back. There was tension between the circumcision of Moses' son (Exodus 4:25) so this could have brought on that separation.

By that time clearly Moses has the new wife. Yes, that is correct; he already had number two, who was the Cushite woman so he was married to two women at the same time. But, there is a twist to the tale where Moses could have already been married to this woman before he left Egypt.

Now Josephus also records the marriage of Moses to an Ethiopian woman. Moses was still in Egypt so this could be the first marriage of Moses adding to the equation meaning he could have had three wives in total at different times. He did not reconcile the marriage with Adoniah. He married this princess Tharbis before he left Egypt so she is his first wife in reality. Then he later married Zipporah when he fled from Egypt, his first wife would have gone back to Cush and later joined with him during his sojourn with the Israelites. So, it was consistent that Zipporah was wife number three if we account Adoniah as number two but she is not counted as a Torah Ketubah wife, and Moses always had two wives. So, when the Cushite princess rejoined Moses that is when Miriam and Aharon would have become angry at this reunion.

We do not hear anything about Tharbis upon Moses' departure from Egypt. So it would be second guessing what actually happened, but our view is she was the one mentioned in Numbers 12 where YHWH upheld his marriage to her and did not discard it.

Tharbis was the daughter of the king of the Cushite people and she happened to see Moses as he led the army near the walls, and fought with great courage; and admiring the subtlety of his undertakings, and believing him to be the author of the Egyptians' success, she fell deeply in love with him; and upon the prevalence of that passion, sent to him the most trustworthy of all her servants to discourse with him about their marriage. He thereupon accepted the offer, on condition she would procure the giving up of the city; and gave her the Continued in next section

2 And they said, Has YHWH indeed spoken only by Mosheh (Musa)? Has he not spoken also by us? And YHWH heard it.

3 Now the man Mosheh (Musa) was very meek, above all the men which were upon the face of the earth.

4 And YHWH spoke immediately
with Mosheh (Musa), and with Aharon, and to Miriam, Come out you three into the Tent of the appointed times. And they three went.

5 And YHWH came down in the pillar of the cloud, and stood in the door of the Tent, and called Aharon and Miriam: and they both came forth.

6 And he said, Hear now my words: If there be a prophet among you, I YHWH will make myself known to him in a vision, and will speak to him in a dream.

7 My servant Mosheh (Musa) is not so, who is trustworthy in all mine Beyth (house).

8 With him will I speak mouth to mouth, and not in dark speeches; and the similitude of YHWH shall he behold: why then were you not afraid to speak against my servant Mosheh (Musa)?

9 And the anger of YHWH burned hot against them; and He departed.

10 And the cloud departed from off the Tent; and, behold, Miriam became leprous, white as snow: and Aharon looked upon Miriam, and, behold, she was leprous.[1]

Footnotes

[1] Miriam was black in colour and of African ethnicity she was struck with leprosy the colour of white skin as Judgment. There are times when YHWH has chosen his prophets such as Moses, and other people YHWH speaks to, who become arrogant in thinking. Well, we are no less than Moses as prophets. Here a lesson is taught to Israel. Moses had a particular mission, and that mission was not for Aharon and certainly not for Miriam. This is not to say that he singled out Miriam because she was a woman, and did not say anything to Aharon. She was struck with leprosy, because she was being taught a lesson, not to usurp authority and slander a man close to YHWH. The sin of slander is grievous, but many do it out of contempt for others and jealousy. Some people would not be able to enter the kingdom because of this unrepented sin both against YHWH and the man or woman they slandered!

We are shown that both Moses and Aharon were in a position to speak to YHWH, but YHWH has different levels of relationships with different people. Verse six makes this very clear, each person at his own level. Verse seven shows us that Moses was trustworthy in all his house, or 'trusted' in the Royal house of the great King. Sometimes there are people who stand in the prophet's position, but they are not wholly trustworthy. This was not the picture YHWH gave of Moses. We know that Aharon was forced in this regard, as he helped build the Golden Calf, falling into the sin of the 'majority are right view' or fearful of the majority. This later caused the Israelites to commit idolatry.

Aharon was spared at this time, because he was dressed in his priestly garments. If YHWH had put leprosy on Aharon, he would have been unclean for 7 days, and would have to live outside the camp as Miriam had to. That would have sent the wrong message to the whole nation of Israel. So, Continued in next section

assurance of an oath to take her to be his wife; and that when he had once taken possession of the city, he would not break his oath to her. No sooner was the agreement made, but it took effect immediately; and when Moses had cut off the Cushites he gave thanks to Elohim and consummated his marriage, and led the Egyptians back to their own land. (2:252-253) Josephus. For the full article see: http://www.forever-israel.com under Debates.

11 And Aharon said to Mosheh (Musa), Alas, my master, I beseech you, lay not the sin upon us, wherein we have done foolishly, and wherein we have transgressed.[1]

12 Please let her not be as one dead,[2] of when coming out of our mother's womb with our flesh half consumed.[3]

YHWH was merciful to Aharon, because he was a man of peace and humility also.

[1] This is classical Lashon hara known as 'Evil Speech'; this incident is particularly vile in the Torah in Numbers 12:1, where Miriam joined hands with Aaron to slander Moses. Although, YHWH may speak to individuals in different ways, that does not give anyone, the authority, to circumvent YHWH's relationship with one another. This is the sin that Miriam and Aaron committed of Lashon Hara (evil speech) against Moses and it was displeasing to YHWH. People think they can speak against Torah polygyny and they feel they are justified by today's corrupt society model where such evil things as same gender marriages are permitted by the local and national laws.

The same problem Moses had to endure for following the forefathers' lifestyle. Well, in YHWH's sight it is not justified to slander righteous Torah believers for polygyny as he has made plural marriages Holy and no man or woman can call it a sin, thereby slandering our forefathers Abraham, Isaac and Jacob. Many other matters can arise which cause people to sin by slandering such as some women in our society running loose slandering YHWH's men for various reasons. The true reason is they are rebelling against YHWH's authority and have unclean spirits vexing them is because of their disobedience to Torah and they need prayer and rescue!

[2] Note pale white also the colour devoid of blood connotes death, while today people foolishly glorify the colour white as a better colour this is in contrast to the original Hebrews who were of black colour and African ethnicity.

[3] This is one of the Tikkunei Soferim that was made to correct the text as the Continued in next section

13 And Mosheh (Musa) cried to YHWH saying, Heal her now, O El (The Power), I beseech you.

14 And YHWH said to Mosheh (Musa), If her father had but spit in her face,[4] should she not be ashamed seven days? Let her be shut out from the camp seven days, and after that let her be received in again.

15 And Miriam was shut out from the camp seven days: and the people journeyed not till Miriam was brought in again.

16 And afterward the people removed from Khezeroth, and pitched in the wilderness of Paran.

Torah Parsha 37 Shalach Lekha, WeDavar 13:1-15:41
Haftarah Yahushua 2:1-24

Chapter 13
1 And YHWH spoke to Mosheh (Musa), saying,

2 Send You men, that they may search the land of Kanan, which I give to the children of Israel: of every tribe of their ahvot (fathers) shall you send a man, everyone a ruler among them.

3 And Mosheh (Musa) by the commandment of YHWH sent them from the wilderness of Paran: all those men who were *the* heads of the children of Israel.

4 And these were their names: of the tribe of Reuven, Shammua the son of Zaccur.

Masorets saw it fit. We have corrected it to the original text.
[4] To spit in someone's face is to show utter contempt.

5 Of the tribe of Shimeon, Shaphat the son of Hori.

6 Of the tribe of Yahudah, Kalev the son of Yepune'yah.

7 Of the tribe of Yskhar (Issachar), Igal the son of Yosef.

8 Of the tribe of Efrayim, Oshea[1] the son of Nun.

9 Of the tribe of Benyamin, Palti the son of Raphu.

10 Of the tribe of Zevulun, Gaddi'el the son of Sodi.

11 Of the tribe of Yosef, namely, of the tribe of Manasheh, Gaddi the son of Susi.

12 Of the tribe of Dan, Ammi'el the son of Gemalli.

13 Of the tribe of Asher, Sethur the son of Michayah'el.

14 Of the tribe of Naphtali, Nahbi the son of Vophsi.

15 Of the tribe of Gawd, Geu'el the son of Machi.

16 These are the names of the men which Mosheh (Musa) sent to spy out the land. And Mosheh (Musa) called Oshea the son of Nun Yahushua.[2]

17 And Mosheh (Musa) sent them to spy out the land of Kanan, and said to them, Get up this way southward, and go up into the mountain:

18 And see the land, what it is; and the people that dwell therein, whether they be strong or weak, few or many;

19 And what the land is that they dwell in, whether it be good or bad; and what cities they be that they dwell in, whether in tents, or in strongholds;

20 And what the land is, whether it be fat or lean, whether there be wood therein, or not. And you be of good courage, and bring of the fruit of the land. Now the time was the time of the first ripe grapes.

21 So they went up, and searched the land from the wilderness of Zin to Rehob, as men come to Hamath.

22 And they ascended by the south, and came to Khevron; where Ahiman, Sheshai, and Talmai, the children of Anak, were. (Now Khevron was built seven years before Zoan in Mitzrayim (Egypt)).

23 And they came to the brook of Eshkol, and cut down from there a branch with one cluster of grapes,[3] and they bare it between two upon a staff; and they brought of the pomegranates, and of the figs.

24 The place was called the brook Eshkol, because of the cluster of grapes which the children of Israel cut down from thence.

25 And they returned from searching of the land after forty days.

26 And they went and came to Mosheh (Musa), and to Aharon, and to all the congregation of the children of Israel, to the

Footnotes
[1] Oshea became Yahushua by Moses who renamed him to show us who gave him the rescue, as it was YHWH by adding a Yud and Wah to his name. Yud signifies YHWH's right hand of rescue. Wah is the picture of a hook connecting between earth and shamayim.
[2] Names changed from Oshea meaning rescue to Yah who is Rescue. Adding the Yud and Wah.

Footnotes
[3] The grapes were very large sized. Drash of the goodness of the land under YHWH's Torah.

wilderness of Paran, to Kadesh; and brought back word to them, and to all the congregation, and showed them the fruit of the land.

27 And they told him, and said, We came to the land where you sent us, and it indeed flows with milk and honey; and this is the fruit of it.

28 Nevertheless the people be strong that dwell in the land, and the cities are walled, and very great: and moreover we saw the children of Anak there.[1]

29 The Amaleki dwell in the land of the south: and the Khitee, and the Yavusi (Jebusites), and the Amoree, dwell in the mountains: and the Kanani dwell by the sea, and by the coast of Yardan (Jordan).

30 And Kalev silenced the people before Mosheh (Musa),[2] and said, Let us go up at once, and possess it; for we are well able to overcome it.[3]

31 But the men that went up with him said, We be not able to go up against the people; for they are stronger than we.

32 And they brought up an evil report of the land which they had searched to the children of Israel, saying, The land, through which we have gone to search it, is a land that devours its inhabitants; and all the people that we saw in it are men of a great stature.

33 And there we saw the Nephillim, the sons of Anak, which came from the Nephillim[4] and we were in our own sight as grasshoppers, and so we were in their sight.

Chapter 14

1 And all the congregation lifted up their voice, and cried; and the people wept that night.

2 And all the children of Israel murmured against Mosheh (Musa) and against Aharon: and the whole congregation said to them, Would Elohim that we had died in the land of Mitzrayim (Egypt)! Or would Elohim we had died in this wilderness!

3 And wherefore has YHWH brought us to this land, to fall by the sword, that our wives and our children should be a prey? Were it not better for us to return into Mitzrayim (Egypt)?

4 And they said one to another, Let us make a captain, and let us return into Mitzrayim (Egypt).

5 Then Mosheh (Musa) and

Footnotes
[1] Ten of the spies brought a bad report.
[2] The people started to murmur as usual.
[3] Caleb as his name suggests is big hearted, its also in modern Hebrew means "dog". Caleb wants to go up and do YHWH's business. Caleb though originally was not from Israel but was added as a witness to the tribe of Yahudah and so represents full Torah compliance and no defeatist attitude. While Joshua is from the tribe of Efrayim, who represents the second witness of YHWH to His truth and trustworthiness for both houses of Israel. Both will one day fight the giants, the drash for the Islamic nations against Tiny Israel, the end time battle where Christians and the Hebrew nation of Israel will join hands together. See reference book Islam Peace or Beast Rabbi Simon Altaf www.forever-israel.com.

Footnotes
[4] When the evil malakhim were killed the spirits became demonic forces and it could be that these same ones later inhabited women, and these women again gave birth to giants. These were subdued, and eradicated later by Caleb. Malakhim do not die as humans, but their spirits become demons, only the bodies disintegrate!

Aharon fell on their faces before all the assembly of the congregation of the children of Israel.

6 And Yahushua the son of Nun, and Kalev the son of Yepune'yah, which were of them that searched the land, tore their clothes:

7 And they spoke to all the company of the children of Israel, saying, The land, which we passed through to search it, is an exceeding good land.

8 If YHWH delight in us, then he will bring us into this land, and give it us; a land which flows with milk and honey.[1]

9 Do not rebel against YHWH, neither fear the people of the land; for they are food[2] for us: their defense is departed from them, and YHWH is with us: Do not be fearful of them.

10 But all the congregation threatened to stone them with stones. And the glory of YHWH appeared in the Tent of the appointed times before all the children of Israel.[3]

11 And YHWH said to Mosheh (Musa), How long will this people provoke me? And how long will it be that they believe me, for all the signs which I have performed among them?[4]

12 I will smite them with the pestilence, and disinherit them, and will make of you a greater nation and mightier than they.

13 And Mosheh (Musa) said to YHWH, Then the Mitzrim (Egyptians) shall hear it, (for You brought up this people in your might from among them.)

14 And they will tell it to the inhabitants of this land: for they have heard that You YHWH are among this people, that You YHWH are seen face to face, and that your cloud stands over them, and that You go before them, by day time in a pillar of a cloud, and in a pillar of fire by night.

15 Now if You shall kill all this people as one man, then the nations which have heard the fame of you will speak, saying,

16 Because YHWH was not able to bring this people into the land which he swore to them, therefore he has slain them in the wilderness.

17 And now, I beseech you, let the Power of my YHWH[5] be Great, according to as You have spoken, saying,

[6]

18 YHWH is longsuffering, and of great loving-kindness, forgiving iniquity and sin, and by no means clearing the guilty, visiting the iniquity of the ahvot (fathers) upon the children to the third and fourth generation.

19 Pardon, I beseech you, the iniquity of this people according to the greatness of your loving-kindness, and as You have forgiven this people, from Mitzrayim (Egypt) even until now.

20 And YHWH said, I have pardoned according to your word:[1]

21 But as truly as I live, all the earth shall be filled with the glory of YHWH.

22 Because all those men which have seen my glory, and my miracles, which I did in Mitzrayim (Egypt) and in the wilderness, and have tested me now these ten times,[2] and have not obeyed my voice;

23 Surely they shall not see the land which I swore to their ahvot (fathers), neither shall any of them that provoked me see it:[3]

24 But my servant Kalev, because he had another ruakh (Spirit) with him, and has followed me completely, I will bring him into the land into which he went; and his descendants shall possess it.

25 (Now the Amaleki and the Kanani dwelt in the valley.) Tomorrow turn around, and turn towards the wilderness by the way of the Sea of Reeds.

26 And YHWH spoke to Mosheh (Musa) and to Aharon, saying,

27 How long shall I bear with this evil congregation, which murmurs against me? I have heard the murmurings of the children of Israel, which they murmur against me.

28 Say to them, As truly as I live, says YHWH, as you have spoken in my ears, so will I do to you:

29 Your carcasses shall fall in this wilderness; and all that were registered of you, according to your whole number, from twenty years old and upward, which have murmured against me,[4]

30 Be sure you will not come into the land, concerning which I swore to make you dwell therein, except Kalev the son of Yepune'yah, and Yahushua the son of Nun.

31 But your little ones, whom you said would become victims of war, them will I bring in, and they shall enjoy the land which you have despised.

32 But as for you, your carcasses, they shall fall in this wilderness.

33 And your children shall wander in the wilderness forty years, and suffer your untrustworthiness, until your dead bodies are wasted away in the wilderness.

the Torah but more so we see the number ten for judgment and mercy the two sides of the sefirotic tree that describes Ahdahm Kadmon.
[1] Moses became a redeemer for Israel.
[2] The number of the Sefirotic tree.
[3] Sin has a price.

Footnotes
[4] This did not mean that their rescue was taken away but that they were punished on a physical level for their disobedience.

34 After the number of the days in which you searched the land, even forty days, each day for a year, shall you bear your iniquities, even forty years, and you shall know what enmity means with me.

35 I YHWH have said, I will surely do it to all this evil congregation, that are gathered together against me: in this wilderness they shall be consumed, and there they shall die.[1]

36 And the men, which Mosheh (Musa) sent to search the land, who returned, and made all the congregation to murmur against him, by bringing in slander[2] upon the land,

37 Even those men that did bring up the evil report[3] upon the land, died by the plague[4] before YHWH.

38 But Yahushua the son of Nun, and Kalev the son of Yepune'yah, which were of the men that went to search the land, lived still.

39 And Mosheh (Musa) told these sayings to all the children of Israel: and the people mourned greatly.

40 And they rose up early in the morning, and climbed up into the top of the mountain, saying, Behold, we be here, and will go up to the place which YHWH has promised: for we have transgressed.

41 And Mosheh (Musa) said, why now do you violate the commandment of YHWH? But it shall not prosper.

42 Do not go up, for YHWH is not among you; that you be not smitten before your enemies.

43 For the Amaleki and the Kanani are there before you, and you shall fall by the sword: because you are turned away from YHWH, therefore YHWH will not be with you.

44 But they presumed to go up to the hill top: nevertheless the ark of the Covenant of YHWH, and Mosheh (Musa), departed not out of the camp.

45 Then the Amaleki came down, and the Kanani which dwelt in that hill, and attacked them, and drove them back as far as Khurma.

Chapter 15

1 And YHWH spoke to Mosheh (Musa), saying,

2 Speak to the children of Israel, and say to them, When you be come into the land of your habitations, which I give to you,

3 And will make an offering by

Footnotes

[1] Physical judgment is set and cannot be changed.

[2] In Judaism today, slandering someone is considered a very bad sin. However, Christians, and so called Torah spectators, relish in gossiping about other believers and spreading false rumours. YHWH will have the last laugh.

[3] Calling good evil does not please YHWH, and many brethren are into this kind of slander against one another. This should stop or you will face retribution from YHWH both here and in the coming age.

[4] It does not matter whether you call yourself a Christian or Torah believer but evil is rewarded with evil not good. We must change our behaviour to what YHWH wants it to be and stop becoming like the world and its evil ways of siding with the majority. This is what happened to Israel when they sided with the majority, and propagated what was good as evil. The end result was that they were not allowed to enter the land.

fire to YHWH, a burnt offering, or a sacrifice in performing a vow, or in a freewill offering, or in your Moe'dim, to make a sweet savour to YHWH, of the herd, or of the flock:

4 Then shall he that offers his offering to YHWH bring a grain offering of a tenth deal of flour mingled with the fourth part of a hin of oil.

5 And the fourth part of a hin of wine for a drink offering shall You prepare with the burnt offering or sacrifice, for one lamb.

6 Or for a ram, You shall prepare for a grain offering two tenth deals of flour mingled with the third part of a hin of oil.

7 And for a drink offering You shall offer the third part of a hin of wine, for a sweet savour to YHWH.

8 And when You prepare a bullock for a burnt offering, or for a sacrifice in performing a vow, or shalom offerings to YHWH.

9 Then shall he bring with a bullock a grain offering of three tenth deals of flour mingled with half a hin of oil.

10 And You shall bring for a drink offering half a hin of wine, for an offering made by fire, of a sweet savour to YHWH.

11 Thus shall it be done for one bullock, or for one ram, or for a lamb, or a kid.

12 According to the number that you shall prepare, so shall you do to everyone according to their number.

13 All that are born of the country shall do these things after this manner, in offering an offering made by fire, of a sweet savour to YHWH.

14 And if a foreigner sojourn with you, or whosoever be among you in your generations, and will offer an offering made by fire, of a sweet savour to YHWH; as you do, so he shall do.

15 One ordinance shall be both for you of the congregation, and also for the foreigner that dwells with you, an ordinance forever in your generations: as you are, so shall the foreigner be before YHWH.

16 One Torah and one manner shall be for you, and for the foreigner that dwells with you.[1]

17 And YHWH spoke to Mosheh (Musa), saying,

18 Speak to the children of Israel, and say to them, When you come into the land where I bring you,

19 Then it shall be, that, when you eat of the Lakhem (bread) of the land, you shall offer up a heave offering to YHWH.

20 You shall offer up a roti of the first of your dough for a heave offering: as you do the heave offering of the threshing floor, so shall you present it.

21 Of the first of your dough you shall give to YHWH a contributory offering in your generations.

22 And if you have erred, and not observed all these commandments, which YHWH has spoken to Mosheh (Musa),

23 Even all that YHWH has commanded you by the hand of Mosheh (Musa), from the day

Footnotes
[1] There is only one Torah for both. It's not this is for the Hebrew people and that is for us mentality.

that YHWH commanded Mosheh (Musa), and henceforward among your generations;

24 Then it shall be, if anything be committed in ignorance outside the knowledge of the congregation, that all the congregation shall offer one young bullock for a burnt offering, for a sweet savour to YHWH, with his grain offering, and his drink offering, according to the manner, and one kid of the goats for a sin offering.

25 And the kohen (priest) shall make atonement for all the congregation of the children of Israel, and it shall be forgiven them; for it is ignorance: and they shall bring their offering, a sacrifice made by fire to YHWH, and their sin offering before YHWH, for their ignorance:

26 And it shall be forgiven all the congregation of the children of Israel, and the foreigner that dwells among them; seeing all the people were in ignorance.

27 And if anyone transgresses through ignorance, then he shall bring a female goat of the first year for a sin offering.

28 And the kohen (priest) shall make atonement for the soul that transgresses ignorantly, when he transgresses by ignorance[1] before YHWH, to make atonement for him; and it shall be forgiven him.

29 You shall have one Torah for him that transgresses through ignorance, both for him that is born among the children of Israel, and for the foreigner that lives among them.

30 But the person that commits sins deliberately,[2] whether he be born in the land, or a foreigner, the same insults YHWH; and that person must be cut off from among his people.

31 Because he has despised the word of YHWH, and has broken his commandment, that soul shall utterly be cut off; his iniquity shall be upon him.

32 And while the children of Israel were in the wilderness, they found a man that gathered sticks upon the Sabbath day.

33 And they that found him gathering sticks brought him to Mosheh (Musa) and Aharon, and to all the congregation.

34 And they put him in a ward,[3] because it was not declared what should be done to him.

35 And YHWH said to Mosheh (Musa), The man shall be surely put to death: all the congregation shall stone him with stones outside the camp.[4]

36 And all the congregation brought him outside the camp, and stoned him with stones, and he died; as YHWH commanded Mosheh (Musa).

37 And YHWH spoke to Mosheh (Musa), saying,

38 Speak to the sons of Israel, and command them that they

Footnotes

[1] There was no sacrifice for intentional sins, we needed YHWH's favor.

[2] Deliberate wilful sin and its penalty was death and still is unless YHWH forgives by his mercy.

[3] Enclosure to hold people for punishment.

[4] Sin was expunged outside the camp. Not keeping the Sabbath was and still is a sin.

make tzitzits[1] in the four corners of their garments throughout their generations, and that they put upon the fringe of the borders a thread of blue:[2]

39 And it shall be to you for a fringe, that you may look upon it,

Footnotes

[1] Tzitzits is a commandment for all the sons of Israel to wear today not just Hebrew Israel and also Christians, who say they believe in the Messiah of Israel. The Hebrew term 'bnai Israel,' is more accurately translated, 'sons of Israel,' not children, because the word 'bnai' has the Hebrew root 'ben,' which means son. The sons are responsible for building up their households, so the tzitzits only really apply to sons not daughters.

In fact, we do not find women wearing tzitzits in the first century, and this fact is well understood in Judaism. Messianics do not understand that only the sons of Israel are commanded to wear them.

The daughters in Israel are <u>never</u> counted separately. If we as sons are commanded to wear any symbol to represent YHWH then this was the tzitzit. Today many run around wearing crosses, chamsa's and Torah scrolls, while the other paraphernalia was never commanded. The cross is a well known pagan symbol of Tammuz in Babylon. The only people who do not seem to know this fact are unfortunately the Christians! The chamsa is a sign of Torah or of the five books of Moses. The Shia Muslims have it on their flag too. The fish symbol that Christians display on their cars is part of Dagon, the false deity of the Philistines. By using the symbol of the tzitzits, we also acquire understanding about the Two Houses of Israel that would be dispersed to the four corners of the world. The four corners on the garment as the four compass points, North, South, East and West. They show us the dispersion of Israel did indeed occur. The garment is the drash for the world. We also get the name of YHWH from the Hebrew gametria as 'YHWH Akhad' (YHWH is one), from our creed in Deuteronomy 6:4. These tzitzits also give us the understanding of the 613 commandments in the Torah.

[2] Royal sign of the Messiah!

and remember all the commandments of YHWH and do them; and that you seek not after your own heart and your own eyes, after which you use to go a whoring:

40 That you may remember, and do all my commandments,[3] and be Holy to Your POWER.

41 I am YHWH Your POWER, which brought you out of the land of Mitzrayim (Egypt), to be Your POWER: I am YHWH Your POWER.

Torah Parsha 38 Korach, WeDavar 16:1-18:32
Haftarah: Shemuel Alef 11:14-12:22

Chapter 16

1 Now Korakh, the son of Yshari, the son of Kohath, the son of Levi, and Dathan and Abiram, the sons of Eliab, and On, the son of Peleth, sons of Reuven, took men:

2 And they rose up before Mosheh (Musa), with certain of the children of Israel, two hundred and fifty princes[4] of the assembly, famous in the congregation, men of renown:

3 And they gathered themselves together against Mosheh (Musa)

Footnotes

[3] What sets us apart, is obeying YHWH's Torah, otherwise, we are just like the heathens.

[4] It is a bad idea that by organising a majority, you think you can defeat the righteous servants of YHWH. Whatever you do, do not face a prophet of YHWH, else you may not live to tell the tale as Korakh learned the hard way. Korakh, means bald, having no covering. These people sadly showed their true colours, they were bald with no covering spiritually speaking.

and against Aharon, and said to them, You take too much upon you, seeing all the congregation are Holy, everyone of them, and YHWH is among them: wherefore then lift you up yourselves above the congregation of YHWH?

4 And when Mosheh (Musa) heard it, he fell upon his face:

5 And he spoke to Korakh and to all his company, saying, Even tomorrow YHWH will show who are His, and who is Holy; and will cause him to come near to him: even him whom he has chosen will he cause to come near to Him.

6 This do take you censers, Korakh, and all his company;

7 And put fire therein, and put incense in them before YHWH tomorrow: and it shall be that the man whom YHWH will choose, he shall be Holy: you take too much upon you, you sons of Levi.

8 And Mosheh (Musa) said to Korakh, Hear, I pray you, you sons of Levi:

9 It might seem a small thing to you, that the Elohim of Israel has separated you from the congregation of Israel, to bring you near to himself to do the service of the Tent of YHWH, and to stand before the congregation to minister to them.

10 And he has brought you near to him, and all your brethren the sons of Levi with you: and yet you seek the priesthood also?

11 For which cause both You and all your company are gathered together against YHWH and what is Aharon, that you murmur against him?

12 And Mosheh (Musa) sent to call Dathan and Abiram, the sons of Eliab: which said, we will not come up:

13 Is it a small thing that You have brought us up out of a land that flows with milk and honey, to kill us in the wilderness, except You make yourself altogether a prince over us?

14 Moreover You have not brought us into a land that flows with milk and honey[1], or given us inheritance of fields and vineyards: will You now put out the eyes[2] of these men? We will not come up.

15 And Mosheh (Musa) was very angry, and said to YHWH, Respect not their offering: I have not taken one ass from them, neither have I hurt one of them.

16 And Mosheh (Musa) said to Korakh, Be You and all your company before YHWH, You, and they, and Aharon, tomorrow:

17 And take every man his censer, and put incense in them, and bring it before YHWH every man and his censer, two hundred and fifty censers;[3] You also, and Aharon, each of you his censer.

Footnotes

[1] They accused Moses of lying. Well, actually the accusation is not against Moses but YHWH. When you accuse His prophets you accuse Him directly. This behaviour is shameful and even occurs today amongst many alleged Torah people and non-Torah Christianity.

[2] Accusing Moses of plucking the eyes out is to say removing someone's Faith because the eyes everyone sees and the reference here is that the Faith of these people, went only as far as miracles go. When the miracles stopped their Faith stopped. While Faith should be based on the trust we have in YHWH.

[3] Two hundred and fifty leaders plus their supporters

18 And they took every man his censer, and put fire in them, and laid incense thereon, and stood in the door of the Tent of the appointed times with Mosheh (Musa) and Aharon.

19 And Korakh gathered all the congregation against[1] them to the door of the Tent of the appointed times: and the glory of YHWH appeared to all the congregation.

20 And YHWH spoke to Mosheh (Musa) and to Aharon, saying,

21 Separate yourselves from among this congregation, that I may consume them in a moment.

22 And they fell upon their faces, and said, O El (The Power), the Elohim of the ruachot (spirits) of all flesh, shall one man sin, and will You be wroth with all the congregation?

23 And YHWH spoke to Mosheh (Musa), saying,

24 Speak to the congregation, saying, move away from the tents of Korakh, Dathan, and Abiram.

25 And Mosheh (Musa) rose up and went to Dathan and Abiram; and the elders of Israel followed him.

26 And he spoke to the congregation, saying, Depart, I beseech you, from the tents of these wicked men, and touch nothing of their's, lest you be consumed in all their sins.[2]

27 So they got up from the tents of Korakh, Dathan, and Abiram, on all sides: and Dathan and Abiram came out, and stood in the door of their tents, and their wives, and their sons, and their little children.

28 And Mosheh (Musa) said, Hereby you shall know that YHWH has sent me to do all these works; for I have not done them of my own mind.[3]

29 If these men die the common death of all men, or if they be visited after the visitation of all men; then YHWH has not sent me.

30 But if YHWH make a new thing, and the earth opens her mouth, and swallows them up, with all that appertain to them, and they go down quick into She'ol[4]; then you shall understand that these men have provoked YHWH.

31 And it came to pass, as he had made an end of speaking all these words, that the ground opened that was under them:

32 And the earth opened her mouth, and swallowed them up, and their Batiym (houses), and all the men that pertained to Korakh, and all their goods.[5]

33 They, and all that pertained to them, went down alive into She'ol[6], and the earth closed

Footnotes

[1] Korakh did not reject Moses the lawgiver but he rejected YHWH. The sin was grievous.

[2] YHWH times His judgment and it will be swift.

[3] Sometimes men are accused of acting on their own, but really their Faith should show they are sent and not acting on their own self will.

[4] Hell has different levels

[5] Everyone went to hell including the wives and children. Any evil man or woman, who stands against YHWH's Torah and commandments will be dealt with by YHWH himself, be forewarned.

[6] She'ol has two main compartments, one for the wicked dead and the other called Continued in next section

upon them: and they perished from among the congregation.

34 And all Israel that were round about them fled at the cry of them: for they said, lest the earth swallow us up also.

35 And there came out a fire from YHWH, and consumed the two hundred and fifty men that offered incense.[1]

36 And YHWH spoke to Mosheh (Musa), saying,

37 Speak to El'ezar the son of Aharon the kohen (priest), that he take up the censers out of the burning, and scatter the fire some distance away; for they are Holy.

38 The censers of these transgressors against their own souls, let them make them broad plates for a covering of the altar: for they[2] offered them before YHWH, therefore they are Holy: and they shall be a sign to the children of Israel.

39 And El'ezar the kohen (priest) took the brazen censers, wherewith they that were burnt had offered; and they were made broad plates for a covering of the altar:

40 To be a remembrance to the children of Israel, that no foreigner, which is not of the seed of Aharon, come near to offer incense before YHWH; that he be not as Korakh,[3] and as his

company: as YHWH said to him by the hand of Mosheh (Musa).

41 But tomorrow all the congregation of the children of Israel murmured against Mosheh (Musa) and against Aharon, saying, You have killed the people of YHWH.[4]

42 And it came to pass, when the congregation was gathered against Mosheh (Musa) and against Aharon, that they looked toward the Tent of the appointed times: and, behold, the cloud covered it, and the glory of YHWH appeared.

43 And Mosheh (Musa) and Aharon came before the Tent of the appointed times.

44 And YHWH spoke to Mosheh (Musa), saying,

45 Get away from among this congregation, that I may consume them as in a moment. And they fell upon their faces.

46 And Mosheh (Musa) said to Aharon, Take a censer, and put fire therein from off the altar, and put on incense, and go quickly to the congregation, and make atonement for them: for there is wrath gone out from YHWH; the plague is begun.

Footnotes

[4] These Israelites did not yet understand reality and were still deceived by those that had died. The dead were not the people of YHWH but were spiritually deceived and deceiving others. 'Anybody who hates YHWH's prophets and hate His Torah are not YHWH's people by definition of Torah, as they are considered rebellious.' If someone claims to be a prophet of YHWH but does not know His name or calls Him, the title for Baal such as the 'Lord,' such a person cannot be considered His prophet as all of YHWH's prophets knew Him by name.

paradise where the righteous are kept until the resurrection.

[1] YHWH judged those that were judging Moses and cursing him down.

[2] This is a scary incident of Israelites going to hell fire to burn.

[3] Bald and without spiritual covering, that is how some people live their lives.

47 And Aharon took as Mosheh (Musa) commanded, and ran into the midst of the congregation; and, behold, the plague was begun among the people: and he put on incense, and made atonement for the people.

48 And he stood between the dead and the living; and the plague was stayed.

49 Now they that died in the plague were fourteen thousand and seven hundred, beside them that died about the matter of Korakh.

50 And Aharon returned to Mosheh (Musa) to the door of the Tent of the appointed times: and the plague was stayed.

Chapter 17

1 And YHWH spoke to Mosheh (Musa), saying,

2 Speak to the children of Israel, and take of everyone of them a rod according to the Beyth (house) of their ahvot (fathers), of all their princes according to the Beyth (house) of their ahvot (fathers) twelve rods: You write every man's name upon his rod.

3 And You shall write Aharon's name upon the rod of Levi: for one rod shall be for the head of the Beyth (house) of their ahvot (fathers).

4 And You shall lay them up in the Tent of the appointed times before the testimony, where I will meet with you.

5 And it shall come to pass, that the man's rod, whom I shall choose, shall blossom: and I will make to cease from me the murmurings of the children of Israel, whereby they murmur against you.

6 And Mosheh (Musa) spoke to the children of Israel, and each of their princes gave him a rod, one for each prince, according to their ahvot (fathers) houses, even twelve rods: and the rod of Aharon was among their rods.

7 And Mosheh (Musa) laid up the rods before YHWH in the Tent of witness.

8 And it came to pass, that on the next day when Mosheh (Musa) went into the Tent of witness; and, behold, the rod of Aharon for the Beyth (house) of Levi was budded, and brought forth buds, and bloomed blossoms, and yielded almonds.[1]

9 And Mosheh (Musa) brought out all the rods from before YHWH to all the children of Israel: and they looked, and every man took his rod.

10 And YHWH said to Mosheh (Musa), Bring Aharon's rod again before the testimony, to be kept for a sign against the rebels;[2] and that You shall put away their murmurings from me, that they do not die.

11 And Mosheh (Musa) did so: as YHWH commanded him, so did he.

12 And the children of Israel spoke to Mosheh (Musa), saying, behold, we will die, we will perish, we all perish.

13 Whosoever comes anywhere

Footnotes

[1] This rod was passed down from Ahdahm and was taken from the tree of life which was an almond tree hence why we see Almonds on it.

[2] This was to show who is on YHWH's side and who isn't.

near the Tent of YHWH shall die: shall we be consumed with death?

Chapter 18

1 And YHWH said to Aharon, You and your sons and your father's Beyth (house) with you shall be responsible for any desecration of the sanctuary: and You and your sons with you will be held responsible for any impropriety in your priestly work.

2 And your brethren also of the tribe of Levi, the tribe of your father, bring with you, that they may be joined to you, and minister to you: but you and your sons with you shall minister before the Tent of witness.

3 And they shall keep your charge, and the charge of all the Tent: only they shall not come near the vessels of the sanctuary and the altar, that neither they, nor you also, die.

4 And they shall be joined to you, and keep the charge of the Tent of the appointed times, for all the service of the Tent: and a foreigner shall not come near to you.

5 And you shall keep the charge of the sanctuary, and the charge of the altar: that there be no wrath any more upon the children of Israel.

6 And I, behold, I have taken your brethren the Lewim from among the children of Israel: to you they are given as a gift[1] from YHWH, to do the service of the Tent of the appointed times.

7 Therefore You and your sons with you shall keep your kohen's (priest) office for everything of the altar, and within the veil; and you shall serve: I have given you the kohen's (priest) office to you as a gift for service and the foreigner that comes near shall be put to death.

8 And YHWH spoke to Aharon, Behold, I also have given you the charge of mine love offerings of all the Holy things of the children of Israel; to you have I given them by reason of the anointing, and to your sons, by an ordinance forever.

9 This shall be yours for the most Holy things, reserved from the fire: every offering of their's, every grain offering of their's, and every sin offering of their's, and every trespass offering of their's, which they shall render to me, shall be most Holy for you and for your sons.

10 In the most Holy place, You shall eat it; every male shall eat it, this shall be Holy to you.

11 And this is yours; the love offering of their grain, with all the wave offerings of the children of Israel: I have given them to you, and to your sons and to your daughters with you, by a statute forever: everyone that is ritually pure[2] in your Beyth (house) shall

Footnotes
[1] The Levitical priests are a gift even today, wherever they will be they will serve YHWH and His people with Torah truths.

Footnotes
[2] Those Lewites who were not ritually pure were not allowed to enter the Temple in fact no person even a non-Levite could enter the Temple if unclean. These particular offerings were only allowed to be eaten by the Lewites and their families who were not unclean ritually as it was an important issue
Continued in next section

eat of it.

12 All the best of the oil, and all the best of the wine, and of the wheat, the first-fruits of them which they shall offer to YHWH, them have I given you.

13 And whatsoever is first ripe in the land, which they shall bring to YHWH, shall be yours; everyone that is clean in your Beyth (house) shall eat of it.

14 Everything devoted in Israel shall be yours.

15 Everything that opens the womb in all flesh, which they bring to YHWH, whether it be of men or beasts, shall be yours: nevertheless the Bekhor (firstborn) of man You shall redeem, and the Bekhor (firstborn) of unclean animals[1] You shall redeem.

16 And those that are to be redeemed from a month old shall You redeem, according to your estimation, for the money of five shekels, after the shekel of the sanctuary, which is twenty gerahs.

17 But the Bekhor (firstborn) of a cow, or the Bekhor (firstborn) of a sheep, or the Bekhor (firstborn) of a goat, You shall not redeem; they are Holy: You shall sprinkle their blood upon the altar, and shall burn their fat for an offering made by fire, for a sweet savour to YHWH.

18 And the flesh of them shall be yours, as the wave breast and as the right shoulder are yours.

19 All the love offerings of the Holy things, which the children of Israel offer to YHWH, have I given you, and your sons and your daughters with you, by a statute forever: it is a Covenant of salt[2] forever before YHWH to you and to your descendants with you.

20 And YHWH spoke to Aharon, You shall have no inheritance in their land, neither shall You have any part among them: I am your part and your inheritance among the children of Israel.

21 And, behold, I have given the children of Levi all the tenth in Israel for an inheritance, for their service which they serve, even the service of the Tent of the appointed times.

22 Neither must the children of Israel henceforth come near the Tent of the appointed times, lest they bear sin, and die.

23 But the Lewim shall do the service of the Tent of the appointed times, and they shall bear their iniquity: it shall be a statute forever throughout your generations, that among the children of Israel they have no inheritance.

24 But the tithes of the children of Israel, which they offer as a

Footnotes

[2] The salt is used to preserve food and the salt can act as a chemical in other uses such as when it snows a lot you can throw it on the ground and in freezing cold temperatures it can melt the ice quicker.

A newborn baby is also washed in salt to remove and kill the bacteria. So here the usage of the salt is important as it was used in sacrifices. Salt is for us to know that YHWH's Covenants are preserved forever.

during Tabernacle and Temple times for the Qorban offerings.
[1] This law applies to unclean animals such as people owning horses and donkey's e.g. the mare giving birth to young ones.

heave offering to YHWH, I have given to the Lewim to inherit: therefore I have said to them, Among the children of Israel they shall have no inheritance.

25 And YHWH spoke to Mosheh (Musa), saying,

26 Thus speak to the Lewim, and say to them, when you take of the children of Israel the tithes which I have given you from them for your inheritance, then you shall offer up for a love offering of it for YHWH, even a tenth part of the tithe.

27 And your love offering shall be reckoned to you, as though it were the wheat of the threshing floor, and as the fullness of the winepress.

28 Thus you also shall offer a love offering to YHWH of all your tithes, which you receive of the children of Israel; and you shall give there YHWH's love offering to Aharon the kohen (priest).

29 Out of all your gifts you shall offer every heave offering of YHWH, of all the best there, even the Holy part there out of it.

30 Therefore You shall say to them, When you have heaved the best there from it, then it shall be counted to the Lewim as the **Increase** of the threshing floor, and as the **Increase** of the winepress.

31 And you shall eat it in every place, you and your households: for it is your reward for your service in the Tent of the appointed times.

32 And you shall bear no sin by reason of it, when you have heaved from it the best of it: neither shall you pollute the Holy things of the children of Israel, lest you die.

Torah Parsha 39 Chukat, WeDavar 19:1-22:1
Haftarah: Shoftim 11:1-33

Chapter 19

1 And YHWH spoke to Mosheh (Musa) and to Aharon, saying,

2 This is the ordinance of the Torah which YHWH has commanded, saying, Speak to the children of Israel, that they bring you a red heifer without spot, wherein there is no blemish, and has never been yoked.

3 And you shall give her to El'ezar the kohen (priest), that he may bring her forth outside the camp, and one shall slaughter her before his face:

4 And El'ezar the kohen (priest) shall take of her blood[1] with his finger, and sprinkle of her blood directly before the Tent of the appointed times seven times:

5 And one shall burn the heifer in his sight; her skin, and her flesh, and her blood, with her excrement, shall he burn:

6 And the kohen (priest) shall take cedar wood, and hyssop, and scarlet, and cast it into the midst of the burning of the heifer.

7 Then the kohen (priest) shall wash his clothes, and he shall bathe his flesh in mayim, and afterward he shall come into the camp, and the kohen (priest)

Footnotes
[1] Note, Yahushua is a "Type" and Shadow of the Red Heifer, he takes upon the sin and becomes rituly unclean. We cannot expand here due to the length of this teaching.

shall be unclean[1] until the evening.

8 And he that burns her shall wash his clothes in mayim, and bathe his flesh in mayim, and shall be unclean until the evening.

9 And a man that is clean shall gather up the ashes of the heifer, and lay them up outside the camp in a clean place, and it shall be kept for the congregation of the children of Israel for a mayim of menstruation/separation: it is for impurity.[2]

10 And he that gathers the ashes of the heifer shall wash his clothes, and be unclean until the evening: and it shall be to the children of Israel, and to the foreigner that lives among them, for a statute forever.

11 He that touches the dead body of any man shall be unclean seven days.

12 He shall purify himself with it on the third day, and on the seventh day he shall be clean: but if he does not purify himself the third day, then the seventh day he shall not be clean.

13 Whosoever touches the dead body of any man that is dead, and does not purifies himself, defiles the Tent of YHWH; and that soul shall be cut off from Israel: because the mayim of separation was not sprinkled

upon him, he shall be unclean; his uncleanness is still upon him.

14 This is the Torah, when a man dies in a tent: all that come into the tent, and all that is in the tent, shall be unclean seven days.

15 And every open vessel, which has no covering bound upon it, is unclean.

16 And whosoever touches one that is slain with a sword in the open fields, or a dead body, or a bone of a man, or a grave, shall be unclean seven days.

17 And for an unclean person they shall take of the ashes of the burnt heifer of purification for sin, and running mayim shall be put into a vessel:

18 And a clean person shall take hyssop, and dip it in the mayim, and sprinkle it upon the tent, and upon all the vessels, and upon the persons that were there, and upon him that touched a bone, or one slain, or one dead, or a grave:

19 And the clean person shall sprinkle upon the unclean on the third day, and on the seventh day: and on the seventh day he shall purify himself, and wash his clothes, and bathe himself in mayim, and shall be clean at evening.

20 But the man that shall be unclean, and shall not purify himself, that soul shall be cut off from among the congregation, because he has defiled the sanctuary of YHWH: the mayim of separation has not been sprinkled upon him; he is unclean.

21 And it shall be an everlasting

Footnotes

[1] Extraordinary sacrifice in which the Kohen became unclean. The Red Heifer and its ash cleansed the most severe form of sins, but the person doing the sacrifice, and the one gathering the ash, became unclean.

[2] The Hebrew word Chatat here refers to impurity.

statute to them, that he that sprinkles the mayim of separation shall wash his clothes; and he that touches the mayim of separation shall be unclean until even.

22 And whatsoever the unclean person touches shall be unclean; and the soul that touches it shall be unclean until evening.

Chapter 20

1 Then came the children of Israel, even the whole congregation, into the wilderness of Zin[1] in the first month: and the people abode in Kadesh; and Miriam died there, and was buried there.

2 And there was no mayim for the congregation: and they gathered themselves together against Mosheh (Musa) and against Aharon.

3 And the people contended with Mosheh (Musa), and spoke, saying, if only would Elohim had killed us too when our brethren died before YHWH?

4 And why have you brought up the congregation of YHWH into this wilderness, that we and our cattle should die there instead?

5 And why have you made us to come up out of Mitzrayim (Egypt), to bring us in to this evil place? It is not a place of seed, or of figs, or of vines, or of pomegranates; neither is there any mayim to drink.

6 And Mosheh (Musa) and Aharon went from the presence of the assembly to the door of the Tent of the appointed times, and they fell upon their faces: and the glory of YHWH appeared to them.

7 And YHWH spoke to Mosheh (Musa), saying,

8 Take the rod, and you gather the assembly together, You, and Aharon your brother, and declare my word upon the rock[2] before their eyes; and it shall give forth mayim, and You shall bring forth to them mayim out of the rock: so You shall give the congregation and their beasts drink.

9 And Mosheh (Musa) took the rod from before YHWH as he commanded him.

10 And Mosheh (Musa) and Aharon gathered the congregation together before the rock, and he said to them, hear now, you rebels; should we now bring you mayim out of this rock?

11 And Mosheh (Musa) lifted up his hand, and with his rod he struck the rock twice[3]: and the mayim came out abundantly, and the congregation drank, and their beasts also.

12 And YHWH spoke to Mosheh (Musa) and Aharon, because you believed me not, to set me apart in the eyes of the children of Israel, therefore you shall not bring this congregation into the land which I have given them.

13 This is the mayim of Meribah;[4] because the children of

Footnotes

[1] Saudi Arabia.

[2] We can use our speech with the power of YHWH behind us to glorify YHWH in many places of the world, declaring His word brings life to the dead and healing to the sick. Moses was about to declare the glory of YHWH through a rock and the rock giving water is an incredible miracle of itself. However, it shows us something greater that the rock being an inanimate object, but in reality our Rock is YHWH. Moses was not asked to generate a conversation with the rock, as some may think from the text. He was asked to declare the word of YHWH, upon the rock, and so he did.

[3] Moses should have struck the rock only once but by striking it twice that displeased YHWH.

[4] The Hebrew word 'Meribah' means Strife. This was a future prophetic picture of Saudi Arabia, an evil place from where a large world religion was to arise and it would
Continued in next section

Israel contended[1] with YHWH and he was sanctified in them.

14 And Mosheh (Musa) sent messengers from Kadesh to the King of Edom, Thus says your brother Israel, You know all the travail that has befallen us:

15 How our ahvot (fathers) went down into Mitzrayim (Egypt), and we have dwelt in Mitzrayim (Egypt) a long time; and the Mitzrim (Egyptians) vexed us, and our ahvot (fathers):

16 And when we cried to YHWH he heard our voice, and sent his Malakh, and has brought us forth out of Mitzrayim (Egypt): and, behold, we are in Kadesh, a city in the edge of your border:

17 Let us pass, I beseech you, through your country: we will not pass through the fields, or through the vineyards, neither will we drink of the mayim of the wells: we will go by the King's high way, we will not turn to the right hand nor to the left, until we have passed your borders.

18 And Edom said to him, you shall not pass by me, lest I come out against you with the sword.

19 And the children of Israel said to him, we will go by the high way: and if I or my livestock drink any of your mayim, then I will pay for it: let me only pass through on foot and nothing else.

20 And he said you shall not go through. And Edom came out against him with much people, and with a strong hand.

21 Thus Edom refused to give Israel passage through his border: wherefore Israel turned away from him.

22 And the children of Israel, even the whole congregation, journeyed from Kadesh, and came to Mount Hor.

23 And YHWH spoke to Mosheh (Musa) and Aharon in Mount Hor, by the coast of the land of Edom, saying,

24 Aharon shall be gathered to his people: for he shall not enter into the land which I have given to the children of Israel, because you rebelled against my word at the mayim of Meribah.[2]

25 Take Aharon and El'ezar his son, and bring them up to Mount Hor:

26 And remove Aharon clothes, and put them upon El'ezar his son: and Aharon shall be gathered to his people, and he shall die there.

27 And Mosheh (Musa) did as YHWH commanded: and they

cause strife in the world and bitterness. Today many people are divided over the Muslim nations, while some Muslims take up the Jihad doctrine and fight the east and the west and bring chaos and disorder and bitterness into many families' lives.

'Islam came out of the country of Saudi Arabia, and it has in the past and it is even today causing much bitterness.'

This is what this prophecy was telling us if we have eyes to see it while many of us are still walking in the imagination of our hearts. We need to repent and turn to the Torah.

[1] Israel contended and this is a remez (hint) that many families will contend with their children when they obey Torah they parents may object.

Footnotes
[2] There is always a cost for sin even if YHWH forgives us, and we have to bear the consequences as we see here by those closest to YHWH.

went up into Mount Hor in the sight of all the congregation.

28 And Mosheh (Musa) took Aharon's clothes off, and put them upon El'ezar his son; and Aharon died there in the top of the Mount: and Mosheh (Musa) and El'ezar came down from the Mount.

29 And when all the congregation saw that Aharon was dead, they mourned for Aharon thirty days,[1] even all the Beyth (house) of Israel.

Chapter 21

1 And when King Arad the Kanani, who dwelt in the south, heard that Israel came by the way of the spies; then he fought against Israel, and took some of them prisoners.

2 And Israel vowed a vow to YHWH, and said, If you will indeed give this people into my hand, then I will utterly destroy their cities.

3 And YHWH listened to the voice of Israel, and gave up the Kanani; and they utterly destroyed them and their cities: and he called the name of the place Khurma.[2]

4 And they journeyed from Mount Hor by the way of the Sea of Reeds, to compass the land of Edom: and the souls of the people became impatient because of the journey.

5 And the people contended against Elohim, and against Mosheh (Musa), why have You brought us up out of Mitzrayim (Egypt) to die in the wilderness? For there is no Lakhem (bread), neither is there any mayim; and our soul hates this worthless food.[3]

6 And YHWH sent poisonous snakes among the people, and they bit the people; and many people of Israel died.

7 Therefore the people came to Mosheh (Musa), and said, we have transgressed, for we have contended against YHWH, and against you; pray to YHWH, that he may take away the serpents from us. And Mosheh (Musa) prayed for the people.

8 And YHWH said to Mosheh (Musa), You make a bronze snake, and set it upon a pole: and it shall come to pass, that everyone that is bitten, when he looks upon it, shall have life[4].

9 And Mosheh (Musa) made a serpent of brass, and put it upon a pole, and it came to pass, that if a serpent had bitten any man, when he looked upon the serpent of bronze, he lived.

10 And the children of Israel set forward, and pitched in Oboth.

11 And they journeyed from Oboth, and pitched at Iye-ha barim, in the wilderness which is before Moav, toward the sun

Footnotes
[1] The custom was to mourn for 30 days.
[2] It was called Zephath before this.

Footnotes
[3] The Hebrew word 'Qiloqel' meaning 'good for nothing' and 'Lakhem' meaning food in general, they complained against Manna as light and not of substance and chewy like the meat. They despised the malakh's food sent by YHWH and wanted earthly substance.
[4] The healing was by Faith. The bronze serpent was hung from a pole, while anyone who looked at it and believed, on the words of Moses would receive life.

rising.

12 From there they moved, and pitched in the valley of Zared.

13 From there they moved again, and pitched on the other side of Arnon, which is in the wilderness that comes out of the coasts of the Amoree: for Arnon is the border of Moav, between Moav and the Amoree.

14 Wherefore it is said in the scrolls[1] of the wars of YHWH, what he did in the Waheb at supha the wadi[2] of Arnon,

15 And at the stream of the brooks that goes down to the dwelling of Ar, and lies upon the border of Moav.

16 And from there they went to Beer: that is the well whereof YHWH spoke to Mosheh (Musa), Gather the people together, and I will give them mayim.

17 Then Israel sang this song, Spring up, O well; We sing to it:

18 The princes dug the well, the nobles of the people digged it, by the direction of the Torah-giver, with their staves. And from the wilderness they went to Mattanah:

19 And from Mattanah to Nahali'el: and from Nahali'el to Bamoth:

20 And from Bamoth in the valley, that is in the country of Moav, to the top of Pisgah, which looks toward Yeshimon.

21 And Israel sent messengers to Sikhon King of the Amoree, saying,

22 Let me pass through your land: we will not turn into the

fields, or into the vineyards; we will not drink of the mayim of the well: but we will go along by the King's high way, until we be pass your borders.

23 And Sikhon would not allow Israel to pass through his borders: but Sikhon gathered all his people together, and went out against Israel into the wilderness: and he came to Yahtsa, and fought against Israel.

24 And Israel killed him with the edge of the sword, and captured his land from Arnon to Yabbok,[3] even to the children of Ammon: for the border of the children of Ammon was strong.

25 And Israel took all these cities: and Israel dwelt in all the cities of the Amoree, in Kheshbon, and in all the villages there after.

26 For Kheshbon was the city of Sikhon the King of the Amoree, who had fought against the former King of Moav, and taken all his land out of his hand, even to Arnon.

27 Wherefore they that speak in proverbs say, Come into Kheshbon, let the city of Sikhon be built and prepared:

28 For there is a fire gone out of Kheshbon, a flame from the city of Sikhon: it has consumed Ar of Moav, and the masters of the high places of Arnon.

29 Woe to you, Moav! You are undone, O people of Chemosh:[4] he has given his sons that escaped, and his daughters, into

Footnotes
[1] Written by some ancient writers
[2] Stream of water.

Footnotes
[3] A river in Jordan.
[4] False deity that required the sacrifice of children.

captivity to Sikhon King of the Amoree.

30 We have shot at them; Kheshbon is perished even to Dibon, and we have laid them waste even to Nophah, which reaches to Medeva.

31 Thus Israel dwelt in the land of the Amoree.

32 And Mosheh (Musa) sent to spy out Yaazer, and they took all the villages there and drove out the Amoree that were there.

33 And they turned and went up by the way of Bashan and Og[1] the King of Bashan went out against them, him and all his people to the battle at Edrei.

34 And YHWH said to Mosheh (Musa), Fear him not: for I have given him into your hand, and all his people, and his land; and You shall do to him as You did to Sikhon King of the Amoree,

Footnotes

[1] He was last of the giants ruling a province of Arabia, (note the region of Arabia was much larger than today) his bed measured thirteen and a half feet by six feet wide (Deut 3:11). There is a hint here to the religion of Islam a giant religion in stature rising out and spreading to the whole world. Islam will obstruct the children of Israel, both Christians and the Hebrew people who will have to fight it in these coming last days. With the help of YHWH it will be brought low but Islam will not be eradicated completely in the first millennium as Muslim nations will go up to the three great feasts to Jerusalem, Zechariah 14:16. The city Edrei was the place where when Hebrew people were driven out of Medina in Saudi Arabia came and settled, at that time the city was called 'Adra'at by the Arabs. Jerome confirms this was a famous city of the Arabs at one time and it was about 24 miles from Botsrah. At his time it was called Adara (De locis Heb. fol. 87. I & 92. M). This should explain why YHWH cast judgment on Mount Seir in Ezekiel 35:2 where the Zionists will be judged.

which dwelt at Kheshbon.

35 So they killed him, and his sons, and all his people, until there was none left alive: and they possessed his land.

Chapter 22

1 And the children of Israel set forward, and pitched in the plains of Moav on this side of Yardan (Jordan) by Yerikho.

Torah Parsha 40 Balak, WeDavar 22:2-25:9
Haftarah: Micah 5:6-6:8

2 And Balak the son of Zippor saw all that Israel had done to the Amoree.

3 And Moav was terrified of the people, because they were many[2] and Moav was distressed because of the children of Israel.

4 And Moav said to the elders of Midian, Now shall this company eat up all that are round about us, as the ox eats up the grass of the field. And Balak the son of Zippor was King of the Moavi at that time.

5 He sent messengers therefore to Bilam [3] the son of Beor to

Footnotes

[2] Israel multiplied fast with polygamous marriages as their standard lifestyle. Very few people in Israel were into monogamous only marriages as thought by many today. The monogamous model of marriage was setup by the Roman/Greek church in the fourth century CE because of the hatred and anti-Semitic attitudes towards the Hebrew people. Many believers in the 1st century assemblies also practiced polygamy, which was spoken of and written by the anti-Semitic writers such as Justin Martyr.

[3] He was a magician and wise man who worked for Pharaoh earlier and ran away when the plagues started to hit Egypt.

Pethor, which is by the Farat (Euphrates) river in the land Amaw,[1] to call him, saying, Behold, there is a people come out from Mitzrayim (Egypt): behold, they cover the face of the earth,[2] and they abide over against me:

6 Come now therefore, I beseech you, curse me this people; for they are too mighty for me: perhaps I will prevail, that we may slay them, and that I may drive them out of the land: for I know that he whom You **Bless** is **Blessed**, and he whom You curse is cursed.

7 And the elders of Moav and the elders of Midian departed with the fee of divination in their hand; and they came to Bilam, [3] and spoke to him the words of Balak.

8 And he said to them, Lodge here this night, and I will bring you word again, as YHWH shall speak to me: and the princes of Moav abode with Bilam.[4]

9 And Elohim came to Bilam, and said, What men are these with you?[5]

10 And Bilam said to Elohim, Balak the son of Zippor, King of Moav, has sent to me, saying,

11 Behold, there is a people come out of Mitzrayim (Egypt), which covers the face of the land:[6] come now, curse me them; perhaps I shall be able to conquer them, and drive them out.

12 And Elohim said to Bilam, You shall not go with them; You shall not curse the people: for they are **Blessed**.[7]

13 And Bilam rose up in the morning, and said to the princes of Balak, go back into your land: for YHWH refused[8] to give me

Footnotes

[1] Some translations render this, 'Sons of his people.'

[2] Israelites named as covering the whole earth.

[3] They came with money to persuade him to curse Israel. This was Balaam's fatal flaw, he was a seer but a false prophet as are many in churches, which may converse with YHWH but have no real relationship. He asked them to stay the night so he could take the money and curse Israel.

[4] The word 'Balaam,' has the meaning, the people of 'Bel,' this is a false deity spoken of in Jeremiah 50:2 and Isaiah 46.1. So this man was a kind of double agent who worked for money and would be a prophet for hire for anyone who needed him. This man is the picture of the ecumenical church today that would feed Israel to the dogs (gentiles) for Continued in next section

money and give their land to the Muslim radicals for peace.

[5] YHWH plays with Balaam as He knows the heart of Balaam is full of greed and selfishness.

[6] Balaam is foolish as he knew that they were Israelites and it was YHWH bringing them out. While he was present there in Egypt and saw all the signs, here he pretends like he is not sure.

[7] YHWH told Balaam, Israel is increased by the Contractual agreements set with the Patriarchs and they could not be cursed. Even if Balaam had succeeded in cursing other people he was not to prevail against Israel. The word increased here means 'protected' 'enriched,' 'rescued' both materially, physically and spiritually from all things. The Rebbim discuss this. So we see here Balaam asking YHWH can I **Bless** them also. YHWH said NO, they do not need your increasing, you two faced man, for My Increasing is enough.

[8] Balaam reluctantly got up and said YHWH refused it while it was in his own heart to curse Israel some way. He was crafty and had thought to circumvent the increases another way but was asking the king for more money.

permission to go with you.

14 And the princes of Moav rose up, and they went to Balak, and said, Bilam refused to come with us.

15 And Balak sent yet again princes, more, and more honourable than they.

16 And they came to Bilam, and said to him, Thus says Balak the son of Zippor, Let nothing, I beseech you, hinder you from coming to me:[1]

17 For I will promote you to very great respect,[2] and I will do whatsoever You say to me: come therefore, I beseech you, curse me this people.

18 And Bilam answered and said to the servants of Balak, If Balak would give me his Beyth (house) full of silver and gold,[3] I cannot go beyond the word of YHWH my POWER,[4] to do less or more.

19 Now therefore, I beseech you, stay here also this night,[5] that I may know what YHWH will say to me more.

20 And the Word[6] from Elohim came to Bilam at night, and said to him, If the men come to call you, rise up, and go with[7] them; but yet the word which I shall say to you, that shall You do.

21 And Bilam rose up in the morning, and saddled his ass, and went with the princes of Moav.

22 And Elohim's anger[8] was kindled because he went: and the Malakh YHWH stood in the way[9] for an adversary against him. Now he was riding upon his ass, and his two servants[10] were with him.

23 And the ass saw the Malakh YHWH standing in the way, and his sword drawn in his hand: and the ass turned aside out of the way, and went into the field: and Bilam beat the ass, to turn her into the way.

24 But the Malakh YHWH[11] stood in a path of the vineyards,[12]

Footnotes
[1] Balak thought Balaam needed more money. He was partly right, as Balaam was looking for a pretext and more money and we will see the money will do the trick but he acted foolishly.
[2] He offered to make him an officer of his court with great wealth as an enticement.
[3] He was actually saying if you give me these things I might just do it anyway.
[4] YHWH was not his Elohim else why would he be in Egypt against Israel! Even today, many people who call upon God and not YHWH only serve mammon as Balaam did.
[5] Why would he ask them to stay and speak to YHWH again since YHWH had already spoken? The reason was that he was greedy and looking for a way out. It's like the Televangelists looking to make loads of money any which way they can by deceiving the masses of people.

Footnotes
[6] Torah
[7] YHWH is sarcastically saying to go, but not really giving him permission to go.
[8] This is because YHWH never gave him permission but since Balaam wanted to do this due to greed he was all set to go.
[9] Ha derech – The way is the practice of Torah.
[10] Targum of Jonathan says they were Jannes and Jambres, the magicians of Egypt. Remember, Balaam himself was one of the magicians present in Egypt at the time before he ran away. He was a coward at heart and he ran away with his sons. See book of Yashar.
[11] The Metatron.
[12] We have two choices either to walk in 'the way' of the King or to walk away. Here a sod hidden teaching can be seen where the donkey can see what the correct path is but the intelligent person Balaam cannot. This is Continued in next section

a wall being on this side, and a wall on that side.

25 And when the ass saw the Malakh YHWH, she thrust herself to the wall, and crushed Bilam's foot against the wall: and he beat her again.

26 And Malakh YHWH went further, and stood in a narrow place,[1] where was no way to turn either to the right hand or to the left.

27 And when the ass saw the Malakh YHWH, she fell down under Bilam:[2] and Bilam's anger was kindled, and he beat the ass with a staff.

28 And YHWH opened the mouth of the ass, and she said to Bilam, What have I done to you, that You have beaten me these three times?

29 And Bilam said to the ass, Because You have mocked me: I wish if there was a sword in my hand, for I would kill you now.[3]

30 And the ass said to Bilam, Am not I your ass, upon which You have been riding ever since I was yours to this day? Have I ever refused to do what you asked? And he said, No.

31 Then YHWH opened the eyes of Bilam, and he saw the Malakh YHWH standing in The WAY[4], and his sword[5] drawn in his hand: and he bowed down his head, and fell flat on his face.[6]

32 And the Malakh YHWH[7] said to him, why have You beaten your ass these three times? Behold, I went out to withstand you, because your way [8] is perverse before me:

33 And the ass saw me, and turned from me these three times: unless she had turned from me, surely now also I would have killed you, and rescued her alive.

34 And Bilam said to the Malakh YHWH, I have transgressed; for I knew not that You stood in The WAY[9] against me: now therefore,

Footnotes

[4] The WAY of YHWH.

[5] Sword of truth/Torah.

[6] This will happen to all wrong theologies one day when they will fail. Those who hate Israelites and teach anti-Semitic teachings and replacement theology that says we are now Israel and Israel has no more Blessings. The real Hebrews are amongst the nations who are not even acknowledged the Black Africans while another people the sons of Japheth are trumped as the Semites. This is a deception many have fallen into.

[7] Metatron

[8] Sod hidden meaning here is the church has been teaching about doing away with 'the Torah,' which is a perverse teaching in many Churches. Also, churches claim to be worshipping 'God,' yet many do not even know the true name is YHWH. See our footnote in the HTHS Tanak in Isaiah 65:11

[9] Many in the Church system will realise, on the day of resurrection how wrong they were in disobeying Torah and casting out Jews as Continued in next section

how many times intelligent people can become foolish in their thinking. The vineyard is the sod teaching for Messiah being the vine and we being the branches. While Balaam is the archetype for the false church, false preachers leading people away from Torah today.

[1] Sod meaning narrow for the narrow path of Torah, which is Torah keeping. Or, the wide gates of the Church who eat unclean food and do not keep Torah, and blaspheme YHWH by bringing his name to naught.

[2] The donkey was bowing before YHWH that is why it fell, even the animal had more sense than Balaam.

[3] When false prophets are found out they cannot find a way out so they curse and abuse the people by lying and we see the sod here.

if it displeases you, I will go back.

35 And the Malakh YHWH said to Bilam, Go with the men: but only the word that I shall speak to you, which You shall speak. So Bilam went with the princes of Balak.

36 And when Balak heard that Bilam was come, he went out to meet him to a city of Moav, which is in the border of Arnon, which is in the utmost coast.

37 And Balak said to Bilam, Did I not sincerely send to you to call you? Why would You not come on to me? Am I not able indeed to promote you to respect?[1]

38 And Bilam said to Balak, Behold, I have come to you: have I now any power at all to say[2] any thing? The word that Elohim puts in my mouth, that shall I speak.

39 And Bilam went with Balak, and they came to Kiryath-huzoth.

40 And Balak offered oxen and sheep, and sent to Bilam, and to the princes that were with him.

41 And it came to pass on the next day, that Balak took Bilam, and brought him up into the high places of Baal,[3] that there he might see the utmost part of the people.

Chapter 23

1 And Bilam said to Balak, Build me here seven altars, and prepare me here seven oxen[4] and seven rams.

2 And Balak did as Bilam had spoken; and Balak and Bilam offered on every altar a bullock and a ram.

3 And Bilam said to Balak, Stand by your burnt offering, and I will go: peradventure YHWH will come to meet me: and whatsoever he shows me I will tell you. And he went to a deserted height.[5]

4 And Elohim met Bilam: and he said to him, I have prepared seven altars, and I have offered upon every altar a bullock and a ram.[6]

5 And YHWH put a word in Bilam's mouth, and said, Return to Balak, and thus You shall speak.

6 And he returned to him, and, behold, he stood by his burnt sacrifice, he, and all the princes of Moav.

Footnotes

[4] This was a heathen practice for worship of the planets as Balaam was a magician, so he thought by adding to the number of Altars he would somehow appease YHWH. But, since YHWH first instructed Adam to build an altar, he has only allowed one altar for sacrifice, not seven. YHWH also did not allow His altar to be cut by instruments so Balaam did not know this and allowed these altars to be cut out of stone by instruments. He was covering all bases, like people do today, who say, if I worship all false elohim in the world, I just might get to the right one. So when I die, one of them will rescue me. This is why he offered 7 bulls instead of one.

[5] The false prophets of the nations believed that deserted places carry the Holy presence, although they mostly carry demonic spirits instead.

[6] Note; YHWH in the next verse does not accept nor acknowledge Balaam's heathen sacrifices but tells him what he needs to do, to the point.

unbelievers and will lose all their rewards as a result.

[1] Here the term respect means to bribe by money hence why the term respect is wrong to use for believers.

[2] Balaam is making an excuse only by mouth and blaming YHWH.

[3] These were Baal worshippers.

7 And he took up his parable, and said, Balak the King of Moav has brought me from Aram, out of the mountains of the east, saying, Come, curse me Yakov, and come, defy Israel.

8 How shall I curse, whom El (The Power) has not cursed? [1] Or how shall I denounce, whom YHWH has not denounced?[2]

9 For from the top of the rocks I see him, and from the hills I behold him: behold, the people shall dwell alone, and shall not be reckoned among the nations.

10 Who can count the dust[3] of Yakov, and the number of the fourth part of Israel? Let me die the death of the Righteous,[4] and let my last end be like his!

11 And Balak said to Bilam, What have You done to me? I took you to curse my enemies, and, behold, You have **Blessed** them altogether.

12 And he answered and said, Must I take heed not to speak that which YHWH has put in my mouth?

13 And Balak said to him, Come, I beseech you, with me to another place, from where You may see them: You shall see but a small part of them, and shall not see them all: and curse me them from there.

14 And he brought him into the field of Zophim, to the top of Pisgah, and built seven altars, and offered a bullock and a ram on every altar.[5]

15 And he said to Balak, Stand here by your burnt offering, while I meet YHWH there.

16 And YHWH met Bilam, and put a word in his mouth, and said, Go again to Balak, and say thus.

17 And when he came to him, behold, he stood by his burnt offering, and the princes of Moav with him. And Balak said to him, What has YHWH spoken?

18 And he took up his parable, and said, Rise up, Balak, and hear; hearken to me, You son of Zippor:

19 El (The Power) is not a man, that he should lie; neither the son of man, that he should repent: has he said, and shall he not do it? Or has he spoken, and shall he not make it good?[6]

20 Behold, I have received orders to **Bless**: and he has **Blessed** them; and I cannot reverse it.[7]

Footnotes

[1] Beresheeth (Genesis) 12:3.

[2] No one has the right or power to curse Israel, YHWH has increased them eternally. If you hate true Israel then you will be hated by YHWH and if you love true Israel then you will receive Love, it's a simple formula. Israel is all of the community of brethren who believe in and serve YHWH, along with true Hebrew Israel who is not yet back in the land. 1948 is not the gathering of the true Hebrews but only gentiles who usurped the land by deception, see Gen 9:26-27.

[3] The multiplication of Israel in the nations and polygamy would be one tool. You cannot multiply by having one child in one family. This is the Roman/Greek failed model of Christianity.

[4] Balaam did not die a righteous death.

[5] See what Balaam was doing was a heathen custom of seven altars and seven ox for sacrifice.

[6] YHWH repeats that he is not like man to change his mind. What He said about Israel is written and sealed, no one can change it.

[7] Israel is Blessed even if people hate her so they must learn to reap the increases by being obedient to the Torah. Balaam is actually saying I wish I could curse them but Continued in next section

21 He has not beheld iniquity in Yakov, neither has he seen perverseness in Israel: YHWH his Elohim is with him, and the shout of a King is among them.

22 El (The Power) brought them out of Mitzrayim (Egypt); he has as it were the strength of a wild bull.[1]

23 Surely there is no enchantment against Yakov, neither is there any divination[2] against Israel: according to this time it shall be said of Yakov and of Israel, What has El (The Power) wrought!

24 Behold, this people shall rise up as a great lion, and soar as an eagle;[3] he shall not lie down until he eat of the prey, and drink the blood of the slain.

25 And Balak said to Bilam, Neither curse them at all, nor **Bless** them at all.

26 But Bilam answered and said to Balak, I told you before, saying, All that YHWH speaks to me, that I must do?

27 And Balak said to Bilam, Come, I beseech you, I will bring you to another place; perhaps it will please Elohim that You may curse me them from there.

28 And Balak brought Bilam to the top of Peor that looks toward Yeshimon.

29 And Bilam said to Balak, Build me here seven altars, and prepare me here seven bullocks and seven rams.[4]

30 And Balak did as Bilam had said, and offered a bullock and a ram on every altar.

Chapter 24

1 And when Bilam saw that it pleased YHWH to **Bless** Israel, he went not, as at other times, to seek to do sorcery, but he set his face toward the wilderness.

2 And Bilam lifted up his eyes, and he saw Israel encamped tribe by tribe; and the Ruakh (Spirit) of Elohim came upon him.

3 And he took up his parable, and said, Bilam the son of Beor has said, and the man whose eyes are open has said:

4 He has said, which heard the words of El (The Power), which saw the vision of the El-Shaddai, falling into a trance, but having his eyes open:

YHWH speaks Blessings to Israel out of Bilam a gentile's mouth

5 How goodly are your tents,[5] O

Footnotes

[4] See footnote WeDabar (Numbers) 23:14

[5] These tents are the homes of Israelites who were practicing a lifestyle that YHWH appointed, such as plural marriages. However, anyone who hates this lifestyle hates YHWH's ordinances. In the Babylonian Talmud Baba Batra 60a they asked what was so "goodly" about these tents. They answered that the doors of each individual tents did not face each other so that no family could see another family front door. Each home protected its own privacy and also the privacy of others was protected in the arrangement of the tents.
Continued in next section

I cannot. Real Israel is not yet fully in the land.

[1] A wild bull with two horns, which is drash for the two Houses of Israel with the strength given to propagate seed.

[2] If you are a believer and serve Him with righteousness then no magic or spell can come against you.

[3] The word here Aryeh is wrong to be translated lion, it should be an eagle same as Gen 49:9.

Yakov, and your tabernacles,[1] O Israel.

6 As the valleys are they spread forth, as gardens by the river's side, as the trees of aloes which YHWH has planted, and as cedar trees beside the mayim.

7 He shall pour the mayim out of his buckets, and his seed shall be in many mayim,[2] and his King shall be exalted over Agag,[3] and his kingdom shall be exalted.

8 It is El (The Power) Who

Israel lived under Roman occupation in the first century which had a spy system to keep an eye on troublesome dissidents. King Balak was troubled by the household privacy in thinking how dare these people keep secrets from the king. Balaam was made to utter the privacy was "goodly" and delightful. You can imagine if one Israelite man had eight wives and fifty-two children how the neighbors today would talk, tale bare and try to backstab the Israelite people in plural marriages. This is why it is important to keep your household matter private and personal and not advertise to the jealous gentile world.

This prophecy will come down as a curse on all those who oppose YHWH, because the other way to go would be the lifestyle of adultery and whoring, which many in the churches have adopted alongside the world. We find this happened when Balaam goes against YHWH's plan for Israel to multiply their children through biblical polygamy, when he instructed Balak how to bring Israel down. Balaam directs Balak to bring in foreign women to seduce Israel. So instead of receiving an increase, Israel would receive punishment instead. Rebbim have stated in the sefer ha aggadah page 97 chapter 113 Start quote. 'The Elohim of these people hates whoring and as it happens these people are very fond of linen garments (having grown accustomed to them in Egypt).

Listen I have useful counsel for you. Make tents partitioned by hanging draperies and put harlots inside old ones in the front part and young ones in the rear, and let them sell linen garments. So all the way from snowcapped Hermon (In the North) to Beth-ha-veshimot (In the South), Balak erected such tents and placed harlots inside-old ones in the front and young ones in the rear. Whenever an Israelite ate, drank, and became mellow, and went out for a stroll in the market place, an old harlot would say to him 'are you not interested in linen garments?' She would offer them at the going price, while the young harlot in the rear of the tent offered them for less.'

After two or three sales, the young harlot would say, 'you are now like one of the Continued in next section

family. Sit down and select any garment you desire.' Near her, there would be a cooler filled with Ammonite wine, which is strong and stimulates the body to lascivious thought. Then she would say, 'will you have a cup of wine?' After he drank, his passion aroused, he would say, 'Yield to me.' Then at that, the harlot would take her idols from her bosom and say '(first) worship this.' He 'but I am a Yahudi.' Then she 'what difference does that make? You need to do more then uncover yourself.' {He did not know that was the way the idol was worshipped.}

'What is more, I will not satisfy you until you reject the Torah of Moses your teacher.' End quote.

[1] This is a future prophecy which Rebbim know about that means how good are your synagogues/assemblies, places of worship of Israel.

[2] Prophecy of numerically multiplying via many nations and via the method of Biblical mandated polygamy as Israel's seed will be in many nations. This means that an Israelite will have more than one wife and produce children. The prophecy in Isaiah is not allegorical alone but in the pashat, it shows that seven gentile women from the ten scattered tribes will come and marry one man.

[3] A clear prophetic voice where we can see Agag is the giant representative of the End-Times Islamic beast and the kingdom they will build will be very large. Not to worry, for Israel will be greater and more exalted than Agag and the end result of Agag was death. It will be the same end result for those who oppose and fight against Israel.

brought him forth out of Mitzrayim (Egypt): he has as it were the strength of a young bull: he shall eat up the nations his enemies, and shall break their bones, and pierce them through with his arrows.[1]

9 He couched, he swooped down as an attacking eagle, and as a great lion: who shall stir him up? Those who **Bless** you will be **Blessed** and those who curse you will be cursed.[2]

10 And Balak's anger was kindled against Bilam, and he beat his hands together:[3] and Balak said to Bilam, I called you to curse my enemies, and, instead, You have **Blessed** them these three times.

11 Therefore now flee from here to your place: I thought to promote you to great respect; but, behold, YHWH has kept you back from respect.

12 And Bilam said to Balak, did I not speak to your messengers and said this.

13 If Balak would give me his Beyth (house) full of silver and gold, I cannot go beyond the commandment of YHWH, to do either good or bad of mine own mind; but whatever YHWH says, that will I speak?

Footnotes

[1] This sees its fulfillment in Psalm 127:5 when an Israelite warrior is shown his quiver full of arrows. The arrows are his children and are from numerous wives. This is the picture of such men like King David and the other kings who had many children from their wives who will one day stand up and fight the enemy of radical Islamic nations.

[2] A renewal of the promises in Beresheeth (Genesis) 27:29. The word Ar-yeh should be translated as an attacking eagle.

[3] A sign of disappointment and anger.

14 And now, behold, I go to my people: come therefore, and I will advertise you what this people shall do to your people in the latter days.

15 And he took up his parable, and said, Bilam the son of Beor has said, and the man whose eyes are open has said:

16 He has said, which heard the words of El (The Power), and knew the knowledge of the most High, which saw the vision of the Almighty, who falls down but having eyes wide open.

17 I shall see him, but not now: I shall behold him, but not near: there shall come a Star[4] out of Yakov, and a Sceptre[5] shall rise out of Israel, and shall smite the corners of Moav, and destroy all the children of Sheth.[6]

Footnotes

[4] The Star of King Messiah to come in the future.

[5] The prophecy of King Messiah to smite and destroy all nations (Islamic) who are against Israel.

[6] See my article on the sons of Sheth. These are radical Islamists who will be removed at the End of Days by the battle of Armageddon. The future Messiah is mentioned as a star (Kokab) meaning He is also described as a Sceptre (King).

The corners or mouth of the nations that will be battered around Israel, are the nations such as Jordan, Egypt, Syria and Lebanon, who will have a marked destruction at the time of the End when the King of Kings will batter them. The idea presented in WeDabar (Numbers) 24:17 in the ancient Hebrew reveals the following.

A King will rise out of the 12 tribes of Israel, in other words Yahudah (Beresheeth Genesis 49:10) will give us this king. This king was set to come at a distant future from the time when the prophecy was spoken. How can a king batter the brow of Moav when Moav was not a full force to deal with at that time
Continued in next section

18 And Edom shall be a possession, Seir also shall be a possession for his enemies; and Israel shall do valiantly.

19 Out of Yakov shall come he that shall have dominion, and shall destroy him that remained of the city.

20 And when he looked on Amalek, he took up his parable, and said, Amalek was the first of the nations; but his latter end shall be that he perishes forever.

21 And he looked on the Qeny, and took up his parable, and said, Strong is your dwelling place, and You put your nest in a rock.

22 Nevertheless the Qeny shall be wasted, until Asshur shall carry you away captive.

23 And he took up his parable, and said, Alas, who shall live when El (The Power) does this!

24 And ships shall come from the coast of Kittim,[1] and shall afflict Asshur, and shall afflict Eber, and he also shall perish forever.

25 And Bilam rose up, and went and returned to his place: and Balak also went his way.

Chapter 25
1 And Israel abode in Shittim,

and also the Messiah would not come during Balaam's time? Balaam's language is like hide and seek, one minute 'I see him' and then 'not' etc and then he speaks about the future destruction of the sons of Sheth which are the radical Islamists and the Edomite, political Zionists for occupiers. The term Sheth illustrates the occupation of the land.
[1] These are European nations that will come and fight alongside Israel. See Islam, Peace or Beast by Simon Altaf www.forever-israel.com

and the people began to commit whoredom with the daughters of Moav.[2]

2 And they called the people to the sacrifices of their powers: and the people did eat, and bowed down to other powers.

3 And Israel joined himself to Baal-peor: and the anger of YHWH was kindled against Israel.

4 And YHWH said to Mosheh (Musa), Take all the heads of the people, and hang them up before YHWH against the sun, that the fierce anger of YHWH may be turned away from Israel.

5 And Mosheh (Musa) said to the judges of Israel, execute everyone the men that were joined to Baal-peor.

6 And, behold, one of the children of Israel came and brought to his brethren a Midiani woman in the sight of Mosheh (Musa), and in the sight of all the congregation of the children of Israel, who were weeping before the door of the Tent of the appointed times.

7 And when Phinekas, the son of El'ezar, the son of Aharon the kohen (priest), saw it, he rose up from among the congregation, and took a javelin in his hand;

8 And he went after the man of Israel into the alcove,[3] and thrust both of them through, the man of Israel, and the woman through

Footnotes
[2] See footnote Num 24:5
[3] The place or brothel where harlots were kept, selling linen clothes and giving free wine and the Israelites were openly committing sexual acts of indecency by being seduced by the women through drink.

her belly. So the plague was stayed from the children of Israel.

9 And those that died in the plague were twenty four thousand.

Torah Parsha 41 Pinchas, WeDavar 25:10-29:40
Haftarah: Melekhim Alef 18:46-19:21

10 And YHWH spoke to Mosheh (Musa), saying,

[1]

11 Phinekas, the son of El'ezar, the son of Aharon the kohen (priest), has turned my wrath away from the children of Israel, while he manifested much zeal for my sake among them, that I consumed not the children of Israel in my jealousy.

12 Wherefore say, Behold, I give to him my Covenant of shalom.[2]

13 And he shall have it, and his descendants after him, even the Covenant of an everlasting priesthood; because he

manifested zeal for his Elohim, and made an atonement for the children of Israel.

14 Now the name of the Y'sraeli that was slain, even that was slain with the Midiani woman, was Zimri, the son of Salu, a prince of a chief Beyth (house) among the Shimoni.

15 And the name of the Midiani woman that was slain was Kozbi, the daughter of Zur; he was head over a people, and of a chief Beyth (house) in Midian.

16 And YHWH spoke to Mosheh (Musa), saying,

17 Bring trouble to the Midianites, and smite them:

18 For they troubled you with their wiles, where they have beguiled you in the matter of Peor, and in the matter of Kozbi, the daughter of a prince of Midian, their sister, which was slain in the day of the plague for Peor's sake.[3]

Chapter 26

[4]

1 And it came to pass after the plague, that YHWH spoke to Mosheh (Musa) and to El'ezar the son of Aharon the kohen (priest), saying,

2 Take the sum of all the congregation of the children of Israel, from twenty years old and upward, throughout their ahvot (fathers)'s Beyth (house), all that are able to go to war in Israel.

Footnotes
[1] The small yud. Picture of distinction. Phinekhas did something of distinction that averted disaster in Israel when Balaam suggested to Balaak that he should seduce the sons of Israel through women and this brought on the plague, because of the whoring. YHWH gave the Covenant of shalom to Phinekhas who was a Levite in the line of Aharon his grandfather and it indicates that our small things done through our hands can sometimes mean a big thing to YHWH so we must not stop doing what is right.
[2] This is a Pledge of friendship and peace while the world would call this an act of murder, but he saved the Israelites from destruction. When we do what is right in YHWH's sight it is never wrong to do good.

Footnotes
[3] It was Balaam who taught them to do this so YHWH's wrath fell on Israel.
[4] The gap in verse 1, it draws attention to what is being said and what happened like a 'moment of silence.'

3 And Mosheh (Musa) and El'ezar the kohen (priest) spoke with them in the plains of Moav by Yardan (Jordan) near Yerikho, saying,

4 Take the sum of the people, from twenty years old and upward; as YHWH commanded Mosheh (Musa) and the children of Israel, which went forth out of the land of Mitzrayim (Egypt).

5 Reuven, the eldest son of Israel: the children of Reuven; Khanokh, of whom comes the Mishpakha (family) of the Khanokhi: of Pallu, the Mishpakha (family) of the Pal'lui:

6 Of Khetsron, the Mishpakha (family) of the Khetsroni: of Carmi, the Mishpakha (family) of the Carmi.

7 These are the Mishpakhot (families) of the Reuveni: and they that were registered of them were forty three thousand seven hundred and thirty.

8 And the sons of Pallu; Eliab.

9 And the sons of Eliab; Nemu'el, and Dathan, and Abiram. This is that Dathan and Abiram, which were famous in the congregation, who contended against Mosheh (Musa) and against Aharon in the company of Korakh, when they contended against YHWH.

10 And the earth opened her mouth, and swallowed them up together with Korakh, when that company died, what time the fire devoured two hundred and fifty men: and they became a sign.

11 The descendants of Korakh did not die.

12 The sons of Shimeon after their Mishpakhot (families): of Nemu'el, the Mishpakha (family) of the Nemu'eli: of Yamin, the Mishpakha (family) of the Yaminites: of Yaken, the Mishpakha (family) of the Yakhini:

13 Of Zerakh, the Mishpakha (family) of the Zarhi: of Shaul, the Mishpakha (family) of the Sha'uli.

14 These are the Mishpakhot (families): of the Shimoni, twenty two thousand and two hundred.

15 The children of Gawd after their Mishpakhot (families): of Zephon, the Mishpakha (family) of the Zephoni: of Haggi, the Mishpakha (family) of the Khaggi: of Shuni, the Mishpakha (family) of the Shuni:

16 Of Ozni, the Mishpakha (family) of the Ozni: of Eri, the Mishpakha (family) of the Eri:

17 Of Arod, the Mishpakha (family) of the Arodi: of Areli, the Mishpakha (family) of the Areli.

18 These are the Mishpakhot (families): of the children of Gawd according to those that were registered of them, forty thousand and five hundred.

19 The sons of Yahudah were Er and Onan: and Er and Onan died in the land of Kanan.

20 And the sons of Yahudah after their Mishpakhot (families) were; of Shelah, the Mishpakha (family) of the Shelni: of Phratz, the Mishpakha (family) of the Pharatzi: of Zerakh, the Mishpakha (family) of the Zarkhi.

21 And the sons of Phratz were; of Khetsron, the Mishpakha (family) of the Khetsroni: of Khamul, the Mishpakha (family) of the Khamuli.

22 These are the Mishpakhot

(families) of Yahudah according to those that were registered of them, seventy six thousand and five hundred.

23 Of the sons of Yskhar (Issachar) after their Mishpakhot (families): of Tola, the Mishpakha (family) of the Tolai'e of Puwwah,[1] the Mishpakha (family) of the Puni:

24 Of Yashub, the Mishpakha (family) of the Yashubi: of Shimron, the Mishpakha (family) of the Shimroni

25 These are the Mishpakhot (families) of Yskhar (Issachar) according to those that were registered of them, sixty four thousand and three hundred.

26 Of the sons of Zevulun after their Mishpakhot (families): of Sered, the Mishpakha (family) of the Sardi: of Elon, the Mishpakha (family) of the Eloni: of Yakhle'el, the Mishpakha (family) of the Yakhle'eli.

27 These are the Mishpakhot (families) of the Zebuluni according to those that were registered of them, sixty thousand and five hundred.

28 The sons of Yosef after their Mishpakhot were Manasheh and Efrayim.

29 Of the sons of Manasheh: of Makhir, the Mishpakha (family) of the Makhiri and Makhir begat Gil'ad of Gil'ad come the Mishpakha (family) of the Gil'ad.

30 These are the sons of Gil'ad of Yeezer, the Mishpakha (family) of the Ye'ezeri of Khlek, the Mishpakha (family) of the Khleki:

Footnotes
[1] Same as in Genesis 46:13, spelt differently here in the Hebrew.

31 And of Asri'el, the Mishpakha (family) of the Asri'eli: and of Shkhem, the Mishpakha (family) of the Shekhemi:

32 And of Shemida, the Mishpakha (family) of the Shemidai: and of Khefer, the Mishpakha (family) of the Kheferi.

33 And Tselof'khad the son of Khefer had no sons, but daughters: and the names of the daughters of Tselof'khad were Makhlah, and Noakh, Hoglah, Milkah, and Tirzah.

34 These are the Mishpakhot (families) of Manasheh, and those that were registered of them, fifty-two thousand and seven hundred.

35 These are the sons of Efrayim after their Mishpakhot (families): of Shuthelakh, the Mishpakha (family) of the Shuthelakhi: of Bakr, the Mishpakha (family) of the Bakry: of Takhan, the Mishpakha (family) of the Takhani.

36 And these are the sons of Shuthelakh of Eran, the Mishpakha (family) of the Erani.

37 These are the Mishpakhot (families) of the sons of Efrayim according to those that were registered of them, thirty two thousand and five hundred. These are the sons of Yosef after their Mishpakhot (families).

38 The sons of Benyamin after their Mishpakhot (families): of Bela, the Mishpakha (family) of the Belaites: of Ashbel, the Mishpakha (family) of the Ashbelites: of Akhiram, the Mishpakha (family) of the Akhirami:

39 Of Shupham, the Mishpakha

(family) of the Shuphamites: of Khupam, the Mishpakha (family) of the Khupami.

40 And the sons of Bela were Ard and Naaman: of Ard, the Mishpakha (family) of the Ardi: and of Naaman, the Mishpakha (family) of the Naami.

41 These are the sons of Benyamin after their Mishpakhot (families): and they that were registered of them were forty five thousand and six hundred.

42 These are the sons of Dan after their Mishpakhot (families): of Shukham, the Mishpakha (family) of the Shukhami. These are the Mishpakhot (families) of Dan after their Mishpakhot (families).

43 All the Mishpakhot (families) of the Shukhami, according to those that were registered of them, were sixty-four thousand and four hundred.

44 Of the children of Asher after their Mishpakhot (families): of Yimna, the Mishpakha (family) of the Yimny: of Yesui, the Mishpakha (family) of the Yesuy: of Bereyah, the Mishpakha (family) of the Beriy.

45 Of the sons of Bereyah: of Kheber, the Mishpakha (family) of the Khebery: of Malkhi'el, the Mishpakha (family) of the Malkhi'ely.

46 And the name of the daughter of Asher was Sarah.

47 These are the Mishpakhot (families) of the sons of Asher according to those that were registered of them; who were fifty three thousand and four hundred.

48 Of the sons of Naphtali after their Mishpakhot (families): of

Yahze'el, the Mishpakha (family) of the Yakhats'eli: of Guni, the Mishpakha (family) of the Guny:

49 Of Yetser, the Mishpakha (family) of the Yetsery: of Shillem, the Mishpakha (family) of the Shillemi.

50 These are the Mishpakhot (families) of Naphtali according to their Mishpakhot (families): and they that were registered of them were forty five thousand and four hundred.

51 These were the registered of the children of Israel, six hundred thousand and one thousand seven hundred and thirty.

52 And YHWH spoke to Mosheh (Musa), saying,

53 To these the land shall be divided for an inheritance according to the number of names.

54 To many You shall give the more inheritance, and to few You shall give the less inheritance: to everyone shall his inheritance be given according to those that were registered of him.

55 Not withstanding the land shall be divided by Lot according to the names of the tribes of their ahvot (fathers) they shall inherit.

56 According to the Lot shall the possession there be divided between many and few.

57 And these are they that were registered of the Lewim after their Mishpakhot (families) of Gershon, the Mishpakha (family) of the Gershoni of Kohath, the Mishpakha (family) of the Kohathi of Merari, the Mishpakha (family) of the Merarites.

58 These are the Mishpakhot (families) of the Lewim the

Mishpakha (family) of the Libni, the Mishpakha (family) of the Khebroni, the Mishpakha (family) of the Makhli, the Mishpakha (family) of the Mushi, the Mishpakha (family) of the Korathi. And Kohath begat Amram.

59 And the name of Amram's wife was Yeh'kobad,[1] the daughter of Levi, whom her mother bare to Levi in Mitzrayim (Egypt) and she bare to Amram, Aharon and Mosheh (Musa), and Miriam their sister.

60 And to Aharon was born Nadav, and Avihu, El'ezar, and Ithamar.

61 And Nadav and Avihu died, when they offered profaned fire[2] before YHWH.

62 And those that were registered of them were twenty three thousand, all males from a month old and upward: for they were not registered among the children of Israel, because there was no inheritance given them among the children of Israel.

63 These are they that were registered by Mosheh (Musa) and El'ezar the kohen (priest), who registered the children of Israel in the plains of Moav by Yardan (Jordan) near Yerikho.

64 But among these there was not a man of them whom Mosheh (Musa) and Aharon the kohen (priest) registered, when they registered the children of Israel in the wilderness of Sinai.

65 For YHWH had said of them,

They shall surely die in the wilderness. And there was not left a man of them, rescue Kalev the son of Yepune'yah, and Yahushua the son of Nun.[3]

Chapter 27

1 Then came the daughters of Tselof'khad, the son of Khefer, the son of Gil'ad, the son of Makhir, the son of Manasheh, of the Mishpakhot (families) of Manasheh the son of Yosef: and these are the names of his daughters; Makhlah, Noakh, and Hoglah, and Milkah, and Tirzah.

2 And they stood before Mosheh (Musa), and before El'ezar the kohen (priest), and before the princes and all the congregation, by the door of the Tent of the appointed times, saying,

3 Our father died in the wilderness, and he was not in the company of them that gathered themselves together against YHWH in the company of Korakh; but died in his own sin, and had no sons.

4 Why should the name of our father be done away from among his Mishpakha (family), because

Footnotes
[1] Amram was Moses' dad and he also had another wife from whom he got Hur who is not listed here.
[2] See Vayikra (Leviticus) Chapter 10:1

[3] Only Caleb and Yahushua ben Nun who represented the tribes of Yahudah and Efrayim were left of the first generation of Israelites to enter the land. None of the others from that generation made it due to their lack of obedience. Many Christians will not make it into the land due to the same, and those that make it with one foot in the church and the other foot in the world will not have very good status. They will be predominantly slaves in the kingdom to Israel. If you want to be a slave in the kingdom keep disobeying Torah and this is a sure way to get slave status for eternity.

he has no son? Give to us therefore a possession among the brethren of our father.

[1]

5 And Mosheh (Musa) brought their cause before YHWH.

6 And YHWH spoke to Mosheh (Musa), saying,

7 The daughters of Tselof'khad speak right: You shall surely give them a possession of an inheritance among their father's brethren; and You shall cause the inheritance of their father to pass to them.[2]

8 And You shall speak to the children of Israel, saying, If a man die, and have no son, then you shall cause his inheritance to pass to his daughter.

9 And if he has no daughter, then you shall give his inheritance to his brethren.

10 And if he has no brethren, then you shall give his inheritance to his father's brethren.

11 And if his father have no brethren, then you shall give his inheritance to his kinsman that is next to him of his Mishpakha (family), and he shall possess it: and it shall be to the children of Israel a statute of judgment, as YHWH commanded Mosheh (Musa).

12 And YHWH said to Mosheh (Musa), Go up into this Mount Abarim, and see the land which I have given to the children of Israel.

13 And when You have seen it, You also shall be gathered to your people, as Aharon your brother was gathered.

14 For you rebelled against my commandment in the wilderness of Zin, in the strife of the congregation, to sanctify me at the mayim before their eyes: that is the mayim of Meribah in Kadesh in the wilderness of Zin.

15 And Mosheh (Musa) spoke to YHWH, saying,

16 Let YHWH, the Elohim of the ruachot (Spirits) of all flesh, set a man over the congregation,

17 Which may go out before them, and which may go in before them, and which may lead them out, and which may bring them in; that the congregation of YHWH be not as sheep which have no shepherd.

18 And YHWH said to Mosheh (Musa), Take Yahushua the son of Nun, a man in whom is the Ruakh (Holy Spirit), and lay your hand upon him;[3]

19 And set him before El'ezar the kohen (priest), and before all the congregation; and give him a

Footnotes

[1] The enlarged Nun - The nun signifies life and hence our inheritance. The daughters who had no inheritance but their inheritance was preserved even though there was no male counterpart. It speaks of our inheritance with YHWH and Israel that YHWH has preserved.

[2] Justice and equity prevails in YHWH's kingdom. Women are not mistreated as in other cultures. They are highly respected and honoured if they are obedient to YHWH. Even though they were the daughters of the man who was killed for his sin of breaking the Sabbath by collecting wood in Numbers 15:32, YHWH does not refuse his children the right of their inheritance.

Footnotes

[3] The laying on of hands is not a new church practice, it has its root in Israelite Torah culture.

charge in their sight.

20 And You shall delegate some of your authority upon him, that all the congregation of the children of Israel may be obedient.

21 And he shall stand before El'ezar the kohen (priest), who shall ask counsel for him after the judgment of Urim before YHWH at his word shall they go out, and at his word they shall come in, both he, and all the children of Israel with him, even all the congregation.

22 And Mosheh (Musa) did as YHWH commanded him: and he took Yahushua, and set him before El'ezar the kohen (priest), and before all the congregation:

23 And he laid his hands upon him, and gave him a charge, as YHWH commanded by the hand of Mosheh (Musa).

Chapter 28

1 And YHWH spoke to Mosheh (Musa), saying,

2 Command the children of Israel, and say to them, My offering, and my Lakhem (bread) for my sacrifices made by fire, for a sweet savour to me, shall you Guard to offer to me in their due season.

3 And You shall say to them, This is the offering made by fire which you shall offer to YHWH; two lambs of the first year without spot day by day, for a continual burnt offering.

4 The one lamb shall You offer in the morning, and the other lamb shall You offer in the evening;

5 And a tenth part of an ephah of flour for a grain offering, mingled with the fourth part of a hin of beaten oil.

6 It is a continual burnt offering, which was appointed in Mount Sinai for a sweet savour, a sacrifice made by fire to YHWH.

7 And the drink offering there shall be the fourth part of a hin for the one lamb: in the Holy place shall You cause the strong wine to be poured to YHWH for a drink offering.

8 And the other lamb shall You offer at evening:[1] as the grain offering of the morning,[2] and as the drink offering there, You shall offer it, a sacrifice made by fire, of a sweet savour to YHWH.

9 And on the Sabbath day two lambs of the first year without spot, and two tenth deals of flour for a grain offering, mingled with oil, and the drink offering there:

10 This is the burnt offering of every Sabbath, beside the continual burnt offering, and his drink offering.

11 And in the beginnings of your months you shall offer a burnt offering to YHWH; two young bullocks, and one ram, seven lambs of the first year without spot;

12 And three tenth deals of flour for a grain offering, mingled with oil, for one bullock; and two tenth deals of flour for a grain offering, mingled with oil, for one ram;

13 And a several tenth deal of flour mingled with oil for a grain offering to one lamb; for a burnt offering of a sweet savour, a

Footnotes
[1] Evening time prayers called Maariv.
[2] Morning prayers called Shahkhrit.

sacrifice made by fire to YHWH.

14 And their drink offerings shall be half a hin of wine to a bullock, and the third part of a hin to a ram, and a fourth part of a hin to a lamb: this is the burnt offering of every month throughout the months of the year.

15 And one kid of the goats for a sin offering to YHWH shall be offered, beside the continual burnt offering, and his drink offering.

16 And in the fourteenth day of the first month is the Passover of YHWH.

17 And in the fifteenth day of this month is the khag (The appointed celebration time): seven days shall matzah (unleavened bread) be eaten.

18 In the first day shall be a miqra kodesh;[1] you shall do no manner of servile work[2] therein:

19 But you shall offer a sacrifice made by fire for a burnt offering to YHWH; two young bullocks, and one ram, and seven lambs of the first year: they shall be to you without blemish:[3]

20 And their grain offering shall be of flour mingled with oil: three tenth deals shall you offer for a bullock, and two tenth deals for a ram;

21 A several tenth deal shall You offer for every lamb, throughout the seven lambs:

22 And one goat for a sin offering, to make atonement for you.

23 You shall offer these beside the burnt offering in the morning, which is for a continual burnt offering.

24 After this manner you shall offer daily, throughout the seven days, the food of the sacrifice made by fire, of a sweet savour to YHWH: it shall be offered beside the continual burnt offering, and his drink offering.

25 And on the seventh day you shall have a miqra kodesh;[4] you shall do no servile work.

26 Also in the day of the bikkurim (Firstfruit), when you bring a new grain offering to YHWH, after your Shavuot (Pentecost), you shall have a miqra kodesh;[5] you shall do no servile work:

27 But you shall offer the burnt offering for a sweet savour to YHWH; two young bullocks, one ram, seven lambs of the first year;

28 And their grain offering of flour mingled with oil, three tenth deals to one bullock, two tenth deals to one ram,

29 A several tenth deal to one lamb, throughout the seven lambs;

30 And one kid of the goats, to make atonement for you.

31 You shall offer them beside the continual burnt offering, and his grain offering, (they shall be to you without blemish) and their drink offerings.

Footnotes
[1] Holy assembly gathering
[2] We are commanded to take the day off from any work.
[3] Since there is not a Temple where we can offer sacrifices, yet we offer praise and worship in respect to YHWH.
[4] Holy gathering and a compulsory day off.
[5] This is a special day off to assemble and praise and worship YHWH.

Chapter 29

1 And in the seventh month, on the first day of the month, you shall have a miqra kodesh;[1] you shall do no servile work: it is a day of blowing the shofarim[2] to

Footnotes

[1] Holy assembly to praise and worship YHWH.

[2] The ancient calendar used was the Khnokian (Enoch's) Calendar but it was forcefully stopped by the Greeks when they invaded Israel. Hence the Luni/solar one started see below.

Yom Teruah – Day of Trumpets. The Hebrew people call this day, Rosh Hashanna, and call it the new civil year.

http://en.wikipedia.org/wiki/Hebrew_calendar

The Hebrew calendar (הלוח העברי ha'luach ha'ivri), or Hebrew calendar, is a lunisolar calendar used today predominantly for Hebrew religious observances which started as a custom and not commandment, as the original calendar was the Hanok one. It determines the dates for Hebrew holidays and the appropriate public reading of Torah portions, yahrzeits (dates to commemorate the death of a relative), and daily Psalm reading, among many ceremonial uses. In Israel, it is an official calendar for civil purposes and provides a time frame for agriculture.

Originally the Hebrew calendar was used by Yahudim for all daily purposes, but following the conquest of Jerusalem by Pompey in 63 BCE (see also Iudaea province), Yahud began additionally following the imperial civil calendar, which was decreed in 45 BCE, for civic matters such as the payment of taxes and dealings with government officials.

The Hebrew calendar has evolved over time. For example, until the Tannaitic period, the months were set by observation of a new crescent moon, with an additional month added every two or three years to keep Passover in the spring, again based on observation of natural events, namely the ripening of barley to reach the stage of "aviv" (nearly ripened crop).[1] Through the Amoraic period and into the Geonic period, this system was displaced by mathematical
Continued in next section

rules. The principles and rules appear to have been settled by the time Maimonides compiled the Mishneh Torah.

Because of the roughly eleven-day difference between twelve lunar months and one solar year, the length of the Hebrew calendar year varies in a repeating 19-year Metonic cycle of 235 lunar months, with an intercalary lunar month added according to defined rules every two or three years, for a total of 7 times per 19 years. Seasonal references in the Hebrew calendar reflect its development in the region east of the Mediterranean and the times and climate of the Northern Hemisphere. The Hebrew calendar year is longer by about 6 minutes and 25+25/57 seconds than the present-day mean solar year, so that every 224 years, the Hebrew calendar will fall a full day behind the modern solar year, and about every 231 years it will fall a full day behind the Gregorian calendar year.

The present counting method for years use the Anno Mundi epoch (Latin for "in the year of the world", לבריאת העולם), abbreviated AM or A.M. and also referred to as the Hebrew era. Hebrew year 5770 began on 19 September 2009 and ended on 8 September 2010. Hebrew year 5771 (a leap year) began on 9 September 2010 and ends on 28 September 2011.

Structure
The Hebrew calendar is a lunisolar calendar, or fixed lunar year, based on twelve lunar months of twenty-nine or thirty days, with an intercalary lunar month added seven times every nineteen years (once every two to three years) to synchronize the twelve lunar cycles with the slightly longer solar year. Each Hebrew lunar month starts with the new month. Although originally the new lunar crescent had to be observed and certified by witnesses, the timing of the new month is now determined mathematically.

Concurrently there is a weekly cycle of seven days, mirroring the seven-day period of the Book of Genesis in which the world is created. The names for the days of the week, like those in the Creation story, are simply the day number within the week, with Shabbat being the seventh day. The Hebrew day always runs from sunset to the next
Continued in next section

sunset; the formal adjustments used to specify a standard time and time zones are not relevant to the Hebrew calendar.

The twelve regular months are: Nisan (30 days), Iyar (29 days), Sivan (30 days), Tammuz (29 days), Abbah (30 days), Elul (29 days), Tishrei (30 days), Cheshvan (29 or 30 days), Kislev (29 or 30 days), Tevet (29 days), Shevat (30 days), and Adar (29 days). In the leap years (such as 5771) an additional month, Adar I (30 days) is added after Shevat, and the regular Adar is referred to as "Adar II".

The first month of the festival year is Nisan. 15 Nisan is the start of the festival of Pesach, corresponding to the full moon of Nisan. Pesach is a spring festival associated with the barley harvest,[2] so the leap-month mentioned above is intercalated periodically to keep this festival in the northern hemisphere's spring season. Since the adoption of a fixed calendar, intercalations in the Hebrew calendar have been at fixed points in a 19-year cycle. Prior to this, the intercalation was determined empirically:

The year may be intercalated on three grounds: 'aviv [i.e.the ripeness of barley], fruits of trees, and the equinox. On two of these grounds it should be intercalated, but not on one of them alone.[3]

The Bible designates Nisan, which it calls Aviv (Exodus 13:4), as the first month of the year (Exodus 12:2). At the same time, the season of the fall Festival of Booths (Sukkoth), is called "the end of the year" (Exodus 23:16). The Sabbatical year in which the land was to lie fallow, necessarily began at the time the winter barley and winter wheat would have been sown, in the fall. The Gezer calendar, an Israelite or Canaanite inscription ca. 900 BCE, also begins in the fall.

Modern practice follows the scheme described in the Mishnah: Rosh Hashanah, which means "the head of the year", and is celebrated in the month of Tishrei, is "the new year for years."[4] This is when the numbered year changes, and most Yahudi today view Tishrei as the de facto beginning of the year.
Continued in next section

Conversion between Hebrew and civil calendars
The list below gives a time which can be used to determine the day the Hebrew ecclesiastical (spring) year starts over a period of nineteen years:

7.36 1/18 A.M. Tuesday, 16th March, 2010
5.08 14/18 A.M. Monday, 4th April, 2011
1.57 8/18 P.M. Friday, 23rd March, 2012
10.46 2/18 P.M. Tuesday, 12th March, 2013
8.18 15/18 P.M. Monday, 31st March, 2014
5.07 9/18 A.M. Saturday, 21st March, 2015
2.40 4/18 A.M. Friday, 8th April, 2016
11.28 16/18 A.M. Tuesday, 28th March, 2017
8.17 10/18 P.M. Saturday, 17th March, 2018
5.50 5/18 P.M. Friday, 5th April, 2019
2.38 17/18 A.M. Wednesday, 25th March, 2020
11.27 11/18 A.M. Sunday, 14th March, 2021
9.00 6/18 A.M. Saturday, 2nd April, 2022
5.49 P.M. Wednesday, 22nd March, 2023
3.21 13/18 P.M. Tuesday, 9th April, 2024
12.10 7/18 A.M. Sunday, 30th March, 2025
8.59 1/18 A.M. Thursday, 19th March, 2026
6.31 14/18 A.M. Wednesday, 7th April, 2027
3.20 8/18 P.M. Sunday, 26th March, 2028
Every nineteen years this time is 2 days, 16 hours, 33 1/18 minutes later in the week. That is either the same or the previous day in the civil calendar, depending on whether the difference in the day of the week is three or two days. If 29th February is included fewer than five times in the nineteen - year period the date will be later by the number of days which corresponds to the difference between the actual number of insertions and five. If the year is due to start on Sunday, it actually begins on the following Tuesday if the following year is due to start on Friday morning. If due to start on Monday, Wednesday or Friday it actually begins on the following day. If due to start on Saturday, it actually begins on the following day if the previous year was due to begin on Monday morning.

1.^ Talmud, Sanhedrin 11b
2.^ Josephus, Antiquities 3.248-251, Loeb Classical Library, 1930, pp. 437-438.
3.^ Tosefta Sanhedrin 2.2, Herbert Danby, Trans., Tractate Sanhedrin Mishnah and Tosefta, Society for Promoting Christian
Continued in next section

you.

2 And you shall offer a burnt offering for a sweet savour to YHWH; one young bullock, one ram, and seven lambs of the first year without blemish:

3 And their grain offering shall be of flour mingled with oil, three tenth deals for a bullock, and two tenth deals for a ram,

4 And one tenth deal for one lamb, throughout the seven lambs:

5 And one kid of the goats for a sin offering, to make atonement for you:

6 Beside the burnt offering of the month, and his grain offering, and the daily burnt offering, and his grain offering, and their drink offerings, according to their manner, for a sweet savour, a sacrifice made by fire to YHWH.

7 And you shall have on the tenth day of this seventh month a miqra kodesh;[1] and you shall afflict your souls: you shall not do any work therein:

8 But you shall offer a burnt offering to YHWH for a sweet savour; one young bullock, one ram, and seven lambs of the first year; they shall be to you without blemish:

9 And their grain offering shall be of flour mingled with oil, three tenth deals to a bullock, and two tenth deals to one ram,

10 A several tenth deal for one lamb, throughout the seven lambs:

11 One kid of the goats for a sin offering; beside the sin offering of atonement, and the continual burnt offering, and the grain offering of it, and their drink offerings.

12 And on the fifteenth day of the seventh month[2] you shall have a miqra kodesh;[3] you shall do no servile work, and you shall keep a khag (The appointed celebration time) to YHWH seven days:

13 And you shall offer a burnt offering, a sacrifice made by fire, of a sweet savour to YHWH; thirteen young bullocks, two rams, and fourteen lambs of the first year; they shall be without blemish:

14 And their grain offering shall be of flour mingled with oil, three tenth deals to every bullock of the thirteen bullocks, two tenth deals to each ram of the two rams,

15 And a several tenth deal to each lamb of the fourteen lambs:

16 And one kid of the goats for a sin offering; beside the continual burnt offering, his grain offering, and his drink offering.

17 And on the second day you shall offer twelve young bullocks, two rams, fourteen lambs of the first year without spot:

18 And their grain offering and their drink offerings for the bullocks, for the rams, and for the lambs, shall be according to their number, after the manner:

Knowledge, London and New York, 1919, p. 31. Also quoted in Sacha Stern, Calendar and Community: A History of the Hebrew Calendar Second Century BCE-Tenth Century CE, Oxford University Press, 2001, p. 70.
4.^ Mishna, Rosh Hashana 1:1

[1] Yom Kippurim – A day to fast 25 hours and to take time off work.

Footnotes
[2] Sukkot – Khag, celebration of Tabernacles.
[3] Holy gathering.

19 And one kid of the goats for a sin offering; beside the continual burnt offering, and the grain offering there, and their drink offerings.

20 And on the third day eleven bullocks, two rams, fourteen lambs of the first year without blemish;

21 And their grain offering and their drink offerings for the bullocks, for the rams, and for the lambs, shall be according to their number, after the manner:

22 And one goat for a sin offering; beside the continual burnt offering, and his grain offering, and his drink offering.

23 And on the fourth day ten bullocks, two rams, and fourteen lambs of the first year without blemish:

24 Their grain offering and their drink offerings for the bullocks, for the rams, and for the lambs, shall be according to their number, after the manner:

25 And one kid of the goats for a sin offering; beside the continual burnt offering, his grain offering, and his drink offering.

26 And on the fifth day nine bullocks, two rams, and fourteen lambs of the first year without spot:

27 And their grain offering and their drink offerings for the bullocks, for the rams, and for the lambs, shall be according to their number, after the manner:

28 And one goat for a sin offering; beside the continual burnt offering, and his grain offering and his drink offering.

29 And on the sixth day eight bullocks, two rams, and fourteen lambs of the first year without blemish:

30 And their grain offering and their drink offerings for the bullocks, for the rams, and for the lambs, shall be according to their number, after the manner:

31 And one goat for a sin offering; beside the continual burnt offering, his grain offering, and his drink offering.

32 And on the seventh day seven bullocks, two rams, and fourteen lambs of the first year without blemish:

33 And their grain offering and their drink offerings for the bullocks, for the rams, and for the lambs, shall be according to their number, after the manner:

34 And one goat for a sin offering; beside the continual burnt offering, his grain offering, and his drink offering.

35 On the eighth day you shall have a solemn assembly: you shall do no servile work therein:

36 But you shall offer a burnt offering, a sacrifice made by fire, of a sweet savour to YHWH: one bullock, one ram, seven lambs of the first year without blemish:

37 Their grain offering and their drink offerings for the bullock, for the ram, and for the lambs, shall be according to their number, after the manner:

38 And one goat for a sin offering; beside the continual burnt offering, and his grain offering and his drink offering.

39 These things you shall do to YHWH in your appointed times, beside your vows,[1] and your freewill offerings, for your burnt offerings, and for your grain offerings, and for your drink offerings, and for your shalom offerings.

40 And Mosheh (Musa) told the children of Israel according to all that YHWH commanded Mosheh (Musa).

Chapter 30
Torah Parsha 42 Mattot,
WeDavar 30:1-32:40
Haftarah Yirmeyahu 1:1-2:3

1 And Mosheh (Musa) spoke to the heads of the tribes concerning the children of Israel, saying, This is the thing which YHWH has commanded.

2 If a man vow a vow to YHWH, or swear an oath to bind his soul with a bond; he shall not break his word, he shall do according to all that proceeds out of his mouth.[2]

3 If a woman also vow a vow to YHWH, and bind herself by a bond, being in her father's Beyth (house) in her youth;

4 And her father hears her vow, and her bond wherewith she has bound her soul, and her father shall hold his shalom at her: then all her vows shall stand, and every bond wherewith she has bound her soul shall stand.

5 But if her father disallow her in the day that he hears; not any of her vows,[3] or of her bonds wherewith she has bound her soul, shall stand: and YHWH shall forgive her, because her father disallowed her.

6 And if she had at all a husband, when she vowed, or uttered anything out of her lips, wherewith she bound her soul;

7 And her husband heard it,[4] and held his shalom at her in the day that he heard it then her vows shall stand, and her bonds wherewith she bound her soul shall stand.

8 But if her husband disallowed her on the day that he heard it; then he shall make her vow which she vowed, and that which she uttered with her lips, wherewith she bound her soul, of none effect: and YHWH shall forgive her.

9 But every vow of a widow, and of her that is divorced, wherewith they have bound their souls, shall stand against her.

10 And if she vowed in her husband's Beyth (house), or bound her soul by a bond with an oath;

11 And her husband heard it, and held his shalom at her, and disallowed her not: then all her vows shall stand, and every bond wherewith she bound her soul shall stand.

12 But if her husband has utterly made them void on the day he

Footnotes

[1] If you count all the days, there were seventy bulls offered for the nations. Please see the book, The Feasts of YHWH, the Elohim of Israel- by Rabbi Simon Altaf www.forever-israel.com.

[2] All vows in YHWH's name are binding and must be fulfilled.

[3] If a woman made a vow and her father hears it, he can annul it but he can leave it and let it be fulfilled.

[4] A husband also has the authority to annul a vow made by his wife upon hearing it.

heard them; then whatsoever proceeded out of her lips concerning her vows, or concerning the bond of her soul, shall not stand: her husband has made them void; and YHWH shall forgive her.

13 Every vow, and every binding oath to afflict the soul, her husband may establish it, or her husband may make it void.

14 But if her husband altogether hold his shalom at her from day today; then he establishes all her vows, or all her bonds, which are upon her: he confirms them, because he held his shalom at her in the day that he heard them.

15 But if he shall in any way make them void after that he has heard them; then he shall bear her iniquity.

16 These are the statutes, which YHWH commanded Mosheh (Musa), between a man and his wife, between the father and his daughter, being yet in her youth in her father's Beyth (house).

Chapter 31

1 And YHWH spoke to Mosheh (Musa), saying,

2 Avenge the children of Israel of the Midianites: afterward shall You be gathered to your people.

3 And Mosheh (Musa) spoke to the people, saying, Arm some of yourselves to the war, and let them go against the Midianites, and avenge YHWH of Midian.

4 Of every tribe a thousand, throughout all the tribes of Israel, shall you send to the war.

5 So there were given out of the thousands of Israel, a thousand of every tribe, twelve thousand armed for war.

6 And Mosheh (Musa) sent them to the war, a thousand of every tribe, them and Phinekas the son of El'ezar the kohen (priest), to the war, with the Holy instruments, and the shofarim to blow in his hand.

7 And they warred against the Midianites, as YHWH commanded Mosheh (Musa); and they slew all the males.

8 And they slew the Kings of Midian, beside the rest of them that were slain; namely, Evi, and Rekem, and Zur, and Khur, and Reba, five Kings of Midian: Bilam also the son of Beor they slew with the sword.[1]

9 And the children of Israel took all the women of Midian captives, and their little ones, and took the spoil of all their cattle, and all their flocks, and all their goods.

10 And they burnt all their cities wherein they dwelt, and all their goodly castles, with fire.

11 And they took all the spoil, and all the prey, both of men and of beasts.

12 And they brought the captives, and the prey, and the spoil, to Mosheh (Musa), and El'ezar the kohen (priest), and to the congregation of the children of Israel, to the camp at the plains of Moav, which are by Yardan (Jordan) near Yerikho.

Footnotes
[1] They killed Balaam because he came to collect the reward for the twenty four thousand Israelites he caused to die. These were victims of the lechery of Balaam and his scheme to cause Israel to whore with the foreign Jordanian women.

13 And Mosheh (Musa), and El'ezar the kohen (priest), and all the princes of the congregation, went forth to meet them outside the camp.

14 And Mosheh (Musa) was very angry with the officers of the host, with the captains over thousands, and captains over hundreds, which came from the battle.

15 And Mosheh (Musa) said to them, Have you rescued all the women alive?

16 Behold, these caused the children of Israel, through the counsel of Bilam, to commit trespass against YHWH in the matter of Peor, and there was a plague among the congregation of YHWH.

17 Now therefore kill every male among the little ones, and kill every woman that has known man by lying with him.[1]

18 But all the female children, that have not known a man by lying with him, keep alive for yourselves.

19 And you abide outside the camp seven days: whosoever has killed any person, and whosoever has touched any slain, purifies both yourselves and your captives on the third day, and on the seventh day.

20 And purify all your raiment, and all that is made of skins, and all work of goats' hair, and all things made of wood.

21 And El'ezar the kohen (priest) said to the men of war which went to the battle, This is the ordinance of the Torah which YHWH commanded Mosheh (Musa);

22 Only the gold, and the silver, the brass, the iron, the tin, and the lead,

23 Every thing that may abide the fire, you shall make it go through the fire, and it shall be clean: nevertheless it shall be purified with the mayim of separation: and all that abides not the fire you shall make to go through the mayim.

24 And you shall wash your clothes on the seventh day, and you shall be clean, and afterward you shall come into the camp.

25 And YHWH spoke to Mosheh (Musa), saying,

26 Take the sum of the plunder that was captured, both of man and of beast, You, and El'ezar the kohen (priest), and the chief ahvot (fathers) of the congregation:

27 And divide the prey into two parts; between them that took the war upon them, who went out to battle, and between all the congregation.

28 And levy a tribute to YHWH of the men of war which went out to battle: one soul of five hundred, both of the persons,

Footnotes

[1] These women had been defiled by worshipping false elohim and would lead Israel and others astray. The adulterers in Israel were killed and these Midianite women were partners in that idolatry. Now according to the Torah law, both the male and female must die. This is why these women had to be killed and the kids were the product of that adultery. The kids also would have grown up to do the same and in their death they would only go back to YHWH, who would not send the children to hell. The virgin women were given a chance since they could be married and brought to the Covenant of YHWH.

and of the cattles, and of the asses, and of the sheep:

29 Take it of their half, and give it to El'ezar the kohen (priest), for a heave offering of YHWH.

30 And of the children of Israel's half, You shall take one portion of fifty, of the persons, of the cattles, of the asses, and of the flocks, of all manner of beasts, and give them to the Lewim, which keep the charge of the Tent of YHWH.

31 And Mosheh (Musa) and El'ezar the kohen (priest) did as YHWH commanded Mosheh (Musa).

32 And the spoils of war, being the rest of the plunder which the men of war had caught, was six hundred thousand and seventy five thousand sheep,

33 And seventy two thousand cattle,

34 And sixty one thousand asses,

35 And thirty two thousand persons in all, of women that had not known man by lying with him.

36 And the half, which was the portion of them that went out to war, was three hundred and thirty-seven thousand five hundred sheep.

37 And YHWH's tribute of the sheep was six hundred and seventy five.

38 And the cattle were thirty six thousand; of which YHWH's tribute was seventy two.

39 And the asses were thirty thousand and five hundred; of which YHWH's tribute was sixty one.

40 And the persons were sixteen thousand; of which YHWH's tribute was thirty two persons.

41 And Mosheh (Musa) gave the tribute, which was YHWH's contribution offering, to El'ezar the kohen (priest), as YHWH commanded Mosheh (Musa).

42 And of the children of Israel's half, which Mosheh (Musa) divided from the men that warred,

43 Now the half that pertained to the congregation was three hundred thousand thirty seven thousand and five hundred sheep,

44 And thirty six thousand cattle,

45 And thirty thousand five hundred asses,

46 And sixteen thousand persons.

47 Even of the children of Israel's half, Mosheh (Musa) took one portion of fifty, both of man and of beast, and gave them to the Lewim, which kept the charge of the Tent of YHWH; as YHWH commanded Mosheh (Musa).

48 And the officers, who were over thousands of the host, the captains of thousands, and captains of hundreds, came near to Mosheh (Musa):

49 And they said to Mosheh (Musa), Your servants have taken the sum of the men of war which are under our charge, and there lacks not one man of us.

50 We have therefore brought an offering for YHWH, what each man has received, of jewels of gold, chains, and bracelets, rings, earrings, and tablets, to make atonement for our souls before YHWH.

51 And Mosheh (Musa) and El'ezar the kohen (priest) took the gold of them, even all wrought jewels.

52 And all the gold of the offering that they offered up to YHWH, of the captains of thousands, and of the captains of hundreds, was sixteen thousand seven hundred and fifty shekels.

53 For the men of war had taken spoil, every man for himself.

54 And Mosheh (Musa) and El'ezar the kohen (priest) took the gold of the captains of thousands and of hundreds, and brought it into the Tent of the appointed times, for a memorial for the children of Israel before YHWH.

Chapter 32

1 Now the children of Reuven and the children of Gawd had a very great multitude of cattle: and when they saw the land of Yatzer, and the land of Gil'ad, that, behold, the place was a place for cattle;

2 The children of Gawd and the children of Reuven came and spoke to Mosheh (Musa), and to El'ezar the kohen (priest), and to the princes of the congregation, saying,

3 Ataroth, and Dibon, and Yatzer, and Nimrah, and Kheshbon, and Elealeh, and Shebam, and Nebo, and Beon,

4 Even the country which YHWH smote before the congregation of Israel is a land for cattle, and your servants have cattle:

5 Wherefore, said they, if we have found favour in your sight, let this land be given to your servants for a possession, and bring us not over Yardan (Jordan).

6 And Mosheh (Musa) said to the children of Gawd and to the children of Reuven, would your brethren go to war, and shall you sit here?

7 And why do you discourage the heart of the children of Israel from going over into the land which YHWH has given them?

8 Thus did your ahvot (fathers), when I sent them from Kadesh-barnea to see the land.

9 For when they went up to the valley of Eshkol, and saw the land, they discouraged the heart of the children of Israel, that they should not go into the land which YHWH had given them.

10 And YHWH's anger was kindled the same time, and he swore, saying,

11 Surely none of the men that came up out of Mitzrayim (Egypt), from twenty years old and upward, shall see the land which I swore to Abraham, to Ytshak, and to Yakov; because they have not fully followed me:

12 Except Kalev the son of Yepune'yah the Kenezi, and Yahushua the son of Nun: for they have fully followed YHWH.

13 And YHWH's anger was kindled against Israel, and he made them wander in the wilderness forty years, until all the generation, that had done evil in the sight of YHWH, was consumed.

14 And, behold, you are risen up in your ahvot (fathers) instead, a brood of transgressors, to ignite the fierce anger of YHWH toward Israel again.

15 For if you turn away from

after him, he will yet again leave them in the wilderness; and you shall destroy all this people.

16 And they came near to him, and said, We will build sheepfolds here for our cattle, and cities for our little ones:

17 But we ourselves will go ready armed before the children of Israel, until we have brought them to their place: and our little ones shall dwell in the fenced cities because of the inhabitants of the land.

18 We will not return to our houses, until the children of Israel have inherited every man his inheritance.

19 For we will not inherit with them on the other side Yardan (Jordan), or forward; because our inheritance is fallen to us on this side Yardan (Jordan) eastward.

20 And Mosheh (Musa) said to them, If you will do this thing, if you will go armed before YHWH to war,

21 And will go all of you armed over Yardan (Jordan) before YHWH, until he has driven out his enemies from before him,

22 And the land be subdued before YHWH: then afterward you shall return, and be guiltless before YHWH, and before Israel; and this land shall be your possession before YHWH.

23 But if you will not do so, behold, you have transgressed against YHWH: and be sure your sin will find you out.

24 Build your cities for your little ones and folds for your sheep; and do that which has proceeded out of your mouth.

25 And the children of Gawd and the children of Reuven spoke to Mosheh (Musa), saying, Your servants will do as my master commands.

26 Our little ones, our wives, our flocks, and all our cattle, shall be there in the cities of Gil'ad:

27 But your servants will pass over, every man armed for war, before YHWH to battle, as my master says.

28 So concerning them Mosheh (Musa) commanded El'ezar the kohen (priest), and Yahushua the son of Nun, and the chief ahvot (fathers) of the tribes of the children of Israel:

29 And Mosheh (Musa) said to them, If the children of Gawd and the children of Reuven will pass with you over Yardan (Jordan), every man armed to battle, before YHWH, and the land shall be subdued before you; then you shall give them the land of Gil'ad for a possession:

30 But if they will not pass over with you armed, they shall have possessions among you in the land of Kanan.

31 And the children of Gawd and the children of Reuven answered, saying, As YHWH has said to your servants, so will we do.

32 We will pass over armed before YHWH into the land of Kanan, that the possession of our inheritance on this side Yardan (Jordan) may be ours.

33 And Mosheh (Musa) gave to them, even to the children of Gawd, and to the children of Reuven, and to half the tribe of Manasheh the son of Yosef, the kingdom of Sikhon King of the

Amoree, and the kingdom of Og King of Bashan, the land, with the cities there in the coasts, even the cities of the country roundabout.

34 And the children of Gawd built Dibon, and Ataroth, and Aroer,

35 And Atroth, Shophan, and Yaazer, and Yogbehah,

36 And Beth-nimrah, and Beth-haran, fenced cities: and folds for sheep.

37 And the children of Reuven built Kheshbon, and Elealeh, and Kiryathaim,

38 And Nebo, and Baal-meon, (their names being changed,) and Shibmah: and gave other names to the cities which they built.

39 And the children of Makhir the son of Manasheh went to Gil'ad, and took it, and dispossessed the Amoree which was in it.

40 And Mosheh (Musa) gave Gil'ad to Makhir the son of Manasheh; and he dwelt therein.

41 And Yair the son of Manasheh went and took the small towns there, and called them Khavuth-Yair.

42 And Nobah went and took Kenath, and the villages there, and called it Nobah, after his own name.

Torah Parsha 43 Maasei, WeDavar 33:1-36:13
Haftarah: Yirmeyahu 2:4-28, 3:4 & 4:1-2

Chapter 33

1 These are the journeys of the children of Israel, which went forth out of the land of Mitzrayim (Egypt) with their armies under the hand of Mosheh (Musa) and Aharon.

2 And Mosheh (Musa) wrote their goings out according to their journeys by the commandment of YHWH and these are their journeys according to their goings out.

3 And they departed from Rameses in the first month, on the fifteenth day of the first month; on the day after the Protection (Passover) the children of Israel went out with a high hand in the sight of all the Mitzrim (Egyptians).

4 For the Mitzrim (Egyptians) buried all their Bekhor (firstborn), which YHWH had smitten among them: upon their powers also YHWH executed judgments.

5 And the children of Israel removed from Rameses, and pitched in Succoth.

6 And they departed from Succoth, and pitched in Etham, which is in the edge of the wilderness.

7 And they removed from Etham, and turned again to Pi-ha hiroth, which is before Baal-zephon: and they pitched before Migdol.

8 And they departed from before Pi-ha hiroth, and passed through the midst of the sea into the wilderness, and went three days' journey in the wilderness of Etham, and pitched in Marah.

9 And they removed from Marah, and came to Elim and in Elim were twelve fountains of mayim, and seventy palm trees; and they pitched there.

10 And they removed from Elim,

and encamped by the Sea of Reeds.

11 And they removed from the Sea of Reeds, and encamped in the wilderness of sin.

12 And they took their journey out of the wilderness of sin, and encamped in Dophkah.

13 And they departed from Dophkah, and encamped in Alush.

14 And they removed from Alush, and encamped at Rephidim, where was no mayim for the people to drink.

15 And they departed from Rephidim, and pitched in the wilderness of Sinai.

16 And they removed from the wilderness of Sinai, and pitched at Kibroth-hattaavah.

17 And they departed from Kibroth-hattaavah, and encamped at Khezeroth.

18 And they departed from Khezeroth, and pitched in Rithmah.

19 And they departed from Rithmah, and pitched at Rimmon-parez.

20 And they departed from Rimmon-parez, and pitched in Livnah.

21 And they removed from Livnah, and pitched at Rissah.

22 And they journeyed from Rissah, and pitched in Kehelathah.

23 And they went from Kehelathah, and pitched in Mount Shapher.

24 And they removed from Mount Shapher, and encamped in Haradah.

25 And they removed from Haradah, and pitched in Makheloth.

26 And they removed from Makheloth, and encamped at Tahath.

27 And they departed from Tahath, and pitched at Tarah.

28 And they removed from Tarah, and pitched in Mithcah.

29 And they went from Mithcah, and pitched in Hashmonah.

30 And they departed from Hashmonah, and encamped at Moseroth.

31 And they departed from Moseroth, and pitched in Bene-yaakan.

32 And they removed from Bene-yaakan, and encamped at Hor-hagidgad.

33 And they went from Hor-hagidgad, and pitched in Yotbathah.

34 And they removed from Yotbathah, and encamped at Ebronah.

35 And they departed from Ebronah, and encamped at Etzyon-gaber.

36 And they removed from Etzyon-gaber, and pitched in the wilderness of Zin, which is Kadesh.

37 And they removed from Kadesh, and pitched in Mount Hor, in the edge of the land of Edom.

38 And Aharon the kohen (priest) went up into Mount Hor at the commandment of YHWH, and died there, in the fortieth year after the children of Israel were come out of the land of Mitzrayim (Egypt), in the first day of the fifth[1] month.

39 And Aharon was a hundred and twenty-three years old when he died in Mount Hor.

40 And King Arad the Kanani, which dwelt in the south in the land of Kanan, heard of the coming of the children of Israel.

41 And they departed from Mount Hor, and pitched in Zalmonah.

42 And they departed from Zalmonah, and pitched in Punon.

43 And they departed from Punon, and pitched in Oboth.

44 And they departed from Oboth, and pitched in Iye-ha barim, in the border of Moav.

45 And they departed from Iim, and pitched in Dibon-Gawd.

46 And they removed from Dibon-Gawd, and encamped in Almon-diblathaim.

47 And they removed from Almon-diblathaim, and pitched in the mountains of Abarim, before Nebo.

48 And they departed from the mountains of Abarim, and pitched in the plains of Moav by Yardan (Jordan) near Yerikho.

49 And they pitched by Yardan (Jordan), from Beth-yesimoth even to Abel-shittim in the plains of Moav.

50 And YHWH spoke to Mosheh (Musa) in the plains of Moav by Yardan (Jordan) near Yerikho, saying,

51 Speak to the children of Israel, and say to them, When you are passed over Yardan (Jordan) into the land of Kanan;

52 Then you shall drive out all the inhabitants of the land from before you, and destroy all their engraved stones, and destroy all their molten images, and demolish all their high places:

53 And you shall dispossess the inhabitants of the land, and dwell therein: for I have given you the land to possess it.

54 And you shall divide the land by Lot for an inheritance among your Mishpakhot (families) and to the more you shall give the more inheritance, and to the fewer you shall give the less inheritance: each man's inheritance shall be in the place where his Lot falls; according to the tribes of your ahvot (fathers) you shall inherit.

55 But if you will not drive out the inhabitants of the land from before you; then it shall come to pass, that those which you let remain of them shall be pricks in your eyes, and thorns in your sides, and shall trouble you in the land wherein you dwell.[2]

56 Moreover it shall come to pass, that I shall do to you, as I thought to do to them.

Chapter 34

1 And YHWH spoke to Mosheh (Musa), saying,

2 Command the children of Israel, and say to them, When you come into the land of Kanan;

Footnotes

[1] This is the month of ABBAH, which is during the months of July/August. This was the time frame of Aharon's death, not Israel's release from Egypt, which took place in the month of Abib (Nisan). He died on Mount Hor but was buried in Mosera, Devrim (Deuteronomy 10:6).

Footnotes

[2] Because of their lack of obedience Israel suffers to this day from the radical Palestinians who are like thorns and pricking briers.

(this is the land that shall fall to you for an inheritance, even the land of Kanan with the coasts there.)

3 Then your south quarter shall be from the wilderness of Zin along by the coast of Edom, and your south border shall be the outmost coast of the salt sea[1] eastward:

4 And your border shall turn from the south to the ascent of Akrabbim, and pass on to Zin: and the going forth there shall be from the south to Kadesh-barnea, and shall go on to Hazar-addar, and pass on to Azmon:

5 And the border shall fetch a compass from Azmon to the river of Mitzrayim (Egypt), and the goings out of it shall be at the sea.

6 And as for the western border, you shall even have the great sea[2] for a border: this shall be your west border.

7 And this shall be your north border: from the great sea you shall point out for you Mount Hor:

8 From Mount Hor you shall point out your border to the entrance of Hamath; and the goings forth of the border shall be to Zedad:

9 And the border shall go on to Ziphron, and the goings out of it shall be at Hazar-enan this shall be your north border.

10 And you shall point out your east border from Hazar-enan to Shepham:

11 And the coast shall go down from Shepham to Riblah, on the east side of Ain; and the border shall descend, and shall reach to the side of the sea of Kinnereth[3] eastward:

12 And the border shall go down to Yardan (Jordan), and the goings out of it shall be at the salt sea: this shall be your land with the coasts there round about.

13 And Mosheh (Musa) commanded the children of Israel, saying, This is the land which you shall inherit by Lot, which YHWH commanded to give to the nine tribes, and to the half tribe:

14 For the tribe of the children of Reuven according to the Beyth (house) of their ahvot (fathers), and the tribe of the children of Gawd according to the Beyth (house) of their ahvot (fathers), have received their inheritance; and half the tribe of Manasheh have received their inheritance:

15 The two tribes and the half tribe have received their inheritance on this side Yardan (Jordan) near Yerikho eastward, toward the sun rising.

16 And YHWH spoke to Mosheh (Musa), saying,

17 These are the names of the men which shall divide the land to you: El'ezar the kohen (priest), and Yahushua the son of Nun.

18 And you shall take one prince of every tribe, to divide the land by inheritance.

19 And the names of the men are these: Of the tribe of Yahudah, Kalev the son of Yepune'yah.

Footnotes
[1] Dead Sea.
[2] Mediterranean Sea.

Footnotes
[3] The Sea of Galilee.

20 And of the tribe of the children of Shimeon, Shemuel the son of Ammihud.

21 Of the tribe of Benyamin, Elidad the son of Chislon.

22 And the prince of the tribe of the children of Dan, Bukki the son of Yogli.

23 The prince of the children of Yosef, for the tribe of the children of Manasheh, Hanni'el the son of Ephod.

24 And the prince of the tribe of the children of Efrayim, Kemu'el the son of Shiphtan.

25 And the prince of the tribe of the children of Zevulun, Elizaphan the son of Parnach.

26 And the prince of the tribe of the children of Yskhar (Issachar), Palti'el the son of Azzan.

27 And the prince of the tribe of the children of Asher, Ahihud the son of Shelomi.

28 And the prince of the tribe of the children of Naphtali, Pedah'el the son of Ammihud.

29 These are they whom YHWH commanded to divide the inheritance to the children of Israel in the land of Kanan.

Chapter 35

1 And YHWH spoke to Mosheh (Musa) in the plains of Moav by Yardan (Jordan) near Yerikho, saying,

2 Command the children of Israel, that they give to the Lewim of the inheritance of their possession cities to dwell in; and you shall give also to the Lewim suburbs for the cities roundabout them.

3 And the cities shall they have to dwell in; and the suburbs of them shall be for their cattle, and for their goods, and for all their beasts.

4 And the suburbs of the cities, which you shall give to the Lewim, shall reach from the wall of the city and outward a thousand cubits[1] round about.

5 And you shall measure from outside the city on the east side two thousand cubits, and on the south side two thousand cubits, and on the west side two thousand cubits, and on the north side two thousand cubits; and the city shall be in the midst: this shall be to them the suburbs of the cities.

6 And among the cities which you shall give to the Lewim there shall be six cities for refuge, which you shall appoint for the person who has killed unintentionally,[2] that he may flee there: and to them you shall add forty two cities.

7 So all the cities which you shall give to the Lewim shall be forty and eight cities: them shall you give with their suburbs.

8 And the cities which you shall give shall be of the possession of the children of Israel: from them that have many you shall give many; but from them that have

Footnotes

[1] 500 Yards.

[2] Someone who committed manslaughter by accident could take refuge in these cities and would not be punished. His accidental sin would be purged by the death of the High Priest, see footnote in verse 25. That if a human High Priest could pay the penalty for sin by his own death for a man who has killed someone by accident. However this is only for a Levite Kohen, Yahushua on the other hand paid for the sins of all those that came into the New Covenant.

few you shall give few: everyone shall give of his cities to the Lewim according to his inheritance which he inherited.

9 And YHWH spoke to Mosheh (Musa), saying,

10 Speak to the children of Israel, and say to them, When you be come over Yardan (Jordan) into the land of Kanan;

11 Then you shall appoint yourself cities to be cities of refuge for you; that the person who kills unintentionally may flee there, who has killed someone accidentally.

12 And they shall be to you cities for refuge from the avenger; that the manslayer die not, until he stand before the congregation in judgment.

13 And of these cities which you shall give six cities shall you have for refuge.

14 You shall give three cities on this side of Yardan (Jordan), and three cities shall you give in the land of Kanan, which shall be cities of refuge.

15 These six cities shall be a refuge, both for the children of Israel, and for the foreigner, and for the sojourner among them: that everyone that kills any person unawares may flee there.

16 And if he has smitten him with an instrument of iron, so that he dies, he is a murderer: the murderer shall surely be put to death.

17 And if he has smitten him with throwing a stone, with which he may die, and he dies, he is a murderer: the murderer shall surely be put to death.

18 Or if he smites him with a hand weapon of wood, wherewith he may die, and he dies, he is a murderer: the murderer shall surely be put to death.

19 The revenger of blood himself shall slay the murderer: when he meets him, he shall slay him.

20 But if he thrust him because of hatred, or waited to kill him by ambush, that he die;

21 Or in enmity smite him with his hand, that he dies he that smote him shall surely be put to death; for he is a murderer: the revenger of blood shall slay the murderer, when he meets him.

22 But if he thrust him suddenly without enmity, or throws an object at him without lying in wait,

23 Or with any stone, wherewith a man may die, seeing him not, and cast it upon him, that he die, and was not his enemy, neither sought his harm:

24 Then the congregation shall judge between the slayer and the revenger of blood according to these judgments:

25 And the congregation shall rescue the slayer out of the hand of the revenger of blood, and the congregation shall restore him to the city of his refuge, where he was fled: and he shall abide in it to the death of the Kohen ha Gadol (High Priest),[1] which was anointed with the Holy oil.

26 But if the slayer shall at any

Footnotes

[1] The death of the High Priest would expunge his guilt. The same way we were all destined to hell but the Torah can give us life if we swear to uphold the Covenants and do the works of Torah as our father Abraham did. Do not follow after gentile systems of salvation which are falsehoods.

time come outside the border of the city of his refuge, where he was fled;

27 And the revenger of blood finds him outside the borders of the city of his refuge, and the revenger of blood kill the slayer; he shall not be guilty of blood:

28 Because he should have remained in the city of his refuge until the death of the Kohen ha Gadol (High Priest): but after the death of the Kohen ha Gadol (High Priest) the slayer shall return into the land of his possession.

29 So these things shall be for a statute of judgment to you throughout your generations in all your dwellings.

30 Whoever kills any person, the murderer shall be put to death by the mouth of witnesses:[1] but one witness shall not testify against any person to cause him to die.

31 Moreover you shall take no satisfaction for the life of a murderer, which is guilty of death: but he shall be surely put to death.

32 And you shall take no satisfaction for him that is fled to the city of his refuge, that he should come again to dwell in the land, until the death of the Kohen ha Gadol (High Priest).

33 So you shall not pollute the land wherein you are: for blood it defiles the land: and the land cannot be cleansed of the blood that is shed therein, but by the blood of him that shed it.

Footnotes
[1] At least two witnesses or three are needed to confirm a case.

34 Defile not therefore the land which you shall inhabit, wherein I dwell: for I YHWH dwell among the children of Israel.

Chapter 36

1 And the chief ahvot (fathers) of the Mishpakhot (families) of the children of Gil'ad, the son of Makhir, the son of Manasheh, of the Mishpakhot (families) of the sons of Yosef, came near, and spoke before Mosheh (Musa), and before the princes, the chief ahvot (fathers) of the children of Israel:

2 And they said, YHWH commanded my master to give the land for an inheritance by Lot to the children of Israel: and my master was commanded by YHWH to give the inheritance of Tselof'khad our brother to his daughters.

3 And if they be married to any of the sons of the other tribes of the children of Israel, then shall their inheritance be taken from the inheritance of our ahvot (fathers), and shall be put to the inheritance of the tribe whereunto they are received: so shall it be taken from the Lot of our inheritance.

4 And when the Yahubel of the children of Israel shall be, and then shall their inheritance be put to the inheritance of the tribe whereunto they are received: so shall their inheritance be taken away from the inheritance of the tribe of our ahvot (fathers).

5 And Mosheh (Musa) commanded the children of Israel according to the word of YHWH, saying, The tribe of the sons of

Yosef has said well.

6 This is the thing which YHWH will command concerning the daughters of Tselof'khad, saying, Let them marry to whom they think best; only to the Mishpakha (family) of the tribe of their father shall they marry.

7 So shall not the inheritance of the children of Israel remove from tribe to tribe: for everyone of the children of Israel shall keep himself to the inheritance of the tribe of his ahvot (fathers).

8 And every daughter, that possessed an inheritance in any tribe of the children of Israel, shall be wife to one of the Mishpakha (family) of the tribe of her father, that the children of Israel may enjoy every man the inheritance of his ahvot (fathers).

9 Neither shall the inheritance remove from one tribe to another tribe; but everyone of the tribes of the children of Israel shall keep himself to his own inheritance.

10 Even as YHWH commanded Mosheh (Musa), so did the daughters of Tselof'khad.

11 For Makhlah, Tirzah, and Hoglah, and Milkah, and Noakh, the daughters of Tselof'khad, were married to their father's brothers' sons:

12 And they were married into the Mishpakhot (families) of the sons of Manasheh the son of Yosef, and their inheritance remained in the tribe of the Mishpakha (family) of their father.

13 These are the commandments and the judgments, which YHWH commanded by the hand of Mosheh (Musa) to the children of Israel in the plains of Moav by Yardan (Jordan) near Yerikho. ת

The Fifth Book of Mosheh (Musa)

Devrim (Deuteronomy)
דברם
Many words were spoken

Torah Parsha 44 Devrim, Devrim 1:1-3:22
Haftarah: Yeshayahu 1:1-27

Chapter 1

1 These be the words which Mosheh (Musa) spoke to all Israel on this side Yardan (Jordan) in the wilderness, in the plain over against the Sea of Reeds, between Paran, and Tophel, and Laban, and Khezeroth, and Dizhab.

2 There are eleven days' journey from Horev by the way of Mount Seir to Kadesh-barnea.

3 And it came to pass in the fortieth year, in the eleventh month,[1] on the first day of the month, that Mosheh (Musa) spoke to the children of Israel, according to all that YHWH had given him in commandment to them;

4 After he had slain Sikhon the King of the Amoree, which dwelt in Kheshbon, and Og the King of Bashan, who dwelt at Ashtaroth in Edrei:

5 On this side of the Yardan (Jordan), in the land of Moav, began Mosheh (Musa) to declare this Torah, saying,

6 YHWH our POWER spoke to us in Horev, saying, You have dwelt long enough in this Mount:

7 Turn and set on your journey, and go to the Mount of the Amoree, and to all the places near thereunto, in the plain, in the hills, and in the vale, and in the south, and by the seaside, to the land of the Kanani, and to Lebanon to the great river, the river Farat (Euphrates).

8 Behold, I have set the land before you: go in and possess the land which YHWH swore to your ahvot (fathers), Abraham, Ytshak, and Yakov, to give to them and to their seed after them.

9 And I spoke to you at that time, saying, I am not able to sustain you by myself.

10 YHWH Your POWER has multiplied you, and, behold, you are this day as the stars of shamayim for multitude.

11 YHWH Elohim of your ahvot (fathers) make you a thousand times[2] so many more as you are, and **Increase** you, as he has promised you.

12 How can I myself alone bear your pressure, and your burden, and your strife?

13 Take your wise men, and with understanding, and known among your tribes, and I will make them rulers over you.

14 And you answered me, and said, the thing which you have spoken is good for us to do.

Footnotes
[1] Biblical month of Shevat.

[2] If we multiply this literal number into four million people including men, women and children that came out of Egypt we arrive at a figure of four billion. We do know that YHWH's word is true, and many people in the world today may carry Hebrew blood without knowing about it.

15 So I took the chief of your tribes, wise men, and known, and made them heads over you, captains over thousands, and captains over hundreds, and captains over fifties, and captains over tens, and officers among your tribes.

16 And I charged your judges at that time, saying, hear the causes between your brethren, and judge with Righteousness between every man and his brother, and the foreigner that is with him.

17 You shall not show partiality for persons in judgment; but you shall hear the small as well as the great; you shall not be intimidated by the face[1] of the man; for the judgment belongs to Elohim and if it is too difficult a case then bring it to me, and I will hear it.

18 And I commanded you at that time all the things which you should do.

19 And when we departed from Horev, we went through all that exceedingly dangerous wilderness, which you saw by the way of the mountain of the Amoree, as YHWH our POWER commanded us; and we came to Kadesh-Barnea.

20 And I said to you, you have come into the Mountain of the Amoree, which YHWH our POWER will give to us.

21 Behold, YHWH Your POWER has laid the land before you: go up and possess it, as

Footnotes
[1] The word panayim in the Hebrew here reflects status in society. This would be one who is rich and well known so that Righteousness can still be conducted.

YHWH Elohim of your ahvot (fathers) has said to you; do not be afraid, neither be discouraged.

22 And you came near to me everyone of you, and said, we will send men before us, and they shall spy out the land, and bring us a report by what way we should go in, and into what cities we shall come.

23 And the saying pleased me well: and I took twelve men of you, one of a tribe:

24 And they prepared and went up into the mountain, and came to the valley of Eshkol, and searched it out.

25 And they took of the fruit of the land in their hands, and brought it down to us, and brought us word again, and said, It is a good land which YHWH our POWER will give us.

26 Not withstanding you would not go up, but rebelled against the commandment of YHWH Your POWER:

27 And you complained in your tents, and said, because YHWH hated us, he has brought us out of the land of Mitzrayim (Egypt), to hand us over to the Amoree, to destroy us.

28 What is going to happen to us? Our brethren have discouraged our heart, saying, the people are greater and taller than we; the cities are great and walled up to shamayim; and moreover we have seen the sons of the Anakim there.

29 Then I said to you, do not be terrified, neither be afraid of them.

30 YHWH Your POWER who

Devrim (Deuteronomy)

goes before you, he shall fight for you, according to all that he did for you in Mitzrayim (Egypt) before your eyes;

31 And in the wilderness, where You had seen how YHWH Your POWER bore you, as a man will bear his son, in all the way that you went, until you came into this place.

32 Yet in this thing you did not believe YHWH Your POWER,

33 Who went in the way before you, to search you out a place to pitch your tents in, in fire by night, to show you by what way you should go, and in a cloud by day.

34 And when YHWH heard this He was angry, and took an oath, saying,

35 Surely there shall not one of these men of this evil generation see that good land, which I swore to give to their ahvot (fathers),

36 Except Kalev[1] the son of Yepune'yah; he shall see it, and to him will I give the land that he has set his foot upon, and to his children, because he has completely followed YHWH.

37 Also YHWH was angry with me for your sakes, saying, you also shall not go in there.

38 But Yahushua the son of Nun, which stands before you, he shall go in there: encourage him: for he shall cause Israel to inherit it.[2]

39 Moreover your children, which you said would die on the way, and your children, which in that day had no knowledge between good and evil, they shall go in there, and to them will I give it, and they shall possess it.

40 But as for you, turn back, and take your journey into the wilderness by the way of the Sea of Reeds.

41 Then you answered and said to me, we have transgressed against YHWH, we will go up and fight, according to all that YHWH our POWER commanded us. And when you had girded on every man his weapons of war, you were ready to go up into the hill.

42 And YHWH said to me, Say to them, do not go up, neither fight; for I am not with you; as you will be defeated.

43 So I spoke to you; and you would not hear, but rebelled against the commandment of YHWH, and you went up proudly into the Mountain.

44 And the Amoree, which dwelt in that mountain,[3] came out against you, and chased you, as bees do, and drove you back in

Footnotes
[1] Caleb was from the tribe of Judah, therefore he enters the land first. This is the sign of Judah, who would inherit the land. The order is important, Yahudah is mentioned first showing us Yahudah will enter in the land first followed by Efrayim (Yahushua, the son of Nun was from the from the tribe of Efrayim). This happened with a small group of Yahudah entering to live in Ysra'el in 1960s the people in Dimona the Black Hebrews.

Footnotes
[2] The sign for Efrayim and his inheritance yet to come.
[3] Present site of Jerusalem is not the Jerusalem of the Yavusi which King David captured and built a city and dwelt therein. So please note there are two Jerusalems, one of the Amorites, and one of the Jebusites as can be seen here. See Yahushua 10:5.

Seir, even to Khurma.

45 And you returned and wept before YHWH; but YHWH would not listen to your voice, nor give any attention to you.

46 So you stayed in Kadesh many days, according to the days that you stayed there.

Chapter 2

1 Then we turned, and set out for our journey into the wilderness by the way of the Sea of Reeds, as YHWH instructed me: and we went around Mount Seir many days.

2 And YHWH spoke to me, saying,

3 You have gone around this mountain long enough: now turn northward.

4 And command the people, saying, You are to pass through the coast of your brethren the children of Esaw, which dwell in Seir; and they shall be afraid of you: take good heed to yourselves therefore:

5 Meddle not with them; for I will not give you any of their land, no, not so much as a foot breadth; because I have given Mount Seir to Esaw for a possession.

6 You shall buy food from them for money, that you may eat; and you shall also buy mayim of them for money, that you may drink.

7 For YHWH Your POWER has **Blessed** you in all the works of your hand: he knows your walking through this great wilderness: these forty years YHWH Your POWER has been with you; You have lacked nothing.

8 And when we passed by from our brethren the children of Esaw, which dwelt in Seir, through the way of the plain from Eilat, and from Etzyon-gaber, we turned and passed by the way of the wilderness of Moav.

9 And YHWH said to me, do not harass the Moavi, neither provoke them to war: for I will not give you of their land for a possession; because I have given Ar to the children of Lot for a possession.

10 The Emim[2] dwelt therein in times past, a people great, and many, and tall, as the Anakim;

11 Which also were accounted giants, as the Anakim; but the Moavi call them Emim.

12 The Khurim also dwelt in Seir beforetime; but the children of Esaw succeeded them, when they had destroyed them from before them, and dwelt in their stead; as Israel did to the land of his possession, which YHWH gave to them.

13 Now rise up, said I, and get you over the wadi zered. And we went over the wadi zered.

14 And the space, in which we came from Kadesh-Barnea, until we came over the wadi zered, was thirty eight years; until all the generation of the men of war were wasted out from among the

Footnotes
[1] We see the scribal gap again in verse 8. This is a pause to show us what follows.
[2] Rephaites are a people who were very tall like giants. Og was also from the same race Dev 3:11.

host, as YHWH had sworn to them.

15 For indeed the hand of YHWH was against them, to destroy them from among the host, until they were consumed.

16 So it came to pass, when all the men of war were consumed and dead from among the people,

17 That YHWH spoke to me, saying,

18 Today you are going to cross the border of Moav. That is Ar.[1]

19 And when You come nigh over against the children of Ammon, do not contend with them, nor meddle with them: for I will not give you of the land of the children of Ammon any possession; because I have given it to the children of Lot for a possession.

20 (That also was accounted a land of giants: giants dwelt therein in old time; and the Ammonim call them Zamzumim;

21 A people great, and many, and tall, as the Anakim; but YHWH destroyed them before them; and they succeeded them, and dwelt in their stead:

22 As he did to the children of Esaw, which dwelt in Seir, when he destroyed the Khuri[2] from before them; and they succeeded them, and dwelt in their stead even to this day:

23 And the Avim which dwelt in Hazerim, even to Azzah, the Kaphtorim, which came forth out

Footnotes
[1] A Moabite city on the Arnon River due east of the Dead Sea.
[2] Another race of giants.

of Caphtor, destroyed them, and dwelt in their stead.)

24 Get up, take your journey, and pass over the river Arnon: behold, I have given into your hand Sikhon the Amoree, King of Kheshbon, and his land: begin to possess it, and engage him for war.

25 This day will I begin to put the dread of you and the fear of you upon the nations that are under the whole shamayim, who shall hear report of you, and shall shiver and shake because of you.

26 And I sent messengers out of the wilderness of Kedemoth to Sikhon King of Kheshbon with words of shalom, saying,

27 Let me pass through your land: I will go along by the high way, I will neither turn to the right hand nor to the left.

28 You shall sell me food for money that I may eat; and give me mayim for money, that I may drink: only I will pass through on my feet;

29 (As the children of Esaw which dwell in Seir, and the Moavi which dwell in Ar, did to me;) until I shall pass over Yardan (Jordan) into the land which YHWH our POWER gives us.

30 But Sikhon King of Kheshbon would not let us pass by him: for YHWH Your POWER hardened his ruakh, and made his heart obstinate, that he might give him into your hand, to this very day.

31 And YHWH said to me, Behold, I have begun to give Sikhon and his land before you: begin to possess, that You may inherit his land.

32 Then Sikhon came out against us, he and all his people, to fight at Yahtsa.

וּנֶ[כ

33 And YHWH our POWER handed him before us; and we struck him down with his sons, and all his people.

34 And we took all his cities at that time, and utterly destroyed the men, and the women, and the little ones, of every city, we left none to remain.

35 Only the cattle we took for a plunder to ourselves, and the spoil of the cities which we took.

36 From Aroer, which is by the brink of the river of Arnon, and from the city that is by the river, even to Gil'ad, there was not one city too strong for us, YHWH our POWER gave all to us:

37 Only to the land of the children of Ammon You came not, nor to any place of the river Yabbok, nor to the cities in the mountains, or wherever YHWH our POWER had forbidden us.

Chapter 3

1 Then we turned, and went up the way to Bashan: and Og [2] the King of Bashan came out against us, he and all his people, to battle at Edrei.

2 And YHWH said to me, Fear him not: for I will give him, and all his people, and his land, into your hand; and You shall do to him as You did to Sikhon King of the Amoree, who dwelt at Kheshbon.

3 So YHWH our POWER gave into our hands Og also, the King of Bashan, and all his people: and we struck him down until not a single survivor was left.

4 And we took all his cities at that time, there was not a city which we took not from them, sixty cities, all the region of Argob, the kingdom of Og in Bashan.

5 All these cities were fenced with high walls, gates, and bars; beside unwalled towns a great many.

6 And we utterly destroyed them, as we did to Sikhon King of Kheshbon, utterly destroying the men, women, and children, of every city.

7 But all the cattle, and the spoil of the cities, we took for a prey to ourselves.

8 And we took at that time out of the hand of the two Kings of the Amoree the land that was on this side Yardan (Jordan), from the river of Arnon to Mount Khermon.

9 Which Khermon the Sidonim call Sirion; and the Amoree call it Shenir;

10 All the cities of the plain, and all Gil'ad, and all Bashan, to Salkha and Edrei, cities of the kingdom of Og in Bashan.

עֶרֶ**שׂ**[3]

Footnotes

[1] The large Kaf signifies the picture of a sling in the ancient Hebrew script therefore this shows Sihon being struck down through the power of YHWH.

[2] A giant.

Footnotes

[3] The sin is raised for the word of bed. This reveals his large bed was seen as his symbol of power by the people around him since he was a giant so the raising of the letter sin Continued in next section

11 For only Og King of Bashan remained of the remnant of giants; behold, his sarcophagus was made of iron; is it not in Rabbath of the children of Ammon? Nine cubits[1] was the length there, and four cubits the breadth of it, after the cubit of a man.

12 And this land, which we possessed at that time, from Aroer, which is by the river Arnon, and half Mount Gil'ad, and the cities there, gave I to the Reuveni and to the Gaddi.

13 And the rest of Gil'ad, and all Bashan, being the kingdom of Og, gave I to the half tribe of Manasheh; all the region of Argob, with all Bashan, which was called the land of giants.

14 Yair the son of Manasheh took all the country of Argob to the coasts of Geshuri and Ma'Akati; and called them after his own name, Bashan-Khavuth-yair, to this day.

15 And I gave Gil'ad to Makhir.

16 And to the Reuveni and to the Gaddi I gave from Gil'ad even to the river Arnon half the valley, and the border even to the river Yabbok, which is the border of the children of Ammon;

17 The plain also, and Yardan (Jordan), and the coast there, from Kinnereth even to the sea of the plain, even the salt sea, under Asdat-pisgah eastward.

18 And I commanded you at

that time, saying, YHWH Your POWER has given you this land to possess it: you shall pass over armed before your brethren the children of Israel, all that are meet for the war.

19 But your wives, and your little ones, and your cattle, (for I know that you have much cattle,) shall abide in your cities which I have given you;

20 Until YHWH has given victory to your brethren, as well as to you, and until they also possess the land which YHWH Your POWER has given them beyond Yardan (Jordan) and then shall you return every man to his possession, which I have given you.

21 And I commanded Yahushua at that time, saying, Your eyes have seen all that YHWH Your POWER has done to these two Kings: so shall YHWH do to all the kingdoms where you are going.

22 You shall not fear them: for YHWH Your POWER He shall fight for you.

Torah Parsha 45 Va'etchanan, Devrim 3:23-7:11
Haftarah: Yeshayahu 40:1-26

23 And I besought YHWH at that time, saying,

24 O Adoni YHWH, You have begun to show your servant your greatness, and your mighty hand: for what El (Power) is there in shamayim or in earth, that can do according to your works, and according to your strength?

25 I beseech you, let me go

---

reveals his brightness or glory that he was known for was taken away.

[1] 13.5 feet long and six feet wide. Og was believed to be a 13 foot tall giant.

over, and see the good land that is beyond Yardan (Jordan), that goodly mountain, and Lebanon.

26 But YHWH was angry with me for your sakes, and would not listen to me: and YHWH said to me, enough of this; speak no more to me of this matter.

27 Get up into the top of Pisgah, and take a good look westward, and northward, and southward, and eastward, for You will not be allowed to go over the Yardan (Jordan).

28 But charge Yahushua, and encourage him, and strengthen him: for he shall go over before this people, and he shall cause them to inherit the land which You shall see.

29 So we abode in the valley over against Beth-peor.

Chapter 4

1 Now therefore listen, O Israel, to the statutes and to the judgments, which I teach you, for to do them, that you may live, and go in and take over the land which YHWH Elohim of your ahvot (fathers) has given you.

2 You shall not add[1] to the word which I command you, neither shall you diminish from it, that you may keep the commandments of YHWH Your POWER which I command you.

3 Your eyes have seen what YHWH did because of Baal-peor: for all the men that followed Baal-peor, YHWH Your POWER has

destroyed[2] them from among you.

4 But you that did remain trustworthy to YHWH Your POWER are alive everyone of you this day.[3]

5 Behold, I have taught you statutes and judgments, even as YHWH my POWER commanded me, that you should do so in the land which you are about to enter and possess.

6 And you shall guard them and do them; for this is your wisdom[4] and your understanding in the sight of the nations, which shall hear all these statutes, and say, Surely this great nation is a wise and understanding[5] people.

7 For what nation is there so great, who has Elohim so close to them, as YHWH our POWER is in all things that we call upon him for?

8 And what nation is there so great, that has statutes and judgments so Righteous as all this Torah,[6] which I set before

Footnotes
[1] We must not add on to YHWH's laws, see Mishle (Proverbs) 30:6; Deuteronomy 12:32.

Footnotes
[2] Doctrines of seduction that many in the churches engage in such as, saying it is ok to eat unclean meats and breaking YHWH's rules to appease denominationalism. Forcing people not to wear makeup, jewelry things which are permitted by Torah.
[3] The only thing that guarantees us life on this earth is our trustworthiness to YHWH's Torah. The rest is commentary.
[4] Man made wisdom is foolishness while guarding and keeping the commandments of YHWH is what really sets us apart and makes us wise and understanding people.
[5] This is speaking about Torah keepers and certainly not Sunday Christians.
[6] Israel as a tiny nation that has defied many bigger Islamic nations roundabout by being trustworthy to YHWH and His Torah, while many Christian nations fell and today have
Continued in next section

you this day?

9 Only pay careful attention lest You forget the things which your eyes[1] have seen, and lest they depart from your heart all the days of your life: but teach them to your sons, and your sons' sons;

10 Specially the day that You stood before YHWH Your POWER in Horev, when YHWH said to me, Gather to me the people together, and I will make them hear my words, that they may learn to fear me all the days that they shall live upon the earth, and that they may teach their children.

11 And you came near and stood under the mountain; and the mountain burned with fire to the midst of shamayim, with darkness, clouds, and thick darkness. [2]

12 And YHWH spoke to you out of the midst of the fire: you heard the voice of the words, but saw no similitude;[3] only you heard a voice.

13 And he declared to you his Covenant,[4] which he commanded you to perform, even ten commandments; and He[5] wrote them upon two tablets of stone.

14 And YHWH commanded me at that time to teach you statutes and judgments, that you might do them in the land where you go over to enter and possess it.

15 Take you therefore good heed to yourselves; for you saw no manner of similitude on the day that YHWH spoke to you in Horev out of the midst of the fire:

16 Lest you corrupt yourselves, and make you a graven image, the similitude of any figure, the likeness of male or female, [6]

17 The likeness of any animal [7] that is on the earth, the likeness of any winged fowl that flies in the air,

18 The likeness of any thing that crawls on the ground, the likeness of any fish[8] that is in the mayim beneath the earth.

19 And lest You lift up your eyes to shamayim, and when You see the sun, and the moon, and the stars, even all the host of shamayim, should be driven to

become Islamic. Just look at Egypt, Lebanon, Sudan, and Algeria as some examples. YHWH has been trustworthy to Israel because of His Covenants. The Christian nations have a hide incident of wickedness causing their fall.

[1] We have a tendency to forget miracles but our Faith must be steadfast irrespective of miracles or not. This was one of Israel's chief problems they saw with their eyes but later forgot all about it and went whoring elsewhere.

[2] Light can only be seen in darkness; hence the glory of YHWH was manifested.

[3] No one ever saw YHWH's real form and lived.

Footnotes

[4] Also known as the Sinaitic Covenant

[5] YHWH

[6] Any form of idol worship whether Mary's statue or some other statues such as of a cow, horse, snake or dog is forbidden as these were worshipped by heathen nations and today many still continue this practice.

[7] Some nations worship animals and call them elohim yet they are only made with hands by humans to earn money.

[8] Some heathen nations worship sea creatures as elohim.

pay homage to them,[1] and serve them, which YHWH Your POWER has divided to all nations under the whole shamayim.

20 But YHWH has taken you, and brought you forth out of the iron furnace, even out of Mitzrayim (Egypt), to be to him a people of inheritance, as you are this day.

21 Furthermore YHWH was angry with me for your sakes, and swore that I should not go over Yardan (Jordan), and that I should not go in to that good land, which YHWH Your POWER gives you for an inheritance:

22 But I must die in this land, I must not go over Yardan (Jordan): but you shall go over, and possess that good land.

23 Take heed to yourselves, lest you forget the Covenant of YHWH Your POWER[2], which he made with you, and make you a graven image, or the likeness of any thing, which YHWH Your POWER has forbidden you.

24 For YHWH Your POWER is a consuming fire, even the jealous El (Power).

25 When You shall produce children, and grandchildren, and you shall have remained long in the land, and shall corrupt yourselves, and make a graven image, or the likeness of any thing, and shall do evil in the sight of YHWH Your POWER, to provoke him to anger:

26 I call the shamayim and the earth to witness against you this day, that you shall soon utterly perish from off the land whereunto you go over Yardan (Jordan) to possess it; you shall not prolong your days upon it, but shall utterly be destroyed.

27 And YHWH shall scatter you among the nations, and you shall be left few in number among the heathen,[3] where YHWH shall lead you.

28 And there you shall serve powers, the work of men's hands, wood and stone, which neither see, nor hear, nor eat, nor smell.[4]

29 But if from now on You shall seek YHWH your POWER, You shall find him, if You seek him with all your heart and with all your soul.

30 In the latter days, when days of distress come upon you, and if You will turn around to repentance to YHWH Your POWER, and shall be obedient to his voice;[5]

31 For YHWH Your POWER is a merciful El (Power); he will not forsake you, [6] neither destroy you, nor forget the Covenant of

Footnotes

[1] Some nations worshipped the moon and the stars, some today even worship the sun and worship fire.

[2] Many people in churches need to learn what a Covenant is as they do not understand neither do they obey the commandments set by YHWH.

[3] YHWH did scatter them and we find the Hebrew people were left few in number amongst the Muslim nations. However, Northern Israel was absorbed into the nations and they lost their identity.

[4] Many are doing this today running after national heathen elohim.

[5] Keeping Torah

[6] Israel is already marked for rescue.

your ahvot (fathers) which he swore to them.

32 For ask now of the days that are past, which were before you, since the day that Elohim created man upon the earth, and ask from the one side of shamayim to the other, whether there has been any such thing as this great thing is, or has been heard like it?

33 Did ever people hear the voice of Elohim speaking out of the midst of the fire, as You have heard, and live?[1]

34 Or has Elohim before tried to take a nation from the midst of another nation, by trials, by signs, and by wonders, and by war, and by a mighty hand, and by a stretched out arm, and by great terrors, according to all that YHWH Your POWER did for you in Mitzrayim (Egypt) before your eyes?

35 Only you were picked so, that You might know that YHWH he is Elohim; there is none else beside him.

36 Out of shamayim he made you to hear His voice, that he might instruct you: and upon earth he showed you his great fire; and You heard his words out of the midst of the fire.

Footnotes
[1] Israel was and is the only nation with the special Covenants that YHWH formed. Yes there are Israelites out of the land but YHWH does not know or have any agreement with heathens but only with Israelites even while they are in the nations. Many Christians, who are in the nations, are unaware that they are biological Israel. First Denominationalism was Satan's way of keeping people separated, and fighting over little things. YHWH does not recognize any denomination but Israel.

37 And because He loved your ahvot (fathers), therefore he chose their seed after them,[2] and brought you out in his sight with his mighty power out of Mitzrayim (Egypt);

38 To drive out nations from before you greater and mightier than You are, to bring you in, to give you their land for an inheritance, as it is this day.

39 Realize this from today, and carefully consider it in your heart, that YHWH he is Elohim in the shamayim above, and upon the earth beneath: there is none else.

40 You shall keep therefore his statutes, and his commandments, which I command you this day, that it may go well with you, and with your children after you, and that You may prolong your days upon the earth, which YHWH Your POWER gives you, forever.

41 Then Mosheh (Musa) selected three cities on this side Yardan (Jordan) toward the sun rising;

42 Anyone who accidentally killed someone without hatred might flee there, and that fleeing into one of these cities he might be safe.

43 Namely, Behtser in the wilderness, in the plain country, of the Reuveni; and Ramoth in Gil'ad, of the Gawdi; and Golan in Bashan of the Manasshites.

44 And this is the Torah which Mosheh (Musa) set before the children of Israel:

Footnotes
[2] He indeed loved our forefathers and our patriarchal order that some hate today.

45 These are the testimonies, and the statutes, and the judgments, which Mosheh (Musa) spoke to the children of Israel, after they came forth out of Mitzrayim (Egypt),

46 On this side Yardan (Jordan), in the valley over against Beth-peor, in the land of Sikhon King of the Amoree, who dwelt at Kheshbon, whom Mosheh (Musa) and the children of Israel smote, after they were come forth out of Mitzrayim (Egypt):

47 And they possessed his land, and the land of Og King of Bashan, two Kings of the Amoree, which were on this side Yardan (Jordan) toward the sun rising;

48 From Aroer, which is by the bank of the river Arnon, even to Mount tsiyon, which is Khermon,

49 And all the plain on this side Yardan (Jordan) eastward, even to the sea of the plain, under the springs of Pisgah.

Chapter 5

1 And Mosheh (Musa) called all Israel, and said to them, Hear, O Israel, the statutes and judgments which I speak in your ears this day, that you may learn them, and keep, and do them.

2 YHWH our POWER made a Covenant with us in Horev.[1]

3 YHWH made not this Covenant with our ahvot (fathers), but with us, even us, who are all of us here alive this

day.

4 YHWH talked with you face to face in the Mount out of the midst of the fire,

5 I stood between YHWH and you at that time, to bring you the word of YHWH[ ]: for you were afraid by reason of the fire, and went not up into the Mount; saying,

The Decalogue repeated by YHWH

6 [Alef] I am YHWH Your POWER, which brought you out of the land of Mitzrayim (Egypt), from the Beyth (house) of slavery.

7 [Bet] You shall have no other powers before me.

8 You shall not make you any graven image,[3] or any likeness of any thing that is in shamayim above, or that is in the earth beneath, or that is in the mayim beneath the earth:

9 You shall not bow down[4] yourself to them, nor serve them: for I YHWH Your POWER am a Devoted El (Power), visiting the iniquity of the ahvot (fathers) upon the children to the third and

Footnotes
[2] The word Devar in Hebrew or Memra in Aramaic is the personification of YHWH through Torah.
[3] No idol to represent our POWER YHWH in shamayim. This is a practice the nations do and these idols do not answer and are without any authority or power. They cannot even blow a fly from themselves.
[4] Bowing down to any man made statue is a grave sin and that includes bowing down to Mary's statue as many do.

Footnotes
[1] This was the Ten Commandments only.

fourth generation[1] of them that hate me,

10 And showing loving-kindness to thousands of them that love me and keep my commandments.[2]

11 [Gimmel] You shall not Lift up the name of YHWH Your POWER *in oaths* falsely; YHWH will not hold him guiltless who Lifts his name and falsifies it.[3]

12 [Dalet] Guard the Sabbath day to set it apart, as YHWH Your POWER has commanded[4] you.

13 Six days You shall labour, and do all your work:

14 But the seventh day is the Sabbath of YHWH Your POWER: in it You shall not do any work, You, nor your son, nor your daughter, nor your male-servant, nor your maidservant,[5] nor your ox, nor your ass, nor any of your

cattle,[6] nor your foreigner that is within your gates; that your male-servant and your maidservant may rest as well as You.

15 And remember that You were a servant in the land of Mitzrayim (Egypt), and that YHWH Your POWER brought you out of there through a mighty hand and by a stretched out arm: therefore YHWH Your POWER commanded you to keep the Sabbath day.[7]

16 [Heh] Respect your father and your mother, as YHWH Your POWER has commanded you; that your days may be prolonged, and that it may go well with you, in the land which YHWH Your POWER is about to give you.

17 [Wah] You shall not murder.

18 [Zayin] Neither shall You commit adultery.

19 [Chet] Neither shall You steal.

20 [Tet] Neither shall You bear false witness against your neighbour.[8]

21 [Yud] Neither shall You desire your neighbour's wife, neither shall You covet your neighbour's Beyth (house), his field, or his male-servant, or his maidservant, his ox, or his ass, or any thing that is your neighbour's.

22 These words YHWH spoke to all your assembly in the Mount

Footnotes

[1] This is still true today for those who hate YHWH. Usually, their children grow up to hate YHWH too, so the judgments pass to the children. But, if the children repent the judgments would not pass on to them. They can break the curse by repenting and asking for forgiveness for what their forefathers did.

[2] If you want the mercy of YHWH then Keep the Torah of Moses.

[3] To falsify it and to bring it to nothing. This is not about taking the name incorrectly or pronouncing it wrong but about using it in oaths or dishonoring it by not being accountable to it.

[4] It is YHWH's Sabbath and not man's to decide on what day it should be. The 7th day is the Sabbath. Sunrise to Sunset.

[5] Even servants are to be given Sabbath off, so you cannot have gentiles working while you rest. Halacha does permit gentiles to work if the work was given to them prior to the Sabbath commencing.

Footnotes

[6] Even animals are to be given rest.

[7] Israel was released on a high Holy Sabbath day from Egypt that was on Passover.

[8] Many in and outside the churches bearing false witness, yet this is very evil when brother or sister speaks lies against another for gain, pride and ego.

out of the midst of the fire, of the cloud, and of the thick darkness, with a great voice: and he added no more. And he wrote them in two tables of stone, and gave them to me.

23 And it came to pass, when you heard the voice out of the midst of the darkness, (for the mountain did burn with fire,) that you came near to me, even all the chiefs of your tribes, and your elders;

24 And you said, Behold, YHWH our POWER has showed us his glory and his greatness, and we have heard his voice out of the midst of the fire: we have seen this day that Elohim will talk with man, and he lives.[1]

25 Now therefore why should we die? For this great fire will consume us: if we hear the voice of YHWH our POWER any more, then we shall die.

26 For who is there of all flesh, that has heard the voice of the living Elohim speaking out of the midst of the fire, as we have, and lived?

27 You go near, and hear all that YHWH our POWER shall say: and speak to us all that YHWH our POWER shall speak to you; and we will hear it, and do it.

28 And YHWH heard the voice of your words, when you spoke to me; and YHWH said to me, I have heard the voice of the words of this people, which they

have spoken to you: they have well said all that they have spoken.

29 O that there were such a heart in them, that they would fear me, and keep all my commandments always, that it might be well with them, and with their children forever!

30 Go say to them, return into your tents again.

31 But as for you, stand here by me, and I will speak to you all the commandments, and the statutes, and the judgments, which You shall teach them, that they may do them in the land which I give them to possess it.

32 You shall observe to do therefore as YHWH Your POWER has commanded you: you shall not turn aside to the right hand or to the left.[2]

33 You shall have your Halaka[3] in all the halachot[4] which YHWH Your POWER has commanded you, that you may live, and that it may be well with you, and that you may prolong your days in the land which you shall possess.

Chapter 6

1 These are the commandments, the statutes, and the judgments, which YHWH

Footnotes
[1] The Israelites were under the impression that even hearing the voice of YHWH would kill a man but this was not so.

[2] The words Right and the Left, too much to the right means too much tendency to the judgment side, while too much to the left is tendency to the mercy side. We must be balanced in the middle united by the middle pillar of the sefirotic tree.
[3] Commandment keeping.
[4] Commandments of Torah that YHWH expects every Israelite to keep. Dispensationalism is the disease that has caused many to go into error over Torah.

Your POWER commanded to teach you, that you might do them in the land where you are going to enter and possess it:

2 That You might fear YHWH Your POWER, to keep all his statutes and his commandments, which I command you, You, and your son, and your grandson, all the days of your life; and that your days may be prolonged.[1]

3 Hear therefore, O Israel, and observe to do[2] it; that it may be well with you, and that you may **Increase** mightily, as YHWH Elohim of your ahvot (fathers) has promised you, in the land that flows with milk and honey.

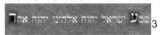[3]

Footnotes
[1] If you want a long life then practice Torah.
[2] Hear and Do is the motif for Torah keeping.
[3] The enlarged Hebrew letter Ayin and the raised Dalet in the text.
The ayin stands for the legs and we know we were to 'hear and do'. This means we are to walk the walk to obey Torah while many just talk with no action. Ad in Hebrew also stands for a witness, if you reverse the letters and append a Tav you get Da'at דעת which is knowledge given to you/us by Em Chockmah.

You cannot hear through the legs but you hear through the ears and establish through the heart. If we look and establish our Faith by our walk (legs), then we will not fall. If your Faith is built upon miracles then the chances are that it is not based on a firm foundation since miracles can be falsified or at best only give momentary comfort. Just look back to Egypt where false miracles were performed by the magicians to outdo Moses' while real miracles performed by YHWH became a remembrance. To 'Hear and Do' is a term that really means we will obey the commandments in the Torah.

Continued in next section

The Shma, our creed [4] HEAR O' ISRAEL

שמע ישראל 𐤀𐤋𐤄𐤍𐤅 יהוה אחד

Shma, Israel, YHWH elohenu, YHWH Akhad

4 Hear, O Israel: YHWH our Supreme One YHWH is Akhad:

5 And You shall love YHWH Your POWER with all your heart, and with all your soul, and with all your might.

6 And these words, which I command you this day, shall be in your heart:

7 And You shall teach them diligently to your children, and shall talk of them when You sit in your Beyth (house), and when You walk by the way, and when You lie down, and when You rise up.[6]

8 And You shall bind them for a

The letter Dalet is raised and the picture for a mouth which means loud speech and points us back to the shofarim sounds of when YHWH spoke on Mount Sinai which reveals remembrance to the Torah forever about keeping and obeying the Torah. However, many in the world are still hearing false speeches of other religions looking for ways to eternal life because they do not hear the mouth or speech of YHWH. This verse is repeated by the Orthodox Jewish/Israelite people twice daily and it contains the signature of YHWH. The ayin is also raised.
[4] The Hebrew people recite this twice daily during their prayers. This is our creed and we should recite this **twice** daily in our prayers.
[5] Two YHWH's in the same line shows us the juxtaposition of the Father.
[6] Three daily prayers, the Shachrit Morning Prayer, the afternoon prayer (Mincha) and the Ma'ariv prayer in the evening according to rabbinic Judaism, While the Temple services were twice daily.

sign upon your hand,[1] and they shall be for a remembrance between your eyes.

9 And You shall write them upon the posts of your Beyth (house),[2] and on your gates.

10 And it shall be, when YHWH Your POWER shall have brought you into the land which he swore to your ahvot (fathers), to Abraham, to Ytshak, and to Yakov, to give you great and goodly cities, which You did not build,

11 And houses full of all good things, which You filled not, and wells dug, which You did not dig, vineyards and olive trees, which You did not plant; when You shall have eaten and be full;

12 Then beware lest You forget YHWH, which brought you forth

out of the land of Mitzrayim (Egypt), from the Beyth (house) of slavery.[3]

13 You shall fear YHWH Your POWER, and serve him, and shall swear by his name.[4]

14 You shall not go after other elohim, of the elohim of the people which are round about you;[5]

15 For YHWH Your POWER is a jealous El (Power) among you lest the anger of YHWH Your POWER be kindled against you, and destroy you from off the face of the earth.

16 You shall not tempt YHWH Your POWER, as you tempted him in Massah.

17 You shall diligently keep the commandments of YHWH Your POWER, and his testimonies, and his statutes, which he has commanded you.

18 And You shall do that which is right and good in the sight of YHWH: that it may be well with you, and that You may go in and possess the good land which YHWH swore to your ahvot (fathers),

19 To cast out all your enemies from before you, as YHWH has spoken.

20 And when your son asks you in the latter times, saying, What

Footnotes

[1] The tefillin or phylacteries to bind on the hands which was introduced by the Rabbis later but the actual words to bind to hand for a sign is not about a box but to judge righteously. The sign of the right hand is the action of judging, which means judge mercifully so that others see that in us that we are merciful people. The word tatafot means remembrance between your eyes is that Torah or the laws of YHWH are forever in our head to guide us how to operate in the Torah. In our ancient culture the metaphor is to wear a bracelet and to wear a piece of jewelry between our foreheads as women wear in the east. So we are to carry the Torah remembrance as a precious piece of Jewelry to us forever.

[2] This should be the Ten Commandments affixed on a plate on the right side of the door and not the Jewish invented box of late derivation. Although if you decide to put the modern Mezuzah up that is fine but the original command was to put the Ten Commandments up.

Footnotes

[3] When we were saved, we were really in the Beyth (house) of slavery, no matter what religious background we may come out of. It's only Torah that truly sets us free.

[4] We are commanded to swear only in His name for taking any oaths.

[5] The people or the religion that is roundabout Israel today is Islam, so taking the name of Allah in ignorance.

mean the testimonies, and the statutes, and the judgments, which YHWH our POWER has commanded you?

21 Then You shall say to your son, We were Pharaoh's bondmen in Mitzrayim (Egypt);[1] and YHWH brought us out of Mitzrayim (Egypt) with a mighty hand[2]:

22 And YHWH sent signs and wonders, great and sore, upon Mitzrayim (Egypt), upon Pharaoh, and upon all his household, before our eyes:

23 And he brought us out from there, that he might bring us in, to give us the land which he swore to our ahvot (fathers).

24 And YHWH commanded us to do all these statutes, to fear YHWH our POWER, for our good always, that he might preserve us alive, as it is at this day.[3]

25 And it shall be our Righteousness, if we observe to do all these commandments before YHWH our POWER, as he has commanded us.

Chapter 7

1 When YHWH Your POWER shall bring you into the land where You go in to possess it, and He has cast out many nations before you, the Khitee, and the Girgashi, and the Amoree, and the Kanani, and the Perzee, and the Khuvi, and the Yavusi, seven nations greater and mightier than You;

2 And when YHWH Your POWER shall hand them before you; You shall conquer them, and utterly destroy them; You shall make no Covenant with them, nor show loving-kindness to them:

3 Neither shall You make marriages with them; your daughter You shall not give to his son,[4] nor his daughter shall You take to your son.

4 For they will turn away your son from following me, that they may serve other Elohim, so will the anger of YHWH be kindled against you, and destroy you suddenly.

5 Instead this is what you must do to them; you shall tear down their altars, and shatter down their pillars, and cut down their asherah[5] poles,[6] and burn their idols.

6 For You are a Holy people to YHWH Your POWER: YHWH Your POWER has chosen you to be a treasured possession to himself, above all the people that are over the whole face of the earth.

7 YHWH did not set his love upon you, nor choose you, because you were more in number than any people; for you

Footnotes
[1] Pharaoh is a depiction also of Satan and the coming anti-Messiah from Turkey.
[2] Drash for the King Messiah.
[3] The commandments were not given to pick and choose as many Christians do.

Footnotes
[4] It is forbidden to marry outside the community of believers, however, one could be converted and you could marry them in Torah.
[5] The word 'Easter' comes from this Hebrew word.
[6] The cross is also a Babylonian symbol and must not be in any place of worship.

were the fewest of all people:[1]

8 But because YHWH loved you, and because he would keep the oath which he had sworn to your ahvot (fathers), has YHWH brought you out with a mighty hand, and redeemed you out of the Beyth (house) of slavery, from the hand of Pharaoh King of Mitzrayim (Egypt).

9 Know therefore that YHWH Your POWER, he is Elohim, the trustworthy El (Power), which keeps Covenant and unmerited favour with them that love him and guard His commandments to a thousand generations;[2]

10 And repays them that hate him to their face, to destroy them: he will not be slack to him that hates him, he will repay him to his face.

11 You shall therefore keep the commandments, and the statutes, and the judgments, which I command you this day, to do them.

Torah Parsha 46 Akev, Devrim 7:12-11:25
Haftarah: Yeshayahu 49:14-51:3

12 Therefore it shall come to pass, if you listen to my voice to these judgments, and guard, and

do them,[3] that YHWH Your POWER shall guard you into the Covenant and unmerited favour which he swore[4] to your ahvot (fathers):

13 And he will love you, and **Bless** you, and multiply you:[5] he will also **Bless**[6] you with many children[7] and the fruit of your land, your wheat, and your wine, and your oil, the offspring of your oxen, and the flocks of your sheep, in the land which he swore to your ahvot (fathers) to give you.

14 You shall be **Blessed** above all people: there shall not be male or female barren among you, or among your cattle.

15 And YHWH will take away from you all sickness, and will put none of the evil diseases of Mitzrayim (Egypt), which You know about, but will lay them upon all them that hate you.

16 And You shall conquer all the people which YHWH Your POWER shall give you; your eye shall have no pity upon them: neither shall You serve their

Footnotes
[1] Israel is still few in number due to the mixing and will be brought back in full numbers.
[2] Remez hint of His prophetic return. Also a thousand generations does not mean it would end at the second Temple, because by then a thousand generations had not passed!
[3] Keep and do is the idiomatic expression for Torah keeping.
[4] The Hebrew word is Shubah, meaning that YHWH has sworn unto self seven times, the Covenant is irrevocable and must be fulfilled. Rescue is already guaranteed with unmerited favour unto Israel if they obey Torah.
[5] This will be a large extended family, implying many wives as in a patriarchal lifestyle and many children.
[6] The **Blessing** only comes via Patriarchal plural marriage and not gentile serial monogamy.
[7] The **Blessing** of many children entails plural marriages, which Israel understood and practiced it in ancient times.

433

powers;[1] for that will be a trap for you.

17 If You shall say in your heart, These nations are more than I; how can I dispossess them?

18 You shall not be afraid of them: but shall well remember what YHWH Your POWER did to Pharaoh, and to all Mitzrayim (Egypt);

19 The great temptations which your eyes saw, and the signs, and the wonders, and the mighty hand, and the stretched out arm, whereby YHWH Your POWER brought you out: so shall YHWH Your POWER do to all the people of whom You are afraid.

20 Moreover YHWH Your POWER will send the hornet among them, until they that are left, and hide themselves from you, be destroyed.

21 You shall not be afraid of them: for YHWH Your POWER is among you, a mighty El (Power) and awesome.

22 And YHWH Your POWER will expel these nations before you by little and little: You may not destroy them all at once, lest the animals of the field overrun you.

23 But YHWH Your POWER shall give them to you, and shall destroy them with a mighty destruction, until they be destroyed.

Footnotes
[1] Any power or gentiles that can bind us and that includes their marriage laws, licenses etc. Powers here can also be related to men who hold authority to enforce certain state laws that can trap us from breaking YHWH's commandments.

24 And He shall give their Kings into your hand, and You shall destroy their name from under shamayim: there shall no man be able to stand before you, until You have destroyed them.

25 The graven images of their powers you shall burn with fire: You shall not desire the silver or gold that is on them, nor take it to you, lest You be entrapped therein: for it is a Ritual Defilement to YHWH your POWER.

26 Neither shall You bring any Ritual Defilement into your Beyth (house), lest You become object of the Holy wrath and You must abhor it; for it is a detestable thing.

Chapter 8

1 All the commandments which I command you this day you shall observe to do, that you may live, and exceedingly **Increase**, and go in and possess the land which YHWH swore to your ahvot (fathers).

2 And You shall remember all the way which YHWH Your POWER led you these forty years in the wilderness, to humble you, and to prove you, to know what was in your heart, whether You would guard His commandments, or not.

3 And he humbled you, and suffered you to hunger, and fed you with manna, which You knew not, neither did your ahvot (fathers) know; that he might make you know that man will not live by Lakhem (bread) only,[1] but by every word that proceeds out of the mouth of YHWH will man live.

4 Your clothes did not wear out, neither did your feet swell, these forty years. [2]

5 You shall also consider in your heart, that, as a man chastens his son, so YHWH Your POWER chastens you.[3]

6 Therefore You shall keep the commandments of YHWH Your POWER, to keep the Halaka (commandments) of His halachot (ways of Torah)[4] and to fear him.

7 For YHWH Your POWER brings you into a good land, a land of brooks of mayim, of fountains and depths that spring out of valleys and hills;

8 A land of wheat, and barley, and vines, and fig trees, and pomegranates; a land of oil, olive, and honey;

9 A land wherein You shall eat Lakhem (bread) without scarcity, You shall not lack any thing in it;

a land whose stones are iron, and out of whose hills You can mine copper.

10 When You have eaten and are full, then You shall *thank* YHWH for the Blessing for Your POWER for the good land which He has given you.[5]

11 Beware that You forget not YHWH Your POWER, in not keeping his commandments, and his judgments, and his statutes, which I command you this day: [6]

12 Lest when You have eaten and are full, and have built good houses, and dwelt therein;

13 And when your herds and your flocks multiply, and your silver and your gold is multiplied, and all that You have is multiplied;

14 Then your heart be lifted up, and You forget YHWH Your POWER, which brought you forth out of the land of Mitzrayim (Egypt), from the Beyth (house) of slavery;

15 Who led you through that great and terrible wilderness,

Footnotes

[1] We need Torah for our very beings, without Torah we will starve spiritually to death. Torah gives life and is the living waters we need.

[2] Amazing miracle that neither the clothes nor the shoes wore out.

[3] YHWH loves us so he has the right to chasten us.

[4] All the commandments in the Torah are valid for all times. As for the Temple related sacrifices, these we are not able to do now without a Temple. However, we are able to do the others which do not require a Temple. We can follow the lead of the prophet Dani'el who kept them while in exile in Iraq. When the millennial temple is built in the millennium, then the sacrifices will resume.

Footnotes

[5] The Jewish people say a prayer after being full as YHWH commanded us to eat then be thankful. The benediction before meals is very short. The long prayer before meals is unscriptural and not done by the Hebrews. This is the Christian pagan way of doing a long prayer before.

[6] Even though YHWH repeats Himself so many times about obedience, many who belong to churches do not want to know and obey the Torah, so judgment is coming on them. There is a repercussion for not keeping the commandments. The results are that there will be no rewards in the Kingdom to come and no positions of authority. What they will receive is the status of a slave for disobedience. Not to mention missed opportunity for the first resurrection also.

wherein were poisonous snakes, and scorpions, and drought, where there was no mayim; who brought you forth mayim out of the rock of flint;[1]

16 Who fed you in the wilderness with manna, which your ahvot (fathers) knew not, that he might humble you, and that he might prove you, to do you good at your latter end;

17 And You say in your heart, My ability and the strength of my hand has gotten me this wealth.

18 But You shall remember YHWH Your POWER: for it is He that gives you power to get wealth, that he may establish His Covenant which he swore to your ahvot (fathers), as it is this day. [2]

19 And it shall be, if You do at all forget YHWH Your POWER,

Footnotes

[1] There is an amazing sod (hidden) mystery in this. Hebrew Israel gives thanks after they are full and not before meals as Christians do. Here we are shown a very interesting picture, that YHWH has already accepted all of Israel. The mention of poisonous snakes and scorpions is a picture of the world that Hebrew Israel is right now facing. These are the satanic forces such as radical Islam, and other oppressors of the world system, but Israel gives thanks right at the end of the meal. Why at the end? So they glorify YHWH, when He saves them, completely, through His Sent Messiah in the future. They come to experience His goodness first, and see the fullness before they all give thanks to YHWH for what is yet to come. We are shown a glimpse of that in Zechariah 12:10 when Hebrew Israel cry. The Covenants require this deal on YHWH's end to be upheld which He will.

[2] Our wellbeing, our wealth, in fact everything we have is dependent on the trustworthiness of YHWH to the Covenant He made with our forefathers. We only receive the **Increase** by being part of that Covenant and fulfilling the obligations of it.

and do the halachot of other powers, and serve them, and pay homage to them, I testify against you this day that you shall surely be destroyed. [3]

20 As the nations which YHWH destroyed in front of you, so shall you perish; because you would not be obedient to the voice of YHWH Your POWER.

Chapter 9

1 Shma (Listen) Israel[4] You are to pass over Yardan (Jordan) this day, to go in to possess nations greater and mightier than yourself, cities great and fenced up to shamayim,

2 A people great and tall, the children of the Anakim, whom You know about, and of whom You have heard say, Who can stand before the children of Anak.[5]

3 Understand therefore this day, that YHWH Your POWER is he who goes over before you; as a consuming fire he shall destroy them, and he shall bring them down before your face: so You shall drive them out, and destroy them quickly, as YHWH has said to you.

4 Do not say in your heart, after that YHWH Your POWER has cast them out from before you, saying, For my Righteousness [6]

Footnotes

[3] They will perish from lack of **Increase**.
[4] Pay attention to something very important.
[5] Common proverb, who can stand before the children of the giants. Targum of Jonathan.
[6] Self boasting in Israel is not considered good. Even when YHWH destroys our

Continued in next section

YHWH has brought me in to possess this land: but for the wickedness of these nations YHWH will drive them out from before you.

5 Not for your Righteousness, or for the uprightness of your heart, do You go to possess their land: but for the wickedness of these nations YHWH Your POWER will drive them out from before you, and that He may perform the word which YHWH swore to your ahvot (fathers), Abraham, Ytshak, and Yakov.

6 Understand therefore, that YHWH Your POWER does not give you this good land to possess it for your Righteousness; for You are a stubborn people.

7 Remember, and forget not, how You provoked YHWH Your POWER to wrath in the wilderness: from the day that You did depart out of the land of Mitzrayim (Egypt), until you came to this place, you have been rebellious against YHWH.

8 Also in Horev you provoked YHWH to wrath, so that YHWH was angry with you to have destroyed you.

9 When I was gone up into the Mount to receive the tables of stone, even the tables of the Covenant[1] which YHWH made with you, then I abode in the Mount forty days and forty nights, I neither did eat Lakhem (bread) nor drink mayim.[2]

10 And YHWH gave to me two tables of stone written with the finger of Elohim; and on them was written according to all the words, which YHWH spoke with you in the Mount out of the midst of the fire in the day of the assembly.

11 And it came to pass at the end of forty days and forty nights, that YHWH gave me the two tables of stone, even the tables of the Covenant.

12 And YHWH said to me, Arise, go down quickly from hence; for your people[3] which You have brought forth out of Mitzrayim (Egypt) have corrupted themselves; they are quickly turned aside out of the way[4] which I commanded them; they have made themselves a molten image.

13 Furthermore YHWH spoke to me, saying, I have seen this people, and, behold, they are a stubborn people:

14 Let me alone, that I may finish them off, and blot out their name from under shamayim: and I will make of you a nation

enemies we are to remember the reasons why, because of their sin and not our good deeds. YHWH's mercy to these idolatrous nations had ended, due to their endless wickedness. The price of wickedness will bring both troubles here, and in the world to come.

Footnotes

[1] The Ten Commandments.

[2] Moses fasted with the help from YHWH for forty days and forty nights. This is not lent and has nothing to do with it.

[3] Because the people transgressed, YHWH dispossesses the people and calls them Moses' people.

[4] Ha Derech – The Way, to eternal life is the Torah.

mightier and greater than they.

15 So I turned and came down from the Mount, and the Mount burned with fire: and the two tables of the Covenant were in my two hands.

16 And I looked, and, behold, you had transgressed against YHWH Your POWER, and had made yourselves a molten calf: you had turned aside quickly out of the WAY which YHWH had commanded you.

17 And I took the two tables, and cast them out of my two hands, and broke them before your eyes.

18 And I fell down before YHWH, as at the first, forty days and forty nights,[1] I did neither eat Lakhem (bread), nor drink mayim, because of all your sins which you sinned, in doing wickedly in the sight of YHWH, to provoke him to anger.

19 For I was afraid of the anger and hot displeasure, wherewith YHWH was extremely angry against you to destroy you. But YHWH listened to me at that time also.

20 And YHWH was very angry with Aharon to have destroyed him: and I prayed for Aharon also the same time.

21 And I took your sin, the calf which you had made, smashed it and then burnt it with fire, and ground it very small, even until it was as small as dust: and I cast the dust there into the stream that descended out of the Mount.

22 And at Teberah, and at Massah, and at Kibroth-hattaavah, you provoked YHWH to wrath.

23 Likewise when YHWH sent you from Kadesh-Barnea, saying, go up and possess the land which I have given you; even then you rebelled against the commandment of YHWH Your POWER, and you believed Him not, nor paid any attention to his voice.

24 You have been rebellious against YHWH from the day that I took pity of you.

25 Thus I fell down before YHWH forty days and forty nights,[2] as I fell down at the first; because YHWH had said he would destroy you.

26 I prayed therefore to YHWH, and said, O Adoni YHWH, destroy not your people and your inheritance, which You have redeemed through your greatness, which You have brought up out of Mitzrayim (Egypt) by your mighty hand.[3]

27 Remember your servants, Abraham, Ytshak, and Yakov; look not to the stubbornness of this people, nor to their wickedness, nor to their sin:

28 Lest the country from where You brought us out say, Because

Footnotes
[1] Moses fasted again the second time for forty days praying and interceding for Israel's stubbornness, so Moses fasted for 80 full days in total.
[2] Two separate fasts of 40 days and 40 nights, the illusion here is to eighty Yom Kipporim. This could be the time they were in Egypt when they could not perform their annual feasts.
[3] Sign of Gevurah (strength) the right side.

YHWH was not able to bring them into the land which He promised them, and because He hated them, He has brought them out to destroy them in the wilderness.

29 Yet they are your people[1] and your inheritance, which You brought out by your Mighty Power and by your stretched out arm.

Chapter 10

1 At that time YHWH said to me, carve out for yourself two tables of stones like the ones before, and come up to me into the Mount, and make yourself an ark of wood.

2 And I will write on the tables the words that were in the first tables which You broke, and You shall put them in the ark.

3 And I made an ark of shittim wood, and carved out two tables of stone like to the first, and went up into the Mount, having the two tables in mine hand.

4 And he wrote on the tables, according to the first writing, the Ten Commandments, which YHWH spoke to you in the Mount out of the midst of the fire in the day of the assembly: and YHWH gave them to me.

5 And I turned myself and came down from the Mount, and put the tables in the ark which I had made; and there they be, as YHWH commanded me.

6 And the children of Israel took their journey from Beeroth of the children of Yaakan to Mosera: there Aharon died,[2] and there he was buried; and El'ezar his son ministered in the kohen's (priest) office in his stead.

7 From there they journeyed to Gudgodah; and from Gudgodah to Yotbathah, a land of rivers of mayim.

8 At that time YHWH separated the tribe of Levi, to bear the ark of the Covenant of YHWH, to stand before YHWH to minister to him, and to Benefit in his name, to this day.

9 Therefore Levi has no part or

Footnotes

[1] Moses switches the motif to they are your people and pleading the Covenant.

[2] Where did Aaron die, at Mount Hor Num 20:27 or here at Mosera?

Rashi
And the children of Israel journeyed from the wells of B'nei Ya'akan to Moserah: What is the relevance of this here? Furthermore, did they really journey from the wells of B'nei Ya'akan to Moserah? Was it not from Moserah that they came to the wells of B'nei Ya'akan, as it is said, "And they journeyed from Moseroth [and encamped in B'nei Ya'akan]" (Num. 33:31) ? Moreover, [why does it say:] "there Aaron died"? Did he not die at Mount Hor? If you calculate it, you will find eight stations from Moseroth to Mount Hor! However, [the answer is that] this is also part of the reproof [introduced in Deut. 1:1 and continued through here]: [In effect Moses said,] This, also, you did. When Aaron died on Mount Hor at the end of the forty years and [consequently] the clouds of the Divine Glory departed, you were afraid of the [impending] war with the king of Arad. So you appointed a leader to return to Egypt, and you went back eight stations until B'nei Ya'akan, and from there to Moserah. There, the sons of Levi battled with you. They slew some of you, and you some of them, until they forced you to return by the way you had retreated. From there, you returned to Gudgodah, which is Hor Hagidgad (Num. 33:32).

Devrim (Deuteronomy)

inheritance with his brethren, YHWH is his inheritance, accordingly as YHWH Your POWER promised him.

10 And I stayed in the Mount, according to the first time, forty days and forty nights; and YHWH listened to me at that time also, and YHWH would not destroy you.

11 And YHWH said to me, Arise, take your journey before the people, that they may go in and possess the land, which I swore to their ahvot (fathers) to give to them.

12 And now, Israel, what will YHWH Your POWER require of you, but to fear YHWH Your POWER, to keep the Halaka in His way, and to love him, and to serve YHWH Your POWER with all your heart and with all your soul,

13 To keep the commandments of YHWH, and his statutes, which I command you this day for your good?

14 Indeed shamayim and the highest shamayim belong to YHWH Your POWER, the earth also, with all that is there in.

15 Only YHWH had a delight[1] in your ahvot (fathers) to love them,

and he chose their seed after them, even you above all people, as it is this day.

16 Therefore, Circumcise the foreskin of your heart, and do not be stubborn anymore.

17 For YHWH Your POWER is the Supreme Power of the powers, and Master of masters, a great El (Power), a strong, and awesome One, who respects not persons,[2] nor takes reward:

18 He will execute the judgment of the fatherless and widow, and loves the foreigner, in giving him food and raiment;

19 You should Love the foreigner: for you were foreigners in the land of Mitzrayim (Egypt).

20 You shall fear YHWH Your POWER; him shall You serve, and to him shall You cling, and swear by His name.[3]

21 He is your praise, and he is Your POWER, that has done for you these great and terrible things, which your eyes have seen.

22 Your ahvot (fathers) went down into Mitzrayim (Egypt) seventy persons; and now YHWH Your POWER has made you as the stars of shamayim for multitude.

Chapter 11

1 Therefore You shall love YHWH Your POWER, and keep his charge, and his statutes, and his judgments, and his

Footnotes

[1] YHWH delighted in our forefathers including their lifestyles. The Patriarchal marriage model practiced by our forefathers, whom many call evil today are standing to be judged. They are committing a grave sin against YHWH, calling Him a liar. They will stand accountable on the Day of Judgment and will have to answer for their sin. This is because they have judged Torah, in fact the Torah will judge them and find them guilty and reckless.

Footnotes

[2] This is in regards to positions in society yet YHWH does regard Israel as special.
[3] We are only to swear or take oaths in YHWH's name.

commandments, all the days.

2 And know you this day: for I speak not with your children which have not known, and which have not seen the chastisement of YHWH Your POWER, His greatness, His mighty hand, and His stretched out arm,

3 And His miracles, and His acts, which he did in the midst of Mitzrayim (Egypt) to Pharaoh the King of Mitzrayim (Egypt), and to all his land;

4 And what he did to the army of Mitzrayim (Egypt), to their horses, and to their chariots; how he made the mayim of the Sea of Reeds to overflow them as they pursued after you, and how YHWH has destroyed them to this day;

5 And what he did to you in the wilderness, until you came into this place;

6 And what he did to Dathan and Abiram, the sons of Eliab, the son of Reuven: how the earth opened her mouth, and swallowed them up, and their households, and their tents, and all the substance that was in their possession, in the midst of all Israel:

7 But your eyes have seen all the great acts of YHWH which he did.

8 Therefore shall you keep all the commandments which I command you this day, that you may be strong, and go in and possess the land, where you go to possess it;

9 And that you may prolong your days in the land, which YHWH swore to your ahvot (fathers) to give to them and to their seed, a land that flows with milk and honey.

10 For the land, where You are going in to possess it, is not as the land of Mitzrayim (Egypt), from where you came out, where You sowed your seed, and watered it with your feet, as a garden of herbs:

11 But the land, where you go to possess it, is a land of hills and valleys, and drinks mayim of the rain of shamayim:

12 A land which YHWH Your POWER cares for: the eyes of YHWH Your POWER are always upon it, from the beginning of the year even to the end of the year.

13 And it shall come to pass, if you listen carefully to my commandments which I command you this day, to love YHWH Your POWER, and to serve him with all your heart and with all your soul,

14 That I will give you the rain of your land in his due season, the first rain and the latter rain,[1] that You may gather in your wheat, and your wine, and your oil.

15 And I will send grass in your fields for your cattle, that You may eat and be full.

16 Take heed to yourselves, that your heart be not deceived, and you turn aside, and serve other powers, and pay homage to them;

17 And then YHWH's wrath be ignited against you, and he shut

Footnotes
[1] A remez (hint) of the early and later rains were about the outpouring of the Holy Spirit on Pentecost, in Israel 2000 years ago.

up the shamayim, that there be no rain, and that the land yield not her fruit; and lest you perish quickly from off the good land which YHWH gives you.

18 Therefore shall you lay up these my words in your heart and in your soul, and bind them for a sign upon your hand, that they shall be for a remembrance between your eyes.

19 And you shall teach them your children, speaking of them when You sit in your Beyth (house), and when You walk by the way, when You lie down, and when You rise up.[1]

20 And You shall write them upon the door posts of your Beyth (house), and upon your gates:

21 That your days may be multiplied, and the days of your children, in the land which YHWH swore to your ahvot (fathers) to give them, as the days of shamayim upon the earth.

22 For if you shall carefully keep all these commandments which I command you, to do them, to love YHWH Your POWER, to walk in all his Halaka (commandments), and to cling to him;

23 Then will YHWH drive out all these nations from before you, and you shall possess greater nations and mightier than yourselves.

24 Every place whereon the soles of your feet shall tread shall be yours: from the wilderness and Lebanon, from the river, the river Farat (Euphrates), even to the uttermost sea shall your coast be.

25 There shall no man be able to stand before you: for YHWH Your POWER shall lay the fear of you and the dread of you upon all the land that you shall tread upon, as he has said to you.

Torah Parsha 47 Re'eh, Devrim 11:26-16:17
Haftarah: Yeshayahu 54:11-55:5

26 Behold, I set before you this day a Blessing and a curse;

27 A Blessing, if you obey the commandments of YHWH Your POWER, which I command you this day:

28 And a curse,[2] if you will not obey the commandments of YHWH Your POWER, but turn aside out of the way[3] which I command you this day, to go after other powers, which you have not known.

29 And it shall come to pass, when YHWH Your POWER has brought you in to the land where You are going to possess it, that You shall put the Blessing upon Mount Gerizim, and the curse upon Mount Ebal.[4]

Footnotes
[2] The curse of Torah is upon all those who do not obey it that includes all denominations of Christianity. See Deuteronomy 27:26. Though they live as they are in favor but it is evident favor starts in Genesis one verse one.
[3] The way here is the way of the world.
[4] The Targum of Jonathan is 'you shall set six tribes on Mount Gerizim, and six tribes on

Continued in next section

Footnotes
[1] Commandment to pray three times daily, this occurs and matches with the three sacrificial times of the Tent meetings.

30 Are they not on the other side Yardan (Jordan), by the way where the sun goes down, in the land of the Kanani, which dwell in the wilderness plains over against Gilgal, beside the terebinth trees of Moreh?

31 For you shall pass over Yardan (Jordan) to go in to possess the land which YHWH Your POWER is going to give you, and you shall possess it, and dwell therein.

32 And you shall obey all the statutes and judgments which I set before you this day.

Chapter 12

1 These are the statutes and judgments, which you shall observe to do in the land, which YHWH Elohim of your ahvot (fathers) will give you to possess it, all the days that you live upon the earth.

2 You shall utterly destroy all the places, wherein the nations which you shall possess served their powers, upon the high mountains, and upon the hills,

Mount Ebal.' The two mountains are set as witnesses. Its drash to the two Covenants of the Sinaitic Covenant and the New Covenant under Yahoshua (Jesus of Nazareth) the Messiah. Its sod (hidden) meaning is to the exile that Israel will go through being dispersed in the nations as the Mountain is a symbol of a kingdom. Mount Gerizim historically was used by the Samaritans to worship YHWH and they are related to the 10 Northern tribes who ended up going into exile into the Assyrian Empire. The town Shkhem is near Gerizim where the Samaritans built their Temple with their own priesthood.

and under every green etz (tree):[1]

3 And you shall overthrow their altars, and break their pillars, and burn their asherah poles with fire; and you shall hew down the graven images of their powers, and destroy the names of them out of that place.[2]

4 You shall not do so to YHWH Your POWER.

5 But to the place which YHWH Your POWER shall choose out of all your tribes to put his name[3] there, even to his habitation shall you seek, and there You shall enter:

6 and there you shall bring your burnt offerings, and your sacrifices, and your tithes, and heave offerings of your hand, and your vows, and your freewill offerings, and the Bekhor (firstborn) of your herds and of your flocks:

7 And there you shall eat before YHWH Your POWER, and you shall rejoice in all that you put your hand to, you and your households, wherein YHWH Your POWER has Blessed you.

8 You shall not do after all the things that we do here this day, every man whatsoever is right in his own eyes.[4]

9 For you are not as yet come to the rest and to the inheritance,

Footnotes
[1] They served their false elohim under these objects
[2] YHWH instructs us not to use the names of any false elohim.
[3] Jerusalem
[4] Everyone thinks he is right but our right is not measured by everyone's own opinions, but by Torah.

which YHWH Your POWER will give you.

10 But when you go over the Yardan (Jordan), and dwell in the land which YHWH Your POWER gives you to inherit, and when He gives you rest from all your enemies round about, so that you dwell in safety;

11 Then there shall be a place which YHWH Your POWER shall choose to cause his name to dwell there; there shall you bring all that I command you; your burnt offerings, and your sacrifices, your tithes, and the heave offering of your hand, and all your choice vows which you vow to YHWH:

12 And you shall rejoice before YHWH Your POWER, you, and your sons, and your daughters, and your menservants, and your maidservants, and the Levite that is within your gates; forasmuch as he has no part nor inheritance with you.

13 Take heed to yourself that You offer not your burnt offerings in every place that You see:

14 But in the place which YHWH shall choose in one of your tribes, there You shall offer your burnt offerings, and there You shall do all that I command you.

15 Notwithstanding You may slaughter and eat meat[1] in all your gates, whatsoever your soul desires, according to the **Blessing** of YHWH Your POWER which he has given you:

the ritually unclean[2] and the ritually clean may eat there too, as of the gazelle, and as of the deer.

16 Only you shall not eat the blood; you shall pour it upon the earth as mayim.

17 You may not eat within your gates the tithe of your wheat, or of your wine, or of your oil, or the Bekhor (firstborn) of your herds or of your flock, nor any of your vows which You have vowed, nor your freewill offerings, or heave offering of your hand:

18 But You must eat them before YHWH Your POWER in the place which YHWH Your POWER shall choose, You, and your son, and your daughter, and your male-servant, and your maidservant, and the Levite that is within your gates: and You shall rejoice before YHWH Your POWER in all that You put your hands to.

19 Take heed to yourself that You forsake not the Levite as long as You live upon the earth.

20 When YHWH Your POWER shall enlarge your border, as he has promised you, and You shall say, I will eat meat, because your soul longs to eat meat; You may eat meat, whatsoever your soul desires.

21 If the place which YHWH Your POWER has chosen to put his name there be too far from you, then You shall slaughter of

Footnotes
[1] Kosher meat.

Footnotes
[2] This is not talking about eating pigs or unclean animals but those that are ceremonially defiled can eat common meats that are kosher.

your herd and of your flock, which YHWH has given you,[1] as I have commanded you, and You shall eat in your gates whatsoever your soul desires.

22 Even as the gazelle and the deer is eaten, so You shall eat them: the unclean[2] and the clean shall eat of them alike.

23 Only be sure that You eat not the blood: for the blood is the life; and You may not eat the life with the flesh.[3]

24 You shall not eat it; You shall pour it upon the earth as mayim.

25 You shall not eat it; that it may go well with you, and with your children after you, when You shall do that which is right in the sight of YHWH.

26 Only your Holy things which You have, and your vows, You shall take, and go to the place which YHWH shall choose:

27 And You shall offer your burnt offerings, both meat and the blood, upon the altar of YHWH Your POWER: and the blood of your sacrifices shall be poured out upon the altar of YHWH Your POWER, and You

shall eat the meat.

28 Observe and hear all these words which I command you, that it may go well with you, and with your children after you forever, when You do that which is good and right in the sight of YHWH Your POWER.

29 When YHWH Your POWER shall cut off the nations from before you, where You go to possess them, and You succeed them, and dwell in their land;

30 Take heed to yourself that You are not entrapped by following them, after that they be destroyed from before you; and that You inquire not after their powers, saying, How did these nations serve their powers? Even so will I do likewise.

31 You shall not do so to YHWH Your POWER: for every Ritual Defilement is to YHWH, which he hates, have they done to their powers; for even their sons and their daughters they have burnt in the fire to their powers.

32 Whatever things I command you, observe to do it: You shall not add thereto, nor diminish from it.

Chapter 13

1 If there arise among you a prophet, or a dreamer of dreams, and gives you a sign or a miracle comes to pass,

2 And the sign or the miracle that came to pass, about which he spoke to you, saying, Let us go after other powers, which You have not known, and let us serve

Footnotes

[1] Kosher variety, Israelites never breed pigs or any of the other unclean animals.

[2] This is kosher food that became unclean. For instance, if a person comes in contact with the dead and becomes unclean, then touches the animal meant for sacrifice, it would be considered unclean. That meant that the kosher animal was no longer fit to be offered for sacrifice. It could still be slaughtered and eaten at home.

[3] The blood carried all the toxins so the blood must never be consumed plus this was an act done by heathens and is still done to this day, and is a most unhygienic practice to eat blood.

them;[1]

3 You shall not listen to the words of that prophet, or that dreamer of dreams: for YHWH Your POWER is testing you, to know whether you love YHWH Your POWER with all your heart and with all your soul.

4 You shall keep the Halaka (commandments) of YHWH Your POWER, and fear him, and guard His commandments, and obey his voice, and you shall serve him, and cling to him.

5 And that prophet, or that dreamer of dreams, shall be put to death; because he has spoken to turn you away from YHWH Your POWER, who brought you out of the land of Mitzrayim (Egypt), and redeemed you out of the Beyth (house) of slavery, to draw you out of the way which Halaka YHWH Your POWER commanded that you keep. So shall You put the evil away from among you.

6 Suppose your own full brother,[2] or your son, or your daughter, or your beloved wife, or your friend, which are very close to you, entertain you by secretively, saying, Let us go and serve other powers,[3] which You have not known, You, nor your ahvot (fathers);

7 Namely, of the powers of the people which are roundabout you, near to you, or far off from you, from the one end of the country even to the other end of the world;[4]

8 You shall not consent to them, nor listen to them; neither shall your eye pity him, neither shall You spare, neither shall You conceal him:[5]

9 But You shall surely kill him; your hand shall be first upon him to put him to death,[6] and afterwards the hand of all the people.

10 And You shall stone him with stones, that he die; because he has sought to thrust you away from YHWH Your POWER, which brought you out of the land of Mitzrayim (Egypt), from the Beyth (house) of slavery.

11 And all Israel shall hear, and fear, and shall do no more any such wickedness as this is among you.

12 If You shall hear say in one of your cities, which YHWH Your POWER has given you to dwell there, saying,

13 Certain men, the children of Belial, are gone out from among you, and have withdrawn the inhabitants of their city, saying,

Footnotes

[1] This would apply to any prophet who is not a prophet of YHWH.

[2] In Israel's polygamous society it was very common to have brothers and sisters from other mothers living together with you.

[3] Someone asks you to go to the Mosque or go to the Church to abrogate the Torah, while Yahushua the Messiah taught the Books of Moses and upheld the Covenants.

Footnotes

[4] Travelling to the pilgrimage sites of the gentiles is forbidden such as Lourdes, the Vatican, Mecca for Hajj etc.

[5] YHWH forbids us to worship any other elohim. While many who profess to be believers and sit in churches today, are quite happy to marry unbelievers. They even sit in ceremonies dedicated to false elohim.

[6] This happened only after the Judges pronounced the people guilty.

Let us go and serve other powers, [1] which you have not known;

14 Then shall You inquire, and make search, and ask diligently; and, behold, if it be truth, and the thing certain, that such Ritual Defilement is wrought among you;

15 You shall surely smite the inhabitants of that city with the edge of the sword, destroying it utterly, and all that is therein, and the cattle there, with the edge of the sword.

16 And You shall gather all the spoil of it into the midst of the street there, and shall burn the city, and all its plunder as a burnt offering to YHWH Your POWER: and it shall be a heap of ruins forever; it shall not be built again.

17 And there shall cling none of the cursed thing to your hand: that YHWH may turn from the fierceness of his anger, and show you loving-kindness, and have compassion upon you, and multiply you, as he has sworn to your ahvot (fathers);

18 When You shall listen to the voice of YHWH Your POWER, to guard all His commandments which I command you this day, to do that which is upright in the eyes of YHWH Your POWER.

Chapter 14

1 You are the children of YHWH Your POWER: you shall not cut yourselves, [2] nor make your forehead bald for the dead.

2 For You are a Holy people to YHWH Your POWER, and YHWH has chosen you to be a special treasure to himself, above all the nations that are upon the earth.

3 You shall not eat any Ritually Defiled [3] thing.

4 These are the animals which you shall eat: the ox, the sheep, and the goat, [4]

5 The deer, and the fallow deer, and the antelope, and the wild goat, and the mountain sheep, and the wild ox, and the gazelle.

6 And you may eat animals that have its hoof divided and chews the cud.

7 However the following animals you shall not eat that chew the cud or have divided hoofs such as the camel, and the hare, and the rabbit: for they chew the cud, but divide not the hoof; therefore they are unclean to you.

8 And the pig, [5] because its hoof is divided, but it does not chew the cud, it is unclean to you: you shall not eat of their meat, nor touch their dead carcass.

9 These you shall eat of all that

Footnotes
[1] Any power, any false gods that the nations have made are forbidden to us as they can trap us into breaking the commandments of the Torah see Deut 7:16.
[2] We must avoid what the heathen do for the dead when they mourn them. Part of their custom is to cut themselves.
[3] Yet Christendom will not stop eating pigs and other unclean species such as shellfish, crabs and lobsters, which are all forbidden in Torah.
[4] YHWH starts to name kosher animals so that we cannot make a mistake of what is clean and unclean.
[5] Strictly unclean and must not be eaten under any circumstances.

are in the mayim: all that have fins and scales[1] shall you eat:

10 And whatever has no fins and scales you may not eat; it is unclean to you.

11 Of all clean birds you shall eat.

12 But these are they of which you shall not eat: the eagle, and the vulture, and the black vulture,

13 And the red kite, and the falcon, and the buzzard after its kind,

14 And every raven after his kind,

15 And the owl, and the night hawk, and the cuckoo, and the hawk after his kind,

16 The little owl, and the great owl, and the swan,

17 And the pelican, and the carrion vulture, and the fisher owl,

18 And the stork, and the heron after her kind, and the hoopoe, and the bat.

19 And every crawling thing that flies is unclean to you: they shall not be eaten.

20 But of all clean fowls you may eat.

21 You shall not eat of any thing that dies of itself: You shall give it to the foreigner that is in your gates,[2] that he may eat it; or You may sell it to an alien: for You are a Holy people to YHWH Your

POWER. You shall not grow a young goat in her mother's milk.[3]

22 Tithe, so that you become wealthy[4] all the **Increase** of your seed, that the field[5] brings forth year by year.

23 And You shall eat before YHWH Your POWER, in the place which he shall choose to place his name there, the tithe of your wheat, of your wine, and of your oil, and the Bekhor (firstborn) of your herds and of your flocks; that You may learn to fear YHWH Your POWER always.

24 And if the way be too long for you, so that You are not able to carry it; or if the place be too far from you, which YHWH Your POWER shall choose to set his name there, when YHWH Your POWER has Blessed you:

25 Then shall You turn it into money, and bind up the money in your hand, and shall go to the

Footnotes

[1] Eat any fish with fins and scales. It should be noted that certain fish such as the Ray are unclean, and many people may not know this, but some other varieties like Shark and Dolphin are also unclean.

[2] Things which were meant to be kosher but did not bleed properly due to dying in some way such as being hunted.

[3] See footnote Exo 34:26. The context here is that you will not sell the firstborn animal to the gentiles as its reserved for YHWH, meaning the priesthood that will be given the kid to slaughter it. In times of NO Temple the firstborn kid should be given to the Priest at the Gate, meaning in the country with other Hebrews in the Diaspora as a gift towards remembering YHWH's laws even in the absence of the Temple.

[4] The Hebrew word ma'aser is using twice to indicate this is mandatory and no excuses should be offered as the tithing allows one to be increased and Blessed. This is known as the second tithe. Tithe only belongs to the Lewites.

[5] Here the field represents any work that you do to bring money in. In the ancient times the crops that were harvested from which this tithe was paid annually FOR THE SECOND TITHE.

place which YHWH Your POWER shall choose:

26 And You shall bestow that money for whatsoever your soul desires to eat,[1] for oxen, or for sheep, or for wine, or for strong drink, or for whatsoever your soul desires: and You shall eat there before YHWH Your POWER, and You shall rejoice, You, and your household,

27 And the Levite[2] that is within your gates: you shall not forsake him;[3] for he has no part nor inheritance with you.[4]

28 At the end of three years[5] You shall bring forth all the tithe of your ma'aser (goods) the same year, and shall lay it up within your gates:[6]

29 And the Levite, because he has no part nor inheritance with you, and the foreigner, and the

fatherless, and the widow, which are within your gates, shall come, and shall eat and be satisfied; that YHWH Your POWER may Bless you in all the work of your hand which You do.

Chapter 15

1 At the end of every seven years You shall make a cancellation of debt.[7]

2 And this is the manner of the release: Every creditor that lends to his neighbour shall release it; he shall not exact it of his neighbour, or of his brother; because it is called YHWH's release.[8]

3 Of a foreigner You may exact it again: but that which is yours with your brother your hand shall release;

4 Rescue until there shall be no poor among you; for YHWH shall greatly **Bless** you in the land which YHWH Your POWER gives you for an inheritance to possess it:

5 Only if You carefully pay attention to the voice of YHWH Your POWER, to observe to do all these commandments which I command you this day.

6 For YHWH Your POWER **Blessed** you, as he promised you: and You shall lend to many nations, but You shall not borrow; and You shall reign over many

Footnotes

[1] Kosher foods

[2] Torah teachers, who teach Torah should be taken care of and treated with much more respect then they are presently given. The First tithe is for the Kohen priests. People ask who should we tithe to today, it must be the same Levite teachers first followed by Torah teachers of any other tribe who can receive love offerings only.

[3] The Tithe belongs to the Levite teachers first and foremost.

[4] It is forbidden to give any tithes to a church that teaches a lawless gospel. If a church is teaching the laws of Elohim and helping poor people such as widows and orphans then they deserve to receive the love offering as long as they are working to bring the kingdom of YHWH into being but no tithe can be given them still. Find a Levite to give the tithe to if you want a true increase.

[5] This is known as the third tithe which was done every three years.

[6] See footnote Devrim (Deut) 26:12

Footnotes

[7] Schmita – the year of release. All borrowed money must be forgiven and no more debt is due.

[8] All debts owed between Israelites are to be released, but the debts that the gentiles owe to Israelites are not released.

nations, but they shall not reign over you.[1]

7 If there be among you a poor man of one of your brethren within any of your gates in your land which YHWH Your POWER has given you, You shall not harden your heart, nor shut your hand from your poor brother:

8 But You shall open your hand wide to him, and shall surely lend him sufficient for his need, in that which he wants.

9 Beware that there be not a thought in your wicked heart, saying, The seventh year, the year of release, is at hand; and your eye be evil against your poor brother, and You give him nothing; and he cry to YHWH against you, and it will be a sin against you.

10 Surely give him, and your heart shall not be grieved when You give to him: because for this YHWH Your POWER shall **Bless** you in all your works, and in all that You put your hand to.

11 For the poor shall never cease out of the land: therefore I command you, saying, You shall open your hand wide to your brother, to your poor, and to your needy, in your land.

12 And if your brother, an Abrahu (Hebrew) man, or an Abrahu (Hebrew) woman, be sold to you, and serve you six years; then in the seventh year You

shall let him go free from you.[2]

13 And when You send him out free from you, You shall not let him go away empty:

14 You shall furnish him liberally out of your flock, and out of your floor, and out of your winepress: of that wherewith YHWH Your POWER has **Blessed** you, You shall give to him.

15 And You shall remember that You were a slave in the land of Mitzrayim (Egypt), and YHWH Your POWER redeemed you: therefore I command you this thing today.

16 And it shall be, if he say to you, I will not go away from you; because he loves you and your Beyth (house), because he is well with you;

17 Then You shall take an awl, and thrust it through his ear to the door, and he shall be your servant forever. And also to your maidservant You shall do likewise.

18 It shall not seem hard to you, when You send him away free from you; for he has been worth a double hired servant to you, in serving you six years: and YHWH Your POWER shall **Increase** you in all that You do.

19 All the Bekhor (firstborn) males that come of your herd and

Footnotes

[1] Israel's destiny is to rule and reign those that are Torah obedient and in anticipation of the future Messiah to keep Torah commandments.

[2] It is okay for Israelites to keep servants in the home on Covenants but not as the world does in keeping classic slaves in chains. The servants are treated very fairly and not chained to the bed so to speak. They can come and go within the stipulations of the Covenant. The reason for this is to tell the nations, about YHWH and evangelize people in the home or business.

of your flock You shall sanctify to YHWH Your POWER: You shall do no work with the Bekhor (firstborn) of your bullock, nor shear the Bekhor (firstborn) of your sheep.

20 You shall eat it before YHWH Your POWER year by year in the place which YHWH shall choose, You and your household.

21 And if there be any blemish therein, as if it be lame, or blind, or have any ill blemish, You shall not sacrifice it to YHWH Your POWER.

22 You shall eat it within your gates: the unclean and the clean person shall eat it alike, as the gazelle, and as the deer.

23 Only You shall not eat the blood of them;[1] You shall pour it upon the ground as mayim.

The appointed Celebration times of YHWH for true Israel and those that do not Guard and Do the Celebrations they will be considered lawless and will not be restored.
Chapter 16

1 Guard intently[2] the new month

of Abib, and keep the Protection (Passover) to YHWH Your POWER: for in the month of Abib YHWH Your POWER brought you forth out of Mitzrayim (Egypt) by night.

2 You shall therefore sacrifice the Protection (Passover) to YHWH Your POWER, of the flock and the herd, in the place which YHWH shall choose to place his name there.

3 You shall eat no leavened Lakhem (bread) with it; seven days shall You eat matzah therewith, even the Lakhem (bread) of affliction; for You came forth out of the land of Mitzrayim (Egypt) in haste: that You may remember the day when You came forth out of the land of Mitzrayim (Egypt) all the days of

It is important to note that one cannot determine the molad or black moon hence observation of the moon is necessary but the moon months lose roughly ten days each year making the years out of sync as per Khanok's prophecy.

The other verse that gives credibility to the possibility of the Khanokian method is the one in First Samuel 20:5. This is where King David is talking about the New month coming the next day, which shows us that in King David's time they had a way of knowing the arrival of the New month with a calendar which was based on the Khanok Calendar. We also know that in the time of the first century Temple, the moon was confirmed by looking at the crescent and by this time they had switched to a pure lunar calendar but in the times of the Patriarchs the calendar was Solar based on the Equinox each year. The Temple priesthood also checked back using a calendar, which the Temple priests had in their possession to confirm dates of the Passover, and the Biblical New Year, this is thought to be the Elder Hillel Calendar.

Footnotes

[1] One might ask how you can eat blood while in reality you can only drink it. The answer is simple, many nations take the blood of animals and put it into rotis and mixes and they then eat it like that.

[2] The Hebrew word here is more accurately translated 'Guard intently,' as a soldier, the month of Abib as that determines the month of Passover and the beginning of the new biblical year. There is a lot of debate whether this is to be a conjunction or crescent. However if the Khanok's Calendar was in effect that then removes the observation of the crescent but if not then it would require to look at the crescent.

Continued in next section

your life.

4 And there shall be no leavened Lakhem (bread) seen with you in all your coast seven days; neither shall there anything of the meat, which You sacrificed the first day at dusk, remain after dawn (*New Day*).[1]

5 You may not sacrifice the Protection (Passover) within any of your gates, which YHWH Your POWER gives you:

6 But at the place which YHWH Your POWER shall choose to place his name in, there You shall sacrifice the Protection (Passover) at dusk, at the going down of the sun, at the season that You came forth out of Mitzrayim (Egypt).

7 And You shall roast and eat it in the place which YHWH Your POWER shall choose: and You shall come in the morning, and go to your tents.

8 Six days You shall eat unleavened Lakhem (bread): and on the seventh day shall be an appointed assembly to YHWH Your POWER: You shall do no work therein.

9 Seven weeks shall You number to you: begin to number the seven weeks from such time as You begin to put the sickle to the wheat.

10 And You shall keep khag ha Shavuot (The appointed celebration time of Pentecost) for YHWH Your POWER with a tribute of a freewill offering of your hand, which You shall give to YHWH Your POWER, according to as YHWH Your POWER has **Increased** you:

11 And You shall rejoice before YHWH Your POWER, You, and your son, and your daughter, and your male-servant, and your maidservant,[2] and the Levite that is within your gates, and the foreigner, and the fatherless, and the widow, that are among you, in the place which YHWH Your POWER has chosen to place his name there.

12 And You shall remember that You were a slave in Mitzrayim (Egypt): and You shall observe and do these statutes.

13 You shall observe khag ha Sukkot (The appointed celebration time of Tabernacles) seven days, after that You have gathered in your wheat and your wine:

14 And You shall rejoice in your khag (The appointed celebration time), You, and your son, and your daughter, and your male-servant, and your maidservant,[3] and the Levite, the foreigner, and the fatherless, and the widow,

Footnotes
[1] Torah days begin sunrise and not at sunset as can be seen from the passage, the 14th Nissan was the end of the day as the Passover Protection sacrifice was to be offered at dusk just before evening considered the end of the daylight hours and the meat eaten until dawn and any remaining meat was to be burned and disposed in the ground.

Footnotes
[2] Female Concubines or lesser wives of the man. Israelites are commanded to live a Patriarchal lifestyle.
[3] Concubines which are lesser wives allowed by the Torah as kosher but shunned by gentiles who are into Satanic Greco/Roman monogamy. We do not follow gentile laws!

that are within your gates.

15 Seven days shall You keep a Holy khag (The appointed celebration time) to YHWH Your POWER in the place which YHWH shall choose: because YHWH Your POWER shall **Bless** you in all your **Increase**, and in all the works of your hands, therefore You shall surely rejoice.

16 Three times in a year shall all your males appear before YHWH Your POWER in the place which he shall choose; in khag ha Matzot (The appointed celebration time of Unleavened Bread), and in khag ha Shavuot (The appointed celebration time of Pentecost), and in khag ha Sukkot (The appointed celebration time of Tabernacles) and they shall not appear before YHWH empty:[1]

17 Every man shall give as he is able, according to the **Blessing** of YHWH Your POWER which he has given you.

Torah Parsha 48 Shoftim, Devrim 16:18-21:9
Haftarah: Yeshayahu 51:12-52:12,

18 You will make Judges and officers in all your gates, which YHWH Your POWER gives you, throughout your tribes: and they shall judge the people with Righteous judgment.

19 You shall not distort the

judgment; nor you shall regard a persons standing, neither take a bribe: for a bribe will blind the eyes of the wise [judges], and pervert the words of judgments'.

20 Justice, Justice You will pursue,[2] that you may live, and inherit the land which YHWH Your POWER gives you.

21 You shall not plant any tree as an asherah *image* near to the altar of YHWH Your POWER, which You shall make for you.

22 Neither shall You set up any graven-image; which YHWH Your POWER hates.

Chapter 17

1 You shall not sacrifice to YHWH Your POWER any bullock, or sheep, wherein is blemish, or any other defect: for that is a Ritual Defilement to YHWH Your POWER.

2 If there be found among you, within any of your gates which YHWH Your POWER has given you, man or woman, that has worked wickedness in the sight of YHWH Your POWER, in transgressing His Covenant,

3 And has gone and served other powers, and worshipped them, either the sun, or moon, or any of the host of shamayim, which I have not commanded;

4 And it has been reported to you and you have made diligent

Footnotes
[1] On these three major feasts; Unleavened Bread, Pentecost and Tabernacles the commandment was for Israelites to appear in Jerusalem annually with a gift.

[2] Many dance around the Abbah's Torah but the Abbah directs our attention to not just talk about how nice Torah is but we must rigorously pursue judgments everyday of our life. Find Lewites in our gates (cities, countries) and follow their instructions, who are the guarders of Torah.

enquiries and the report is true that Ritual Defilement has occurred in Israel:

5 Then shall You bring forth that man or that woman, which has committed that wicked thing, to your gates, even that man or that woman, and shall stone them with stones, till they die.

6 At the mouth of two witnesses, or three[1] witnesses, shall he that is worthy of death be put to death; but at the mouth of one witness he shall not be put to death.

7 The hands of the witnesses shall be first upon him[2] to put him to death, and afterward the hands of all the people. So You shall put the evil away from among you.

8 If there arise a matter too hard for you in judgment, between blood and blood, between plea and plea, and between stroke and stroke, being matters of controversy within your gates: then shall You arise, and get up into the place which YHWH Your POWER shall choose;

9 And You shall come to the kohenim the Lewim, and to the judge that shall be in those days, and inquire; and they shall show you the sentence of judgment:[3]

10 And You shall do according to the sentence, which they of that place which YHWH shall choose shall show you; and You shall observe to do according to all that they inform you:

11 According to the sentence of the Torah which they shall teach you, and according to the judgment which they shall tell you, You shall do: You shall not decline from the sentence which they shall show you, to the right hand, nor to the left.[4]

12 And the man that does not pay attention, and will not listen to the kohen (priest) that stands to minister there before YHWH Your POWER, or to the judge, even that man shall die: and You shall put away the evil from Israel.

13 And all the people shall hear, and fear, and do no more presumptuously.

14 When You have come into the land which YHWH Your POWER gives you, and shall possess it, and shall dwell therein, and shall say, I will set a King over me, like as all the nations that are about me;[5]

15 You shall in any wise set him King over you, whom YHWH Your POWER shall choose: one

Footnotes

[1] For anything in Israel, a two or three witness true report must be established. This is to prevent injustice to the individuals.

[2] The witness had to cast the first stone upon the one being killed so that this affirms the reliability of the witness.

[3] We had the great court of the Sanhedrin which had a number of judges to decide matters. See Leviticus 20:14 footnote.

Footnotes

[4] The symbols of the right and left are quite important in Torah. They signify the right being the side of Judgment and Strength and the left the side of mercy, love and victory. If one side becomes too heavy then that can cause unbalanced decisions. Both sides need to be balanced by the middle-pillar. So this is how the whole of the scrolls use the term the Right and the Left.

[5] This literally happened and came to pass as Israel wanted a king over her and the prophet Samuel made Saul king over them. First Sam 10:1

from among your brethren shall You set King over you:[1] You may not set a foreigner over you, which is not your brother.

16 But he shall not accumulate horses for himself, nor cause the people to return to Mitzrayim (Egypt), to the end that he should accumulate horses:[2] for as much as YHWH has said to you, You shall henceforth return no more that way.[3]

17 Neither shall he greatly **Increase** many wives[4] for

himself, that his heart turn not away: neither shall he **Increase** a great amount of silver and gold for himself.[5]

18 And it shall be, when he sits upon the throne of his kingdom, that he shall write him a copy of this Torah[6] in a scroll out of that which is before the kohenim the Lewim:

19 And it shall be with him, and he shall read therein all the days of his life: that he may learn to fear YHWH his Elohim, to keep all the words of this Torah and these statutes, to do them:

20 That his heart be not lifted up above his brethren, and that he

Footnotes

[1] The first king was Saul from the tribe of Benyamin. Israel was to only set kings within the twelve tribes and no outsider could be king.

[2] A king cannot be without an army so he was allowed to have an army with thousands of horses. But the idea here of accumulation or multiplication with the word Rabbah is not about multiplying at all. It must be understood that in context its not that you cannot have 2000 or 10,000 horses, but that you must trust YHWH.

[3] Note the mention of Egypt is important as it clearly shows that the Pharaoh thought himself like Elohim hence Egypt is mentioned.

[4] This is the same principle as in verse 16. The king can have many wives because Israel was a polygamous society and that is the only way they could multiply and **Increase** the seed in the earth. The idea here is that you must not **Increase** wives to forget YHWH. You could have five wives or fifteen wives and that would not be a problem as long as you could provide for their needs and be able to serve YHWH. This does not break the concept of Yesod Ha Briah, which is the idea of men and not YHWH.

The case of King Solomon having one thousand wives shows us the problem was not the 1000 wives contrary to most scholar's opinions or biases but the fact that they turned his heart away from YHWH because they were heathen. So even If you Continued in next section

being a believer marry a non-believer, and she turns your heart away from Elohim as can happen then that one wife is too much.

We have a perfect example in the scrolls of this one wife, who caused folly in Israel with King Ahab and his wife Jezebel. She did more damage in Israel bringing in Baalism then any other woman. Proving that one wrong wife was too much. Whereas if King Ahab had married twenty righteous women there would have been no problem.

Context is important. In Israel the argument is not whether polygamy is allowed or not but it is a reality we live. Even in the coming messianic kingdom there will be polygamy. See Isaiah 4:1, which tells us that the ratio will be seven women to one man.

[5] There is no problem with having large amounts of silver and gold, since King Solomon used this to build the Temple for YHWH. The problem is what you do with the silver and gold. Do you spend all your time thinking of it, and forget YHWH? Don't make an idol of what you have. YHWH must always come first.

[6] A king was to act with righteous within the set requirement of the Torah.

turn not aside from the commandment, to the right hand, or to the left:[1] to the end that he may prolong his days in his kingdom, he, and his children, in the midst of Israel.

Chapter 18

1 The kohenim the Lewim, and all the tribe of Levi, shall have no part nor inheritance with Israel: they shall eat the offerings of YHWH made by fire, and his inheritance.

2 Therefore shall they have no inheritance among their brethren: YHWH is their inheritance, as He has said to them.

3 And this shall be the kohenim due from the people, from them that offer a sacrifice, whether it be ox or sheep; and they shall give to the kohen (priest) the shoulder, and the two cheeks, and the stomach.

4 The bikkurim (first-fruit) also of your wheat, of your wine, and of your oil, and the first of the fleece of your sheep, shall You give him.

5 For YHWH Your POWER has chosen him out of all your tribes, to stand to minister in the name of YHWH, him and his sons forever.

6 And if a Levite come from any of your gates out of all Israel, where he sojourned, and come with all the desire of his mind to the place which YHWH shall choose;

7 Then he shall minister in the name of YHWH his Elohim, as all his brethren the Lewim do, which stand there before YHWH.

8 They shall have like portions to eat, beside that which comes from the sale of his family's inheritance.

9 When You have come into the land which YHWH Your POWER gives you, You shall not learn to do the Ritual Defilement of those nations.[2]

10 There shall not be found among you any one that sacrifices his son or his daughter in the fire, or that predicts horoscopes, or a medium calling up ruachot (spirits), or an omen reader or a sorcerer.

11 Or a magician casting spells, or a medium with familiar ruachot (spirits), or a conjurer, or one speaking to the ruachot (spirits) of the dead.

12 For all that do these things are Ritual Defilement practices to YHWH: and because of these Ritual Defilement practices YHWH Your POWER will drive them out from before you.

13 You shall be blameless before YHWH Your POWER.

14 For these nations, which You shall possess, listened to astrologers, and to omen readers: but as for you, YHWH Your POWER has not permitted you to do this.

Footnotes
[1] See notes on Devrim 17:11

Footnotes
[2] Abortion and birth control are types of these and we find many women in our society are getting cervical cancer due to birth-control pills. YHWH knew better so we need to pay attention to His words. There is nothing wrong with contraception but it must be taken with caution.

15 YHWH Your POWER will raise up for you a Prophet from among you, your brethren, like me; you shall listen to him;[1]

16 According to all that You desired of YHWH Your POWER in Horev in the day of the assembly, saying, Let me not hear again the voice of YHWH my POWER, neither let me see this great fire any more, that I die not.

17 And YHWH said to me, They have spoken well that which they have spoken.

18 I will raise them up a Prophet[2] from among their brethren,[3] like you,[4] and will put my words in his[5] mouth; and he shall speak to them all that I shall command him.

19 And it shall come to pass, that whosoever will not listen to my words which he shall speak in my name,[6] I will personally require it of him.

20 But the prophet, which shall presume to speak a word in my name, which I have not commanded him to speak, or that shall speak in the name of other powers, even that prophet shall die.

21 And if You say in your heart, How shall we know the word which YHWH has not spoken?

22 When a prophet speaks in the name of YHWH, if the thing follows not, nor comes to pass, that is the thing which YHWH has not spoken, but the prophet has spoken it presumptuously: You shall not be afraid of him.

Chapter 19

1 When YHWH Your POWER has cut off the nations, whose land YHWH Your POWER gives you, and You succeed them, and dwell in their cities, and in their houses;

2 You shall separate three cities for yourselves in the midst of your land, which YHWH Your POWER gives you to possess it.

3 You shall prepare a road way, and divide the coasts of your land, which YHWH Your POWER gives you to inherit, into three parts, that any person who kills another accidentally may find protection there.

4 And this is the case of the one

Footnotes

[1] This is all the righteous prophets of YHWH who would warn Israel not to commit idolatry. This can fit Yahushua the Messiah into the prophethood as He taught Torah and repentance to turn to YHWH.

[2] This was not Muhammad as the Muslims claim. See Islam peace or beast written by Rabbi Simon Altaf.

[3] The prophet the Hebrew word is Navi (נָבִיא) and not Ha-Navi so its not relating to a singular figure but to all future prophets of Israel who would speak the words of YHWH and be YHWH's mouthpiece so to speak and do miracles likewise. See Isaiah 59:21 and Jeremiah 1:9. The term here is related to establishing the office of a prophet as to who can be a prophet and who cannot. In Deut 18 Israel was being warned not to indulge in black magic, sorcery, mediums for their answers to prayers but look to the guidance of the prophets. Jesus, Yahushua could fit the prophet spoken of in Deuteronomy 18:15.

[4] Same black colour as Mosheh (Musa).

[5] The Office of Prophet which applies to all future called out prophets teaching Torah and are greater than the king of the land.

Footnotes

[6] He must come in the name of YHWH, as all prophets did.

Devrim (Deuteronomy)

who kills accidentally, who shall flee there, and that he may live: Whosoever kills his neighbour accidentally, for whom he has no hatred;

5 As when a man goes into the wood with his neighbour to cut wood, and he raises the axe to cut down the etz (tree), and his axe head cuts loose from its holding, and strikes his neighbour, that he dies as a result; he shall flee to one of those cities, and live:

6 Lest the avenger of the blood pursue the one who killed accidentally, while his heart is hot, and overtake him, because the way is long, and slay him; whereas this is not a capital case inasmuch as he hated him not before the accident.

7 Wherefore I command you, saying, You shall separate three cities for you.

8 And if YHWH Your POWER enlarge your coast, as he has sworn to your ahvot (fathers), and give you all the land which he promised to give to your ahvot (fathers);

9 If You shall keep all these commandments to do them, which I command you this day, to love YHWH Your POWER, and to walk always in His ways; then shall You add three cities more for you, beside these three:

10 That innocent blood be not shed in your land, which YHWH Your POWER gives you for an inheritance, and so blood be upon you.

11 But if any man hate his neighbour, and lie in wait for him, and rise up against him, and wound him mortally that he die, and then flee into one of these cities:

12 Then the elders of his city shall send and fetch him from there, and hand him over to the avenger of blood, that he may die.[1]

13 Your eye shall not pity him, but You shall put away the guilt of innocent blood from Israel, that it may go well with you.

14 You shall not remove your neighbour's landmark, which have been defined according to your inheritance, which You shall inherit in the land that YHWH Your POWER gives you to possess it.

15 One witness shall not rise up against a man for any iniquity, or for any sin, in any sin that he transgresses: at the mouth of two witnesses, or at the mouth of three witnesses, shall the matter be established.

16 If a false witness rise up against any man to testify against him that which is wrong;

17 Then both the men, between whom the controversy is, shall stand before YHWH, before the kohenim and the judges, which shall be in those days;

Footnotes
[1] YHWH is just, this particular crime was deliberate and planned therefore he could not take refuge in the cities like the one who killed by accident. YHWH does not want people to be punished unjustly as our societal laws often fail to measure the correct dose of justice. In the disapora wherever the Lewites are found in exile there the cities will be counted as the cities of refuge for safety.

18 And the judges shall make diligent inquiry:[1] and, behold, if the witness be a false witness, and has testified falsely against his brother;

19 Then shall you do to him, as he had thought to have done to his brother: so shall You put the evil away from among you.

20 And those which remain shall hear, and fear, and shall henceforth commit no more any such evil among you.

21 And your eye shall not pity; but life shall go for life, eye for eye, tooth for tooth, hand for hand, foot for foot.[2]

Chapter 20

1 When You go out to battle against your enemies, and see horses, and chariots, and a people more than You, be not afraid of them: for YHWH Your POWER is with you, who brought you up out of the land of Mitzrayim (Egypt).

2 And it shall be, when you have come into the battle field, that the kohen (priest) shall approach and speak to the people,

3 And shall say to them, Hear, O Israel, you approach this day to battle against your enemies: let not your hearts faint, fear not, and do not tremble, neither be terrified because of them;

4 For YHWH Your POWER is He who goes with you, to fight for you against your enemies, to rescue you.

Footnotes
[1] See footnote Vayikra (Lev) 20:2
[2] This is not plucking out the eyes of each other, but measured justice.

5 And the officers shall speak to the people, saying, What man is there that has built a new Beyth (house),[3] and has not dedicated it? Let him go and return to his Beyth (house), lest he die in the battle, and another man dedicate it.

6 And what man is he that has planted a vineyard, and has not yet eaten of it? Let him also go and return to his Beyth (house), lest he die in the battle, and another man eat of it.

7 And what man is there that has betrothed a wife,[4] and has not taken her? Let him go and return to his Beyth (house), lest he dies in the battle, and another man takes her.

8 And the officers shall speak further to the people, and they shall say, What man is there that is fearful and fainthearted? Let him go and return to his Beyth (house), lest his brethren's heart faint as well as his heart.

9 And it shall be, when the officers have made an end of

Footnotes
[3] When the Greek Armies were expelled from the Temple in the Maccabean times, the festival of Chanukah began to be celebrated by the Hebrew people, to show the rededication of the Temple following its desecration by Antiochus IV Epiphanes (1 Maccabees 4:36-61). The same Hebrew word Chanukah is used here to show a religious use of the property being sanctified in the name of YHWH. Israelites when they purchase or acquire land and houses must dedicate the belongings to YHWH as ultimately He is the owner and we are only sojourners.
[4] Betrothal was a marriage and still is. Deu 24:5 says the husband needs to spend one year with his wife before embarking on a battle.

speaking to the people, that they shall make captains of the armies to lead the people.

10 When You come near a city to fight against it, then offer it terms of shalom.

11 And it shall be, if they accept the offer of shalom, and open it to you, then it shall be, that all the people that is found therein shall become your labourers, and they shall serve you.

12 And if it will make no shalom with you, but will make war against you, then You shall besiege it:

13 And when YHWH Your POWER has given them to you into your hands, You shall kill every male there with the edge of the sword.[1]

14 But the women, and the little ones, and the cattle, and all that is in the city, even all the plunder there, You shall take into yourself; and You shall eat the plunder of your enemies, which YHWH Your POWER has given you.

15 Thus shall You do to all the cities which are very far off from you, which are not of the cities of these nations.

16 But of the cities of these people, which YHWH Your POWER will give you for an inheritance, You must not allow any living being.

17 But You shall utterly destroy them; namely, the Khitee, and the Amoree, the Kanani, and the Perzee, the Khuvi, and the Yavusi; as YHWH Your POWER has commanded you:

18 That they teach you not to do after all their Ritual Defilements, which they have done [2] to their powers; so should you sin against YHWH Your POWER.

19 When You shall besiege a city a long time, in making war against it to take it, You shall not destroy the etzim (trees) there by forcing an axe against them: for You may eat of them, and You shall not cut them down for the etz (tree) of the field is man's life to employ them in the siege:

20 Only the etzim (trees) which You know that they be not etzim (trees) for food, You shall destroy and cut them down; and You shall build siege-works against the city that makes war with you, until it be subdued.

Chapter 21

1 If one be found slain in the land which YHWH Your POWER gives you to possess it, lying in the field, and it be not known who has killed him:

2 Then your elders and your judges shall come forth, and they shall measure to the cities which are round about him that is dead:

3 And it shall be, that the city which is next to the slain man, even the elders of that city shall take a heifer, which has not done

Footnotes
[1] This means only if they refuse the terms of peace then the reverse is that they want war and will fight to the end. So shall it be.

Footnotes
[2] These nations committed gross evil deeds such as burning their children alive, burying them alive, cutting off their flesh, bestiality and many other evil deeds.

any work, and which has not drawn in the yoke;

4 And the elders of that city shall bring down the heifer to a valley with flowing water, which is neither plowed nor sown, and shall strike off the heifer's neck there in the valley:

5 And the kohenim the sons of Levi shall come near; for them YHWH Your POWER has chosen to speak to him, and to **Bless** in the name of YHWH; and by their word shall every controversy and every stroke be tried:

6 And all the elders of that city, that are next to the slain man, shall wash their hands over the heifer that is beheaded in the valley:

7 And they shall answer and say, Our hands have not shed this blood, neither have our eyes seen it.

8 Be merciful, O YHWH, to your people Israel, whom You have redeemed, and lay not innocent blood to your people of Israel's charge. And the blood shall be forgiven them.

9 So shall You put away the guilt of innocent blood from among you, when You shall do that which is right in the sight of YHWH.

Torah Parsha 49 Ki Teze, Devrim 21:10-25:19
Haftarah: Yeshayahu 52:13-54:10

10 When You go forth to war against your enemies, and YHWH Your POWER has given them into your hands, and You

have taken them captive,

11 And see among the captives a beautiful woman, and you find her attractive, that You would like to have her to be your wife;[1]

12 Then You shall bring her home to your Beyth (house); and she shall shave her head,[2] and trim her nails;

13 And she shall remove the clothing before being captured, and shall remain in your Beyth (house), and have a period of mourning for her father and her mother a full month: and after that You may have sexual relationship with her, and become her husband, and she shall be your wife.

14 And it shall be, if You have no delight in her, then You shall send her off where she will;[3] but

Footnotes

[1] Remember polygamy is YHWH's allowance to propagate seed. In this instance this was not a soldier who is single but could be one who already has a wife and children at home and takes another wife.

[2] Symbol of putting away her old life and customs. When she is taken from 'captivity,' meaning she was in false worship and in her old satanic ways but now she has her head shaven to indicate that she is no longer under the authority of her old husband whether widow or single because her old husband was her false elohim that she has been released from. The new husband now covers her with a fresh covering, puts on the garment of favor on her, takes her to be his wife and she grows on new hair and of course wearing a new Hebrew head-covering to show new life, respect and protection of her husband.

[3] This means if there was an issue in the marriage then a divorce could be sought early in the marriage provided there was ground for fraud or putting away for certain reasons. One such reason could be that she was formally married and you did not know this or she did not tell you. However, after Continued in next section

You shall not sell her at all for money, You shall not make merchandise of her, because You have humiliated[1] her.

15 If a man has two wives,[2] one beloved, and another loved-less,[3] and they have born him children, both the beloved and the loved-less; and if the Bekhor (firstborn) son was on the one that was loved-less:

16 Then it shall be, when he makes his sons to inherit that which he has, that he may not make the son of the beloved Bekhor (firstborn) before the son of the loved-less,[4] which is indeed the Bekhor (firstborn):[5]

17 But he shall acknowledge the son of the loved-less for the Bekhor (firstborn), by giving him a

double portion[6] of all that he has: for he is the beginning of his strength; the right of the Bekhor (firstborn) is his.

18 If a man has a stubborn and rebellious son, which will not obey the voice of his father, or the voice of his mother, and that, when they have chastened him, will not listen to them:

19 Then shall his father and his mother lay hold on him, and bring him out to the elders of his city, and to the gate of his place;

20 And they shall say to the elders of his city, This our son is stubborn and rebellious, he will not obey our voice; he is a glutton, and a drunkard.

21 And all the men of his city shall stone him with stones[7] that he dies: so shall You put evil away from among you; and all Israel shall hear, and fear.

22 And if a man have committed a sin worthy of death, and he be to be put to death, and You hang him on an etz (tree):

23 His body shall not remain all night upon the etz (tree), but You shall in any wise bury him that day; (for he that is hanged is accursed of Elohim;) that your land be not defiled, which YHWH Your POWER gives you for an inheritance.

Chapter 22
1 You shall not see your brother's ox or his sheep go

you marry her she reveals this news which means she cannot be your wife. So she has to be divorced as this is adultery unless her former husband is dead.
[1] The woman was divorced and would be feeling rejected in ancient society and even in many present societies, so our conduct towards women must be above reproach.
[2] Clear case for polygamy allowed by YHWH.
[3] Most bible translations use the word 'hate' which is incorrect in its Hebrew usage. The word in Hebrew means to love less not to hate as we understand the English language.
[4] See Gen 29:31.
[5] This is what happened with Sarah and Hagar already so the law is clarified. The firstborn son of the principle wife e.g. Sarah was favoured above Hagar's son because she was the principle wife. Even though Hagar's son was born first but could not be favoured above Isaac as we see in the Torah. The same principle applies here. Just because your first wife hates you and your second one loves you that does not mean you show favouritism to the children of the second wife, the sons of the first wife being principle must come first.

Footnotes
[6] The son of the principle wife number one.
[7] This will happen after proper judgment is passed by the judges holding seat to commit judgment.

astray, and hide yourself from them: You shall in any case bring them again to your brother.

2 And if your brother be not near to you, or if You know him not, then You shall bring it to your own Beyth (house), and it shall be with you until your brother seek after it, and You shall restore it to him again.

3 In like manner shall You do with his ass; and so shall You do with his raiment; and with all lost thing of your brother's, which he has lost, and You have found, shall You do likewise: You may not refuse to get involved.

4 You shall not see your brother's ass or his ox fall down by the way, and hide yourself from them: You shall surely help him to lift them up again.

5 The woman shall not wear that which is men's clothing, neither shall a man put on women's clothing: for all that do so are Ritually Defiled[1] before YHWH Your POWER.

6 If a bird's nest chance to be before you in the way in any etz (tree), or on the ground, whether they be young ones, or eggs, and the mother bird is sitting upon the young, or upon the eggs, You shall not take the mother bird with the young:

7 But You shall in any wise let the mother bird go, and take the young to you; that it may be well with you, and that You may prolong your days.

8 When You build a new Beyth (house), then You shall make a guard-rail for your roof, that You bring not blood upon your Beyth (house), if any man fall from there.

9 You must not plant your vineyard with different seeds: lest the fruit of your seed which You have sown, and the fruit of your vineyard, be defiled.[2]

10 You shall not plow with an ox and an ass yoked together.

11 You shall not wear clothes, as of woolen and linen meshed together.

12 You shall make yourselves tassels[3] on your four corner garment.

13 If any man takes a wife, and has sexual relations with her, and hate her,

14 And shows hatred towards her, and brings up an evil name upon her, and say, I took this woman, and when I came to her, I found her not a maid:[4]

15 Then shall the father of the damsel, and her mother, take and

Footnotes

[1] A woman is to be submitted to a man but when a woman in Israel wears man's clothing she takes on the role of the man and the roles swap. The Abbah does not want the swapping of Roles as the man is the head, the woman the subordinate to the man who lives in Torah. This causes Spiritual Defilement causing the woman to fall so low as not to uphold the Torah and causes her household to be defiled. Its for her benefit the Abbah said not to do so. She must also be attached to a Torah righteous man.

Footnotes

[2] YHWH does not want Israel to mix the seed in the same field. This is similar to adulteration which is forbidden.

[3] These are tzitzits, Israel was commanded to wear them that means Christians also. Numbers 15:37-38.

[4] Accuses her of not being a virgin which would be considered a fraud in Israel.

bring forth the evidence of the damsel's virginity to the elders of the city in the gate:

16 And the damsel's father shall say to the elders, I gave my daughter to this man to wife, and he hates her;

17 And, behold, he has given occasions of speech against her, saying, I found not your daughter a maid; and yet this is the evidence of my daughter's virginity. And they shall spread the cloth before the elders of the city.

18 And the elders of that city shall take that man and discipline him;

19 And they shall fine him with a hundred shekels of silver, and give them to the father of the damsel, because he has brought up shame upon a virgin of Israel: and she shall be his wife; he may not divorce her all his days.[1]

20 But if this thing be true, and the evidence of virginity[2] be not found for the damsel:

21 Then they shall bring out the damsel to the door of her father's Beyth (house), and the men of her city shall stone her with stones that she die:[3] because she

has wrought folly in Israel, to play the whore in her father's Beyth (house): so shall You put evil away from among you.

22 If a man be found lying with a woman married to a husband, then they shall both die, both the man that lay with the woman, and the woman: so shall You put away evil from Israel.[4]

23 If a damsel that is a virgin be betrothed to a husband, and a man find her in the city, and lie with her;[5]

24 Then you shall bring them both out to the gate of that city, and you shall stone them with stones that they die; the damsel, because she cried not, being in the city; and the man, because he has humiliated his neighbour's wife: so You shall put away evil from among you.

25 But if a man find a betrothed damsel in the field, and the man force her, and lie with her: then the man only that lay with her shall die:

26 But to the damsel You shall do nothing; there is in the damsel no sin worthy of death: for as when a man rises against his neighbour, and slays him, even so is this matter:

27 For he found her in the field, and the betrothed damsel cried,

Footnotes

[1] This was a false charge for which he cannot divorce her. This could be done in the early phase of marriage if the woman was found to be impure then the marriage could be annulled. Please see article on divorce and remarriage http://www.forever-israel.com/BM/marriage-divorce.html

[2] Bloodstained clothes i.e., the bed sheet on the night of the marriage.

[3] This was extreme hatred on the part of the husband who suspected his wife of wrong doing but could not forgive her. YHWH found a way to quell the hatred of the man, but Continued in next section

the woman in such a society would be an outcast and be mistreated for the rest of her life. YHWH allowed her to be put to death to go back to him. Sleeping around is a capital crime!

[4] Death for the sin of adultery.

[5] A betrothal meant marriage in Biblical customs so the woman could not sleep with another man as that would be adultery.

and there was none to rescue her.

28 If a man find a damsel that is a virgin, who is not betrothed, and overpowers her, and rapes her, and they are discovered;

29 Then the man that raped her shall give to the damsel's father fifty shekels of silver, and she shall be his wife; because he has violated her, he may not divorce her all his days.[1]

30 A man shall not take his father's wife,[2] nor discover his father's skirt.

Chapter 23

1 He that has crushed testicles, or has severed genitals, shall not enter into the congregation of YHWH. [3]

2 An illegitimate person shall not enter into the congregation of YHWH; even to his tenth generation shall he not enter into the congregation of YHWH.

3 An Ammonite or Moabite shall not enter into the congregation of YHWH; even to their tenth generation shall they not enter into the congregation of YHWH forever:

4 Because they met you not with Lakhem (bread) and with mayim in the way, when you came forth out of Mitzrayim (Egypt); and because they hired against you Bilam the son of Beor of Pethor of Mesopotamia, to curse you.

5 Nevertheless YHWH Your POWER refused to listen to Bilam; but YHWH Your POWER turned the curse into a **Blessing** to you, because YHWH Your POWER loved you.

6 You shall not seek their shalom nor their prosperity all your days forever.

7 You shall not hate an Edomite; for he is your brother: You shall not hate an Egyptian; because You were a foreigner[4] in his land.

8 The children that are begotten of them shall enter into the congregation of YHWH in their third generation.

9 When your armies go forth against your enemies, then keep yourselves from anything impure.

10 If there be among you any man, that is not clean by reason of nocturnal emission, then he shall go outside the camp, he may not come into the camp:

11 But it shall be, when evening comes, he shall wash himself with mayim: and when the sun is down, he shall come into the camp again.

Footnotes

[1] This may be considered a harsh penalty on the girl to have to live with the man who raped her. However, consent was sought from both the girl and the father before they would have to officially marry. But in middle-eastern society, most rape victims would kill themselves so this was actually a more humane option. Other considerations need to be made such as what if she was pregnant, then what is to be done with the baby. In this case it makes sense that the marriage option would work.

[2] A concubine who would be the stepmother of the boy.

[3] See footnote Lev 21:20.

Footnotes

[4] Why are these two particularly singled out not to be hated? This is because the Edomi are from Esaw who was Jacob's brother and if you recall Yshmael's mother was one, and he got mixed with them.

12 You shall have a place also outside the camp, where You shall go for latrine:

13 And You shall have a spade upon your weapon; and it shall be, when You will go to the latrine, You shall dig with the spade and cover your excrement.

14 For YHWH Your POWER walks in the midst of your camp, to rescue you, and to give up your enemies before you; therefore your camp shall be Holy: that he sees no unclean thing in you, and turn away from you.

15 You shall not give back to his master the servant which is escaped from his master to you:

16 He shall dwell with you, even among you, in that place which he shall choose in one of your gates, where he likes best: You shall not oppress him.

17 There shall be no female cultic prostitute[1] of the daughters of Israel, nor a male cultic prostitute of the sons of Israel.

18 You shall not bring the wages of a female prostitute, or the wages of a dog,[2] into the Beyth (house) of YHWH Your POWER for any vow you have made for both these are abhorrent practices to YHWH Your POWER.

19 You shall not charge interest for loan of money to your brother; for loan of money, loan of food, or loan of any type no interest to be charged:

20 To a foreigner You can lend with interest; but to your Brother You shall not lend money with interest: that YHWH Your POWER may **Bless** you in all that You set your hand to in the land where You go to possess it.

21 When You shall vow a vow to YHWH Your POWER, You shall not be slack to pay it: for YHWH Your POWER will surely require it of you; and it would be a sin if you don't.

22 But if You shall refrain to vow, it shall not be a sin to you.

23 That which you have spoken must be honored even a freewill offering, accordingly as You have vowed to YHWH Your POWER, which You have promised with your mouth.

24 When You come into your neighbour's vineyard, then You may eat grapes as much as you like; but You must not take away any in your vessel.[3]

25 When You come into the standing wheat of your neighbour, then You may pluck the ears with your hand; but You shall not move a sickle to your neighbour's standing wheat.

Chapter 24

1 When a man has taken a wife, and married her, and it come to

Footnotes

[1] The term qadeshah signifies a female Temple prostitute who was forbidden as the heathens used these often.

[2] See note on verse 17 as the Hebrew term 'dog' here was the euphemism for a male prostitute, and in the nations they used them as well.

[3] It's assumed that if you are hungry you can eat your fill, but taking some away would mean you came with the intent to steal, which is forbidden.

pass that she find no favour in his eyes, because he has found some uncleanness[1] in her: then let him write her a bill of divorcement, and give it in her hand, and send her out of his Beyth (house).[2]

Footnotes

[1] The Hebrew word Ervah Dvar means some sexual impropriety such as a past affair or something similar. It can also be whoring.

[2] The word for 'favour' in verse one is 'chen' and means 'favour,' 'favor,' 'elegance' and 'acceptance.' When a husband finds out that his wife had slept with someone before she married him, he becomes angry and thus has no more 'favour' or 'elegance' or charm towards his wife. Sadly this happens a lot in the Eastern culture and men can become very cruel to their wives. This can be witnessed first hand in the Islamic culture where Muslims can even kill their wives for this type of thing and this can create lifelong feuds between clans. In Israel YHWH allowed a hot headed man to cool himself down therefore a provision was made that if proven, it did not lead to divorce as most think but the DEATH OF THE WOMAN. Life is precious so we must think; is this what we want for the sake of our hatred to kill someone else! If it takes the death of someone that you thought you loved to pacify your anger, and then something is probably not right with this type of person.

It is again a provision for what to do when a husband has lost his love for his wife and is burning with hatred. Many Christians and other people discover the divorce law here but this is not about divorce, yet YHWH is showing us here, how to deal with the uncleanness that a husband has found in his wife or it has been made known to him after the marriage has been consummated. For me this is not dealing with divorce at all as we all thought but the same principle as in Deuteronomy 22:13. Where a husband finds no favour for his wife and could not love her any longer, and he started to hate his wife. Then, he becomes one husband whose heart has become hard. So, he puts his wife away quietly rather than the public fanfare as we read in the Devrim (Deuteronomy) 22:13-17 scenario.
Continued in next section

2 And when she is departed out of his Beyth (house), she may go and be another man's wife.[3]

3 And if the latter husband hates her as well, and writes her a bill of divorcement, and gives it in her hand, and sends her out of his Beyth (house); or if the latter husband die, which took her to be his wife;

4 Her former husband, who sent her away, may not take her again to be his wife, after that she is ritually impure;[4] for that is a Ritual Defilement before YHWH and You shall not cause the land to sin, which YHWH Your POWER gives you for an inheritance.

5 When a man has taken a new wife, he shall not go out to war, neither shall he be charged with any business: but he shall be free at home one year, and shall cheer up his wife[5] which he has

For more, please see the article on divorce. http://www.forever-israel.com/BM/marriage-divorce.html

[3] Early stage of marriage allowed it to be terminated on the pretext of fraud so she could get married to another man. Normally Hebrew marriages can never be terminated unless the husband dies, as it is an unto death Covenant.

[4] All Israelite marriages are Holy. Because he sent her out and she went and slept with another husband then she can never come back to the former. She could have come back had she not remarried and slept with another husband/man. A wife that has been sent away must be done so for a period of one year, her repentance then seen and she allowed to return if she has not defiled herself with another man. If she has then she can no longer return.

[5] Israelite marriages are allowed to be nurtured for one year while the couple get to know each other and also have their first
Continued in next section

taken.

6 No man shall take the lower or the upper millstone to pledge: for he takes a man's life to pledge.[1]

7 If a man be found stealing any of his brethren of the children of Israel, and makes merchandise of him, or sold him; then that thief shall die; and You shall put evil away from among you.

8 Take heed in the disease of leprosy, that You observe diligently, and do according to all that the kohenim the Lewim shall teach you: as I commanded them, so you shall observe to do.

9 Remember what YHWH Your POWER did to Miriam by the way, after that you were come forth out of Mitzrayim (Egypt).

10 When You decide to lend your brother any thing, You shall not go into his Beyth (house) to fetch his pledge.

11 You shall stand outside, and the man to whom You decided to lend shall bring out the pledge out to you.

12 And if the man be poor, You shall not sleep with his pledge:

13 In any case You shall respect the pledge when the sun goes down, that he may sleep in

his own clothes, and **Bless**[2] you: and it shall be Righteousness to you before YHWH Your POWER.

14 You shall not oppress a hired servant that is poor and needy, whether he be of your brethren, or the foreigners that are in your land within your gates:

15 At his day You shall give him his hire, neither shall the sun go down upon it; for he is poor, and set his heart upon it: lest he cry against you to YHWH, and it will be a sin to you.

16 The ahvot (fathers) shall not be put to death for the children, neither shall the children be put to death for the ahvot (fathers): each man shall be put to death for his own sin.

17 You shall not pervert the judgment of the foreigner, nor of the fatherless; nor take a widow's clothes to pledge:

18 But You shall remember that You were slaves in Mitzrayim (Egypt), and YHWH Your POWER redeemed you there: therefore I command you to do this thing.

19 When You cut down your harvest in your field, and have forgotten a sheaf in the field, You shall not go again to fetch it: it shall be for the foreigner, for the fatherless, and for the widow: that YHWH Your POWER may **Bless** you in all the work of your hands.

20 When You beat your olive etz (tree), You shall not go over the boughs again: it shall be for

child together when the wife needs the love and care of the husband by her side.

[1] Guarantees for a loan such as ones pledge of some valuable asset that he needs to survive with such as if one grows wheat and then pledges and puts down his wheat factory to someone else. Then how will he thresh his wheat and make flour out of it? The Arabs had four millstones; one fixed to do the grinding of the wheat the upper millstone and the other three portable possibly to pledge.

Footnotes

[2] The poor man will say good words that will carry weight in Elohim's court.

the foreigner, for the fatherless, and for the widow.

21 When You gather the grapes of your vineyard, You shall not glean it afterward: it shall be for the foreigner, for the fatherless, and for the widow.

22 And You shall remember that You were a slave in the land of Mitzrayim (Egypt): therefore I command you to do this thing.

Chapter 25

1 If there be a controversy between men, and they go to court for judgment, that the judges may judge them; then they shall justify the innocent, and condemn the guilty.

2 And it shall be, if the wicked man be worthy to be beaten, that the judge shall cause him to lie down, and to be beaten before his face, according to his fault, by a certain number.

3 Forty stripes[1] he may give him, and not exceed: lest, if he should exceed, and beat him above these with many stripes, then your brother should seem vile to you.

4 You shall not muzzle the ox when he treads out the wheat.

5 If brethren dwell together, and one of them die, and his wife had no child, from the dead brother, she shall not marry outside to a foreigner: her husband's brother

shall go in to her,[2] and take her to him to be his wife, and perform the duty of a husband's brother to her.

6 And it shall be that the Bekhor (firstborn) which she bears shall succeed in the name of his brother which is dead, that his name be not put out of Israel.

7 And if the man refuses to take his brother's wife, then let his brother's wife go up to the gate to the elders, and say, My husband's brother refuses to raise up to his brother a name in Israel, he will not perform the duty of my husband's brother.

8 Then the elders of his city shall call him, and speak to him: and if he stands to it, and says, I do not want to take her to be my wife;

9 Then shall his brother's wife come to him in the presence of the elders, and loose his shoe from off his foot,[3] and spit in his face,[4] and shall answer and say, so shall it be done to that man that will not build up his brother's

Footnotes
[1] Rav Sha'ul was striped five times by the Yahudim for his Torah disobedience so it would be 39 minus 1, Second Corinthians 11:24

Footnotes
[2] This is called 'Levirate Marriage.' This is commanded polygamy even if the brother is married and has children. Then YHWH orders the brother who is alive to take his brother's wife as an additional wife. The reason was to give sons to the dead brother by marrying his sister in law who has no son. This way the children could get the dead brother's name and the dead man's progeny may continue in Israel.
[3] This is a symbolic act of the shoe being upon the ground so to say, he could not have his brother's inheritance.
[4] To show contempt because the brother refuses to raise sons for his dead brother and take her as his second wife.

Devrim (Deuteronomy)

Beyth (house).[1]

10 And his name shall be called in Israel, The Beyth (house) of him that has his shoe untied.[2]

11 When two men fight together and the wife of the one draws closer to help her husband being beaten and grabs the genitals of the other man;

12 Then You shall cut off her hand, your eye shall not pity her.[3]

13 You shall not have different stone weights, a great and a small.

14 You shall not have in your Beyth (house) different measuring containers, a great and a small.

15 But You shall have an accurate and right stone weight, and an accurate and right measuring container that your days may be lengthened in the land which YHWH Your POWER gives you.

16 For all that do such things, and all that do wickedly, are Ritually Defiled before YHWH Your POWER.

17 Remember what Amalek did to you by the way, when you were come forth out of Mitzrayim (Egypt);

18 How he met you by the way, and tried to cut off the rear,[4] even all that were tired behind you, when You were faint and weary; and he feared not Elohim.

19 Therefore it shall be, when YHWH Your POWER has given you rest from all your enemies round about, in the land which YHWH Your POWER gives you for an inheritance[5] to possess it, that You shall blot out the remembrance of Amalek from under shamayim; You shall not forget it.

Torah Parsha 50 Ki Tavo, Devrim 26:1-29:9
Haftarah: Yeshayahu 60:1-22

Chapter 26

1 And it shall be, when You have come into the land which YHWH Your POWER is about to give you for an inheritance, and possess it, and dwell in it;

2 That You shall take of the first of all the fruit of the earth, which You shall bring of your land that YHWH Your POWER is about to give you, and shall put it in a

Footnotes

[1] What you sow that you must reap. One who refuses to raise up a son for his brother.

[2] A certificate was issued to her by the standing Rebbim and Judges that she was now free to marry anyone else in Israel as this man had disgraced himself in public.

[3] This is seen to be offensive as she could have crushed his testicles and he would lose the ability to have any more children so the act by the woman is considered a grave offence. The case would be taken to the judges and there was actually no case of cutting of an actual hand as in Israel people were not deliberately made cripple but a sum of money was exchanged as blood money. This is the same as eye for an eye, tooth for a tooth Shemoth (Exo) 21:24 where no eye or tooth was plucked. The right hand signifies strength so here it shows too much strength can act in judgment against the other person. This is the right side of YHWH.

[4] They struck those who were old and young who could not keep up. Shemoth (Exodus) 17:8-16

[5] Israel is an eternal inheritance not just for a season.

470

basket, and shall go to the place which YHWH Your POWER shall choose to place his name there.

3 And You shall go up to the kohen (priest) that shall be in those days, and say to them, I profess this day to YHWH Your POWER, that I have come into the country which YHWH swore to our ahvot (fathers) to give us.

4 And the kohen (priest) shall take the basket out of your hand, and set it down before the altar of YHWH Your POWER.

5 And You shall speak and say before YHWH Your POWER, An Aramaen[1] was ready to destroy my father, and he[2] went down into Mitzrayim (Egypt), and sojourned there with a few, and became there a nation, great, mighty, and numerous in numbers:[3]

Footnotes

[1] The 'Aramean,' reference here is to Laban (Beresheeth - Genesis 25:20).

[2] Children of Israel.

[3] You cannot be numerous if you have a husband and a wife plus two children each. Israel's average was eight wives and fifty six children in each family or one wife and several concubines as lesser wives to give birth to children. Look at Divre HaYamim Bet (2 Chronicles 13:21) where Abiyah had 14 wives and 38 children, also see Divre HaYamim Bet (2 Chronicles) 11:21 where Rehab'am had 78 wives and had 88 children.

The Arabs and Muslims have carried this model today, while the Israelites shy away from their national calling.

All the Patriarchal people were from Mesopotamia and became Hebrews, meaning 'the ones who crossed over.' But the Hebrew people or Israel as a whole with all twelve tribes (including Efrayim's 10 non-Hebrew tribes) are descendants of these people. Anyone who will join Israel today by Continued in next section

6 And the Mitzrim (Egyptians) evil entreated us, and afflicted us, and laid upon us hard bondage:

7 And when we cried to YHWH Elohim of our ahvot (fathers), YHWH heard our voice, and looked on our affliction, and our labour, and our oppression:

8 And YHWH brought us forth out of Mitzrayim (Egypt) with a mighty hand, and with an outstretched arm, and with great terribleness, and with signs, and with wonders:

9 And he has brought us into this place, and has given us this land, even a land that flows with milk and honey.

10 And now, behold, I have brought the bikkurim (first-fruit) of the land, which You, O YHWH, have given me. And You shall set it before YHWH Your POWER, and pay homage before YHWH Your POWER:

11 And You shall rejoice in every good thing which YHWH Your POWER has given to you, and to your Beyth (house), You, and the Levite, and the foreigner that is among you.

12 When You have made an end of tithing all the tithes of your

confession and acceptance of the Covenants in the Torah will become a full Hebrew, not half or not spiritual. These are joined by the oath in front of two elders.

When Jacob was invited to live in Egypt and then his descendants decided to stay there and as a polygamous group of people, they became many in number which threatened the Pharaoh's kingdom. Hence why we see they were worried about what to do with them. So, they enforced slavery on Israel.

Increase the third year,[1] which is the year of tithing, and have given it to the Levite, the foreigner, the fatherless, and the widow, that they may eat within your gates, and be filled;

13 Then You shall say before YHWH Your POWER, I have brought away the Holy things out of mine Beyth (house), and also have given them to the Levite, and to the foreigner, to the fatherless, and to the widow, according to all your commandments which You have commanded me: I have not transgressed your commandments, neither have I forgotten them:

14 I have not eaten anything while in mourning, neither have I removed anything while I was unclean, nor offered anything of it to the dead: but I have obeyed the voice of YHWH my POWER, and have done according to all that You have commanded me.

15 Look down from your Holy dwelling, from shamayim, and **Bless** your people Israel, and the land which You have given us, as You swore to our ahvot (fathers), a land that flows with milk and honey.

16 This day YHWH Your POWER has commanded you to do these statutes and judgments: You shall therefore guard and do them with all your heart, and with all your soul.

17 You have declared to YHWH this day to be Your POWER, and to keep His halachot in his ways, and to keep his statutes, and his commandments, and his judgments, and to obey His voice:

18 And YHWH has declared to you this day to be his treasured possession as he has promised you, and that You should guard all his commandments;

19 And to elevate you above all nations which He has made, in praise, and in name, and in respect; and that You may be a Holy people to YHWH Your POWER, as he has spoken.

Chapter 27

1 And Mosheh (Musa) with the elders of Israel commanded the people, saying, Guard all the commandments which I command you this day.

2 And it shall be on the day when you shall pass over Yardan (Jordan) to the land which YHWH Your POWER gives you, that You shall erect together great stones,[2] and plaster them with plaster:

3 And You shall write upon them all the words of this Torah, when You have passed over, that You may go in to the land which YHWH Your POWER gives you, a land that flows with milk and honey; as YHWH Elohim of your ahvot (fathers) has promised you.

4 Therefore it shall be when you have gone over the Yardan (Jordan), that you shall erect

Footnotes
[1] There was a three yearly tithe. The three years are counted from the seventh year. When the land lay fallow, this was also known as the poor people's tithe. Also mentioned in Deuteronomy 14:28.

Footnotes
[2] In Mount Ebal and not Jordan

these stones, which I command you this day, in Mount Ebal, and You shall plaster them with plaster.

5 And there shall You build an altar to YHWH Your POWER, an altar of stones: You shall not lift up any iron tool upon them.

6 You shall build the altar of YHWH Your POWER of whole stones: and You shall offer burnt offerings thereon to YHWH Your POWER:

7 And You shall offer shalom offerings, and shall eat there, and rejoice before YHWH Your POWER.

8 And You shall write upon the stones all the words of this Torah very plainly.

9 And Mosheh (Musa) and the kohenim the Lewim spoke to all Israel, saying, Be Silent and pay close attention, O Israel; this day You have become the people of YHWH Your POWER.

10 You must listen[1] carefully to the voice of YHWH Your POWER, and do His commandments and his statutes, which I command you this day.

11 And Mosheh (Musa) commanded the people the same day, saying,

12 These shall stand upon Mount Gerizim to speak **Blessings** over the people, when you have come over the Yardan (Jordan); Shimeon, and Levi, and Yahudah, and Yskhar (Issachar), and Yosef, and Benyamin:

13 And these shall stand upon

Mount Ebal to curse; Reuven, Gawd, and Asher, and Zevulun, Dan, and Naphtali.

14 And the Lewim shall speak, and say to all the men of Israel with a loud voice,

15 Cursed be the man that makes any graven or molten image, or something Ritually Defiled before YHWH, the work of the hands of the craftsman, and puts it in a secret place. And all the people shall answer and say, Amen.

16 Cursed be he that disrespects[2] his father or his mother. And all the people shall say, Amen.

17 Cursed be he that removes his neighbour's boundary markers. And all the people shall say, Amen.

18 Cursed be he that makes the blind to wander out of the way. And all the people shall say, Amen.

19 Cursed be he that perverts judgment of the foreigner, fatherless, and widow. And all the people shall say, Amen.

20 Cursed be he that lies with his father's wife; because he uncovers his father's nakedness. And all the people shall say, Amen.

21 Cursed be he that commits

Footnotes

[1] 'Listen and do means,' to obey Torah

[2] It does not matter whether your parents are believers or unbelievers, disrespect will bring on the curse. This disrespect is in general obedience in day to day living. However, if they tell you to obey other elohim, you are only to serve YHWH and this is not counted as disrespect to parents as you can tell them lovingly that you will not follow after their idols.

bestiality. And all the people shall say, Amen.

22 Cursed be he that lies with his sister, the daughter of his father, and also the daughter of his mother.[1] And all the people shall say, Amen.

23 Cursed be he that lies with his mother in law. And all the people shall say, Amen.

24 Cursed be he that kills his neighbour secretly. And all the people shall say, Amen.

25 Cursed be he that takes reward to kill[2] an innocent person. And all the people shall say, Amen.

26 Cursed be he that does not continue in all the words of this Torah to do them.[3] And all the people shall say, Amen.

Chapter 28

1 And it shall come to pass, if You shall listen carefully to the voice of YHWH Your POWER, to Guard[4] and to do all his commandments which I command you this day, that YHWH Your POWER will elevate you high above all nations of the world:[5]

2 And all these **Blessings** shall come on you, and overtake you, if You shall listen carefully to the voice of YHWH Your POWER.

3 Blessed shall You be in the city, and **Blessed** shall You be in the field.

4 Blessed shall you be the fruit of your body[6], and the fruit of your ground, and the fruit of your cattle, the calves of your herds, and the flocks of your sheep.

5 Blessed shall be your basket[7] and your store.

6 Blessed shall You be when You come in, and **Blessed** shall You be when You go out.[8]

7 YHWH shall cause your enemies that rise up against you to be struck down before you: they shall come out against you one way, and flee before you seven ways.[9]

Footnotes

[1] Brothers and sisters from polygamous relations clearly defined.

[2] This is speaking of a hit man who is hired to murder someone.

[3] Anyone even claiming to be a believer who does not continue in all the words of the Torah is still under a curse even if he claims to be in the Messiah. There are many curses written in the Torah and there are also many favorable Blessings, in order to reap these you have to 'hear and do,' the words of this Torah.

[4] The word 'shomer' here means to protect and to obey the commandments. The protection is like your own property and right. Do you guard His commandments like you guard your son and daughter or your most material prized possession? The meaning behind this is like a solider standing
Continued in next section

with a machine gun guarding and fighting for his country and the rights of his nation.
[5] YHWH will also raise up Israel first in the order of resurrection, so the idea in the ancient Hebrew 'Elyon,' to be elevated is not just an elevation here but also elevation ahead of the world. In ancient Hebrew it means to be 'led by the hand of YHWH'.
[6] Child birth is related to Torah obedience.
[7] First-fruits – Targum of Jonathan.
[8] 'Come in and go out' is an idiomatic expression to mean anything you do in life. Any business or employment conducted by Israelites will be **Blessed** as long as the Torah is obeyed.
[9] This only happened when Israel obeyed the Torah otherwise their enemies defeated them such as the Assyrians and Babylonians.

8 YHWH shall command the **Blessing** upon you in your storehouses, and in all that You set your hand to; and he shall **Bless** you in the land which YHWH Your POWER gives you.

9 YHWH shall establish you as a Holy people to himself, as He has sworn to you, if You shall Guard[1] the commandments of YHWH Your POWER, and walk in his ways.

10 And all people of the world shall see that You are called by the name of YHWH;[2] and they shall be afraid of you.

11 And YHWH shall make you plenteous in goods, in the fruit of your body,[3] and in the fruit of your cattle, and in the fruit of your ground, in the land which YHWH swore to your ahvot (fathers) to give you.

12 YHWH shall open to you his good treasure, the shamayim to give the rain to your land in his season, and to **Bless** all the work of your hand: and You shall lend to many nations, and You shall not borrow.[4]

13 And YHWH shall make you the head, and not the tail; and You shall be above only, and You shall not be beneath; if You carefully listen to the commandments of YHWH Your POWER, which I command you this day, to Guard and to do them:

14 And You shall not go aside from any of the words which I command you this day, to the right hand, or to the left,[5] to go after other elohim to serve them.

15 But it shall come to pass, if You will not listen to the voice of YHWH Your POWER, to Guard and to do all His commandments and His statutes which I command you this day; that all these curses shall come upon you, and overtake you:

16 Cursed shall You be in the city, and cursed shall You be in the field.

17 Cursed shall be your basket and your store.

18 Cursed shall be the fruit of your body, and the fruit of your land, the calves of your herd, and the flocks of your sheep.[6]

19 Cursed shall You be when

Footnotes

[1] If you guard, means, to obey the commandments not simply going to church once a week to satisfy your Pastor's denomination laws. Torah obedience is commanded and not obligatory and many Christians need to learn this fact and state of play.

[2] YHWH is the only Name under shamayim and no other NAME can compete.

[3] Israelite people especially chiefs practiced polygamy having a minimum of two wives in the North/South axis while common Israelites in ancient times also practiced polygamy extensively so had many children.

[4] How come many people who claim to know YHWH are constantly down? This is because Continued in next section

they are disobedient to Torah. If you want to rise up then obey, obey and obey and YHWH will bring you out of adversity.

[5] See footnote Shemoth (Exodus) 29:20.

[6] The only people to be grazing sheep and cattle were the Asian/Africans and it was very common for these people to graze sheep and cattle. Europeans did not do this, in fact they were well known for looting and robbing other people's foods. Read the history of the Anglo/Saxon people and Scandinavians who conducted raids by ships to loot for food and were known as common thieves.

You come in, and cursed shall You be when You go out.

20 YHWH shall send upon you cursing, confusion, and oppose you, in all that You set your hand to do, until You be destroyed, and until You perish quickly; because of the wickedness of your doings, whereby You have forsaken me.

21 YHWH shall make the pestilence cling to you,[1] until he have consumed you from off the land, where You go to possess it.

22 YHWH will punish you with consumption,[2] and with a fever, and with an inflammation, and with an extreme burning, and with the sword, and with blasting, and with mildew;[3] and they shall pursue you until You perish.

23 And your shamayim that is over your head shall be bronze, and the earth that is under you shall be iron.[4]

24 YHWH shall make the rain of your land powder and dust: from shamayim shall it come down upon you, until You be destroyed.

25 YHWH shall cause you to be defeated before your enemies: You shall go out one way against them, and flee seven ways before them becoming an object of terror and shall be removed into all the nations of the world.[5]

26 And your carcasses shall become food on to the birds of the air, and to all the wild animals of the earth, and no man shall be there to scare them away.

27 YHWH will punish you with the boils of Mitzrayim (Egypt), and with the tumors, and with the scab, and with the itch, from which You cannot be healed.

28 YHWH shall punish you with madness, and blindness, and confusion of heart:

29 And You shall grope at noonday, as the blind grope in darkness, and You shall not prosper in your ways: and You shall only be oppressed and continually robbed, and no man can rescue you.

30 You shall betroth a wife, and another man shall lie with her: You shall build a Beyth (house), and You shall not dwell therein: You shall plant a vineyard, and shall not gather the grapes there.

31 Your ox shall be slain before your eyes, and You shall not eat there: your ass shall be violently taken away from before your face, and shall not be restored to you: your sheep shall be given to your enemies, and You shall have none to rescue them.[6]

Footnotes
[1] You will get plagued with diseases.
[2] Such as Diabetes.
[3] This is an Idiomatic expression to mean, to strip you step by step of your goods, so things just do not go right, e.g. you start a business and it fails, you try another and it fails until you have lost all your money.
[4] Look at footnote 6 and 7 on Vayikra (Lev) 26:19.

Footnotes
[5] This happened to Israel for disobedience, the judgment of YHWH had mercy built in which allowed them to scatter and fill the nations. The melo ha goyim Beresheeth (Genesis) 48:19.
[6] This is literally happening in Pakistan and places like Nigeria and the common issue is not that the nation is hostile because of something the believer has done, but the common thread is they do not obey YHWH Continued in next section

32 Your sons and your daughters shall be given to another people,[1] and your eyes shall look, and fail with longing for them all the day long: and there shall be no might in your hand.

33 The fruit of your land, and all your labours, shall a people which You knows not eat up; and You shall be only oppressed and crushed always.

34 So that You shall become insane from seeing all this.

35 YHWH shall smite you in the knees, and in the shoulders, with incurable boils, from the sole of your feet to the top of your head.

36 YHWH shall bring you, and your King which You shall set over you, to a heathen nation which neither You nor Your ahvot (fathers) have known; and there shall You serve other powers, of wood and stone.[2]

37 And You shall become an astonishment, a proverb, and an occasion of horror, among all the peoples[3] where YHWH shall scatter you.

38 You shall carry much seed out into the field, and shall gather but little in; for the locust[4] shall

Footnotes

and His Torah. Christians are disobedient, and they wonder what is going on. Many Christian families that have daughters have had them forcefully taken away and then converted. Lands have been confiscated and not returned; people have been put in jails with a false charge. All these things are occurring not because they are disobedient to Torah pure and simple!

The Pastor's will not tell you this because they lack knowledge of YHWH's laws and are taught Western Christianity, which wrongly teaches that the Torah is abolished (interpreting Sha'ul's epistles which are blatant lies). They further exacerbate the problem by introducing pagan feasts and eating unclean foods and not understanding the difference between clean and unclean. Israel did not keep Christianity as a Faith, either we learn to walk in our forefathers' ways or perish, the choice is clear. Obey and be **Blessed** or suffer and die. If our forefathers who were disobedient perished in the wilderness then what chance do we have?

[1] Gentile Sephardim converted Jews that enslaved biological Israel. Aaron Lopez born in 1731 and died in 1782 was at birth called Duarte Lopez his Portuguese name but he was one of the wealthiest Sephardi Jewish merchant in Newport, Rhode Island. He commissioned many black slave ships and traded heavily in slaves.

[2] The people who were carried from Africa were brought to Europe and America including their kings and humiliated there. They had never seen these white faces before. The Africans even today paint evil as white so the faces of Black men and women are painted white to depict evil spirits.

[3] Israelites will be reviled all over the world.

[4] There is a sod (hidden) meaning here of future issues with Torahlessness with the Islamic nations who will be numerous like the locusts. The Hebrew word 'Arbeh' for locust can also mean a Desert roaming creature like a Bedouin Arab. Hence they will attack you or come to your lands which many Islamic nations have done and attack Christians for Torahlessness. Get the book World War III – Unmasking the End Times Beast Page 158 The word used by the Rebbim for locust is 'arbeh,' which they refer to the 'desert creature' and use also synonymously for the Arabs.

The Hebrew word used is 'arbeh' and one can understand why the Rebbim used this for the Arabs as the desert-roaming creatures. It is a foregone conclusion that the Arabs will come up in the end-times to try and destroy Israel with other Islamic nations and that YHWH will crush them on the mountains of Israel. It is our job to warn them so that some may repent. However, the last battle is not only a battle that will wake up Israel, but also rescue Muslims who

Continued in next section

consume it.

39 You shall plant vineyards, and dress them, but shall neither drink of the wine, nor gather the grapes; for the scarlet worms shall eat them.

40 You shall have olive etzim (trees) throughout all your coasts, but You shall not anoint yourself with the oil; for your olive shall cast its fruit.

41 You shall give birth to sons and daughters, but You shall not enjoy them; for they shall go into

are left. Ultimately it involves rescue of both peoples, the Arabs and the Yahudim, since both in their present state without Torah are lost.

Let me show you another understanding in the Aramaic in Daniel 2:43 where he describes the fourth kingdom. Daniel shows us that this kingdom will be strong yet divided and we see this fracture in the Islamic Empire today. But they will unite to try and destroy Israel as a confederacy, just as the scrolls dictates. One thing is 100% certain; that YHWH is trustworthy and everything He said has so far has come to pass and the rest will be fulfilled in its due course.

Daniel 2:43 'As you saw iron mixed with ceramic clay, they will mingle with the seed of men; but they will not adhere to one another, just as iron does not mix with clay.'

The Aramaic word for 'mix' is 'Arab.' Do you see how YHWH is trying to show us that it is the Arabs who will mix with the seed of men, i.e. intermarriages, plus the spread of Islam globally, that will produce the end-time empire? Although 'arbah' can also mean the number four (4). So another allegoric (drash) reading of this could be that the four beast mix in the Middle East is in this SAME region that will produce this last empire. Since this is the SAME geographic region for all these 4 beast empires, as both Daniel 7 and Revelation 13:2 clearly dictate.

captivity.[1]

42 All your etzim (trees) and fruit of your land shall the locust consume.

43 The foreigner that is within you shall get up above you very high; and You shall come down very low.

44 He shall lend[2] to you, and You shall not lend to him: he shall be the head, and You shall be the tail.

45 Moreover all these curses shall come upon you, and shall pursue you, and overtake you, till You be destroyed; because You did not listen to the voice of YHWH Your POWER, to guard His commandments and his statutes which he commanded you:

46 And they shall be upon you for a sign and for a wonder, and upon your seed forever.

47 Because You served not YHWH Your POWER with joyfulness, and with gladness of heart, for the abundance of all things;

48 Therefore shall You serve your enemies which YHWH shall send against you, in hunger, and in thirst, and in nakedness, and in want of all things: and he shall put a yoke of iron upon your neck, until he has destroyed you.

49 YHWH shall bring a heathen

Footnotes

[1] Not necessarily physical captivity but also spiritual, as they will take on other false religions and be lost that way.

[2] Prophecy of gentiles, who are the moneylenders of this world. They control many banks and governments, institutions such as the IMF, World Bank and the Federal Reserve are owned by them.

nation against you from far, from the end of the earth, as swift[1] as the eagle[2] flies; a heathen nation whose tongue You shall not understand;

50 A heathen nation of fierce countenance, which shall not regard the person of the old, nor show favour to the young.

51 And he shall eat the fruit of your cattle, and the fruit of your land, until You be destroyed. which also shall not leave you either wheat, wine, or oil, or the calves from your herd, or flocks of your sheep, until they have destroyed you:

52 And he shall besiege you in all your gates, until your high and fenced walls come down, wherein You trusted, throughout all your land: and they shall besiege you in all your gates throughout all your land, which YHWH Your POWER has given you.

53 And You shall eat the fruit of your own body,[3] the flesh of your sons and of your daughters, which YHWH Your POWER has given you, in the siege,[4] and in the desperate straits, wherewith your enemies shall distress you:

54 So that the man that is tender among you, and very delicate, his eye shall be evil toward his brother, and toward his beloved wife, and toward the remnant of his children which he shall leave:

55 So that he will not give to any of them of the flesh of his children whom he shall eat: because he has nothing left him in the siege, and in the desperate straits, where your enemies shall distress you in all your gates.

56 The tender and delicate woman among you, which would not adventure to set the sole of her foot upon the ground for delicateness and tenderness, her eye shall be evil toward her beloved husband, and toward her son, and toward her daughter,

57 And toward her young one that came out from her womb, and toward her children which she shall bear: for she shall eat them for want of all things secretly in the siege and straightness, wherewith your enemy shall distress you in your gates.

58 If You will not Guard to do all the words of this Torah that are written in this book, that You may

Footnotes
[1] The nation to come were Romans who attacked and were dreadful. The second attack occurred by the Islamists. The stallions of the Muslims were known for their swiftness and so were the Turkic ones. Such were called the Byerly Turk, the Darley Arabian and the Godolphin Barb with famous and pure Arab bloodlines. The remez (hint) is also of how quickly they will conquer many countries of the world, presently we have fifty two majority Muslim nations.
[2] Eagle was a sign of both the Romans who later inhabited England and Americans both of these countries were involved in the slave trade enslaving Hebrews.
[3] The Talmud calls this "the after birth (Niddah 24)."

Footnotes
[4] This happened once with the Assyrian and Babylonian siege when the Hebrew people ate their children for food. Both of these regions are now occupied and controlled by Islamic nations who hate Israel.

fear[1] this glorious and fearful name, YHWH Your POWER;

59 Then YHWH will harden your afflictions, and the afflictions of your descendants, even great plagues, and these will continue a longtime, and also severe enduring illnesses.

60 Moreover he will bring upon you all the diseases of Mitzrayim (Egypt), which You were afraid of; and they shall cling to you.

61 Also every sickness, and every plague, which is not written in the book of this Torah, them will YHWH bring upon you, until You be destroyed.

62 And you shall be left few in number, whereas you were as the stars of shamayim for multitude; because You would not obey the voice of YHWH Your POWER.

63 And it shall come to pass, that as YHWH rejoiced over you to do you good, and to multiply you; so YHWH will rejoice over you to destroy you, and to bring you to naught; and you shall be plucked from off the land where You go to possess it.

64 And YHWH shall scatter you among all people, from the one end of the earth even to the other; and there You shall serve other powers,[2] which neither You nor your ahvot (fathers) have known, even tree[3] and stone.

65 And among these nations shall You find no ease, neither shall the sole of your feet have rest: but YHWH shall give you there a trembling heart, and failing of eyes, and sorrow of mind:

66 And your life shall hang in doubt before you; and You shall fear day and night, and shall have no assurance of your life.[4]

67 In the morning You shall say, would Elohim it was evening. And in the evening you will say, would Elohim it was morning. For the fear of your heart where you shall fear, and for the sight of your eyes which You shall see.

68 And YHWH shall bring you into Mitzrayim (Egypt) again with ships, by the way whereof I spoke to you, You shall see it no more again: and there you shall be sold to your enemies for bondmen and bondwomen, and no man shall buy you. [5]

Footnotes

[1] We must learn to fear YHWH as a righteous and awesome judge.

[2] False deities of this world and religions.

[3] Christians using the cross of Tammuz from Babylon is sinful. Other people's worshipping stones as gods is idolatry. While our fathers Continued in next section

knew nothing of bowing to the cross of Tammuz is idolatry in all it's forms. Christendom removed our people from Torah and proclaimed a 'white' Messiah though the Torah was suppressed in Christendom and hidden away by Rome and by Christendom's unrighteous Church fathers to this day. This is why all black and other mixed Hebrews must come to their senses and return to the Torah.

[4] You can have assurance of life the minute you change your mind and start to obey Torah and repent.

[5] This has noting to do with modern slavery in ships that many ignorantly claim. Josephus and Diodorus both have written about these events, that when Titus took Jerusalem (70 CE), all the Yahudim over seventeen years old, both men and women, were sent by ships into Egypt to labour in the mines. They were sold as slaves there Continued in next section

but since the slave market was so full no one wanted to buy them so many perished as a result.

(Josephus Book VI, Chapter IX, Section 2) And now, since his soldiers were already quite tired with killing men, and yet there appeared to be a vast multitude still remaining alive, Caesar gave orders that they should kill none but those that were in arms, and opposed them, but should take the rest alive. But, together with those whom they had orders to slay, they slew the aged and the infirm; but for those that were in their flourishing age, and who might be useful to them, they drove them together into the temple, and shut them up within the walls of the court of the women; over which Caesar set one of his freed-men, as also Fronto, one of his own friends; which last was to determine everyone's fate, according to his merits. So this Fronto slew all those that had been seditious and robbers, who were impeached one by another; but of the young men he chose out the tallest and most beautiful, and reserved them for the triumph; and as for the rest of the multitude that were above seventeen years old, he put them into bonds, and sent them to the Egyptian mines Titus also sent a great number into the provinces, as a present to them, that they might be destroyed upon their theatres, by the sword and by the wild beasts; but those that were under seventeen years of age were sold for slaves. Now during the days wherein Fronto was distinguishing these men, there perished, for want of food, eleven thousand; some of whom did not taste any food, through the hatred their guards bore to them; and others would not take in any when it was given them. The multitude also was so very great, that they were in want even of corn for their sustenance.

(Book VI, Chapter IX, Section 3) The Number Of Captives, And Of Those That Perished In The Siege. Now the number of those that were carried captive during the whole war was collected to be ninety-seven thousand ; as was the number of those that perished during the whole siege, eleven hundred thousand * , the greater part of whom were indeed of the same nation, [with
Continued in next section

the citizens of Jerusalem,] but not belonging to the city itself; for they were come up from all the country to the feast of unleavened bread, and were on a sudden shut up by an army , which, at the very first, occasioned so great a straightness among them, that there came a pestilential destruction upon them, and soon afterward such a famine as destroyed them more suddenly. And that this city could contain so many people in it is manifest by that number of them which was taken under Cestius, who being desirous of informing Nero of the power of the city, who otherwise was disposed to contemn that nation, entreated the high priests, if the thing were possible, to take the number of their whole multitude. So these high priests, upon the coming of their feast which is called the Passover, when they slay their sacrifices, from the ninth hour to the eleventh, but so that a company not less than belong to every sacrifice, (for it is not lawful for them to feast singly by themselves,) and many of us are twenty in a company, found the number of sacrifices was two hundred and fifty-six thousand five hundred; which, upon the allowance of no more than ten that feast together, amounts to two millions seven hundred thousand and two hundred persons that were pure and Holy; for as to those that have the leprosy, or the gonorrhoea, or women that have their monthly courses, or such as are otherwise polluted, it is not lawful for them to be partakers of this sacrifice; nor indeed for any foreigners neither, who come hither to worship.

(Book VI, Chapter X, Section 1) That Whereas The City Of Jerusalem Had Been [Six] Times Taken Formerly, This Was The Second Time Of Its Desolation. A Brief Account Of Its History

And thus was Jerusalem taken, in the second year of the reign of Vespasian, on the eight day of the month Gorpieus [Elu]. It had been taken five* times before, though this was the second time of its desolation; for Shishak, the king of Egypt, and after his Antiochus, and after him Pompey, and after him Sosius and Herod took the city, but still preserved it; but before all these, the king of Babylon conquered it, and made it desolate,
Continued in next section

Chapter 29

1 These are the words of the Covenant, which YHWH commanded Mosheh (Musa) to make with the children of Israel in the land of Moav,[1] beside the

one thousand four hundred and sixty-eight years and six months after it was built. But he who first built it was a potent man among the Canaanites, and is in our tongue called [Melchizedek] the righteous King, for such he really was; on which account he was [there] the first priest of God, and first built a temple, [there,] and called the city Jerusalem, which was formerly called Salem. However, David, the king of the Yahudim, ejected the Canaanites, and settled his own people therein. It was demolished entirely by the Babylonians, four hundred and seventy-seven years and six months after him. And from king David, who was the first of the Yahudim who reigned therein, to this destruction under Titus, were one thousand one hundred and seventy-nine years; but from its first building, till this last destruction, were two thousand one hundred and seventy-seven years; yet hath not its great antiquity, nor its vast riches, nor the diffusion of its nation over all the habitable earth, nor the greatness of the veneration paid to it on a religious account, been sufficient to preserve it from being destroyed. And thus ended the siege of Jerusalem.

[1] This is the New Covenant being established with Moses Rebenu. The words 'beside' indicate this is a New Covenant but encompassing what was contained in the Sinaitic Covenant (10 Commandments only and no animal sacrifices). Well respected Hebrew Rabbi's such as famous Rabbi Moses ben Maimon (Rambam) and Rabbi Shlomo Yitzhak (Rashi) also said that this was to be a different Covenant separate from Horeb which is the same one mentioned in Jeremiah 31:31, which Christians cite so freely without understanding. However, they do not realise that it was not made with Yirmeyah but with Moses Rebenu and Israel at Mount Nebo and finds it's place right here in the Torah. YHWH's Covenants overlap and run interchangeably like flights at an airport to different destinations. Just because a
Continued in next section

Covenant which He made with them in Horev.

2 And Mosheh (Musa) called to all Israel, and said to them, You have seen all that YHWH did before your eyes in the land of Mitzrayim (Egypt) to Pharaoh, and to all his servants, and to all his land;

3 The great judgments which your eyes have seen, the signs, and those mighty miracles:

4 Yet YHWH has not given you a heart to know, and eyes to see, and ears to hear,[2] to this day.

5 And I have led you forty years in the wilderness: your clothes have not worn out, and your sandals on your feet have not deteriorated.

6 You have eaten no Lakhem (bread), neither have you drunk wine or strong drink: that you might know that I am YHWH Your POWER.

7 And when you came to this place, Sikhon the King of Kheshbon, and Og the King of Bashan, came out against us for war, and we defeated them:

8 And we took their land, and gave it for an inheritance to the Reuveni, and to the Gawdi, and to the half tribe of Manasheh.

flight is going to India does not mean it cancels out the flight to Pakistan. No Covenant is ever annulled or terminated itself. They all run parallel.

[2] Showing Israelites stubbornness in their ways, 'ears to hear' the term means to rebel against the given 'Faith.' So, if you do not obey Torah and believe like today's disobedient Christians then you certainly do not have ears, the ones that are needed to obey Torah.

9 Guard therefore the words of this[1] Covenant, and do them, that you may prosper in all that you do.

Torah Parsha 51 Nizavim, Devrim 29:10-30:20
Haftarah: Yeshayahu 61:10-63:9

10 You stand this day all of you before YHWH Your POWER; your captains of your tribes, your elders, and your officers, with all the men of Israel,

11 Your infants, your wives, and the foreigner that are in your camp, from the wood cutters to the mayim carriers.

12 That You should enter into Covenant[2] with YHWH Your POWER, and into his oath, which YHWH Your POWER makes with you this day.

13 That he may establish you today for a people to himself, and that He may be to you a Elohim, as He has said to you, and as He has sworn to your ahvot (fathers), to Abraham, to Ytshak, and to Yakov.

14 Neither with you only do I make this Covenant and this oath;

15 But with him that stands here with us this day before YHWH our POWER, and also with him that is not here with us this day:[3]

16 For you know how we have dwelt in the land of Mitzrayim (Egypt); and how we came through the nations which you passed by;

17 And you have seen their idolatrous practices, and their idols, wood and stone, silver and gold, which were among them:

18 Lest there should be among you man, or woman, or Mishpakha (family), or tribe, whose heart turns away this day from YHWH our POWER, to go and serve the powers of these nations; lest there should be among you a root that produces poisonous and bitter fruit;

19 And if it comes to pass, when he hears the words of this curse, that he speaks **Blessing** for himself in his heart, saying, I shall have shalom, though I keep my Halaka (commandments) with a rebellious heart,[4] the watered ground with the parched:[5]

20 YHWH will not be willing to forgive[6] him, but then the anger

Footnotes

[1] The New Covenant was formed at Mount Nebo in today's Jordan.

[2] The Covenant was effectively being made with Israel, they were given another chance.

[3] This is the New Covenant with all present and future believers. The Covenant is not Continued in next section

finished but is in three stages. This was the first stage.

[4] This is the categorical state of most in Christianity. The majority of them walk in utter rebellion and trying to **Increase** self while sticking to the pagan ways of their forefathers popularly known as the church fathers. Our task in life is not to behave like this and **Bless** self, because when we are walking Torah then YHWH will **Bless** us and not self.

[5] Idiomatic expression to mean whatever this person touches will be cursed that includes friendships and business and he will bring judgment on whole nations if he be a king or leader.

[6] The person not willing to obey the Torah will NOT be forgiven by YHWH no matter what he or she claims, Not even The Continued in next section

of YHWH and his jealousy shall arouse against that man, and all the curses[1] that are written in this book shall lie upon him, and YHWH shall blot out his name[2] from under shamayim.

21 And YHWH shall separate him to evil out of all the tribes of Israel, according to all the curses of the Covenant that are written in this scroll of the Torah.

22 So that the generation to come of your children that shall rise up after you, and the foreigner that shall come from a far land, shall say, when they see the plagues of that land, and the sicknesses which YHWH has laid upon it;

23 And that the whole land there

Messiah can save such a person as he has rejected the basic requirement to enter the Covenants of receiving the Torah. The Torah makes a very strict reading "Lo Yowe YHWH Shalakh." The Master is not willing to forgive such a person.

[1] The Torah has many curses. Our own obedience will lift those curses, but if we remain in disobedient living, constantly breaking the 7th day Sabbath, and not keeping the seven annual appointed times (feasts), then the Torah curses remain upon us. Even irrespective of chasing after the Messiah would make no difference to the person.

[2] Ultimately resulting in eternal death. The same way Lilith the first wife of Adam's name was blotted out of the Holy writings because of her rebellion. The world as we know it is regenerated in a polygamous relationship out of Adam's second wife Khawa known to men as Eve and his other wives. YHWH will remove the names from the book of life of the disobedient soles. Yahushua the Messiah on the other hand came to make and ratify the New Covenant that tied back to Abraham. The only guarantee of redemption is acceptance of the Torah, see Deut 30:19.

is brimstone, and salt, and burning, that it is not sown, nor does it bear, nor any grass grows therein, like the overthrow of Sedom, and Amorah (Gomorrah), Admah, and Zevoim, which YHWH overthrew in his anger, and in his indignation:

24 Even all nations shall say, why has YHWH done thus to this land? What is the meaning of this heated great anger?

25 Then men shall say, Because they have forsaken the Covenant of YHWH Elohim of their ahvot (fathers), which he made with them when he brought them forth out of the land of Mitzrayim (Egypt):

26 For they went and served other powers, and worshipped them, powers whom they knew not, and whom He had not given to them:

27 And the anger of YHWH was blazing against this land, to bring upon it all the curses that are written in this scroll:

[3]

28 And YHWH rooted them out of their land in anger, and in wrath, and in great indignation, and cast them into another land, as it is this day.

[4]

Footnotes
[3] The enlarged Lamed. This shows that as Moses was leading the sheep of Israel, the Messiah king would also gather. In the ancient script the Lamed is the picture of the lion for Yahudah.
[4] In Verse 29 we see the jots again. These jots remind us that we must look to YHWH and His Torah in order to get correct
Continued in next section

29 The Hidden-Torot[1] belongs to YHWH our POWER; but that revealed to us and to our children as a witness[2] forever that WORK and DO[3] all the words[4] of this Torah.

Chapter 30

1 And it shall come to pass, when all these things have come upon you, the **Blessing** and the curse, which I have set before you, and You shall call them to mind among all the nations, where YHWH Your POWER has driven you,

2 And shall return[5] to YHWH Your POWER, and shall obey his voice according to all that I command you this day, You and your children, with all your heart, and with all your soul;

3 That then YHWH Your

POWER will turn your captivity, and have compassion upon you, and will return and gather you from all the nations, where YHWH Your POWER has scattered you.[6]

4 If any of you be driven out to the outmost parts of shamayim, from even there will YHWH Your POWER gather you, and from there will He fetch you:

5 And YHWH Your POWER will bring you into the land which your ahvot (fathers) possessed, and You shall possess it; and He will do you good, and multiply you above your ahvot (fathers).

6 And YHWH Your POWER will circumcise your heart,[7] and the heart of your descendants, to love YHWH Your POWER with all your heart, and with all your soul, that You may live.

7 And YHWH Your POWER will put all these curses upon your

Footnotes

instructions for life. It shows each generation will have to preserve the Torah of YHWH.
[1] YHWH hides many things in the Torah some he will reveal to us that which we need and yearn for. Those things that belong to YHWH the hidden things are available to the Lewites since YHWH is their heritage hence they can tap into those things through YHWH
[2] The Hebrew word Ad is for a "witness" forever.
[3] Without obedience and doing the commandments Israelites will get no where. The Torah is not to put on the shelf but to do the working hence the term Le'asot. Not all the children of Israel will be a witness but only those that obey the Torah.
[4] Not a single word of the Torah is to be suppressed or annulled, the words of the Torah are immensely powerful and must be understood to be performed, which will give powerful results to the true Israelites.
[5] Hebrews must return to Torah. Turning away from sin and turning back to Torah. If we do not then there is no restoration.

[6] This shows a prophecy that the ten tribes the Black/Brown Hebrews will make teshuvah (Repentance back to Torah keeping) and be one day gathered back to the land. Of course, not all will be gathered but only the remnant. However all will be raised who died, please see our footnotes in Ezekiel 37.
[7] It is YHWH who gives the new birth with what we term born from above. It is not new but an ancient term. While many today make it sound like a new buzzword, it is not new at all. When you walk with YHWH, you must come to Him with a full repentant heart to turn to Torah and He will circumcise it and give you the new birth. That happens via the Keter (crown), the King, passing through the Middle-Pillar, to the feet, the Malchut, reaching into the (Kingdom). This is the path even Balaam's donkey saw where the Malakh YHWH was standing on the narrow path (Numbers 22:24), the middle path, not to the right or to the left.

enemies, and on them that hate you, who persecuted you.

8 And You shall return and obey the voice of YHWH, and do all his commandments which I command you this day.

9 And YHWH Your POWER will make you plenteous in every work of your hand, in the fruit of your body, and in the fruit of your cattle, and in the fruit of your land, for good: for YHWH will again rejoice over you for good, as He rejoiced over your ahvot (fathers):

10 If You shall carefully listen to the voice of YHWH Your POWER, to guard His commandments and his statutes which are written in this scroll of the Torah, and if You Return[1] to YHWH Your POWER with all your heart, and with all your soul.

11 For this commandment which I command you this day, it is not hidden from you, neither is it far off.[2]

12 It is not in the shamayim, that You should say, Who shall go up for us to the shamayim, and bring it to us, that we may hear it, and do it?[3]

13 Neither is it beyond the sea, that You should say, Who shall go over the sea for us, and bring it to us, that we may hear it, and do it?

14 But the word[4] is very near to you, in your mouth, and in your heart, that You may do it.

15 See, I have set before you this day life[5] and good, and death and evil;

16 In that I command you this day to love YHWH Your POWER, to walk in His Halaka, and to guard His halachot and his statutes and his judgments, that You may live and multiply: and YHWH Your POWER shall **Bless** you in the land where You go to possess it.

17 But if your heart turn away, so that You will not hear, but shall be drawn away, and pay homage to other powers, and serve them;

18 I declare to you this day, that you shall surely perish, and that you shall not prolong your days upon the land, where You pass over the Yardan (Jordan) to go to possess it.

19 I call the shamayim[6] and the earth to record this day against you, that I have set before you life[7] and death[8], **Blessing** and curse: therefore choose **LIFE**,[9]

Footnotes
[4] The Torah
[5] Idiomatic expression, 'life,' for Torah keeping.
[6] Idiomatic expression for upper Jerusalem and lower Jerusalem and the most Holy Place in the Hekel as witness against the people of YHWH.
[7] Torah Keeping
[8] Lawlessness is not keeping Torah and will lead to early physical death for many and lack of Increases. However for a fuller explanation see our HTHS Bible edition Ezekiel 37.
[9] The word 'life' here means to choose to be regenerated by YHWH who wants to give it
Continued in next section

Footnotes
[1] Full obedience to the Torah as best as possible.
[2] The idea that many Christians are taught that the Torah is hard to keep or impossible is an error they live with to this day.
[3] The Torah is easy and not hard to keep if one is diligent.

that both You and your seed may live:

20 That You may love YHWH Your POWER, and that You may obey his voice, and that You may cling to him: for He is your life,[1] and the length of your days: that You may dwell in the land which YHWH swore to your ahvot (fathers), to Abraham, to Ytshak, and to Yakov, to give them.

Torah Parsha 52 Vayelech, Devrim 31:1-31:30
Haftarah: Hoshea 14:1-9, Yoel 2:11-27

Chapter 31

1 And Mosheh (Musa) went and spoke these words to all Israel.

2 And he said to them, I am a hundred and twenty years old this day; I can no more go out and come in: also YHWH has said to me, You shall not go over this Yardan (Jordan).

3 YHWH Your POWER, He will go over before you, and he will destroy these nations from before you, and You shall possess them: and Yahushua, he shall go over before you, as YHWH has said.

4 And YHWH shall do to them as he did to Sikhon and to Og, Kings of the Amoree, and to the land of them, whom he destroyed.

5 And YHWH shall give them up before your face, that you may do to them according to all the commandments which I have commanded you.

6 Be strong and of a good courage, fear not, nor be afraid of them: for YHWH Your POWER, He it is that will go with you; He will not fail you, nor forsake you.

7 And Mosheh (Musa) called to Yahushua, and said to him in the sight of all Israel, Be strong and of a good courage: for You must go with this people to the land which YHWH has sworn to their ahvot (fathers) to give them; and You shall cause them to inherit it.

8 And YHWH, He it is that will go before you; He will be with you, He will not fail you, neither forsake you: fear not, neither be dismayed.

9 And Mosheh (Musa) wrote this Torah, and gave it to the kohenim the sons of Levi, which carried the ark of the Covenant of YHWH, and to all the elders of Israel.

10 And Mosheh (Musa) commanded them, saying, At the end of every seven years,[2] in the appointed time of the year of suspension of labour, in khag ha Sukkot (The appointed celebration time of Tabernacles),

11 When all Israel is come to appear before YHWH Your POWER in the place which He shall choose,[3] You shall read this Torah before all Israel in their hearing.

which many incorrectly term 'born again', it should be born from above.

[1] Here YHWH clarified that he is life, meaning we must believe in His Torah or suffer the consequences.

Footnotes

[2] The Shimita when it was commanded to leave the ground fallow for one year each seven years.

[3] The Temple in Jerusalem.

12 Gather the people together, men, and women, and children, and the foreigner that are within your gates, that they may hear, and that they may learn, and fear YHWH Your POWER, and Guard to do all the words of this Torah:[1]

13 And that their children, which have not known anything, may hear, and learn to fear YHWH Your POWER, as long as you live in the land where you go over the Yardan (Jordan) to possess it.

14 And YHWH said to Mosheh (Musa), Behold, your days approach that You must die: call Yahushua, and present yourselves in the Tent of the appointed times, that I may give him a charge. And Mosheh (Musa) and Yahushua went, and presented themselves in the Tent of the appointed times.

15 And YHWH appeared in the Tent in a pillar of a cloud: and the pillar of the cloud stood over the door of the Tent.

16 And YHWH said to Mosheh (Musa), Behold, You shall sleep with your ahvot (fathers); and this people will rise up, and go whoring after the powers of the strangers of the land, where they go to be among them, and will forsake me, and break My Covenant which I have made with them.

17 Then my anger shall be kindled against them in that day, and I will forsake them, and I will hide my face from them, and they shall be devoured, and many evils and troubles shall befall them; so that they will say in that day, Are not these evils come upon us, because our POWER is not among us?

18 And I will surely hide my face in that day for all the evils which they shall have worked, in that they are turned to other powers.

19 Now therefore you write this song for you, and teach it the children of Israel: put it in their mouths, that this song may be a true report for me against the children of Israel.

20 For when I shall have brought them into the land which I swore to their ahvot (fathers), that flows with milk and honey; and they shall have eaten and filled themselves, and become fat; then will they turn to other powers, and serve them, and provoke me, and break My Covenant.

21 And it shall come to pass, when many evils and troubles are befallen them, that this song shall testify against them as a witness; for it shall not be forgotten out of the mouths of their descendants: for I know their imagination which they go about, even now, before I have brought them into the land which I swore.

22 Mosheh (Musa) therefore wrote this song the same day, and taught it the children of Israel.

23 And he gave Yahushua the son of Nun a charge, and said, Be strong and of a good courage:

Footnotes
[1] There is only <u>one</u> law (Torah) for ALL of the people. And there is no such thing as the Torah for Hebrew Israel and a different Torah for the rest of the gentile/Efrayim world.

for You shall bring the children of Israel into the land which I swore to them: and I will be with you.

24 And it came to pass, when Mosheh (Musa) had made an end of writing the words of this Torah in a scroll, until they were finished,

25 That Mosheh (Musa) commanded the Lewim, which carried the ark of the Covenant of YHWH, saying,

26 Take this scroll of the Torah, and put it in the side of the ark of the Covenant of YHWH Your POWER, that it may be there for a witness against you.

27 For I know your rebellion, and your stubbornness: behold, while I am yet alive with you this day, you have been rebellious against YHWH; and how much more after my death?

28 Gather to me all the elders of your tribes, and your officers, that I may speak these words in their ears, and call shamayim and earth to record against them.

29 For I know that after my death you will utterly corrupt yourselves, and turn aside from the way which I have commanded you; and evil will befall you in the latter days; because you will do evil in the sight of YHWH, to provoke Him to anger through the work of your hands.

30 And Mosheh (Musa) spoke in the ears of all the congregation of Israel the words of this song, until they were ended.

Torah Parsha 53 Ha'azinu, Devrim 32:1-52

Haftarah: Shemuel Bet 22:1-22:51

Chapter 32

1 Give ear, O you shamayim, and I will speak; and hear, O earth, the words of my mouth.

2 My doctrine shall drop as the rain, my speech shall drip as the dew, as the small rain upon the tender herb, and as the showers upon the grass:

3 Because I will publish the name of YHWH: ascribe you greatness to our Supreme One.

4 He is the Rock, His work is complete: for all His Halachot (commandments) are Righteous; El (The Power) of Truth and without iniquity, just and right is He.

5 They have corrupted themselves, their spot is not the spot of his children: they are a perverse and crooked generation.

[1]

6 Is this how you pay YHWH, O foolish and unwise people? Is not He your father that has bought you? Has He not made you, and established you?

7 Remember the days of old,

Footnotes
[1] The beginning letter of the Torah that was raised was the 'Bet,' meaning to build the House of YHWH or YHWH building His house. The letter here represents the glory of YHWH as it is the letter Heh, which is not only for the Ruakh of YHWH, which is both the mother (Cochmah) that came from the Father but also the Heh reveals to us the glory of YHWH and His breath or life giving force. One day it will shine over Israel when the whole world at the End of Days will go to Israel to pay homage to the great King of Kings.

consider the years of many generations: ask your father, and He will show you; your elders, and they will tell you.

8 When the most High divided to the nations their inheritance, when he separated the sons of Ahdahm, He set the bounds of the people according to the number of the sons of Israel.[1]

9 For YHWH's portion is His people; Yakov is the Lot of his inheritance.

10 He found him in a wilderness land, and in the waste howling wilderness; he led him about, He instructed him, He continually guarded him as the pupil of His eye.

11 As an eagle stirs up her nest, flutters over her young, spreads abroad her wings, takes them, and bears them on her wings:

12 So YHWH alone did lead him, and there was no strange el (power) with him.

13 He made him ride on the high places of the earth, that he might eat the **Increase** of the fields; and he made him to suck honey out of the rock, and oil out of the flinty rock;

14 Butter from the herd, and milk of sheep, with fat of lambs, and rams of the breed of Bashan, and goats, with the fat, kernels of wheat; and You did drink the pure wine of the grapes.

15 But Yeshurun waxed fat, and kicked: You are waxen fat, You are grown thick, You are covered with fatness; and then he forsook Elohim who made him, the Rock of his salvation with contempt.

16 They provoked Him to jealousy with strange powers, with Ritual Defilement they provoked Him to anger.

17 They sacrificed to demons, not to powers; to powers whom they knew not, to new powers that came newly up, whom your ahvot (fathers) feared not.

18 Of the Rock that gave you birth, You are unmindful, and have forgotten El (The Power) that formed you.

19 And when YHWH saw it, He abhorred them, because of the provoking of his sons, and of his daughters.

20 And he said, I will hide my face from them, I will see what their end shall be: for they are a very perverse generation, children in whom there is no faith.

21 They have moved me to jealousy with el (power); they have enraged me to anger with their futilities:[2] and I will move them to jealousy with those which are not a people; I will provoke them to anger with a nation that is slow to learn.

22 For a fire is kindled in my anger, and shall burn to the lowest She'ol,[3] and shall consume the earth with her **Increase**, and set on fire the foundations of the mountains.

23 I will **Increase** their disasters; I will spend mine

Footnotes

[1] All other texts have the wording "according to the sons of Elohim".

[2] Referring to false elohim.

[3] Lowest parts of hell where rebellious malakhim are kept in chains.

arrows upon them.

24 They shall be burnt with hunger, and devoured with burning heat, and with bitter destruction: I will also send wild animals upon them, with the poison of serpents of the dust.

25 The sword outside, and terror within, shall destroy both the young man and the virgin, the suckling also with the man of gray hairs.

26 I said, I would scatter them into corners, I would make the remembrance of them to cease from among men:

27 Was it not that I considered the taunt of their enemies, lest their adversaries misunderstand, and lest they should say, Our hand is high, and YHWH has not done all this.

28 For they are a nation void of counsel, neither is there any understanding in them.

29 O that they were wise, that they understood this, that they would consider their latter end!

30 How should one chase a thousand, and two put ten thousand to flight, except their Rock had sold[1] them, and YHWH had shut them up?

31 For their rock is not as our Rock, even our enemies themselves being judges.

32 For their vine is of the vine[2]

of Sedom, and of the fields of Amorah (Gomorrah): their grapes are grapes of gall, their clusters are bitter:

33 Their wine is the poison of dragons, and the cruel venom of asps.

34 Is not this laid up in store with me, and sealed up among my treasures?

35 To me belongs vengeance, and recompense; their feet shall slide in due time: for the day of their calamity is at hand, and the things that shall come upon them make haste.

36 For YHWH shall judge His people, and is grieved for His servants, when he sees that their power is gone, and there is no one left, whether confined or set free.

37 And he shall say, Where are their powers, their rock in whom they trusted,

38 Which did eat the fat of their sacrifices, and drank the wine of their drink offerings? Let them rise up and help you, and be your protection.

39 See now that I, even I, am He, and there is no Elohim with me: I kill, and I make alive; I wound, and I heal: neither is there any that can rescue out of My hand.

40 For I lift up my hand to

Footnotes

[1] The comparison is of the End-Times battle that Israel will fight with Radical Islam where Israel will literally be outnumbered by the Muslim nations of the world. The only difference is YHWH has not sold them out!

[2] The residents of Sodom and Gomorrah were rich but became complacent and did not care for the poor or needy, they lived in Continued in next section

lawlessness. The analogy here is to the Muslim nations who are very rich with their oil but in their richness they do not care for the poor and lawlessness abides in their nations. Just as Sodom and Gomorrah were destroyed by fire and brimstone YHWH will destroy the oil rich nations of the Gulf and they will also burn with smoke.

shamayim, and say, I live forever.

41 If I sharpen my glittering sword, and my hand will take hold on judgment; I will render vengeance to my enemies, and will reward them that hate me.

42 I will make my arrows drunk with blood, and my sword shall devour flesh; and that with the blood of the slain and of the captives, from the beginning of revenges upon the enemy.

43 Be glad, O shamayim, with him, and let all the heavenly sons pay homage to him. Be glad, O goyim (nations), with his people, and let all the malakhim of Elohim prevail for him. For he will avenge the blood of his sons and take revenge and repay the enemies with a sentence, and he will repay those who hate, and the Adoni (Lord: Master) shall cleanse the land of his people.[1]

44 And Mosheh (Musa) came and spoke all the words of this song in the ears of the people, he, and Hoshea (Joshua) the son of Nun.

45 And Mosheh (Musa) made an end of speaking all these words to all Israel:

46 And he said to them, Set your hearts to all the words which I testify among you this day, which you shall command your children to Guard to do, all the words of this Torah.

47 For it is not a worthless word for you; because it is your life:[2] and by this word you shall prolong your days in the land, where you go over the Yardan (Jordan) to possess it.

48 And YHWH spoke to Mosheh (Musa) the very same day, saying,

49 Get up into this mountain Abarim, to Mount Nebo, which is in the land of Moav, that is over against Yerikho; and behold the land of Kanan, which I give to the children of Israel for a possession:

50 And die in the Mount where You go up, and be gathered to your people; as Aharon your brother died in Mount Hor, and was gathered to his people:

51 Because you trespassed against me among the children of Israel at the mayim of Meribah-Kadesh, in the wilderness of Zin; because you sanctified me not in the midst of the children of Israel.

52 Yet You shall see the land before you; but You shall not go there to the land which I give the children of Israel.

Torah Parsha 54 Vezot Ha'Brachu, Devrim 33:1-34:12
Haftarah: Yahushua 1:1-18

Chapter 33
1 And this is the **Blessing**, wherewith Mosheh (Musa) the

Footnotes
[1] The correct reading from the Septuagint. Israel will get a cleansing in the future when the fake European chosen people are removed and the real ones brought in. These are the haters of YHWH because they deliberately mistranslated his texts, omitted important details and called themselves chosen. If you remove his words he will remove You be warned.

Footnotes
[2] Keeping Torah is life, meaning eternal life and should be joyous.

man of Elohim **Blessed** the children of Israel before his death.

2 And he said, YHWH came from Sinai, and rose up from Seir to them; he shined forth from Mount Paran, and he came with ten thousands of his Holy ones: from his right hand[1] went a royal decree for them.[2]

3 Yes, he loved the people; all his Holy kedoshim (saints) are in your hand: and they sat down at your feet; everyone shall receive of your words.[3]

4 Mosheh (Musa) commanded us a Torah, even the inheritance of the congregation of Yakov.

5 And he was King in Yeshurun, when the heads of the people and the tribes of Israel were gathered together.

6 Let Reuven live, and not die; and let not his men be few.[4]

7 And this is the **Blessing** of Yahudah: and he said, Hear, YHWH, the voice of Yahudah,[5]

and bring him to his people: let his hands be sufficient for him; and You be a help against his enemies.

8 And of Levi he said, Let your Thummim and your Urim be with your favoured one, whom You did prove at Massah, and with whom You did strive at the mayim of Meribah;[6]

9 Who said to his father and to his mother, I have not seen him; neither did he acknowledge his brethren, nor knew his own children: for they have observed your word, and kept your Covenant.

10 They shall teach Yakov your judgments, and Israel your Torah: they shall put incense before you, and whole burnt sacrifice upon your altar.[7]

11 Bless YHWH, his might, and accept the work of his hands: smite through the loins of them that rise against him, and of them that hate him, that they rise not again.

12 And of Benyamin he said, The beloved of YHWH shall dwell in safety by him; and YHWH shall cover him all the day long, and he shall dwell between his chest.

13 And of Yosef he said, **Blessed** of YHWH be his land, for the precious things of shamayim, for the dew, and for

Footnotes

[1] He came from Mount Paran an area in Arabia with Judgment, hence why the right hand of YHWH is mentioned.

[2] The Right hand here is the Master Yahushua, the area Paran you should read Northern Arabia and where YHWH will use the Islamic fighters to come out to destroy many areas of the world, its written and none can change it. For Mount Paran read the Kingdom of Islam. Let those who have ears understand.

[3] Sat down at His feet to learn Torah.

[4] Reuben to help Judah indicated in the next verse.

[5] Judah's voice to be preeminent before the others, YHWH will hear his voice first when in distress as YHWH did when the Kings of Israel were in trouble and from the tribe of Continued in next section

Judah they were heard by the Holy One of Israel.

[6] The tribe of Levi did not complain like the rest at Meribah.

[7] The tribe of Levi.

the deep that couches beneath,[1]

14 And for the precious fruits brought forth by the sun, and for the precious things put forth by the moon,

15 And for the chief things of the ancient mountains, and for the precious things of the lasting hills,

16 And for the precious things of the earth and fullness there, and for the good will of him that dwelt in the bush: let the **Increase** come upon the head of Yosef, and upon the top of the head of him that was separated from his brethren.

17 His glory is like the Bekhor (firstborn) of his bullock, and his horns are like the horns of wild ox: with them he shall push the people together to the ends of the earth: and they are the ten thousands of Efrayim, and they are the thousands of Manasheh.[2]

18 And of Zevulun he said, Rejoice, Zevulun, in your going out; and, Yskhar (Issachar), in your tents.

19 They shall call the people to the mountain; there they shall offer sacrifices of Righteousness: for they shall suck of the abundance of the seas, and of treasures hid in the sand.

20 And of Gawd he said, **Blessed** be he that enlarges Gawd: who dwells as a lioness,

and tears the arm with the crown of the head.

21 And he has selected the best portion for himself,[3] because there, in a portion of the lawgiver, was he seated; and he came with the leaders of the people,[4] he did the Righteousness of YHWH, and his judgments with Israel.[5]

22 And of Dan he said, Dan is a lion's whelp: he shall leap from Bashan.

23 And of Naphtali he said, O Naphtali, satisfied with favour, and full with the **Blessing** of YHWH: You possess the west and the south.

24 And of Asher he said, Let Asher be **Blessed** with children; let him be acceptable to his brethren, and let him dip his foot in oil. [6]

25 Your sandals shall be iron and bronze; and as your days, so shall your strength be.[7]

26 There is none like to the El (Power) of Yeshurun, who rides

Footnotes

[1] Already realised oil resources for Yosef in the scattered ten tribes who ended up in different parts of the world.

[2] These are the ten tribes that literally will become billions and the fullness of the gentiles. This is the prophecy given to Yosef by his father Jacob in Beresheeth (Genesis) 48:19.

Footnotes

[3] This was partially fulfilled in Numbers 32:1 when Gawd and Reuben took the fertile parts of Yatzer and Gilead for themselves because they had a lot of cattle.

[4] They came to Moses and asked to stay on the east side of the Jordan and to inherit that portion of the land which they saw fit. The lawgiver is Moses not the tribe of Gawd.

[5] They came to fight for Israel and then went back to their inherited portions of the land.

[6] Asher is an African nation with oil.

[7] They will fight many nations and bring judgment to them from YHWH. They have already gone to war with Iraq twice and ruled other nations before, this is all part of the prophecy. They will fight another major war with Iran together and then will take on many Muslims nations in war. See Islam, peace or Beast www.forever-israel.com.

upon the shamayim in your help, and in his excellency on the sky.

27 The eternal Elohim is your refuge, and underneath are the everlasting arms: and he shall thrust out the enemy from before you; and shall say, Destroy them.

28 Israel then shall dwell in safety alone: the fountain of Yakov shall be upon a land of wheat and wine; also his shamayim shall drop down dew.

אשריך ישראל[1]

29 Happy are You, O Israel: who is like to you, O people rescued by YHWH, the shield of your help, and who is the sword of your excellency! And your enemies shall be found liars to you; and You shall tread upon their high places.

Chapter 34

1 And Mosheh (Musa) went up from the plains of Moav to the mountain of Nebo, to the top of Pisgah, that is over against Yerikho. And YHWH showed him all the land of Gil'ad, to Dan,

2 And all Naphtali, and the land of Efrayim, and Manasheh, and all the land of Yahudah, to the utmost sea,

3 And the south and the plain of the valley of Yerikho, the city of palm etzim (tree), to Tzoar.

4 And YHWH said to him, This is the land which I swore to Abraham, to Ytshak, and to Yakov, saying, I will give it to your seed: I have caused you to see it with your eyes, but You shall not go over there.

5 So Mosheh (Musa) the servant of YHWH died there in the land of Moav, according to the word of YHWH.

6 And he buried him in a valley in the land of Moav, over against Beth-peor: but no man knows of his sepulcher to this day.

7 And Mosheh (Musa) was a hundred and twenty years old when he died[2] his eye was not dim, nor his natural force abated.

8 And the children of Israel wept for Mosheh (Musa) in the plains of Moav thirty days[3] so the days of weeping and mourning for Mosheh (Musa) were ended.

9 And Yahushua the son of Nun was full of the Ruakh (Spirit) of wisdom; for Mosheh (Musa) had laid his hands upon him:[4] and the children of Israel listened to him, and did as YHWH commanded Mosheh (Musa).

10 And there arose not a prophet since in Israel like to Mosheh (Musa), whom YHWH knew face to face,

11 In all the signs and the wonders, which YHWH sent him

Footnotes
[1] The Alef for the word Ashrekha Israel is enlarged. In ancient Hebrew this is the picture of a Lion revealing End of Days for Israel will be like a lion amongst the nations and no longer under slavery in the nations (Mic 5:8).

[2] Moses died on the same day he was born which is Adar 7 and this is the day that Aman miscalculated to kill the Hebrew people in the month of Adar.
[3] Hebrew custom is to mourn for thirty days. This is the same mentioned for Aharon his brother in Numbers 20:29.
[4] The laying on of hands is an ancient Israelite practice not a new Christian one as many think.

to do in the land of Mitzrayim
(Egypt) to Pharaoh, and to all his
servants, and to all his land,

12 And in all that mighty hand,
and in all the great terror which
Mosheh (Musa) showed in the
sight of all Israel (Israel). [1] ת

CHAZAK CHAZAK
VENITCHAZEK

**Be strong, Be strong and
may we be strengthened!**

**Israel will rise again
Hallelu'Yah**

**Rise Up Israel repent and
return back to the Torah for the
Master YHWH/Yahushua is
with you and restoring you
back to Him**

Footnotes
[1] When we take the first character of the
word Beresheeth in the book of Genesis and
the last character from the book of
Deuteronomy, which is the letter L from the
word Israel we arrive at the Hebrew word
Lev looking backwards. which means the
heart. The Torah is the HEART of Elohim.

Covenants of Israel

Table of Covenants

7. A Covenant with the animals also in the millennium in Israel Hosea 2:18
6.   Covenant of peace with Israel yet future in the millennium   Ezek 37:27
5. The Davidic   Covenant Second Samuel 7:10-16
4.   New Covenant, Jeremiah 31:31, Luke 22.20
3. The Sinaitic   Covenant Exodus 24:7
2. The Abrahamic Covenant (Circumcision) Genesis 12:3,7; 15:4; 17:7
1. The Noahic Covenant Genesis 9:1, 11-13

Now as we see the Covenants seem to be upside down but actually they are stacked on top of each other just as YHWH decided. Each Covenant is tightly supported by the one beneath it. There is no concept of removing one to add another. Any theology that teaches us that we are to do so is untrue.

Maps

Ancient map of the Middle-East, there was no Red Sea before the Flood of Noakh so Ysra'el was correctly in North-East Africa and still is.

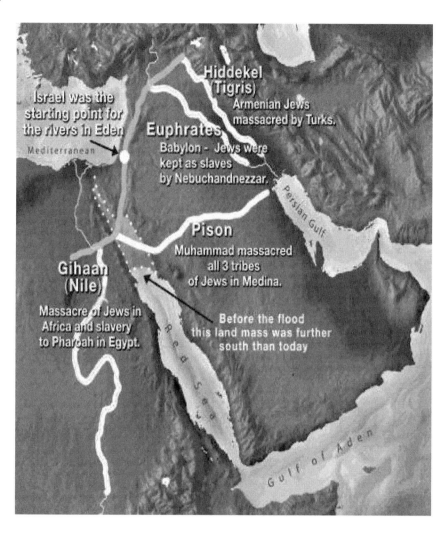

Israel was the starting point for the rivers in Eden

Hiddekel (Tigris)
Armenian Jews massacred by Turks.

Euphrates
Babylon - Jews were kept as slaves by Nebuchandnezzar.

Pison
Muhammad massacred all 3 tribes of Jews in Medina.

Gihaan (Nile)
Massacre of Jews in Africa and slavery to Pharoah in Egypt.

Before the flood this land mass was further south than today

Mediterranean

Persian Gulf

Red Sea

Gulf of Aden

Present Map of Middle-East

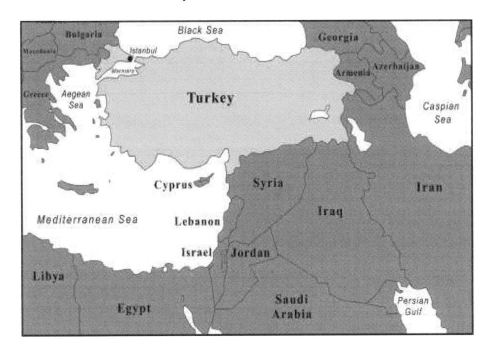

Egyptian Empire

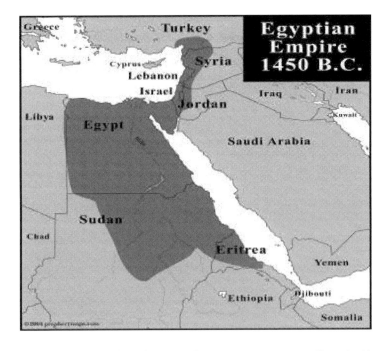

Birthplace of Avraham that has an important connection to the End of Days and the Radical Islamic beast and the Anti-Messiah. He was not born in Iraq as often thought but in South-Eastern Turkey.

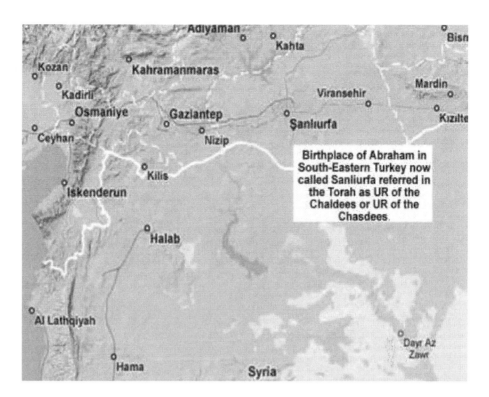

Birthplace of Abraham in South-Eastern Turkey now called Sanliurfa referred in the Torah as UR of the Chaldees or UR of the Chasdees.

Yahoshua 24:3 And I took your father Avraham from the other side of the river,[1] and led him throughout all the land of Kanan, and multiplied his seed, and gave him Ytshak (Isaac).

The word Hebrew/Ivri was derived out of the civilsation that one time ruled in what is today known as India/Pakistan. The word Harappa from where we get Hipiru or Abrahu, Hebrew. This is an Indo/Hebrew dialect.

The Indus Valley Civilization (also known as the **Harappan** culture) has its earliest roots in cultures such as that of Mehrgarh, approximately 6000 BCE. The two greatest cities, Mohenjo-daro and **Harappa**, emerged circa 2600 BCE along the Indus River valley in Punjab and Sindh.

Footnotes
1 Clear proof Avraham came from Eastern Turkey, his ancestors came from Beyond from India/Pakistan region.

Map of Islamic nations and the coming war – Please see World War III series – Unmasking the End times Beast for further illumination at www.Forever-Israel.com.

Kenya, Ethiopia and Nigeria are engulfed in radicalism but are not Islamic nations but will play important parts in the End of Days. The Northern parts of Ethiopia will get taken over by Islamists in the future. If Ethiopia was to fall completely to Islam then so will Kenya but prophetically speaking neither nation is marked for a fall in the End of Days.

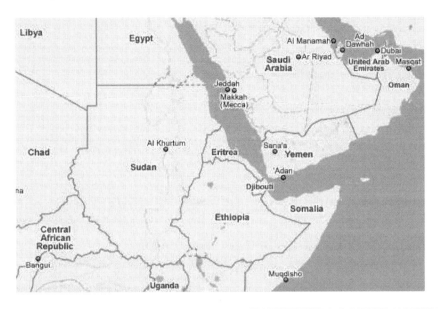

Formation of the Tribes around the Tent

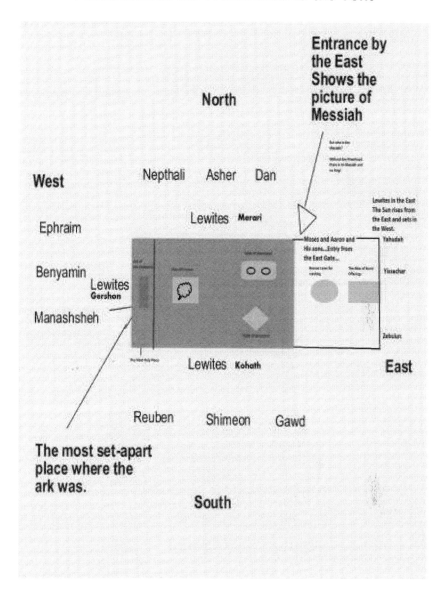

North

Entrance by the East Shows the picture of Messiah

West

Nepthali   Asher   Dan

Lewites   Merari

Ephraim

Benyamin

Lewites Gershon

Manashsheh

Lewites   Kohath

East

Reuben   Shimeon   Gawd

The most set-apart place where the ark was.

South

503

The Ancient and Modern Hebrew Alphabet

Letter Name	Ancient Hebrew Pictograph	Ancient meaning	Printed Hebrew	Numeric Value
Alef		A man	א	1
Bet		A House	בּ	2
Vet (Soft sound)			ב	
Gimmel		Hand/Arm	ג	3
Dalet		Mouth	ד	4
Heh		Breath/No strils	ה	5
Wah		Feather	ו	6
Zayin		Knife	ז	7
Khet		Bosom/conceal/Darkness/Black	ח	8
Tet		Spade	ט	9
Yud		Eye	י	10
Kaf		Sling	פ	
Kaf			כ	20
Khaf Sofit			ך	
Lamed		Lion	ל	30
Mem		Water	מ	40
Mem Sofit			ם	
Nun		Cup	נ	

Nun Sofit			ן	50
Samech	🌙	Moon	ס	60
Ayin		Legs/action	ע	70
Pey		Mouth/head	פ	80
Feh			פ	80
Feh Sofit			ף	
Tzadie		Two horned beast	צ	90
Tzadie Sofit			ץ	90
Kuf		Oar	ק	100
Resh		Bird	ר	200
Shin		Crown/Sun	שׁ	300
Sin			שׂ	
Tav		Tree	ת	400

Modern Hebrew Vowels

Cholam Shva Segol Tsere Patach Kamatz

Chataf Chataf Chataf
Segol Patach Kamatz Shuruk Kubbutz Chirik

Hebrew Glossary

YHWH (YHWH)	The set-apart name of Elohim
Alef	Alpha or equivalent of A
Ahdahm Kadmon	Primordial man
Ahvot (fathers)	Fathers or forefathers
Abbah, or ABBAH in modern Hebrew	Father
Beresheeth	Genesis
Beyth	House
Binah	Understanding
Batiym (houses)	Houses
Bikkurim	Firstfruit
WeDavar	Numbers
Khag ha Matzot	The Celebration of Unleavened Bread
Chametz	Leavened
Cochmah	Wisdom
Devrim	Deuteronomy
Derech	Way or the way (Truth, commandments of Torah
Dalet	Door (Modern Hebrew)
Divre Yamim	Ascribed to the book of Chronicles
Etz	Tree
Etzim	Trees
Eretz	Land, Country, Province, whole world
Ein Sof or Ain Sof	The Master of the

	Universe (YHWH)
Elohim	Powers YHWH or can be applied to false Elohim in the singular or plural such as polytheism
El	Mighty one
Goy or Goyim	Gentile/Gentiles/Heathens a non Israelite
Gevurot/Gevurah	Strength
Halaka	Commandments, procedures set by YHWH
ha'Ahdahm	Used for Adam and the humanity
Hod	Majesty, beauty
Keter	Crown
Kohen/Kohenim	Priest/priests
Lakhem Panayim	Bread of His faces
Lakhem (bread)	Bread
Ma'aseh Shalekhim	Acts of the Emissaries
Mattityahu	Matthew
Melek	King
Melekhim I and II	One and two Sovereigns
Mikvah	Ritual Immersion
Mayim	Water or waters
Melo Ha Goyim	Multitude of Gentile nations
Middle-Pillar	Term for the sefirotic tree
Mishpakha	Family
Mishpakhot	Families
Netzach	Victory
Pesach	Passover
Qahal or Qahalim	Assembly or Assemblies
Rosh	Head or summit of a Mount

Shamayim	The lofties or shamayim the place many call heaven.
Shemoth	Exodus
Shavuot	Celebration of Pentecost
Tavilah/Tavilotym	Immersion or ritual washing
Tifereth	Esteem
Tzadik	Upright, Right-ruling, Redeemed
Toroh/Torot	Instructions, teachings
Tov	Good
We'Yikra	Leviticus
Yahukhannan	John
Ytshak	Isaac
Yshmael	Ishmael
Zera	Seed – Used in Torah for Descendants or offspring or just a seed to sow in a field. It is also used for a man or male member in as zara.

TORAH PARASHOT (Torah Portions)

Hebrew Title	English	Readings (Torah/Haftorah)
Torah Parsha 1 **Beresheeth**	In the Beginning	Beresheeth 1:1-6:8, Yeshayahu 42:5-43:21
Torah Parsha 2 **Noakh**	Concealed Pouring	Beresheeth 6:9-11:32, Yeshayahu 54:1-55:5
Torah Parsha 3 **Lekh Lekha**	Get Yourself out	Beresheeth 12:1-17:27, Yeshayahu 40:27-41:16
Torah Parsha 4 **Va'eira**	And He Appeared	Beresheeth 18:1-22:24, Melekhim Bet 4:1-37
Torah Parsha 5 **Chayei Sarah**	Life of Sarah	Beresheeth 23:1-25:18, Melekhim Alef 1:1-31
Torah Parsha 6 **Toldot**	Generations	Beresheeth 25:19-28:9, Malaki 1:1-2:7
Torah Parsha 7 **VaYetze**	And He Went Out	Beresheeth 28:10-32:3, Hoshea 12:13-14:9
Torah Parsha 8 **WaYishlakh**	And He Sent	Beresheeth 32:4-36:43, Ovadiyah 1:1-21
Torah Parsha 9 **VaYeshev**	And He Settled	Beresheeth 37:1-40:23, Amos 2:6-3:8
Torah Parsha 10 **Miketz**	At the End Of	Beresheeth 41:1-44:17, Melekhim Alef 3:15-4:1
Torah Parsha 11 **VaYigash**	And He Drew Near	Beresheeth 44:18-47:27, Ykhezkiel 37:15-28
Torah Parsha 12 **VaYekhi**	And He Lived	Beresheeth 47:28-50:26, Melekhim Alef 2:1-12
Torah Parsha 13 **Shemot**	Names	Shemoth 1:1-6:1, Yeshayahu 27:6-28:13 & 29:22-23
Torah Parsha 14 **Wa'yera**	And I Appeared	Shemoth 6:2-9:35, Ykhezkiel 28:25-29:21
Torah Parsha 15 **Bo**	Enter / Go	Shemoth 10:1-13:16, Yirmeyahu 46:13-28
Torah Parsha 16 **B'shalakh**	When He Let Go	Shemoth 13:17-17:16, Shoftim 4:4-5:31
Torah Parsha 17 **Yithro**	Jethro	Shemoth 18:1-20:26, Yeshayahu 6:1-7:6 & 9:5-6

Torah Parsha 18 Mishpatim	Judgements	Shemoth 21:1-24:18, Yirmeyahu 33:25-26 & 34:8-22
Torah Parsha 19 Terumah	Offerings	Shemoth 25:1-27:19, Melekhim Alef 5:12-6:13
Torah Parsha 20 Tetzaveh	You Shall Command	Shemoth 27:20-30:10, Ykhezkiel 43:10-27
Torah Parsha 21 Ki Tisa	When You Elevate	Shemoth 30:11-34:35, Melekhim Alef 18:1-39
Torah Parsha 22 Wa' Yachel	And He Assembled	Shemoth 35:1-38:20, Melekhim Alef 7:40 – 7:50
Torah Parsha 23 Pekudei	Accounts Of	Shemoth 38:21-40:38, Melekhim Alef 7:51-8:21
Torah Parsha 24 We'Yikra	And He Called	We'Yikra 1:1-6:7, Yeshayahu 43:21-44:23
Torah Parsha 25 Tzav	Command	We'Yikra 6:8-8:36, Yirmeyahu 7:21-8:3 & 9:23-24
Torah Parsha 26 Shemeni	Eighth	We'Yikra 9:1-11:47, Shemuel Bet 6:1-7:17
Torah Parsha 27 Tazria	Leprosy	We'Yikra 12:1-13:59, Melekhim Bet 4:42-5:19
Torah Parsha 28 Metzora	Cleansing the Leper	We'Yikra 14:1-15:33, Melekhim Bet 7:3-20
Torah Parsha 29 Acharei Mot	After the Death	We'Yikra 16:1-18:30, Amos 9:7-15
Torah Parsha 30 Kedoshim	Set-apart Ones	We'Yikra 19:1-20:27, Ykhezkiel 22:1-16
Torah Parsha 31 Emor	Say	We'Yikra 21:1-24:23, Ykhezkiel 44:15-31
Torah Parsha 32 Behar	On the Mount	We'Yikra 25:1-26:2, Yirmeyahu 32:6-27
Torah Parsha 33 Bechukkotai	In My Statutes	We'Yikra 26:3-27:34, Yirmeyahu 16:19-17:14
Torah Parsha 34 Bemidbar	In Wilderness	WeDavar 1:1-4:20, Hoshea 1:10-2:20
Torah Parsha 35 Naso	Elevate	WeDavar 4:21-7:89, Shoftim 13:2-25
Torah Parsha 36	In Your	WeDavar 8:1-12:16,

Beha'alotcha	Going Up	Zechariah 2:10-4:7
Torah Parsha 37 Shelakh Lekha	Send For Yourself	WeDavar 13:1-15:41, Yehoshua 2:1-24
Torah Parsha 38 Korakh	Bald – no covering	WeDavar 16:1-18:32, Shemuel Alef 11:14-12:22
Torah Parsha 39 Chukat	Statutes	WeDavar 19:1-22:1, Shoftim 11:1-33
Torah Parsha 40 Balak	Balak	WeDavar 22:2-25:9, Micah 5:6-6:8
Torah Parsha 41 Pinchas	Mouth of a Serpent	WeDavar 25:10-29:40, Melekhim Alef 18:46-19:21
Torah Parsha 42 Matot	Tribes	WeDavar 30:1-32:42, Yirmeyahu 1:1-2:3
Torah Parsha 43 Massei	Stages	WeDavar 33:1-36:13, Yirmeyahu 2:4-28, 3:4 & 4:1-2
Torah Parsha 44 Devrim	Many words	Devrim 1:1-3:22, Yeshayahu 1:1-27
Torah Parsha 45 Wah'Etchanan	And I Pleaded	Devrim 3:23-7:11, Yeshayahu 40:1-26
Torah Parsha 46 Ekev	On the Heel Of	Devrim 7:12-11:25, Yeshayahu 49:14-51:3
Torah Parsha 47 Re'eh	See	Devrim 11:26-16:17, Yeshayahu 54:11-55:5
Torah Parsha 48 Shoftim	Judges	Devrim 16:18-21:9, Yeshayahu 51:12-52:12
Torah Parsha 49 Ki Tetse	When You Go Out	Devrim 21:10-25:19, Yeshayahu 52:13-54:10
Torah Parsha 50 Ki Tavo	When You Enter In	Devrim 26:1-29:9, Yeshayahu 60:1-22
Torah Parsha 51 Nitsavim	You are Standing	Devrim 29:10-30:20, Yeshayahu 61:10-63:9
Torah Parsha 52 Wa'Yelech	And He Went	Devrim 31:1-31:30, Hoshea 14:1-9, Yoel 2:11-27
Torah Parsha 53 Ha'azinu	Give Ear	Devrim 32:1-52, Shemuel Bet 22:1-22:51
Torah Parsha 54 Vezot	And They increased	Devrim 33:1-34:12, Yahoshua 1:1-18

Ha'Brachu		

YHWH's Festival Date

Kislev 25 – Tevet 3	**Feast of Dedication** Commonly Known as Chanukah
	A non-commanded festival – *not mandatory...*
Kislev 24	**Shabbat** Torah Parsha 9 Vayeshev (And He Settled)
(Shabbat & Feast of Dedication)	**& Feast of Dedication** Eve (Erev Chanukah) – *1 Candle*
	Torah: Beresheeth (Genesis) 37:1-40:23
	Haftarah: Amos (Amos) 2:6-3:8
Kislev 25	**Feast of Dedication** (Chanukah Day 1) *2 Candles*
	WeDavar (Numbers) 7:1-17
Kislev 26	**Feast of Dedication** (Chanukah Day 2) *3 Candles*
	WeDavar (Numbers) 7:18-23
Kislev 27	**Feast of Dedication** (Chanukah Day 3) *4 Candles*
	WeDavar (Numbers) 7:24-29
Kislev 28	**Feast of Dedication** (Chanukah Day 4) *5 Candles*
	WeDavar (Numbers) 7:30-35
Kislev 29	**Feast of Dedication** (Chanukah Day 5) *6 Candles*
	WeDavar (Numbers) 7:36-41
Tevet 1	**Feast of Dedication** (Chanukah Day 6) *7 Candles*
	WeDavar (Numbers) 7:42-47
Tevet 2	**Shabbat** Torah Parsha 10 Miqeitz

	(At The End Of)
(Shabbat & Chanukah)	Torah: Beresheeth (Genesis) 41:1-44:17 Haftarah: Melekhim Alef (1st Kings) 3:15-4:1 **And Feast of Dedication** (Chanukah Day 7) *8 Candles*
	Torah: WeDavar (Numbers) 7:48-53 Haftarah: Zechariyah (Zechariah) 2:14-4:7
Tevet 3	**Feast of Dedication** (Chanukah Day 8) WeDavar (Numbers) 7:54-8:4
Adar 14	**Purim (Feast of Lots)** – (Non-commanded festival – *not mandatory*)
	Shemoth (Exodus) 17:8-16
14 Nisan	**Erev Pesach** – Seder tonight
	Refer to *African-Israel Hebraic Siddur* – "Passover Aggadah
Nisan 15 through Nisan 21 [22, Nisan in the Diaspora]	**Passover (Pesach/Matzot)** **Unleavened Bread** (Khag HaMatzot)
Nisan 15	Torah: Shemoth (Exodus) 12:21-51
(Pesach/Matzot Day 1)	WeDavar (Numbers) 28:16-25
	Haftarah: Yahoshua (Joshua) 3:5-7, 5:2-6:1, 6:27
Nisan 17	Chol Hamoed **Passover** I
(Pesach/Matzot Day 3)	Torah: Shemoth (Exdous) 13:1-16
	WeDavar (Numbers) 28:19-25
Nisan 18	Chol Hamoed **Passover** II –
(Pesach/Matzot Day 4)	Torah: Shemoth (Exodos) 22:24-23:19
	WeDavar (Numbers) 28:19-25
Nisan 19	**Shabbat** - Chol Hamoed **Passover** III -
(Pesach/Matzot Day 5)	Note: Shir HaShirim (Song of Songs)

	is read before the Torah
	Torah: Shemoth (Exodus) 33:12-34:26
	WeDavar (Numbers) 28:19-25
	Haftarah: Y'chezki'el (Ezekiel) 36:37-37:14
Nisan 20	Chol Hamoed **Passover** IV
(Pesach/Matzot Day 6)	Torah: WeDavar (Numbers) 9:1-14, 28:19-25
Nisan 21	**Passover / Unleavened Bread** Day Seven (Ysrael)
(Pesach/Matzot Day 7)	Torah: Shemoth (Exodus) 13:17-15:26
	WeDavar (Numbers) 28:19-25
	Haftarah: Shemuel Bet (Second Samuel) 22:1-51
Next Day of weekly Sabbath after Unleavened Bread always on a Sunday	**First Fruits (Bikkurim)** – *Omer: Day 1*
(Yizkhor)	
	Torah : Devrim (Deuteronmy) 15:19-16:17 WeDavar (Numbers) 28: 19-25 Haftarah: Yeshayahu (Isaiah) 10:32-12:6
50 Days Omer Count	Some groups celebreate Pentecost on Sivan 6
	The Ingathering Harvest…(*End of Omer Count – 50 Days*)
Sunrise	**Shavuot (Pentecost)** 1st Day – Feast of Weeks
	Torah: Devrim (Deuteronomy) 15:19-16:17 WeDavar (Numbers) 28:26-31 Haftarah: Chabaqquk (Habakkuk) 3:1-19

	Shavuot (Pentecost) 2st Day (Reading if you are outside of Ysrael)
	Torah: Devrim (Deuteronomy) 15:19-16:17 WeDavar (Numbers) 28:26-31 Haftarah: Chabaqquk (Habakkuk) 3:1-19
	Destruction of the First Temple and Herod's Temple (*Optional for Hebrew Yisraelites*)
	Morning: Devrim (Deuteronomy) 4:25-40 Yirmeyahu (Jeremiah) 8:13-9:23 Afternoon: Shemoth (Exodus) 32:11-14, 34:1-10. Yeshayahu (Isaiah) 55:6-56:8
Tishrei 1 Sunrise	**Trumpets (Yom Teruah)** Rosh Hashanah Day I
	Torah: Beresheeth (Genesis) 21:1-34 WeDavar (Numbers) 29:1-6 Haftarah: Shemuel Alef (1st Samuel) 1:1-2:10
Tishrei 2 (Outside Ysrael)	**Trumpets (Yom Teruah)** Rosh Hashanah Day II
	Torah: Beresheet (Genesis) 22:1-24 WeDavar (Numbers) 29:1-6. Haftarah: Yirmeyahu (Jeremiah) 31:1-19
Tishrei 9 Evening	**Erev Yom Kippur (Atonement)**
	25 hour fast begins no food and water
Tishrei 10 Daytime	**Yom Kippur (Atonement) and Shabbat**
	Morning: We'Yikra (Leviticus) 16:1-34 WeDavar (Numbers) 29:7-11 Yeshayahu (Isaiah) 57:14-58:14 Afternoon: We'Yikra (Leviticus) 18:1-30 Yonah (Jonah) 1:1-4:11

	Mikah 7:18-20
Tishrei 15 – Tishrei 21	**Sukkoth (Feast of Tabernacles)**
	(No work Day 1 and Day 7)
Tishrei 15 Sunrise	**Sukkoth** Day 1
	Torah: We'Yikra (Leviticus) 22:26 – 23:44
	WeDavar (Numbers) 29:12-16 Haftarah: Zechariyah 14:1-21 Book of Koheleth (Ecclesiastes)
Tishrei 16	**Sukkoth** Day 2
	Melekhim Alef (1 Kings) 8:2-21
Tishrei 17	**Shabbat and** Chol Hamoed **Sukkoth** I (Sukkoth Day 3)
	Torah Parsha: Shemoth (Exodus) 33:12-34:26 We' Davar (Numbers) 29:17-22 Haftarah: Y'chezki'el (Ezekiel) 38:18-39:16
Tishrei 18	Chol Hamoed **Sukkoth** II (Sukkoth Day 4)
	WeDavar (Numbers) 29:20-28
Tishrei 19	Chol Hamoed **Sukkoth** III (Sukkoth Day 5)
	WeDavar (Numbers) 29:23-31
Tishrei 20	Chol Hamoed **Sukkoth** IV (Sukkoth Day 6)
	WeDavar (Numbers) 29:26-34
Tishrei 21	**Sukkoth** Day 7 – Hoshana Raba (Great Supplication)
	WeDavar (Numbers) 29:26-34
Tishrei 22	**Shemini Atzeret** – Solemn Assembly on the 8th
(Ysrael)	Day of Sukkot…also Simchat Torah

	in Israel
	Torah: Devrim (Deuteronomy) 14:22-16:17 WeDavar (Numbers) 29:35-30:1 Haftarah: Melekhim Alef (1st Kings) 8:54-9:1
Tishrei 23 (Outside Y'srael)	**(Simchat Torah** – Joy of the Torah) Torah: Devrim (Deuteronomy) 33:1-34:12 Beresheeth (Genesis) 1:1-2:3 WeDavar (Numbers) 29:35-30:1 Haftarah: Yahoshua (Joshua) 1:1-18
Kislev 25- Tevet 2	**Feast of Dedication** Commonly Known as Chanukah A non-commanded festival – *not mandatory…*
Kislev 24	**Feast of Dedication Eve** (*Erev* Chanukah) – *1 Candle*
Kislev 25	**Feast of Dedication** (Chanukah Day 1) *2 Candles*
	WeDavar (Numbers) 7:1-17
Kislev 26	**Feast of Dedication** (Chanukah Day 2) *3 Candles*
	WeDavar (Numbers) 7:18-23
Kislev 27	Torah: Beresheeth (Genesis) 41:1-44:17
Shabbat and Feast of Dedication	Haftarah: Melekhim Alef (1st Kings) 3:15-4:1
	And **Feast of Dedication** (Chanukah Day 3) *4 Candles*
	Torah: WeDavar (Numbers) 7:24-29
	Haftarah: Zechariyah (Zechariah) 2:14-4:7
Kislev 28	**Feast of Dedication** (Chanukah Day 4) *5 Candles*

	WeDavar (Numbers) 7:30-35	
Kislev 29	**Feast of Dedication** (Chanukah Day 5) *6 Candles*	
	WeDavar (Numbers) 7:36-41	
Kislev 30	**Feast of Dedication** (Chanukah Day 6) *7 Candles*	
	WeDavar (Numbers) 7:42-47	
Tevet 1	**Feast of Dedication** (Chanukah Day 7) *8 Candles*	
	WeDavar (Numbers) 7:48-53	
Tevet 2	**Feast of Dedication** (Chanukah Day 8)	
	WeDavar (Numbers) 7:54-8:4	

(1)   For an in-depth understanding of YHWH's Festivals, please refer to "The Feasts of YHWH the Elohim of Israel" by Rebbe Simon Altaf available for purchase at http://www.african-israel.com.

(2)   The "Passover Aggadah" is contained in the following siddur, African-Israel Hebraic Siddur by Rebbe Simon Altaf and is available for purchase on the following website http://www.african-israel.com/ or Amazon.

Annual Festivals

	Note: All festivals start Sunrise day and only Yom Kippur starts sunset as it a day and a half.	
	Torah days begin sunrise	
Holiday	**Dates**	**Description**
Rosh Hashana	**Tishri 1**	The Civil New Year
Civil New Year		
Yom Kippur	**Tishri 9 -10**	Day of Atonement, 25

Day of Atonement		hours fast beginning one hour before sunset finishes to the next sunset
Sukkot	**Tishri 15-21**	Feast of Tabernacles
Shemini Atzeret **Rabba Hoshana**	Tishri 22	Eighth Day of Assembly
Simchat Torah **Rejoicing of the Torah**	**Tishri 23-24**	2 Days of Celebrating the Torah in the Diaspora
Hanukah **Dedication**	**Kislev 25**	The Festival of Lights
Purim	**Adar 15-16**	Purim
Pesach **Passover**	**Nissan Aviv 14**	Passover - No work April 3 and April 10
Bikkurim (First-fruits)	Aviv 16	
Second Passover for missed people	**Iyar 14**	**Those who missed it due to taking part in a funeral**
Shavuot (Pentecost)	**Sivan 6 or Sivan 7**	Ysrael is born as a nation, chosen into a Covenant and the Torah is given
Tish'a B'Abbah Fast of commemoration	*ABBAH 9*	*The Ninth of Abbah, fast commemorating tragedies befallen the Hebrew nation including the two Temples being destroyed (Not mandatory fast)*

Date and historical timelines of the Scrolls

Book name	Approximate time	Author
The Torah **Beresheeth (Genesis)**	The Torah Written 1400 BC, time of Ahdahm and Khawa 6000 BC, history of Genesis – Ahdahm to Avraham alone spans 1948 years.	Moses and the last chapter of Devrim completed by Yehoshua the son of Nun
Shemoth (Exodus)	1445 BC	Moses
We'Yikra (Leviticus)	1440 BC	Moses
WeDavar (Numbers)	1444 BC	Moses
Devarim (Deuteronomy)	1400 BC	Moses, ending composed by Yahoshua Ben Nun

World War III – Unmasking the End-Times Beast
World War III – Salvation of the Jews
World War III – The Second Exodus, Ysrael's return journey home
Dear Muslim – Meet YHWH the God of Abraham
The Feasts of YHWH, the Elohim of Israel
What is Truth?
Yeshua or Isa?
Hidden Truths Hebraic Scrolls Complete with Commentary
(Complete 66 books)
Hidden Truths Hebraic Scrolls Tanak
Hidden Truths Hebraic Scrolls Brit Chadasha (NT)
Hidden Truths Hebraic Scrolls Torah
Beyth Yehoshua – The Son of Tzadok, The Son of Dawud
Islam, Peace or Beast
Sefer Yashar (The Book of Yashar the upright ones)
Seferim Khanokh (The Books of Enoch)
Yehoshua – The Black Messiah
Hebrew Wisdom, Kabbalah
Apocrypha and Pirket Avot (Ethics of the Fathers)
Forever-Israel Siddur, Daily living prayers
What Else Have They Kept From Us?
Patriarchal Marriage, Ysrael's right-ruling way of life, Methods and practice
Who Am I? A book for children to find their identity as Hebrews.
Hebrew Letters, The Power to have prayers answered
Hidden Truths Hebraic Scrolls Compendium Guide, Secrets of the Hebrew Scrolls, Commentaries for explaining Scriptural texts unleashed
Now That I know I am a Hebrew
Why The Objections That The New Testament Is Not Scripture And Jesus Not The Messiah
Religious Confusion, and the Everlasting Path to the Torah

Torah Appendix

HBYH Sopherim Tikkunim

There were 134 places where the scribes in Israel made changes in the text from YHWH to Adoni in the masoretic text. They have made documentation of this which then allows us to rectify the text back. It is understood that in ancient culture Sovereigns were highly respected and therefore the scribes did not see fit in these places for YHWH to be addressed by name. However this is not for us to decide and to repair the text as this creates obscurity of the set-apart name, a doctrine of the Pharisees, which developed post Babylonian exile.

-> Beresheeth 18:3,27,30,32; 19:18; 20:4.
-> Shemoth 4:10,13; 5:22; 15:17; 34:9,9.
-> WeDavar 14:17.

For further reading: The Masorah of Biblia Hebraica Struttgartensia by Kelley, Mynatt and Crawford and Anchor Bible Dictionary; Introduction to the Massoretic-Critical Edition of the Hebrew Bible, by C. Ginsburg.

HB1 (Beresheeth 1:1 on Elohim)

Why did YHWH not reveal His name in the very first verse of Genesis and why did He reveal the word Elohim (אלהים)?

Who is the saviour?

__Beresheeth__ Bara Elohim Alef-Tav ha shamayim v'et ha eretz
   1:1 In the beginning Elohim/Powers created the shamayim and the land.

This sums up the answer that the Creator Elohim (אלהים) is technically the Saviour.

The Hebrew word Elohim means (Powers/Lights) so it encompasses the whole court of God in other words the true Heavenly Court.

The word Elohim is used to describe judgment and justice this is crucial to understand, while the name YHWH is used to describe the merciful side of God or Yasha the saving Arm but where did the saving Arm come from?

So when isolated passages are provided such as Isa 43:11 or John 3:16 they do not match the criteria of the COURT. Salvation/Rescue issued out of the COURT that we know as **Elohim**.

So who is the Saviour? Elohim (The heavenly court where judgment and justice issues from)

When a poor woman who is in a village calls out what she calls out to? What if a poor dying hungry child? Would they call out to Jesus who they do not know, would they perhaps call out to Allah if they were Muslims then does that mean their salvation is not there? What if they knew no God and just called out to the Creator of the Universe?

Is Elohim so cruel not to acknowledge the cries of a child that is starving? A woman that is lowly? This is what the foolish religionists in Christianity will teach you but what does the Torah say;

Who did Avraham appeal to for justice?

Beresheeth (Gen) 18:25 ...Shall not the Judge (השפט) of all the earth do right?

So Avraham referenced him as The JUDGE (Ha Shofet). So where does judgment issue from? ELOHIM (The Court with all the Ruhkhots).

As Israel was chosen and redeemed at the very beginning before even Creation therefore Elohim is the Saviour, the throne room or the courtroom where Judgment and justice issues from.

Remember Avraham said Khalelah Lakh Ha-Shofet Kul ha-Eretz Lo Y'esah Mishpat...Shall not the Judge of all the earth do right?

I am sure by now a Lot of people are scratching their heads how can this be.

Its elementary my dear look at what God describes, the answer lies in the underlying wisdom revealed.

When Adam and everything else was created it says by necessity **Created Elohim** (meaning He established a Court), Bara Elohim. This is where God did not reveal himself as anything but Elohim. He hid himself basically. Get it? So while everyone is trying to fit their prophet and God as the saviour

Our God hid himself. He concealed himself. Adam was not shown who Elohim is. Remember Elohim is the COURT. Adam did not meet the whole court. This would be The Ten lights, Abbah, the Ruakh, the Son and the Seven Rachamim (Spirits).

Next Adam is revealed YHWH (Gen 2:4), then he sees YHWH walking and talking in the Garden (Gen 3:8).

Beresheeth (Gen) 2:4...אלהים יהוה עשׂות

Elohim YHWH Asot...

Literally one can read; Elohim (COURT) announces YHWH. The Hebrew word Asot here can mean to BROADCAST OR ANNOUNCE.

In other words Justice and Judgment which is Elohim that has revealed YHWH as a merciful judge.

Why merciful?

Because YHWH means typological meaning is "mercy" SO wherever you see the word YHWH written it means the Creator is revealing his merciful side or Khesed (loving-kindness) that is on the left side of God but when we look at it.

Remember when we wash our hands and pour water on it we pour water on the right hand first 3 times. When we take our shoes off we take off left foot off first. This means we are acting our the Loving-kindness side or mercy to others first.

Revelation to Avraham..
Beresheeth (Gen) 12:1
ויאמר יהוה אל־אברם
We'Yomar YHWH El Avraham

Note now what is being revealed to Avraham

The word YHWH is used which means the mercy side of God is revealed to our forefather Avraham.

Shemoth (Exo) 24:10...אלהי ישׂראל ותחת רגליו

Elohee Ysrael WeTakhat Raglev.

When the 70 elders of Israel see God they are only shown the FEET but not the rest of God.

So what do we have? We have Adam sees only the invisible Powers/Lights (Elohim/Judgment/Court) followed by YHWH (mercy) because of his fall.

Avraham has been given mercy so sees (YHWH).

The Elders of Ysrael see the feet of Elohee. This word Elohee here is plural. This means this takes us back to Genesis 1:1 THE COURT/Judgment. Ysrael see the feet only but actually faces the full COURT. This means our people Ysrael by seeing the FEET are revealed that they need to kneel to the FEET for that is where God's wisdom (Chockmah) rests in the Sefirotic tree.

South East Asian Muslims often say "Jannat mah kay pao may" (Heaven is in the mother's feet). Well that saying is not far wrong as Malkhut (symbol for the Holy Spirit) in the sefirotic tree where the Kingdom is in the feet or Em Chokmah is the Kingdom itself.

Since the Torah emanated out of the Creator therefore Torah being a feminine noun means it was representative symbol for the Ruakh Ha Kadosh or Holy Spirit the mother figure in the Godhead. The seven rachmim each are a symbol of the seven annual festivals one festival for each Spirit of El.

Now do you see the importance our Abbah has placed in the feminine? Therefore one who blasphemes the feminine side of God removes his salvation. The same way if we have mother and father and we disrespect our mother put her down, slap her around we have effectively removed our salvation.

This is why the Muslim saying that heaven is in the feet of mother is not far wrong.

In order to receive salvation or even be worthy of it the first thing fix your relation with your parents, hence why it is one of the commandments given. Usually you find the sons who are close to their parents are the best candidates to reap the benefits of above.

So next time you need to address who is the Savior. It actually emanates out of the COURT called (ELOHIM).

The Talmud teaches us the following about the Hebrew words YHWH Elohim (Lord, God) as follows:

> .... THE LORD GOD [MADE EARTH AND HEAVEN]. This may be compared to a king who had some empty glasses. Said the king: ' If I pour hot water into them, they will burst; if cold, they will Covenant [and snap]. ' What then did the king do? He mixed hot and cold water and poured it into them, and so they remained [unbroken]. Even so, said the Holy One, benevolent is He: ' If I create the world on the basis of mercy alone, its sins will be great; on the basis of judgment alone, the world cannot exist. Hence I will create it on the basis of judgment and of mercy, and may it then stand!' Hence the expression,' THE LORD GOD. (Midrash Rabbah - Genesis XII:15)

> *Woe to the wicked who turn the Attribute of Mercy into the Attribute of Judgment. Wherever the Tetragrammaton ['Lord] is employed it connotes the Attribute of Mercy, as in the verse, The Lord, the Lord God, merciful and gracious (Ex. XXXIV, 6), yet it is written, And the Lord saw that the wickedness of man was great (Gen. VI, 5), And it repented the Lord that he had made man (ib. 6), And the Lord said: I will blot out man (ib. 7). Happy are the right-ruling who turn the Attribute of Judgment into the Attribute of Mercy. Wherever Elohim (God) is employed it connotes the Attribute of Judgment: Thus: Thou shalt not revile Elohim- God (Ex. XXII, 27); the cause of both parties shall come before Elohim-God (ib. 8); yet it is written, And Elohim heard their groaning, and Elohim remembered His Covenant (ib. II, 24); And Elohim remembered Rachel (Gen. XXX, 22); AND ELOHIM REMEMBERED NOAH. (Midrash Rabbah - Genesis XXXIII:3).*

May the Most High Elohim Increase all those that obey and uphold his Torah and listen to his Kohanim.

Rabbi Simon Altaf HaKohen

Some Important History

The Jews taken as slaves by Rome.

True Israel taken slaves by the Assyrians.

A Hebrew Musician, notice the facial features and braided hair with braided beards. Ancient Israel was of darker skins not much different from Cushites, however if you look carefully at ancient Hebrew noses they do not match many modern black Negro people, which means there's considerable mix of Hamites who are also Negroes and are not part of true Israel. However this does not preclude mixing of nations in Israel with all colours including white. Anyone who claims Israel heritage based on black skin alone cannot be taken seriously but the most marked Character in an Israelite is of the Love for Torah as they took the Covenant from the God of Israel at Mount Sinai.

A brown skinned Israelite with woolly hair. Early Israelites put the tzitzits also on the circle of their lower garments.

The Arch of Titus

The Menorah taken from Jerusalem in 1st Century CE

Hand Washing cup (Al-Natalat) found in Qumran 100-250 BCE

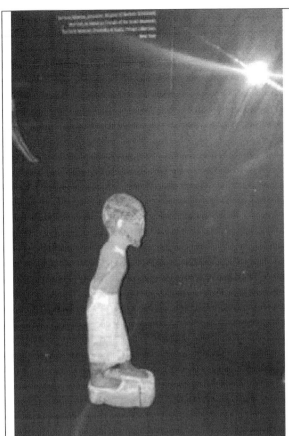

**Israel Museum Ancient Cannanite figure
1550-1070 BCE**

The 72 Names of God

והו	ילי	סיט	עלם	מהש	ללה	אכא	כהת
הזי	אלד	לאו	ההע	יזל	מבה	הרי	הקם
לאו	כלי	לוו	פהל	נלך	ייי	מלה	חהו
נתה	האא	ירת	שאה	ריי	אום	לכב	ושר
יהו	להח	כוק	מנד	אני	חעם	רהע	ייז
ההה	מיכ	וול	ילה	סאל	ערי	עשל	מיה
והו	דני	החש	עמם	ננא	נית	מבה	פוי
נמם	ייל	הרח	מצר	ומב	יהה	ענו	מחי
דמב	מנק	איע	חבו	ראה	יבם	היי	מום

Notes...